# Creating Literacy Instruction for All Children in Grades Pre-K to 4

**Thomas G. Gunning**

*Central Connecticut State University, Adjunct Professor*
*and*
*Southern Connecticut State University, Emeritus*

Boston    New York    San Francisco
Mexico City    Montreal    Toronto    London    Madrid    Munich    Paris
Hong Kong    Singapore    Tokyo    Cape Town    Sydney

*To my grandchildren:*

*Alex and Paige Gunning and Andrew Thomas Pizzuto*

Series Editor: Aurora Martínez-Ramos
Editorial Assistant: Katie Freddoso
Senior Marketing Manager: Elizabeth Fogarty
Editorial-Production Administrator: Karen Mason
Editorial-Production Services: Helane M. Prottas
Photo Research: Helane M. Prottas/Posh Pictures

Cover Coordinator: Linda Knowles
Cover Designer: Susan Paradise
Composition and Prepress Buyer: Linda Cox
Manufacturing Buyer: Megan Cochran
Electronic Composition: Dayle Silverman/Silver Graphics

For related titles and support materials, visit our online catalog at www.ablongman.com.

Between the time Website information is gathered and then published, it is not unusual for some sites to have closed. Also, the transcription of URLs can result in unintended typographical errors. The publisher would appreciate notification where these errors occur so that they may be corrected in subsequent editions.

**Library of Congress Cataloging-in-Publication Data**

Gunning, Thomas G.
    Creating literacy instruction for all children in grades pre-K to 4/Thomas G. Gunning.
        p. cm.
    Includes bibliographical references and index.
    ISBN 0-205-35683-4 (pbk.)
        1. Language arts (Early childhood) I. Title.

LB1139.5.L35G86 2003
372.6--dc21

2003040351

Printed in the United States of America
10 9 8 7 6 5 4 3 2 1   RRD-IND   08 07 06 05 04 03

Photo credits begin on page 590 which constitutes a continuation of the copyright page.

# Brief Contents

# Special Features

# Contents

## 3  Fostering Emergent/Early Literacy  *84*

## 4  Teaching Phonics, High-Frequency Words, and Syllabic Analysis  *158*

## 5 Building Vocabulary 246

## 6 Comprehension: Theory and Strategies *294*

## 7 Comprehension: Text Structures and Teaching Procedures *342*

# 8 Reading Literature 386

# 9 Approaches to Teaching Reading 414

## 10 Writing and Reading 448

# 11 Diversity in the Classroom 488

# 12 Creating and Managing a Literacy Program 504

Teaching literacy is in large measure a matter of making choices: Should you use basal readers or children's books, or both? Should you teach children to read whole words or to sound out words letter by letter, or both? Should you have three reading groups or four, or no groups? The answers depend on your personal philosophy, your interpretation of the research, the level at which you are teaching, the kinds of students you are teaching, community preferences, and the nature of your school's or school district's reading program.

This book has been written to help you discover approaches and techniques that fit your teaching style and your teaching situation. Its aim is to present as fairly, completely, and clearly as possible the major approaches and techniques that research and practice have indicated to be most effective. This book also presents the theories behind the methods, so you will be free *to choose, adapt, and/or construct* those approaches and techniques that best fit your style and teaching situation.

According to Howard Gardner, the multiple intelligence theorist, the purpose of education is to "enhance understanding" (Harvey, 2002). He recounts the story of his daughter who, despite being an A student in physics, was dismayed when she was unable to explain the physics behind a coin toss. Taking Gardner's remarks and his daughter's experience to heart, I have attempted in this text to build understanding. One example of this attempt to build understanding is the inclusion of information on the articulation of speech sounds. If you know how speech sounds are formed, you can understand why young children spell *bed* as BAD and *train* as CHRAN. Understanding can lead to more effective teaching. In teaching the spelling of the word *train*, you will not urge students to listen to the sounds they hear in *train* to spell it correctly because you will realize that they hear /ch/ at the beginning of the word. Instead you will explain that *train* is spelled with a *tr.* In the short term, building understanding makes for harder reading. Understanding how speech sounds are formed is fairly technical. In the long term, the reading is easier. Knowing how speech sounds are formed will help you to better understand sections on spelling, phonological awareness, and phonics. The text also explains cognitive development, differences between the Spanish and English writing systems, and other topics that will foster a deeper understanding of teaching techniques.

Although the text emphasizes approaches and techniques, methods are only a portion of the equation. Reading is not just a process; it is also very much a content area. What students read does matter, and, therefore, I have provided recommendations for specific children's books and other reading materials. Appendix A lists more than 1200 high-quality children's books by grade level. The basic premise of this book is that the best reading programs are a combination of effective techniques and plenty of worthwhile reading material.

Because children differ greatly in their backgrounds, needs, and interests, the book offers a variety of suggestions for both techniques and types of books to be used. The intent is to provide you with sufficient background knowledge of teaching methods, children's books, and other materials to enable you to create effective instruction for all the children you teach, whether they are rich or poor; bright, average, or slow; with disabilities or without; urban or suburban; or from any of the diverse cultural and ethnic groups that compose today's classrooms.

This book also recognizes that reading is part of a larger language process; therefore, considerable attention is paid to oral language development, writing and the other language arts, especially as these relate to reading instruction. Whether reading or writing is being addressed, emphasis is on making the student the center of instruction. For instance, activities are recommended that allow students to choose writing topics and reading materials. Approaches that foster a personal response to reading are also advocated. Just as you are encouraged by this text to create your own reading instruction, students must be encouraged to create their own literacy.

Because of the impact of the standards movement and related assessment issues, a full chapter is devoted to assessment (Chapter 2).

With classrooms becoming increasingly diverse, the emphasis has been placed on helping struggling readers and writers and English language learners. Chapters 3–11 conclude with a "Help for Struggling Readers and Writers" section. Emphasis has also been placed on programs of intervention and the role of the classroom teacher in working with struggling read-

ers and writers. This text endorses the viewpoint that a well-prepared classroom teacher is capable of effectively instructing most struggling readers and writers. To prevent problems, the text stresses providing students with carefully planned direct instruction in both reading and writing.

To assist you as you construct a framework for teaching reading and writing, a number of features that readers and reviewers found most valuable have been included.

■ Each chapter begins with an **Anticipation Guide,** which invites you to take inventory of your current ideas and opinions about chapter topics. Review your answers to this guide after reading the chapter, and note how your ideas may have changed.

■ **Using What You Know** is a brief introduction to each chapter that helps you relate your prior knowledge and the information presented in previous chapters to the chapter you are about to read.

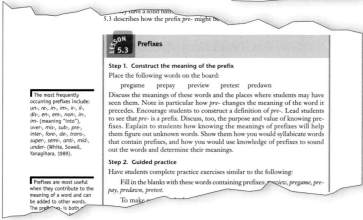

### ANTICIPATION GUIDE

Complete the anticipation guide below. It will help to activate your prior knowledge so that you interact more fully with the chapter. It is designed to probe your attitudes and beliefs about important and sometimes controversial topics. There are often no right or wrong answers; the statements will alert you to your attitudes about reading instruction and encourage you to become aware of areas where you might require additional information. At the end of the chapter, you might respond to the anticipation guide again to see if your answers have changed in light of what you have read. For each of the following statements, put a check under "Agree" or "Disagree" to show how you feel. Discuss your responses with classmates before you read the chapter.

|  | | Agree | Disagree |
|---|---|---|---|
| **1** | Before children learn to read, they should know the sounds of most letters. | ____ | ____ |
| **2** | Reading should not be fragmented into a series of subskills. | ____ | ____ |
| **3** | Oral reading should be accurate. | ____ | ____ |
| **4** | Teach phonics after children have learned to read about one hundred words. | ____ | ____ |
| **5** | Reading short passages and answering questions about them provide excellent practice. | ____ | ____ |
| **6** | Mistakes in oral reading should be ignored unless they change the sense of the passage. | ____ | ____ |

### USING WHAT YOU KNOW

This chapter provides a general introduction to literacy instruction in preschool and grades K–4. Before reading the chapter, examine your personal knowledge of the topic so that you will be better prepared to interact with the information. Sometimes, you may not realize what you know until you stop and

...ey have a solid basis. 5.3 describes how the prefix *pre-* might be

**LESSON 5.3  Prefixes**

**Step 1. Construct the meaning of the prefix**

Place the following words on the board:

  pregame    prepay    preview    pretest    predawn

Discuss the meanings of these words and the places where students may have seen them. Note in particular how *pre-* changes the meaning of the word it precedes. Encourage students to construct a definition of *pre-*. Lead students to see that *pre-* is a prefix. Discuss, too, the purpose and value of knowing prefixes. Explain to students how knowing the meanings of prefixes will help them figure out unknown words. Show them how you would syllabicate words that contain prefixes, and how you would use knowledge of prefixes to sound out the words and determine their meanings.

**Step 2. Guided practice**

Have students complete practice exercises similar to the following:

  Fill in the blanks with these words containing prefixes: *preview, pregame, prepay, predawn, pretest.*

  To make...

The most frequently occurring prefixes include: *un-, re-, in-, im-, ir-, il-, dis-, en-, em-, non-, in-, im-* (meaning "into"), *over-, mis-, sub-, pre-, inter-, fore-, de-, trans-, super-, semi-, anti-, mid-, under-* (White, Sowell, Yanagihara, 1989).

Prefixes are most useful when they contribute to the meaning of a word and can be added to other words. The pref... *in-* is both ...

■ Additional model teaching **Lessons** have been provided that encompass nearly every area of literacy instruction.

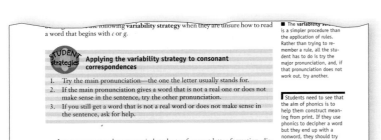

■ Key strategies, such as analyzing unknown words or summarizing a paragraph, which students can use to become independent learners, are outlined step by step and highlighted by the heading **Student Strategies.**

■ Practice and application activities have been identified as **Reinforcement Activities.** Activities that involve reading and writing for real purposes have been stressed.

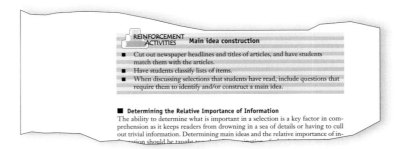

■ **Children's Reading Lists** appear in all chapters as a resource for titles that reinforce the particular literacy skills being discussed.

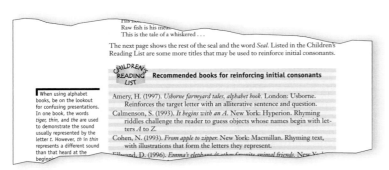

■ To help make the descriptions of teaching techniques come alive, examples of good teaching practices have been placed throughout the book in a feature entitled **Exemplary Teaching.** All are true-life accounts; many have been drawn from the memoirs of gifted teachers, while others were garnered from newspaper reports or the author's observations.

■ Marginal annotations throughout the text provide the reader with interesting, practical, handy advice and guidance. Because of the movement toward inclusive classrooms, suggestions for teaching students of varying abilities—including students with reading or learning disabilities—are presented in the body of the text and in marginal annotations with the heading **Adapting Instruction for Struggling Readers and Writers.** Suggestions are also made throughout the text for assisting students who are still acquiring English. Marginal annotations for these students are entitled **Adapting Instruction for English Language Learners.** Other headings include **Using Technology, Involving Parents,** and **Building Language.** There are also many untitled annotations on specific topics that elaborate on the text discussion. Key terms are highlighted in the text and appear, with their definitions, in the margin.

---

In what ways were the biggest dinosaurs alike? In what ways were they different?

*Elaborating*

How do you know that Professor Rodolfo is determined and hard-working? In your mind, picture Argentinosaurus. What does Argentinosaurus look like? What is the area where Argentinosaurus lives like? What sounds do you hear?

*Monitoring*

Did you find any confusing parts? Did you run into any words that you couldn't read or whose meanings you didn't know? If so, what did you do? Can you summarize each dinosaur's ma...

**ADAPTING INSTRUCTION for *STRUGGLING READERS and WRITERS***

There is a tendency to give struggling readers mostly lower-level questions. Be sure to include some higher-level questions, but provide scaffolding and prompts as necessary.

---

...about a tiger, point to a picture of the tiger. When introducing a unit on magnets, hold up a magnet every time you use the word; point to the poles each time you mention them. Supplement oral directions with gestures and demonstrations. Think of yourself as an actor in a silent movie who must use body language to convey meaning.

■ **Use Print**

Use print to support and expand the oral-language learning of English learners. Label items in the room. Write directions, schedules, and similar information about routines on the chalkboard. As you write them, read them orally (Sutton, 1989). Also encourage students to write:

Provide experiences in which language is greatly contextualized (as, for example, a field trip, a science experiment, role playing, planning a class party, solving a puz- Use print ... these activities as a natural extension of the or...

**ADAPTING INSTRUCTION for *ENGLISH LANGUAGE LEARNERS***

Because of limited English, ELLs may have difficulty fully explaining what they know about a selection they have read. They may mispronounce words whose meanings they know. The key element is whether students are getting meaning from these words, not whether they are pronouncing them correctly. In one study, students...

---

**USING TECHNOLOGY**

Information about the major basal series is available on the following sites:

Harcourt School Publishers
http://www.hbschool.com/

Houghton Mifflin
http://www.eduplace.com/

Macmillan/McGraw-Hill
http://www.mmhschool.com/teach/reading/index.html

Open Court

contents of the anthology are mo... provide a base of materials for all students to move thr... ...ave diverse interests and abilities and progress at different rates. Although basal selections are meant to be of high quality, they will not all be of interest to all students. The sports biography that delights one child is a total bore to another. A second shortcoming has to do with the way basal readers are assembled: They are anthologies and often contain excerpts from whole books. For example, the fourth-grade reader from a typical series contains "The Diary of Leigh Botts," a delightful tale of a budding young writer that is excerpted from Beverly Cleary's 1983 Newbury Award winner, *Dear Mr. Henshaw*. If reading the excerpt is worthwhile, reading the whole book should be even better.

There is also the question of pacing and time spent with a selection. Students often move through basals in lockstep fashion. Part of the problem is the nature of the teacher's guides; they offer too much of a good thing. Stories and even poems are overtaught. There are too many questions asked before a selection is read, too many asked after the piece has been read, and too many follow-up activities. A class might spend three to five days on a thousand-word story. To be fair, the guides do present activities as choices. Teachers can choose those that they wish to ... ...hers may even be provided a choice of ways of

---

**AND WRITERS**

Struggling readers and writers do best when given a systematic program in word analysis skills (Foorman et al., 1998). Although most students will grasp word analysis skills regardless of the approach used to teach them, at-risk learners need direct, clear instruction (Snow, Burns, & Griffin, 1998). For students who are struggling, this text recommends word building, with one important adaptation. When presenting a pattern, emphasize the components of the pattern. As explained in the sample lesson, say the parts of a pattern word. When adding *p* to *et* to form *pet*, say, "When I add /p/ to /et/, I get the word *pet*." Then point out each letter and the sound it represents. Pointing to *p* say /p/, pointing to *e* say /e/, pointing to *t* say /t/. Then say the word as a whole. Later, after adding *et* to *p* to form *pet*, again say the word in parts and then as a whole. Pointing to *p*, say the sound /p/. Pointing to *e*, say the sound /e/. Pointing to *t*, say the sound /t/. Then say the word as a whole. Have students say the word in parts and as a whole. Saying the individual sounds in a word helps the students to note all the sounds in the word and the letters that represent them. It also fosters phonemic awareness, which develops slowly in many struggling readers. In addition, some struggling read-

syllable words and multisyllabic words can be found at http://www.resourceroom.net/OGLists/wordlists.asp.

**INVOLVING PARENTS**

Parents might want to know what to do if their children ask for help with a word. Having them simply tell their children unknown words is the safest, least frustrating approach (Topping, 1989). But in some situations, you may want to have them encourage their children in the use of specific strategies.

---

**BUILDING LANGUAGE**

In conferences, ask open-ended questions, such as "Tell me about your book. What do you like best about it?" Use wait time to help students develop their responses more fully. Model the use of literary language as you ask such questions as, "How did the author build suspense in the story? How did she develop the characters? How did she make them seem real?"

...are not to be...

An individual conference begins with some ...tions designed to ... ...dent at ease and to get a general sense of the student's understanding of the boo... Through questioning, the teacher also attempts to elicit the child's personal response to the text and encourages the child to relate the text to her or his own life. The teacher poses questions to clear up difficulties and to build comprehension—and concepts, if necessary—and reviews difficult vocabulary. In addition, the teacher assesses how well the student understood the book, whether she or he enjoyed it, and whether she or he is able to apply the strategies and skills that have been taught. The teacher notes any needs the student has and may provide spontaneous instruction or give help later. To prepare for individual conferences, students choose a favorite part of the book to read to the teacher and also give a personal assessment of the book, telling why they did or did not like it or what they learned from it. Students also bring words, ideas, or items they want clarified or questions that they have about the text. In addition, students may be asked to complete a generic response sheet or a specific response sheet geared to the book they have read. Figures 9.1 and 9.2 present ...response forms that include items designed to elicit a

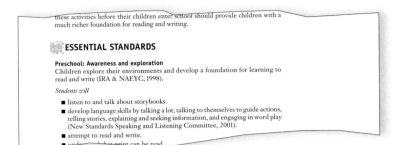

these activities before their children enter school should provide children with a much richer foundation for reading and writing.

### ESSENTIAL STANDARDS

**Preschool: Awareness and exploration**
Children explore their environments and develop a foundation for learning to read and write (IRA & NAEYC, 1998).

*Students will*

- listen to and talk about storybooks.
- develop language skills by talking a lot, talking to themselves to guide actions, telling stories, explaining and seeking information, and engaging in word play (New Standards Speaking and Listening Committee, 2001).
- attempt to read and write.
- understand what print can be read.

■ An **Essential Standards** section lists specific literacy curriculum goals so students and professors can focus on key objectives.

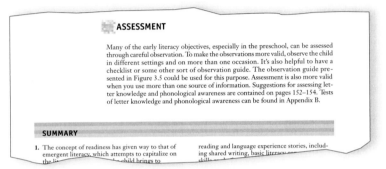

### ASSESSMENT

Many of the early literacy objectives, especially in the preschool, can be assessed through careful observation. To make the observations more valid, observe the child in different settings and on more than one occasion. It's also helpful to have a checklist or some other sort of observation guide. The observation guide presented in Figure 3.5 could be used for this purpose. Assessment is also more valid when you use more than one source of information. Suggestions for assessing letter knowledge and phonological awareness are contained on pages 152–154. Tests of letter knowledge and phonological awareness can be found in Appendix B.

### SUMMARY

1. The concept of readiness has given way to that of emergent literacy, which attempts to capitalize on the literacy concepts and skills a child brings to reading and language experience stories, including shared writing, basic literacy concepts and skills such as...

■ **Assessment** sections provide specific focus on evaluation issues and ideas for individual chapters.

*Help I'm a Prisoner in the...*
*Little House in the Big Woods* by Laura Ingalls Wilder
*Charlotte's Web* by E. B. White

**Benchmark passage:** *Charlotte's Web* by E. B. White
The next day was foggy. Everything on the farm was dripping wet. The grass looked like a magic carpet. The **asparagus** patch looked like a silver forest.

### ACTION PLAN

1. Become acquainted with national, state, and local standards and expectations.
2. Set standards or goals for your program. Translate goals or standards into measurable objectives.
3. Align materials and instructional activities with your objectives.
4. Align assessment with objectives and instruction. For each objective, you need formal and/or informal assessment devices so that you can tell whether objectives are being achieved.
5. Begin assessment by finding out where students are and what their strengths and needs are. This can be done with an IRI, emergent literacy measure, or other devices.
6. Screen students for specials needs. Students identified as struggling should be given diagnostic tests to be used to plan interven-

cess. Guide them so they can self-assess. Involve them in the setting of standards and creation of rubrics. Make adjustments in the program as required.
8. At year's end, administer an outcomes measure. This could be another form of the IRI or other measures that you administered at the beginning of the year. As part of your assessment, use information yielded by district-required or state or national tests.
9. Do not overtest. Don't give a test if it is not going to provide useful information or if you are not going to use the information. Make sure that students are tested on the appropriate level.
10. Make sure that there is a match between students' reading levels and the materials that they...

■ **Action Plan,** at the end of each chapter, lists specific steps that students might take to implement the assessment and teaching suggestions discussed in the chapter.

■ Each chapter concludes with a brief **Summary** and activities designed to extend the student's understanding of key concepts and provide suggestions for practical applications in a section entitled **Extending and Applying.** In a feature entitled **Developing a Professional Portfolio,** students are provided with suggested activities to help them create and maintain a portfolio, which might be used as a device for documenting and assessing their professional development. **Developing a Resource File,** provides practical suggestions for assembling assessment and instructional activities and materials.

## ORGANIZATION OF THE TEXT

The text's organization has been designed to reflect the order of the growth of literacy. Chapter 1 stresses constructing a philosophy of teaching reading and writing. Chapter 2 presents techniques for evaluating individuals and programs so that readers come to see assessment as an integral part of instruction. Chapters 3 and 4 discuss emergent literacy and basic decoding strategies, including phonics, syllabic analysis, and high-frequency words. Chapter 5 presents advanced word-recognition skills and strategies: morphemic analysis, dictionary skills, and techniques for building vocabulary. Chapters 6 and 7 are devoted to comprehension: Chapter 6 emphasizes comprehension strategies that students might use; Chapter 7 focuses on text structures and teaching procedures and covers application of comprehension skills in the content areas. Chapter 8 takes a step beyond comprehension by focusing on responding to literature and fostering a love of reading.

Chapters 3 through 8, which emphasize essential reading strategies, constitute the core of the book. Chapters 9 through 12 provide information on creating a well-rounded literacy program. Chapter 9 describes approaches to teaching reading. Chapter 10 explains the process approach to writing and discusses how reading and writing are related. Chapter 11 suggests how previously presented strategies might be used with children from diverse cultures and those with special needs or who are struggling with reading. Chapter 12 pulls all the topics together in a discussion of principles for organizing and implementing a literacy program. Also included in the final chapter is a section on technology and its place in a program of literacy instruction.

This text, designed to be practical, offers detailed explanations, and often examples of application, for every major technique or strategy. Numerous suggestions for practice activities and reading materials are also included. I hope that this book will furnish you with an in-depth knowledge of literacy methods and materials so that you will be able to construct lively, effective reading and writing instruction for all the students you teach.

## SUPPLEMENTS FOR INSTRUCTORS AND STUDENTS

**Instructor's Manual with Test Bank and Transparency Masters:** For each chapter, the instructor's manual features a series of Learner Objectives, a Chapter Overview, suggestions for Before, After, and During Reading, a list of suggested Teaching Activities, and suggestions for Assessment. There is a Test Bank, which contains an assortment of multiple-choice, short essay, and long essay questions for each chapter. This supplement has been written completely by the text author, Tom Gunning.

## ALLYN AND BACON SUPPLEMENTS FOR LITERACY

In addition to the supplements available with *Creating Literacy Instruction for All Children in Grades Pre-K to 4*, Allyn and Bacon offers an array of student and instructor supplements on the overall topic of literacy. All are available with this textbook.

**Allyn & Bacon Digital Media Archive for Literacy:** This CD-ROM offers still images, video clips, audio clips, weblinks, and assorted lecture resources that can be incorporated into multimedia presentations in the classroom.

**Professionals in Action: Literacy Video:** This 90-minute video consists of 10- to 20-minute segments on Phonemic Awareness, Teaching Phonics, Helping Students Become Strategic Readers, Organizing for Teaching with Literature, Discussions of literacy and brain research with experts. The first four segments provide narrative along with actual classroom teaching footage. The final segments present, in a question-and-answer format, discussions by leading experts in the field of literacy.

**Allyn & Bacon Literacy Video Library:** Featuring renowned reading scholars Richard Allington, Dorothy Strickland and Evelyn English, this three-video library addresses core topics covered in the Literacy classroom: reading strategies, developing literacy in multiple intelligences classrooms, developing phonemic awareness, and much more.

**VideoWorkshop for Reading:** A new way to integrate video for maximized learning! This total teaching and learning system includes quality classroom video footage on an easy-to-use CD-ROM plus a Student Learning Guide and an Instructor's Teaching Guide—both with textbook-specific Correlation Grids. The result? A program that brings textbook concepts to life with ease and that helps students understand, analyze, and apply the objectives of the course. VideoWorkshop is not sold separately and is available only as a FREE value-pack option with this textbook. (Special package ISBN required from your representative.)

**Allyn & Bacon PowerPoint Presentation for Elementary Reading Methods:** Available on the Web at http://www.ablongman.com/ppt. This PowerPoint presentation includes approximately 100 slides that cover a range of reading topics: assessment, building vocabulary, comprehension instruction and theory, developing literacy programs, diversity and special needs, reading and learning to read, using literature, and emergent early literacy, among others.

**Allyn & Bacon Transparency Package for Reading Methods:** This set includes 100 full-color transparencies that cover a myriad of reading topics.

**CourseCompass Content for Elementary Reading Methods:** CourseCompass, powered by Blackboard, is the most flexible online course management system on the market today. By using this powerful suite of online tools in conjunction with Allyn & Bacon's preloaded textbook and testing content, you can create an online presence for your course in under 30 minutes. You can find course objectives, lecture outlines, quizzes, essay activities, tests and a glossary of key terms in reading that you can adapt for your course. In addition, you will find weblinks providing access to a wealth of resources in the field of reading. Log on at http://www.coursecompass.com and find out how you can get the most out of this dynamic teaching resource.

**Research Navigator™ Guide for Education with Access Code:** Designed to help students select and evaluate research from the Web to find the best and most credible information available. The booklet contains:

- A practical and to-the-point discussion of search engines
- Detailed information on evaluating online sources
- Citation guidelines for Web resources

- Web activities for Education
- Web links for Education
- A complete guide to Research Navigator™ (access code required)

Allyn & Bacon's new Research Navigator™ is the easiest way for students to start a research assignment or research paper. Complete with extensive help on the research process and three exclusive databases of credible and reliable source material including EBSCO's ContentSelect Academic Journal Database, *New York Times* Search by Subject Archive, and "Best of the Web" Link Library. Research Navigator™ helps students make the most of their research time quickly and efficiently. Each Research Navigator Guide contains an access code allowing individual users entry into this wonderful resource for research assistance.

**Allyn & Bacon LiteracyZone SuperSite (Access code required)** (http://www.ablongman.com/literacy) A website with a wealth of information for pre-service and in-service teachers—whether you want to gain new insights, pick up practical information, or simply connect with one another! It includes State Standard Correlations; Teaching Resources; Ready-to-Use Lesson Plans and Activities for All Grade Levels; Subject-specific Web links for further research and discovery; Information in A&B professional titles to help you in your teaching career; Up-to-date "In the News" features and Discussion Forum, and much more.

**Speak with your representative about obtaining these supplements for your class!**

## ACKNOWLEDGMENTS

I am indebted to Aurora Martínez, acquisitions editor at Allyn and Bacon, who provided thoughtful suggestions as well as support and encouragement. I am also grateful to Beth Slater and Katie Freddoso, editorial assistants at Allyn and Bacon, for their patient and timely assistance.

My wife, Joan, offered both thoughtful comments and continuous encouragement. I deeply appreciate her loving assistance.

T. G.

# Creating Literacy Instruction for All Children in Grades Pre-K to 4

# 1

# The Nature of Literacy and Today's Children

Complete the anticipation guide below. It will help to activate your prior knowledge so that you interact more fully with the chapter. It is designed to probe your attitudes and beliefs about important and sometimes controversial topics. There are often no right or wrong answers; the statements will alert you to your attitudes about reading instruction and encourage you to become aware of areas where you might require additional information. At the end of the chapter, you might respond to the anticipation guide again to see if your answers have changed in light of what you have read. For each of the following statements, put a check under "Agree" or "Disagree" to show how you feel. Discuss your responses with classmates before you read the chapter.

|  |  | *Agree* | *Disagree* |
|---|---|---|---|
| **1** | Before children learn to read, they should know the sounds of most letters. | _____ | _____ |
| **2** | Reading should not be fragmented into a series of subskills. | _____ | _____ |
| **3** | Oral reading should be accurate. | _____ | _____ |
| **4** | Teach phonics after children have learned to read about one hundred words. | _____ | _____ |
| **5** | Reading short passages and answering questions about them provide excellent practice. | _____ | _____ |
| **6** | Mistakes in oral reading should be ignored unless they change the sense of the passage. | _____ | _____ |

## USING WHAT YOU KNOW

This chapter provides a general introduction to literacy instruction in preschool and grades K–4. Before reading the chapter, examine your personal knowledge of the topic so that you will be better prepared to interact with the information. Sometimes, you may not realize what you know until you stop and think about it. Think over what you know about the nature of reading. What do you think reading is? What do you do when you read? What do you think the reader's role is? Is it simply to receive the author's message, or should it include some personal input? How about writing? What processes do you use when you write?

How would you go about teaching reading and writing to today's students? What do you think the basic principles of a literacy program should be? What elements have worked especially well in programs with which you are familiar?

## THE NATURE OF READING

"Awake! Awake!" These are the first words I remember reading. But the words were as magical as any I have read since. Even after all these years, I still have vivid memories of that day long ago in first grade when reading came alive for me, and, indeed, awakened a lifetime of reading and a career as a reading teacher.

**Reading** is, first and foremost, magical, as those who recall learning to read or have witnessed their students discover the process will attest. It opens the door to a vast world of information, fulfillment, and enjoyment. After having learned to read, the person is never quite the same.

### Importance of Language

As magical as it may be, reading is our second major intellectual accomplishment. Our first, and by far, most important, intellectual accomplishment is our acquisition of language. Without language, of course, there would be no reading. Reading is very much a language activity and, ultimately, our ability to read is limited by our language skills. We can't read what we can't understand. Even if we can pronounce words we don't understand because of superior phonics skills, we are not reading. Reading is a process in which we construct meaning from print. Without meaning, there is no reading.

### Developing Language

Social interaction is an absolute requirement for language development. In order to learn language and progress from one stage to another, children must interact with others. Both the quantity and quality of the interaction are important. In a longitudinal study of children in Bristol, England, Wells (1986) found that children exposed to the most language heard ten times as many words as those exposed to the least amount. As might be expected, those exposed to more language were generally at a higher level of development.

However, the quality of the interaction is more important than the quantity. Children did best in one-to-one situations in which an adult discussed matters that were of interest and concern to the child or the two talked over a shared activity.

It is also essential that the adult adjust his or her language so as to take into consideration and compensate for the child's limited linguistic ability, something parents seem to do intuitively.

In his extensive study, Wells (1986) found that some parents intuitively provided maximum development for their children's language. Far from being directors of what their children said, these parents were collaborative constructors of meaning. Careful listeners, they made genuine attempts to use both nonverbal and verbal clues so as to understand what their children were saying. Through careful listening and being actively involved in the conversation, parents were able to help the children extend their responses so that both knowledge of the world and linguistic abilities were fostered. In this book, high-quality social interactions of the type conducted by the best parents are emphasized. Language, of course, has an effect on cognitive development.

> Adults clarify and extend children's ideas and provide additional information and advanced vocabulary, which lift children's thinking to higher levels (Raines & Isbell, 1994).

## Role of Cognitive Development

Many of the practices advocated in literacy education are based on the work of Jean Piaget and L. S. Vygotsky, the two leading developmental theorists of modern times. Vygotsky, a Russian psychologist, stressed the social nature of language and learning and the important role that adults play in both. Piaget, a Swiss psychologist, stressed stages of cognitive development and the unique nature of children's thinking.

*E*xpert guidance helps children improve their reading and writing.

### ■ Jean Piaget

Piaget concluded that children's thinking is qualitatively different from adults' thinking and that it evolves through a series of hierarchical stages. He believed that children's thinking developed through direct experience with their environment. Through adaptation or interaction with the environment, the child builds psychological structures or schemes, which are ways of making sense of the world. Adaptation includes two complementary processes: **assimilation** and **accommodation.** Through assimilation, the child interprets the world in terms of his schemes. Seeing a very small dog, he calls it a "doggie" and assimilates this in his dog scheme. Seeing a goat for the first time, the child might relate it to his dog scheme and call it a "doggie." Later, realizing that there is something different about this creature, he may accommodate his "doggie" scheme and exclude the goat and all creatures with horns. Thus, he has refined his dog scheme. To Piaget, direct experience rather than language was the key determiner of cognitive development.

> ■ **Assimilation** is the process of incorporating new ideas into existing ones.

> ■ **Accommodation** is the process by which concepts or schema are modified or new ones created to accommodate new knowledge.

### ■ L. S. Vygotsky

Although both Piaget and Vygotsky believed that children need to interact with the world around them, Vygotsky stressed the importance of social factors in cognitive development (1962). In a theory that has become a keystone for instruction, Vygotsky distinguished between actual and potential development. Actual development is a measure of the level at which a child is developing. In a sense, it is a measure of what the child has learned up to that point. Potential development is a measure of what the child might be capable of achieving. The difference between the two is known as the **zone of proximal development.** As explained by Vygotsky (1978), the zone of proximal development is "the distance between the actual developmental level as determined by independent problem solving and the level of potential development as determined through problem solving under adult guidance or in collaboration with more capable peers" (p. 84). In other words, the zone of proximal development is the difference between what a child can do on his or her own and what the child can do with help.

> ■ The **zone of proximal development** is the area between independent performance and potential as determined through problem solving under guidance of an adult or more capable peer.

Focusing on the importance of interaction with adults or knowledgeable peers, Vygotsky's theory is that children learn through expert guidance. In time, they internalize the concepts and strategies employed by their mentors and so, ultimately, are able to perform on a higher level. The support, guidance, and instruction provided by an adult is known as **scaffolding** (Bruner, 1975, 1986).

Ideally, instruction should be pitched somewhat above a child's current level of functioning. Instruction and collaboration with an adult or more capable peers will enable the child to reach the higher level and ultimately function on that level. Instruction and interaction are key elements. The overall theories of evaluation and instruction presented in this book are grounded in the concepts of actual and potential development and the zone of proximal development.

> ■ **Scaffolding** refers to the support and guidance provided by an adult that helps a student function on a higher level.

Implications based on an integration of the theories of Piaget and Vygotsky are listed below:

> | Vygotsky neglected the importance of other ways of learning. Children can and do learn through nonverbal imitation and self-discovery (Berk, 1997).

■ Provide students with hands-on experiences and opportunities to make discoveries.

- Be aware and plan for individual differences. Because children have different experiences and come from different backgrounds, they develop at different rates.
- Children learn best when activities are developmentally appropriate. Careful observation of processes the child is using provides insight into the child's level of development.
- Classrooms should be rich in verbal guidance. Interaction with the teacher and peers fosters learning.

## Importance of Experience

Although based on language, reading is also experiential. One second-grade class was reading a story that took place in a laundromat. None of the children had ever been to a laundromat or even heard of one, so they found the story confusing. Reading is not so much getting meaning from a story as it is bringing meaning to it. The more the reader brings to a story, the more she or he will be able to take away. For example, the child who can't seem to sit still will readily empathize with the boy in *Sit Still* (Carlson, 1996). In this instance, reading evokes an emotional response as well as an intellectual one.

## Importance of the Students' Culture

Living as we do in a multicultural, pluralistic society, it is important for us to explore and understand the literacy histories of our pupils. We have to ask such questions as these: In students' culture(s), how are reading and writing used? What values are placed on them? What are the ways in which the students have observed and participated in reading and writing? Is literacy in their environment primarily a group or an individual activity? Given this information, the school should build on the children's experiences and develop and reinforce the skills and values important to their culture(s) as well as those important to the school.

## THE READER'S ROLE IN THE READING PROCESS

What is the reader's role in the reading process? In the past, it was defined as being passive, getting the author's meaning. Today, reading requires a more active role—the reader must construct meaning from text. The model of transmission of information in which the reader was merely a recipient has given way to transactional theory, a two-way process involving a reader and a text:

> Every reading act is an event, or a **transaction,** involving a particular reader and a particular pattern of signs, a text, and occurring at a particular time in a particular context. Instead of two fixed entities acting on one another, the reader and the text are two aspects of a total dynamic situation. The "meaning" does not reside ready-made "in" the text or "in" the reader but happens or comes into being during the transaction between reader and text. (Rosenblatt, 1994, p. 1063)

- **Transaction** refers to the relationship between the reader and the text in which the text is conditioned by the reader and the reader is conditioned by the text.

In her study of how students read a poem, Rosenblatt (1978) noted that each reader was active:

> He was not a blank tape registering a ready-made message. He was actively involved in building up a poem for himself out of his responses to text. He had to draw on his past experiences with the verbal symbols. . . . The reader was not only paying attention to what the words pointed to in the external world, to their referents; he was also paying attention to the images, feelings, attitudes, associations, and ideas that the words and their referents evoked in him. (p. 10)

The type of reading, of course, has an effect on the transaction. The reader can take an efferent or an aesthetic **stance.** When reading a set of directions, a science text, or a math problem, the reader takes an **efferent** stance, the focus being on obtaining information that can be carried away (*efferent* is taken from the Latin verb *efferre*, "to carry away"). In the **aesthetic** stance, the reader pays attention to the associations, feelings, attitudes, and ideas that the words evoke.

Does it make any difference whether reading is viewed as being transmissional, transactional, or somewhere in between? Absolutely. If reading is viewed as transmissional, students are expected to stick close to the author's message. If reading is viewed as transactional, students are expected to put their personal selves into their reading, especially when encountering literature. From a transactional perspective, building background becomes especially important because it enriches the transaction between reader and text. Personal response and interpretation are at the center of the reading process. The reader's role is enhanced when a transactional view prevails.

## APPROACHES TO READING INSTRUCTION: WHOLE VERSUS PART LEARNING

Just as there are philosophical differences about the role of the reader, there are differences in approaches to teaching reading. On one end of the continuum are those who espouse a subskills, or bottom-up, approach, and on the other end are those who advocate a **holistic,** top-down approach. In between are the interactionists. Where do you fit on the continuum? Go back to the anticipation guide at the beginning of the chapter. Take a look at how you answered the six statements. If you agreed with only the odd-numbered ones, you are a bottom-up advocate. If you agreed with only the even-numbered statements, you are a top-downer. If your answers were mixed, you are probably an interactionist.

### Bottom-Uppers

In the **bottom-up approach,** children literally start at the bottom and work their way up. First, they learn the names and shapes of the letters of the alphabet. Next, they learn consonant sounds, followed by simple and then more complex vowel correspondences. As Carnine, Silbert, and Kameenui (1990) explain: "Our position is that many students will not become successful readers unless teachers identify the

---

■ **Stance** refers to the position or attitude that the reader takes. The two stances are aesthetic and efferent.

■ **Efferent** refers to a kind of reading in which the focus is on obtaining or carrying away information from the reading.

■ **Aesthetic** is a type of reading in which the reader focuses upon experiencing the piece: the rhythm of the words, the past experiences these call up (Rosenblatt, 1978, p. 10).

■ **Holistic** refers to the practice of learning through the completion of whole tasks rather than fragmented subskills and fragments of reading and writing.

■ **Bottom-up approach** refers to a kind of processing in which meaning is derived from the accurate, sequential processing of words. The emphasis is on the text rather than the reader's background knowledge or language ability.

essential reading skills, find out what skills students lack, and teach those skills directly" (p. 3).

Bottom-up procedures are intended to make learning to read easier by breaking complex tasks into their component skills. Instruction proceeds from the simple to the complex. In essence, there are probably no 100-percent bottom-uppers among reading teachers. Even those who strongly favor phonics recognize the importance of higher-level strategies.

## Top-Downers

A **top-down approach,** as its name indicates, starts at the top and works downward. Learning to read is seen as being similar to learning to speak; it is holistic and natural through immersion. Subskills are not taught because it is felt they fragment the process and make learning to read more abstract and difficult (K. Goodman, 1986). One of the most influential models of reading is that proposed by Ken Goodman (1994). According to Goodman, readers use their background knowledge and knowledge of language to predict and infer the content of print. Readers "use their selection strategies to choose only the most useful information from all that is available" (Goodman, 1994, p. 1125). When reading the sentence "The moon is full tonight," the reader can use his or her knowledge of the moon, context clues, and perhaps the initial consonants *f* and *t* to reconstruct *full* and *tonight*. According to Goodman's theory, it is not necessary for the reader to process all the letters of *full* and *tonight*. However, in order to make use of background knowledge, context clues, and initial consonant cues, the reader must consider the whole text. If the words *full* and *tonight* were read in isolation, the reader would have to depend more heavily on processing all or most of the letters of each word.

## Interactionists

Most practitioners tend to be more pragmatic than either strict top-downers or dyed-in-the-wool bottom-uppers and borrow practices from both ends of the continuum. These **interactionists** teach skills directly and systematically—especially in the beginning—but they avoid overdoing it, as they do not want to fragment the process. They also provide plenty of opportunities for students to experience the holistic nature of reading and writing by having them read whole books and write for real purposes.

## IMPORTANCE OF LITERACY MODELS

Why is it important to be aware of different models of teaching reading? For one thing, it is important that you formulate your own personal beliefs about reading and writing instruction. These beliefs will then be the foundation for your instruction. They will determine the goals you set, the instructional techniques you

---

Bottom-up theorists claim that when reading, we process nearly every word and virtually every letter in the words. Samuels (1994) concludes that novice readers process words letter by letter but that experienced readers may process words holistically or break words down into their components. Context fosters both speed and accuracy of word recognition.

■ **Top-down processing** refers to deriving meaning by using one's background knowledge, language ability, and expectations. The emphasis is on the reader rather than the text.

In Goodman's model, students use three cuing systems: semantic, syntactic, and graphophonic. Semantic cues derive from our past experiences, so that we construct meaning by bringing our background of knowledge to a story. Syntactic cues derive from our knowledge of how the structure of language works. Graphophonics cues refer to our ability to sound out words or recognize them holistically. Based on their use of these cues, students predict the content of the text, confirm or revise their predictions, and reread if necessary.

■ **Interactionists** hold the theoretical position that reading involves processing text and using one's background knowledge and language ability.

To clarify one's philosophy of teaching, ask: "What are my instructional practices and why am I doing what I'm doing?" Examining your practices, should help you uncover your beliefs.

**USING TECHNOLOGY**

Controversies such as "Is reading top down or bottom up?" are often explored on the Web sites of professional organizations, such as the International Reading Association's Web site: **http://www.ira.org**

This book takes the position that all sources of information—semantic, syntactic, background knowledge, and letter-sound relationships—are essential when processing text and emphasizes the use of both context and phonics. However, the text also agrees that even in mature reading, nearly all words are processed.

**USING TECHNOLOGY**

To find the results of the latest National Assessment in reading and other areas, consult: National Center for Educational Statistics: **http://nces.ed. gov/ indihomeasp**

use, the materials you choose, the organization of your classroom, the reading and writing behaviors you expect students to exhibit, and the criteria you use to evaluate students. For instance, whether you use children's books or a basal, how you teach phonics, and whether you expect flawless oral reading or are satisfied if the student's rendition is faithful to the sense of the selection will depend upon your theoretical orientation (DeFord, 1985).

Having a theoretical orientation helps in another way. It provides a means of examining what you do in your teaching. You may find that you are not walking your talk—your practices might not fit in with your beliefs. According to Ross (cited in DeFord, 1985), the ability to implement your beliefs is dependent on the clarity of those beliefs and your ability to see a connection between them and what you do in your classroom.

## APPROACH TAKEN BY THIS TEXT

This book draws heavily on research in cognitive psychology, combines an interactionist point of view with a holistic orientation, and takes an integrated approach. Both the bottom-up and top-down approaches are step by step (Kamhi & Catts, 1999). In the bottom-up model, the reader progresses from letter to sound to word. In the top-down process, the reader proceeds from sampling of language cues to prediction and to confirmation. However, in an integrated approach, the processes occur in parallel fashion. For instance, when students decode words, four processors are at work: orthographic, phonological, meaning, and context (Adams, 1990, 1994). The orthographic processor is responsible for perceiving the sequences of letters in text. The phonological processor is responsible for mapping the letters into their spoken equivalents. The meaning processor contains one's knowledge of word meanings, and the context processor is in charge of constructing a continuing understanding of the text (Stahl, Osborne, & Lehr, 1990). The processors work simultaneously and both receive information and send it to the other processors; however, the orthographic and phonological processors are always essential participants. Context may speed and/or assist the interpretation of orthographic and phonological information but does not take its place (see Figure 1.1). When information from one processor is weak, another may be called on to give assistance. For instance, when a word such as *lead* is encountered, the context processor provides extra help to the meaning and phonological processors in assigning the correct meaning and pronunciation.

In an integrated model, both top-down and bottom-up processes are used. However, depending on circumstances, bottom-up or top-down processes are emphasized. If one is reading a handwritten note in which some words are illegible, top-down processes are stressed as the reader uses knowledge of language and knowledge of the world to fill in what is missing. If reading unfamiliar proper names or words in isolation, bottom-up processes are emphasized.

In an integrated approach, reading is considered an active, constructive process, with the focus on the reader, whose experiences, cultural background, and point

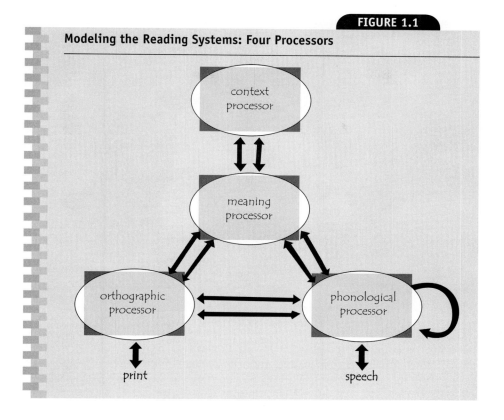

**FIGURE 1.1**

**Modeling the Reading Systems: Four Processors**

of view will play a part in her or his comprehension of a written piece. The focus is on cognitive processes or strategies used to decode words and understand and remember text: using phonics and context to decipher unknown words, activating one's knowledge of a topic, predicting meaning, summarizing, and visualizing.

Stress is also placed on teaching strategies in context and holistically applying them to children's books, periodicals, ads and other real-world materials, and content area textbooks. It recommends a balanced approach in which systematic instruction and immersion in reading and writing play complementary roles.

##  STATUS OF LITERACY

Our best readers are improving. The top 25 percent of students are achieving higher scores than ever (Barton, 2001). Unfortunately, the bottom 25 percent are doing worse than ever. The gap between the best and the poorest readers in fourth grade is widening, as is the gap between minority students and white students. In a study of reading achievement of fourth-graders, only three of thirty-two states showed

Based on National Assessment results, some 37 percent of fourth-graders read below a basic level. For children living in poverty, the figure is 60 percent. A basic level indicates partial mastery of skills required for fourth-grade reading (Barton, 2001).

*E*xtensive reading is necessary for growth in literacy.

**READ.WRITE.THINK**
http://www.
readwritethink.org/
sitefeatures.html
Features a listing of
IRA/NCTE standards and
lessons geared to those
standards.

**USING TECHNOLOGY**
The best source of infor-
mation about standards
is Standards for
Education
http://edstandards.
org/Standards.html
which offers a wealth of
information about cur-
riculum frameworks and
standards and provides
links to each state so
you can examine your
state's standards.

an improvement in the scores of the lowest 25 percent. In twelve states, scores de-clined. The gap between white and minority students increased in six states and declined in just one (Barton, 2001). The gap between boys and girls is also in-creasing, with boys lagging, especially in the lower grades.

## NO CHILD LEFT BEHIND

To raise the achievement of all students but especially those who are struggling with reading, the United States has embarked on a campaign to raise the literacy levels of all its students. Billions of dollars have been poured into intervention programs, summer school, after-school instruction, and research. Never before has there been such an intense commitment to "leaving no child behind." The com-mitment has a standards and an assessment component. The logic behind stan-dards is that once there is "broad agreement on what students should know and be able to do, then everything else in the system (i.e., assessments, professional devel-opment, materials, school structures) could be directed toward achieving these stan-dards. It was a systemic approach that included *all* elements rather than the piecemeal approach of the past" (Valencia & Wixson, 2001, p. 204).

All states are required to have standards. In many instances, literacy standards are based on the broad goals of national organizations such as the International Reading Association and the National Council of Teachers of English (1996). Students are assessed in terms of state or district standards. In addition, beginning in 2002–2003, tests aligned with state standards must be administered in grade spans 3–5, 6–9, and 10–12. Starting in 2005–2006, all public school students in grades three through eight must be assessed in reading on a yearly basis. Students, especially those who have fallen behind, are expected to show an improvement. Otherwise, schools that fail to make adequate progress in closing the gap will be penalized. Standards have even made it down to the preschool and kindergarten levels. Headstart children are expected to be able to identify ten letters of the alphabet. Many states and school districts have standards for kindergarten. In some instances, students are retained or placed in a transition class if they don't know the letters of the alphabet, beginning letter-sound relationships, and some high-frequency words. Because of the overwhelming concern with standards, assessment, and lifting the levels of the lowest performing students, these themes will be emphasized throughout this text.

## Scientifically Based Literacy Instruction

Because reading achievement has remained essentially unchanged over the past two decades and because the gap between the reading achievement of the poor and middle-class students is substantial, there has been a call for programs that are scientifically based. Reading First, for example, is an initiative designed to raise the literacy achievement of students in grades K–3, the crucial years for literacy development. Under the initiative, all states are eligible to apply for substantial grants. However, as part of their application they must show that they will be including key elements shown to be part of scientifically based successful reading programs: phonological awareness, phonics, fluency, vocabulary, and comprehension. Scientific evidence is interpreted as meaning studies in which Method A has been compared with Method B and/or a control group and found to be statistically superior.

The International Reading Association (2002) uses the term *evidence-based* rather than *scientifically based. Evidence-based* is a broader term and includes qualitative studies as well as the more scientifically based studies that include comparison of experimental and control groups.

As a teacher, you should become acquainted with the major findings of literacy research so that you can construct a literacy program that is based on research, and you can assess whether new techniques or materials that you are thinking about trying are supported by research. You should also assesses the research base to see if it is applicable to your students and your situation. A technique that works well on a one-to-one basis may not be effective with small groups. Of course, research doesn't answer all the instructional questions that arise. You need to become a teacher-researcher so that you can test out methods and materials and have a better basis for selecting those that are most effective in your situation. You also need to assess all aspects of your program with a view to replacing or improving elements that aren't working and adding elements that are missing.

Insofar as possible, the suggestions made in this text are evidence-based. However, in some instances they are based on personal experience or the experience of others. Teaching literacy is an art as well as a science.

Based on their review of standards, Valencia and Wixson (2001) concluded that standards-based reform is a way to "address the inequities of the past and raise the ceiling for all" (p. 210).

**USING TECHNOLOGY**
Reading First **http://www.ed.gov/offices/OESE/readingfirst/** contains information on this program for children in grades K–3.

**USING TECHNOLOGY**
*What Is Evidence-Based Reading Instruction?* Available online at **http://www.reading.org/positions/evidence_based.html**, this site provides a summary of a position statement of the International Reading Association (June 2002).

**USING TECHNOLOGY**
Research reported in the *Report of the National Reading Panel* has been judged to be scientifically based. The report contains many of the basic principles of teaching reading. The report is free and may be ordered at **http://www.nationalreadingpanel.org/Publications/.**

### Influence of Reading First

Reading First, a component of No Child Left Behind, has as its goal that students will be proficient readers by the end of third grade. To accomplish that goal some 5 billion dollars has been allocated for programs that have already begun and that will last until 2010 or longer. Most of the money will be spent at the classroom level. Although Reading First is designed primarily for underachieving readers living in poverty, it has the potential to change the way all students in the primary grades are taught. States that are awarded the grants are encouraged to advocate the use of scientific methods with all primary students. Because of the influence Reading First is having and will continue to have on primary reading instruction, this text will devote extra space to exploring the provisions of this program and its implications for instruction. Ways of meeting Reading First requirements will be discussed along with controversial issues.

## A READING AND WRITING PROGRAM FOR TODAY'S STUDENTS

The world is growing ever more complex, and so the demands for literacy are increasing. Functioning in today's global society requires a higher degree of literacy than did functioning in yesterday's pre-information-superhighway society. Requirements for tomorrow's citizens will be higher yet. Today's and tomorrow's

*S*tudents do their best when they feel involved and have interesting materials and activities.

readers need to be selective and efficient. Bombarded with information, students must be able to select the information that is important to them. They must also be efficient.

What kind of program will help meet the literacy needs of today's students? That is a question that the remainder of this book will attempt to answer. However, when all is said and done, the ten principles discussed below, if followed faithfully, should make a difference in determining such a program.

**1.** *Children learn to read by reading.* Learning to read is a little like learning to drive a car—instruction and guidance are required. In addition to instruction and guidance, novice readers, like novice motorists, require practice. They must read a variety of fiction and nonfiction books, newspapers, and magazines to become truly skilled. In a way, each book or article makes a child a better reader. As Hirsch (1987) pointed out, children must have a broad background in a variety of areas in order to be able to understand much of what is being written and said in today's world. For example, a child who has read the fable "The Boy Who Cried Wolf" will have the background necessary to understand a story that includes the sentence "Frank cried wolf once too often." Reading is not simply a matter of acquiring and perfecting skills, it also requires accumulating vocabulary, concepts, experiences, and background knowledge.

To provide the necessary practice and background, children's books are an essential component of a reading program. Unfortunately, large numbers of students are alliterate: They *can* read, but they *do* not, at least not on a regular basis. In a recent study, only 44 percent of a large sample of fourth-graders reported reading on a daily basis; however, 60 percent of these same children watched three or more hours of television each day (Mullis, Campbell, & Farstrup, 1993). Responding to a reading attitude questionnaire, the Motivation to Read Profile (Gambrell, Codling, & Palmer, 1996), 17 percent of the students reported that they would rather clean their rooms than read, 10 percent said that people who read are boring, and 14 percent stated that they would spend little time reading when they grew up.

It is not surprising that those who do the most reading on their own are the most proficient readers (Anderson, Wilson, & Fielding, 1988; Applebee, Langer, & Mullis, 1988; Mullis, Campbell, & Farstrup, 1993). While it is true that better readers read more partly because reading is easier for them, Anderson, Wilson, and Fielding's (1988) analysis of data suggests a cause–effect relationship. Students are better readers because they read more.

The case for including children's books in a reading program is a compelling one. First, as just noted, those who read more, read better. Second, research suggests that students who read widely and are given some choice in what they read have a more favorable attitude toward reading (Cline & Kretke, 1980). In addition, all types of students—able readers, at-risk children, bilingual students—benefit from an approach that incorporates children's books. Based on their review of research, Tunnell and Jacobs (1989) concluded that programs using children's books achieve dramatic levels of success and are particularly effective with disabled and uninterested readers.

Reading First schools require and are charged with constructing "reading and library programs that provide student access to a wide array of engaging reading materials, including both expository and narrative texts" (U.S. Department of Education, 2002, p. 38).

Using children's books in the reading program not only leads to an opportunity for a greater enjoyment of reading but also builds skill in reading. In addition, allowing some self-selection should produce students who can and do read. To assist you in choosing or recommending books for your students, lists of appropriate books are presented throughout the text along with a description of several extensive lists of leveled books (see Chapter 2). Chapter 2 also describes a number of devices for leveling or assessing the difficulty level of books. Appendix A presents more than 1,200 titles listed by suggested grade level.

**2.** *Reading should be easy—but not too easy.* Think about it this way: If children find reading difficult, they will acquire a distaste for it and will simply stop reading except when they have to. Because of inadequate practice, they will fall farther behind, and their distaste and avoidance will grow. In addition, students will be unable to apply the strategies they have been taught, and learning will be hampered if the text is too difficult (Clay, 1993a). As Fry (1977a) put it years ago, make the match. Give students a book that they can handle with ease. Research by Berliner (1981) and Gambrell, Wilson, and Gantt (1981) suggested that students do best with reading materials in which no more than 2 to 5 percent of the words are difficult for them.

**3.** *Instruction should be functional and contextual.* Do not teach skills or strategies in isolation—teach a word-attack skill because students must have it to decipher words. For example, teach the prefix *pre-* just before the class reads a selection about prehistoric dinosaurs. Students learn better when what they are being taught has immediate value. Suggestions for lessons that are both functional and contextual are presented throughout this book.

**4.** *Make connections.* Build a bridge between children's experiences and what they are about to read. Help them see how what they know is related to the story or article. Students in Arizona reading about an ice hockey game may have no experience either playing or watching the sport. However, you could help create a bridge of understanding by discussing how hockey is similar to soccer, a sport with which they probably are familiar. You should also help students connect new concepts to old concepts. Relate reading, writing, listening, and speaking—they all build on each other. Reading and talking about humorous stories can expand students' concept of humor and remind them of funny things that have happened to them. They might then write about these events. Also build on what students know. This will make your teaching easier, since you will be starting at the students' level. It will also help students make a connection between what they know and what they are learning.

**5.** *Promote independence.* Whenever you teach a skill or strategy, ask yourself: How can I teach this so students will eventually use it on their own? How will students be called upon to use this skill or strategy in school and in the outside world? When you teach students how to summarize, make predictions, or use context, phonics, or another skill or strategy, teach so that there is a gradual release of responsibility (Pearson & Gallagher, 1983). Gradually fade your instruction and guidance so that students are applying the skill or strategy on their own. Do the same with the selection of reading materials. Although you may discuss ways of choosing books with the class, you ultimately want students to reach a point where they select their own books.

**6.** *Believe that all children can learn to read and write.* Given the right kind of instruction, virtually all children can learn to read. There is increasing evidence that the vast majority of children can learn to read at least on a basic level. Over the past two decades, research (Reading Recovery Council of North America, 2001) has shown that Reading Recovery, an intensive twelve- to twenty-week early intervention program, can raise the reading levels of about 82 percent of the lowest achievers to that of average achievers in a class. In the United States, Reading Recovery has been used in forty-nine states and has helped more than 700,000 students. Reading Recovery uses an inclusive model:

> It has been one of the surprises of Reading Recovery that all kinds of children with all kinds of difficulties can be included, can learn, and can reach average-band performance for their class in both reading and writing achievement. Exceptions are not made for children of lower intelligence, for second-language children, for children with low language skills, for children with poor motor coordination, for children who seem immature, for children who score poorly on readiness measures, or for children who have already been categorized by someone else as learning disabled. (Clay, 1991, p. 60)

Using highly trained teachers and one-on-one instruction, Reading Recovery is costly in terms of money and personnel. However, carefully planned, conscientiously implemented early intervention programs have also been shown to work with small groups of youngsters. Working with the lowest 20 percent of first-grade readers, teachers were able to raise the achievement of approximately 75 percent of the students to a level at which it was felt that they could function adequately in second grade (Hiebert & Taylor, 2000). Intervention programs are especially effective when systematic phonics is featured along with lots of reading and writing (Santa & Høien, 1999). An important aspect of these efforts is that supplementary assistance is complemented by a strong classroom program. These results demonstrate the power of effective instruction and the belief that all children can learn to read. Actually, a quality program will prevent most problems. A national committee charged with making recommendations to help prevent reading difficulties concluded, "Excellent instruction is the best intervention for children who demonstrate problems learning to read" (Snow, Burns, & Griffin, 1998, p. 33).

In virtually every elementary school classroom, there are a number of struggling readers and writers. Classroom teachers estimate that as many as one student out of four is reading more than one year below grade level (Baumann, Hoffman, Duffy-Hester, & Ro, 2000). Teachers also report that their greatest challenge is working with struggling readers. Fortunately, today's teachers have a strong commitment to helping struggling readers (Baumann, Hoffman, Duffy-Hester, & Ro, 2000). Although classroom teachers receive support from specialists, they usually bear the primary responsibility for helping struggling readers. Fortunately, however, all

**ADAPTING INSTRUCTION for *STRUGGLING READERS and WRITERS***
Classroom teachers are taking increased responsibility for helping struggling readers and writers. Suggestions for working with struggling readers and writers are made throughout the text.

of today's basal reading programs offer suggestions and materials for helping struggling readers.

Given the large number of struggling readers and writers in today's elementary schools, this text has numerous suggestions for helping these students and concludes each instructional chapter with a section entitled "Help for Struggling Readers and Writers," which discusses steps classroom teachers might take to help underachieving students.

**7.** *The literacy program should be goal oriented and systematic.* In keeping with the current concern for articulating and teaching to high standards, this text provides suggested grade-by-grade content standards for each of the major instructional areas: emergent literacy, phonics and other word analysis skills and strategies, vocabulary, comprehension, reading in the content areas, study skills, and writing. These objectives are presented at the end of each appropriate chapter in a panel entitled "Essential Standards."

**8.** *Build students' motivation and sense of competence.* Students perform at their best when they feel competent, view a task as being challenging but doable, understand why they are undertaking a task, are given choices, feel a part of the process, and have interesting materials and activities. For many students, working in a group fosters effort and persistence. Students also respond to knowledge of progress. They work harder when they see that they are improving, and they are also energized by praise from teachers, parents, and peers, especially when that praise is honest and specific (Schunk & Zimmerman, 1997; Sweet, 1997; Wigfield, 1997). The aim of a literacy program is to produce engaged readers and writers. Engaged readers and writers are motivated, are knowledgeable, and have mastered key strategies. They also do well when working with others (Guthrie & Wigfield, 1997).

**9.** *Ongoing assessment is an essential element in an effective literacy program.* Teachers need to know how students are progressing so they can give extra help or change the program, if necessary. Assessment need not be formal. Observation can be a powerful assessment tool. However, assessment should be tied in to the program's standards and should result in improvement in students' learning. In each chapter in which instructional objectives are stated, suggestions are made for assessing those objectives. Suggestions for assessment can also be found in annotations in the margins and in Chapter 2. In addition, there are several assessment instruments in Appendix B.

**10.** *Build students' language proficiency.* Reading and writing are language based. Students' reading levels are ultimately limited by their language development. Students can't understand what they are reading if they don't know what the words mean or get tangled up in the syntax of the piece. One of the best ways to build reading and writing potential is to foster language development. In study after study, knowledge of vocabulary has been found to be the key element in comprehension. Students' listening level has also been found to be closely related to students' reading level. The level of material that a student can understand orally is a good gauge of the level that a student can read with understanding. While fostering language development is important for all students, it is absolutely essential for students who are learning English as a second language.

# HIGHLY EFFECTIVE TEACHERS

In the 1960s the U.S. Department of Education spent millions of dollars in an attempt to find out which method of teaching reading was the best (Bond & Dykstra, 1967; Graves & Dykstra, 1997). More than a dozen approaches were studied. There was no clear winner. No one method was superior in all circumstances. What the researchers did find was that the teacher was key. Teachers using the same methods got differing results. Some teachers were simply more effective than others.

What are the characteristics of effective teachers? Over the past decade, a number of top researchers have visited the classes of teachers judged to be highly effective. Their students read more books and wrote more stories. Virtually all read on or above grade level. Their writing skills were surprisingly advanced. They also enjoyed school. On many occasions observers watched in surprise as students skipped recess so they could continue working on an activity. Their work was more appealing to them than play.

## Caring and High Expectations

Perhaps the most outstanding characteristic of highly effective teachers is that they cared for their students and believed in them (Pressley, Allington, Wharton-McDonald, Block, & Morrow, 2001). They were genuinely convinced that their students could and would learn and acted accordingly. In writing, for instance, typical first-grade teachers believed that writing was difficult for young students and expected their students would be able only to produce pieces of writing composed of a sentence or two by year's end (Wharton-McDonald, 2001). Their expectations were discouragingly accurate. By year's end most students in their classes were producing narratives that consisted of one to three loosely connected sentences with little attention to punctuation or capitalization.

Highly effective teachers had higher expectations. They believed that first-graders were capable of sustained writing. By year's end they expected a coherent paragraph that consisted of five or even more sentences, each of which started with a capital letter and ended with a period. And that's the kind of writing their students produced. Students have a way of living up to or down to teachers' expectations.

However, the highly effective teachers realized that high expectations are in the same category as good intentions; they need to be acted upon. High expectations were accompanied by the kind of instruction that allowed students to live up to the high expectations. Highly effective teachers were also superior motivators. The teachers created a feeling of excitement about the subject matter or skill areas they teach (Ruddell, 1995).

## Balanced Instruction

As students evidenced a need for instruction, teachers were quick to conduct a mini-lesson. A student attempting to spell *boat*, for instance, would be given an on-the-spot lesson on the *oa* spelling of long *o*. However, essential skills were not relegated to opportunistic teaching. Key skills were taught directly and thoroughly but were related to the reading and writing that students were doing

## Extensive Instruction

Effective teachers used every opportunity to reinforce skills. Wherever possible connections were made between reading and writing and between reading and writing and content area concepts. Often students would develop or apply science and social studies concepts in their writing.

## Scaffolding

Exemplary teachers scaffold students' responses. Instead of simply telling students answers, teachers use prompts and other devices to help students reason their way to the correct response.

## Classroom Management

Highly effective teachers were well organized. Routines were well established and highly effective. The core of their management was building in students a sense of responsibility. Students learned to regulate their own behavior. One of the things that stood out in the rooms of highly effective classes was the sense of purpose and orderliness. There was a 90–90 rule: 90 percent of the students were engaged in productive activity 90 percent of the time. The greatest proportion of time was spent with high-payoff activities. When students composed illustrated booklets, for instance, the bulk of their time was spent researching and composing the booklets. Only a minimum of time was spent illustrating them.

Students learned how to work together. The classroom atmosphere was one of cooperation rather than competition. Effort was emphasized. Praise and reinforcement were used as appropriate. Students were also taught to be competent, independent learners. They were taught strategies for selecting appropriate level books and for decoding unfamiliar words and for understanding difficult text. Their efforts were affirmed, so that they would be encouraged to continue using strategies. "Jonathan, I liked the way you previewed that book before selecting it to read. Now you have a better idea of what it is about and whether it is a just-right book for you."

## High-Quality Materials

The best teachers used the best materials. Students listened to and read classics as well as outstanding contemporary works from children's literature. There was a decided emphasis on reading. Classrooms were well stocked with materials, and time was set aside for various kinds of reading: shared, partner, and individual.

## Matching of Materials and Tasks to Student Competence

Highly effective teachers gave students materials and tasks that were somewhat challenging but not overwhelming. Teachers carefully monitored students and made assignments on the basis of students' performance. If the book students were reading seemed to have too many difficult words and concepts, students were given an easier book. If they mastered writing a brief paragraph, they were encouraged to write a more fully developed piece. However, they were provided with the assistance and instruction needed to cope with more challenging tasks.

## Becoming a Highly Effective Teacher

How did highly effective teachers get that way? They worked at it (Day, 2001). They were always seeking better techniques and better materials. To sustain their desire for improvement, they kept up with developments in the field through reading, taking courses, attending workshops and inservices, and reading the professional literature. They also reflected on their teaching and sought the advice of colleagues. When a technique failed to work or materials seemed too hard, they were quick to recognize this and quick to seek a better approach or more effective materials. They looked at new methods and materials in the light of students' needs:

> Exemplary teachers believe that excellent teaching consists of observing and understanding student perspectives on what they are learning, and examining materials in light of how well they fit with a particular child's needs. Rather than promote a method or program for its own sake, they look at it in the light of the specific children in front of them and whether it would be better or worse in meeting a need. (Day, 2001, p. 217)

Although a great variety of topics will be covered in later chapters, the ten primary principles discussed above are emphasized throughout. Teaching suggestions and activities are included for fostering wide reading, keeping reading reasonably easy, keeping reading and writing functional, making connections, setting goals and assessing progress, and, above all, building a sense of competence and promoting independence. This book is based on the premise that virtually all children can learn to read and write.

### ACTION PLAN

1. Construct a personal philosophy of teaching literacy. Note the effects that your philosophy of teaching literacy would have on your approach to teaching, your assessment methods, grouping practices, and choice of learning activities and materials.

2. Create a plan for becoming an effective teacher. What steps will you take to create a high quality program and to continue to develop your ability to teach literacy?

## SUMMARY

1. Reading is an active process in which the reader constructs meaning from text. The school should build on the language and literacy skills that the child has learned at home.

2. In Vygotsky's view, social interaction is an important factor in children's cognitive and language development. More knowledgeable others can help students operate on a higher level of development.

3. Living as we do in a pluralistic society, it is important for the school to build on the literacy activities that are prominent in students' cultures.

4. The type of reading being done can help determine whether the reader takes primarily an efferent or an aesthetic stance.

5. Reading can be viewed as holistic, which is a top-down approach. Reading can also be viewed as composed of a number of subskills, which is a bottom-up approach. A third approach is to describe reading as a balanced interaction between top-down and bottom-up processes, which is the position that this book takes. Interactionists emphasize cognitive strategies rather than subskills, which tend to fragment the process. It is important for teachers to explore their personal beliefs about reading and writing instruction so that they can implement programs rooted in their beliefs and consistent with their philosophies.

6. By creating clear expectations for students and teachers, the standards movement is designed to improve the reading and writing performance of all students, but especially those who are struggling. Although it is bringing additional resources to struggling readers, the standards movement has been criticized because it may lead to teaching to standards-based tests and result in the neglect of important literacy skills.

7. Widespread reading and functional instruction commensurate with children's abilities are essentials of an effective reading program. Also necessary is instruction that helps students make connections and fosters independence. Believing that virtually every child can learn to read and building students' motivation and sense of competence are important factors in an effective literacy program, as are setting goals; systematic, direct instruction; ongoing assessment, and building student's language proficiency. However, a highly effective teacher is the key to effective instruction.

## EXTENDING AND APPLYING

1. Analyze your beliefs about teaching reading. Make a list of your major beliefs. Are you a top-downer, a bottom-upper, or an interactionist? Now make a list of your major teaching and reinforcement activities. Do they fit your philosophy? If not, what changes might you make?

2. To find out more about the thinking behind setting literacy goals for students in kindergarten through grade three, read the joint position statement issued by the International Reading Association and the National Association for the Education of Young Children, which can be found in *Young Children*, July 1998, pp. 30–45 and *The Reading Teacher*, October 1998, pp. 193–214.

3. Find out what your state's literacy goals or standards are. Most state departments of education list this information on their Web sites. If so, what are they? How are they assessed?

4. Analyze your activities as you teach a reading lesson or observe a class being taught. Classify the instructional activities as being top down, bottom up, or interactive. Also, note the reactions of the students to the activities. Do they find them interesting? Do they seem to be learning from them?

## DEVELOPING A PROFESSIONAL PORTFOLIO

Many school systems require applicants to submit a portfolio. Some also require new teachers to complete portfolios as part of the evaluation process. Even if a portfolio is not required in your situation, creating and maintaining one provides you with the opportunity to reflect on your ideas about teaching and your teaching practices. It will help you get to know yourself better as a teacher and so provide a basis for improvement. To assist you in creating a portfolio, each chapter will contain suggestions for working on your portfolio.

Set up a professional portfolio. The portfolio should highlight your professional preparation, relevant experience, and mastery of key teaching skills. Using the list compiled in Item 1 of Extending and Applying, draw up a statement of your philosophy of teaching reading and writing.

## DEVELOPING A RESOURCE FILE

As you read about various teaching and assessment procedures in the text, collect resources that will help you implement the procedures and assessments. The resources might be a list of books for reading out loud or a list of Web sites for developing vocabulary. For this chapter, you might collect articles that have helpful suggestions for setting up a literacy program.

2

# Evaluation

## ANTICIPATION GUIDE

*F*or each of the following statements related to the chapter you are about to read, put a check under "Agree" or "Disagree" to show how you feel. Discuss your responses with classmates before you read the chapter.

|  |  | *Agree* | *Disagree* |
|---|---|---|---|
| **1** | Nationwide achievement tests are essential for the assessment of literacy. | _____ | _____ |
| **2** | Setting high standards and assessing student achievement on those standards is a good way to improve the quality of reading and writing instruction. | _____ | _____ |
| **3** | Most writing assessments are too subjective. | _____ | _____ |
| **4** | Today's students take too many tests. | _____ | _____ |
| **5** | The community has a right to know how its schools are doing. | _____ | _____ |
| **6** | Observation yields more about a student's progress in reading and writing than a standardized test does. | _____ | _____ |

## USING WHAT YOU KNOW

*E*valuation is an essential part of literacy learning. It is a judgment by teachers, children, parents, administrators, and the wider community as to whether instructional goals have been met. Evaluation also helps teachers determine what is and what is not working so that they can plan better programs. Self-evaluation gives students more control over their own learning.

What kinds of experiences have you had with evaluation? How has your school work been assessed? Do you agree with the assessments, or do you think they were off the mark? Keeping in mind the current emphasis on balanced reading and writing processes and integration of language arts, what might be some appropriate ways to evaluate the literacy development of today's students?

## THE NATURE OF EVALUATION

■ **Evaluation** is the process of using the results of tests, observations, work samples, and other devices to judge the effectiveness of a program. A program is evaluated in terms of its objectives. The ultimate purpose of evaluation is to improve the program.

In evaluation, we ask, "How am I doing?" so that we can do better. **Evaluation** is a value judgment. We can also ask, "How is the education program doing?" and base our evaluation on tests, quizzes, records, work samples, observations, anecdotal records, portfolios, and similar information. The evaluation could be made by a student while reviewing her or his writing folder or by parents as they look over a report card. The evaluator could be a teacher, who, after examining a portfolio or collection of a student's work and thinking over recent observations of that student, concludes that the student has done well but could do better.

Evaluation should result in some kind of action. The evaluator must determine what that action should be, based on her judgment. The student may decide that he has been writing the same type of pieces and needs to branch out, the parents might decide that their child must study more, and the teacher might choose to add more silent reading time to the program.

### The Starting Point

Evaluation starts with a set of goals. You cannot tell if you have reached your destination if you do not know where you were headed. For example, a teacher may decide that one of her goals will be to instill in children a love of reading. This is a worthy goal, but it is lacking in many programs. How will the teacher decide whether the goal has been reached, and what will the teacher use as evidence? The goal has to be stated in terms of a specific objective that includes, if possible, observable behavior—for example, students will voluntarily read at least twenty minutes a day or at least one book a month. The objective then becomes measurable, and the teacher can collect information that will provide evidence as to whether it has been met.

■ **Standards** are statements of what students should know and be able to do.

▌A composite set of standards is available from the Mid-Central Regional Educational Laboratory (MCREL, 2001). *Content standards and benchmarks for K–12 education.* Available online at **http:// www.mcrel.org/ standards-benchmarks/.** Composite goals are also available from New Standards (National Center on Education and the Economy & The University of Pittsburgh, 1997).

### The Standards Movement

The centerpiece of the standards movement is also the statement of goals or objectives. The **standards** movement grew out of concern for the quality of education in the United States. A National Goals Panel was convened in the late 1980s. A set of broad goals was established. These have now been translated into standards, which are a set of objectives, for every discipline, including reading and writing. The idea behind the standards is that clearly stated objectives should lead to improved instruction, especially if assessment is closely tied to the standards and if there are adequate instructional resources for helping students meet standards.

State standards are available at state departments of education. Key standards are listed as Essential Standards throughout the text in each of the instructional chapters. Ultimately, national and state standards have to be translated, adapted, and revised so that they fit the needs of your students.

Along with standards have come assessment devices for measuring students' progress toward meeting those standards. In many instances, these include a high-stakes test.

## High-Stakes Testing

In 1999, the Board of Directors of the International Reading Association announced its opposition to high-stakes testing. As its name suggests, a **high-stakes test** is one in which an important decision will be based on the outcome of a single test. The decision might be whether the student passes or fails or is placed in a special program. In many areas high-stakes testing begins in kindergarten. Kindergartners who don't know the letters of the aphabet, can't detect rhyme, or are not able to read a list of high-frequency words are retained. The IRA is not opposed to assessment or testing. It is opposed to making critical decisions based on a single test. It is also opposed to the undue influence that high-stakes testing may have on what is taught in the schools.

Instead of being used to assess how well students are doing and providing information for program improvement, high-stakes tests have the potential to dictate curriculum. Instead of teaching what their community has judged to be important, educators might teach what is tested. This has the effect of narrowing the curriculum. Knowing, for instance, that students will be tested on narrative writing in the fourth grade, teachers in the early grades over-emphasize story writing and neglect expository writing. A great deal of time is also spent writing to a prompt because that is the way students will be assessed on the state tests. To combat the misuse of tests, the International Reading Association has made the following recommendations:

Teachers should

- construct rigorous classroom assessments to help outside observers gain confidence in teacher techniques.
- educate parents, community members, and policy makers about classroom-based assessment.
- teach students how tests are structured, but not teach to the test.

Properly implemented, the standards should result in greater learning, especially among those who have underachieved in the past. An essential component of evaluation is improvement of the instructional program. Once strengths and weaknesses are noted, steps should be taken to build on the strengths and repair the weak spots.

## Three Perspectives of Evaluation

Evaluation has three perspectives: self, collaborative others, and society (Short, 1990). The self is the student. The collaborative others are all those who work with the child, including the teacher, peer editor, learning team, and discussion groups. Society

> ■ A **high-stakes test** is one in which the results are used to make important decisions such as passing students, graduating students, or rating a school.

> ▍High-stakes assessment is especially controversial at the early levels. The National Educational Goals Panel (NEGP, 1998) advises against using standardized tests to make high-stakes accountability decisions before grades three or four. Clay (1993a) suggests that students be immersed in school for at least a year before being assessed for intervention. Some children may have had minimal exposure to reading and writing activities. It would be erroneous to assume that these children have difficulty learning (Johnston & Rogers, 2001). A better course of action is to give them the opportunity to learn and see how they do.

includes the parents, the community at large, and officials of the school or school district. Each group may have a different purpose for evaluating and may require different types of evidence. The school board, for instance, may want information on how the students in the district are doing as compared with students in other districts; students may note that they are not doing well on science and social studies tests; and teachers may observe that students are having difficulty applying comprehension strategies to expository text. The students and teacher are using information as cues to improving students' immediate performance. The school board is more concerned with how the district's students are performing as compared with similar schools or how the performance of this year's students compares to that of past students or whether standards are being met.

Because students, teachers, parents, and school boards have differing perspectives, they need different kinds of evaluation information. Although results of norm-referenced tests are frequently used by school boards and state departments of education as a basis for evaluation, they have limited usefulness for teachers. **Norm-referenced tests** rank students' performance by comparing them to a representative sample of students—the norm group—who took the test. Authentic measures are more helpful because they provide insight into students' learning strategies.

## Authentic Assessment

■ **Norm-referenced tests** are ones in which students are compared with a representative sample of students who are the same age or are in the same grade.

■ **Assessment** is the process of gathering data about an area of learning through tests, observations, work samples, or other means.

■ **Authentic assessment** involves using tasks that are typical of the kinds of reading or writing that students perform in school and out.

Changing views of reading and writing have created a need for alternative methods of **assessment.** Alternative forms of assessment are often called **authentic assessment.** The word *authentic* is used because these assessment procedures "reflect the actual learning and instructional activities of the classroom and out-of-school worlds" (Hiebert, Valencia, & Afflerbach, 1994, p. 11). In authentic assessment, students retell or summarize whole texts, as opposed to the kind of objective testing in which students respond to multiple-choice questions asked about short paragraphs. Observations, think-alouds, holistic scoring of writing, anecdotal records, and assembling and evaluating a portfolio are also examples of authentic assessment. Even large-scale assessments are becoming more authentic. Many state and national assessments now use longer passages and ask for constructed responses in which students respond in writing.

## Product versus Process Measures

Authentic assessment emphasizes process rather than product. Product assessment is concerned with what the student has learned. Process assessment seeks to find out how the student learns. Product measures are the number of correct answers on a quiz, the score on a norm-referenced test, the final copy of a composition, or the number of books read. They help teachers assess students' current and past levels of achievement. They provide information on students' reading and writing levels and abilities, the kinds of materials they can read, the kinds of writing they can do, and how well they can spell. Knowing where each student is, the teacher can plan instruction and activities that build on what students have already accomplished.

*O*bservations often reveal more information about students' progress than do traditional paper-and-pencil tests.

Process measures include observing students to see what strategies they use to arrive at a particular answer, to compose a piece of writing, or to study for a test. These measures seek to answer such questions as How do students prepare to read an assignment? Do they reread or use some other strategy when the material they are reading doesn't make sense? Do students select, organize, and elaborate information as they read? If so, how? Having this kind of insight, the teacher is able to redirect errant thought processes, correct poorly applied strategies, or teach needed strategies. Actually, both process and product measures provide useful information. Knowing where a child is and how he or she got there, the teacher is better prepared to map out a successful journey.

# JUDGING ASSESSMENT MEASURES

## Reliability

To be useful, tests and other assessment instruments must be both reliable and valid. **Reliability** is a measure of consistency, which means that if the same test were given to the same students a number of times, the results would be approximately the same. Reliability is usually reported as a coefficient of correlation and ranges from 0.00 to 0.99 or –0.01 to –0.99. The higher the positive correlation, the more reliable the test. For tests on which individual decisions are being based, reliability should be in the 0.90s.

Reliability can also be thought of as generalizability. In observations and other informal approaches to assessment, it means that similar findings have been found by different judges and at different times (Johnston & Rogers, 2001). One way of increasing reliability is by training observers. Another is to have several observations.

■ **Reliability** is the degree to which a test yields consistent results. In other words, if you took the test again, your score would be approximately the same.

A test that is not reliable is of no value. It is the equivalent of an elastic yardstick—the results of measurement would be different each time.

## Validity

In general, **validity** means that a test measures what it says it measures: vocabulary knowledge or speed of reading, for instance. Ultimately, it means that a particular test will provide the information needed to make a decision, such as placing a student with an appropriate level book or indicating specific strengths and weaknesses in comprehension (Farr & Carey, 1986). Johnston and Rogers (2001) contend that unless an assessment practice helps to improve students' learning, it should not occur. Reading tests need content validity, meaning that skills and strategies tested must be the same as those taught. Calfee and Hiebert (1991) define validity with the following question: "Does assessment match what I have taught and the way I have taught it?" (p. 282).

To check for **content validity,** list the objectives of the program and note how closely a particular test's objectives match them. The test selections should be examined, too, to see whether they reflect the type of material that the students read. Also, determine how reading is tested. If a test assesses skills or strategies that you do not cover or assesses them in a way that is not suitable, the test is not valid for your class.

Reading First and some other government programs require assessment measures that have concurrent and predictive validity. Concurrent validity means that an assessment measure correlates with a similar test or other criteria given or occurring at about the same time. Predictive validity means that there is a correlation between the assessment measure and some future behavior. This could be a correlation between phonological awareness in kindergarten and reading comprehension in third grade.

Closely tied to validity are the consequences or uses to which the assessment will be put. If the test assesses only a narrow part of the curriculum, it will be detrimental and thus invalid (Joint Task Force on Assessment, 1994). Assessment measures should also be fair to all who take them. There should be no biased items, and the content should be such that all students have had an equal opportunity to learn it.

## Questions to Be Asked

Essentially, evaluation is the process of asking a series of questions. Specific questions depend on a program's particular goals and objectives. However, some general questions that should be asked about every literacy program include the following:

- Where are students in their literacy development?
- At what level are they reading?
- Are they reading up to their ability level?
- How well do they comprehend what they read?

Whether assessment is formal or informal, through observation or paper-and-pencil testing, reliability is essential. As Farr (1991) observes, "If a test or other means of assessment is not reliable, it's no good. . . . If you stand on the bathroom scale and it registers 132 lbs. one morning, but it's 147 the next morning, and 85 the morning after that, you conclude it's time for a new set of bathroom scales. . . ." (p. 4).

■ **Validity** is the degree to which a test measures what it is supposed to measure, or the extent to which a test will provide information needed to make a decision. Validity should be considered in terms of the consequences of the test results and the use to which the test results will be put.

■ **Content validity** means that the tasks of an assessment device are representative of the subject or area being assessed.

One danger in evaluation is the temptation to gather too much information. Be economical. Do not waste time gathering information you are not going to use.

- How adequate are students' reading vocabularies?
- What comprehension and word-analysis strategies do students use?
- What is the level of students' language development?
- What are their attitudes toward reading?
- Do they enjoy a variety of genres?
- Do they read on their own?
- How well do they write?
- What kinds of writing tasks have they attempted?
- Are students' reading and writing improving?
- Which students seem to have special needs in reading and writing?
- Are these special needs being met?

Answers to these essential questions help teachers plan, revise, and improve their reading and writing programs. The rest of this chapter explores a number of techniques for gathering the assessment information necessary to answer them. Both traditional and alternative means will be used.

#  PLACEMENT INFORMATION

The first question the classroom teacher of reading has to have answered is Where are the students? If they are reading, assessment begins with determining the levels at which they are reading. One of the best placement devices is an **informal reading inventory (IRI).** In fact, if properly given, it will tell just about everything a teacher needs to know about a student's reading. It will also supply useful information about language development, work habits, interests, and personal development.

## Informal Reading Inventory

An informal reading inventory is a series of graded selections beginning at the very easiest level—preprimer—and extending up to eighth grade or beyond. Each level has two selections; one is silent and the other oral. Starting at an easy level, the student continues to read until it is obvious that the material has become too difficult.

An IRI yields information about four levels: independent, instructional, frustration, and listening capacity. The **independent level,** or the free-reading level, is the point at which students can read on their own without teacher assistance. The **instructional level** refers to the point at which students need assistance because the material contains too many unknown words or concepts or their background of experience is insufficient. This is also the level of materials used for teaching. Material at the **frustration level** is so difficult that students cannot read it even with teacher assistance. The fourth level is listening capacity, the highest level at which students can understand what has been read to them. **Listening capacity** is an informal measure of ability to comprehend spoken language. Theoretically, it

---

If students are not yet reading, they can be given an emergent literacy assessment as explained in Chapter 3.

■ An **informal reading inventory (IRI)** is an assessment device in which a student reads a series of selections that gradually increase in difficulty. The teacher records errors and assesses comprehension in order to determine levels of materials that a student can read.

■ The **independent level** is the level at which a student can read without any assistance. Comprehension is 90 percent or higher and word recognition is 99 percent or higher.

■ The **instructional level** is the level at which a student needs teacher help. Comprehension is 75 percent or higher and word recognition is 95 percent or higher.

■ The **frustration level** is the level at which reading material is so difficult that the student can't read it even with help. Frustration is reached when either word recognition is 90 percent or lower or comprehension is 50 percent or lower.

■ **Listening capacity** is the highest level at which students can understand material that is read to them with 75 percent comprehension.

is the level at which students should be able to read if they have all the necessary decoding skills. In practice, a small percentage of students have listening deficiencies, so a listening test might underestimate their true capacity. Younger students also tend to read below capacity because they are still acquiring basic reading skills. As students progress through the grades, listening and reading levels grow closer together (Sticht & James, 1984).

The first informal reading inventories were constructed by teachers and were created using passages from basal readers. This was a good idea because it meant that there was an exact match between the material the student was tested on and the material the student would be reading. Because constructing informal reading inventories is time consuming, most teachers now use commercially produced informal reading inventories. (See Table 2.1.) However, informal reading inventories are available for basal reading programs.

Informal reading inventories can also be geared to children's books. If, for instance, your program emphasizes the reading of children's books, you might designate certain titles as benchmark books and construct questions or retelling activities based on these books. Benchmark books can be used to place students and check their

**TABLE 2.1** Commercial reading inventories

| Name | Publisher | Grades | Added Skill Areas |
|------|-----------|--------|-------------------|
| Bader Reading and Language Inventory | Merrill | 1–12 | phonics, language, spelling, emergent literacy |
| Basic Reading Inventory | Kendall/Hunt | 1–8 | emergent literacy |
| Classroom Reading Inventory | McGraw-Hill | 1–8 | spelling |
| Ekwall/Shanker Reading Inventory | Allyn & Bacon | 1–12 | emergent literacy, word analysis, reading interests |
| English-Español Reading Inventory for the Classroom | Prentice Hall | 1–12 | emergent literacy (has an English-only version) |
| Informal Reading Thinking Inventory | Harcourt | 1–11 | |
| Qualitative Reading Inventory III | Longman | 1–12 | |
| Spanish Reading Inventory | Kendall/Hunt | 1–4 | |
| Stieglitz Informal Reading Inventory | Allyn & Bacon | 1–8 | emergent literacy |
| Texas Primary Reading Inventory | Texas Education Agency | K–3 | emergent literacy, phonics (varies with grade level) (has a Spanish version) |

progress. Sets of benchmark books and accompanying questions are available from basal reader publishers. Or you can construct your own. This chapter lists benchmark books that can be used to judge the difficulty level of children's books. These books can also be used as the basis for an informal reading inventory.

## ■ Determining Placement Levels

Placement levels are determined by having students read two selections, one orally and one silently, at appropriate grade levels. The percentages of oral-reading errors and comprehension questions answered correctly at each level are calculated. This information is then used to determine placement levels. Quantitative data for determining levels are contained in Table 2.2.

To be at the independent level, a reader must have both 99 percent word recognition and 90 percent comprehension. At the instructional level, the reader must have at least 95 percent word recognition and at least 75 percent comprehension. The frustration level is reached when word recognition drops to 90 percent or comprehension falls to 50 percent. Even with 80 percent comprehension and 90 percent word recognition, readers are at the frustration level because they are encountering too many words that they cannot decode. Listening capacity is the level at which students can understand 75 percent of the material that is read to them.

Running records and some other placement devices use lower standards, such as 90 to 95 percent word recognition. It is strongly advised that you stick to the 95 to 98 percent word recognition standard. Research indicates that students do best when they can read at least 95 to 98 percent of the words (Berliner, 1981; Biemiller, 1994; Gambrell, Wilson, & Gantt, 1981). It is also important that the examiner adhere to strict standards when marking word reading errors. Enz (1989) found that relaxing IRI standards resulted in a drop in both achievement and attitude. Students placed according to higher standards spent a greater proportion of time on task, had a higher success rate, and had a more positive attitude toward reading.

## ■ Administering the Word-List Test

Rather than guessing at which grade level to begin the inventory, a teacher can administer a word-list test to locate an approximate starting point. This test consists of a series of ten to twenty words at each grade level. Students read the words in isolation, starting with the easiest and continuing until they reach a level where

The listening portion of the inventory provides only an approximate indication of children's capacity. It would tend to be inaccurate with youngsters who have difficulty paying attention or who lack good listening skills or who are still learning English.

Standards for determining levels, marking symbols, types of misreadings that are counted as errors, and administration procedures vary, depending on the source consulted. The standards used in this book are taken from Johnson, Kress, and Pikulski (1987) and seem to be the most widely used.

**TABLE 2.2** Quantitative criteria for IRI

| Level | Word Recognition in Context (%) | Average Comprehension (%) |
|---|---|---|
| Independent | 99 | 90–100 |
| Instructional | 95–98 | 75–89 |
| Frustration | ≤90 | ≤50 |
| Listening capacity | | 75 |

Increasingly, classroom teachers are administering informal reading inventories. The *Classroom Reading Inventory* (Silvaroli & Wheelock, 2001), which is a streamlined inventory, was specifically designed to be given by classroom teachers and takes approximately twelve minutes to administer.

they get half or more of the words wrong. In a simplified administration of the test, students read the words from their copy of the list and the teacher marks each response on her or his copy as being right or wrong.

In a diagnostic administration, the teacher uses three-by-five cards to flash the words for one second each. When students respond correctly, the teacher moves on to the next word. If the answer is incorrect or if students fail to respond, the teacher stops and lets them look at the word for as long as they wish (within reason). While students examine the missed word, the teacher writes down their response or marks a symbol in the flash (timed) column. If students make a second erroneous response, it is written in the second, or untimed, column. Symbols used to mark word-list tests are presented in Table 2.3. A corrected word-list test is shown in Figure 2.1.

Although used to indicate the starting level for the IRI, a word-list test can yield valuable information about students' reading, especially if a diagnostic administration has been used. By comparing flash and untimed scores, teachers can assess the adequacy of students' sight vocabulary (their ability to recognize words immediately) and their proficiency with decoding. Teachers can note which decoding skills students are able to use and which must be taught. Looking at the performance depicted in Figure 2.1, it is clear that the student has a very limited sight vocabulary. The flash column shows that the student recognized few of the words immediately; the untimed column gives an overall picture of the student's ability to apply decoding skills. The student was able to use initial and final consonants and short vowels to decode words; for example, the student was able to read *wet, king, let,* and *bit* when given time to decode them. However, the student had difficulty with initial clusters; note how the student read *sick* for *stick, sell* for *smell,* and *for* for *floor.*

### ■ Administering the Inventory

The informal reading inventory is started at the level below the student's last perfect performance on the flash portion of the word-list test. If that perfect performance was at the fourth-grade level, the inventory is started at the third-grade level.

An IRI is like a directed reading lesson, except that its main purpose is to assess a student's reading. To administer an IRI, first explain to the student that she will be reading some stories and answering some questions so that you can get

| **TABLE 2.3** | Word-list marking symbols | |
|---|---|---|
| **Word** | **Teacher Mark** | **Meaning** |
| the | ✓ | Correct |
| was | ✓' | Incorrect response or repeated error |
| have | *o* | No response |
| dog | *boy* | Mispronunciation |
| are | *dk* | Don't know |

some information about her reading. Before each selection is read, have the student read its title and predict what it will be about (Johns, 1997). Doing this will help the student set a purpose for reading, and it will give you a sense of the student's prediction ability and background of experience.

The student reads the first selection orally. This is one of the few times in which reading orally without having first read the selection silently is valid. As the student reads, use the symbols shown in Table 2.4 to record her performance. Although many different kinds of misreadings are noted, only the following are counted as errors or **miscues:** mispronunciations, omissions, insertions, and words supplied by the examiner because the student asked the examiner to read them or apparently could not read them on her own. Self-corrected errors are not counted. Hesitations, repetitions, and other qualitative misreadings are noted but not counted as errors. A corrected inventory selection is shown in Figure 2.2.

After the student finishes reading aloud, ask the series of comprehension questions that accompany the selection or ask for an oral retelling (see pp. 51–52 for information on administering a retelling). Then, introduce a silent selection on the same level. Just as with the oral selection, allow a very brief preparation phase and have the student make a prediction. During the silent reading, note finger pointing, head movement, lip movement, and subvocalizing. Symbols for these behaviors are given in Table 2.5. Ask comprehension questions when the student finishes reading. Proceeding level by level, continue to test until the student reaches a frustration level—that is, misreads 10 percent or more of the words or misses at least half the comprehension questions.

When the frustration level has been reached, read to the student the oral and silent selections at each level beyond the frustration level until the student reaches the highest level at which she or he can answer 75 percent of the comprehension questions. This is the student's listening capacity, and it indicates how well the student would be able to read if she or he had the necessary word-recognition skills and related print-processing skills. For children who have limited language skills or background of experience or deficient listening skills, you may have to backtrack and read selections at the frustration level and below. Because students will

## FIGURE 2.1

### A Corrected Word-List Test

| | | Flash | Untimed |
|---|---|---|---|
| 1. | their | *the* | ✓ |
| 2. | wet | *o* | ✓ |
| 3. | king | *o* | ✓ |
| 4. | off | *o* | *dk* |
| 5. | alone | *uh* | *along* |
| 6. | hurt | ✓ | |
| 7. | near | ✓ | |
| 8. | tiger | *tie* | ✓ |
| 9. | stick | *sick* | ✓' |
| 10. | move | *moo* | *more* |
| 11. | let | *o* | ✓ |
| 12. | men | ✓ | |
| 13. | shoe | *o* | ✓ |
| 14. | wish | ✓ | |
| 15. | apple | *o* | *dk* |
| 16. | on | *o* | ✓ |
| 17. | sign | *o* | *o* |
| 18. | bit | *o* | ✓ |
| 19. | smell | *sell* | ✓' |
| 20. | floor | *for* | ✓' |
| Percent correct | | 20% | 60% |

■ A **miscue** is an oral reading response that differs from the expected (correct) response. The term *miscue* is used because miscue theory holds that errors are not random but are the attempts of the reader to make sense of the text.

| TABLE 2.4 | Oral-reading symbols | |
|---|---|---|
| | **Marking** | **Meaning** |
| **Quantitative errors** | the big̶ dog *(bad above big)* | Mispronounced |
| | the ̶b̶i̶g̶ dog | Omitted word |
| | the (ferocious) dog | Asked for word |
| | the big ∧ dog *(bad above)* | Inserted word |
| **Self-correction** | the b̶i̶g̶ dog *(bad✓ above)* | Self-corrected |
| **Qualitative errors** | I hit the ball⊗ and George ran. | Omitted punctuation |
| | The \|\|ferocious dog | Hesitation |
| | <u>the ferocious dog</u> | Repetition |
| | Good morning! ↑ | Rising inflection |
| | Are you reading? ↓ | Falling inflection |
| | W x W | Word-by-word reading |
| | HM | Head movement |
| | FP | Finger pointing |
| | PC | Use of picture clue |

already have been exposed to the lower-level selections, you will have to use alternative selections to test listening comprehension.

After administering the inventory, enter the scores from each level on the inventory's summary sheet (see Figure 2.3). Word-recognition scores are determined by calculating the percentage of words read correctly on each oral selection (number of words read correctly divided by number of words in the selection). If the student made 5 miscues in a 103 word selection, the word-recognition score would be 98/103 = 95.1 percent.

Comprehension is calculated by averaging comprehension scores for the oral and silent selections at each level. Using the numbers on the summary sheet, determine the placement levels. Refer to the criteria in Table 2.2.

### ■ Interpreting the Inventory

After determining the student's levels, examine her or his performance on the inventory to determine word-recognition and comprehension strengths and weaknesses. What kinds of phonics skills can the student use? Is the student able to decode multisyllabic words? Could the student read words that have prefixes or suffixes? Did the student use context? Did the student integrate the use of decoding skills

▌Some inventories recommend counting all miscues as errors. Others suggest counting only those that disrupt the meaning or flow of the passage. It is easier and quicker to count all misreadings but to make note of whether or not they fit the sense of the passage. Deciding whether a miscue is significant is subjective. If standards are too lenient, the student being assessed may end up being placed with a text that is too difficult.

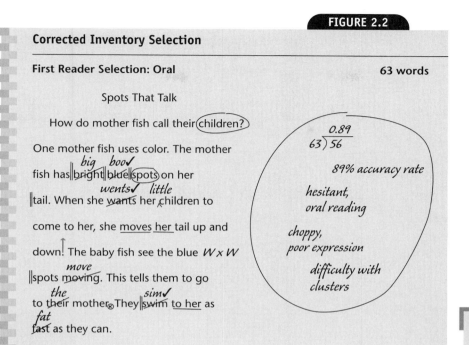

**FIGURE 2.2**

**Corrected Inventory Selection**

**First Reader Selection: Oral**                                      **63 words**

Spots That Talk

How do mother fish call their children?

One mother fish uses color. The mother

fish has bright blue spots on her *big boo✓*

tail. When she wants her children to *wents✓ little*

come to her, she moves her tail up and

down! The baby fish see the blue W x W

spots moving. This tells them to go *move*

to their mother. They swim to her as *the* *sim✓*

fast as they can. *fat*

0.89
63)56

89% accuracy rate

*hesitant,*
*oral reading*

*choppy,*
*poor expression*

*difficulty with*
*clusters*

with context? How did the student's word recognition compare with her or his comprehension? How did the student handle literal and inferential questions? How did comprehension on oral passages compare with comprehension on silent passages? You can also note the quality of the student's responses as she or he answered questions and the way the student approached the tasks. What level of language did the student use to answer questions? What was the student's level of confidence and effort as she or he undertook each task? Through careful observation, you can gain insight into the student's reading processes. For example, you may observe the student decoding unfamiliar words sound by sound or using a combination of context and phonics to handle difficult words. Strengths and weaknesses as well as immediate needs can be noted on the IRI summary sheet.

### ■ Miscue Analysis of IRIs

Students use three cueing systems to decode printed words: syntactic, semantic, and phonic (graphophonic). In other words, they use their sense of how language sounds (syntax), the meaning of the sentence or passage (semantics), and phonics to read. To determine how they are using these systems, analyze their word-recognition errors, or miscues, with a modified **miscue analysis.** On a sheet similar to the one in Figure 2.4, list the students' miscues. Try to list at least ten miscues, but

**BUILDING LANGUAGE**
When students are responding orally to informal reading questions, note the level and quality of their language and use your observations to plan a program of language development.

■ **Miscue analysis** is the process of analyzing miscues in order to determine which cueing systems or combination of cueing systems the student is using: semantic, syntactic, or graphophonic.

**TABLE 2.5**    Silent-reading symbols

| Symbol | Meaning |
|--------|---------|
| HM | Head movement |
| FP | Finger pointing |
| LM | Lip movement |
| SV | Subvocalizing |

**FIGURE 2.3**

## Informal Reading Inventory Summary Sheet

**Word-List Scores**

**Inventory Scores**

| Level | Flash | Untimed | Word recognition (in context) | Comprehension (oral) | Comprehension (silent) | Comprehension (avg.) | Listening capacity |
|---|---|---|---|---|---|---|---|
| PP | 80 | 95 | 100 | 100 | 90 | 95 | |
| P | 70 | 80 | 96 | 100 | 80 | 90 | |
| 1 | 30 | 55 | 89 | 60 | 60 | 60 | |
| 2 | | | | | | | 90 |
| 3 | | | | | | | 80 |
| 4 | | | | | | | 50 |
| 5 | | | | | | | |
| 6 | | | | | | | |
| 7 | | | | | | | |
| 8 | | | | | | | |

| Levels | | Strengths and weaknesses |
|---|---|---|
| Independent | PP | *Strong language development* |
| Instructional | P | *Difficulty with high-frequency* |
| Frustration | 1 | *words and clusters* |
| Listening capacity | 3 | |

do not analyze any that are at or beyond the frustration level. Miscues can be chosen from the independent and instructional levels and from the buffer zone between the instructional and frustration levels (91 to 94 percent word recognition). Also list the correct version of each error. Put a check in the syntactic column if the miscue is syntactically correct—that is, if it is the same part of speech as the word in the text or could be used in that context. Put a check in the semantic column if the miscue makes sense in the sentence. In the graphic column, use a check to show whether the miscue is graphically and/or phonically similar to the text word. It is similar if it contains at least half the sounds in the text word. Also use a check to show whether the beginning, middle, and end of the miscue are similar to the text word. Put a check in the nonword column if the miscue is not a real word. Also indicate corrected miscues with a check in the self-correction column.

Tally each column (as shown in Figure 2.4) and convert tallies to percentages. After tallying the columns, examine the numbers to see whether the student is reading for meaning. Miscues that make sense in the context of the selection, self-corrections, and absence of nonwords are positive signs. They show that the student is reading for meaning. Conversely, the presence of nonwords is a negative sign, as are miscues that do not fit the sense of the passage or the syntax.

Also compare the tallies to see whether the cues are being used in balanced fashion or whether one is being overused or underused. The student could be overusing phonics and underusing semantic context, or vice versa. Draw tentative conclusions about the strategies that the student uses in his or her word recognition. Double-check those conclusions as you observe the student read in the classroom.

As you can see from Figure 2.4, fewer than half of this student's miscues fit the context either syntactically or semantically. Moreover, three of them are nonwords,

**FIGURE 2.4**

## Miscue Analysis

Name: _____   Date: _____

| Miscue | Text | Syntactic similarity | Semantic similarity | Graphic similarity | Beginning | Middle | End | Nonword | Self-correction |
|--------|------|---------------------|---------------------|--------------------|-----------|--------|-----|---------|-----------------|
| gots | gets | ✓ | ✓ | ✓ | ✓ | — | ✓ | | |
| will | with | — | — | ✓ | ✓ | ✓ | — | | |
| ran ✓ | runs | ✓ | ✓ | ✓ | ✓ | — | ✓ | | ✓ |
| balt | ball | — | — | ✓ | ✓ | ✓ | — | ✓ | |
| tricks | kicks | ✓ | — | ✓ | — | ✓ | ✓ | | |
| my | me | — | ✓ | ✓ | ✓ | | — | | |
| trick | trust | ✓ | — | — | ✓ | — | — | | |
| bell | ball | ✓ | — | ✓ | ✓ | — | ✓ | | |
| frain | five | — | — | — | ✓ | — | — | ✓ | |
| grain | gray | — | — | ✓ | ✓ | ✓ | — | | |
| there | that | — | — | — | ✓ | — | — | | |
| eak | each | — | — | ✓ | ✓ | | — | ✓ | |
| **Totals** | | 5 | 3 | 9 | 11 | 4 | 4 | 3 | 1 |
| **Numbers of miscues analyzed** | | 12 | 12 | 12 | | | | 12 | 12 |
| **Percentage** | | 42 | 25 | 75 | | | | 25 | 8 |

and the student had only one self-correction. All indications are that the student is failing to use context clues and is not reading for meaning. The student makes heavy use of phonics, especially at the beginning of words, but must also integrate his or her use of phonics with syntactic and semantic cues. The student also needs to improve his or her use of phonics skills, especially middle and ending elements.

IRIs require training and practice to administer and interpret. In the past, they were generally administered by the school's reading specialist. However, increasingly, classroom teachers are administering IRIs. To make the best possible use of time, classroom teachers might give a streamlined version of an IRI in which they give the full word list test but only administer the oral passages of the inventory and don't administer the listening portion of the IRI. It will also save time if an inventory that contains brief passages is given. Giving a shortened inventory reduces its reliability, so results should be regarded as being tentative and should be verified by observation of the student's performance reading books at the estimated instructional level.

Even if you, as a classroom teacher, never formally administer an IRI, it is still essential that you be familiar with the concept. Knowing the IRI standards for instructional and other levels, you have a basis for evaluating your students' reading performance. If students have difficulty orally reading more than five words out of a hundred, or if their oral and written comprehension seem closer to 50 percent than 75 percent, you may have to check the material they are reading to see whether it is too difficult. On the other hand, if both word recognition and comprehension in everyday reading tasks are close to perfect, you may want to try more challenging materials.

As children struggle with difficult words, you may also want to conduct a mental miscue analysis. By closely observing miscues, you can sense whether students might need added instruction in using context, using phonics, or integrating the two.

## Running Records

Similar to the informal reading inventory and based on K. S. Goodman's (1974) theory of analyzing students' miscues to determine what strategies they are using to decode words, the **running record** has become a popular device for assessing students' progress. Like the IRI, the running record is administered individually. However, only an oral-reading sample is obtained. The running record has two major purposes: to determine whether students' reading materials are on the proper level and to obtain information about the word-recognition processes students are using. To get a fuller assessment of comprehension, some teachers supplement the administration of a running record by having students retell the selection. Teachers often take running records during guided reading, while other students are reading silently.

Although running records may be obtained from older readers, they are most often used to assess the performance of novice readers and are administered daily to Reading Recovery students. As used in Reading Recovery and recommended in

---

Generally, IRIs are given at the beginning of the school year to obtain placement information, when a new student enters the class, or whenever a student's placement is in doubt. They may also be given as pretests and posttests and are often more sensitive indicators of progress than norm-referenced tests.

■ The **running record** is an assessment device in which a student's oral reading errors are noted and classified in order to determine whether the material is on the appropriate level of difficulty and to see which reading strategies the student is using.

To simplify the administration of running records, use IRI marking symbols, and record miscues on photocopies of the selection.

Clay's (1993a) *An Observation Survey of Early Literacy Achievement*, running records are administered according to a standardized format in which students' errors and corrections are recorded on a separate sheet. As adapted for use by classroom teachers, running records may be recorded (as long as the fair-use provision of the copyright laws is adhered to or permission is obtained from the publisher) on a photocopy of the text that the student is using (Learning Media, 1991). To assess whether materials are on a suitable level of difficulty and to determine how well the child makes use of previously presented strategies, take a running record on a text that the student has recently read. To assess the student's ability to handle challenging materials and apply strategies independently, take a running record on material that the student has not read. If the book or article is very brief, take a running record of the whole piece. If the text is lengthy, select a sample of 100 to 200 words. As the student reads orally, record her or his performance with symbols, such as those presented in Table 2.6. However, you may use the IRI symbols if you are more familiar with them. After taking a running record, record the number of words in the selection, number of errors made, error rate, number of self-corrections made, and the accuracy rate.

*R*unning records help teachers monitor students' progress.

Clay (1993a) accepts 90 percent as an adequate accuracy rate; however, 95 percent seems more realistic. Word recognition is emphasized in a running record, so comprehension is not directly checked. However, you may ask the child to retell the story if you wish to obtain information about comprehension.

It is essential that you analyze a student's miscues in order to determine what strategies she or he is using. As you examine the student's miscues, ask the following questions:

- Is the student reading for meaning? Do the student's miscues make sense?
- Is the student self-correcting miscues, especially those that do not fit the meaning of the sentence? Is the student using meaning cues?
- Is the student using visual or sound-symbol cues (phonics)? Are the student's miscues similar in appearance and sound to the target word?
- Is the student using picture cues?
- Is the student integrating cues? Is the student balancing the use of meaning and sound-symbol cues?
- Based on the student's performance, what strategies does she or he need to work on?

For younger readers in the very early stages, note whether they read from left to right or top to bottom and whether there is a voice-print match (the word the

Running records provide indirect evidence of comprehension. "Observation of how a child reads a text—including phrasing, expression, and use of a variety of clues, checking to be sure all sources of information fit to determine when attempts don't make sense—provide evidence of comprehension" (Fountas, 1999, p. 11).

**COMMERCIAL RUNNING RECORDS**

Based on the Reading Recovery model, the Developmental Reading Assessment (Beaver, 1997) functions as an informal reading inventory/running record for students in grades one through three. A Spanish equivalent (Evalucaion Del Desarrollo De LA Lectura) is also available.

**TABLE 2.6** Running record symbols

| Symbol | Text | Example |
|---|---|---|
| Words read correctly are marked with a check mark. | Janice kicked the ball. | ✓  ✓  ✓  ✓ |
| Substitutions are written above the line. | A barn owl hooted. | ✓ *big* ✓  ✓<br>*barn* |
| Self-corrections are marked SC. | A barn owl hooted. | ✓ *big\|sc* ✓  ✓<br>*barn* |
| A dash is used to indicate no response. | I saw her yesterday. | ✓ ✓ ✓  —<br>*yesterday* |
| A dash is used to indicate an insertion of a word. The dash is placed beneath the inserted word. | We saw a big dog. | ✓ ✓ ✓ *bad* ✓<br>— |
| A *T* is used to indicate that a child has been told a word. | Her cat ran away yesterday. | ✓  ✓  ✓  ✓   *T*<br>*yesterday* |
| The letter *A* indicates that the child has asked for help. | A large moose appeared. | ✓  ✓  ✓    *A*<br>*appeared* |
| At times, the student becomes so confused by a misreading that it is suggested that she or he "try that again" (coded TTA). Brackets are put around the section that has been misread, the whole misreading is counted as one error, and the student reads it again for a new score. | The deer leaped over the fence. | ⌐ ✓ ✓ *landed* ✓  ✓ *field* ⌐<br>  *leaped*        *fence*  ⌐ *TTA* |
| A repetition is indicated with an *R*. Although not counted as errors, repetitions are often part of an attempt to puzzle out a difficult item. The point to which the student returns in the repetition is indicated with an arrow. | The deer leaped over the fence. | ✓ ✓ *landed\|sc* ✓  ✓ *field\|sc. R*<br>  *leaped*        *fence.* |

child says matches the one she or he is looking at). For detailed information on analyzing and interpreting running records, see Clay (1993a, 2000) or P. Johnston (1997).

## Group Inventories

Because of the time involved, it may be impractical to administer individual IRIs. However, you may choose to administer a group reading inventory. Information about constructing and administering group reading inventories can be found in *Informal Reading Inventories* (2nd ed.) by Johnson, Kress, & Pikulski (1987). Some reading series contain group reading inventories. There are also three tests that function as group inventories: the Degrees of Reading Power, the Scholastic Reading Inventory, and STAR.

### ■ Degrees of Reading Power (DRP)

Composed of a series of passages that gradually increase in difficulty, the Degrees of Reading Power assesses overall reading ability by having students choose from among five options the one that best completes a portion of the passage from which words have been omitted. Each passage has nine deletions.

As in a traditional IRI, the passages gradually increase in difficulty and encompass a wide range of difficulty so that slow, average, and superior readers' ability may be appropriately assessed. Instead of yielding a grade-level score, the assessment provides a DRP score. The DRP score indicates what level of material the student should be able to read. A complementary readability formula is used to indicate the difficulty level of books in DRP units. Approximate grade equivalents of DRP units are presented in Table 2.7. The main purpose of the DRP is to match students with books that are on their levels.

### ■ The Scholastic Reading Inventory

The Scholastic Reading Inventory, which also uses a modified cloze procedure and can be administered and scored mannually or by computer, yields lexile scores. Lexile units range from about 70 to 1700+. A score of 70 to 200 is about mid-first grade. A score of 1700 would be the level at which difficult scientific journals are written. Approximate grade equivalents of lexile units are presented in Table 2.7.

### ■ STAR

STAR (Advantage Learning Systems), which is administered and scored by a computer and so doesn't require valuable teacher time, has a branching component. The program is set so that if students give correct answers they are given higher level passages, but are given lower level passages if they respond incorrectly. The STAR uses a modified cloze procedure. Students need a reading vocabulary of 100 words in order to be able to take STAR. Testing time is ten minutes or less.

## Word-List Tests

To save time, teachers sometimes administer word-list tests instead of IRIs. Because they require only the ability to pronounce words, these tests neglect comprehen-

**TABLE 2.7** Comparison of readability levels

| Grade Equivalent | DRP | Lexile | Guided Reading | Reading Recovery |
|---|---|---|---|---|
| Emergent/Picture | | | A | 1 |
| Frame/Caption (Early PP) | | | B | 2 |
| High Frequency PP-1 | | | C | 3 |
| Preprimer 2 | | | D | 5–6 |
| Preprimer 3 | 34–36 | | E | 7–8 |
| Primer | 37–39 | 200–300 | F | 9–10 |
| First Reader | 40–43 | 300–400 | H–I | 13–17 |
| Grade 2a | 44–45 | 400–500 | J–K | 18–20 |
| Grade 2b | 46–47 | 400–500 | L–M | |
| Grade 3 | 48–49 | 500–700 | N–P | |
| Grade 4 | 50–51 | 700–800 | Q–S | |
| Grade 5 | 52–53 | 800–900 | T–V | |
| Grade 6 | 54–55 | 900–1000 | W–X | |
| Grade 7 | 56–57 | 1000–1100 | Y | |
| Grade 8 | 58–59 | 1000–1100 | Z | |

sion and may yield misleading levels for students who are superior decoders but poor comprehenders or vice versa. One of the most popular word-list tests is the Slosson Oral Reading Test (SORT). The SORT presents twenty words at each grade level from preprimer through grade twelve. The student is only required to pronounce the words and does not have to know their meanings. Standardized and norm-referenced, the Slosson is also listed as being appropriate for Reading First assessment (Reading First Reading Assessment Committee, 2002).

##  NORM-REFERENCED VERSUS CRITERION-REFERENCED TESTS

### Norm-Referenced Tests

■ **Norm-referenced tests** are those in which students' performance is compared with a norm group, which is a representative sampling of students.

Many traditional tests provide some sort of comparison. In a **norm-referenced test,** students are compared with a representative sample of others who are the same age or in the same grade. The scores indicate whether students did as well as the average, better than the average, or below the average. The norm group typically includes students from all sections of the country, from urban and nonurban areas, and from a variety of racial or ethnic and socioeconomic groups. The group is chosen to be representative of the nation's total school population. However, norm-referenced tests can result in unfair comparisons. Urban schools, for example, should only be compared with other urban schools.

Because norm-referenced tests yield comparative results that are generally used by school boards, school administrators, and the general public, they provide one source of information to assess the effectiveness of the school program. Classroom teachers can also make use of the data to complement information from quizzes, informal tests, and observations. Reading scores indicate an approximate level of achievement. If a measure of academic aptitude has been administered, results can be examined to see whether students are reading up to their expected or anticipated level of achievement. If they are not, the teacher can explore the problem.

The tests can also be used as a screening device. Very high-scoring students may be candidates for a gifted or enriched reading program. Low-scoring students may benefit from input from the reading or learning-disabilities specialist, especially if there is a marked difference between capacity and performance. Subtest scores of individuals can also be analyzed for patterns of strengths and weaknesses. A high-vocabulary, low-comprehension score, for example, is often a sign that a student needs extra instruction in the use of comprehension strategies. A low-vocabulary, high-comprehension score might indicate the need for language development. Occasionally, norm-referenced tests yield surprises. Sometimes children, because of shyness or other factors, hide their talents. Norm-referenced tests occasionally spotlight a student whose abilities have gone unnoticed.

Some school districts have as a goal that all students will be reading on grade level according to the results of a norm-referenced test. This is the same thing as saying that everyone will be at least average. However, norm-referenced tests are created in such a way that half the students in a typical group will score below average. Even if students' scores improve, this won't make the goal achievable. Test publishers periodically renorm their tests so that if scores generally improve, the norms are set higher (Harcourt Educational Measurement, 2000).

Norm-referenced tests have a number of weaknesses. Because they are multiple choice, they don't assess reading the way it is taught or used, and guessing is a factor. They also invite competition and comparison. According to some theorists the most serious problem with standardized tests is that "They are often considered to be the single or at least the most important determinate of students' achievement" (Salinger, 2001, p. 394). When documenting students' progress, teachers tend to use information garnered from standardized tests, even if they have data gathered through informal methods. It is as though teachers don't trust their own judgements (Johnston & Rogers, 2001.) To offset this, teachers need to be more careful and systematic with their classroom assessments.

This book does not recommend administering norm-referenced tests. However, in many school systems, their administration is mandated. If information from these tests is available, you should make use of it along with other sources of data.

## Criterion-Referenced Tests

In contrast to a norm-referenced test, a **criterion-referenced test** compares students' performance with some standard, or criterion. For instance, the criterion

> Norm-referenced tests provide information generally desired by school boards, policymakers, and the public at large. Ease and efficiency of administration and objectivity are appealing factors.

> Norm-referenced tests are not a very good source of information in terms of planning classroom instruction. However, in most instances, the decision to give standardized tests is made by the school board or superintendent's office. Since the tests are being given anyway, teachers might as well make use of the information yielded by the tests.

> ■ A **criterion-referenced test** is one in which the student's performance is compared to a criterion, or standard.

NAEP has been assessing students in grades four, eight, and twelve since 1969. Carefully constructed, the NAEP tests in reading and writing are highly regarded and are the standard against which other tests are evaluated.

on a comprehension test might be answering 80 percent of the questions correctly. The informal reading inventory is criterion-referenced; a student must have at least 95 percent word recognition and 75 percent comprehension to be on the instructional level, for example. Tests that accompany basal readers also tend to be criterion-referenced. Many have a passing score, which is the criterion. Most state tests and the National Assessment of Educational Progress (NAEP) tests are criterion-referenced. The major weakness of criterion-referenced tests is that, all too often, the criterion is set arbitrarily. No one tests it to see whether average students usually answer 80 percent of the items correctly, for example, or whether 80 percent comprehension is adequate in most instances. Sometimes the criterion is set too high. For instance, the NAEP test has been criticized for having standards that are unrealistically high. Although America's fourth-graders outscored every country but Finland on an international test (Elley, 1992), according to NAEP test results, only 67 percent of fourth-graders read at or above the basic level and only 24 percent read at or above the proficient level (Barton, 2001).

A second major shortcoming of criterion-referenced tests is that all too often they do not assess reading skills and strategies in the way students actually use them. For instance, comprehension might be assessed as in norm-referenced tests, with brief passages and multiple-choice questions. Despite these limitations, criterion-referenced tests are generally more useful to teachers than are norm-referenced tests. They indicate whether students have mastered particular skills and so are useful for making instructional decisions.

## REPORTING PERFORMANCE

There are two primary ways of reporting scores: norm-referenced and criterion-referenced. In norm-referenced reporting, a student's performance is compared with that of other students. In criterion-referenced reporting, a student's performance might be described in terms of a standard or expected performance or in terms of the student's goals.

### Norm-Referenced Reporting

■ A **raw score** is the number of correct answers or points earned on a test.

■ The **percentile rank** is the point on a scale of 1 to 99 that shows what percentage of students obtained an equal or lower score. A percentile rank of 75 means that 75 percent of those who took the test received an equal or lower score.

■ A **grade equivalent score** indicates the score that the average student at that grade level achieved.

Tests and other assessment measures yield a number of possible scores. To interpret results correctly, it is important to know the significance of each score. Here are commonly used test scores:

■ **Raw score.** A raw score represents the total number of correct answers. It has no meaning until it is changed into a percentile rank or other score.

■ **Percentile rank.** A percentile rank tells where a student's raw score falls on a scale of 1 to 99. A score at the first percentile means that the student did better than 1 percent of those who took the test. A score at the fiftieth percentile indicates that the student did better than half of those who took the test. A top score is the ninety-ninth percentile. Most norm-referenced test results are now reported in percentiles; however, the ranks are not equal units and should not be added, subtracted, divided, or used for subtest comparison.

- **Grade equivalent score.** The grade equivalent score characterizes a student's performance as being equivalent to that of other students in a particular grade. A grade equivalent score of 5.2 indicates that the student correctly answered the same number of items as the average fifth-grader in the second month of that grade. Note that the grade equivalent score does not tell on what level the student is operating; that is, a score of 5.2 does not mean that a student is reading on a fifth-grade level. Grade equivalent scores are more meaningful when the test students have taken is at the right level and when the score is not more than a year above or a year below average. Because grade equivalent scores are misleading and easily misunderstood, they should be used with great care or not at all.

- **Normal curve equivalents.** Normal curve equivalents (NCEs) rank students on a scale of 1 through 99. The main difference between NCEs and percentile ranks is that NCEs represent equal units and so can be added and subtracted and used for comparing performance on subtests.

- **Stanine.** Stanine is a combination of the words *standard* and *nine*. The stanines 4, 5, and 6 are average points, with 1, 2, and 3 being below average, and 7, 8, and 9 above average. Stanines are useful when making comparisons among the subtests of a norm-referenced test.

- **Scaled scores.** Scaled scores are a continuous ranking of scores from the lowest levels of a series of norm-referenced tests—first grade, for example—through the highest levels—high school. They start at 000 and end at 999. They are useful for tracking long-term reading development through the grades. Lexiles, DRP units, and grade equivalents are also examples of scaled scores.

Grade equivalents and other scaled scores rise over time. However, percentiles, stanines, and normal curve equivalents may stay the same from year to year. If they do, this means that the student is making average progress in comparison with others. For instance, if a student is at the thirty-fifth percentile in third grade and then tests at the thirty-fifth percentile in fourth grade, that means that his relative standing is the same. He continues to do better than 35 percent of the students who took the test. However, if he moves to a higher percentile, this means that he outperformed students who started off with similar scores. If he scores at the fortieth percentile in fourth grade, it means that he is moving up in the relative standings. Now he is doing better than 40 percent of those who took the test.

## Criterion-Referenced Reporting

Criterion-referenced results are reported in terms of a standard, or criterion. For example, the student answered 80 percent of the comprehension questions correctly. Two types of standards now being used in authentic assessment are the benchmark and the rubric, which are descriptive forms of criterion-referenced reporting.

### ■ Benchmarks

A **benchmark** is a written description of a key task that students are expected to perform. For instance, a benchmark for word recognition might be "Uses both con-

---

Grade equivalent scores, which have been opposed by the International Reading Association, are relatively valid when pupils are tested on their instructional level and when extrapolations are limited to a year or two beyond the target grade level.

■ A **normal curve equivalent** is the rank on a scale of 1 through 99 that a score is equal to.

■ A **stanine** is a point on a nine-point scale, with 5 being average.

■ A **scaled score** is a continuous ranking from 000 to 999 of a series of norm-referenced tests from the easiest to the highest-level test.

For additional information about tests, see the *Fifteenth Mental Measurements Yearbook* (Plake, Impara, & Spies, 2003), or *Tests in Print VI* (Murphy, Plake, Impara, & Spies, 2002), which lists more than 4,000 tests. You might also consult the Buros Center for Testing which specializes in test information: **http://www.unl.edu/buros/** or the ERIC site for assessment: **http://ericae.net/.**

■ A **benchmark** is a standard of achievement or written description of performance against which a student's achievement might be assessed.

When setting up benchmarks, it is important not to set up too many tasks.

text and phonics to identify words unknown in print." If adapted to fit your curriculum, the Essential Standards presented in the instructional chapters could be used to create benchmarks. Information on expected level of performance should be added, however.

Benchmarks are useful because they provide a concrete description of what students are expected to do. They provide students, teachers, parents, and administrators with an observable framework for assessing accomplishments and needs. Using benchmarks, the teacher can assess whether the student has mastered key skills and strategies and is ready to move on. Opportunities for assessing benchmark behaviors include observing during shared reading, story discussions, drama, writing activities, and student conferences. Parent conferences during which parents provide information about the child's reading and writing at home offer additional sources of data.

### ■ Rubrics

■ A **rubric** is a description of the traits or characteristics of standards used to judge a process or product.

A **rubric** is a written description of what is expected in order to meet a certain level of performance and is usually accompanied by samples of several levels of performance. For assessing a piece of writing, such samples show the characteristics of an excellent, average, fair, and poor paper. A writing rubric is presented in Table 2.8. Although rubrics are typically used in the assessment of writing tasks, they can also be used to assess combined reading and writing tasks, portfolios, presentations, and projects.

In addition to their use as scoring guides, rubrics can be powerful teaching tools (Popham, 2000). Carefully constructed rubrics describe the key tasks that students must complete or the main elements that must be included in order to produce an excellent piece of work. This helps both the teacher and student focus on key skills. To be effective, rubrics should contain only three to six evaluative criteria so that students and teachers do not get sidetracked by minor details. More important, each evaluative criterion must encompass a teachable skill. For instance, evaluative criteria for a story might include an exciting plot, believable characters, an interesting setting, and the use of vivid language.

**Creating a rubric.** To develop a rubric, first identify the key characteristics or traits of the performance or piece of work to be assessed. For a rubric for a friendly letter, the key traits might include interesting content, chatty style, correct letter format, and correct mechanics. If available, examine finished products to see what their major traits are. Write a definition of each trait. What exactly is meant by "interesting content," "chatty style," "correct letter format," and "correct mechanics"? Develop a scale for the characteristics. It is usually easiest to start with the top performance. If you have examples of students' work, sort them into piles: best, worst, and middle. Look over the best pieces and decide what makes them the best. Look at the poorest and decide where they are deficient. Write a description of the best and poorest performances. Then fill in the middle levels. For the middle levels, divide the remaining papers into two or more piles from best to worst depending upon how many levels you wish to have. However, the more levels you create, the more difficult it becomes to discriminate between adjoining levels. You

**TABLE 2.8**    Rubric for assessing writing

| | Level 4<br>Most Successful | Level 3<br>Upper Half | Level 2<br>Lower Half (Basic) | Level 1<br>Least Successful<br>(Skill Failure) |
|---|---|---|---|---|
| Content | Shows clear under-standing of content. Develops the topic with appropriate detail in each paragraph. | Generally understands content. At least two para-graphs used. Details relate clearly to topic sentence. | Appears to understand the topic. If using more than one paragraph, relation to overall topic may be weak. | Some misunderstand-ing of topic. Usually only one paragraph. Includes material not related to topic. |
| Organization | Organization and sequence of ideas are clear and relate to one another in develop-ment of the overall topic. | Clear organization and sequences of detail. Relationship of para-graphs to major topic not fully developed. | Basically sequential. Some weakness in relating paragraph details to topic sen-tences. | Lacks coherence. Sequencing of ideas may be incorrect. |
| Sentence structure | Uses correct sentence structure, descriptive words, and phrases. Expands sentence pat-terns. Makes few grammati-cal errors. | Basic sentence pat-terns correct. Some difficulty with expanded sentence patterns and grammar. | Uses simple sentences. Errors in grammar when more complex structure is attempted. Some run-on and sen-tence fragments. | Uses basic simple sen-tences. Errors in noun–verb agreement. Infrequent use of modifiers. |
| Mechanics | Capitalization, punctu-ation, and spelling are generally correct. | Few problems with capitalization, punctu-ation, and spelling. | Errors in capitalization, punctuation, and spelling. | Frequent errors in capitalization, punc-tuation, and spelling of words. |
| Word choice | Vocabulary includes some words usually used at a higher level. | Average for grade level. Vocabulary words used correctly. | Simple vocabulary words used, some incorrectly. | Poor word choice. |

From *The Writing Handbook* (p. 19) by the Reading and Communications Arts Department, 1983, Hartford, CT: Hartford Public Schools. Reprinted by permission of the Hartford Board of Education.

may find that four suffice. Evaluate your rubric. Use the following checklist to assess your rubric:

- Does the rubric measure the key traits in the student performance?
- Are differences in the levels clearly specified?
- Does the rubric clearly specify what students are required to do?
- Can the rubric be used as a learning guide by students?
- Can the rubric be used as an instructional guide by the teacher (Chicago Public Schools, 2000)?

Discuss the rubric with students and invite feedback. Through helping with the creation of the rubrics, students form a better idea of what is expected in the task being assessed and also feel more willing to use the rubric because they had a hand

Students should partici-
pate in the creation of
rubrics. Through helping
with the creation of the
rubrics, students form a
clearer idea of what is
expected in their writing.
In one study, students used
these rubrics to assess their
own writing. They also took
part in peer evaluation sessions in which the rubric
was used to judge their
writing. As a result of creating and using the rubric,
students' writing of persuasive pieces showed a significant improvement (Boyle,
1996).

In some assessments, stu-
dents are given materials
on grade level to read and
respond to. Because as
many as one child in four
will be reading significantly
below grade level (Gunning,
1982), this practice is
unfair to underachieving
youngsters. Lower-
achieving readers should be
provided with at least some
items that are on their
instructional level. Test
publishers support the concept of functional level
testing and offer guidelines
for out-of-level assessment.
A general practice is to use
the teacher's estimate or a
quick locator test provided
by the publisher to obtain a
rough estimate of the
child's reading level and to
test the child on that level.

■ **Functional level testing**
is the practice of assigning
students to a test level on
the basis of their reading
ability rather than their
grade level.

in its construction. When fourth-graders used cooperatively created rubrics to assess their writing (Boyle, 1996), their persuasive pieces showed a significant improvement.

Try out the rubric, revise it, and then use it. As you use the rubric with actual
pieces of students' work, continue to revise it.

One source of rubrics might be the key standards for a grade. Teachers can align
their rubrics with key state or local standards (Skillings & Ferrell, 2000). To ease her
students into using rubrics, Ferrell modeled the process. She also had students
create rubrics for everyday activities such as picking the best restaurant. After students caught on to the idea of creating rubrics, she involved them in creating rubrics
for basic writing tasks. To keep the rubrics simple, the class had just three levels:
best, okay, not so good. Later the class created rubrics for more complex tasks.
Sample rubrics can be found at the following Web sites:

The State of Colorado (2000) has developed an online set of general, holistic
scoring rubrics designed for the evaluation of various writing tasks.
http://www.cde.state.co.us/cdeassess/as_rubricindex.htm

Chicago Public Schools (1999) maintain an extensive electronic list of analytic and holistic scoring rubrics that span the broad array of subjects represented from kindergarten through high school.
http://intranet.cps.k12.il.us/Assessments/Ideas_and_Rubrics/
ideas_and_rubrics.html

## FUNCTIONAL LEVEL ASSESSMENT

The typical elementary school class will exhibit a wide range of reading ability.
Just as students need appropriate levels of materials for instruction, they should have
appropriate levels of materials for testing. Most literacy tests cover a limited range.
For instance, a general reading test designed for fourth-graders will mostly have
selections on a fourth-grade level, a selection or two on a third-grade level, and a
few selections beyond the fourth-grade level. A fourth-grader reading on a second-
grade level should not be given a fourth-grade reading test. It would be frustrating
to the student and would yield misleading results. The student should take a test
that includes material on his level of reading ability. This might mean giving the student a test designed for third grade but which includes second-grade material.
Similarly, a second-grade-level test would probably not be appropriate for a second-
grader reading on a fifth-grade level. It would probably lack an adequate ceiling
and so would underestimate the student's true reading ability. Students should be
tested at their **functional level,** which is not necessarily their grade level. Students
reading significantly above or below grade level should be given out-of-level tests
unless the tests they are taking cover a wide range of levels. Giving students a test
at the wrong level results in erroneous, invalid information. This is true whether
norm-referenced, criterion-referenced, or other assessment is being used.

# OTHER METHODS OF ASSESSMENT

## Retelling

**Retelling** has the potential for supplying more information about a student's comprehension than simply asking questions does. In a retelling, a student is asked to do what the name suggests: The student may retell a selection that has been read to her or him or one that she or he has read. The student may do this orally or in writing. In addition to showing what the reader comprehended, retelling shows what she or he added to and inferred from the text (Irwin & Mitchell, 1983). Free from the influence of probes or questions, retelling demonstrates the student's construction of text and provides insight into her or his language and thought processes. It shows how the student organizes and shapes a response. The teacher can also assess the quality of language used by the student in the retelling.

To administer a retelling, explain to the student what she or he is supposed to do: Read a selection orally or silently or listen to one read aloud. It may be a narrative or expository piece. Tell the student that she or he will be asked to retell the story in her or his own words. Use neutral phrasing, such as "Tell me about the story that you read." For a young child, say, "Pretend I haven't read the story. Tell it to me in your own words." A shy child can use props—such as a puppet—to facilitate the retelling.

If a child stops before retelling the whole selection, encourage her or him to continue or elaborate. When the student is finished, ask questions about any key elements that were not included in the retelling.

### ■ Evaluating Retellings

As the student retells the selection, record it on audiocassette and/or jot down brief notes on the major events or ideas in the order in which the child relates them. Note any recalls that were not spontaneous but were elicited by your questions. Tape recording provides a full and accurate rendition of the retelling but is time consuming.

Retellings can be scored numerically by giving students credit for each major unit that they retell. However, this is a laborious process. Far less time consuming but still useful is noting the major units in the retelling in one column, comments about it in a second column, and a summary and recommendations in a third. Because the main purpose of the retelling is to gain insight into students' reading processes, draw inferences about students' overall understanding of the selection and their ability to use strategies to construct the meaning of the piece. A sample retelling is presented in Figure 2.5.

### ■ Written Retellings

Written retellings can be timesavers, as the teacher can assess the class as a group. Using holistic scoring, the teacher can also assess the quality of the response. It is

Obtaining a valid assessment of the ability and performance of English Language Learners is a problem. ELLs can obtain conversational proficiency in two years or less. However, it may take five years or more for ELLs to learn enough academic English so that they can do as well on tests of academic proficiency as native speakers of English do (Cummins, 2001).

■ **Retelling** is the process of summarizing or describing a story that one has read. The purpose of the retelling is to assess comprehension.

Being less time consuming, informal retellings are more practical for the classroom teacher. Of course, shy children may not perform up to their ability.

Because the person assessing them obviously knows the story, students might provide a contextualized retelling. They may not give the characters names, referring to them as *he* or *she* because they assume that the examiner is familiar with the characters. Knowing that the examiner is familiar with the story, they might omit or abbreviate crucial details (Benson & Cummins, 2000). When using a retelling as an assessment, stress that the students should pretend that they are telling the story to someone who has not read it or heard it.

FIGURE 2.5

**Evaluation of an Oral Retelling**

Name of student: _Jamie S._

| | Retelling | Comments | Summary and recommendations |
|---|---|---|---|
| Elves and the shoemaker | Shoemaker said had only one piece of leather left. Elves made shoes. | Drew inference. Started with story problem. | Good grasp of story. |
| | Man in hat came in. Woman came in. Many people bought shoes. Shoemaker and wife waited up to see elves. | Told story in sequence. | Used structure of story to retell it. |
| | Elves had ragged clothes. Wife made new clothes. Elves thought new clothes looked funny. Elves said would no longer be cobras. Never came back. | Used picture to get information about elves. Misinterpreted passage. Missed _cobblers_. | Didn't go beyond story to suggest why elves started or stopped helping. Failed to use context to help with _cobblers_. Good average performance. Work on context and drawing conclusions. |

As an alternative to a strictly written response, you might invite students to use whatever form they want to retell a selection: semantic map or web, story map, outline, flow chart, diagram, or other graphic organizers. Students, especially those in the early grades, might also respond by drawing an illustration of the story.

important to keep in mind that, whether oral or written, the mode of expression will affect the information students convey. Students may have good knowledge of a selection but find it difficult to express their ideas orally and/or in writing. To obtain a better picture of that knowledge, the teacher might have a class discussion after students have completed their written retellings and compare impressions garnered from the discussion with those from the written versions.

**Structured written retellings.**   In a structured written retelling, the teacher might ask students to read a whole selection and write answers to a series of broad questions. The questions are constructed to assess students' ability to understand major aspects of the text, such as characters, plot, and setting. The questions can also be framed to provide some insight into the strategies students are using. They are scored and analyzed by the teacher.

# Think-Aloud Protocols

**Think-alouds** are used to show the thought processes students use as they attempt to construct meaning. During a think-aloud, the reader explains her thought processes while reading a text. These explanations might come after each sentence, at the end of each paragraph, or at the end of the whole selection. Students' thoughts might be expressed as "news bulletins or play-by-play accounts" of what students do mentally as they read (Brown & Lytle, 1988, p. 96).

> ■ **Think-alouds** are procedures in which students are asked to describe the processes they are using as they engage in reading or another cognitive activity.

## ■ Informal Think-Alouds

Whereas formal think-aloud procedures might be too time consuming, informal think-alouds can be incorporated into individual and small-group reading conferences and classroom activities. For example, the teacher might simply ask students to share their thoughts on a difficult passage or question or to tell what strategies they used. Think-aloud questions can include the following:

- Tell me how you figured out that hard word.
- Tell me how you got the answer to that question.
- What were you thinking about when you read that selection?
- Pretend that you are an announcer at a sports game. Tell me play by play what was going on in your mind as you read that sentence (or paragraph) (Brown & Lytle, 1988).
- What do you think will happen next in the selection? What makes you think that?
- How did you feel when you read that passage? What thoughts or pictures were going through your mind?

*A*s part of an informal think-aloud, students might be asked to discuss strategies they used to read a difficult passage.

Think-alouds may also be expressed in writing. In their learning logs, students can note the difficulties they encountered in hard passages and describe the processes they used to comprehend the selections. In follow-up class discussions, they can compare their thought processes and strategies with those of other students (Brown & Lytle, 1988). A simple way for students to keep track of perplexing passages is to have students record comprehension problems on sticky notes and place them next to the passages.

## Observation

Teachers learn about children "by watching how they learn" (Y. M. Goodman, 1985, p. 9). As "kidwatchers," teachers are better able to supply the necessary support or ask the kinds of questions that help students build on their evolving knowledge.

### ■ Opportunities for Observations

Observations can be made any time students are involved in reading and writing. Some especially fruitful opportunities for observation include shared reading (What emergent literacy behaviors are students evidencing?), reading and writing conferences (What are the students' strengths and weaknesses in these areas? What is their level of development? How might their progress in these areas be characterized?), and sustained silent reading (Do students enjoy reading? Are they able to select appropriate materials? What kinds of materials do they like to read?). Other valuable observation opportunities include author's circle, literature circle, and sharing periods in general (Australian Ministry of Education, 1990).

## Anecdotal Records

■ An **anecdotal record** is the recording of the description of a significant incident in which the description and interpretation are kept separate.

An **anecdotal record,** is a field note or description of a significant bit of student behavior. It is an observational technique long used by both anthropologists and teachers. Almost any observation that can shed light on a student's literacy endeavors is a suitable entry for an anecdotal record, including notes on strategies, miscues, interests, interactions with others, and work habits (Rhodes, 1990). The anecdotal record should be "recordings of what the child said or did—not interpretations" (Bush & Huebner, 1979, p. 355). Interpretation comes later and is based on several records and other sources of information. It is important to keep in mind that when recording observations of strategy use, the way in which strategies are used may vary according to the nature of the task—the type of story being read, its relative difficulty, and the purpose for reading it. Therefore, it would be helpful to record several observations before coming to a conclusion (Tierney, Readence, & Dishner, 1995). In going over anecdotal records, the teacher should ask what this information reveals about the student and how it can be used to plan her or his instructional program.

To keep track of observations and anecdotal records, you might keep a notebook which has a separate section for each student. Or you might use a handheld computer to record observations, which then can be downloaded into a database,

Teachers may resist keeping anecdotal or other written records because they believe that they will remember the important things that the student does. However, memories are fallible. They may remember only the good things or not so good things that a student does, and thus fail to obtain a balanced view of the pupil.

class management, or assessment management software, such as Learner Profile (Sunburst), which allows you to record and organize observations and other data in terms of standards or objectives.

## Ratings

A structured and efficient way to collect data is through the use of **ratings.** Ratings generally indicate the "degree to which the child possesses a given trait or skill" (Bush & Huebner, 1979, p. 353). The three kinds of ratings are checklists, questionnaires, and interviews. Checklists can use a present–absent scale (a student has the trait or does not have it) or one that shows degrees of involvement. The present–absent scale might be used for traits for which there is no degree of possession, such as knowing one's home address and telephone number. The degree scale is appropriate for traits that vary in the extent to which they are manifested, such as joining in class discussions. Figure 2.6 shows a sample observation checklist designed to assess voluntary reading.

■ **Rating** is the process of estimating the quality of a learning process or product.

## Questionnaires

A good example of a reading attitude **questionnaire** is the Elementary Reading Attitude Survey (ERAS) (McKenna & Kerr, 1990). It includes twenty items designed to measure how students feel about recreational and school reading. ERAS can be read to younger, less-skilled readers; older, more-skilled students can read it themselves. The questionnaire addresses such areas as how children feel when they

■ A **questionnaire** is an instrument in which a subject is asked to respond to a series of questions on some topic.

**FIGURE 2.6**

### Observation Checklist for Voluntary Reading

Name of student: _____     Date: _____

|  | Never | Seldom | Occasionally | Frequently |
|---|---|---|---|---|
| Reads during free time | _____ | _____ | _____ | _____ |
| Visits the library | _____ | _____ | _____ | _____ |
| Reads books on a variety of topics | _____ | _____ | _____ | _____ |
| Recommends books to others in the class | _____ | _____ | _____ | _____ |
| Talks with others about books | _____ | _____ | _____ | _____ |
| Checks out books from the library | _____ | _____ | _____ | _____ |

read a book on a rainy Saturday and how they feel about reading in school. Students respond by circling one of four illustrations of the cartoon Garfield, which range from a very happy to a very sad cat. Another questionnaire that might be used is the Reading Survey section of the MRP (Motivation to Read Profile), which can be found in the March 1996 issue of *The Reading Teacher*. The Survey probes two aspects of reading motivation: self-concept as a reader and value of reading.

Questionnaires can provide information about reading interests, study habits, strategy use, and other areas in reading and writing. They can be forced-choice like ERAS or open-ended and requiring a written response. Questionnaires assessing study habits and skills might cover such topics as how students go about studying for a test, where they study, and how much time they spend doing homework each night.

> ▌Thanks to the generosity of the authors and the cartoon Garfield's creator, Jim Davis, ERAS has not been copyrighted and was presented, ready to duplicate, in the May 1990 issue of *The Reading Teacher*.

## Interviews

> ■ An **interview** is the process of asking a subject a series of questions on a topic.

**Interviews** are simply oral questionnaires. Their advantage is that the teacher can probe a student's replies, rephrase questions, and encourage extended answers and so obtain a wide range of information. An interview can focus on such topics as a student's likes and dislikes about a reading group, preferences with respect to reading materials, and reasons for these attitudes. A good example of an interview is the Conversational Interview section of the Motivation to Read Profiles (Gambrell, Codling, & Palmer, 1996). The Conversational Interview, which complements the Reading Survey, consists of a series of questions about a student's reading interests and habits and possible influences on those habits.

One kind of interview, the process interview, provides insight about the strategies students are using and also helps students become aware of their processes (Jett-Simpson, 1990). The process interview is best conducted informally on a one-to-one basis, but if time is limited, you might ask for written responses to your questions or hold sessions with small groups. Possible process interview questions include the following, which are adapted from Jett-Simpson (1990). Only one or two of these questions should be asked at one sitting.

1. If a young child asked you how to read, what would you tell him or her to do?
2. When you come to a word you don't know, what do you do?
3. How do you choose something to read?
4. How do you get ready for reading?
5. Where do you read or study at home?
6. When a paragraph is confusing, what do you do?
7. How do you check your reading?
8. What do you do to help you remember what you've read?

**USING TECHNOLOGY**

The National Center for Research on Evaluation, Standards, and Student Testing provides information on assessment. **http://cresst96.cse.ucla.edu/**

National Center on Educational Outcomes provides information on assessing students who have disabilities. **http://www.coled.umn.edu/nceo/**

## Conferences

Just as with interviews, conferences can be an excellent source of assessment information. During writing conferences, you might ask questions such as, "What

## Exemplary Teaching

### *Ongoing Assessment*

*T*o make her instruction as fruitful as possible, Pat Loden, a first-grade teacher, bases her instruction on ongoing assessment of students (Morrow & Asbury, 2001). Each day she focuses on two students to assess. During the day she carefully observes these students and records her observations. She keeps running records of their reading, assesses their story retellings, and notes their use of reading strategies. She also has a conference with them and goes over their reading logs. In their reading logs, they record titles and authors of books read and their reading goals for the week. During whole-class activities she makes sure to direct questions to them and notes their responses. She also observes the two focus students as they work

independently. She keeps a file on each student and uses the files when planning instruction, making decisions about placing students in guided reading groups, and before holding conferences with students. Loden also keeps records of conferences she holds during writing workshop. During the conferences she asks questions that help reveal students' thought processes as they write and the strategies they use. Emphasis throughout the assessment is to obtain a deeper understanding of where children are and what processes and strategies they are using so individual and group instructional activities can be planned to further foster their development.

do you like best about writing? What kind of writing do you like to do? What is easy for you in writing? What is hard for you? What are some things that you might do to become an even better writer than you are now? What do you like best about reading? Do you have any favorite authors? Who are they? What is easy for you in reading? What is hard for you? What might you do to become a better reader?"

Questionnaires, interviews, conferences, and ratings completed by students have a common weakness. Their usefulness depends on students' ability and willingness to supply accurate information. Students may give answers that they think the teacher wants to hear. Information gathered from these sources, therefore, should be verified with other data.

## SELF-EVALUATION

The ultimate evaluation is, of course, self-evaluation. Students should be involved in all phases of the evaluation process and, insofar as possible, take responsibility for assessing their own work. Questionnaires and self-report checklists are especially useful for this. Figure 2.7 shows a self-report checklist with which students can assess their use of strategies in learning from text.

Self-assessment should begin early. Ahlmann (1992) noted that by October, her first-graders are already evaluating their own work and that of authors they read. To self-assess, students reflect on their learning, assemble portfolios of their work, list their achievements, and, with the guidance of the teacher, put together a plan for what they hope to achieve.

**FIGURE 2.7**

### Student's Self-Report Checklist on Strategies for Learning from Text

|  | Usually | Often | Sometimes | Never |
|---|---|---|---|---|
| **Before reading, do I** | | | | |
| 1. Read the title, introductory paragraph, headings, and summary? | ___ | ___ | ___ | ___ |
| 2. Look at photos, maps, charts, and graphs? | ___ | ___ | ___ | ___ |
| 3. Think about what I know about the topic? | ___ | ___ | ___ | ___ |
| 4. Predict what the text will be about or make up questions that the text might answer? | ___ | ___ | ___ | ___ |
| **During reading, do I** | | | | |
| 5. Read to answer questions that the teacher or I have made up? | ___ | ___ | ___ | ___ |
| 6. Stop after each section and try to answer my questions? | ___ | ___ | ___ | ___ |
| 7. Use headings, maps, charts, and graphs to help me understand the text? | ___ | ___ | ___ | ___ |
| 8. Try to make pictures in my mind as I read? | ___ | ___ | ___ | ___ |
| 9. Reread a sentence or get help if I don't understand what I am reading? | ___ | ___ | ___ | ___ |
| 10. Use context or the glossary if I don't understand what I am reading? | ___ | ___ | ___ | ___ |
| **After reading, do I** | | | | |
| 11. Review the section to make sure that I know the most important information? | ___ | ___ | ___ | ___ |
| 12. Try to organize the information in the text by creating a map, chart, time line, or summary? | ___ | ___ | ___ | ___ |

In some classes, students complete exit slips on which they talk about what they have learned that day or raise questions that they did not have time to raise in class or were reluctant to raise. Learning logs and journals might perform a similar function. As an alternative, the teacher and the class might design a form on which students tell what they learned in a certain class and list questions that they still have. In reading and writing conferences, part of the discussion should center on skills mastered and goals for the future, and how those goals might be met. These conferences, of course, should be genuinely collaborative efforts so that students' input is shown to be valued.

As students engage in a literacy task, they should assess their performance. After reading a selection, they might ask themselves: How well did I understand this selection? Do I need to reread or take other steps to improve my comprehension? After completing a piece of writing, they should also evaluate their performance. If a rubric has been constructed for the piece of writing, they should assess their work in terms of the rubric.

## Logs and Journals

Reading logs and response journals can also be a part of students' self-evaluation as well as a source of information for the teacher. Reading logs contain a list of books read and, perhaps, a brief summary or assessment. Response journals provide students with opportunities to record personal reactions to their reading. Both reading logs and response journals offer unique insights into students' growing ability to handle increasingly difficult books, their changing interests, and personal involvement with reading.

# EVALUATING WRITING

## Holistic Scoring

What captures the essence of a piece of writing—its style, its theme, its development, its adherence to conventions, its originality? The answer is all of these elements and more. Because of the way the parts of the piece work together, it must be viewed as a whole. In **holistic scoring,** instead of noting specific strengths and weaknesses, a teacher evaluates a composition in terms of a limited number of general criteria. The criteria are used "only as a general guide . . . in reaching a holistic judgment" (Cooper & Odell, 1977, p. 4). The teacher does not stop to check the piece to see whether it meets each of the criteria but simply forms a general impression. The teacher can score a piece according to the presence or absence of key elements. There may be a scoring guide, which can be a checklist or a rubric. (A holistic scoring guide in the form of a rubric is shown in Table 2.8.) The teacher should also use anchor pieces along with the rubric to assess compositions. Anchor pieces, which may be drawn from the work of past classes or from the compositions that are currently being assessed, are writing samples that provide examples of deficient, fair, good, and superior pieces. The teacher decides which of the anchor pieces a student's composition most closely resembles.

■ **Holistic scoring** is a process for sorting or ranking written pieces on the basis of an overall impression of the piece. Sample pieces (anchors) or a description of standards (rubric) for rating the pieces might be used as guides.

### ■ Applying Holistic Scoring

Before scoring the pieces, the teacher should quickly read them all to get a sense of how well the class did overall. This prevents setting criteria that are too high or too low. After sorting the papers into four groups—beginning, developing, proficient, and superior—the teacher rereads each work more carefully before confirming its placement. If possible, a second teacher should also evaluate the papers. This is especially important if the works are to be graded.

## Analytic Scoring

**Analytic scoring** involves analyzing pieces and noting specific strengths and weaknesses. It requires the teacher to create a set of specific scoring criteria. Instead of overwhelming students with corrections, it is best to decide on a lim-

■ **Analytic scoring** is a type of scoring that uses a description of major features to be considered when assessing the piece.

FIGURE 2.8

**Analytic Scoring Guide for a Friendly Letter**

Name of student: _____     Date: _____

| | Beginning | Developing | Proficient | Superior |
|---|---|---|---|---|
| **Content** | | | | |
| Has a natural but interesting beginning. | _____ | _____ | _____ | _____ |
| Includes several topics of interest. | _____ | _____ | _____ | _____ |
| Develops each topic in sufficient detail. | _____ | _____ | _____ | _____ |
| Shows an interest in what's happening to the reader. | _____ | _____ | _____ | _____ |
| Has a friendly way of ending the letter. | _____ | _____ | _____ | _____ |
| **Style** | | | | |
| Has a friendly, natural tone. | _____ | _____ | _____ | _____ |
| **Form** | | | | |
| Follows friendly letter form. | _____ | _____ | _____ | _____ |
| Indents paragraphs. | _____ | _____ | _____ | _____ |
| Is neat and legible. | _____ | _____ | _____ | _____ |
| **Mechanics** | | | | |
| Begins each sentence with a capital. | _____ | _____ | _____ | _____ |
| Uses correct end punctuation. | _____ | _____ | _____ | _____ |
| Spells words correctly. | _____ | _____ | _____ | _____ |

ited number of key features, such as those that have been emphasized for a particular writing activity. Spandel and Stiggins (1997) suggest the following six characteristics: ideas, organization, voice, word choice, sentence fluency, and conventions. Although more time consuming than holistic scoring, analytic scoring allows the teacher to make constructive suggestions about students' writing. An analytic scoring guide for a friendly letter is presented in Figure 2.8.

## Using a Combination of Techniques

In some cases, a combination of holistic and analytic scoring works best. Holistic scoring guards against the teacher's becoming overly caught up in mechanics or stylistics and neglecting the substance of the piece. Analytic scoring provides students with necessary direction for improving their work and becoming more proficient writers. Whichever approach is used, it is important that criteria for assessment be

▌ When reviewing students' papers, there is a tendency to note all errors. However, students do their best when comments are positive and when there is emphasis on one or two areas, such as providing more detail or use of more vivid language. This is especially effective when instruction is geared to the areas highlighted and students revise targeted areas in their compositions (Dahl & Farnan, 1998).

clearly understood. As Dahl and Farnan (1998) note, "When writers lack specific standards and intentions, their ability to reflect on and evaluate their writing is severely compromised. It is not surprising that if writers do not know what they want to accomplish with a particular writing, it will be difficult for them to judge whether they have created an effective composition" (p. 121).

# PORTFOLIOS

Artists, photographers, designers, and others assemble their work in **portfolios** for assessment. Portfolios are now being used in a somewhat modified fashion to assess the literacy growth of elementary and middle school students. Portfolios have a number of advantages. First, they facilitate the assessment of growth over time. Because they provide the teacher with an opportunity to take a broad look at a student's literacy development, they are an appropriate method for assessing holistic approaches. Portfolio assessment can also lead to changes in the curriculum and teaching practices. In Au's (1994) study, for instance, teachers began emphasizing the revision phase of writing when portfolio assessment helped them see that they were neglecting that area. Teachers in Kentucky reported that portfolios were the key element in a program designed to improve writing (Stecher, Arron, Kuganoff, & Goodwin, 1998).

■ A **portfolio** is a collection of work samples, test results, checklists, or other data used to assess a student's performance.

## Types of Portfolios

There are five kinds of portfolios, each performing different functions and containing different kinds of materials: showcase, evaluation, documentation, process, and composite (Valencia & Place, 1994). Like the traditional portfolio used by artists to display their best works, the showcase is composed of works that students have selected as being their best. The focus in the evaluation portfolio is on obtaining representative works from key areas. The samples included might be standardized—that is, based on a common text or a common topic—so that results are comparable across students. A documentation portfolio is designed to provide evidence of students' growth and so might contain the greatest number and variety of work samples. The process portfolio is designed to show how students work, so it includes samples from various stages of a project along with students' comments about how the project is progressing. A composite portfolio contains elements from two or more types of portfolios. For instance, a portfolio designed for district evaluation might contain showcase and process items.

## Writing Samples

Collecting representative pieces from several types of writing assignments gives the teacher a broad view of a student's development. Including pieces written at different times of the year allows the teacher to trace the student's growth. Rough drafts as well as final copies illustrate the student's writing progress and indicate how

*T*eachers periodically review students' portfolios with them.

well the student handles the various processes. Each student might include in her or his portfolio lists of pieces written, major writing skills learned, and current goals. Both student and teacher should have access to the portfolio and should agree on which pieces should be included. Teacher and student should also agree on how to choose what goes into the portfolio.

To help students reflect on their learning and make wise choices about the included pieces, you might have them explain their choices by completing a self-evaluative statement. The statement can be a brief explanation with the heading "Why I Chose This Piece." Initially, reasons for inclusion and comments tend to be vague (Tierney, Carter, & Desai, 1991). However, through classroom discussions and conferences, you should help students explore criteria for including certain pieces rather than others—it tells a good story, it has a beginning that grabs the reader, it has many interesting examples, it seems to flow, and so on.

## Reading Samples

▌A portfolio can demonstrate the power of a reader and a writer. Unbeknownst to the teacher, a student may read dozens or hundreds of books or be a budding author. A reading log or sampling of written pieces should reveal this (Tierney, Carter, & Desai, 1991).

Some teachers use portfolios primarily to assess writing. If you wish to use portfolios to assess reading, include samples of reading. Samples to be included depend on the goals of the program. Valencia (1990) cautioned, "If the goals of instruction are not specified, portfolios have the potential to become reinforced holding files for odds and ends . . . " (p. 339). If a goal of reading instruction is to teach students to visualize, drawings of reading selections might be included. If you have been working on summaries, you may want to see sample summaries. A list of books read might be appropriate for a goal of wide reading. Running records or informal reading inventories might be included to demonstrate fluency, word recognition in context, comprehension, or overall reading development.

At certain points, reading and writing will converge—written summaries of selections and research reports using several sources might count toward both reading and writing goals. Other items that might be placed in the portfolio are checklists, quizzes, standardized and informal test results, learning logs, written reactions to selections, and graphic organizers.

## Reviewing Portfolios

To check on students' progress, periodically review their portfolios. Farr and Farr (1990) suggested that this be done a minimum of four times a year. In order to make the best use of your time and to help students organize their work, you might have them prepare a list of the items included in the portfolio. The portfolio should also contain a list of students' learning objectives. Students might write a cover letter or fill out a form summarizing work they have done, explaining which goals they feel they have met, which areas might need improvement, and what their plans for the future are. A sample portfolio evaluation form is presented in Figure 2.9.

Before you start to review a portfolio, decide what you want to focus on. It could be number of books read, changes in writing, or effort put into revisions. Your evaluation should, of course, consider the student's stated goals; it is also important to emphasize the student's strengths. As you assess the portfolio, consider a variety of pieces and look at the work in terms of its changes over time. Ask yourself: What does the student's work show about her or his progress over the time span covered? What might she or he do to make continued progress?

To save time and help you organize your assessment of the portfolio, you may want to use a checklist that is supplemented with personal comments. A sample port-

> Portfolios have the potential for demonstrating students' growth. As you assess folders, note the areas in which students have done especially well. Also note areas of weakness. In addition, portfolios provide information that shows class as well as individual needs. If the class as a whole is evidencing difficulty with the mechanics of writing, that might be an area in your curriculum that needs special attention.

> Giving students a say in portfolio decisions helps them maintain a sense of ownership (Simmons, 1990). It also fosters a more positive attitude and encourages students to take risks in their writing (Johnson, 1995).

**FIGURE 2.9**

### Portfolio Evaluation by Student

Name: _____     Date: _____

Portfolio Evaluation

What were my goals in reading for this period?

What progress toward meeting these goals does my portfolio show?

What are my strengths?

What are my weaknesses?

What are my goals for improving as a reader?

How do I plan to meet those goals?

What were my goals in writing for this period?

What progress toward meeting these goals does my portfolio show?

What are my strengths as a writer?

What are my weaknesses?

What are my goals for improving as a writer?

How do I plan to meet these goals?

What questions do I have about my writing or my reading?

Portfolios are most useful when goals are clearly stated and specific criteria are listed for their assessment. It is essential, of course, that goals and criteria be understood by students (Snider, Lima, & DeVito, 1994).

folio review checklist is presented in Figure 2.10. Because the objective of evaluation is to improve instruction, students should be active partners in the process. "It follows that . . . assessment activities in which students are engaged in evaluating their own learning help them reflect on and understand their own strengths and needs, and it instills responsibility for their own learning" (Tierney, Carter, & Desai, 1991, p. 7).

**INVOLVING PARENTS**

Parents may feel uncomfortable or even threatened by portfolios. When portfolios are explained, parents prefer them to standardized tests (Tierney, Carter, & Desai, 1991). Tierney, Carter, and Desai (1991) suggested sitting down with parents and explaining the portfolio process to them. This not only helps parents understand the process, it also helps them to see what their role might be.

In Kentucky, teachers reported that the portfolio system was the most influential factor in determining their instructional practice (Stecher, Barron, Kaganoff, & Goodwin, 1998). They also credited the portfolio system with helping them to become better teachers and their students better writers.

**FIGURE 2.10**

**Portfolio Review Checklist**

Name of student: _____   Date: _____

**Voluntary Reading**
   Number of books read  _____
   Variety of books read  _____
   Strengths  _____
   Needs  _____

**Reading Comprehension**
   Construction of meaning  _____
   Extension of meaning  _____
   Use of strategies  _____
   Quality of responses  _____
   Strengths  _____
   Needs  _____

**Writing**
   Amount of writing  _____
   Variety of writing  _____
   Planning  _____
   Revising  _____
   Self-editing  _____
   Content  _____
   Organization  _____
   Style  _____
   Mechanics  _____
   Strengths  _____
   Needs  _____

Comments: _____
_____
_____

# BASAL READER ASSESSMENT

Today's basal readers offer a variety of assessment devices. Tests that accompany each selection or skills checks contained in workbooks can be used as part of a paper-and-pencil formative assessment. There are also numerous suggestions for ongoing, informal assessment through observation or use of checklists. In some instances, these suggestions are accompanied by corrective techniques: For instance, if students have difficulty making inferences, the teacher is provided with a reteaching lesson (Cooper et al., 2001). There are also numerous suggestions for self-assessment by students: "What parts of the selection were difficult for me? Why?" (Cooper et al., 2001). End-of-theme tests are also available, as are benchmark tests designed to be given quarterly. Portfolio systems are also part of the assessment package. One program also includes weekly lessons on test-taking skills (Flood et al., 2001).

# SCREENING AND DIAGNOSTIC INSTRUMENTS AND CLASSROOM-BASED ASSESSMENT

An assessment program should include screening and diagnostic instruments as well as classroom-based assessment. Screening instruments are assessment measures that indicate a possible problem and the need for a more thorough assessment. Group tests of reading can function as screening devices. Low scores indicate a possible difficulty. A quick test of the ability to read lists of words can also function as a screening device. A carefully administered IRI is diagnostic because it yields a depth of information about a student's reading.

Classroom-based instructional assessments indicate whether students are making adequate progress or need more support. In classroom-based assessment, teachers use a variety of techniques for obtaining information about students' performance. Techniques include many of the informal devices presented in this chapter: running records, work samples such as pieces of writing, observations, checklists, anecdotal records, interviews, conferences, questionnaires, and portfolios. Classroom quizzes, basal reader assessments, and tests might also be included. The advantage of classroom-based assessment is that it provides information for planning instruction and making needed changes in a literacy program.

Classroom-based assessment works best when a school system or school and its teachers decide what its standards or objectives are and then decide how to gather information in order to judge whether these standards are being reached. By discussing objectives teachers clarify the schools' goals. In discussing assessment devices, they can address the issues of reliability and validity. What is the most valid way to judge that students are writing in a variety of genres? If a system of scoring written pieces is selected, how will they ensure that teachers' judgments are consistent so that the pieces judged to be proficient by one teacher would be judged proficient by other teachers?

Some programs, such as Reading First, have fairly strict requirements for screening, diagnostic, and ongoing monitoring or classroom-based assessment. Reading First also requires an outcomes measure to assess whether students are making adequate progress. Check to see how these requirements are being implemented in your state.

Assessment systems have been created that align teaching and assessment with objectives and are available commercially. First Steps (Education Department of Western Australia, 1994) is one such system. In addition, a number of school systems have devised classroom-based assessment systems. Check to see if your state or your school district has created an assessment system.

Different assessment systems have differing visions of reading. Some espouse a strong phonics approach. Others favor use of context and a more holistic approach. You might use an existing system as a starting point but modify it to meet your vision of reading and the objectives that you emphasize. This text has a list of standards and suggestions for assessment at the end of each chapter. These could provide a starting point for the construction of a classroom-based assessment system.

## ASSESSING ENGLISH LANGUAGE LEARNERS

Under the No Child Left Behind Act of 2001, the academic progress of every child in grades three through eight will be tested in reading and math, including those learning English. All English Language Learners (ELLs) will be tested annually to measure how well they are learning English. States and individual schools will be held accountable for results.

Apart from state and federal regulations, it is essential that you have information about ELLs' proficiency in literacy in their first language. Students who can read in another language will have learned basic concepts of reading. They will have developed phonological awareness, alphabetical knowledge, and knowledge of phonics. You can build on this knowledge. It is also essential that you have information about the students' proficiency in oral and written English. If students are weak in understanding English, you can plan a literacy program that develops oral language.

Key questions include:
- What is the student's proficiency in speaking her or his first language?
- What is the student's proficiency in speaking English?
- What is the student's proficiency in reading in the first language?
- What is the student's proficiency in reading in English?
- What is the educational background of the student?

The ESL or bilingual specialist should be able to provide information about the students' proficiency in literacy in their first language and also their knowledge of English. If this information is not available, use informal techniques to assess the students' proficiency in reading and writing their first language. Ask students to bring in books in their native tongue and read them to you and then retell the selection in English. Also ask them to bring in a piece of writing that they have done in their native language and read it to you and then retell it in English. Based on the ease with which they read, you can judge whether they are literate in their first language, even if you don't know the language. You might also obtain or construct a list of common words in their language and ask students to read them. Figure

2.11 contains a list of twenty common Spanish words, phonetically respelled and with their English translations. You might use a list such as this to get a very rough idea of the students' reading proficiency. If students can read all or most of these words, they can read at least at a basic level in Spanish. If you are fluent in Spanish, you might administer the Spanish Reading Inventory (Kendall/Hunt) or the English-Español Reading Inventory for the Classroom (Merrill).

To assess students' ability to understand language, point to objects, such as a pen, book, desk, colors, shapes, food, and provide such requests as: Point to the book. Point to the red dot. Point to the square. Point to your knee, your foot, your ear (Law & Eckes, 2002). Start with common objects and progress to more advanced ones: Point to the magnet. Point to the picture of the jet. Real objects work better but you might also use magazine or other photos to assess students' receptive vocabulary. Also request that students follow a series of commands: Stand. Sit. Open the book. Raise your hand, Write your name. To assess expressive vocabulary, have the students identify objects that you point to. Also ask students a series of questions and note how they respond: What is your name? How old are you? Where do you live? Count to ten. Name the colors that I point to. Name the letters that I point to. For a copy of informal language tests for English language learners and additional suggestions for assessment, refer to the text by Law and Eckes, which is listed in the References section.

**FIGURE 2.11**

### Spanish Word List

| Spanish Word | Pronunciation | Meaning |
| --- | --- | --- |
| no | no | no |
| mi | me | my |
| uno | OO-no | one |
| esta | ES-tah | this |
| ella | AY-yah | she |
| señor | sen-YOR | mister |
| leer | lay-AIR | read |
| libro | LEE-bro | book |
| amigo | ah-ME-go | friend |
| pelota | peh-LOH-tah | ball |
| vaca | BAH-kah | cow |
| musica | MYEW-see-kah | music |
| sorpressa | sor-PRES-ah | surprise |
| leopardo | lay-oh-PAR-doh | leopard |
| abuela | ah-BWEH-lah | grandmother |
| bicicleta | bee-see-KLAY-tah | bicycle |
| mañana | mon-YAH-nah | tomorrow |
| primavera | pre-mah-BEAR-ah | spring |
| zapatos | sah-PAH-toes | shoes |
| zoológico | soh-oh-LOH-hee-koh | zoo |

## ASSESSING MATERIALS

Just about the most important instructional decision you will make is selecting the appropriate level of materials for your students. Choose a level that is too easy and students will be bored and unchallenged. Select material that is too difficult and they will be discouraged, have their academic self-concepts demolished, and fail to make progress. Perhaps, worst of all, they will learn to hate reading (Juel, 1994). As noted earlier, students should know at least 95 percent of the words in the materials they are asked to read and should have about 75 percent comprehension.

Publishers of school materials generally provide reading levels for their texts. Using a formula or subjective leveling scale, they estimate that the material is at, for example, a second-. third-, or fourth-grade level, which means that the average second-. third-, or fourth-grader should be able to read it. Or they may use

■ **Readability** is the difficulty level of a selection. A formula may be used to estimate readability by measuring quantitative factors such as sentence length and number of difficult words in the selection. A leveling system may use a number of qualitative factors to estimate the difficulty of the text. Best results are obtained by assessing both qualitative and quantitative factors.

letters or numbers to indicate a level rather than a grade. Some publishers of children's books also supply **readability** levels. If no readability level is indicated for a book that you wish to use, you might check Appendix A, which contains more than 1,200 leveled titles, or you can consult one of the following sources.

## ATOS (Advantage-TASA Open Standard)

ATOS is a new computerized formula that uses number of words per sentence, characters per word, and average grade level of words and analyzes the entire text to estimate the readability of a book and provide a grade-level equivalent. ATOS scores for more than 40,000 trade books are available from Renaissance Learning, the creators of Accelerated Reading, at their Web site: http://www.renlearn.com. Click on Quizzes and enter the title of the book for which you would like to have an ATOS score. ATOS scores are expressed in grade equivalents. First grade is subdivided into a series of levels that are equated with Reading Recovery levels. If the text for which you want a readability estimate is not available, contact Renaissance Learning. They may have the ATOS score. If you provide sample passages from the book, the company will provide an ATOS score for you.

## Lexile Scale

The lexile scale is a two-factor computerized formula that consists of a measurement of sentence length and word frequency. The lexile scale ranges from about 70 to 1700+, with 70 being very easy beginning reading material and 1700 being very difficult reading material of the type found in scientific journals. Table 2.7 provides approximate grade equivalents for lexile scores. A software program for obtaining readability estimates, the *Lexile Analyzer*, is available from MetaMetrics. However, lexile scores for about 25,000 books are available online at http://www. lexile.com/.

## Degrees of Reading Power

The Degrees of Reading Power measures sentence length, number of words not on the Dale List of words known by fourth-graders, and average number of letters per word (Touchstone Applied Science Associates, 1994). Compilations of readability levels expressed in DRP units for content area textbooks can be found on the following Web site: http://www.tasaliteracy.com. DRP readabilities for trade books are available on a piece of easy-to-use software, *BookLink*. DRP units range from 15 for the easiest materials to 85 for the most difficult reading material. Table 2.7 provides approximate grade equivalents for DRP scores.

## Other Readability Formulas

If you are unable to get a readability level from one of these sources, or if you prefer to assess the readability of the text yourself, there are a number of formulas you can apply. One of the easiest to use is the Fry Graph. The Fry Graph bases its estimate on two factors: sentence length and number of syllables in a word. Number of syllables in a word is a measure of vocabulary difficulty. In general, the more syllables a word has, the harder it tends to be. The Fry Readability Graph (Fry, 1977b) is presented in Figure 2.12. A formula that counts the number of hard words but is relatively easy to use is the Primary Readability Formula (Gunning, 2002), which can be used to assess the difficulty level of materials in grades one to four. *The New Dale-Chall Readability Formula* (Chall & Dale, 1995), which also counts the number of hard words, is recommended for grades three and up.

One problem with readability formulas is that they are mechanical and so do not consider subjective factors, such as the density of concepts, use of illustrations, or background required to construct meaning from the text. Readability formulas should be complemented by the use of the subjective factors incorporated in a leveling system (Gunning, 2000b). A leveling system uses subjective or qualitative factors to estimate the difficulty level of materials.

## Leveling Systems

In addition to failing to consider qualitative factors, traditional formulas do not work well at the very beginning levels. Formulas don't consider such factors as usefulness of illustrations and number of lines per page, which are major determinants of the difficulty level of beginning materials. Formulas do indicate with reasonable accuracy that materials are on a first-grade level. However, first-grade reading encompasses a wide range of material that includes counting or color books that have just one or two easy words per page as well as books, such as the Little Bear series, that contain brief chapters and may contain several hundred words. To make fine discriminations among the range of first-grade books, it is necessary to use a leveling system.

Although materials for beginning readers may look similar—large print and lots of illustrations—they incorporate different theories of teaching reading and have different uses (Hiebert, 1999). Early reading materials can be classified as being predictable, high frequency, or decodable. Predictable texts are written in such a way that the student can use illustrations or their knowledge of language to "read" the text. A predictable book might have the sentences "I can run. I can jump. I can sing. I can read," each on a separate page accompanied by an illustration showing each of these actions. The reader gets heavy support from the illustrations and the repeated pattern. Predictable books are excellent for reinforcing concepts of print and giving students the feel of reading, and they can also help English Language Learners (ELLs) learn the patterns of English. Predictable books do a good job of introducing students to reading. Most students will pick up an initial reading vocabulary by repeatedly meeting words in print. However, some will continue to use picture and language clues. The use of predictable text may actually hinder their progress.

Some texts emphasize high-frequency words. Words such as *of, and, the, was,* and *where* occur so often in print that they are said to be high frequency. Most of the predictable books are composed primarily of high-frequency words.

FIGURE 2.12

## Fry's Graph for Estimating Readability

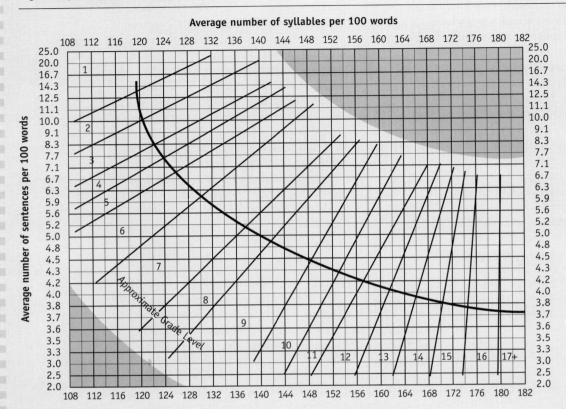

**Average number of syllables per 100 words**

**Expanded Directions for Working Readability Graph**

**1.** Randomly select three (3) sample passages and count out exactly 100 words each, beginning with the beginning of a sentence. Do count proper nouns, initializations, and numerals.

**2.** Count the number of sentences in the 100 words, estimating length of the fraction of the last sentence to the nearest one-tenth.

**3.** Count the total number of syllables in the 100-word passage. If you don't have a hand counter available, an easy way is to simply put a mark above every syllable over one in each word, then when you get to the end of the passage, count the number of marks and add 100. Small calculators can also be used by pushing numeral 1, then the + sign for each word or syllable when counting.

**4.** Enter graph with *average* sentence length and *average* number of syllables; plot dot where the two lines intersect. Area where dot is plotted will give you the approximate grade level.

**5.** If a great deal of variability is found in syllable count or sentence count, putting more samples into the average is desirable.

**6.** A word is defined as a group of symbols with space on either side; thus, *Joe, IRA, 1945,* and *&* are each one word.

**7.** A syllable is defined as a phonetic syllable. Generally, there are as many syllables as vowel sounds. For example, *stopped* is one syllable and *wanted* is two syllables. When counting syllables for numerals and initializations, count one syllable for each symbol. For example, *1945* is four syllables, *IRA* is three syllables, and *&* is one syllable.

Fry's Readability Graph: Clarifications, Validity, and Extension to Level 17 by E. Fry, 1977, *Journal of Reading, 21,* p. 249.

Decodable texts are ones that contain phonics elements that have been taught. A story about a *bug* who lived in a *rug* would be decodable to students who have learned the *-ug* pattern. No text is totally decodable. High-frequency words such as *is*, *are*, and *the* need to be included, as do content words such as *bear* and *hungry* if the story is about a hungry bear.

The most widely used leveling system is based on the predictability of text. Adapting a system that was originally devised for Reading Recovery, Fountas and Pinnell (1996) and Pinnell and Fountas (1999, 2002) have compiled a list of almost 14,000 leveled books for students in kindergarten through grade eight. Books are leveled from A through Z, with A being very beginning reading and Z being eighth-grade reading. Books in Appendix A have been leveled according to both predictability and decodability and take in quantitative as well as qualitative factors.

However, you may wish to use books that have not been leveled, or you may not have access to a listing of leveled books. In that case, you need to be able to level books on your own. To level books, consider key subjective factors and compare passages from the book you are leveling to passages from benchmark books. *The Qualitative Assessment of Text Difficulty* (Chall, Bissex, Conard, & Harris-Sharples, 1996) provides benchmark passages and directions for leveling both fictional and informational books. Or you might use the Basic Leveling Index, which is explained below.

### ■ The Basic Leveling Index

The Basic Leveling Index uses both quantitative and qualitative factors to level books. Subjected to extensive tryouts, it has been used to level several thousand books and compares favorably with other leveling systems (Gunning, 1998b, 2000b). Tryouts suggest that it is more accurate than readability formulas or subjective leveling systems used alone.

**Using the basic leveling system with beginning reading books.** Beginning reading books are more difficult to level than are upper-grade books because they encompass a very wide range of difficulty. The Basic Leveling System has seven beginning-reader-first-grade levels: picture, frame/caption (early preprimer), preprimer one, preprimer two, preprimer three, primer, and first. To determine the difficulty of an early reading text, compare the text being assessed with a benchmark book or the benchmark passage. Ask: Which benchmark book or passage is this text most like? Also consider qualitative factors. Note especially the difficulty level of the words. Would students be able to read them? Remember that they should be able to read about 95 percent of the words. At this level, most of the words will be in their listening vocabulary. Their major task is to pronounce or recognize the printed words. Words such as *the* and *are* appear with high frequency and so are easier to read. Some words such as *cat* and *hat* will be easy to decode. Consider, too, how helpful the illustrations are. Some of the words may be depicted by illustrations. Illustrations might also provide an overview of the text or show signifi-

**Levels correspond to those used by basal readers. Most basal reading systems divide materials into the following levels: three preprimers, a primer, and a first-grade reader. Informal reading inventories typically feature a preprimer, primer, and first-grade level.**

cant portions of it. Consider overall interest of the selection, familiarity of the topic and language, repetition of elements, use of rhyme, and such format factors as number of lines per page. Also consider the length of the text. Short pieces are easier to read than longer ones. Above all, note whether the average beginning reader would have the background of information necessary to read the text. A book about the Vietnam War, no matter how simply written, would be beyond most beginning readers. Watch out, too, for the use of figurative language and allusions that are beyond beginning readers. When estimating difficulty level, be conservative. If you are undecided whether a book is on a primer or first level, place it at the higher level. It's better to give a student a book that is on the easy side rather than one that is too difficult.

Leveling books works best when those leveling the books are carefully trained. Otherwise, it is prone to error. To get a more reliable and more accurate estimate, use a quantitative measure along with the qualitative ones. The key objective factor that determines the difficulty level of early reading materials is vocabulary, or the difficulty the novice reader will experience pronouncing the words in a book. Stories that use a few common words should prove easier to read than those that use a variety of words, including some that do not occur with high frequency. Vocabulary difficulty is measured by counting the number of words that do not appear on the Alphabetical Listing of 500 High-Frequency Words. The list is a compilation of the 500 words that occur with the highest frequency in first-grade textbooks and children's books that are on a first-grade level (see Figure 2.13). It is based on *The Educator's Word Frequency Guide* (Zeno, Ivens, Millard, & Duvvuri, 1995). In tryouts, teachers who used the number of hard words as an aid in determining difficulty level were much more accurate than those who used only subjective factors (Gunning, 1996).

To determine the number of hard words, count the number of words in a selection that do not appear on the high-frequency list. Consider as familiar words on the list to which -s, -es, -d, -ed, or -ing have been added. If the book being analyzed has fewer than 100 words, check all the words. For brief books, those with 300 or fewer words, analyze the entire work in 100-word segments. For longer texts, analyze as many samples as you can. Analyze at least three samples. Select samples from the beginning, middle, and end of the book. The more samples you analyze, the more valid and reliable the estimate of difficulty. Many children's books increase in difficulty so that the latter part of the book has many more hard words than the beginning portions. Average the hard words scores of the passages sampled. Table 2.9 provides estimated levels based on the proportion of hard words per 100 words.

However, the hard words score should *never* be used as the sole determining factor in estimating difficulty level. Qualitative factors should be carefully considered. In tryouts, when subjective factors were considered, changes were made in estimated difficulty levels about one third of the time. For the most accurate results, obtain an objective readability estimate based on the number of words not on the high-frequency list. Using that estimate as an anchor, consider the benchmark passages and qualitative factors. Then use both objective and subjective in-

FIGURE 2.13

## Alphabetical Listing of 500 High-Frequency Words

| | | | | | | | | | |
|---|---|---|---|---|---|---|---|---|---|
| a | book | drop | gave | hurt | made | over | see | table | voice |
| about | both | duck | get | I | make | own | seed | take | wait |
| across | box | each | girl | I'll | man | paint | seem | talk | walk |
| afraid | boy | ear | give | I'm | many | paper | seen | tall | want |
| after | bring | earth | go | I've | mark | park | set | tell | warm |
| again | brother | eat | gone | if | may | part | she | ten | was |
| air | brown | egg | good | in | maybe | party | sheep | than | wasn't |
| all | bus | end | got | inside | me | people | ship | thank | watch |
| alone | but | enough | grandfather | into | mean | pet | shoe | that | water |
| along | by | even | grandma | is | men | pick | shop | that's | way |
| always | cake | ever | grandmother | isn't | might | picture | short | the | we |
| am | call | every | grandpa | it | minute | piece | should | their | we'll |
| an | came | everyone | grass | it's | mom | pig | shout | them | week |
| and | can | everything | great | its | money | place | show | then | well |
| animal | can't | eye | green | jeep | moon | plant | sick | there | went |
| another | cannot | face | ground | job | more | play | side | these | were |
| answer | car | fall | grow | jump | morning | please | sign | they | wet |
| any | care | family | guess | just | mother | pond | sing | thing | what |
| anybody | cat | far | had | keep | mouse | pretty | sister | think | what's |
| anything | catch | farm | hair | kept | move | pull | sit | this | wheel |
| are | change | farmer | hand | kid | much | push | sky | those | when |
| arm | children | fast | happen | kind | must | put | sleep | thought | where |
| around | city | father | happy | king | my | quick | slow | three | which |
| as | clean | feel | hard | kitten | name | quiet | small | through | while |
| ask | climb | feet | has | knew | near | rabbit | smile | time | white |
| at | close | fell | hat | know | need | race | snow | tired | who |
| away | cloud | felt | have | lake | never | rain | so | to | why |
| baby | cold | few | he | last | new | ran | some | toad | wife |
| back | come | find | head | late | next | reach | someone | today | will |
| bad | cook | fine | hear | laugh | nice | read | something | together | wind |
| bag | could | fire | heard | learn | night | ready | sometime | told | window |
| ball | couldn't | first | held | leave | no | real | soon | too | wish |
| be | cow | fish | hello | left | noise | really | sound | took | with |
| bear | cried | fix | help | leg | not | red | spot | top | without |
| because | cry | floor | hen | let | nothing | rest | stand | town | wolf |
| bed | cut | flower | her | let's | now | ride | star | train | woman |
| been | dad | fly | here | letter | of | right | start | tree | won't |
| before | dark | follow | high | light | off | river | stay | tried | wood |
| began | day | food | hill | like | oh | road | step | truck | word |
| behind | did | for | him | line | old | rock | stick | try | work |
| bell | didn't | found | himself | lion | on | room | still | turn | would |
| best | different | four | his | listen | once | run | stood | turtle | write |
| better | do | fox | hit | little | one | sad | stop | two | year |
| big | doctor | friend | hold | live | only | said | store | uncle | yell |
| bike | does | frog | hole | long | open | same | story | under | yellow |
| bird | dog | from | home | look | or | sat | street | until | yes |
| birthday | don't | front | horse | lost | other | saw | sun | up | you |
| black | door | fun | hot | lot | our | say | sure | us | you'll |
| blue | down | funny | house | love | out | school | surprise | use | your |
| boat | drink | game | how | lunch | outside | sea | swim | very | you're |

**TABLE 2.9**  Estimate of readability level based on number of hard words

| Level | Number of Hard Words |
|---|---|
| Picture | All words depicted by illustrations |
| Caption/Frame | Most words depicted by illustrations |
| High frequency PP1 | 1–3 |
| Preprimer 2 | 4–6 |
| Preprimer 3 | 7–8 |
| Primer | 9–10 |
| First | 11–12 |

Objective difficulty level _____

Estimated difficulty level of text (quantitative and qualitative factors) _____

formation to decide on a difficulty level. Use the worksheet in Figure 2.14 to note quantitative and qualitative factors. As you become familiar with using benchmark passages and subjective factors to level books, your estimates will become more accurate and there will be less need to rely on objective measures. However, objective measures provide a helpful check. Listed on the next few pages is a descrip-

**FIGURE 2.14**

**Worksheet for Estimating Difficulty of Grade-One Materials**

Number of hard words depicted by illustrations:

None _____   Some _____   Most _____   All _____

Number of words that would be easy to decode:

None _____   Some _____   Most _____   All _____

Difficulty of vocabulary and concepts

_____ Familiar vocabulary and concepts

_____ One or two unfamiliar words or concepts

_____ Several unfamiliar words or concepts

Familiarity of topic or story line

High _____   Medium _____   Low _____

When compared with benchmark passages or books, what level(s) do the sample passages from the text seem to be most like?

Passage 1 _____

Passage 2 _____

Passage 3 _____

Average  _____

**FIGURE 2.15**

tion of each level and a sample benchmark passage. Words that do not appear on the high-frequency list are boldfaced.

## ■ Picture Level

A single word or phrase is depicted with an illustration. The word *lion*, for instance, is accompanied by a drawing of a lion; the word *three* is accompanied by the numeral three and three dots. The text is so fully and clearly depicted that no reading is required. For some books the student might need to use the initial consonant to help identify the picture. For instance, the student might not know whether a wolf or dog is being depicted. Seeing that the label for the picture starts with a *w*, the student uses knowledge of initial consonants to reason that a wolf is being depicted.

> **Benchmark books:**
> *Colors* by John Burningham
> *Numbers* by Guy Smalley

## ■ Caption/Frame Level

Text is illustrated so that the reader can use pictures to identify most but not all of the words. Caption level books feature frame sentences, which are easy sentences, such as: "I can ____, I am ____, or ____ can swim," that are repeated throughout the text. The name of the object, animal, or person that completes the frame is depicted. The student would need to know initial consonants and the few high-frequency words that make up the frame.

**FIGURE 2.16**

*Benchmark books:*
*Have You Seen My Cat?* by Eric Carle
*My Barn* by Craig Brown
*Cat on the Mat* by Brian Wildsmith

*Benchmark passage:* I see _____ .

### ■ Preprimer 1 (Easy, High-Frequency Words)

Similar to caption level but there are a greater number of different words used and more reading is required. Illustrations usually depict some or much of text. Requires increased knowledge of high-frequency words and some beginning familiarity with short-vowel patterns, such as *-at* and *-am.*

Hard words: Could be as many as 1–3 words out of 100 not on the high-frequency list.

*Benchmark books:*
*Brown Bear, Brown Bear, What Do You See?* by Bill Martin
*Bugs* by Patricia and Fredrick McKissack

*Benchmark passage*: "The Bad Cat"
**Matt** is sad.
Matt had a hat.
Now **Pat** has **Matt's** hat.

Pat is a cat.
Matt ran after Pat.
But Pat ran away.
Pat ran away with Matt's hat.
Pat is a bad cat.

### ■ Preprimer 2

Similar to preprimer 1 but there are a greater number of different words used and more reading is required. Illustrations usually depict some of the text. Requires increased knowledge of high-frequency words and some familiarity with most of the short-vowel patterns, such as *-at, -op,* and *-et.*

Hard words: Could be as many as 4–6 words out of 100 not on the high-frequency list.

*Benchmark books:*
*Cat Traps* by Molly Coxe.
*The Carrot Seed* by Ruth Krauss.

*Benchmark passage:* "The Red Kangaroo"
Hop! Hop! Hop!
**Kangaroos** like to hop.
The red kangaroo can **hop** the best.
The red kangaroo can hop over you.
The red kangaroo can hop over the top of a **van.**

The red kangaroo is big.
The red kangaroo has big back legs.
Its back legs are very **strong.**
And it has a long **tail.**
The red kangaroo is bigger than a man.
The red kangaroo is the biggest kangaroo of all.

### ■ Preprimer 3

Similar to preprimer 2 but requires increased knowledge of high-frequency words and increased familiarity with short-vowel patterns, such as *-at*, *-op*, and *-et*. Increased use of consonant combinations such as *tr*, *st*, and *sch*.

Hard words: Could be as many as 7–8 words out of 100 not on the high-frequency list.

*Benchmark books:*
*The Foot Book* by Dr. Seuss
*Sleepy Dog* by Harriet Ziefert

*Benchmark passage:* "Best Pet"

"I have the best pet," said **Ted.**
"My dog **barks** and **wags** his **tail** when I come home from school."
"No, I have the best pet," said **Robin.** "I have a cat. My cat **wakes** me up so that I can go to school."
"I have the best pet," said Will. "I have a pet pig.
My pig can do many **tricks.**"
Then Ted said, "We all have the best pet.
I have the pet that is best for me.
Robin has the pet that is best for her.
And Will has the pet that is best for him."

### ■ Primer

Vocabulary is becoming more diverse and illustrations are less helpful. Would need to know high-frequency words and short-vowel and long-vowel patterns *(-ake, -ike, -ope)*. Approximately 9–10 words per 100 not on the high-frequency list. Might also require some knowledge of *r*-vowel *(-ar; -er)* and other-vowel *(-our, –ought)* patterns.

*Benchmark books:*
*And I Mean It Stanley* by Crosby Bonsall
*Jason's Bus Ride* by Harriet Ziefert

*Benchmark passage: The Little Red Hen*

A little red hen lived on a farm with her **chickens.** One day she found a **grain** of **wheat** in the **barnyard.**
"Who will plant this wheat?" she said.

"Not I," said the Cat.

"Not I," said the Duck.

"I will do it **myself**," said the little Red Hen. And she planted the grain of wheat.

When the wheat was **ripe** she said, "Who will take this wheat to the **mill?**"

"Not I," said the Cat.

"Not I," said the Duck.

"I will, then," said the little Red Hen, and she took the wheat to the mill.

When she **brought** the **flour** home, she said, "Who will bake some bread with this flour?" (Only hard words in first 100 words were counted.)

### ■ First Grade

Selections are becoming longer and more complex. Books may be divided into very brief chapters. Would need to know short-vowel, long-vowel, and some of the easier other-vowel (*-ow, -oy, -oo, -aw*), and *r*-vowel patterns (*-ear, -or*). There may also be some easy two-syllable words. Illustrations support text and may depict a hard word or two.

Hard words: 11–12 words not on high-frequency list.

*Benchmark books:*

*The Cat in the Hat* by Dr. Seuss

*Little Bear's Visit* by Else Minark

*Benchmark passage: Johnny Appleseed*

**John Chapman** wore a **tin pan** for a hat. And he was **dressed** in **rags. But** people liked John. He was kind to others, and he was kind to animals.

John loved **apples.** He left his home and headed **west** about 200 years ago. He wanted everyone to have apples. On his back he carried a **pack** of apple seeds. Walking from place to place, John planted his apple seeds. As the years **passed** the seeds **grew** into trees. After planting **hundreds** and hundreds of apple trees, John Chapman came to be called "**Johnny Appleseed.**"

### ■ Leveling Books Beyond the First Grade

If possible, use the Fry Graph, one of the other formulas mentioned, or obtain a readability score from one of the sources mentioned earlier in the chapter. Use the objective readability as an estimate. Compare 100-word passages from the book you are assessing with the benchmark books or passages. Find the passage that is most like the one you are assessing. Pay particular attention to difficulty level of vocabulary, complexity of ideas, and sentence complexity. Be conservative. If undecided between the second- and third-grade level, go with the more difficult level. It does not hurt students to read a book that is on the easy side; it can be very frustrating for them to cope with a book that is too hard. If the book is very brief and has 100 words or fewer, assess the entire book. If the book is longer, assess three sample passages chosen from near the beginning, middle, and end of the book, but avoid using the first page as a sample. Average the three readability levels that you obtain. Also consider the qualitative factors listed in Figure 2.17. In the light of the comparison with the benchmark passages and qualitative factors, you might decide that the objective readability estimate is accurate or you might move it up or down a level.

Listed on the next few pages are descriptions of levels and benchmark passages. The Primary Readability Formula (Gunning, 2002), the *New Dale-Chall Readability Formula* (Chall & Dale, 1995), and qualitative factors were used to estimate readability. Words not on the high-frequency word list are boldfaced for passages on grade two. Words not on the Dale list of words known by fourth-graders are boldfaced for passages on grade three and above.

### ■ Grade 2A

Selections are longer with more involved plots or more detailed explanations. Books are usually divided into chapters. Would need a grasp of basic vowel patterns. Texts have a number of multisyllabic words.

*Benchmark books:*
*Frog and Toad at Home* by Arnold Lobel
*Henry and Mudge, the First Book* by Cynthia Rylant
*Arthur's Funny Money* by Lillian Hoban

Grade 2A is a transition level between the end of first and the beginning of second grade. Some leveling systems and basal reading programs place *Frog and Toad* and *Henry and Mudge* books in first grade; others place them in second grade.

---

**FIGURE 2.17**

### Estimating Difficulty of Materials for Grades Two through Four

Objective level (estimate yielded by formula) _____

| | | | |
|---|---|---|---|
| Background required to read text | familiar | limited amount | considerable |
| Difficulty and density of concepts | easy | average | challenging |
| Difficulty of vocabulary | easy | average | challenging |
| Complexity of language | easy | average | challenging |
| Degree of interest of content | high | average | low |
| Use of graphics and other aids | high | average | low |

When compared with benchmark passages or books, what level(s) do the sample passages from the text seem to be most like?

Passage 1 _____
Passage 2 _____
Passage 3 _____
Average _____

Estimated difficulty level of text (objective and subjective factors) _____

*Benchmark passage:* Arthur's Funny Money *by Lillian Hoban*

It was **Saturday** morning.
**Violet** was **counting numbers** on her **fingers.**
**Arthur** was counting the money in his **piggy bank.**
He counted three **dollars** and **seventy-eight cents.**
"Arthur," said Violet, "do you know numbers?"
"Yes I do," said Arthur. "I am working with numbers right now."
"Well," said Violet, "If I have five **peas** and you take three and give me back
  two, how many peas will I have?"
"All of them," said Arthur. "I don't like peas, so I **wouldn't** take any."
"I know you don't like peas," said Violet. "But I am trying to do a number
  **problem.**"

### ◼ Grade 2B

Sentences are becoming longer and more complex. There is an increase in multi-syllabic words. Notice the high proportion of multisyllabic words in the benchmark passage.

*Benchmark books:*

*Bread and Jam for Frances* by Russell Hoban
*Thank You, Amelia Bedelia* by Peggy Parish
*Stone Soup* by Anne McGovern

*Benchmark passage:* Stone Soup *by Anne McGovern*

"**Soup** from a **stone,**" said the little old **lady. "Fancy** that."
The pot **bubbled** and bubbled.
After a **while,** the little old lady said, "This soup **tastes** good."
"It tastes good now," said the **hungry young** man. "But it would taste better
  with **beef bones.**"
So the little old lady went to get some **juicy** beef bones.
Into the **pot** went the juicy beef bones, and the long, **thin carrots,** and the
  yellow **onions,** and the **round, gray** stone.
"Soup from a stone," said the little old lady. "Fancy that."
The pot bubbled and bubbled.

### ◼ Grade 3

Sentences continue to increase in length, as does the number of mutlisyllabic words.

*Benchmark books:*

*Magic School Bus and the Electric Field* by Joanna Cole
*Molly's Pilgrim* by Barbara Cohen
*Courage of Sarah Noble* by Alice Dalgliesh

*Benchmark passage:* Courage of Sarah Noble *by Alice Dalgliesh*

Now they had come to the last day of the journey. The Indian trail had been
narrow, the hills went up and down. **Sarah** and her father were tired, and
even **Thomas** walked **wearily.**

By late afternoon they would be going home. Home? No, it wasn't really home, just a place out in the **wilderness.** But after a while it would be home. **John Noble** told Sarah it would be. His voice kept leading her on.
"Now we must be about two miles away."
"Now it is surely a mile . . . only a mile."

## ■ Grade 4

Sentences are somewhat longer. Vocabulary is somewhat more advanced and includes words such as *glistened*, *delicate*, and *veil* that might not be in some fourth-graders' listening vocabulary. Greater use of figurative language.

### Benchmark books:

*Help I'm a Prisoner in the Library* by Eth Clifford
*Little House in the Big Woods* by Laura Ingalls Wilder
*Charlotte's Web* by E. B. White

### Benchmark passage: *Charlotte's Web* by E. B. White

The next day was foggy. Everything on the farm was dripping wet. The grass looked like a magic carpet. The **asparagus** patch looked like a silver forest.

## ACTION PLAN

1. Become acquainted with national, state, and local standards and expectations.
2. Set standards or goals for your program. Translate goals or standards into measurable objectives.
3. Align materials and instructional activities with your objectives.
4. Align assessment with objectives and instruction. For each objective, you need formal and/or informal assessment devices so that you can tell whether objectives are being achieved.
5. Begin assessment by finding out where students are and what their strengths and needs are. This can be done with an IRI, emergent literacy measure, or other devices.
6. Screen students for specials needs. Students identified as struggling should be given diagnostic tests that can be used to plan intervention programs.
7. Monitor students' progress on an ongoing basis. Maintain a portfolio of students' work. On a quarterly basis, assess students in more depth. Involve students in the assessment process. Guide them so they can self-assess. Involve them in the setting of standards and creation of rubrics. Make adjustments in the program as required.
8. At year's end, administer an outcomes measure. This could be another form of the IRI or other measures that you administered at the beginning of the year. As part of your assessment, use information yielded by district-required or state or national tests.
9. Do not overtest. Don't give a test if it is not going to provide useful information or if you are not going to use the information. Make sure that students are tested on the appropriate level.
10. Make sure that there is a match between students' reading levels and the materials that they read. Obtain readability information from appropriate sources and put a leveling system into place. Make sure that in determining difficulty levels that you use subjective judgement as well as objective data.

On foggy mornings, **Charlotte's** web was truly a thing of beauty. This morning each thin **strand** was **decorated** with dozens of tiny beads of water. The web **glistened** in the light and made a pattern of **loveliness** and mystery, like a **delicate veil. Lurvy,** who wasn't **particularly** interested in beauty, noticed the web when he came with the pig's breakfast. He noted how clearly it showed up and he noted how big and carefully built it was. And then he took another look and saw something that made him set his pail down. There, in the center of the web, neatly **woven** in block letters, was a message.

## Verifying Readability Levels

The true measure of the difficulty level of a book is the proficiency with which students can read it. Note how well students are able to read books that have been leveled. Based on your observation of students' performance, be prepared to change the estimated difficulty level.

## SUMMARY

1. Evaluation entails making a subjective judgment about the quality of students' work or the effectiveness of a program or some component of it. It is based on data from tests, work samples, and observations. An evaluation is made in terms of goals and objectives and should result in some sort of action to improve deficiencies that are noted or to build on strengths.

2. The standards movement is an attempt to improve the quality of education by setting high but clear standards for all. If assessment and instruction are aligned with the standards, education should be more effective. A controversial component of the standards movement is high-stakes testing. Although testing can highlight needs and result in more resources being allocated to struggling readers, there is concern that high-stakes testing may result in a narrowing of the curriculum by encouraging teaching to the test and spending too much time on test preparation.

3. Placement information is necessary to indicate where the student is on the road to literacy. For a student who is reading, the informal reading inventory is one of the best sources of such information. It taps word recognition and comprehension and yields information about language development and thought processes. It also yields information on four reading levels: independent, instructional, frustration, and listening capacity.

4. In norm-referenced tests students are compared to a representative sample of children who are the same age or in the same grade. Scores are reported in a variety of ways: raw scores, percentile ranks, grade equivalent scores, stanines, normal curve equivalents, and scaled scores.

5. In criterion-referenced tests, students' performance is assessed in terms of a criterion or standard. Because they indicate whether students have mastered a particular skill or strategy, these tests tend to be more valuable than norm-referenced tests for planning programs. Because neither norm-referenced nor criterion-referenced tests are adequate for today's balanced instruction and student-centered assessment in reading and writing, there has been a strong push for authentic assessment. In authentic assessment, students read whole texts and construct responses. Portfolios and observation are widely used components of authentic assessment.

6. Benchmarks and rubrics offer ways of holistically indicating performance. The benchmark is a written description of a key task that students

would be expected to perform. Rubrics provide descriptions of expected or desirable performances as well as unsatisfactory ones.

7. Students should be given tests designed for the level on which they are reading. Tests that are too easy or too hard are invalid and yield erroneous information.

8. Assessment is beginning to catch up with evolving theories of reading and writing instruction. Oral and written retellings, think-alouds, observations, anecdotal records, questionnaires, interviews, and ratings are growing in popularity.

9. Holistic evaluation of writing is based on the premise that, to capture the essence of a piece, it is necessary to consider it as a whole and assess it by forming an overall impression. However, analytic assessment of key elements of the piece provides information that the teacher can use to make specific suggestions to the writer.

10. Portfolios provide a means of assembling a broad range of assessment data. They can include work samples, a list of books read, results of observations, test scores, and other information.

11. Having basic information about English learners' literacy ability in their first language and their knowledge of English will help you plan a more effective program for them.

12. A number of objective readability formulas and several subjective leveling systems are used to estimate the difficulty level of texts. Because formulas neglect such factors as background needed to read a text and leveling systems rely on subjective judgment, it is strongly recommended that both objective and subjective factors be used when estimating the readability of books.

## EXTENDING AND APPLYING

1. Examine the assessment devices in a basal series. Evaluate their content validity and format. Note whether all major areas of reading have been covered, whether guessing is a factor, and whether the devices have been tested and give information on validity and reliability.

2. Create a portfolio system for evaluation. Decide what kinds of items might be included in the portfolio. Also devise a checklist or summary sheet that can be used to keep track of and summarize the items.

3. Find out what the standards are for your state, how they are assessed, and how test results are used. Check the American Federation of Teachers Web site to find out how your state's standards are rated at: http://www.aft.org/edissues/standards/. Explain how you would implement the standards for the grade that you teach or plan to teach.

4. Administer an informal reading inventory or running record to at least one student. Based on the results of the assessment, draw up a list of the student's apparent strengths and needs.

## DEVELOPING A PROFESSIONAL PORTFOLIO

Place in your portfolio any checklists, rubrics, or other similar assessment devices that you have devised and used. Reflect on the effectiveness of these devices.

## DEVELOPING A RESOURCE FILE

Keep a file of observation guides, checklists, sample tests, think-aloud protocols, questionnaires, sample tests, rubrics, and other assessment devices that might be useful. For a wealth of information about literacy assessments go to the Southwest Educational Development Laboratory Web site at: http://www.sedl.org/reading/rad.

3

# Fostering Emergent/ Early Literacy

*F*or each of the following statements, put a check under "Agree" or "Disagree" to show how you feel. Discuss your responses with classmates before you read the chapter.

|  | *Agree* | *Disagree* |
|---|---|---|
| **1** An informal, unstructured program works best in kindergarten. | _____ | _____ |
| **2** Reading books to young children is a better use of instructional time than working on skills. | _____ | _____ |
| **3** Allowing children to spell any way they can is harmful. | _____ | _____ |
| **4** Children at risk should have their literacy development accelerated so that they can catch up. | _____ | _____ |
| **5** The best way for young children to learn reading is through writing. | _____ | _____ |
| **6** Kindergartners should be taught a full program of beginning phonics. | _____ | _____ |

## USING WHAT YOU KNOW

*C*hapter 1 explored the nature of reading, discussed the reading status of children today, and presented ten basic principles for teaching reading. This chapter on emergent literacy is based on those ten principles. The word *literacy* encompasses both writing and reading; *emergent* indicates that the child has been engaged in reading and writing activities long before coming to school. Putting the two concepts together, Sulzby (1989) defined emergent literacy as "the reading and writing behaviors that precede and develop into conventional literacy" (p. 84).

Before reading this chapter, reflect on your personal knowledge of emergent literacy. Have you observed young children as they explored reading and writing? How did they do this? What did their writing look like? What did they learn about reading and writing from their homes and the larger environment? How would you go about fostering emergent literacy?

# UNDERSTANDING EMERGENT LITERACY

■ **Emergent literacy** consists of the reading and writing behaviors that evolve from children's earliest experiences with reading and writing and that gradually grow into conventional literacy.

The term *early literacy* is sometimes used instead of *emergent literacy*. Early literacy suggests that the child already has some knowledge of reading and writing, whereas *emergent literacy* might suggest that the child is merely on the verge of acquiring this knowledge.

Children begin developing literacy long before they enter school. Unless they are disabled, all school-age children have acquired a fairly extensive oral language vocabulary and a sophisticated syntactic system. They have seen traffic signs and billboard advertising, printed messages on television, and printing on cereal boxes. They can tell the McDonald's logo from that of Burger King and distinguish a box of Fruit Loops from one of Captain Crunch. They have seen their parents read books, magazines, newspapers, letters, and bills and have observed them writing notes or letters, filling out forms, and making lists. They may also have imitated some of these activities. Their parents may have read books to them and provided them with crayons, pencils, and other tools of literacy. All children, no matter how impoverished their environment may be, have begun the journey along the path that begins with language acquisition and ends in formal literacy. The teacher must find out where each child is on the path and lead him or her on the way. "The issue," explains Purcell-Gates (1997), "is not getting children ready to learn, but rather creating literacy environments within which the learning they already do on an ongoing basis includes the different emergent literacy concepts needed for school success" (p. 427).

The concept of emergent literacy is rooted in research conducted a number of years ago. Read (1971) reported on a study of early spellers who had learned to spell in an informal manner. The early spellers were preschoolers who were given help in spelling when they asked for it but were otherwise allowed to spell however they wanted. What surprised Read was that these young children, who had no contact with each other, created spelling systems that were remarkably similar and that, although not correct, made sense phonetically. For instance, *er* at the end of a word such as *tiger* was typically spelled with just an *r*, as *tigr*. In this instance, *r* is syllabic; it functions as a vowel and so does not need to be preceded by an *e*. For long vowels, children generally used the letter name, as in *sop* for *soap*, where the name of the letter *o* contains the sound of the vowel. Commenting on his findings, Read stated, "We can no longer assume that children must approach reading with no discernible prior conception of its structure" (p. 34). Landmark studies by researchers in several countries echoed and amplified Read's findings in both reading and writing (Clay, 1972; Ferreiro & Teberosky, 1982; Teale & Sulzby, 1986).

These revelations about children's literacy abilities have a number of implications. First and foremost, we must build on what children already know. In their five or six years before coming to us, they have acquired a great deal of insight into the reading and writing process. Instead of asking whether they are ready, we have to find out where they are and take it from there. We must value and make use of their knowledge.

As children observe parents and peers reading and writing and as they themselves experiment with reading and writing, they construct theories about how these processes work. For instance, based on their experience with picture books, children may believe that pictures rather than words are read. Initially children may believe that letters operate as pictures. They may believe that letters represent objects in much the same way that pictures represent objects. Using this hypothesis, they may reason that *snake* would be a long word because a snake is a long animal. *Mouse* would be a short word because a mouse is a short animal. As children notice long words for little creatures (hummingbird, mosquito) and little words for large creatures (whale, tiger), they assimilate this and make an accommodation by giving up their hypothesis of a physical relationship between size of words and size of objects or creatures represented. They may then theorize that although letters do not represent physical characteristics, they do somehow identify the person or thing named. They may theorize that the first letters of their names belong uniquely to them (Ferreiro, 1986). Children need to see that other people's names may start with the same letters as theirs but that some or all of the other letters are different. When Paige comments that Paul has her letter, Paige might be told that yes she and Paul have the same letter at the beginning of their names and even the same second letter, but the other letters are different. She might also be told that both their names begin with a *p* because they both begin with the same sound /p/.

Before children discover the alphabet principle, they may refine their theories of the purpose of letters and conclude that it is the arrangement of letters that matters. Through exposure to print, they will have noticed that words form patterns and they begin to string letters together in what seem to be reasonable patterns. Usually the words are between three and seven characters long and only repeat the same letter twice (Schickedanz, 1999). Known as mock words, these creations look like real words. After creating mock words, children frequently ask adults what the words say. The adults may attempt sounding out the words and realize that they don't say anything and inform the child of that fact. Realizing that they can't simply string a series of letters together, children may begin asking adults how to spell words or copy words from signs or books. As adults write multisyllabic words for children, they might sound them out as they write each syllable and also say the letters: "An-dy. . . A-N-D-Y spells Andy." Hearing words sounded out, children catch onto the idea that letters represent speech sounds. Since the words they hear have been spoken in syllables as they were written, the children may use one letter to represent each syllable and one letter for the final sound and produce spellings such as *jrf* for *giraffe*.

If you have some insight into students' current schema for the writing system, you can provide the kind of explanation that will help them to move into a higher level of understanding. For children who are moving from a visual or physical hypothesis about how the alphabetical system operates to a phonological one, sounding out words as you spell them provides helpful information. Providing many opportunities to write also helps students to explore the writing system.

## Essential Skills and Understandings for Emergent Literacy

Understanding how print works and the many roles it plays in people's lives is known as the "big picture" (Purcell-Gates, 1997). The big picture is the foundation upon which all other information about reading and writing are built. Children also

For a time, children's concept of letter–sound relationships may be very specific. At age four, my granddaughter Paige told me that she had a friend by the name of Paul in school, and commented, "He has my letter." She had noticed that Paul's name began with a *P*, as did hers. She regarded the letters of her name as being personal and specific. The *P* in *Paige* identified her. She did not realize that *p* represents /p/ and can be used in any word containing a /p/ sound (see Ferreiro, 1986).

Different cultures might value different literacy activities. Therefore, it is important for the teacher to know what kinds of writing and reading activities are stressed in the children's homes and communities so these can be built upon in the classroom.

Having reading and writing materials in the home, being read to, and talking to their caregivers about reading and writing fosters children's formation of the "big picture." The more reading and writing they are exposed to, the more complete and detailed their big pictures become (Purcell-Gates, 1997).

need to become more familiar with the types of language used in books and to acquire a deeper sense of how stories develop. On a more formal level, they need to construct basic **concepts of print,** if they have not already learned them. These concepts of print include the following:

- What we say and what others say can be written down and read.
- Words, not pictures, are read.
- Sentences are made up of words and words are made up of letters.
- Reading goes from left to right and from top to bottom.
- A book is read from front to back.
- What we say is divided into words. (Some students may believe that "How are you?" is a single word, for example.) Students must also grasp the concept of what a word is. Of course, they use words in their oral language, but understanding what a word is occurs on a higher level of abstraction, becoming a metalinguistic, or metacognitive awareness. This means that they must be able to think about language as well as use it.
- Space separates written words. Students must be able to match words being read orally with their written counterparts. Hearing the sentence "The little dog ran," the student must focus on *the*, *little*, *dog*, and *ran* as each word is read.
- Sentences begin with capital letters.
- Sentences end with periods, question marks, or exclamation marks.
- A book has a title, an author, and sometimes an illustrator.

■ **Concepts of print** are understandings about how print works—that printed words represent spoken words, have boundaries, are read from left to right, and so on.

▌Reinforce the concepts of print and print conventions whenever the opportunity presents itself. When writing on the board, emphasize that you are writing from left to right. If you are writing information that students are giving you, tell them that you are writing their words.

*I*nstruction in concepts of print, the alphabet, and phonological awareness should take place within the context of opportunities to read and write for real purposes.

■ Students must also develop phonological awareness and arrive at an understanding of the alphabetic principle. Phonological awareness involves being able to detect rhyming words, to segment words into their separate sounds, and to perceive beginning sounds. Understanding the alphabetic principle means grasping the concept that letters represent sounds.

The rate of children's literacy development varies as does the richness of home environments. A few children will be able to read words or even whole sentences when they enter kindergarten. However, most will still be developing emergent literacy in kindergarten and possibly into first grade; a few may make very slow progress and may still be developing emergent literacy beyond first grade. The activities and procedures explored in this chapter apply to any students who might benefit from them, whether they are in kindergarten, first grade, or beyond. These activities and procedures may even be used with preschool children who are making very rapid progress.

> ■ In a typical kindergarten, there may be a span of as much as five years between the lowest- and highest-functioning children, so that some children will have the skill level of three-year-olds while the most advanced will function like eight-year-olds (Riley, 1996).

## Creating a Literacy-Rich Environment

Regardless of where children are in terms of literacy, an essential step in further development is to create an environment that promotes active reading, writing, listening, and speaking. Getting children to engage in literacy activities is partly a matter of providing an appealing environment. One means of encouragement is simply to have readily available writing instruments, paper of various kinds, and books and periodicals. In a classroom environment that fosters literacy, print is everywhere. Bulletin boards include words as well as pictures. There is a calendar of students' birthdays and other important upcoming events. Aquariums and terrariums are labeled with the names of their inhabitants. Most important of all, students' stories and booklets are displayed prominently. The classroom might have a student-run post office so that children can correspond with each other. If computer equipment is available, students might even make use of e-mail. Label mailboxes with children's names but also include their pictures so students who cannot read can find the mailboxes they are looking for. Be sure to include a mailbox for yourself and anyone who regularly visits the class. To encourage the use of the mailboxes and to model the process of writing a letter, let students observe you as you write notes to parents, to the principal, and to the students. Also, encourage adults to write to your class. Read and post their letters (Jurek, 1995).

Although a classroom can be arranged in many ways to induce children to take part in literacy activities, Morrow (1997) recommended that a variety of centers be set up, including areas for writing, math, social studies, science, music, blocks and other manipulatives, **dramatic play,** and a library. A listening/viewing center and a computing center are also possibilities. If the classroom is small, some of these centers could be combined.

> ■ **Dramatic play** refers to a type of activity in which students play at being someone else: a doctor, a teacher, a firefighter.

The writing center should contain the upper- and lowercase alphabets in manuscript form. Letters, stories, lists, and other models of writing can also be displayed. The materials should be posted at eye level so students can easily make use of them. A selection of writing instruments and paper should be available.

Display books in as many places as you can. For instance, in the science center display books about animal mothers, plants, or whatever topic students are exploring. In the dramatic play center, display books about firefighters, trucks, a doctor's office, or whatever the theme is.

Paper should come in various colors and should be unlined so that students are not unduly concerned with spacing. Small memo pads of paper are also recommended. Writing instruments should include crayons and magic markers, the latter being the choice of most children (Bauman, 1990). If pencils are provided, students should be instructed in using them safely. Other useful items for the writing center are chalkboards, magnetic letters, printing sets, a typewriter, and a computer with an easy-to-use word-processing program. Paste, tape, safety scissors, and staplers are also useful. Reference materials are important. For kindergarten children, such materials could consist primarily of picture dictionaries, both commercially produced and constructed by students.

The library or book corner should feature a wide selection of reading materials attractively displayed, including both commercial and student-written books. Extra copies of a book currently being read by the teacher or other books by the same author or on the same theme should be given a place of prominence. Rockers, cushions, bean-bag chairs, and pieces of rug will give students comfortable places to read. The listening/viewing center should have a wide variety of audiotaped books and videotapes or, if available, CD-ROM versions of favorite stories so that students can follow the text as the story is being read. Multiple copies of audiotapes of favorite books will allow small groups of students to listen to a book together. The dramatic play and housekeeping centers should be stocked with order blanks, note pads, signs, bills, and other realia of literacy. A technology center might include software, such as *Dr. Seuss Kindergarten* (Learning Company), *Arthur's Kindergarten* (Learning Company), *ABC by Dr. Seuss* (Learning Company), or *A to Zap* (Sunburst), that reinforce key themes or skills. In a classroom that fosters literacy, the tools and products of writing and reading abound. A sample floor plan of a literacy-rich environment is presented in Figure 3.1.

## FOSTERING EMERGENT LITERACY

**USING TECHNOLOGY**

*Between the Lions*

*Between the Lions* is an award-winning PBS TV series for children four to seven designed to foster a love of reading and literacy skills. The programs are complemented by a Web site which features a host of supplementary activities including reading stories and playing games. A number of the activities are designed for parents to engage in with their children. Kindergartners who watched the program made impressive gains in essential early literacy skills (Linebarger, 2000). A teaching guide for kindergarten teachers is available.
http://pbskids.org/lions/

An environment that fosters literacy is both physical and attitudinal. Attitudinally, the teacher believes that literacy is a broad-based, naturally occurring process that takes place over a long period of time. Although it can and should be taught, literacy can also be fostered by "setting the scene" and through subtle encouragement. The teacher should lose no opportunity to reinforce literacy concepts. For example, after the class's pet gerbil has been named George, a label containing his name is attached to the cage. While preparing the label, the teacher explains what is being done and shows the class that the letters *G-e-o-r-g-e* spell "George." When students are running software on the computer, the teacher points to the RETURN key and explains what the printing on it means. After turning a page on the calendar, the teacher points to the name of the new month and asks the class to guess what the word is. When a notice is being sent home, the teacher reads it aloud to the class first. If students see any familiar words in the notice, they are encouraged to read them.

Classroom routines are placed on charts. For instance, procedures for using the computer, turning on the tape recorder, and signing out books are posted. Simple

FIGURE 3.1

## Floor Plan for Early Childhood Classroom

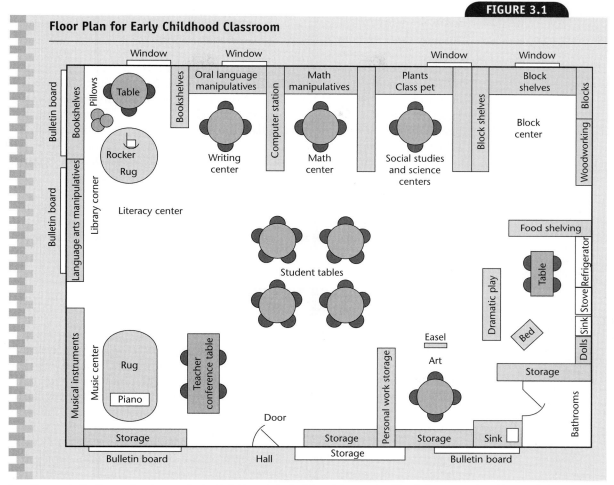

From Morrow, *L. M., Literacy Development in the Early Years,* 3rd ed., ©Copyright 1997 by Allyn & Bacon. Reprinted by permission.

words and illustrations that help convey the meaning of the procedures are used (Jurek, 1995).

Labels and signs should be used generously. Cubbies and coat hooks should be labeled with children's names. Places where supplies are stored should be labeled: paper, paints, crayons. Signs should be used to designate learning centers and key locations in the classroom. Signs should also direct students to wash hands, put away paints when finished, walk, don't run, nurse's office. The room might also have an attendance chart and a helper chart. Students can show that they are present by putting their names in the pockets of the attendance chart. Calendar charts and schedules charts also provide opportunities for discussing print as you talk over the fact that Monday and May both begin with the same letter, which makes an

/m/ sound. Special days such as birthdays and holidays can be marked. On the weather chart, students can place in a pocket cards containing the words *sunny*, *cloudy*, *rainy*, or *snowy*; *cold*, *warm*, or *hot*; *windy* or *calm*. Cards might be illustrated with a picture of the sun or rain to help students identify them. Lists, recipes, and schedules for centers also provide opportunities for reading and writing.

The key is to make use of whatever opportunities are available to foster reading and writing concepts and skills. At snack time, point out the writing on the milk cartons and note that the word *m-i-l-k* spells "milk." On subsequent days you might read the name of the dairy or have students tell you which word says "milk," tell what letter *milk* begins with, or tell what letters *milk* has. Talk about the letters and the words in apple juice and crackers or whatever snack foods children are eating.

Students are also encouraged to write or draw, and the emphasis is on expression and exploration rather than on conventional spelling or handwriting. There is plenty of time for that later. The class library is an active place. Students read books in school and are allowed to take them home. The inevitable torn pages and jelly-stained covers and the occasional lost books are a small price to pay for the development of literacy skills.

## Making Reading and Writing a Part of Classroom Activities

Fostering literacy growth among young children is a matter of making reading and writing a natural part of their classroom activities. One way to increase early literacy experiences is to stock centers with the tools of writing and reading that might naturally appear there. In dramtic play centers, children can make use of these as they take on the roles of adults whom they see in their everyday lives. They also are more likely to role-play literacy tasks if the appropriate materials are available. Christie (1990) recommended that dramatic play centers be supplied with pens, pencils, note pads, diaries, cookbooks, telephone books, picture books, magazines, catalogs, and newspapers—in other words, the kinds of materials that might be found in the typical home. Opportunities for dramatic play that can stimulate reading and writing include the following:

1. Grocery store—creating signs, writing checks or food lists
2. Bank—writing deposit and withdrawal slips and checks
3. Doctor's office—writing prescriptions, making appointments, making bills
4. Restaurant—writing and reading menus, taking food orders, creating signs (Christie, 1990)
5. Post office—writing letters, addressing letters, mailing packages, selling stamps, delivering mail

In planning dramatic play centers, find out what kinds of experiences the children have had and how they have seen literacy function in their environments. For instance, if they are more familiar with fast-food eating places than with restaurants having servers and individual menus, create wall-type menus characteristic of fast-food establishments.

To make dramatic play as valuable as possible, provide an introduction. Discuss the activity or read students a book about it. Show the props and talk about some of the ways that they might be used (Bunce, 1995). Provide prompts or model interchanges in the initial stages or when students seem to be foundering

For dramatic play at a railroad station, the best preparation would be to actually visit a station and take a short trip on a train. Other possibilities include having a conductor visit the class and talk about the things that a conductor does. Viewing videos and listening to informational books about trains would also extend students' knowledge of the topic. You might model some of the oral language that the children would be using. "Where are you going? A ticket to ___ will cost $100. How will you pay for that? Will you pay in cash? Or will you use a credit card? Train Number 5 to Washington will be leaving from track 5. Train Number 5 will be leaving in 10 minutes."

Change the dramatic play center frequently. Possible dramatic play activities include an airport, bus terminal, train station, dock, grocery store, clothing store, toy store, doctor's office, dentist's office, firehouse, police station, recycling station, zoo, circus, movie theater, car wash, campground, beach, fast food restaurant, pizza parlor, delivery truck, warehouse, beauty parlor, barber shop, hospital, post office, office, hotel, library, apartment, aquarium, vet. Possibilities are many and varied. Select the ones that interest and benefit your students the most.

Playing with print is an important part of literacy development through which children can explore the uses of the medium. After scrawling letterlike figures on a piece of paper, one child pretended he was reading a weather report (McLane & McNamee, 1990). Others have been police officers writing tickets, restaurant owners creating menus, store owners writing receipts, parents writing shopping lists, and authors writing books. Children have also pretended to read books to dolls, teddy bears, friends, and younger siblings. "Through play, children may come to feel that they are writers and readers before they actually have the necessary skills to write and read" (McLane & McNamee, 1990, p. 19).

As children learn about literacy skills through playing and observing how members of their families and communities use these skills, they become motivated to learn more about reading and writing so that they can make fuller use of these skills. In learning literacy, function fosters form. Students learn the what and the why of reading and writing as a prelude to learning the details of how to read and write.

## Reading to Students

One of the best ways to develop students' emergent literacy is to read interesting books to them. As the Commission on Reading (Anderson, Hiebert, Scott, &

*O*ne of the best ways to develop students' emergent literacy is to read to them.

▌Whenever possible, use naturally occurring activities to develop literacy. By involving students in an activity in which they explore literacy naturally, you know that you have their attention and their interest. In contrast, they may find instructional activities of a more formal nature to be boring or too difficult. Contrast students experimenting with a word-processing program such as one in which the letters of the alphabet say their names and sounds when their keys are pressed to a more formal lesson in which students say the letter of the alphabet that the teacher points to.

At least twenty minutes a day should be set aside for reading aloud, and this period should be held at a regularly scheduled time.

Wilkinson, 1985) noted, "The single most important activity for building the knowledge required for eventual success in reading is reading aloud to children" (p. 23). Unfortunately, there is incredible variation in the amount of experience children have in being read to. In his study of language development of children, Wells (1986) found that one child, Jonathan, had been read to six thousand times. His parents had read an average of four stories a day to him. On the other hand, Rosie had never had a story read to her before entering school. Not surprisingly, at age ten, Jonathan was doing quite well in school, whereas Rosie ranked last out of thirty-two children studied. Poorer parents and less-well-educated parents are less likely to read to their children. Only 58 percent of parents who lack a high school diploma read to their children three times a week (National Center for Educational Statistics, 1998).

Reading both narrative and informational texts is important. As Dorion (1994) points out, "Narrative is the principal mode through which children understand the world around them" (p. 616). Informational texts build students' background and arouse their curiosity.

Why is being read to so important? Being read to also develops children's vocabulary, expands their experiential background, makes them aware of the language of books, introduces them to basic concepts of print and how books are read, and provides them with many pleasant associations with books. Perhaps most important is the power of books to help children create worlds based on words and story structures (Wells, 1986).

In conversation, the child can use context to help construct the meaning of a situation. For instance, if someone is pointing to a ball and making a throwing motion while saying, "Throw me the ball," then the context of the statement—the pointing, the ball, and the throwing motion—aids understanding. However, in a story, there is no context except for, possibly, illustrations. The child must therefore use language to construct meaning. As parents read storybooks to their children, they provide a bridge between conversation with all its support and the more abstract, noninteractive experience of hearing a story read. Intuitively, parents use the illustrations as well as explanations, gestures, and discussion to help children understand the storybook.

Reading to students helps them comprehend literary language, which is different from conversation. Conversation is concrete, immediate, and contextual. In storybook reading, there is no physical context or clarifying interchanges between author and listener.

Initial readings are highly interactive. Over time, as the child becomes a more sophisticated listener and assimilates the format of storybook reading into her or his own schema or conceptual background, less support is offered by the reader. In the process, however, the child learns invaluable lessons about the language and structure of written text. As they read to their children, parents explain new words and expressions that crop up in storybooks. They also discuss unfamiliar concepts, intuitively relating new concepts to the child's background. Parents do not deliberately set out to teach their children new concepts and words; this happens as a natural part of reading to children. As a result of these interactions, children who are read to the most have the most highly developed language skills. They have larger vocabularies and are better able to narrate an event, describe a scene, and understand the teacher (Strickland & Taylor, 1989).

## INVOLVING PARENTS

If families lack sufficient literacy to read to their children, encourage them to tell stories orally or to talk with their children about the pictures in books.

What kinds of books should be read to children? Books such as *The Very Hungry Caterpillar* (Carle, 1969), *Farms Feed the World* (L. S. Hill, 1997), and *What Do Animals Do in Winter?* (Berger & Berger, 1995) that have a richness of content are excellent choices. They build background. Nursery rhymes and books with repetitive patterns, such as *Are You My Mother?* (Eastman, 1960) and *I Swapped My Dog* (Ziefert,

1998), are also excellent choices. If possible, select books that relate to themes or topics that the class is studying. However, choose books that are on students' level of comprehension and background. A book on ancient Egypt, for instance, would be well beyond the comprehension and background level of most primary age students. If students seem bored or restless while you are reading a book, make sure that the book is of interest to them, is on the proper level, and is not too long and complex. If students have little experience being read to, you may want to start out with brief, easy-to-understand texts and gradually move into longer, more complex books.

Before reading a selection aloud, preview it. Make sure that it is appropriate for your class and that your students will enjoy it. Note places where you might like to stop for a brief discussion. Also practice reading it aloud so that you get the flow of it.

Schedule read-alouds regularly. Don't withhold read-alouds as a punishment. They are too important a part of the curriculum (Campbell, 2001). Set the mood for read-aloud time. To signal the start of a read-aloud, you might play a little tune, ring a bell, or initiate a chant. Or have a puppet make the announcement. Before starting to read, ask students questions that enable them to make connections between their personal backgrounds and the story. For instance, before reading *All the Way Home* (Segal, 1973), which is a humorous tale about a little girl who falls and hurts herself and then cries all the way home, ask students to tell about a time when they fell and hurt themselves. In preparation for reading Eric Carle's (1973) *Have You Seen My Cat?*, discuss experiences that they have had with a lost pet. Such discussion will build essential concepts and background.

Hold up the book that is to be read. Point to and discuss the title. If it lends itself to it, use the title as a predictive device. Have students think about the title and guess what the story might be about. For example, before reading *Ducks Disappearing* (Naylor, 1997), ask them to tell why ducks might disappear.

Point to the author's name. Show a picture of the author, if there is one on the book jacket, and read the author's biography. When reading *Have You Seen My Cat?*, show Carle's picture with his two cats and discuss how the pets may have given him the idea for the book and may also have been models for the drawings. Talk about the methods the author may have used to write the book—for example, did the author write it in pen on pads of paper or type it? Emphasize the fact that stories can be written down and then read by others.

As you read a book, stop periodically to review what has happened, and encourage children to discuss the book with you and to make some predictions. Younger children will need more frequent stops, and their story conversations may be less focused. After you have finished reading, talk over whether their predictions came true. For example, when reading *Too Many Books* (Bauer, 1984), a story of a girl who accumulated a houseful of books, you might ask, "What do you think Marylou will do with all those books?" Encourage students to modify predictions, if necessary, and make new ones.

Hold the book so that students can see the illustrations as you read the selection. Discuss and ask questions about them. Looking at a picture in *Too Many*

■ When choosing informational books, use children's interest and curiosity as your guide. What kinds of questions do they have? Do they want to know where fog comes from or where dinosaurs lived? Are they curious about rainbows or clouds or cows?

*Books*, you might ask, "What is different about Marylou's house?" Point to pictures as you read a book. This will illustrate words and concepts that might be unfamiliar to students. By pointing to the illustration of an unfamiliar word rather than stopping and defining it, you maintain the flow of the story. Another way of handling difficult words is to simply supply a brief meaning. When reading the book *The Relatives Came* (Rylant, 1985), you might explain that relatives are people in the family: mother, father, uncles, aunts, cousins, grandma, and grandpa, too. Dramatizing and highlighting onomatopoeia can also help provide meanings for words. For instance, when reading *The Cat in the Hat* (Seuss, 1957) emphasize the sounds of *bump* and *thump* as you read these words. You might even make bumping and thumping sounds (Schickedanz, 1999).

### ■ Developing Story Structure

Reading to children develops a sense of story as they become familiar with plot development and the interaction of plot, characters, and setting. This familiarity bolsters comprehension, the ability to discuss stories, and the ability to compose stories.

To develop a sense of story structure, discuss with the class literary language, or words and phrases that are frequently used in stories: "once upon a time," "lived happily ever after," "many years ago," and so on. Point out that most stories have a main character, who may be an older person, a young person, or even an animal who talks and acts like a human. Have students identify the main characters in stories they know. Discuss how setting, too, may be an important element.

After students have grasped the concepts of story language and characters, point out that the main characters usually have problems to solve. Give examples from familiar stories. Discuss how Marylou's problem with having too many books and the old man's problem in Wanda Gág's (1928) *Millions of Cats* are similar. Discuss the fact that problems are usually solved in some way. Talk over how that occurred for Marylou and the old man. These kinds of questions not only build comprehension, discussion, and composing skills, they also develop and lay the groundwork for an understanding of literary techniques.

### ■ Building Comprehension

In your discussions about books, ask students a variety of questions, including those that involve important details, sequence, and drawing conclusions or making inferences and that provide a foundation for reading comprehension (Feitelson, Kita, & Goldstein, 1986). Do not use the questions primarily as a technique for gauging depth of understanding but as means for drawing attention to important details or relating details so that a conclusion can be reached or a main idea constructed. For example, after you have read *The Snowy Day* (Keats, 1962), ask students how Peter felt about the snow. Then ask them how they know that Peter liked the snow. Go back over the story if children have difficulty supplying details that back up the conclusion. Think of your discussions as a way of sharing so that books can be more fully understood and enjoyed.

---

Books with subtle character development may be difficult for children who have not had much experience being read to. They may do better with tales in which action is emphasized.

---

**BUILDING LANGUAGE**

Although predictable books allow students to think of themselves as readers, they aren't the best texts for developing language (Dickinson & Smith, 1994). Books that have more complex plots and better developed characters or that delve more deeply into topics offer a richer vocabulary and more opportunities for language development.

### ■ Making Personal Connections

Students will not fully appreciate reading unless the stories touch their lives. Ask questions that involve personal reactions, such as how a story made them feel, what they liked best, whether they have ever met anyone like the main character, or whether they would like to hear a similar book. After reading *Whistle for Willie*, by Ezra Jack Keats (1964), have students describe how Willie felt at the end, and ask them about a time when they may have been proud themselves.

After discussing a story, you may want to provide follow-up or extension activities. Students might listen to a taped version, or they may pretend to read the story to a partner. Pretend reading provides them with the opportunity to use book language. Follow-up activities also include illustrating a portion of the story; watching a videotape, CD-ROM, filmstrip, or videocassette version; or carrying out some activity suggested by the book. After reading *The Gingerbread Boy* (Galdone, 1975), students might have a hunt for a gingerbread man; reading *The Carrot Seed* (Krauss, 1945) might lead to the planting of seeds. Another excellent follow-up is reading another book by the same author.

Mason, Peterman, and Kerr (1988, Fig. 1) suggested using the following general plan when presenting narrative materials:

*Before reading the narrative*

Show the cover of the book to the children. Encourage discussion about the book's content.

Discuss the author and illustrator of the book.

Allow children to discuss their own experiences that are related to those raised in the book.

Discuss the type of text the children will be hearing (folk tale, repetitive story, fables, fantasies, etc.).

Introduce children to the story's main characters and to the time and place in which the story occurs.

Set a purpose for the children to listen to the story, usually what happens to the main character.

*During the reading of the narrative*

Encourage children to react to and comment on the story.

Elaborate on the text, when appropriate, in order to help children understand the written language used in the story and story components, such as the main character's problem, attempts to resolve the problem, and its resolution.

Ask questions, occasionally, to monitor children's comprehension of the story or relevant vocabulary.

Rephrase the text when it is apparent that children are having difficulty with the words or phrases.

At appropriate points in the story, ask children to predict what will happen next.

Allow children to share their own interpretation of a story.

*After reading the narrative*

Review the story components (the setting, problem, goal, and resolution).

Help children make connections between the events of the main character and similar events in their own lives.

Engage children in some kind of follow-up activity, such as a discussion of other books by the same author or illustrator, an art activity, perhaps as simple as drawing a picture about the story, or some other means of active involvement with the story.

For informational books, Mason, Peterman, and Kerr (1988, Fig. 2) recommended the following general plan:

*Before reading the text*

Determine children's level of understanding of the topic presented in the text. Do this by discussing the pictures in the text and having them describe their experiences with the topic. You might also bring in relevant artifacts, such as model trucks when reading a book about trucks. Build background as necessary.

Provide demonstrations and in-context explanations of difficult concepts.

Discuss the relationship between the title and the topic to be addressed.

Set a purpose for listening. This might include finding the answers to questions the children raised in their discussion of the topic.

Provide a link between their experiences with the topic and what they will be learning from the text.

*During the reading of the text*

Ask open-ended questions, such as What did you learn about trucks? Do you think you would like to be a long-distance truck driver? Why or why not? What kind of truck would you most like to drive or ride in?

Ask questions periodically to check their understanding of the text. Questions that actually appear in the text might provide excellent opportunities for discussion and demonstration of the topic.

Through comments about the pictures and through carefully selected questions, help children identify pictures that might represent unfamiliar concepts.

Provide suggestions about activities children might engage in later that will encourage them to further explore the topic.

*After reading the text*

Allow children to ask questions about the text.

Help them see how informational texts can be used to learn more about their own world.

Offer activities that will tie text concepts to children's experiences.

Book reading is particularly effective for developing language when the books are carefully chosen and when there is interaction before, during, and after the book has been read. This is especially true when the readers use cognitively challenging talk. Cognitively challenging talk includes analyzing characters and events, predicting upcoming events, making connections between the text and real-life experiences, discussing or explaining vocabulary words, summarizing portions of the text, eliciting evaluative responses about the text by asking students to tell whether they liked the story or tell who the favorite character was and why (Dickinson & Smith, 1994). Although discussions are important, they shouldn't interrupt the flow of the story. Delay extended discussions until after the story has been read. Otherwise, children are likely to lose interest and become restless.

### ■ Developing Language and Thinking Skills

Being read to and discussing books also builds thinking skills. For instance, one group of kindergartners who were listening to *The Very Hungry Caterpillar* (Carle, 1969) were led through well-planned questions to make inferences about the caterpillar, learned what a cocoon is, and compared the caterpillar's home to that of other animals (Campbell, 2001). The quality of the children's thinking was determined by the quality of the questions and support provided by the teacher.

Because the children liked the book so much, it was read repeatedly. These repeated readings familiarized the children with the book and encouraged them to try the book on their own.

The teacher created a word wall for some key words from the story. With the help of the word wall and their invented spelling, students created stories of their own. Some simply retold a portion of the text. Others wrote about the eating habits of other animals.

Students also learned the days of the week and the numbers one through five, which were highlighted in the story. And, through discussion and other read-alouds, they learned the life cycle of the caterpillar.

Typically, questions are asked about read-alouds that produce only brief responses, often just a single word (Beck & McKeown, 2001). To encourage students to provide elaborated responses, ask open-ended questions. Open-ended questions for *Harry the Dirty Dog* (Zion, 1956) might include: What do we know about Harry? How does what Harry did fit in with what we know about him? Why did the family call Harry a strange dog when they saw him in their backyard? Since students often have a difficult time providing elaborated responses, the teacher might follow up these queries with prompts. Some of the prompts are general: What does that mean? What is that all about? Can you tell me more about that? Would you explain what you mean? Others are specific: What else do we know about Harry? What else did Harry do? Repeating what students said also helps. When students are unable to respond, rereading the portion of the story being queried helps them formulate a response. The key to developing language and thinking skills is to pose questions that elicit more elaborated responses and to provide support through prompts or reading that help students formulate a response.

See the Children's Reading List for a number of books that are recommended for reading aloud.

Students who have been read to will pick up many concepts of print through observing the reading and interacting with the person reading. Children may notice how print functions, ask questions about words and letters, or try to match print with the words being read.

Wells (1986) found book reading to be one of the most productive situations for developing language.

## CHILDREN'S READING LIST — Recommended read-alouds

Angelou, M. (1994). *My painted house, my friendly chicken, and me.* New York: Clarkson N. Potter. An eight-year-old Ndebele girl tells about life in her village in South Africa.

Barnes-Murphy, F. (1994). *The fables of Aesop.* New York: Lothrop. A collection of fables retold from Aesop, including "The Hare and the Tortoise" and "The Ant and the Grasshopper."

Canon, J. (1993). *Stellaluna.* San Diego: Harcourt. After she falls headfirst into a bird's nest, a baby bat is raised like a bird until she is reunited with her mother.

Dorros, A. (1991). *Abuela.* New York: Dutton. While riding on a bus with her grandmother, a little girl imagines that they are carried up into the sky and fly over the sights of New York City.

Eastman, P. D. (1960). *Are you my mother?* New York: Random House. After falling out of its nest, a small bird searches for its mother.

Gershator, D., & Gershator, P. (1995). *Bread is for eating.* New York: Holt. When her son leaves bread on his plate, his mother explains why bread is for eating. And she sings him a song in Spanish.

Greenfield, E. *Honey, I love.* (1978, 1995). New York: HarperCollins. A young girl tells about the many things in her life that she loves.

Hong, L. (1993). *Two of everything.* New York: Whitman. A poor Chinese farmer finds a magic brass pot that doubles whatever is placed inside it.

Keats, E. J. (1962). *The snowy day.* New York: Viking. A small boy has fun in the snow.

Maitland, B. (2000). *Moo in the morning.* New York: Farrar Straus Giroux. A boy and his mother visit an uncle in the country because the city is noisy, but they find that the country has its own noises.

Martin, B., Jr. (1983). *Brown Bear, Brown Bear, what do you see?* New York: Holt. A brown bear, blue horse, purple cat, and other creatures are asked to tell what they see.

Marzollo, J. (1997). *Once upon a springtime.* New York: Scholastic. A fawn is born in spring, and as the months pass, grows.

McCloskey, R. (1941). *Make way for ducklings.* New York: Viking. With the assistance of a kindly police officer, a mother duck and her brood waddle from the Charles River to the pond in Boston's Public Garden.

Sturges P. (1999). *The little red hen (makes a pizza).* New York: Philomel. The little red hen attempts to make the best pizza.

Literally thousands of books make enjoyable, worthwhile read-alouds. An excellent source of both titles and techniques for reading aloud is Trelease's (2001)

*The New Read-Aloud Handbook*, 5th ed. (New York: Penguin). Other sources of read-aloud titles include the following:

Barrera, R. B., Thompson, V. D., & Dressman, M. (Eds.). (1997). *Kaleidoscope: A multicultural booklist for grades K–8* (2nd ed.). Urbana, IL: NCTE.

Children's Book Committee at the Bank Street College of Education (1999). *Books to read aloud*. New York: Author.

Children's Book Committee at the Bank Street College of Education (2001). *The best children's books of the year*. New York: Author.

Freeman, J. (1995). *More books kids will sit still for, a read-aloud guide*. New Providence, NJ: Bowker.

Indiana Library Federation (2001). *Read-aloud books too good to miss*. http://www.ilfonline.org/Programs/ReadAloud/readaloud.htm

Lipson, E. R. (2000). *The New York Times parent's guide to the best books for children* (3rd ed.). New York: Three Rivers Press.

If students have not been read to on a regular basis, schedule extra read-aloud sessions. When read to systematically on a one-to-one basis, economically disadvantaged preschoolers demonstrate a greater involvement with stories and increase the number and complexity of their questions and comments. Together with fostering a sense of story, the sessions apparently develop oral language and social skills (Morrow, 1988). Working with groups of five, Klesius and Griffith (1996) implemented interactive storybook reading with kindergarten children whose language development was below that of the other students in the class and who were not responsive to whole-class read-aloud sessions. In addition to developing overall literacy skills, the children "discovered that books are a source of enchantment and wonder" (p. 560).

> **ADAPTING INSTRUCTION for *STRUGGLING READERS and WRITERS***
>
> In Maxie Perry's urban prekindergarten, Perry has enlisted the services of volunteers and aides to read to individual children. Because some of the volunteers have limited reading skills themselves and lack confidence, she supplies sensitive guidance and suggestions (Strickland & Taylor, 1989).

## A Theme Approach

Instruction is most beneficial when connections are made. Creating units helps to build connections. A unit topic might be transportation. The theme might be: We travel in different ways. Activities revolve around the themes. In dramatic play, students manage bus stations, airports, docks, railroad stations, and a taxi company. Read-alouds include books about the various kinds of transportation: *Cars, Boats, Planes* (Emberley, 1987), *Toad on the Road* (Shade & Buller, 1992), *Cars* (Rockwell, 1984), *Boat and Ships from A to Z* (Alexander, 1961), *School Bus* (Crews, 1984), *The Adventures of Taxi Dog* (Barracca, 1990), *Jamie Goes on an Airplane* (Kremetz, 1986), *Airport* (Barton, 1982). Students also sing songs and recite rhymes related to the unit theme: "Row, Row, Row Your Boat," "Wheels on the Bus." Instruction is also most beneficial when you have specific objectives. If you want to foster language and literacy skills, you need to specify these. You might note vocabulary words and structures that you would like students to learn. Vocabulary might include *transportation, highway, airport, luggage, tickets, boarding pass, passengers, fuel, pilot, cabin attendants, driver, captain, port, dock, railroad, train station, engineer, conductor, platform, reservation, track,* and *coach*. Also note literacy objectives and activities. One objective might be to have students read environmental print such as signs and logos. Another might be to become aware of the uses of print and to engage in writing. Activities such as reading signs at the railroad station or advertisements for recognizable products, an illustrated menu in a food car, or illustrated schedules, and writing tickets and credit card slips would help achieve these objectives.

## Emergent Storybook Reading

On one visit with my four-year-old granddaughter Paige, she took me aside and whispered, "I can read." Sitting on the sofa, she "read" *Are You My Mother?* (Eastman, 1960) as she leafed through the pages. Although she was not actually reading the words on the pages—her retelling was guided by the pictures—her voice had the tone and expression of one who is reading aloud rather than of one who is telling a story. Paige was engaged in **emergent storybook reading,** a widespread phenomenon in homes and classrooms where children are read to frequently.

> ■ **Emergent storybook reading** is the evolving ability of a child to read storybooks, which progresses from simply telling a story suggested by the book's illustrations or having heard the book read aloud to reading the book conventionally.

Children who have been read to imitate the process and engage in readinglike behaviors. As a result of being read to, children play with books, often for long periods of time, and gradually learn to reconstruct the stories conveyed in the books that have been read to them. For their pretend reading, or emergent storybook reading, children typically select a favorite storybook, one that has been read to them many times. Children's storybook reading can be placed in any of five broad categories beginning with talking about the illustrations in a storybook (but not creating a story) to actually reading a storybook in conventional fashion. The five categories are presented in Table 3.1.

Encourage students to "read" to themselves, to you, and to each other, even though that reading may be a simple retelling of the story. By providing them with opportunities to interact with books in this way, you will be setting the scene for their con-

*E*ncourage students to read to each other even if they are just pretend reading.

| TABLE 3.1 | Emergent reading of storybooks |
|---|---|
| **Category** | **Description** |
| Attends to pictures but does not create a story | The child simply talks about the illustrations and does not attempt to make connections among the pictures so as to tell a story. |
| Uses pictures to create an oral story | Using the storybook's illustrations, the child creates a story. However, the child's expression and intonation are those of telling rather than reading a story. |
| Uses pictures to create a combined oral/reading story | Using the storybook's illustrations, the child retells a story. Portions of the retelling sound like oral storybook reading; however, other portions sound like an oral retelling of the story or are conversational. |
| Uses pictures to create a literary retelling | Using the storybook's illustrations, the child creates a literary rendition of a story. In wording, expression, and intonation, it sounds like the reading of a storybook. The reading may be verbatim but is not just memorized. The verbatim rendition is conceptual. The child uses knowledge of the specific events in the story to help recall the wording of the story (Sulzby, 1985). |
| Uses print to read | Ironically, the first subcategory here may be a refusal to read. As a child attempts to use print rather than pictures, the child may realize that she or he cannot decipher the print and therefore might say, "I don't know the words." In the second subcategory, the child pays attention to known aspects of print, such as a few known words or a repeated phrase. |

Based on Classification Scheme for Children's Emergent Reading of Favorite Storybooks (simplified version) (pp. 137–138) by E. Sulzby (1992). In J. W. Irwin & M. A. Doyle (Eds.), *Reading/Writing Connections, Learning from Research.* Newark, DE: International Reading Association.

struction of more advanced understandings about the reading process. You might provide ten minutes a day for reading time. Schedule it to follow your read-aloud segment so that students can choose to read or retell a book that you have just read. Students can read alone, to you, or to a classmate. Explain to them that they do not have to read like grownups; they can read in their own way (Sulzby & Barnhart, 1992). You might also provide a read-aloud center where students can read to a doll or stuffed animal or read along with a taped or CD-ROM version of a story.

Observe children as they read to themselves (young children's "silent" reading is generally audible), to a stuffed animal, to a friend, or to you. Observing children's storybook reading will provide insight into their understanding of the reading process, which has implications for instruction. If children do not use storybook intonation, for example, they may not have a grasp of the language of books and so may need to be read to more often (Sulzby & Barnhart, 1992). Until they have a sense of literary language, children may have difficulty grasping the concept that the printed words on a page convey the story and can be read aloud.

## Using Shared Book Experiences

An excellent way to help students construct concepts of print (words are made up of letters, sentences are made up of words, reading goes from left to right and top to bottom, etc.) and other essential understandings is the **shared book experience.** Shared book experience is modeled on the bedtime story situation in which

■ When young children play at reading, they rehearse the special things a reader does, such as turning the pages, inspecting the pictures, and pausing to savor or to return to particular moments (Learning Media, 1991).

■ **Shared book experience,** which is also known as shared reading, is the practice of reading repetitive stories, chants, poems, or songs, often in enlarged text, while the class follows along or joins in.

## *Exemplary Teaching*

### *Shared Reading with Big Books*

*H*aving seen the effectiveness of the traditional bedtime story, Don Holdaway (1979), a primary teacher, reading clinician, and consultant in Auckland, New Zealand, decided to duplicate this experience in a kindergarten classroom. Here is his account of trying out a big book—which he calls an "enlarged book"—for the first time:

> Now we bring out our first enlarged book—a version of *The Three Billy Goats Gruff*. We choose this partly because of the strongly emotional language of the repetitive section which may draw the children into prediction and participation even on the first reading. The children are delighted with the enormous book and many keep their eyes glued on it as we use a pointer to follow the story as we read. Sure enough, on the second occasion of the "Trip, trap!"

and the "Who's that tripping over my bridge?" some of the children chime in, encouraged by the invitational cues we give off. They are delighted in the closing couplet, "Snip, snap, snout, This tale's told out," and want to say it for themselves. (p. 66)

The big book was a smashing success. After a period of experimentation and revision of the program, Holdaway concluded that the results seemed "more hopeful than we might at first have supposed" (p. 79). The shared experience apparently began a cycle of success in which the reading of high-quality literature led to more positive and enjoyable teaching, which led to a greater degree of attention and higher level of personal satisfaction among pupils, which, in turn, led to higher levels of achievement.

---

■ A **big book** is a book large enough so that all the words can be seen by all the members of the group or class. A typical size is fifteen by nineteen inches.

**ADAPTING INSTRUCTION for *STRUGGLING READERS* and *WRITERS***
Share-read books that are shorter and easier so students will be better able to follow along. After a shared reading (as compared to a traditional oral reading of a storybook), students, in general, had richer retellings and were more enthusiastic; however, the average and below-average youngsters benefit most (Combs, 1987).

a parent or grandparent reads to a child, and, through observation and interaction, the child discovers the purpose of and satisfaction provided by books and begins to construct basic concepts of print (Holdaway, 1979). In order to make the print visible to a group, enlarged text or multiple copies are used. There are several ways of providing enlarged text. Holdaway (1979) suggested using a **big book,** an oversized book measuring approximately fifteen by nineteen inches, in which the text is large enough so that students can follow the print as the teacher reads. Alternatives to a big book include using an opaque projector or an overhead projector and transparencies or carefully printing parts of the text on story paper or the chalkboard.

Before reading a big book, introduce the selection by discussing the title and cover illustration. Invite students to predict what the story might be about, build background and interest, and set a purpose for reading it. If it is a story that has already been shared with the class, the purpose can grow out of the original reading and discussion. Perhaps some details were not clear, and so children need to listen carefully to those parts. Or they may simply enjoy hearing a certain tale over and over again. The purpose also could lead to deeper involvement with the characters. Say, for example, that you have made a big book out of *Good as New* (Douglas, 1982), the story of a badly damaged teddy bear that was refurbished by its owner's grandfather. Students might imagine that they are the child who owns the bear. Have them read along with you and describe how they feel when K. C. cries for the bear. As the story progresses, ask them what they think when K. C. plays with the bear and treats it very roughly. What do they feel when the bear is just about ruined?

As you read, point to the words so that students have a sense of going from left to right and also begin to realize that printed words have spoken equivalents. Also discuss key happenings, and clarify confusing elements and have students revise or make new predictions. However, do not interrupt the flow of the reading. Focus should be on having students enjoy the experience. After you have shared a book, discuss it with the class, just as you would after reading a book orally to them.

### ■ Successive Readings

One goal of shared reading is to involve the students more deeply in the reading. If the book that you have shared with students is one they would like to read again, conduct a second shared reading. During this second reading, encourage students to join in by reading refrains, or repeated phrases, sentences, or words that are readily predictable from context or illustrations. They can do this chorally as a group or as individual volunteers. In these subsequent shared readings,

*S*hare reading a big book is an excellent way to introduce beginning reading skills.

continue to point to each word as you read it so that students can see that you are reading individual words. During a second reading of the book *Are You My Mother?* (Eastman, 1960), read the repeated sentence, "Are you my mother?" pointing to each word as you read it. Have volunteers read the sentence. Again, point to each word as the sentence is being read. Then read the story once more. Tell students that you are going to read the story, but they are going to help. As you come to "Are you my mother?" pause and have the class read the sentence in unison as you point to each word. Schedule the book for additional readings with choral reading of the repeated sentence. From time to time, have individual volunteers read the line. During follow-up reading of *Rosie's Walk* (Hutchins, 1987), one teacher began introducing students to concepts of words and letters. Pointing to the first page, she asked the students what the page said. Because the story had been read to them previously, they were able to say that it told that Rosie the hen went for a walk. The teacher asked them to find the word *hen* and point to it with a pointer and to tell what letters were in *hen* (Campbell, 2001). Students might also talk about names of classmates that begin with *h* or other *h* words in the story.

Once a big book has been shared, have students engage in follow-up activities. Some may choose to listen to a taped version of the book while reading a regular-size edition of the big book. A small group may want to read the big book once more, with one of their members assuming the role of teacher. Some may want to read to partners, while still others may want to listen to a new story in the listening center or draw an illustration related to the big book. Some may want to look at Komori's (1983) *Animal Mothers*, which uses realistic paintings to show how animal mothers get their babies to travel with them. Viewing a filmstrip, videotape, CD-

■ Predictable books invite children to chime in as the adult is reading (Schickedanz, 1999). Knowing letters and beginning sounds helps a child to point to words. If the text is a memorized one, the child can recite a line of print, but while she is reciting a word, she thinks of the beginning sound of the word and the letter that represents that sound. This enables her to point to words as she reads (Schickedanz, 1999). Until a child knows beginning sounds and letters, following along with a shared reading may be difficult and unprofitable. Reading aloud to these children might be a more appropriate activity.

ROM, or Web site on animal mothers and their young may be another option. Later, the class might compose a group-experience story based on observations of how the class's mother gerbil cares for her young. Some students may want to dictate an individual story telling how their cats or dogs cared for their young. Some students may want to compose their own stories, using drawings and **invented spellings.** Invented spellings reflect the evolving concept of how letter–sound relationships should be represented and include items such as "I KN RT" for "I can write."

To help students get started, you might put three or four key words from the story on the classroom wall or bulletin board. After sharing *Rosie's Walk* (Hutchins, 1987), one class took a walk around the school grounds to see what they could see. Students then wrote a story about their walk (Campbell, 2001). Words from the story that might be put on the wall include: *walk, saw, for.* The students' individual stories were collected in a book. Each student was given two pages. The students' version was pasted on the right-hand page. The student's story was rewritten in large, easy to read, correctly spelled manuscript on the left-hand page, so that other students could read the book.

Periodically, introduce other repetitive selections. They need not be stories—poems, rhymes, songs, and even jump rope chants are suitable. Some of these selections may be in big books; others can be written on the chalkboard or on chart paper. As students' understanding of print develops, introduce additional concepts: Point out that words are composed of letters, talk about the sounds in words, discuss words that rhyme or begin with the same sound, and help students see that some words begin with the same letter and the same sound. Also discuss **print conventions,** such as punctuation marks, capital letters, and quotation marks. And, whenever introducing a new selection, point out the title and author's name.

## Using the Language Experience Approach

**Language experience** stories can also be used to introduce the visual aspects of reading. They may be used instead of or in conjunction with big books and may be created by students working in groups or by individuals. As the name suggests, language experience is based on real-life experiences. For instance, the story in Figure 3.2 began with a class trip to a nearby apple orchard. When they returned to school, the students discussed the orchard and drew pictures to illustrate their trip. Pictures often result in more focused, coherent stories because they encapsulate the child's experience (Platt, 1978). The teacher (or an aide) discusses each child's picture, after which the child dictates a story about it. As the teacher writes the child's dictated story, the teacher tells the student what he or she is doing. Then the teacher reads the story back and asks if that is what the child wanted to say. The teacher invites the child to add to the story or make other changes.

■ **Invented spelling** is the intuitive spelling that novices create before learning or while learning the conventional writing system. Invented spelling is also known as temporary, developmental, or transitional (Strickland, 1998). These terms indicate that this spelling marks a passing stage in the child's development.

■ **Print conventions** refer to generally accepted ways of putting words on a page, such as arranging words from left to right and using capital letters and end punctuation.

■ **Language experience** is an approach to literacy teaching in which one or a group of students dictates a story, which is then used as a basis for reading and writing instruction.

**FIGURE 3.2**

### Language Experience Story

The Apple Orchard

We went to the apple orchard.
I saw apples on the trees.
I saw a big red apple on the ground.

Miguel

Once any requested changes have been made, the teacher again reads the story. Then the teacher and the child read the story together. After this shared reading, the child is invited to read his or her story to the teacher. Aided by the drawing and the familiarity of the experience, children usually are able to read their stories.

Individual stories are gathered into books, which children are encouraged to take home and read to their parents. During the school year, students may create anywhere from one to a dozen books, depending on their interest in the activity and their emerging skills.

## Shared Writing

In **shared writing,** which is modeled on experience stories and shared reading, both teacher and student compose a story (Martin, 1995). Just as in traditional language experience, the class writes about experiences they have had or books that have been read to them. Often, a shared reading of a favorite book sets the stage for the class's writing. After share reading Sarah Albee's *I Can Do It* (1997), in which the muppets tell about some of the things they can do, the class composed a story about things they can do. In addition to suggesting content, students also participated in the actual writing. The teacher encouraged students to spell or write initial consonants, parts of words, or even whole words. One strategy that these novice writers are encouraged to use is knowledge of the spellings of their names. For instance, Carl was able to supply the first letter of *can* because *can* begins like *Carl*, and Roberto was able to supply the first letter of *ride*.

In shared writing, the teacher emphasizes reading for meaning and basic concepts of print. For instance, after adding a word to a story, the teacher goes back and reads the portion of the sentence that has been written so far. Focused on the details of the writing of a word, students may have lost the sense of the sentence. Going back over what has been written helps the students keep the story in mind and also helps them make a one-to-one match between written and spoken words. After, for example, adding "ride" to "Roberto can," the teacher rereads all that has been written of the sentence: "Roberto can ride." As part of the scaffolding, the teacher also asks such questions as the following:

Where do we begin writing?

How many words are there in our sentence?

Say the word slowly. What sounds do you hear?

Can you write the letter that stands for that sound?

Here is sample dialog to show how shared writing might be implemented:

*Teacher:* "What are some things that you can do?"

*Maria:* "I can ride a bike."

*Teacher:* "How shall we write that in our story?"

*Felicia:* "Maria can ride a bike."

*Teacher:* "How many words are in that sentence?"

*Reginald:* "Five."

---

**ADAPTING INSTRUCTION for *ENGLISH LANGUAGE LEARNERS***

For individual stories, write the story just as the student says it, even if the grammar is not correct or the student uses both English and his native language. For group stories, use correct grammar or students may be confused.

■ In a **shared writing,** students may tell the teacher what letter(s) to write or may actually write them in the piece.

Shared writing is sometimes known as interactive writing, especially if students are writing parts of words or whole words.

**ASSESSING STUDENTS' PROGRESS**

As students participate in shared writing, note what they can do. Can they supply initial or final consonants? Do they seem to know most of the consonant correspondences? Or do they just know the consonants that their names begin with? Can they read some words? What do your observations suggest about the type of instruction they might need?

*Teacher:* "What is the first word?"

*Jason:* "Maria."

*Teacher:* (pointing to spot on chalkboard) "Maria, will you write your name here?"

*Teacher:* (pointing to and reading "Maria") "What goes next?"

*Thomas:* "Can."

*Teacher:* "How many sounds does *can* (teacher stretches out word) have?"

*James:* "Three."

*Teacher:* "How does *can* (emphasizes first sound) begin? Who has a name that begins like *can*?"

*Carl:* "I do."

*Teacher:* "How does your name begin?"

*Carl:* "With a *c*."

*Teacher:* "Would you write a *c* here?" (Judging that the students would not be able to spell the short *a* sound, the teacher adds an *a* and says, "What should we add to /ca/ to make *can*?"

*Class:* "N."

*Teacher:* "Whose name has an *n*?"

*Nan:* Mine does.

*Teacher:* (After *n* has been added, she says, pointing to each word) "Maria can. What can Maria do?"

*Class:* "Ride a bike."

*Teacher:* "How many sounds does *ride* (teacher stretches out word) have?"

*Cynthia:* "Three."

*Teacher:* "How does *ride* (emphasizes first sound) begin? Whose name begins like *ride*?"

*Roberto:* "My name. Roberto begins like *ride*."

*Teacher:* "What other sounds do you hear in *ride*? What comes after *rrr*?"

*Carl:* "I–duh."

*Teacher:* "What letter spells /ī/?"

*Carl:* "That's easy. *I* spells /ī/."

*Teacher:* "What letter spells /d/?"

*Carl:* "D."

*Teacher:* "Can you write *i-d* for us?"

*Carl:* "I can write *i*, but I forget how *d* goes."

*Teacher:* "Can you find *d* on the alphabet chart?"

*Teacher:* (After adding an *e* to the *d* on the end of the word, she asks,) "Who will point to and read what we have written so far?"

The teacher continues until the story is completed.

Finished pieces are placed on the walls. The teacher share-reads the pieces. As students become familiar with the pieces, they are encouraged to read the walls.

▌For additional examples of shared writing, see chapters on interactive writing in I. C. Fountas & G. S. Pinnell (eds.), (1999). *Voices in word matters.* Portsmouth, NH: Heinemann.

▌Students are asked to point to the words they read to make sure that they are processing individual words and not just reciting a portion of the text that they have memorized.

## Exemplary Teaching

### Shared Writing in Kindergarten

*U*sing a series of informal assessment devices, Paige Ferguson determined that only half of her kindergarten students could write their names and only two knew the letters of the alphabet. Given the children's low level of literacy development, she decided to use shared writing with them. As part of their literature unit, she read Paul Galdone's (1975) *The Gingerbread Boy* to the class. The class then took a walking tour of the school to find hidden gingerbread boys. After returning to the classroom, the class began creating a shared story. The story consisted of listing the places where they found the gingerbread boys.

Building on the students' knowledge of the sounds and letters in their names, the teacher introduced other sounds and letters as the class created additional shared stories. To reinforce the children's awareness of separate words, she had one student point to each word in the story while the other children read it. As the year progressed, the children learned to hear the separate sounds in words and represent these sounds with letters. They also learned to write in a variety of formats. They wrote shared letters to pen pals, retold stories, made lists, and summarized scientific observations that they had made.

In addition to writing interactively, the children wrote independently each day. Shared writing provided a foundation for their independent writing. They also reread the shared stories that had been hung up around the room. When assessed in the spring, the students demonstrated dramatic progress. They showed growth in phonemic awareness, knowledge of letter–sound relationships, alphabet knowledge, concepts of print, and writing. Most could also read some beginning first-grade-level books (Button, Johnson, & Furgerson, 1996).

Lists of color, number, and other common words and students' names are also placed on the wall in alphabetical order. Students are encouraged to use these lists and the stories placed on the wall to help them with pieces that they write independently. Because shared writing is a group project, stories are written in standard spelling. When students write independently, they use invented spelling but are encouraged to use words from the wall. Their writing typically contains conventional spellings drawn from lists and stories on the walls.

> Until recently, writing was viewed as being more difficult and advanced than reading, so children were taught to write after they learned to read. However, reading and writing are now seen as developing simultaneously and as being interrelated.

## A New Concept of Writing

Traditionally, writing was not taught until after students started reading. Often, it was equated with handwriting, copying, and spelling instruction. However, writing is not simply a matter of forming letters (Holdaway, 1979); it is a way of representing the world, progressing from apparently random scribbles to meaningful marks to increasingly more conventional letters and spellings. From their first day in school, children should be encouraged to write as best they can in whatever way they can, whether by drawings, letterlike forms, or invented spellings.

Teachers should encourage them to write and draw, should accept and support their efforts, and should resist correcting "errors." Teachers should model the process, allowing students to see them writing on the chalkboard, chart paper, word processor, notepaper, and so on. Attempts at writing lead to discoveries about the alphabetic system that help students gain essential insights into both writing and reading.

## Formation of Speech Sounds

Knowing how speech sounds are formed will help you to do a better job teaching phonological awareness, phonics, and spelling. It will help you to understand why *train* is frequently spelled CHRAN and why *girl* is often spelled GRIL and why clusters such as the *st* in *stop* and the *sp* in *spot* are often misread.

### ■ Consonant Formation

Consonants are formed by obstructing or interfering in some way with the flow of breath. In English there are twenty-five consonant sounds (see Table 3.2). Consonants can be distinguished by place and manner of articulation and voice. Say the consonant sounds in Table 3.2. As you do so, focus on the formation of each one. Notice that you are using your tongue, lips, and teeth, and that the consonants are formed in various parts of your mouth, nose, and throat. In addition, consonants are either voiced or voiceless. A voiced consonant is one that is accompanied by a vibration of the vocal cords. Thus /b/ is voiced but /p/ is not. If you say /b/ and /p/, you will notice that both have the same manner and place of articulation. The only difference between them is that one is voiced and the other is not.

### ■ Vowel Formation

Vowels are articulated with tongue, lips, and teeth. Vowels are classified according to where they are articulated. Say each of the vowel sounds in Table 3.3. What do

**TABLE 3.2**  Consonants: Place and manner of articulation

| | Lips (Labials) | Lips & Teeth (Labio-dentals) | Tongue betweeen Teeth (Dentals) | Tongue behind Teeth (Aveolars) | Roof of Mouth (Palatal-velars) | Back of Mouth (Velars) | Throat (Glottal) |
|---|---|---|---|---|---|---|---|
| **Stops** Voiced Voiceless | b (barn) p (pot) | | | d (deer) t (time) n (now) | | g (gate) k (kite) | |
| **Nasals** | m (me) | | | | | ng (sing) | |
| **Fricatives** Voiced Voiceless | | v (van) f (fan) | th (thin) <u>th</u> (this) | z (zipper) s (sight) | zh (azure) sh (ship) | | h (horse) |
| **Africatives** Voiced Voiceless | | | | | j (jug) ch (chip) | | |
| **Semivowels (glides)** | | | | | y (yacht) | w (we)  hw (whale) | |
| **Liquids** | | | | l (lion)  r (ride) | | | |

| TABLE 3.3 | American English vowels | | |
|-----------|-------------------------|---|---|
| | **Front** | **Central** | **Back** |
| High | ē (beat) | | ōō (boot) |
| | i (bit) | | oo (book) |
| Mid | ā (bait) | u (but) | ō (boat) |
| | e (bet) | schwa | |
| Low | a (bat) | | aw (bought) |
| | | o (bottle) | |
| | | i(bite)   oy   ow (combinations of vowel sounds) | |

you notice about their articulation? What happens to your tongue as you say the various vowels? Notice that your tongue moves from the very front of your mouth to the back. Your tongue also moves lower in your mouth as you say /ē/, /i/, /ā/, /e/, /a/, /ī/, /o/, /oo/, /ōō/ and then begins to move up. Starting with /ē/, your lips are parted as though you were smiling. Gradually, your lips become rounded. The sounds /oy/ and /ow/ are not placed on the chart because they include two sounds.

### ■ Effect of Environment on Speech Sounds

Except for words like *I* and *oh*, most speech sounds don't appear in isolation. They have speech sounds coming before or after them. Often speech sounds are altered by the sounds surrounding them (Moats, 2000).

**Nasalization.**    Nasal consonant sounds such as /m/, /n/, and /ng/ are partially absorbed by the preceding vowel and sometimes the consonant after it so that a word like *ant* may sound like /at/. Because of nasalization, it is difficult to segment the sounds in *sand* and *pan* and similar words. There is also an increased possibility that words like *ant* and *sand* will be spelled without the nasal consonant and will be spelled: *at*, and *sad*.

**Affrication.**    The phonemes /ch/ and /j/ are known as affricatives. In an affricative, a stop of breath is followed by a fricative. A fricative is a consonant sound that is produced through friction as in /v/ or /f/. The phonemes /t/ and /d/ are affricated when they appear before a sound such as /r/ so that /t/ sounds like /ch/ and /d/ sounds like /j/ as in *train* and *drum*. In the process of articulating an /r/, the mouth naturally forms a /ch/ or a /j/. Because of affrication, *train* is often spelled CHRAN and *drum* JUM or JM by children who are focusing on the sounds they hear.

**Aspiration**.    Holding a piece of paper a few inches from your mouth, say *pit* out loud. Now say *tip*. When you said *pit*, the paper moved but not when you said *tip*. The pronunciation of *pit* was accompanied by aspiration. Aspiration is a puff of air as when you articulate /h/. The voiceless stop consonants /p/, /t/, and /k/ are usually aspirated when they come at the beginning of a word or syllable. Voiceless stops are not aspirated when they come at the end of a word or syllable or are the second sound in a cluster as in *spot*, *stop*, or *scare*. Being unaspirated they are harder to detect so children have more difficulty identifying final sounds and the second sound in a cluster. Students might have a more difficult time segmenting the sounds in words that have unaspirated stops. Because the unaspirated forms may sound like their voiced counterparts, /p/ is often spelled as *b*, /t/ as *d*, and /k/ as *g* as in *pig* for *pick*, *cub* for *cup*, *sgar* for *scare*, and *sbot* for *spot* (Moats, 2000).

**Vowel Blending.** Some vowels are difficult to detect because they blend in with the consonant that follows them. This is especially true of /l/ and /r/ as in *will* and *girl*. Children may spell *bird* as *brid*, not because they are confusing the sequence of sounds but because the /i/ and /r/ are blended and the *r* sound dominates. This also explains the GRIL spelling of *girl*, where the /l/ sound dominates. Segmenting the sounds in these words can be difficult. When students have difficulty spelling these words, encouraging them to sound them out may be counterproductive. If they spell what they hear, chances are they will misspell the words (Moats, 2000). This is also true of words like *train* and *drum* and *dress*. These elements need to be taught as onset-rime patterns. By teaching the rime as a unit, students aren't asked to separate the sounds in words like *third* or *fort*.

### ■ Development of Spelling

When does writing start? At the age of eighteen months, average toddlers will make marks on paper (Gibson & Levin, 1974). By age three, scribbling is no longer random or unorganized (Harste, Woodward, & Burke, 1984). Because it proceeds in a straight line across the page and may be composed of up-and-down or curved marks, it resembles genuine writing. In time, children may create letterlike figures, may use a combination of numbers and letters, and may eventually use letters. Along the way, they discover the concept of sign (Clay, 1972)—that is, they arbitrarily use a graphic element to represent an idea or a word, a syllable, or a sound. For example, the child may use the letter *b* or *x* or a self-created letterlike form to represent the word *ball*.

The earliest spelling is **pre-alphabetic** (pre-phonemic). At this stage, children realize that letters are used to create words but have not caught on to the alphabetic principle—that is, that letters represent sounds. At age four, Paul Bissex used strings of letters to cheer his mother up. The letters were a random selection and were designed to convey the messages "Welcome home" in one instance and "Cheer up" in another (Bissex, 1980).

The next stage of spelling is the early **alphabetic** (letter name) stage, as children start putting the alphabetic principle to work. Single letters may at first represent whole words but later may stand for syllables and then represent single sounds (Ferreiro, 1986). For instance, the letter *k* may be used to represent the word *car*. In later phases of this stage, a child may add the final consonant, spelling car as *KR*. Some consonant combination spellings may at first seem to have no connection to their sounds: *tr* is frequently spelled *CH*, and *dr* may be spelled *JR*. Try saying "train." Listen very carefully to the initial sound. The beginning sound is actually /ch/. Likewise, the *d* in *dr* combinations has a /j/ sound. The child is spelling what she or he hears (Read, 1971).

■ In the **pre-alphabetic** stage, students use letters but don't realize that the letters represent sounds.

■ The **alphabetic** stage is also known as the letter name stage because students use the names of the letters to figure out the sounds they represent. The name of *b*, for instance, contains its sound.

In time, the child begins representing vowel sounds. In the alphabetic (letter name) stage, students continue to employ a strategy in which a letter is used to represent the sound heard in the letter's name, so *late* would be spelled *LAT* and *feet* would be spelled *FET*. This works for most consonants and long vowels but not for short ones, as the names of short vowels do not contain their pronunciations. To spell short vowels, children employ the "close to" tactic, in which they use the long-vowel name that is closest to the point in the mouth where the short vowel to be spelled is articulated. For instance, short *e* is formed very close to the point where long *a* is articulated, so the child spells short *e* with an *A*, as in *BAD* for *bed*. Based on the "close to" tactic, short *i* is spelled with an *E* (*SET* for *sit*), short *o* with an *I* (*HIP* for *hop*), and short *u* with an *O* (*BOT* for *but*) (Read, 1971).

As they are exposed to standard spellings in books and environmental print, children begin to notice that spelling incorporates certain conventions—that final *e* is used to mark long vowels, for instance. They enter the **consolidated alphabetic (within word pattern)** stage in which they begin to consolidate visual or orthographic elements along with sound elements in their spelling (Henderson, 1990). Their spelling is no longer strictly guided by sound. Although their spelling may not always be accurate, they begin to use final *e* markers and double vowel letters to spell long vowel sounds. They may spell *mean* as *MEEN* or *MENE*. However, they begin to spell short vowels accurately. As children progress through this stage, their spelling becomes conventional, and ultimately they move into the stages of syllable juncture and derivational constancy, which are advanced stages of conventional spelling involving multisyllabic words (Henderson, 1990). See Table 3.4 for examples of the major stages of spelling.

As can be seen from the description of the stages of spelling, spelling is not merely a matter of memorizing words. Spelling is conceptual and involves three levels of understanding: alphabetic, pattern, and meaning. At the alphabetic level, students understand that letters represent sounds. At the pattern level, they realize that letters often form patterns, as in the spelling of *load* and *rope* when long *o* is spelled with an *oa* and *o-e*. At the meaning level, students conclude that meaning

■ The **consolidated alphabetic** stage is sometimes known as the within word pattern or orthographic stage because students are beginning to see patterns such as final e and double vowel letters.

| **TABLE 3.4** | Stages of spelling | |
|---|---|---|
| **Age** | **Stage** | **Example** |
| 18 months | Random scribbling | ⌒⌒⌒⌐ |
| 3 years | Wordlike scribbling | ∿∿‿ |
| 4–5 years | Prephonemic writing | L W I Ɔ |
| 4–6+ years | Early alphabetic (early letter name) | W L |
| 5–7+ years | Alphabetic (letter name) | W A L |
| 6–7+ years | Consolidated alphabetic (within word pattern) | who le |
| 8–10+ years | Syllable juncture | whaling |
| 10–20+ years | Derivational constancy | aquatic |

may govern a word's spelling so that words that have a similar meaning have a similar spelling even though their pronunciations may differ: *sign/signature* (Bear & Templeton, 1998).

As they have more experience with writing, children develop a deeper understanding of the spelling system. They begin to use visual and meaning features to spell words instead of just relying on sound characteristics. Instruction is most effective when it matches the student's stage of development. For instance, a student in the early letter name (alphabetic) stage would have difficulty with final *e* words. She or he might be able to memorize the spelling of *note* but would not understand the final *e* principal and so wouldn't apply it to other words.

To determine students' spelling stage, analyze samples of their writing. You might also use the Elementary Spelling Inventory (Bear & Barone, 1989), presented in Table 3.5. The inventory presents twenty-five words that increase in difficulty and embody key elements of the stages. Start with the first word and continue testing until the words become too difficult. Ask students to spell as best they can

**TABLE 3.5** The elementary spelling inventory (with error guide)

| Stages | Early Letter Name | Letter Name | Within Word Pattern |
|---|---|---|---|
| 1. bed | b bd | bad | bed |
| 2. ship | s sp shp | sep shep | sip ship |
| 3. drive | jrv drv | griv driv | drieve draive drive |
| 4. bump | h bp bmp | bop bomp bup | bump |
| 5. when | w yn wn | wan whan | wen when |
| 6. train | j t trn | jran chran tan tran | teran traen trane train |
| 7. closet | k cs kt clst | clast clost clozt | clozit closit |
| 8. chase | j jass cs | tas cas chas chass | case chais chase |
| 9. float | f vt ft flt | fot flot flott | flowt floaut flote float |
| 10. beaches | b bs bcs | bechs becis behis | bechise beches beeches beaches |
| | | | |
| 11. preparing | | | preparng preypering |
| 12. popping | | | popin poping |
| 13. cattle | | | catl cadol |
| 14. caught | | | cot cote cout cought caught |
| 15. inspection | | | inspshn inspechin |
| 16. puncture | | | pucshr pungchr puncker |
| 17. cellar | | | salr selr celr seler |
| 18. pleasure | | | plasr plager plejer pleser plesher |
| 19. squirrel | | | scrl skwel skwerl |
| 20. fortunate | | | forhnat frehnit foohinit |
| | | | |
| 21. confident | | | |
| | | | |
| 22. civilize | | | |
| 23. flexible | | | |
| 24. opposition | | | |
| 25. emphasize | | | opasiun opasishan opozcison opishien opasitian |

Note: The Preliterate Stage is not presented here.

because even partially spelled words reveal important information about the student's spelling. Before administering the inventory, explain to students that you want to see how they spell words. Tell them that some of the words may be hard, but they should do the best they can. Say each word, use it in a sentence, and say the word once more.

Using the error guide, carefully analyze the students' performance. Most novice readers will be in the early alphabetic (letter name) stage. However, a few might be in a more advanced stage, and some may be in the prephonemic stage. Often, students move back and forth between adjacent stages. Figure 3.3 shows examples of a child's use of invented spelling in kindergarten and in first grade.

### ■ Forms of Emergent Writing

Children's writing develops through seven forms, beginning with drawing and ending with conventional spelling. These forms include the spelling stages depicted in Table 3.2 but go beyond spelling to include the writer's intentions. The major

| **TABLE 3.5** The elementary spelling inventory (with error guide) *(continued)* | |
|---|---|
| **Syllable Juncture** | **Derivational Constancy** |
| 11. preparing prepairing preparing | |
| 12. popping | |
| 13. catel catle cattel cattle | |
| 15. inspecshum inspecsion inspection | |
| 16. punksher punture puncture | |
| 17. seller sellar celler cellar | |
| 18. plesour plesure | pleasure |
| 19. scqoril sqrarel squirle squirrel | |
| 20. forchenut fochininte fortunet | fortunate |
| 21. confadent confedint confedent confadent conphident confiadent confiedent confendent confodent confident | |
| 22. sivils sevelies sivilicse cifillazas sivelize sivalize civalise civilise civilize | |
| 23. flecksibl flexobil fleckuble flecible flexeble flexibel flaxable flexibal flexable | flexible |
| 24. opasition oppasishion oppisition | oposision oposition opposition |
| 25. infaside infacize emfesize emfsize imfasize ephacise empasize emphasise | emphizize emphasize |

FIGURE 3.3

**A Student's Invented Spelling in Kindergarten and First Grade**

(a) Kindergarten

(b) First Grade

From stories written by Anne Lincoln. Used by permission

| TABLE 3.6 | Forms of emergent writing |
|---|---|
| **Form** | **Description** |
| Drawing | The drawing is not an illustration for a story but is the story itself. The child reads the drawing as though it were text. |
| Scribbling | The scribbling resembles a line of writing. It may have the appearance of a series of waves or, in a more advanced representation, may resemble a series of letterlike forms. |
| Letterlike forms | Letterlike forms resemble manuscript or cursive letters and are generally written as separate forms rather than the continuous forms seen in scribbling. They are not real letters, and care needs to be taken that poorly formed real letters are not placed in this category. |
| Prephonemic spelling | The child writes with real letters, but the letters are a random collection or a meaningless pattern, such as repeating the same letter. Although the letters are real, they do not represent sounds. |
| Copying | The child copies from print found in his or her environment: signs, labels, etc. One child copied from a crayon box but, when asked to read his piece, told a story that had nothing to do with crayons (Sulzby, 1989). |
| Invented spelling | Students make use of the alphabetic principle. The letters they write represent sounds. Initially, one letter may represent a whole word. Over time, there is a gradual movement to conventional spelling. See Table 3.2 for a chart of spelling stages, including the several stages of invented spelling. |
| Conventional spelling | Student's spelling is conventional. |

Based on Appendix 2.1, Forms of Writing and Rereading from Writing, Example List (pp. 51–63) by E. Sulzby (1989). In J. M. Mason (Ed.), *Reading and Writing Connections.* Boston: Allyn & Bacon.

forms of emergent writing described in Table 3.6 are based on research completed with kindergarten students (Sulzby, Barnhart, & Hieshima, 1989).

At the beginning of the kindergarten year, many children are operating on a scribble level. Some continue to use that form throughout the year. However, even though some students cling to a scribble form of writing, the scribbles at the end of the year are more advanced than those created at the beginning of the year. How can one scribbled story be more advanced than another? Although, on the surface, two scribbled stories may seem very similar, they may have very different meanings for their creators. In children's writing, there may be more on the page than meets the eye. Sulzby (1989) cautions, "One can only judge the quality of the form of writing by comparing it with the rereading a child uses with it" (p. 51).

After students write stories in whatever form or forms they choose, they are asked to read them. Just as in emergent storybook readings, described in Table 3.1, students reread their pieces on a variety of levels of sophistication. A child asked to reread a scribble story may simply retell a story that apparently has no connection with the scribbles. Another child may read the scribble as though she is reading conventional writing. The child's voice may incorporate the intonation of a story. She may even point to the scribbles as they are read as though pointing to a line of words. When the child comes to the end of the scribbles, her reading ceases. When asked to reread the scribbles, the child may use exactly the same words to retell the tale. In a sense, the student is reading the scribbles. Categories of rereading are presented in Table 3.7.

**ASSESSING STUDENTS' PROGRESS**

Through observation and discreet probing, find out where children are in their writing development. Some may be drawing or scribble writing. Others may have advanced into invented or even conventional spelling. Also note how children approach the task of writing. Do they jump right in, or are they hesitant and unsure?

| TABLE 3.7 | Rereading from emergent writing |
|---|---|
| **Category** | **Description** |
| Null | The child refuses to read the story he or she has written, says that he or she cannot read it, or comments that nothing was written or the story does not say anything. |
| Labeling/describing | The child supplies labels or a description instead of reading. The child says, "Cat," or, "This is a cat." A one-word response is a label; a sentence response is a description. |
| Dialogue | The child only responds if you ask questions, so the interchange takes on a question–answer format. The question–answer interchange may be initiated by the child. |
| Oral monologue | The child tells a story in the style of an oral retelling. It does not have the characteristics of the reading of a piece of writing. |
| Written monologue | The reading sounds as though the child is reading from a written piece. It has the sound and flow of oral reading of written text, but the child is not actually reading from the written piece. |
| Naming letters | The child names the letters that have been written. |
| Aspectual/strategic reading | The child is beginning to attend to the writing and may attempt to sound out some words and phrases while skipping others. The child may read the written piece while looking at the written words, but the written words may not completely match up with what the child is reading. |
| Conventional | The child uses the written words to read. The rendition may sound like written monologue, but the main difference is that the child is deciphering the written words while reading. |

Based on Appendix 2.1, Forms of Writing and Rereading from Writing, Example List (pp. 51–63) by E. Sulzby (1989). In J. M. Mason (Ed.), *Reading and Writing Connections.* Boston: Allyn & Bacon.

---

**ASSESSING STUDENTS' PROGRESS**

Children use different forms of writing for different tasks. When writing brief pieces, kindergarten children tend to use conventional spelling. When writing a long story, they may scribble.

Invented spelling contributed to the progress made by at-risk first-graders in acquiring phonological awareness and phonics (Santa & Høien, 1999).

## ■ Encouraging Children to Write

Whether they are drawing, scribbling, copying, creating invented spellings, or entering into a transitional phase, children should be encouraged to write. The program should be informal but functional. The first prerequisite is that each student should realize that she or he has something to say. Whatever a student produces should be accepted and valued.

The teacher's role should be an active one, modeling the writing process at every opportunity. When the teacher is writing a note to parents explaining a field trip, the children should be shown what the teacher is doing. They should see the teacher create signs for the room, draw up a list of supplies, complete a book order, and write messages on the board. Seeing real writing done for real purposes is especially important for students who may not have seen their parents do much writing.

Invitations to write should be extended to the children. The teacher might ask them to write about things they like to do. The teacher should model the process by writing a piece that tells what he or she likes to do. Students should then be encouraged to write as best they can or in any way they can. If they wish, they can draw pictures showing what they like to do, or they may both draw and write. The teacher should show samples of the various ways that children write—including scribbling, random letter strings, drawings, and invented spellings—and explain that each student is to write in her or his own way.

During the year, the students should engage in several writing projects, such as letters or invitations to family members and friends, stories, accounts of personal experiences, and lists. After writing a piece, a child should read it to an adult, who might want to transcribe it on another sheet of paper if the original is not readable. Transcriptions should be kept with the written pieces in a writing folder, which becomes a file of the child's writing development. As Sulzby and Barnhart (1992) commented,

> Many people are still shocked at the ease with which children at kindergarten age (or younger) write, when we invite them and if we accept the forms of writing they prefer. From working with and observing hundreds of classrooms, we can say confidently that all kindergartners reared in a literate culture like our own can and will write. (pp. 125–126)

### ■ Real Writing for Real Purposes

Emphasis in a writing program for young children is on writing a variety of pieces for a variety of reasons. Young children adopt different strategies for different tasks. They might use invented spelling when compiling a list but use scribble writing for a lengthy tale (Martinez & Teale, 1987). Real-life activities have the effect of motivating them to use more sophisticated techniques.

Functional writing tasks have proven especially effective in facilitating students' development. This became apparent in the first year of the Kindergarten Emergent Literacy Program, an experimental program that included daily writing. When writing invitations for the class's Thanksgiving feast, many children, who until that time had used scribble writing, chose to use random strings of letters or even to attempt to spell words (Martinez & Teale, 1987). Other effective writing activities include making lists, writing names, and using routines.

**Making lists.** One writing activity on which young children thrive is making lists. Clay (1975) called the motivation for this activity the inventory principle. Novice writers enjoy creating an inventory of letters or words that they can write. Suggested assignments include making lists of friends, family members, favorite foods, places visited, favorite toys, and so on.

**Writing names.** One of the first words that a child learns to spell is his or her name. Special attention should be given to this task, because once children learn their names, they frequently use the letters to spell other words. Thus, each name becomes a source of known letters that can be used in various sequences and combinations (Temple, Nathan, Temple, & Burris, 1993).

Take full advantage of children's interest in their names. Put name tags on their cubbyholes, coat hooks, and/or shelf spaces. Ask the children to sign all their written work. When scheduling individuals for activities or assignments, write

> Modeling is an important part of children's early writing attempts. In writing letters and notes, they imitate what they have seen parents, teachers, and older siblings do.

> For additional suggestions for using children's names to teach phonics, see Cunningham, P. M., & Hall, D. P. (1997). *Month-by-month phonics for first grade*. Greensboro, NC: Carson-Dellosa.

As students are learning to compose morning messages, you might supply frame sentences until they catch onto the idea and are able to write their reports on their own. Frame sentences might include "Today is ____. Today the class is going to ___. My news is ____." (Morrow & Asbury, 2001).

**ADAPTING INSTRUCTION for STRUGGLING READERS and WRITERS**

Encouraging students to spell a word the way it sounds helps them to make discoveries about the spelling system. If they don't know how to begin, help them go through a word sound by sound and talk about the letters that spell those sounds. For words like *train, drum, girl,* and *bird,* where the words are not spelled the way they sound, explain to children that these are "tricky" spellings.

If, when dictating a story, children pause between words, this is a sign that they can segment a sentence into words (Oken-Wright, 1998).

Students need lots of practice with sounding out. When using sounding out, first-graders failed to represent all the sounds in half the words. Second-graders did somewhat better, but failed to represent all the sounds in one-third of the words (Rittle-Johnson & Siegler, 1999).

their names on the chalkboard so that they become used to seeing and reading their own names, as well as those of the other children.

**Using routines.** Whenever possible, use routines to demonstrate literacy lessons. The Kamehameha School in Honolulu, Hawaii, uses a device known as the morning message to impart literacy skills (Kawakami-Arakaki, Oshiro, & Farran, 1989). Written by the teacher, the morning message gives the date and important information about the day's activities. Messages in the beginning of the year are relatively simple, but they become increasingly complex to match the growth in children's skills. A November message might be "Today is Monday, November 12. We will go to the firehouse this morning." The teacher reads it aloud and encourages the students to read along with her. At this juncture, the teacher wants the children to see that writing is functional (it conveys important information), that one reads from left to right and top to bottom, and that written messages are made up of individual words and leters. Later, longer messages are written, and more sophisticated skills—such as the concepts that words are made up of sounds and that certain sounds are represented by certain letters—are stressed. As students learn letter–sound relationships, the writing can be more interactive. Students can be asked to tell what letter the words begin with or even spell out high-frequency words that they may have learned.

Students can also be encouraged to add to the morning message. This assures them that what they have to say is important. These additions also help students and teacher get to know each other better, as the students' contributions might include major family events such as the birth of siblings or the death of grandparents and other news of personal importance.

### ■ Help with Spelling

Children should be encouraged to use their knowledge of letter–sound relationships to create spellings, even if the spellings are not accurate. You can foster this process by showing students how to elongate sounds as they spell them. One question that arises in a program emphasizing invented spelling is what to do when children ask how to spell a word. The advice offered most often is to encourage them to spell it as best they can or to say the word very slowly—to stretch it out—and work out the spelling. You might ask, How does the word start? What letter comes first? What letter comes next? The idea is to have students develop their own sense of the spelling system. If you spell words for students, they will begin to rely on your help instead of constructing their own spellings. Keep in mind that students' invented spellings reflect their understanding of the spelling system. Words that they create belong to them in a way that words that are spelled for them do not (Wilde, 1995).

Providing access to standard spelling could take the form of having picture dictionaries available; placing some frequently requested words on the board; posting word lists of animals, families, colors, foods, or other related words; labeling items; or creating a word wall (see Chapter 4). It could also mean providing assistance when students are unable to work out the spelling of a word and you believe that providing help will further their development. Occasionally, you might have students attempt to spell the word as best they can and then write the conventional spelling above their attempt, saying, "Here's how we usually spell ____. Look how close you came" (Ruddell & Ruddell, 1995, p. 103). Any help that you supply should take into account the student's understanding of the spelling system. If, for instance, the child spells *truck* with *CH*, you should say, "Truck sounds like it begins with a *ch* as in *Charles*, but it begins with a *t* as in *Tim* and an *r* as in *Raymond*" (Wilde, 1995).

Although students are encouraged to explore the writing system through invented spellings, they should be held accountable for any letter relationships they have been taught. If students have been taught initial *m* or *s*, they should be held accountable for spelling these sounds, although you might provide some prompting such as modeling the process of sounding out the first sound so as to be better able to perceive it (Invernizzi, Meier, Swank, & Juel, 2001).

Whatever you do, have a clear policy—one based on your beliefs about invented spelling. Be sure to explain your policy to both students and their parents. Parents should understand that one reason for encouraging children to write before they can spell conventionally is that it gives them a reason to learn the real system, the "code."

### ■ Dictation in the Writing Program

Although students should be encouraged to write as best they can, they may choose to dictate on occasion, such as when they are expressing heartfelt feelings or recounting events that touch them deeply. The content may be so intense that they cannot handle both it and the form. For example, one young student, who usually wrote on her own, chose to dictate when she told the story of how her mother had been involved in a serious auto accident. Both teacher-initiated and child-initiated writing and **dictation** are vital elements of a literacy program, as "they provide process as well as content for beginning reading" (Fields, Spangler, & Lee, 1991, p. 52).

Dictation helps children see the relationship between speaking and writing. They can see that if they speak too fast, the scribe has a difficult time keeping up. Over time, they learn to pace their dictation so that it matches the scribe's ability to record it. Of course, the scribe can also point out letters, words, and sentences as he writes so that the child is better able to see the relationship between written and spoken language. One thing that should be made clear is the role of dictation. The teacher does not want to create the impression that she is writing because the student cannot. The teacher should explain that dictating is another way of writing. In addition to being used to capture emotional stories that individuals have to tell, dictated writing can also be used to record a group experience (Sulzby, Teale, & Kamberelis, 1989).

## Planned Instruction of Essential Understandings

Setting the stage for developing reading and writing is important and arranging for many opportunities to read and write is vital, but explicit instruction should

**INVENTED SPELLING**
The best teachers encourage invented spelling in the beginning stages of learning literacy. However, as the teachers introduce students to phonics elements and high-frequency words in reading and spelling, they begin holding students responsible for the correct spelling of words incorporating those items (Wharton-McDonald, 2001).

▌ Up until the age of six, formal handwriting instruction may not be appropriate for most children. Before the age of six, most children have not developed the fine motor control needed to form letters accurately. The best course of action is to offer handwriting tips and models but not to pressure children into a performance that is still beyond them.

▌ If, when dictating a story, children pause between words, this is a sign that they can segment a sentence into words (Oken-Wright, 1998).

■ **Dictation** is the process of recounting an experience orally and having someone else write down the words.

With the acceptance of invented spelling, dictation of experience stories has been deemphasized. However, children's dictated pieces are more fully developed than those that they compose themselves. When content is essential, dictation is the better approach.

The two best predictors of future success in reading are phonemic awareness and letter knowledge.

Children generally know more uppercase letters than lowercase ones. Uppercase letters are easier to learn, and adults generally write in uppercase when writing for children.

When should the alphabet be introduced? "As soon as the child is encouraged to write his name, his attention is being directed to letters. Often the first two or three letters that occur in his name become distinctive because of these efforts" (Clay, 1991, pp. 266–267).

also be a key element in the literacy program. This is especially true when students are struggling.

Direct instruction should take place within the context of the kinds of reading and writing activities that are being explored in this chapter. Two areas in which students are most likely to need direct instruction are phonological awareness (ability to detect rhyme and beginning sounds, ability to hear separate sounds in words) and the alphabetic principle (the system by which speech sounds are represented by letters). In fact, the major cause of difficulty in learning to read is a deficiency in these areas (Adams, 1990).

Children vary greatly in knowledge of the alphabet and phonological awareness. In the fall of 1998, trained assessors conducted standardized, one-on-one assessments with a representative sample of about 22,000 kindergartners (West, Denton, & Germino-Hausken, 2000). A majority of entering kindergartners (66 percent) can recognize letters of the alphabet by name, whether they are upper- or lowercase. However, most kindergartners cannot point to letters representing sounds at the beginning or end of simple words, read basic words in isolation, or read more complex words in the context of a sentence. Only about two children out of a hundred can read high-frequency words. And only about one in a hundred can read sentences (see Table 3.8). However, children raised in poverty are less proficient. Only 41 percent of children whose caregivers are receiving welfare benefits can identify the letters of the alphabet.

### ■ Learning the Letters of the Alphabet

Although it seems logical that students would learn letters by memorizing their shapes, that is not the way it happens. They learn to tell one letter from another and to identify particular letters by noting distinctive features such as whether lines are curved or slanted, open or closed (Gibson, Gibson, Pick, & Osser, 1962). To perceive distinctive features, students must be given many experiences comparing and contrasting letters. When introducing letters, teachers should present at least two at a time so that students can contrast them. It is also a good idea to present letters that have dissimilar appearances—*s* and *b*, for instance. Presenting similar letters such as *b* and *d* together can cause confusion. It is recommended, too, that upper- and lowercase forms of the letters be introduced at the same time, because students will see both in their reading.

Using names is a good way to introduce the alphabet. Discuss the fact that names are made up of letters. Write your name on the board, and talk about the letters in it. Explain that your first and last names begin with capital letters and that the other letters are lowercase. Write the names of some students, perhaps those that

| **TABLE 3.8** | Percentage of kindergartners passing each reading proficiency level |
| --- | --- |

| Letter Recognition | Beginning Sounds | Ending Sounds | High-Frequency Words | Words in Context |
| --- | --- | --- | --- | --- |
| 66 | 29 | 17 | 2 | 1 |

begin with the first three or four letters of the alphabet, and then move to other letters on succeeding days.

To emphasize a letter, ask students to raise their hands if their name has that letter—*m*, for example. Ask them to spell out their names; give assistance if they need it. Write the names on the board—*Manuel, Marcella,* and *Tom,* for example—and have students tell where the *m* is in each name.

Create signs for the class: "Writing Center," "In," "Out," and so on. Let students see you make the signs, and talk about the letters you used. Bring in familiar objects, such as cereal boxes, signs, and posters, and discuss the words printed on them and the letters that make up the words.

Obtain a computer or a typewriter or both. Keyboards invite exploration of the alphabet. If you are using *Dr. Peet's Talk/Writer* (Interest-Driven Learning), which has speech capability, the name of the letter will be pronounced when the child presses the key. Whole words are spoken when the space bar is pressed. *Dr. Peet's Talk/Writer* also has an ABC Discovery module that introduces the alphabet. In one activity, students are prompted to find the letter *P.* When they press the *P* key, they are shown the letter *P* in upper- and lowercase, and a picture of two polar bears, and they hear a song that says, "*P* is for polar bear." Stamp printing sets, magnetic letters, and felt letters also encourage working with the alphabet.

Use games such as alphabet walk to teach the names of the letters of the alphabet. Place large alphabet cards on the floor. Begin playing music. As the music plays, students walk. When the music stops, they stop. Hold up an alphabet card. Ask the student who is standing on that card to identify it. If students are working on letter sounds, ask the student to tell what sound the letter makes and to name some word that begins with that sound (Invernizzi, Meier, Swank, & Juel, 2001).

As with all learning activities, proceed from the concrete to the abstract. Letters by their very nature are abstract; when they are in the contexts of names, signs, and labels, they are more concrete than letters in isolation.

Display a model alphabet so that students can see how letters are formed. Provide each child with his or her own alphabet to refer to as needed. At this point, do not emphasize letter formation. Students who are overly conscious of forming their letters perfectly will have a difficult time moving beyond that task to writing.

Read to the class some of the many alphabet books that are available. *A to Zoo Subject Access to Children's Picture Books,* 6th ed., (Lima & Lima, 2002) lists more than 300 alphabet books. Some of these are listed in the following Children's Reading List. Look for books that present the letters clearly. Overly ornate letters may be aesthetically pleasing, but they can be distracting and confusing. Many of these books show words containing the beginning sound that a particular letter frequently represents. Do not emphasize these letter–sound relationships, as they require advanced skill. Focus instead on the appearance of each letter and how it differs from a similarly formed letter—for example, how *y* is different from *t*. Point out that letters have two forms—capital and lowercase. Avoid the words *little* and *big* so that children do not use size to determine whether a letter is upper- or lowercase. When possible, choose alphabet books that present both forms.

▌The two kinds of typeface are serif and sans serif. A serif is a small line used to complete a stroke in a letter. Sans serif type lacks these strokes. Serif type is more distinctive and easier to read. However, the *a*s and *g*s in sans serif type are similar to the *a*s and *g*s in manuscript and so may be easier for emergent readers to identify.

## CHILDREN'S READING LIST    Alphabet books

Aylesworth, J. (1991). *Old black fly.* New York: Holt. Rhyming text follows a mischievous black fly through the alphabet as he has a very busy day.

Ehlert, L. (1989). *Eating the alphabet.* New York: Harcourt. Drawings of foods beginning with the letter being presented are labeled with their names in both upper- and lowercase letters.

Hoban, T. (1982). *A, B, see!* New York: Greenwillow. Upper case letters are accompanied by objects in silhouette that begin with the letter shown.

Howland, N. (2000). *ABC Drive!* Boston: Clarion. While going for a drive with his mother, a boy encounters an ambulance, bus, and other ABC items.

Musgrove, M. (1976). *Ashanti to Zulu.* New York: Dial. This Caldecott winner gives information about African tribes as it presents the alphabet.

Onyefulu, I. (1993). *A is for Africa.* New York: Dutton. Color photos and a brief paragraph using the target letter show everyday life in Africa.

Scarry, R. (1973). *Richard Scarry's find your ABC.* New York: Random. Each letter is illustrated with numerous objects and creatures whose names contain the letter.

Shirley, G. C. (1991). *A is for animals.* New York: Simon & Schuster. Illustrations and information are provided about animals whose names begin with the target letter.

Wood, J. (1993). *Animal parade.* New York: Bradbury. A parade starts with an aardvark, an antelope, and other animals whose names begin with *A* and proceeds through the rest of the letters of the alphabet.

## REINFORCEMENT ACTIVITIES    Alphabet knowledge

- Have children create their own alphabet books.
- Help children create name cards. Explain that names begin with capital letters but that the other letters in a name are lowercase.
- Make a big book of the alphabet song, and point to the letters and words as children sing along.
- If children are using classroom computers, teach the letters of the alphabet as you teach them keyboarding skills.
- Encourage students to write as best they can. This will foster learning the alphabet as they move from using pictures and letterlike forms to real letters to express themselves.
- As you write messages, announcements, or stories on the board, spell out

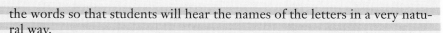

the words so that students will hear the names of the letters in a very natural way.

- Sing songs, such as "Bingo," that spell out words or use letters as part of their lyrics.
- Read books such as *Chicka Chicka Boom Boom* (Martin & Archambault, 1989), in which letters play a prominent role.
- Most important, provide an environment in which the child is surrounded by print. Encourage students to engage in reading and writing activities. These might include "reading" a wordless picture book, using a combination of drawings and letterlike figures to compose a story, creating some sort of list, using invented spelling to write a letter to a friend, exploring a computer keyboard, or listening to a taped account of a story. Interaction with print leads to knowledge of print. The ability to form letters improves without direct instruction (Hildreth, 1936). However, complement providing opportunities to learn with systematic instruction. Learning the alphabet is too important to be left to chance.

### ■ Building Phonological Awareness

For children, the sounds in words blend so that words seem like the continuation of a single sound. In their natural environment, children do not have to deal with individual sounds; however, the ability to detect speech sounds in words is absolutely crucial for literacy development. Without the ability to abstract separate sounds, they will not be able to understand, for example, that the letter *b* stands for the sound /b/ heard at the beginning of *ball*. They will not even be able to consider a beginning sound because they will not be able to abstract it from the word itself. These children will also have difficulty with rhyme because of their inability to abstract the ending sounds. They may be able to write a few letters, but their writing will not evolve beyond the early alphabetic stage because they will be unable to isolate the sounds of words.

Savin (1972) stated, "In the present author's experience everyone who has failed to learn to read even the simplest prose by the end of first grade has been unable to analyze syllables into phonemes" (p. 321). (**Phonemes** are individual speech sounds. The word *cake* has four letters but three phonemes: /k/, /ā/, /k/.) Savin's assertion was echoed by Elkonin (1973), a Russian psychologist, who maintained that being able to analyze the sounds of words "is the most important prerequisite for the successful learning of reading and writing" (p. 571).

Instruction in **phonemic awareness** has been found to improve performance in word reading and spelling (Ehri, et al., 2001). All students benefited from instruction in phonological awareness, even older disabled readers. However, young at-risk readers benefited the most. In a long-term study, students in the lowest twentieth percentile on a test of phonemic awareness were more than three years behind their classmates at the end of fifth grade (Torgesen, Wagner, & Rashotte, 1994). Although suggestions for teaching phonological awareness are

Phonological awareness is not the same as speech discrimination. Speech discrimination is the ability to discriminate the sounds of language, such as being able to tell the difference between *bat* and *hat*. Students having adequate speech discrimination may have difficulty with phonological awareness. Speech discrimination does not require abstracting sounds, whereas phonological awareness does (Snow, Burns, & Griffin, 1998).

■ A **phoneme** is the smallest unit of sound that distinguishes one word from another. *Pit* is different from *pat* because of the difference in the phonemes /i/ and /a/.

■ **Phonemic awareness** is the consciousness of individual sounds in words. It is the realization that a spoken word is composed of a sequence of speech sounds.

Phonemic awareness . . . demands that the child ignore meaning and attend to the word's form. This requires a new perspective, a change in the way the child "looks at" a word (Gough, Larson, & Yopp, 2001).

featured in this chapter on emergent literacy, students should be taught phonological awareness as long as they need it. Instruction in phonological awareness should be a continuing feature of instruction in phonics.

For many children, acquiring phonemic awareness is difficult (Snow, Burns, & Griffin, 1998). What makes detecting sounds in words difficult? Two elements: metalinguistic awareness and **coarticulation.** Metalinguistic awareness requires students to reflect on language on an abstract level, to treat language as an object of thought. Coarticulation is a feature of language that makes listening and speaking easy but makes reading difficult. For instance, when saying the word *cat*, you do not say /k/, /a/, /t/; you coarticulate the phonemes: As you form the /k/, you also form the /a/, and as the /a/ is being formed, you coarticulate the final sound /t/. Because of coarticulation, *cat* is a blend of sounds, rather than three separate sounds. Coarticulation makes it easier to form and perceive words. However, because the sounds in the words are coarticulated, they seem to be one continuous sound and so are difficult for young children to pry apart (Liberman & Shankweiler, 1991).

Language is the foundation for **phonological awareness**. The larger children's vocabularies and the better their articulation of speech sounds, the easier it is for them to acquire phonological awareness. Initially children learn words as wholes. The ability to segment individual sounds in words apparently develops as children's vocabularies grow and as they acquire larger numbers of words that have similar pronunciations, such as *cat, can, cap,* and *cab* (Metsala, 1999). Distinguishing among these words means that they must be able to segment words into smaller units of pronunciation. It is theorized that children segment words by syllables and segment syllables by onset and rime. Children with large vocabularies will have more words represented by syllable and onset and rime or sound by sound (Metsala, 1999). Because they have elements that occur more frequently, some words will be easier to rhyme or segment than others. Children are better at rhyming *at* words than *ud* words. In other words, students are more successful saying that *cat* and *rat* rhyme than they are saying that *bud* and *mud* rhyme. There are more *at* words than *ud* words, so children know more *at* words and so have had more experience noting differences among them. Words that children learn early and word elements such as *at* that have a large number of examples are easier for students to learn (Metsala, 1999). For novice readers, begin phonological awareness instruction with patterns that contain very basic words that students have learned early and also patterns that encompass many words. These are words that are more likely to have segmented representations in the children's memory (Goswami, 2001).

If students' vocabularies are limited, they may have difficulty with phonemic awareness. Students may also have difficulty with phonemic awareness if their pronunciation of sounds lacks accuracy and distinctiveness (Elbro, 1998). Fostering language development lays a foundation for phonological awareness.

**Word play.**   One of the best ways to develop phonological awareness is to have fun with words. As students play and experiment with language, they become aware of it on a more abstract level. They begin to think of words as words and

---

■ **Coarticulation** is the process of articulating a sound while still articulating the previous sound—for instance, saying /oy/ while still articulating /t/ in *toy*.

Speaking of coarticulation, Murray (1998) points out, the spoken word *train* is heard as a single sound. Even if played at a very slow speed, we would not hear a series of distinct phonemes /ch/, /r/, /ā/, and /n/, but rather a continuous /chrān/.

■ **Phonological awareness** is the consciousness of the sounds in words. It includes the ability to detect rhyme and separate the sounds in words. It is a broad term and includes the concept of phonemic awareness.

become aware of the sounds of language on an abstract level. In addition to playing games with words in the classroom, read books that have fun with words, especially those that call attention to the parts of words.

An excellent book for developing phonological awareness is *Jamberry* (Degan, 1983), in which both real and nonsense words are formed by adding *berry* to a variety of words. After reading the tale to students, have them create berry words. *Don't Forget the Bacon!* (Hutchins, 1976) is another good choice for developing phonological awareness. Afraid that he will forget an item on his shopping list (six farm eggs, a cake for tea, and a pound of pears), the child rehearses the list as he heads for the store. Unfortunately, as he rehearses it, he makes substitutions in some of the words so that "a cake for tea" becomes "a cake for me" and later "a rake for leaves." Read the story to students, and discuss how the boy kept changing the sounds. This will build their awareness of sounds in words. Also have them role-play the child rehearsing the shopping list so that they can see firsthand how the sounds in the words are changed (Griffith & Olson, 1992). In *The Hungry Thing Goes to a Restaurant* (Slepian & Seidler, 1992), initial sounds are substituted. When the Hungry Thing orders a meal, the staff can't understand what he wants when he orders things such as bapple moose and spoonadish. As you read the story, have students guess what the Hungry Thing was ordering (apple juice and tuna fish). Other books that play with sounds include most of the Dr. Seuss books and the sheep series by Shaw (including *Sheep in a Jeep*, *Sheep on a Ship*, and *Sheep in a Shop*).

**Developing the concept of rhyme.** Because longer units are easier to perceive than individual speech sounds, a good place to begin to develop phonological awareness is through rhymes, which are the easiest of the phonological awareness tasks (Yopp, 1988). Read nursery rhymes and other rhyming tales to the students to help them develop the ability to detect rhyme. In a study conducted in Great Britain, children who knew nursery rhymes were better at detecting rhyme and also did better in early reading than those who had no such knowledge (Maclean, Bryant, & Bradley, 1987). At first, just read the nursery rhymes and rhyming tales so that the children enjoy the stories and the sounds. They may memorize some of the rhymes if they wish. Books that might be used to introduce and reinforce the concept of rhyme are listed in the Children's Reading List.

### CHILDREN'S READING LIST — Rhyming books

Barrett, J. (2000). *I knew two who said moo*. New York: Atheneum. Features humorous sentences containing words that rhyme with the number words *one* to *twenty*.

Cameron, P. (1961). *"I can't," said the ant*. New York: Coward. With the help of an army of ants and some spiders, an ant helps repair a broken teapot amid the encouragement of the kitchen's inhabitants.

---

*Although some students may pick up phonemic awareness through interaction with print, most need direct instruction.*

*There is a reciprocal relationship between phonemic awareness and reading. Being able to detect phonemes helps the child learn to read. The act of reading fosters growth in phonemic awareness.*

**INVOLVING PARENTS**

Parents can help their children develop phonemic awareness by playing word games with them, reading rhyming stories to them, and reciting traditional nursery rhymes and singing songs.

dePaola, T. (1985). *Tomie dePaola's Mother Goose.* New York: Putnam. Traditional verses are accompanied by dePaola's lighthearted illustrations.

Fox, M. (1993). *Time for bed.* Orlando, FL: Harcourt. Mother animals and a human mother lull their babies to sleep.

Hague, M. (1993). *Teddy Bear Teddy Bear.* New York: Morrow. In this action rhyme, Teddy Bear is asked to do such things as turn around, touch the ground, and show his shoe.

Harwayne, S. (1995). *Jewels, children's play rhymes.* Greenvale, NY: Mondo. Features twenty play rhymes from around the world. Includes brief poems, as well as action, game, jump rope, and song rhymes.

Hoberman, M. A. (1997). *One of each.* Boston: Little, Brown. Oliver Tolliver learns to share with friends.

Jewell, N. (1996). *Silly times with two silly trolls.* New York: HarperCollins. Two silly trolls are confused by the word *here*, have fun making up poems, and don't catch on to the fact that their clock has stopped.

Lobel, A. (1986). *The Random House book of Mother Goose.* New York: Random House. More than 300 nursery rhymes are presented.

Marzollo, J. (1990). *Pretend you're a cat.* New York: Dial. Rhyming verses ask the reader to purr like a cat, scratch like a dog, leap like a squirrel, and so on.

Raffi. (1987). *Down by the bay.* New York: Crown. Song celebrates silly rhymes: "Did you ever see a whale with a polka-dot tail, Down by the bay?"

Samuells, J. (2003). *A nose like a hose.* New York: Scholastic. A little elephant has a very long nose.

Wong, E. Y. (1992). *Eek! There's a mouse in the house.* Boston: Houghton Mifflin. After the discovery of a mouse in the house, larger and larger animals are sent in after one another, with increasingly chaotic results.

**ADAPTING INSTRUCTION for *ENGLISH LANGUAGE LEARNERS***

When working with ELLs, focus on speech sounds that are common to both languages and avoid sounds that students might not be familiar with until they have had a chance to learn them. Spanish has no short *a, i,* or *u,* but does have the long vowels. Start phonological awareness with words containing long vowels. See Table 11.1 for an overview of differences between English and Spanish.

Discuss any rhyming stories that you read to the children, thereby building a background of literacy. In time, discuss the concept of rhyme itself. Lead students to see that the last word in one line has the same ending sounds as the last word in another line. Reread some of the nursery rhymes aloud, emphasizing the rhyming words. Explain what rhyming words are, using examples such as *rake/cake, bell/well, ice/mice,* and so on. Also build rhymes with students. Using the element *an,* here is how a rhyme might be built. Say "an." Have students say "an." Explain to students that you are going to make words that have *an* in them. Say "c-an," emphasizing the *an* portion of the word. Ask students if they can hear the *an* in *c-an.* Holding up a picture of a can, have them say *can* and listen to the *an* in *c-an.* (By using pictures, you are reducing the burden on students' memories.) Hold up a picture of a pan. Have students tell what it is. Tell students that *p-an* has *an* in it. Ask them if they can hear the *an* in *f-an* as you hold up a picture of a fan. Introduce *man* and *van* in the same way. Ask students if they can tell what sound is the same in *can, pan, man, fan*, and *van*. Stress the *an* in each of these words. Explain that *can, pan, man, fan* and *van* rhyme because they all have *an* at the end. Invite students to suggest other words that rhyme with *can: tan, Dan, Jan, plan, ran* (Gunning, 2000c). Build other rhymes in similar fashion. Illustrations for rhyming words can be found at Webbing into Literacy: http://curry.edschool.virginia.edu/go/wil/home.html. This site has a variety of excellent materials and suggestions for teaching rhyming.

### REINFORCEMENT ACTIVITIES  The concept of rhyme

- Have students supply the final rhyming word of a couplet:

  There was an old lady who lived in a shoe. She had so many children she didn't know what to _____.

  I like to run. It's so much _____.

- Students can compose a rhyming pictionary in which they paste on each page illustrations of words that rhyme. A typical page might include pictures of a man, a can, a fan, and a pan. Pictures might come from old magazines, workbooks, or computer clip art, or they can be drawn.

- Read a rhyming story or verse to students. Pause before the rhyming word and have them predict what the word might be.

- Have students sort cards containing illustrations of objects whose names rhyme. Begin by providing a model card (cat) and having students arrange rhyming cards under it (bat, rat, hat). Provide students with cards that do not rhyme with *cat* as well as those that do. Later, have students sort two or three rhyming patterns at the same time. Discuss students' sorting.

- Play the game I Spy using rhyming clues. "I spy something that rhymes with *walk* and *talk*" (chalk) (Ericson & Juliebo, 1998).

- Sing traditional songs that have a strong rhyming element. After singing a song once, have students listen to a second singing to detect rhyming words. Also sing all of two rhyming lines except the last word, and let students say or sing the missing word.

- Use pictures to show rhymes. Give each student three pictures whose names will rhyme with the names of pictures that you hold up. Give them pictures of a hat, a pen, and a bug, for instance. Discuss the names of the three pictures. Hold up pictures that rhyme with one of the students' three pictures. Say the picture's name and have students say it. Have them hold up the picture that rhymes with the one you are holding up. Ask, which one of your pictures, hat, pen, or bug, rhymes with *rat*? The students would hold up a picture showing a hat. After students have held up their pictures, affirm their responses. Say, "Yes, you are right, *hat* and *rat* do rhyme. They both have an *at* sound." Note which children are able do this fairly easily and which seem to be unsure or look to see which picture the other students are holding up. These students may need additional instruction. If students have difficulty, give them just two pictures to select from. Illustrations for this activity can be found at Webbing into Literacy.

■ Play rhyming concentration. Place six pairs of rhymes face down. Players turn over a card, say its name, and then try to turn over a picture that rhymes with it. Turning over another card, the player says its name, says the name of the card originally turned over, and tells whether they rhyme. If the player succeeds in making a match, she says the name of each card and says that they rhyme. If the player fails to find a rhyme, she turns the cards face down, and the next player takes his turn. The game ends when all the cards have been picked up. The winner is the person with the most rhyming pairs. Illustrations for this activity can be found at Webbing into Literacy.

■ Read rhyming riddles to students. The answer to the riddle is two rhyming words. Provide clues if needed.

What do you call a rug where a kitten might take a nap? (cat mat)

What do you call a dog or cat that has been out in the rain? (wet pet)

What do you call an insect that lives in rugs? (rug bug)

### ■ Blending

Through blending, students create words by combining word parts. Blending builds on students' ability to rhyme and prepares them for segmenting or noting the beginning sounds in words. In the activities below, students blend onsets and rimes. The onset is the consonant or consonant cluster preceding the rime: *f-, pl-, scr-*. The rime is the pattern's vowel and any consonants that follow it: *-o, -at, -ot, -een*. Using a hand puppet, tell students that the puppet says its words in parts. Instead of saying *moon* the way we do, it says *m-oon*; so we have to help him by putting the parts of the word together. Have students help put the following words together: *m-an, s-and, h-at, r-at, r-an*. Present the words in groups of four. In order to actively involve all students, provide each student with a set of pictures showing the four words. When you say the word to be blended, students choose the picture that shows the word and hold it up. By observing students, you can tell who is catching on and who is struggling. Discuss the names of the pictures before beginning the activity so that students know them:

cat, hat, bat, rat

can, man, pan, fan

king, ring, wing, ball

lock, rock, sock, mop

pie, tie, tire, bus

After students have held up the picture for the word being blended, have them say the word. Affirm students' efforts but correct wrong responses. For a correct response, you might say, "Hat. That is correct. When you put /h/ and /at/ together, you get *hat*." For an incorrect response, you might say, "That was a good try. But when I put /f/ and /an/ together, I get *fan*. You say it, 'f-an—fan.'" After students have completed a group, go through it again. Encourage them to put the words together faster. If students have difficulty with the activity, provide assistance or go back to rhyming activities.

Have students solve riddles that incorporate both rhyming and blending: "I'm thinking of a word that begins with /m/ and rhymes with *pan*

. . . begins with /h/ and rhymes with *pot*.
. . . begins with /s/ and rhymes with *wing*.
. . . begins with /r/ and rhymes with *king*.

### ■ Perceiving Beginning Consonant Sounds

Students will have difficulty learning phonics if they are unable to perceive the sounds of beginning consonants. For example, if a child confuses the sound /p/ with the sound /d/, when he or she is taught the letter that represents /p/, the child may actually associate it with the sound /d/, or vice versa.

To introduce the concept of beginning sounds, read and discuss *The Story of Z* (Modesitt, 1990), if possible. Tired of being last, *Z* leaves the alphabet so that children say things such as, "Can we go to the oo and see the ebras?" Have students supply the missing beginning sound and tell what the sound is. Using the same technique employed in *The Story of Z*, hold up objects or pictures of objects or creatures and ask such questions as "Is this an ee? (while holding up a picture of a bee). What is it? What sound did I leave off?" While holding up a pen, ask, "Is this an en?" Do the same with other objects and pictures. Also, or as an alternative introduction, read aloud alliterative stories or alphabet books such as *Emma's Elephant & Other Favorite Animal Friends* (Ellwand, 1996), which features alliterative captions, or *Flatfoot Fox and the Case of the Bashful Beaver* (Clifford, 1995), which has a character who speaks in alliterative sentences.

Some other alliterative books that might be used to reinforce the idea of beginning consonant sounds are listed in the following Children's Reading List. At first, simply read such a book as you would any other picture book, showing pictures and discussing content. Then, lead students to see that many of the words begin with the same sound and let them read some selections along with you. For instance, read the following from *Nedobeck's Alphabet Book* (Nedobeck, 1981):

> Little Leonard Lion climbs a
> Ladder to mail a Love Letter to Lori.

Also read the *L* page from Judith Gwyn Brown's (1976) *Alphabet Dreams:*

> My name is Lucy,
> And my husband's name is Lee.
> We live in a log,
> And we sell lamps.

Rhyming and detecting beginning sounds are close in difficulty. Some students may actually find that noting that two words begin with the same sound is easier than detecting rhyme (Gough, Larson, & Yopp, 2001).

Books such as *Hoot and Holler* (Brown, 2001), in which two owl friends learn to overcome their shyness, can be used to develop a foundation for phonological awareness as children hear the alliterative names of the main characters and the drawn out *hoo-oot* as Hoot searches for Holler and as friends call out the words *you-hoo* and *too-hoo*.

## Alliterative books for reinforcing beginning consonants

Bandes, H. (1993). *Sleepy river.* New York: Philomel. A canoe ride at nightfall provides a Native American mother and child glimpses of the ducks, fireflies, bats, and other wonders of nature.

Base, G. (1987). *Animalia.* New York: Harry N. Abrams. Each letter is illustrated and accompanied by an alliterative phrase, such as "Lazy lions lounging in the local library."

Bayer, J. (1984). *A my name is Alice.* New York: Dial. The well-known jump rope rhyme that is built on letters of the alphabet is illustrated with animals from all over the world.

Cole, J. (1993). *Six sick sheep.* New York: Morrow. A collection of all kinds of tongue twisters.

Geisel, T. S. (1973). *Dr. Seuss's abc.* New York: Random. Letters of the alphabet are accompanied by an alliterative story and humorous illustrations.

Kellogg, S. (1987). *Aster Aardvark's alphabet adventures.* New York: Morrow. A highly alliterative story accompanies each letter.

Knutson, K. (1993). *Ska-tat.* New York: Macmillan. Children describe playing in the colorful, crunchy autumn leaves as the leaves fall to the ground.

Schwartz, A. (1972). *Busy buzzing bumblebees and other tongue twisters.* New York: HarperCollins. A fun collection of tongue twisters.

Steig, J. (1992). *Alpha beta chowder.* New York: HarperCollins. An alliterative humorous verse for each letter of the alphabet is presented.

Stevenson, J. (1983). *Grandpa's great city tour.* New York: Greenwillow. Letters in upper- and lowercase are accompanied by numerous unlabeled objects whose names begin with the sound commonly associated with the letter being presented.

## REINFORCEMENT ACTIVITIES  The concept of beginning sounds

- Recite traditional alliterative pieces such as "Peter Piper picked a peck of pickled peppers" and have students attempt to repeat them. See *The Little Book of Big Tongue Twisters* by Foley Curtis (1977) or *Six Sick Sheep: 101 Tongue Twisters* by Calmerson and Cole (1993) for examples of alliterative pieces to accompany nearly every beginning sound. After reading each piece, give students examples of what is meant by "begin with the same sound," and then have them tell which words begin with the same sound.

- Say a word, and have students supply other words that begin with the

**USING TECHNOLOGY**

Tongue twisters tested with students can be found at: Wallach and Wallach's Tongue Twisters.
http://www.auburn.edu/~murraba/twisters.html

same sound. Discuss students' names that begin with the same sound, such as Benjamin, Barbara, and Billy.

- Play the game I Spy with students. Tell them that you spy something whose name begins like the word *boat*. Encourage them to say the names of objects in the classroom that begin like *boat*. If necessary, give added clues: It has covers; it can be read.

- Using a troll doll or puppet, have it say that only people whose names begin like the name *Sandy* (or whatever name you choose) may cross the bridge. Supply names, and have students tell which persons would be allowed to cross (Stahl, 1990).

- Have students sort cards containing illustrations of objects whose names begin with the same sound (ball, boy, banana, baby). Sorts can be closed or open. In a closed sort, you provide a model (illustration of a ball). In an open sort, you provide the items (illustrations of /b/ words and /s/ words), and children decide how to sort them. Be sure to model sorting.

- Encourage students to stretch out the sounds of words as they write them, saying *soap* as "sss-ooo-ppp." This helps build awareness of separate sounds in words as well as perception of beginning sounds. It also helps students determine how to spell words.

## ■ Segmenting Words

After students have developed some sense of rhyme, blending, and initial sounds, introduce the concept of **segmenting,** or separating words into sounds. This can be done as you lead the class in reading a big book, an experience story, or the morning message. Choose two-phoneme words whose sounds are easily discriminated, and then elongate the words and discuss their sounds. For instance, after reading Goldilocks and the Three Bears, stretch out the words *he, me, see,* and *she* and help students abstract the separate sounds. After students can segment two-phoneme words, move onto words that have three phonemes. Focus on words that have **continuants** such as /s/ or /m/, because these are easier to say and detect than stops such as /b/ and /d/, which distort following vowels more than continuants do. Also teach those sounds that students will need to know to read and spell words. If the first words they are going to learn are *see* and *me,* teach /s/ and /m/.

As students try their hand at spelling, encourage them to stretch out words so they can hear the sounds. As you write on the board, say the separate sounds that correspond to the letters so that students can hear them. As you write, "Bob has a new pet," say, "B-o-b h-a-z uh n-oo p-e-t." After students have begun to catch on to the concept of sounds, say words slowly and ask them to tell how many sounds are in them.

If students experience difficulty learning to segment words, you might try a technique designed by Blachman et al. (1994) known as Say It and Move It. As students say a sound in a word, they move a blank tile down the page. Looking at a picture of a man, the student would say /m/ while moving a first tile, /a/ while moving a second tile, and /n/ while moving a third tile. Later, the students use a

- **Segmenting** is dividing a word into its separate sounds—*cat* is /k/, /a/, /t/.

- **Continuants** are consonant sounds that are articulated with a continuous stream of breath: /s/, /f/, /h/, /w/, /m/, /r/, /l/, and /n/.

▎Stretching out the sounds of words works best with continuants.

**FIGURE 3.4**

### Elkonin Boxes

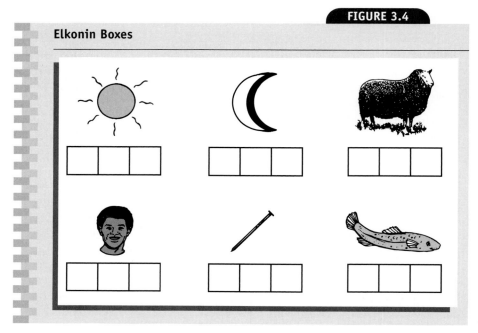

Source: *Word Building: Beginnings* by T. Gunning, 1994. New York: Phoenix Learning Resources. Reprinted by permission of Galvin Publications

procedure suggested by Elkonin (1973) and widely used in intervention programs. Elkonin attempted to make the abstract skill of segmenting more concrete by using drawings and markers. The student is given a drawing of a short word, below which are blocks that correspond to the number of sounds in the word. Below a drawing of the word *sun*, for instance, there would be three blocks, as in Figure 3.4. Tokens are placed in the blocks to represent the three sounds in *sun*. To introduce the technique, carry out the steps outlined in Lesson 3.1. As students learn letter–sound relationships, they might fill in the blocks with the letters that represent the sounds.

## LESSON 3.1 Elkonin phonemic segmentation technique

**Step 1.**

Explain the task, model it, and guide the child through it.

**Step 2.**

Give the child a drawing of the sun. Remind the child to say the word that names the picture and to stretch the word out so she or he can hear the separate sounds. If the child has difficulty noting the sounds, very carefully and

According to Elkonin (1973), five- and six-year-olds who used his technique were able to learn to segment words.

deliberately pronounce the word. Emphasize each sound, but do not distort the word.

### Step 3.

Have the child put a marker in each square while saying each sound. The child says /s/ and puts a marker in the first block, then says /u/ and puts a marker in the second block, and finally puts a marker in the third block while saying /n/.

### Step 4.

Using the blocks tells the child how many separate sounds there are in a word. As the child becomes more proficient, eliminate the blocks and markers and have him or her simply tell how many sounds are in a word.

Once a child begins to catch on to the concept of segmenting, you might record a word's letters in the appropriate blocks. The child then puts markers on the letters that represent the segmented sounds.

### ■ Forming Sounds

Being aware of articulation fosters phonological awareness. Skjelford (1976, 1987) found that students did better when they were trained to prolong continuant sounds such as /s/ and /f/ and to stress plosives such as /p/, /b/, and /t/. In segmentation tests students often said the word silently before responding. The harder the word to segment, the more they repeated the word.

The easiest sounds to perceive are continuants because they are articulated with a continuous stream of breath: /f/, /h/, /l/, /m/, /n/, /w/, /r/, /s/, /sh/, /th/, /t͟h/, /v/, /z/, /zh/, /sh/. Other consonant sounds cannot be continued: /b/, /d/, /p/, /ch/, /j/, /k/, /t/, and /y/. To emphasize continuants such as /s/ or /m/, students can simply elongate the sound as in "ssssun" and "mmmman." For sounds that cannot be elongated, students may use a process known as iteration, in which they repeat the sound as in "g-g-g goat."

Sounds differ according to where they are formed, how they are formed, and whether they are voiced or unvoiced (see Tables 3.2 and 3.3). Demonstrating how and where sounds are formed helps students become aware of separate sounds. For instance, for the sounds /b/ or /p/, have them note how their lips make a popping sound. For /t/ or /d/, have them notice how they use their tongues to make the sound. For /f/ or /v/, they might note the use of teeth and lips. For /th/, they might note the use of teeth and tongue. For /n/, they might note the use of tongue and nose. For /m/, they might note how their lips come and stay together to make the sound and how the nose is used. They could see what happens when they hold their noses and try to articulate one of the nasals: /m/, /n/, or /ng/. Students might note, too, that some sounds—the stops—pop out: /b/, /d/, /k/, /g/, /p/, /t/, but the continuants are articulated with a continuous stream of breath. Students might note that /p/ and /b/ are both produced in the same way and in the same part of the mouth. However, *b* is voiced—the larynx vibrates when it is articulated—and *p* is not.

---

**ADAPTING INSTRUCTION for *STRUGGLING READERS and WRITERS***

Elkonin blocks can be used informally. If a student is struggling with the spelling of a word, draw one box for each sound so the student can see how many sounds the word has. Encourage the student to spell any sounds he or she can and give help with the rest.

---

**ADAPTING INSTRUCTION for *ENGLISH LANGUAGE LEARNERS***

English Language Learners have a difficult time segmenting words because they are still learning the words and sounds of the language. Blending sounds is easier because the separate sounds are pronounced for them. Use blending as a way of building an awareness of separate sounds in words.

---

If children cannot abstract the separate sounds in *hat* or the beginning sound of *ball*, they may learn to read a few words by sheer rote memory but will not be able to sound out words.

Having phonemic aware-
ness means that the stu-
dent must be able to
abstract the sound from a
real word and use it to read
that word. Seeing the letter
m, a student could say /m/
but he could not say and
blend /m/ and /ē/ when he
saw the word *me*. Though
he could say /m/ for the
letter *m,* he could not apply
this to a real word. He was
unable to manipulate
phonemes and so lacked
genuine phonemic aware-
ness.

Most consonants occur in voiced and unvoiced pairs: /d/–/t/, /g/–/k/, /z/–/s/, /v/–
/f/, /zh/ (pleasure)–/sh/, /j/–/ch/, /th/ (that)–/th/ (think), with the first sound in each
pair being the voiced one. The sound /h/ is formed by forcing air through an
opening in the larynx, the glottis (Gunning, 2000).

In the LIPS (Lindamood Phoneme Sequencing) Program (Lindamood &
Lindamood, 1998), students are taught to become aware of the speech articulation
movements involved in creating sounds by analyzing the way they form sounds.
For instance, students can tell that there are three phonemes in the word *meat* because three movements are needed to articulate the word: lips closing for /m/, lips
opening in a smile for /ee/, and tongue tapping the roof of the mouth for the final
/t/. Sounds are given names based on the way they are formed. Sounds such as /p/
and /b/, for instance, are known as lip poppers. In the NewPhonics program (Birnbaum,
1999), which is designed for kindergartners, students are shown photos of faces of
children articulating speech sounds. The photographs were each given a descriptive
label, such as the "itchy nose card" for the short-*i* sound, and a description of fa-
cial characteristics involved in the production of that phoneme. Helping children
become aware of how sounds are formed may help them better perceive and then
separate sounds in words, especially if they are struggling with this concept. However,
this instruction can be informal and need not involve intensive study of how sounds
are formed. Learning how sounds are articulated is a means to an end and not an
end in itself.

How much phonemic
awareness is needed before
students are able to grasp
phonics? Stahl (1998)
asserts that the ability to
segment or perceive initial
consonants is sufficient.

Phonemic awareness may be learned through interaction with print, through
specific training in segmenting and other skills, or through some combination of the
two. Watson (1984) concluded that an underlying cognitive factor may be necessary for the development of phonemic awareness that is above and beyond what is
required to develop listening and speaking skills. Thus, students who are skilled users
of language may not acquire phonemic awareness, even when working with print,
without some sort of intervention.

### ■ Integrating Phonological Awareness and Phonics

Although phonological awareness is an essential skill, it should be taught in functional fashion. Because it is so important, there is a tendency in some programs to
teach phonological awareness in isolation and to teach more phonological awareness than is necessary. Phonological awareness is most effective when students
learn to segment and identify phonemes as part of learning to read and write
rather than as an isolated skill (Bus & van Ijzendoorn, 1999; Vandervelden &
Siegel, 1997). Because the letters in a word represent the word's sounds, working
with letters is a way of marking sounds. "Learning to attend to letters in words
and relating these to how words sound appeared to make explicit the underlying
phonemic structure" (Vandervelden & Siegel, 1997, p. 78). In a series of studies, students taught by an integrated approach outperformed those who are taught either
phonological awareness or phonics in isolation. "Letters may draw the child's attention to the sounds in spoken words, and a distinct visual symbol for each phoneme
may anchor the phonemes perceptually" (Bus & van Ijzendoorn, 1999, p. 412).

Instruction should also be geared to the students' level of understanding and need to know. Apparently, students do not need a high level of phonological awareness before being able to tackle phonics. Being able to detect rhyme and perceive and segment beginning sounds should be enough to get them started on learning initial consonant correspondences (Stahl, 1998). As they study initial consonant correspondences, they can do so in such a way that their phonemic awareness is enhanced. Stretching out sounds as they spell words ("mmmaaannn"), making new words by changing the initial consonant (making *hat* from *cat* by substituting *h* for *c* in the word *cat*), and similar activities build phonemic awareness.

If students are about to be instructed in final consonants, that is the time to teach them to segment or isolate final sounds. If they are about to learn vowel sounds, they need to be able to segment all the sounds in a word (Stahl, 2001). Some skills, such as deleting a sound from a word (say *sting* without the /t/) may be beyond what is necessary. On the other hand, phonological awareness should be an integral part of phonics and spelling lessons. Students can't learn to decode or spell sounds if they cannot detect them. Apparently, each phoneme needs to be understood individually. It is possible for a child to be able to abstract initial /s/ from a word but not initial /m/. When teaching a new phonics element such as *m* = /m/, be sure to teach students how to detect the sound /m/ at the beginning of *m* words (Stahl & McKenna, 2002). One reason students struggle with consonant clusters such as *st* or *bl* is that they may have difficulty segmenting the separate sounds in the clusters. Part of teaching students how to decode clusters is teaching them how to segment the sounds in a cluster. Students also do better when they are taught in small groups and when only key skills are emphasized (Ehri et al., 2001). Placing students in small groups means that that they can be taught according to their needs and that they get more individualized attention.

> Integrating phonological awareness and instruction in phonics and spelling is the most effective way to foster early literacy. After learning to identify and/or segment initial sounds, students should use this knowledge to read and spell words that begin with the sound taught.

### ■ Speech-to-Print Phonics

One highly successful integrated phonological awareness/phonics program used speech-to-print recognition. Students were required only to recognize the printed form of a word spoken by the teacher. This is a relatively easy task and is highly recommended for use with students who are struggling with other approaches. The teacher presents a letter–sound correspondence, such as *m* = /m/, and shows students two cards—one of which contains a word that incorporates the correspondence. The teacher then asks students to point to the word that contains that correspondence. After two correspondences have been presented, the students are shown two words, one of which contains the correspondence just taught and one of which contains a correspondence previously taught. For instance, having taught the correspondences *s* = /s/ and *m* =/m/, the teacher presents the words *man* and *sun* and asks students to point to the word that says *man*. After a third correspondence has been taught, students choose from all three. However, as additional correspondences are introduced, drop one so that students are not required to choose from more than three correspondences. Choose correspondences whose letter names are known by students. An adapted lesson is presented in Lesson 3.2.

> At-risk students who took part in speech-to-print recognition activities of this type improved in phonemic awareness, letter- sound recognition, and the ability to learn new words (Vandervelden & Siegel, 1997).

**Sample lesson: Speech-to-print: Introducing the correspondence *m* = /m/**

### Step 1. Phonemic Awareness

Teach the correspondence *m* = /m/. You might do this with a storybook such as *Moo in the Morning* (Maitland, 2000). Read the book aloud and discuss it. Talk about the words *moo* and *morning* and how they begin with the same sound. Emphasize the sound of /m/ as you say *moo* and *morning*. Stress the way that the lips are pressed together to form the sound /m/. Show pictures of a man, moon, mouse, monkey, mirror, and mop. Have students say the name of each item. Repeat the names of the items, emphasizing the beginning sound as you do so. Ask students to tell what is the same about *man, moon, mouse, monkey, mirror,* and *mop*. Help students to see that they all begin with the same sound. Explain that *man, moon, mouse, monkey, mirror,* and *mop* begin with /m/. Have students say the words.

### Step 2. Letter–Sound Integration

Write the words *man* and *moon* on the board. Stress the sounds as you write the letters that represent them. Explain that the letter *m* stands for the sound /m/ heard at the beginning of *mmman* and *mmmoon*. If any of your students' names begin with /m/, write their names on the board, too: *Maria, Martin, Marisol,* again emphasizing the beginning sound as you do so.

### Step 3. Guided Practice

Assuming that the correspondences *s* = /s/ and *f* = /f/ have been introduced, present groups of word cards similar to the following.

Ask: Which word says *man*? (*man, sun,* and *fish* are on cards)

After each correct response, ask questions similar to the following: "How do you know this word says *man*?" If the student says, "because it begins with the letter *m*," ask, "What sound does *m* stand for?" If the student says he chose the word because it begins with an /m/ sound, ask what letter stands for /m/. In that way students will make connections between the letters and the sounds they represent. If the student has given an incorrect response, read the word that was mistakenly pointed to and then point to the correct word and read it: "No, this word is *sun*. It begins with the letter *s*. *S* makes a /s/ sound. This is the word *man*. It begins with the letter *m*. *M* makes the /m/ sound that you hear at the beginning of *man*." Proceed to additional word groups. To make the activity more concrete, you might have the students place a plastic letter on the word they have identified, placing an *m* on *man*, for example.

| | |
|---|---|
| Which word says *sun*? | man sun fish |
| Which word says *fish*? | man sun fish |
| Which word says *me*? | me see five |
| Which word says *five*? | me see five |

| Which word says *see*? | me see five |
| Which word says *mat*? | mat sat fat |
| Which word says *fat*? | mat sat fat |
| Which word says *sat*? | mat sat fat |
| Which word says *mat*? | mat sat fat |
| Which word says *mad*? | mad sad fad |
| Which word says *sad*? | mad sad fad |

Go through the words in groups of three several times or until students seem to have some fluency with the words.

### Step 4. Guided Spelling

In guided spelling, the teacher carefully articulates the words and the student spells it with a set of plastic letters. Initially, the student might simply select from three plastic letters the one that spells the beginning sound. Later, as the student learns to spell whole words, he might be asked to spell two- or three-letter words and would be given the letters in mixed-up order.

### Step 5. Practice and Application

Have students read and write stories that contain the phonic elements that have been taught.

See Building Literacy for additional speech-to-print lessons at: http://www.thomasgunning.org

### ■ Introducing Other Consonant Correspondences

After students have mastered the first set of consonants, gradually introduce additional correspondences. Taking distinctiveness and overall utility into consideration, the following correspondences are recommended: $r = $ /r/, $b = $ /h/, $b = $ /b/, $n = $ /n/, $p = $ /p/, $c = $ /k/, $d = $ /d/, $t = $ /t/, $w = $ /w/, $g = $ /g/, $k = $ /k/. After students have learned initial consonants, they are introduced to final consonants and make matches based on both the initial and final consonants. For instance, presenting the students with the word cards *cat*, *can*, and *cap*, the teacher would say, "Which word spells *can*? Which word spells *cat*? Which word spells *cap*?"

Later, vowel correspondences would be introduced. After vowels have been introduced, choices would be made on the basis of vowels. Given the word cards *bit*, *bet*, and *but*, the students would be asked, "Which word spells *but*? Which word spells *bet*? Which word spells *bit*?"

An informal way to use speech-to-print phonics is to say a sound and have students choose from three letters the one that represents that sound. To make the task more challenging, have students write the letter that represents the sound.

Encourage students to attempt to spell words. As students attempt to spell words, they focus on the sounds of words and make discoveries about the spelling system (Clark, 1988).

## Fostering Language Development

Although both home and school play key roles in developing a child's language and literacy skills, they do so in somewhat different ways.

**ASSESSING STUDENTS' PROGRESS**

To assess students' language development, observe the range of their vocabularies and the complexity of their sentence structures. Observe children in informal situations as well as formal ones. Children who say little in class might be talkative when playing.

The school is by necessity more formal and structured than the home; however, there should be continuity between home and school. The school should build on the language and literacy skills and understandings that children have learned at home. It should make use of the learning strategies that children are accustomed to using and the techniques employed by the best parents. As Wells (1986) states,

> As far as learning is concerned, therefore, entry into school should not be thought of as a beginning, but as a transition to a more broadly based community and to a wider range of opportunities for meaning making and mastery. Every child has competencies, and these provide a positive base from which to start. The teacher's responsibility is to discover what they are and to help each child extend and develop them. (pp. 68–69)

To ease the transition from home to school and to make full use of the knowledge and skills that the child brings to school, it is important that the school resemble a rich, warm home environment, using techniques employed by the parents in such homes. In his comparison of home and school conversations, Wells (1986) concluded that home conversations were far richer. At school, the teacher dominates conversations, saying approximately three times as much as the children do. Teachers ask more questions—often of a quizlike nature—make more requests, initiate conversations more often, and choose the topic to be talked about more frequently. Because the teacher dominates conversations and discussions, both the amount and complexity of students' contributions are drastically reduced. Syntax is less complex, vocabulary is more restricted, and utterances are briefer. Busy answering the teacher's many questions and requests, the students have limited opportunities to make a genuine contribution. Teachers are also only half as likely as parents to help children extend their statements (Wells, 1986).

To foster children's language development, try the following (Wells, 1986):

**ADAPTING INSTRUCTION for *ENGLISH LANGUAGE LEARNERS***

Understanding a new language is easier than speaking it. To help ELLs bridge the gap between understanding words and speaking them, use prompts to help them formulate what they would like to say. Also focus on the meaning of what they say and not the form.

- Listen very carefully to what the student has to say. Try to see the world from the child's point of view. Do not run away with the topic. For instance, if a child mentions a trip to the zoo, find out what it was about the trip that intrigued her or him. Do not launch into a detailed description of your last trip to the zoo.
- Be open to what children want to talk about. Do not follow a preconceived plan for the direction you want the discussion to take. When discussing a story that you have read to the children, let them tell you what they liked best about it. Do not tell them what they should like best, and, of course, give them the freedom not to like it at all.
- Help students extend their responses by making encouraging comments.
- Provide students with opportunities to initiate conversations and ask questions.
- Although whole-class discussions are valuable, they do not allow for much interaction. As often as possible, arrange for small-group and one-on-one discussions.
- When you respond to students, use language that is on or slightly above their level.

■ Students are active learners who are using what they know to try to make sense of their world. Use their comments and questions to help them construct meaning.

■ Give the children something to talk about. Take trips to the zoo or museum. Plant seeds and raise fish or hamsters. Have lots of experiences so that children have lots to talk about. But don't make the mistake of having the experience and not talking about it. It is through talk that students form concepts about what makes plants grow or why hippos at the zoo spend just about all their time in the water. Children develop language and concepts when they talk about what they have experienced.

■ Foster conversations among children. One way children learn that talking is satisfying is by having enjoyable interchanges with other children. Fostering conversations can build language as well as social skills. Sometimes teachers see themselves as the molders or builders of language. While this is so, teachers should also see themselves as the facilitators of language and encourage conversations and discussions among children whenever possible.

■ Build upon children's talk. Whenever possible, have one-on-one conversations with children. Make certain that children have equal access. Often the quiet children, those who need one-on-one conversation the most, are given the least. In conversations, ask questions that require extended answers. Also ask real questions. Ask questions that you don't already know the answer to. When replying to young children's statements or questions, elaborate. In answer to the statement, "The dog is barking," you might reply, "Yes, the dog is barking. Perhaps it is hungry or maybe it is lonely. It wants its owner to come home and play with it" (Bunce, 1995).

## Assisting English Language Learners

Children vary in the rate at which they learn a second language. Aptitude for learning language varies. Some children have an easier time learning a second language. In addition, there are social and psychological factors. More outgoing children will learn a second language more rapidly, as will children who are highly motivated (Tabors, 1997). Children face a double bind when learning a second language. In order to learn a language, they must be socially accepted by their peers so that they can learn language from them. But to be socially accepted, they need to be able to speak to the other children. Age also has an impact on children's language development. Young children have less language to learn. However, they also have less cognitive capacity than older children, so they may take longer to learn a second language.

When they find themselves in a situation in which English is spoken, English Language Learners (ELLs) may continue to use their native tongue. When they find that this isn't working, many students enter a nonverbal period, which may last a few weeks, a few months, or even an entire year. Students use gestures and other nonverbal strategies in order to communicate. Gradually, the children use increasingly complex English to communicate. At first, ELLs learn object names:

*blocks, water, paint, books.* They might also use commands or comments such as *stop, OK, uh-oh, please, yes, no, hi, bye-bye.* They also pick up a series of useful expressions or routine statements, such as "Good morning. What's happening? How did you do this?" They progress to useful sentence structures, such as "I want __" or "I like __" in which they supply a variety of words to complete the statement.

In order to cope with the demands of the setting, ELLs use a number of strategies. These include:

- Join a group and act as though they know what is going on. This might mean joining a group that is playing with toy cars or building with blocks. ELLs participate by watching the activities of the others.
- Connect what they see with what people are saying. If the teacher holds up a round object and says *ball* several times, they assume that the name of the round object is ball.
- Learn some words and expressions and use them. Even though ELLs know very little of the language, they become part of a social group by making the most of what they do know and so will have the opportunity to expand their language.
- Find and use sources of help. Finding an adult or a friend who will teach them new words or expressions and help resolve confusions will foster language development (Tabors, 1997).
- Use a copying strategy. Not fully understanding directions or the complexity of an assignment, English learners often imitate their English-speaking classmates. They look to see how they are doing a workbook page or might even copy a sentence composed as part of a writing assignment. This may be viewed by the teacher and classmates as a coping strategy and, thus, tolerated (Weber & Longhi-Chirlin, 2001). When not copying from others, students often copied words that were written around the room or copied words from stories they had read. Expression of their own ideas was very limited.

ELLs should be encouraged to ask questions or seek help when they don't understand what they are being taught or what they are supposed to do. English learners are often confused by assignments or explanations or don't know what question the teacher is asking because they don't understand enough of the language (Weber & Longhi-Chirlin, 2001). English learners can do better in small groups because they are in a less intimidating environment and have the opportunity to ask peers for help.

The good news is that English learners placed in an English-speaking classroom can and do make progress. They develop speaking, listening, reading, and writing skills when their teachers believe that they can learn and present them with meaningful instruction and activities, even though the teachers do not have any training teaching ELLs. Although the students have some success, they would more than likely do even better if teachers were trained or took special steps to assist the English learners in their classes (Weber & Longhi-Chirlin, 2001). Some techniques for helping students learn English include modeling, running commentary, expansions, and redirects.

### ■ Modeling

The teacher models the element that the student is having difficulty with or needs to learn. For instance, to model the use of *this* and *I* and *these* and *are*, you might say, "This is my pencil. These are my pencils. This is my book. These are my books." The student is offered the opportunity to use the constructions but is not required to do so. He may need more time to assimilate the structures.

### ■ Running Commentary

In a running commentary, you take the role of a sports announcer and describe a process that you are carrying out (Bunce, 1995). "To make a paper bag puppet, first I ___ then I ___ and then I ___." The running commentary helps acquaint students with vocabulary and sentence structure. Since it accompanies an activity, it is concrete. It also provides insight into the teacher's thought processes and problem-solving strategies. Running commentary should be used selectively. If overused, the running commentary could be overwhelming to students. It is best used when a process or activity is being demonstrated.

### ■ Expansion

In an expansion, you repeat the student's statement but supply a missing part. Thus if a student says, "Car red," you would say, "Yes, the car is red." This affirms the student's comment but also gives the student a model of a more advanced form (Bunce, 1995).

### ■ Redirect

In a redirect, you encourage a student who has asked you a question or made a request to direct that to another student. If a student says he wants to play with the blocks, but Martin is playing with them, you direct him to ask Martin. If necessary, you provide a prompt, "Say to Martin, 'May I play with the blocks?'" This prompting fosters both social and language growth.

## CORE ACTIVITIES FOR BUILDING EMERGENT/EARLY LITERACY

This chapter has presented a number of techniques for building emergent literacy. Listed below are activities that are so highly effective that they should form the core of a literacy program for kindergarten children or other students on an emergent level. These core activities can be supplemented with other activities chosen by the teacher.

- Reading to children
- Shared reading
- Reading (could consist of reading along with a taped book or CD-ROM, reading a wordless or highly predictable book, pretend reading, or reading with a partner)
- Language experience/shared writing

**USING TECHNOLOGY**

For information about literacy programs for young children, refer to CIERA (Center for the Improve-ment of Early Reading Achievement): **http://www.ciera.org**

**ADAPTING INSTRUCTION for *ENGLISH LANGUAGE LEARNERS***

For additional suggestions for working with ELLs, see Chapter 11.

**USING TECHNOLOGY**

For added information about prekindergarten programs, see Prekindergarten Curriculum Guidelines (Texas Education Agency, 2002) at **http://www.tea.state.tx.us/curriculum/early/prekguide.html**

- Independent writing
- Other language/literacy building activities

Once students have a sense of story, understand the purpose and the basic concepts of print, can identify most of the letters of the alphabet, have a sense of rhyme, can segment the sounds in a word, and can perceive rhyme and detect beginning sounds in words, they are prepared for a higher level of instruction. Upcoming chapters contain suggestions for a more intensive and structured approach to reading that fosters children's growth in literacy areas such as phonics, high-frequency words, and other word analysis skills. The next section is devoted to reading in preschool, working with parents, and monitoring emergent literacy.

## READING IN PRESCHOOL

Given the importance of reading and writing, there is a growing movement to include literacy activities in the preschool. The Committee on the Prevention of Reading Difficulties in Young Children recommends that: "Preschool programs . . . should be designed to provide optimal support for cognitive, language, and social development. . . . However, ample attention should be paid to skills that are known to predict future reading achievement . . ." (Snow, Burns, & Griffin, 1998, p. 9).

A joint committee of the International Reading Association (IRA) and the NAEYC (National Association for the Education of Young Children) (1998) recommended that preschool children build the foundations for learning to read and write. "Failing to give children literacy experiences until they are school-age can severely limit the reading and writing levels they ultimately obtain" (p. 197). The concept of ready to read has been replaced by the concept of preparing to read (Texas Instrument Foundation, Head Start of Greater Dallas, Southern Methodist University, 1996). Essential literacy goals (standards) for the preschool can be found at the end of this chapter. A prudent course would be to avoid formal instruction in literacy. Reading aloud regularly, share reading, setting up dramatic play and reading and writing areas and a classroom library, developing oral language skills, modeling reading and writing, and providing opportunities for children to write, draw, and explore language will naturally develop emergent literacy (Campbell, 1998).

### Federal Initiatives

Although there is much agreement on the curriculum for students in K–12, ideas for preschool education range from programs that are play based and child centered to those that embody direct instruction. The current trend is toward adding academics to early childhood education. Indeed, Head Start is now mandated to performance standards that require that children:

1. Develop print and numeracy awareness
2. Understand and use an increasingly complex vocabulary
3. Develop and demonstrate an appreciation of books

Head Start standards also require that "children know that letters of the alphabet are a special category of visual graphics that can be individually named, recognize a word as a unit of print, identify at least 10 letters of the alphabet, and associate sounds with written words" (Taylor, 2001, p. 2).

## Early Reading First

Early Reading First, which can be implemented in a Head Start setting, is a federal initiative designed to prepare children, especially those at risk, for reading instruction. Its overall purpose is to prepare young children to enter kindergarten with the necessary language, cognitive, and early reading skills to prevent reading difficulties. Key skill areas include:

- Learning the letters of the alphabet
- Learning to hear the individual sounds in words; children need to learn to break words apart into their separate sounds (segmenting) and put sounds together to make words (blending)
- Learning new words and how to use them
- Learning early writing skills
- Learning to use language by asking and answering questions, and by participating in discussions and engaging in conversations
- Learning about written language by looking at books and by listening to stories and other books that are read to them every day (U.S. Department of Education, 2002a)

> **USING TECHNOLOGY**
> Early Reading First
>
> The Early Reading First Web site **http://www.ed.gov/offices/OESE/earlyreading/** Contains information on this program for preschool children.

## Effective Preschool Programs

Low-income four-year-olds showed encouraging gains when stories were read to them on a regular basis and the teacher engaged them in discussions in which they made predictions, reflected on the story, and talked about words (Dickinson & Smith, 1994). When book reading and literacy interactions were enhanced by training the teachers and adding a library of children's books in child care centers for three- and four-year-olds, children outperformed a comparison group on vocabulary, concepts of print, concepts of writing, letter names, and phonemic awareness when assessed in kindergarten (Neuman, 1997).

## Para Los Niños

In Para Los Niños, a child care center in a part of Los Angeles known as Skid Row, a morning language and literacy program was instituted for approximately fifty four-year-old Spanish-speaking preschool children. The program included big-book shared reading, writing and reading centers, and a take-home library for parents. Workshops for parents were held on various aspects of book-handling and home reading and writing activities. Students demonstrated encouraging gains in concepts of print, letter knowledge, and recognition of some phonics elements. Many of the families had also established read-aloud routines at home (Yaden et al., 2001).

This study substantiates the transfer of early language awareness in Spanish to English. Although they were taught literacy skills in Spanish, these skills transferred to English. In fact, the students outscored native speakers of English who had participated in other preschool programs despite the fact that the emergent literacy tests were administered in English.

## LEAP

For students at risk, a well-planned preschool program can mean the difference between success and failure in later schooling. Otherwise, children who start off behind tend to stay behind. The gap between potential and achievement widens as children progress through the grades (Hehir, 2001).

To give poor students in Head Start at the Cone Center (located in a poor section of Dallas, Texas) a boost, supplemental health, nutrition, and social services were added. Teachers and staff provided extended hours each day as well as a year-round program. Despite these additions, which were sponsored by the Texas Instruments Foundation, the children continued to enter kindergarten performing well behind their chronological age. The Texas Instruments Foundation then teamed up with Southern Methodist University (SMU) and a Language Enrichment Activities Program (LEAP) was developed. LEAP emphasizes language development, phonological awareness, knowledge of the letters of the alphabet, basic concepts, and prewriting fine motor skills, skills that would form a foundation for success in kindergarten. The program also included teacher training, workshops for volunteers, and a parent component.

Before the introduction of LEAP, students were operating at the thirtieth percentile. Today, average scores exceed the fiftieth percentile. Commenting on the performance of the graduates of the preschool program, the chair of the kindergarten department at the local elementary school stated, "They can sit for long periods of time. They have fine motor skills, such as using scissors and holding pencils. They understand letter–sound association. . . . We find them to be like mentors to their classmates" (Community Update, 1996, p. 4). Key elements in the instructional program include the following:

- **Language with stories.** Teachers read aloud at least five books a day selected from a thematically organized bibliography of books appropriate for children whose language development is from two to four years. The book is introduced and discussed. Vocabulary and concepts are developed. Connections are made between the book's themes and other classroom activities.
- **Language with words.** Posters of objects and activities are used as a stimulus for developing language. Students listen to, repeat, and produce responses in complete sentences. Teachers develop concepts and vocabulary throughout the day.
- **Language with sounds.** Beginning with their names, children learn to recognize individual words in phrases and sentences. Children also learn to iden-

tify the separate words in compound words and the syllables in two- and three-syllable words. The theory is that before students can learn to identify phonemes, they must learn to identify sentences, clauses, and words.

- **Language with letters.** Children learn the sounds of beginning consonants and the names of the letters that represent those sounds. Children also learn the uppercase letters of the alphabet and learn to sing the alphabet song. Children manipulate objects that have the same beginning sound.
- **Language with ideas.** Children learn shapes, sizes, colors, numbers, plurals, rhymes, opposites, and other concepts.
- **Language with prewriting motor skills.** Children learn the fine motor skills needed for writing.

Personal/social skills are also fostered. Children begin school prepared to learn as opposed to ready to learn (Texas Instruments Foundation, Head Start of Greater Dallas, Southern Methodist University, 1996). Suggestions for setting up such a preschool program can be found at the Texas Instruments Foundation's Web site at http://www.ti.com/corp/docs/company/citizen/foundation/leapsbounds/history.shtml.

## Webbing into Literacy

Webbing into Literacy (http://curry.edschool.virginia.edu/go/wil/home.html) also offers a wealth of resources for developing preschool literacy skills. Webbing into Literacy is a downloadable program designed to provide Head Start teachers with materials and instruction that will foster language development, phonological awareness, alphabet knowledge, and concepts of print. Because the site is designed for preschool students, the goal is exposure and awareness rather than mastery. Activities include shared reading and singing of nursery rhymes, sorting word patterns, and using rhymes to complete riddles. Downloadable materials include rhyme cards containing nursery rhymes, picture card sets containing illustrated rhyming words, riddle rhymes, covers for students' alphabet booklets, and nursery rhymes booklets.

## 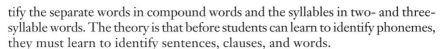 WORKING WITH PARENTS

Because today's emergent literacy practices are different from those parents experienced when they attended school and there was a readiness orientation, it is important that the emergent literacy program be explained to them. Trace the roots of reading and writing, and explain to parents the essential role that they have played and continue to play. Be sensitive to different styles of parenting. Some parents, not having been read to themselves, may not realize the value of reading aloud to their children or, because of limited skills, may not feel able to do it well.

Affirm what parents have done and encourage them to support their children's efforts as best they can. Also, explain each element of the program. Pay special attention to invented spelling and process writing, as these are areas that lend

Parents' ways of interacting with their children are determined by cultural factors. Some parents may read in an authoritative style and fail to interact with the child (Leseman & deJong, 1998). Sessions demonstrating effective read-aloud techniques or even videotapes of read-aloud sessions would be helpful to these parents.

**ADAPTING INSTRUCTION for *ENGLISH LANGUAGE LEARNERS***

Parents of English Language Learners should be encouraged to use the language that they feel most comfortable with. Advising them to speak only English may hinder communication between parents and children.

themselves to misunderstanding. Trace the development of children's writing from drawing and scribbling through invented spelling to conventional writing. Show examples of students' writing. Stress the benefits of early writing, and assure parents that invented spelling is transitory and will not harm their children's spelling.

The joint position statement of the International Reading Association and the National Association for the Education of Young Children (1998) suggests that parents can help emergent readers in the following ways:

- Read and reread narrative and informational stories to children daily.
- Encourage children's attempts at reading and writing.
- Allow children to participate in activities that involve writing and reading (for example, making grocery lists).
- Play games that involve specific directions (such as Simon Says).
- Have conversations with children during mealtimes and throughout the day.

## Family Literacy

■ **Family literacy** has as its overall goal the sharing of reading and writing by a family. Although concerned with helping children become proficient readers and writers, its major goal is the transmission of the family's culture. In one program, parents wrote stories about their experiences that they would then share with their children (Akroyd, 1995).

One highly effective way of assisting children, especially those at risk, fully develop their literacy is to help their parents overcome their own literacy difficulties so that they can then help their children. A **family** or intergenerational **literacy** program can take several forms. Parents and children may attend sessions held after school or during the summer. The parents and children may be given separate programs, or the program may be coordinated in such a way that the parents spend some of the time working directly with their children. In other forms, just the parents attend sessions, but they are taught reading and writing skills, which they pass on to the children. Learning how to read, parents are then prepared to read storybooks to their children or to assist with homework. In a third version, parents are taught ways to enhance their children's reading and writing skills by reading to them, talking with them, or supervising homework. As they learn ways to help their children, parents' literacy skills improve. Parents may also meet in discussion groups to talk over difficulties they are having and ways in which they might help their children.

**INVOLVING PARENTS**

Parents need specific suggestions for helping their children. Don't just suggest that they read books to their children. Provide a list of possible books and tips for reading aloud.

Parents may need ongoing, specific guidance in the use of techniques to build their children's literacy development. Paratore (1995) found that it wasn't enough to provide parents with storybooks and demonstrations on how to read to children. The parents needed many opportunities to observe read-aloud sessions as well as opportunities to practice reading aloud. Discussing their read-aloud sessions and obtaining practical feedback also helped.

## MONITORING EMERGENT LITERACY

Emergent literacy can best be monitored through careful observation. As students read and write, try to get behind the product to the process. As a student is reading, try to determine what he or she is reading. Is the student reading the pictures? Has the student simply memorized the text? Is it some sort of combination? Ask yourself: What is the child attending to? Possibilities include pictures, overall memory of the selection, memorized words or phrases, context, beginning letters, beginning letters and ending letters, all the letters in the word, or a combination of elements. Knowing where the student is, you can build on his or her knowledge and, through scaffolding, lift the student to a higher level. For instance, if the student is simply using picture clues, you can help him or her use highly predictable text along with pictures. A checklist for evaluating a child's use of early reading strategies is presented in Table 3.9.

Note the level of the student's writing. Does the student have a sense of what writing is? Is the student attempting to convey a message? Is the student using invented spelling? Use the checklists in the observation guide in Figure 3.5 to monitor writing, stages of storybook reading, oral language, concepts about reading, interest in reading and writing, and work habits. The observation guide is generic; use only those parts that fit in with your program.

Observation should be broad-based. Dahl (1992) suggests observing strategies that children use in reading and writing, the routines that students engage in every day, and the products of their efforts and the comments that they make about them:

■ **Strategies.** In addition to noting what strategies students use as they attempt to read a text, ask: What strategies do they use as they attempt to write a word? Do they elongate the sounds? Ask a teacher?

■ **Routines.** How do students choose books? What do they do when they write? Do they typically use a book as a model? Do they use a drawing as a story starter?

| TABLE 3.9 | Checklist for evaluating early reading strategies | | |
|---|---|---|---|
| **Strategy** | **Never** | **Seldom** | **Often** |
| 1. Uses pictures exclusively to retell story. | ____ | ____ | ____ |
| 2. Uses pictures and text to retell story. | ____ | ____ | ____ |
| 3. Uses pictures to help with difficult words. | ____ | ____ | ____ |
| 4. Uses memory of entire piece to read story. | ____ | ____ | ____ |
| 5. Uses memory of repeated phrases. | ____ | ____ | ____ |
| 6. Uses context to decipher words. | ____ | ____ | ____ |
| 7. Uses initial consonants and context to decipher words. | ____ | ____ | ____ |
| 8. Uses initial and final consonants and context to decipher words. | ____ | ____ | ____ |
| 9. Uses all or most of each word's parts to decipher words. | ____ | ____ | ____ |
| 10. Uses a variety of cues to decipher words. | ____ | ____ | ____ |

Based on Appendix 2.1, Forms of Writing and Rereading, Example List (pp. 51–63) by E. Sulzby (1989). In J. M. Mason (Ed.), *Reading and Writing Connections*. Boston: Allyn & Bacon.

**FIGURE 3.5**

## Emergent Literacy Observation Guide

Student's name: _____   Age: _____

Date: _____

| Oral language | Below average | Average | Advanced |
|---|---|---|---|
| Uses a vocabulary appropriate for age level | 1 | 2  3  4 | 5 |
| Uses a sentence structure appropriate for age level | 1 | 2  3  4 | 5 |
| Can make himself/herself understood | 1 | 2  3  4 | 5 |
| Listens attentively to directions and stories | 1 | 2  3  4 | 5 |
| Can retell a story in own words | 1 | 2  3  4 | 5 |
| Understands oral directions | 1 | 2  3  4 | 5 |
| Asks questions when doesn't understand something | 1 | 2  3  4 | 5 |

| Concepts about reading | Below average | Average | Advanced |
|---|---|---|---|
| Knows the parts of a book | 1 | 2  3  4 | 5 |
| Understands that the print is read | 1 | 2  3  4 | 5 |
| Can follow a line of print as it is being read | 1 | 2  3  4 | 5 |
| Can point to words as each is being read | 1 | 2  3  4 | 5 |
| Can name letters of the alphabet | 1 | 2  3  4 | 5 |
| Can perceive beginning sounds | 1 | 2  3  4 | 5 |
| Can detect rhyming words | 1 | 2  3  4 | 5 |
| Can tell how many sounds are in a word | 1 | 2  3  4 | 5 |
| Can discriminate between words that have a similar appearance | 1 | 2  3  4 | 5 |
| Recognizes environmental print signs and labels | 1 | 2  3  4 | 5 |
| Can read own name | 1 | 2  3  4 | 5 |

| Interest in reading and writing | Below average | Average | Advanced |
|---|---|---|---|
| Enjoys being read to | 1 | 2  3  4 | 5 |
| Browses among books in class | 1 | 2  3  4 | 5 |
| "Reads" picture books | 1 | 2  3  4 | 5 |
| Asks questions about words, sentences, or other elements in books | 1 | 2  3  4 | 5 |

| Writing | Below average | Average | Advanced |
|---|---|---|---|
| Shows interest in writing | 1 | 2  3  4 | 5 |
| Writes or draws stories or letters | 1 | 2  3  4 | 5 |
| Understands the purpose of writing | 1 | 2  3  4 | 5 |
| Writes to communicate with others | 1 | 2  3  4 | 5 |

**FIGURE 3.5**

### Emergent Literacy Observation Guide *(continued)*

For the most part his/her writing is best described as being at the following level:

| | | |
|---|---|---|
| Unorganized scribbles | _____ | (The scribbles have no perceptible pattern.) |
| Drawings | _____ | (Drawing is the child's primary mode of written expression.) |
| Organized scribbles | _____ | (The scribbles show a pattern. They may be linear.) |
| Letterlike figures | _____ | (The characters aren't real letters, but have some of the features of letters.) |
| Prephonemic spelling | _____ | (The child uses real letters, but the letters have no apparent relationship to the sounds of the words he or she is writing.) |
| Early alphabetic spelling | _____ | (Consonant sounds are spelled; *kitten* may be spelled *KTN*.) |
| Alphabetic spelling | _____ | (Vowels are spelled with letter names; *RAN* for *rain*.) |
| Consolidated alphabetic spelling | _____ | (Vowel markers are used; *RANE* for *rain*.) |
| Standard spelling | _____ | |

| Work habits | Below average | Average | Advanced |
|---|---|---|---|
| Is able to work on own | 1 | 2  3  4 | 5 |
| Works at task until it is finished | 1 | 2  3  4 | 5 |
| Works well with others | 1 | 2  3  4 | 5 |
| Is able to share materials | 1 | 2  3  4 | 5 |
| Is able to take turns | 1 | 2  3  4 | 5 |

- **Products.** What do the illustrations children have made of their reading look like? What do their written pieces look like? Are they scribble writing or using a combination of scribble writing and invented spelling? How are the products changing over time?
- **Comments.** What are children saying about their work? For instance, when Maurice tossed his piece of scribble writing into the wastebasket, his teacher asked him about it. Maurice replied, "My writing doesn't say anything." Maurice realized that he needed another form of writing in order to express meaning. His rejection of his scribble writing was a sign of development (Dahl, 1992). This is the kind of incident of which perceptive anecdotal records are made.

Observations should focus on what the child can do. For instance, the focus of the observation made about Maurice was that he has a new understanding of what is required to represent spoken words in writing.

Notes taken after a discussion has been completed or a reading or writing conference has been held can also offer valuable insights. If the notes are put on gummed labels or sticky notes, they can be entered into a handheld computer or pasted into a looseleaf notebook that contains separate pages for each child .

Because young children's literacy behavior changes rapidly, observations should be ongoing. However, progress should be checked on a more formal basis approximately once a month. In addition to filling out checklists, keep anecdotal records. Note the emergence of significant behaviors, such as the appearance of finger pointing, word-by-word reading, and the use of invented spelling. Briefly describe the behavior and note the date. See Chapter 2 for more information on using checklists and anecdotal records.

## Informal Assessment Measures

> If your program requires a more formal assessment, consider an assessment such as PALS (Ivernizzi, Meir, Swank, & Juel, 2001).

Emergent literacy measures need not be purchased. Teachers can put together a measure that is geared to their own concept of literacy and that meshes with their literacy program. Although it can be a paper-and-pencil test to allow for group administration, an informal type of one-to-one assessment often works better. A sample informal assessment, which is administered individually, follows.

### ■ Letter Knowledge

> A group test of letter knowledge can be found in Appendix A. The group test is somewhat easier because the student only has to select from four letters the one that the teacher names.

Print or type the twenty-six letters of the alphabet on cards. Make a set for uppercase letters and lowercase ones. Mix up the cards and see how many lowercase and uppercase letters the student can name. Assess knowledge of lowercase letters first.

### ■ Writing Sample

Ask the child to write his or her name as best he or she can. If the child can write his or her name, ask the child to write any other words that he or she knows. Ask the child to write a story as best he or she can. In the story, the child might tell about himself or herself and his or her family. This may be done with letterlike forms or drawings or real letters. Note the level of the child's writing and the number of words that he or she can write, if any.

### ■ Print Familiarity

> **ASSESSING STUDENTS' PROGRESS**
>
> The copyright-free Yopp-Singer Test of Phoneme Segmentation can be found in *The Reading Teacher, 49,* pp. 20–29, 1995. The Test of Invented Spelling, which notes how many sounds students are able to represent, can be found in the *Merrill-Palmer Quarterly, 33,* pp. 365–389, 1987.

Give *Have You Seen My Cat?* (Carle, 1973) or a similar book to the child. Discuss the book informally to find out how familiar the child is with print conventions. You might ask, "Have you ever seen this book? What do you think this book is about? How can you tell what the book is about? What do you do with a book?" Open to the first page of the story and say, "I'm going to read this page to you. Show me where I should start reading." (Note whether the child points to the illustration or the first word.) Ask the child if he or she can read any words on the page. Then tell the child that you are going to read the first sentence. Ask him or her to point to each word as you read it. (Note whether the child can do this.) Read the sentence again. Then ask the child to read it. Ask him or her to point to each word as he or she reads it. (Pointing to each word shows whether the child has a concept of separate words.) Point to a line of print and ask, "How many words are in this line?" Point to a word and ask, "How many letters are in this word?"

## *Exemplary Teaching*

### *Using Assessment to Reduce Potential Reading Problems*

*T*he purpose of the Early Intervention Reading Initiative in Virginia is to reduce the number of students in grades kindergarten through three with reading problems by using early diagnosis and acceleration of early reading skills. The initiative provides teachers with a screening tool that helps them determine which students would benefit from additional instruction. Schools are also given incentive funds to obtain additional instruction for students in need.

Students are administered the Phonological Literacy Screening (PALS) instrument. PALS-K (kindergarten) includes measures of rhyme, beginning sounds, alphabet recognition, letter sounds, spelling, concept of word, and word recognition. According to PALS scores, approximately 25 percent of students need additional instruction.

The PALS project makes heavy use of the Internet. When teachers report their scores, they get an immediate summary report. Principals can also get reports for their schools. The site contains 100 instructional suggestions and a listing of materials. Instruction provided to students must be in addition to their regular classroom instruction. When retested in the spring, approximately 80 percent of kindergartners identified as needing added help were making satisfactory progress. Retention is not considered a means of providing additional assistance and is not the purpose of the Early Intervention Reading Initiative.

After screening ninety-two children with PALS, the four kindergarten teachers at the McGuffey School in Virginia found that twenty-three children needed an intervention program. The students worked with a PALS tutor for thirty minutes a day. The focus was on developing phonological awareness, alphabet skills, and beginning consonants. The lesson also included shared reading of nursery rhymes and simple pattern books. This approach was designed to develop awareness of sounds, letter recognition, concept of word, and writing skills. Although all of the students had low overall scores on emergent literacy skills, some were especially weak in rhyming. Others had difficulty with letter recognition or matching beginning sounds. Students were placed in groups of four according to common needs so that instruction would be focused. Skills were introduced in integrated fashion. If the lesson's focus was on beginning sounds, the teacher read aloud a selection that contained the target sounds and discussed them. Students also sorted objects and pictures that shared the target sounds and then attempted to write the name of each object or picture. The lesson ended with a rhyme that contained the target sounds (Invernizzi, Meier, Swank, & Juel, 2001). For more information go to www.edschool. virginia.edu/curry/ centers/pals/home/html.

## Other Measures of Emergent Literacy

One of the best-known measures of print concepts is CAP, or Concepts about Print (Clay, 1982). CAP has twenty-four items and takes only five to ten minutes to administer. The test has two forms: Sand and Stones. The tests are equivalent and consist of a storybook and a series of questions. Clay (1993a) also assembled a battery of reading and writing measures known as the Observation Survey, which can be used to assess emergent reading and early reading behaviors. The Bader Reading and Language Inventory (Bader, 2002) also includes a number of assessment devices for emergent literacy: Concepts about Print, Blending, Segmentation, Letter Knowledge, Hearing Letter Names in Words, and Syntax Matching (being able to match printed with spoken words).

**ASSESSING STUDENTS' PROGRESS**

Tests of letter knowledge, rhyming, and begining sounds can be found in Appendix B.

Tests of phonological awareness may not work well with children younger than five. In a study by Muter and Snowling (1998), tests of phonological awareness given at age five were relatively good predictors of later reading achievement, but when given at age four, the tests failed to provide adequate predictions.

We have no direct measure of phonemic awareness. Each of the assessment tasks has its own cognitive requirements. To blend a string of isolated phonemes, the child must first perceive those phonemes, then hold them in memory while trying to connect them into a word. To detect a rhyme, the child must identify both of the words' rimes, keep them in memory, and then decide if both end with the same rime.

Both the Bader and the CAPS are individually administered. The Phonological Literacy Screening (PALS) is a group test and includes measures of rhyme, beginning sounds, alphabet recognition, letter sounds, spelling, concept of word, and word recognition (Invernizzi, Meir, Swank, & Juel, 2001). Measures of emergent literacy are also included in the teacher's manual of a basal reading series or as a separate item. One advantage of basal tests is that they are geared to the program for which they have been constructed. They are also generally accompanied by suggestions for working with students who do poorly on them.

## Using the Assessment Results

The results of an emergent literacy assessment should help you plan instruction. Generally, an acceptable standard for letter knowledge and phonological awareness is 80 percent. Students falling below that level require additional help. Those who are lacking in print familiarity need more experience with concepts with which they had difficulty. Writing samples are also indicators of emergent literacy concepts. Based on the samples, note where children are on the path to literacy and, according to their level of development, what experiences will be most beneficial.

As indicated earlier, not every ability important to reading can be measured formally or informally. Learning to read requires hard work, perseverance, and a certain degree of maturity. It also demands reasonably good health, sufficient social skills to allow one to work with others, and adequate language skills so that the teacher's instructions and the material to be read can be understood.

## HELP FOR STRUGGLING READERS AND WRITERS

Struggling readers and writers should be carefully assessed to determine their strengths and weaknesses. They should then be taught on a level that is comfortable for them. If students have had limited experience with print, spend extra time reading to them. If possible, have volunteers read individually to them or in small groups and discuss the selections much as a parent would. If students are hesitant to write, encourage them to write as best they can. Model the ways in which young children write, including drawing, and encourage them to pick the kind of writing that they feel they can do. Provide experiences with phonological awareness that are on the appropriate level. If children are having difficulty detecting rhyme or initial sounds, read rhyming or alliterative tales to them and engage in word play activities to build their awareness of the sounds of language. Connect with the home and find out what kinds of literacy activities the children's families engage in. Build on these and provide suggestions for the families for working with the children.

Also, take a preventive approach. As noted earlier, some impoverished families don't spend much time reading to their children or talking with them about letters and words until the children start engaging in these activities at school (Purcell-Gates, 1997). A family literacy or similar program that helped parents engage in these activities before their children enter school should provide children with a much richer foundation for reading and writing.

## ESSENTIAL STANDARDS

### Preschool: Awareness and exploration

Children explore their environments and develop a foundation for learning to read and write (IRA & NAEYC, 1998).

*Students will*

- listen to and talk about storybooks.
- develop language skills by talking a lot, talking to themselves to guide actions, telling stories, explaining and seeking information, and engaging in word play (New Standards Speaking and Listening Committee, 2001).
- attempt to read and write.
- understand that print can be read.
- recognize labels and signs in the environment.
- engage in rhyming and other word play games.
- recognize some letters and letter sounds.
- use letters or letterlike forms to write names and messages.

### Kindergarten: Experimental reading and writing

Students develop oral language and listening skills, learn basic concepts of print, and explore the form and function of reading and writing.

*Students will*

- recognize and write the letters of the alphabet.
- develop phonological awareness: rhyming, beginning sounds, blending, segmentation of words.
- understand basic print concepts: left to right, top to bottom, front to back, spaces between words.
- match spoken words with printed ones.
- learn consonant–sound correspondences.
- learn some short-vowel word families: *-at*, *-am*, *-an*, etc.
- read some high-frequency words and simple stories.
- write their names and use their knowledge of letter–sound relationships to write words, lists, captions for drawings, messages, and stories.
- develop language skills by talking a lot, talking to themselves to guide actions, telling stories, explaining and seeking information, and engaging in word play (New Standards Speaking and Listening Committee, 2001).
- listen to, retell, answer questions about, and respond to stories.

> Most major basal programs introduce initial consonant correspondences and short-vowel patterns at the kindergarten level.

## ACTION PLAN

1. Assess students to see where they are in terms of their literacy development. Assess concepts of print, alphabet knowledge, and phonological awareness. Also note language development and work habits. Plan a program that develops all these areas.
2. Establish a literacy-rich environment.
3. Use oral reading and shared reading to develop background, language and thinking skills, and literacy concepts.
4. Use word games and other activities to develop letter knowledge and phonological awareness. Once students are aware of beginning sounds, tie letters into instruction.

5. Develop emerging writing skills.
6. Involve parents in their children's learning.
7. Make certain that the program is developmentally appropriate. Make sure that preschool, kindergarten, and grade 1 programs are articulated so that one builds on the other.
8. For English Language Learners, develop phonological awareness and beginning literacy skills in the students' native language, if possible. Make extra efforts to build language skills.
9. Monitor children's progress and make any necessary adjustments.

 ## ASSESSMENT

Many of the early literacy objectives, especially in the preschool, can be assessed through careful observation. To make the observations more valid, observe the child in different settings and on more than one occasion. It's also helpful to have a checklist or some other sort of observation guide. The observation guide presented in Figure 3.5 could be used for this purpose. Assessment is also more valid when you use more than one source of information. Suggestions for assessing letter knowledge and phonological awareness are contained on pages 152–154. Tests of letter knowledge and phonological awareness can be found in Appendix B.

## SUMMARY

1. The concept of readiness has given way to that of emergent literacy, which attempts to capitalize on the literacy learning that the child brings to school. To foster literacy, the teacher immerses the class in reading and writing activities.
2. By reading selected books to children, the teacher builds knowledge of story structure and story language, vocabulary, and background of experience. To build language, the school should use techniques to make the child an active partner in conversations and discussions. Through shared

reading and language experience stories, including shared writing, basic literacy concepts and skills are built.
3. Once primarily a matter of copying and learning letter formation, writing in kindergarten is now seen as a valid means of expression. Children are invited to write and spell as best they can.
4. Progress in literacy is closely tied to knowledge of the alphabet and phonological awareness. In most kindergarten literacy programs, language and social development are fostered. In addition,

students are instructed in letter recognition, phonological awareness, concepts of print, initial consonant correspondences, and—in some programs—short-vowel patterns.

5. Parents should be involved in their children's literacy learning.

6. It is now recommended that preschool programs use informal, naturalistic activities to prepare students for learning to read and write. Several pre-

school programs have been shown to be highly beneficial to at-risk learners.

7. A number of formal and informal measures assess emergent literacy.

8. Instruction for struggling readers and writers should build on what students know and focus on areas most important for success in reading and writing.

## EXTENDING AND APPLYING

1. Examine stories written by a kindergarten class. What are some characteristics of children's writing at this age? How do the pieces vary?

2. Read the description of Webbing into Literacy at http://curry.edschool.virginia.edu/go/wil/home.html. Examine the many resources offered. How might these be used in a preparatory literacy program for preschool children?

3. Read the description of LEAP at http://www.ti.com/corp/docs/company/citizen/foundation/leapsbounds/history.shtml. Also read

the handbook entitled *What Suggestions Are Offered for Setting Up A Preschool Program?*"

4. Search out alphabet books, rhyming tales, song books, and other materials that you might use to enhance alphabet knowledge, rhyming, or perception of beginning sounds. Keep an annotated bibliography of these materials.

5. Using the procedures described in this chapter, plan a lesson teaching alphabet letters, rhyming, or beginning sounds. Teach the lesson, and rate its effectiveness.

## DEVELOPING A PROFESSIONAL PORTFOLIO

Reflect on your beliefs about teaching literacy skills in preschool and kindergarten classes. Compose a statement in which you highlight your beliefs and how you might implement them. Teach a lesson as suggested in Item 5 of Extending and Applying above and, if possible, record it on a video or CD-ROM. On a paper copy of the lesson plan, reflect on the effectiveness of the lesson.

## DEVELOPING A RESOURCE FILE

Start and maintain a list of books and other materials that you might use to teach literacy in preschool or kindergarten. Start a file of illustrations and nursery rhymes that you might use to develop phonological awareness.

4

# Teaching Phonics, High-Frequency Words, and Syllabic Analysis

*F*or each of the following statements, put a check under "Agree" or "Disagree" to show how you feel. Discuss your responses with classmates before you read the chapter.

|  |  | *Agree* | *Disagree* |
|---|---|---|---|
| **1** | Before they start to read, students should be taught most of the consonant letters and their sounds. | ____ | ____ |
| **2** | Phonics rules have so many exceptions that they are not worth teaching. | ____ | ____ |
| **3** | Phonics is hard to learn because English is so irregular. | ____ | ____ |
| **4** | The natural way to decode a word is sound by sound or letter by letter. | ____ | ____ |
| **5** | Memorizing is an inefficient way to learn new words. | ____ | ____ |
| **6** | Syllabication is not a very useful skill because you have to know how to decode a word before you can put it into syllables. | ____ | ____ |

## USING WHAT YOU KNOW

*T*he writing system for the English language is alphabetic. Because a series of twenty-six letters has been created to represent the speech sounds of the language, our thoughts and ideas can be written down. To become literate, we must learn the relationship between letters and speech sounds. Chapter 3 presented techniques for teaching the nature and purpose of writing and reading, concepts of print, the alphabet, awareness of speech sounds, and a technique for presenting initial consonants. These techniques form a foundation for learning phonics, which is the relationship between spelling and speech sounds as applied to reading. This chapter covers high-frequency words, some of which may not lend themselves to phonic analysis. In addition, the chapter explores syllabic analysis, which is applying phonics to multisyllabic words, and fluency, which is freedom from word identification problems. This chapter will be more meaningful if you first reflect on what you already know about phonics, syllabic analysis, and fluency.

Think about how you use phonics and syllabic analysis to sound out strange names and other unfamiliar words. Think about how you might teach phonics, and ask yourself what role phonics should play in a reading program.

## RATIONALE AND APPROACHES FOR PHONICS INSTRUCTION

As you read the following sentence out loud, think about the processes you are using.

> In *Palampam Day*, by David and Phyllis Gershator (1997), Papa Tata Wanga offers sage advice to Turn, who refuses to eat because on this day, the food talks back, as do the animals.

In addition to thinking about what the sentence is saying, did you find that you had to use **phonics** and syllabication skills to read *Palampam, Gershator,* and *Tata Wanga?* Phonics skills are absolutely essential for all readers. Most of the words we read are sight words. We've encountered them so many times that we don't need to take time to sound them out. They are in our mental storehouse of words that we recognize automatically. However, we need phonics for names of people or places or events that we have never met in print. Without phonics, we would not be able to read new words.

As adept readers, we use phonics occasionally. Because of our extensive experience reading, we have met virtually all of the word patterns in the language. Although you may have never seen the word *Palampam* before, you have seen the word patterns *pal* and *am*. Chances are you used these patterns to decode *Palampam.* You probably decoded the word so rapidly that you may not even be

■ **Phonics** is the study of speech sounds related to reading.

▌ As adept readers, we apply our skills with lightning speed and process words by patterns of sound. Having read words such as *papa* and *tango,* you may have grouped the letters in *Tata* as "ta-ta" and those in *Wanga* as "Wang (g)a" and pronounced the *as* in *Tata* just as you have the *as* in *papa* and the *ang* in *Wanga* just as you would the *ang* in *tango.*

*T*he purpose of learning phonics is to enable students to decode words that are in their listening vocabularies but that they fail to recognize in print.

conscious of applying your skills. For novice readers, phonics is a key skill. For a period in their development, novice readers may be using phonics in a conscious, deliberate fashion to decode many of the words that they read. In time, after they've had sufficient experience with a word, that word becomes part of their instant recognition vocabulary.

## HOW WORDS ARE READ

Words are read in one of five, often overlapping, ways. They are predicted, sounded out, chunked, read by analogy, or recognized immediately. Predicting means using context by itself or context plus some decoding to read a word. Seeing the letter *w* and using the context "Sam was pulling a red w _____ ," the student predicts that the word missing is *wagon*. Sounding out entails pronouncing words letter by letter or sound by sound (/h/ + /a/ + /t/) and then blending them into a word. As readers become more advanced, they group or chunk sounds into pronounceable units (/h/ + /at/). Readers may also decode a word because it is analogous to a known word. They can read the new word *net* because it is like the known word *pet*. In the fifth process, the words are recognized with virtually no mental effort. Adept readers have met some words so often that they recognize them just about as soon as they see them. These are called sight words because they are apparently recognized at sight (Ehri & McCormick, 1998).

### How High-Frequency Words Are Learned

According to Ehri (1998), learning words at sight entails forging links that connect the written form of the word and its pronunciation and meaning. Looking at the spelling of a word, the experienced reader retrieves its pronunciation and meaning from her mental dictionary or storehouse of words instantaneously. Beginners might look at a word, analyze it into its component sounds, blend the sounds, and say the word. At the same time, they note how the word's letters symbolize single or groups of sounds. Over time, the connections that the reader makes between letters and sounds enable the reader to retrieve the spoken form and meaning of the word just about instantaneously. The reader makes adjustments for irregular words so that certain letters are flagged as being silent or having an unusual pronunciation. "Knowledge of letter–sound relations provides a powerful mnemonic system that bonds the written forms of specific words to their pronunciations in memory" (Ehri & McCormick, 1998, p. 140).

> P. M. Cunningham (1998) notes that "words we have not read before are almost instantly pronounced on the basis of spelling patterns the brain has seen in other words" (p. 199).

## STAGES IN READING WORDS

### Pre-alphabetic Stage

Students go through stages or phases in their use of word analysis skills. Young children surprise their elders by reading a McDonald's sign, soda can and milk carton labels, and the names of cereals. However, for the most part, these children are not translating letters into sounds as more mature readers would do; instead, they are associating "nonphonemic visual characteristics" with spoken words (Ehri, 1994). For instance, a child remembers the word *McDonald's* by associating it with the golden arches and Pepsi is associated with its logo. At times, teachers take advantage of the nonphonemic characteristics of words. They tell students that the word *tall* might be remembered because it has three tall letters and that *camel* is easy to recall because the *m* in the middle of the word has two humps.

In the pre-alphabetic (prephonemic) stage, students learn a word by selective association, by selecting some nonphonemic feature that distinguishes it from other words (Gough, Juel, & Griffith, 1992). For the word *elephant*, it could be the length of the word; or in the word *look*, it could be the two *o*s that are like eyes. The problem with selective association is that students run out of distinctive clues, and the clues that they use do not help them decode new words. Students can learn only about forty words using nonphonic clues (Gough & Hillinger, 1980). In addition, students don't begin to advance in their understanding of the alphabetic nature of the language until they begin to use letter–sound relationships to read words.

Students' invented or spontaneous spelling provides clues to the stage they are in. They may use random letters to represent a word. Or they may even be able to spell their names because they have memorized the letters. As students become aware of individual sounds in words and the fact that letters represent sounds, they move into the second stage of reading, the alphabetic stage (Byrne, 1992).

> Most children in preschool and early kindergarten are in the pre-alphabetic stage.

> Purcell-Gates (1997) concluded that observing and working with print without the support of pictorial clues as provided by labels and signs was more effective in building literacy concepts than was working with signs and labels. When children read signs or labels, they attend to the pictorial portions rather than the print.

## Partial Alphabetic Stage

In the alphabetic (letter name) stage, learners use letter–sound relationships to read words. In the partial alphabetic stage, they may use just a letter or two. They may use only the first letter of a word and combine the sound of that letter with context. For instance, in the sentence "The cat meowed," students may process only the initial *m* and then use context and their experience with cats to guess that the word is *meowed*. Or they may use the first and last letter to decode the word *cat* in "I lost my cat"; so they read the word *cat* as opposed to *cap* or *car*. Students cannot use full decoding because they haven't yet learned vowel correspondences.

In their spontaneous spelling, students in this stage may represent a word by using just the first letter: *K* for *car* or *KR*, the letters that represent the most distinctive sounds in *car*. At the end of this stage, they begin using vowels, but may not spell the words correctly.

## Full Alphabetic Stage

In the full alphabetic stage, students begin to process all letters in the words. As they learn to apply their growing knowledge of letter–sound relationships, their reading may be slow and effortful. Focusing on using their newly learned decoding skills, students cautiously read word by word. Students are "glued to print" (Chall, 1996). The danger at this stage is that too much emphasis will be put on accuracy and sounding out. This could impede students' development. "Too analytical an approach . . . may hold up silent reading comprehension" (Chall, 1996, p. 47). With students glued to print, this is a bottom-up stage. As students build their store of known words, they are better able to see commonalties in words. They note that *cat* and *hat* both have an *at*. Encountering the word *mat*, which they have never seen in print, they can decode it by noting the pronounceable part *at* and blending it with *m*. Or they may use an analogy strategy. Seeing that *mat* is similar to *cat* enables them to read the word.

Students spell vowel sounds in this stage but may not spell them correctly. Because they may not perceive patterns until the end of this stage, they may fail to use final *e* (*hope*) and double vowel letters (*coat*) to represent long-vowel sounds.

## Consolidated Alphabetic Stage

In the consolidated alphabetic (within-word-pattern) stage, students consolidate and process longer and more sophisticated units. For instance, instead of processing *hen* as *h-e-n*, they may divide it into two units: *h+ en*. They process *light* as *l+ ight* and make use of such elements as a final *e* (as in *cape*) to help them determine the pronunciation of a word. In spelling, they begin using final *e* or use two vowel letters to show that a vowel is long.

As students process the same words over and over again, connections are made, and they do not have to read *cat* as /k/ /a/ /t/, or even /k/ /at/. Rather, the printed representation of the word as a whole elicits its spoken equivalent. The printed representation becomes bonded with the spoken equivalent (Perfetti, 1992). As Ehri (1998) explains, "Sight word learning is at root an alphabetic process in which spellings of specific words are secured to their pronunciations in memory" (p. 105). Gough, Juel, and Griffith (1992) explain the process somewhat differently. They believe that just about all the letters in a word are analyzed. Through practice, access speed increases so that even though words are analyzed element by element, this is done so rapidly as to be almost instantaneous. Perfetti (1985) suggests that even when words are recognized immediately, the decoding processes are still at work but are on a subconscious level. This underlying processing verifies our word recognition so that we are alerted when we misread a word. This system also enables us to read words we have never seen before very rapidly.

Regardless of how the process is explained, the end result is the same. In time, nearly all the words expert readers encounter in print are read as "sight" words. They are recognized virtually instantaneously. What makes the instantaneous recognition possible are the connections that have been created between each word's spelling or phonics elements and its pronunciation and meaning. To create this bond between a word's written appearance and its pronunciation and meaning, it is essential that students have many opportunities to encounter the word in print. It is also important that students process the whole word rather than simply look at the initial consonant and guess what the rest of the word is. By processing the whole word, students are creating a stronger, clearer bond between the word and its pronunciation. However, the rate at which individuals create these bonds may vary. Research suggests that there is a processing ability that determines the rate

Spelling and reading experts have chosen different terms to refer to similar stages. The alphabetic stage is the same as the letter name stage. The consolidated alphabetic stage is the same as the within-word-pattern stage.

Because they begin to notice patterns and don't have to process a word letter by letter, students' reading speed and oral fluency begin to improve at this point.

### USING TECHNOLOGY

A talking word processing program such as *Write Out Loud* (Don Johnston) can be used to help children develop phonics. As students type in a word, it is pronounced for them. This kind of program encourages them to explore letter–sound relationships and the sounds of words.

When students miss a word here or there, teachers may get the impression that they do not know their phonics and so may review phonics from the beginning. Students become bored when taught skills they already know. Observe students as they read or give them a test, such as the Word Pattern Survey presented in Appendix B, and see what they know and where they might need help.

"Though the logic and structures of the ortho-graphic systems may be most efficiently built layer by layer, bottom up, from simple to complex, they are useful only as connected at every step to the child's top-down knowledge of lan-guage and meaning" (Adams, 2001, p. 75).

Insufficient familiarity with the spellings and spelling-to-sound corre-spondences of frequent words and syllables may be the single most common source of reading difficul-ties (Stahl, Osborne, & Lehr, 1990).

One major improvement in today's basal reading sys-tems is that the selections carefully reinforce the phonics elements that have been taught. If you have a pre-2000 series, this may not be true.

When infrequent spellings are included, there are more than 300 spellings of the forty-plus sounds of English. Many of these infrequent spellings occur in words borrowed from other languages, as in the long *a* spelling of *exposé* and *beret*.

at which these associations are formed (Torgeson et al., 1997). This means that some students will need more practice than others, and, in some instances, special help.

Having a firmer command of basic phonics skills, students in this stage begin to incorporate top-down strategies. They begin to rely more on "knowl-edge of language, of ideas, and of facts to anticipate meanings as well as new words" (Chall, 1996, p. 47). Students begin using an integrated approach. Their decod-ing also becomes fluent and virtually automatic so that they can devote full at-tention to comprehension.

In the beginning of this stage, students begin using final *e* and double letters to represent long-vowel sounds but may do so incorrectly. By the end of this stage, their spelling has become conventional.

### ■ Implications of Stage Theory

This theory of the stages of reading has two very important implications for the teaching of reading. First, it suggests that nearly all the words we acquire are learned through phonics. Therefore, words to be learned (except for a few highly irregular ones, such as *of* or *one*, and perhaps a few learned in the very beginning) should be taught through a phonics approach rather than through an approach based on vi-sual memory. Most words that have been classified as having irregular spellings are at least partly predictable. For instance, the first and last letters of *was* are reg-ular, as are the first and last letters of *been*. In fact, except for *of*, it is hard to find any word that does not have some degree of spelling–sound predictability. In teaching words, take advantage of that regularity. It will make the words easier to learn and to recognize. And establishing links between letters and sounds helps fix words in memory so that they are eventually recognized instantaneously, or at sight.

The stage theory also implies that instruction should be geared to the stage that a student is in. Students lacking in phonemic awareness may have difficulty with letter–sound instruction unless it incorporates practice with phonemic aware-ness. Whereas using picture clues and memorizing predictable stories is appropri-ate for building emergent literacy, students in the alphabetical stage should be focusing on letters and sounds. This helps foster their decoding ability. Moreover, a student in the alphabetic stage is not ready for the final-*e* pattern as in *pipe* and *late*.

## BASIC PRINCIPLES OF PHONICS INSTRUCTION

Phonics instruction is of no value unless it fulfills some specific conditions. First, it must teach skills necessary for decoding words. Being able to read the short *a* in *hat* is an important skill, but knowing whether the *a* is long or short is not impor-tant; students can guess that the *a* is short without being able to read the word. Noting so-called silent letters is another useless skill. Knowing that the *k* in *knight* is silent does not ensure that a student can read the word.

Second, the skill should be one that students do not already know. One second-grader who was reading a fourth-grade book was put through a second-grade phonics workbook to make sure she had the necessary skills. If students can read ma-terial on a third-grade level or above, they obviously have just about all the phon-ics skills they will ever need.

Finally, the skills being taught should be related to reading tasks in which students are currently engaged or will soon be engaged. For instance, the time to teach that *ee* = /ē/ in words such as *jeep* and *sheep* is when students are about to read a book like *Sheep in a Jeep* (Shaw, 1986). All too often, they are taught skills far in advance of the time they will use them, or well after the relevant selection has been read, with no opportunity to apply the skills within a reasonable amount of time. This is ineffective instruction. Research indicates that children do not use or internalize information unless the skills they have been taught are applicable in their day-to-day reading (Adams, 1990).

In summary, phonics instruction must be functional, useful, and contextual to be of value. It also should be planned, systematic, and explicit (Fielding-Barnsley, 1997; Foorman et al., 1998).

## PHONICS ELEMENTS

Before discussing how to teach phonics, it is important to know the content of phonics. Knowing the content, you are in a better position to decide how to teach phonics elements and in what order these elements might be taught.

The content of phonics is fairly substantial. Depending on the dialect, English has forty or more sounds; however, many of them, especially vowels, may be spelled in more than one way. As a result, children have to learn more than one hundred spellings. The number would be even greater if relatively infrequent spellings were included, such as the *eigh* spelling of /ā/ in *neighbor* or the *o* spelling of /i/ in *women*.

### Consonants

There are twenty-five consonant sounds in English (see Table 4.1). Some of the sounds are spelled with two letters (*ch*urch and *sh*ip) and are known as **digraphs,** but these two letters represent just one sound. The most frequently occurring digraphs are *sh* (*sh*op), *ch* (*ch*ild), -*ng* (si*ng*), *wh* (*wh*ip), *th* (*th*umb), and *th* (*th*at). Common digraphs are listed in Table 4.2.

Some groups of consonants represent two or even three sounds (*st*op, *str*ike). These are known as **clusters** or blends and are listed in Table 4.3. Most clusters are composed of *l*, *r*, or *s* and another consonant or two. Because they are composed of two or more sounds, clusters pose special problems for students. Novice readers have a difficult time discriminating separate sounds in a cluster and often decode just the first sound, the /s/ in /st/, for example.

### Vowels

English has about sixteen vowel sounds. (The number varies somewhat because some dialects have more than others.) Each vowel sound has a variety of spellings. For example, /ā/, which is commonly referred to as long *a*, is usually spelled *a-e*, as in *late*; *a* at the end of a syllable, as in *favor*; or *ai* or *ay*, as in *train* and *tray*. We can say then that the vowel sound /ā/ has four main spellings, two of which are

Although there are forty sounds in English, there are only twenty-six letters. This explains some of the variability in the spelling system.

Go back to Table 3.2 to review the formation of consonant sounds.

■ If you look at the consonant chart in Table 4.1, you will notice that some of the sounds are spelled with two letters. The sound /f/ is usually spelled with *f* as in *fox* but may also be spelled with *ph* or *gh*, as in *photograph*. When two letters are used to spell a single sound, these double letters are known as **digraphs** (*di*, "two"; *graphs*, "written symbols").

■ A **cluster** is composed of two or more letters that represent two or more sounds, such as the *br* in *broom*. Clusters are sometimes called "blends." Because it is difficult to hear the separate sounds in a cluster, this element poses a special difficulty for many students.

How many words can you make by adding vowel letters to the word frame b__t? Here is a list of the 16 English vowels plus 5 *r*-vowels, most of which can be spelled with the b__t frame: *bat, bet, bit, bottle, but, bait, beat, bite, boat, Butte, bought, boot, book, bout, boil, between, Bart, Bert, beard, board, tired.*

**TABLE 4.1** Consonant spellings

| Sound | Initial | Final | Model Word |
|-------|---------|-------|------------|
| /b/ | *b*arn | ca*b*, ro*b*e | ball |
| /d/ | *d*eer | ba*d* | dog |
| /f/ | *f*un, *ph*oto | lau*gh* | fish |
| /g/ | *g*ate, *gh*ost, *gu*ide | ra*g* | goat |
| /h/ | *h*ouse, *wh*o | | hat |
| /hw/ | *wh*ale | | whale |
| /j/ | *j*ug, *g*ym, sol*di*er | a*ge*, ju*dge* | jar |
| /k/ | *c*an, *k*ite, qui*ck*, *ch*aos | ba*ck*, a*ch*e | cat, key |
| /l/ | *l*ion | mai*l* | leaf |
| /m/ | *m*e | hi*m*, co*mb*, autu*mn* | man |
| /n/ | *n*ow, *kn*ow, *gn*u, *pn*eumonia | pa*n* | nail |
| /p/ | *p*ot | to*p* | pen |
| /r/ | *r*ide, *wr*ite | | ring |
| /s/ | *s*ight, *c*ity | bu*s*, mi*ss*, fa*ce* | sun |
| /t/ | *t*ime | ra*t*, jump*ed* | table |
| /v/ | *v*ase | lo*v*e | vest |
| /w/ | *w*e, *wh*eel | | wagon |
| /y/ | *y*acht, on*i*on | | yo-yo |
| /z/ | *z*ipper | ha*s*, bu*zz* | zebra |
| /ch/ | *ch*ip, *c*ello, ques*ti*on | ma*tch* | chair |
| /sh/ | *sh*ip, *s*ure, *ch*ef, ac*ti*on | pu*sh*, spe*ci*al, mi*ssi*on | sheep |
| /th/ | *th*in | brea*th* | thumb |
| /<u>th</u>/ | *<u>th</u>*is | brea*<u>th</u>e* | the |
| /zh/ | a*z*ure, ver*si*on | bei*ge*, gara*ge* | garage |
| /ŋ/ | | si*ng* | ring |

**TABLE 4.2** Common consonant digraphs

| Correspondence | Examples | Correspondence | Examples |
|----------------|----------|----------------|----------|
| *ch* = /ch/ | chair, church | *sh* = /sh/ | shoe, shop |
| *ck* = /k/ | tack, pick | *(s)si* = /sh/ | mission |
| *gh* = /f/ | rough, tough | *th* = /<u>th</u>/ | there, them |
| *kn* = /n/ | knot, knob | *th* = /th/ | thumb, thunder |
| *ng* = /ŋ/ | thing, sing | *ti* = /sh/ | station, action |
| *ph* = /f/ | phone, photograph | *wh* = /w/ | wheel, where |
| *sc* = /s/ | scissors, scientist | *wr* = /r/ | wrench, wrestle |

Go back to Table 3.3 to review the formation of vowel sounds.

**TABLE 4.3** Common consonant clusters

| Initial Clusters | | | | | | | |
|---|---|---|---|---|---|---|---|
| **With *l*** | **Example Words** | **With *r*** | **Example Words** | **With *s*** | **Example Words** | **Other** | **Example Words** |
| *bl* | blanket, black | *br* | broom, bread | *sc* | score, scale | *tw* | twelve, twin |
| *cl* | clock, clothes | *cr* | crow, crash | *sch* | school, schedule | *qu* | queen, quick |
| *fl* | flag, fly | *dr* | dress, drink | *scr* | scream, scrub | | |
| *gl* | glove, glue | *fr* | frog, from | *sk* | sky, skin | | |
| *pl* | plum, place | *gr* | green, ground | *sl* | sled, sleep | | |
| *sl* | slide, slow | *pr* | prince, prepare | *sm* | smoke, smile | | |
| | | | | *sn* | snake, sneakers | | |
| | | | | *sp* | spider, spot | | |
| | | | | *st* | star, stop | | |
| | | | | *sw* | sweater, swim | | |

| Final Clusters | | | | | |
|---|---|---|---|---|---|
| **With *l*** | **Example Words** | **With *n*** | **Example Words** | **Other** | **Example Words** |
| *ld* | field, old | *nce* | prince, chance | *ct* | fact, effect |
| *lf* | wolf, self | *nch* | lunch, bunch | *mp* | jump, camp |
| *lk* | milk, silk | *nd* | hand, wind | *sp* | wasp, grasp |
| *lm* | film | *nk* | tank, wink | *st* | nest, best |
| *lp* | help | *nt* | tent, sent | | |
| *lt* | salt, belt | | | | |
| *lve* | twelve, solve | | | | |

closely related: *ay* appears in final position, and *ai* is found in initial and medial positions; so these two spellings work together.

All the other vowel sounds are similar to /ā/ in having two to four major spellings. Considering correspondences in this way makes vowel spellings seem fairly regular. It is true that /ā/ and other vowel sounds can each be spelled in a dozen or more ways, but many of these spellings are oddities. For instance, the *Random House Dictionary* (Flexner & Hauck, 1994) lists nineteen spellings of /ā/: *ate, Gael, champagne, rain, arraign, gaol, gauge, ray, exposé, suede, steak, matinee, eh, veil, feign, Marseilles, demesne, beret,* and *obey.* Many of these are in words borrowed from other languages.

A chart of vowels and their major spellings is presented in Table 4.4. Note that the chart lists twenty-one vowel sounds and includes *r* vowels, which are combinations of *r* and a vowel so, technically, are not distinct vowels.

## Onsets and Rimes

The **onset** is the consonant or consonant cluster preceding the rime: *b-, st-, scr-*. The **rime** is the pattern's vowel and any consonants that follow it: *-at, -op, -een*. Rimes,

■ **Short vowels** are the vowel sounds heard in *cat, pet, sit, hot,* and *cut*.

■ **Long vowels** are the vowel sounds heard in *cake, sleep, pie, boat,* and *use*.

■ The **onset** is the initial part of a word, the part that precedes a vowel. The onset could be a single consonant (*c+at*), a digraph (*sh+eep*), or a cluster (*tr+ip*). A word that begins with a vowel, such as *owl* or *and,* does not have an onset.

■ The **rime** is the part of a word that rhymes and refers to the *ook* in *look* or the *ow* in *cow*.

| TABLE 4.4 | Vowel spellings | | |
|---|---|---|---|
| | **Vowel Sound** | **Major Spellings** | **Model Word** |
| Short Vowels | /a/ | rag, happen, have | cat |
| | /e/ | get, letter, thread | bed |
| | /i/ | wig, middle, event | fish |
| | /o/ | fox, problem, father | mop |
| | /u/ | bus | cup |
| Long Vowels | /ā/ | name, favor, say, sail | rake |
| | /ē/ | he, even, eat, seed, bean, key, these, either, funny, serious | wheel |
| | /ī/ | hide, tiny, high, lie, sky | nine |
| | /ō/ | vote, open, coat, bowl, old, though | nose |
| | /ū/ | use, human | cube |
| Other Vowels | /aw/ | daughter, law, walk, off, bought | saw |
| | /oi/ | noise, toy | boy |
| | /o͝o/ | wood, should, push | foot |
| | /o͞o/ | soon, new, prove, group, two, fruit, truth | school |
| | /ow/ | tower, south | cow |
| | /ə/ | above, operation, similar, opinion, suppose | banana |
| r Vowels | /ar/ | far, large, heart | car |
| | /air/ | hair, care, where, stair, bear | chair |
| | /i(ə)r/ | dear, steer, here | deer |
| | /ər/ | her, sir, fur, earth | bird |
| | /or/ | horse, door, tour, more | four |

▌Although onsets and rimes seem to be natural units of language, some students may have to process individual sounds before being able to group them into rimes. They may need to learn a = /a/ and t = /t/ before learning the -at rime.

which are also known as phonograms and word families, are highly predictable. When considered by itself, *a* can represent several sounds. However, when followed by a consonant, it is almost always short (*-at, -an, -am*). A list of common rimes is contained in Table 4.5.

## APPROACHES TO TEACHING PHONICS

■ The **analytic approach** involves studying sounds within the context of the whole word so that /w/ is referred to as the "sound heard at the beginning of *wagon.*"

■ The term **synthetic phonics** refers to saying a word sound by sound and then synthesizing the sounds into words.

There are two main approaches to teaching phonics: **analytic** and **synthetic.** In the analytic approach, which is also known as implicit phonics, consonants are generally not isolated but are taught within the context of a whole word. For example, the sound /b/ would be referred to as the one heard in the beginning of *ball* and *boy.* The sound /b/ is not pronounced in isolation because that would distort it to "buh." Although somewhat roundabout, the analytic approach does not distort the sound /b/.

In the synthetic approach, which is sometimes called explicit phonics, words are decoded sound by sound, and both consonant and vowel sounds are pronounced

| TABLE 4.5 | Common rimes | |
|---|---|---|
| | **Vowel Sound** | **Rimes** |
| Short Vowels | /a/ | -ab, -ack, -ad, -ag, -am, -amp, -an, -and, -ang, -ank, -ant, -ap, -ash, -ask, -ast, -at, -atch |
| | /e/ | -ead, -eck, -ed, -ell, -elt, -en, -end, -ent, -ess, -est, -et |
| | /i/ | -ick, -id, -ig, -ill, -im, -in, -ing, -ink, -ip, -ish, -iss, -it |
| | /o/ | -ob, -ock, -od, -og, -op, -ot |
| | /u/ | -ub, -uck, -ud, -udge, -uff, -ug, -um, -ump, -un, -unch, -ung, -unk, -us, -ust, -ut |
| Long Vowels | /ā/ | -ace, -ade, -age, -ake, -ale, -ame, -ane, -ape, -ate, -aid, -ail, -ain, -aste, -ate, -ave, -ay |
| | /ē/ | -e, -ea, -each, -ead, -eak, -eal, -eam, -ean, -ee, -eep, -eet |
| | /ī/ | -ice, -ide, -ie, -ife, -ike, -ile, -ime, -ind, -ine, -ipe, -ite, -ive, -y |
| | /ō/ | -o, -oe, -oke, -old, -ole, -oll, -one, -ope, -ow, -own |
| | /ū/ | -ute |
| Other Vowels | /aw/ | -alk, -all, -aught, -aw, -awl, -awn, -ong, -ought |
| | /oi/ | -oil, -oy |
| | /o͝o/ | -ood, -ook, -ould |
| | /o͞o/ | -ew, -oo, -ool, -oom, -oon, -oot, -ue, -oup |
| | /ow/ | -ouch, -ound, -our, -ouse, -out, -ow, -owl, -own |
| r Vowels | /air/ | -air, -are, -ear |
| | /ar/ | -ar, -ard, -ark, -art |
| | /ər/ | -ir, -ird, -irt, -urt |
| | /e(ə)r/ | -ear, -eer |
| | /i(ə)r/ | -ire |
| | /or/ | -oar, -ore, -ort, -orn |

Note: Rimes containing few examples have been omitted. Because of dialect variation, some rimes (*-og*, for instance) may have more than one pronunciation. Depending upon onset, some rimes will vary in pronunciation: *mash* vs. *wash,* for example.

in isolation. A child decoding *cat* would say, "Kuh-ah-tuh." This approach is very direct, but it distorts consonant sounds, which cannot be pronounced accurately without a vowel. However, Ehri (1991) maintained that artificial procedures, such as saying the sound represented by each letter in a word, may be necessary to help beginning readers decipher words.

For most of the twentieth century, the major basals advocated an analytic approach in which letter sounds were never isolated and there was heavy reliance on the use of the initial consonant of a word and context. Selections were chosen on the basis of topic or literary quality, so they didn't reinforce the phonics elements that had been taught. Today, all of the basals use a systematic approach to phonics in which students are taught to say individual sounds and blend them. However, this book recommends a combination of the analytic and synthetic approaches. Novice readers need to have the target sound highlighted by hearing it in isolation, which is what the synthetic approach does. And they need to hear it in the context of a real word, which is what the analytic approach does.

Phonics instruction can also be part to whole or whole to part. In a whole-to-part approach, students listen to or share-read a selection. From the selection, the teacher draws the element to be presented. After share-reading "Star Light, Star Bright," the teacher might lead students to see that *bright, might,* and *light* contain the *ight* pattern. After discussing the pattern, students then read a selection such as *Sleepy Dog* (Ziefert, 1984) that contains the element. In a part-to-whole approach, the teacher presents the *ight* pattern in preparation for reading *Sleepy Dog.* Both approaches prepare students for an upcoming selection. However, the whole-to-part approach also helps students to relate the element to a familiar selection and words that they have seen in print (Moustafa & Maldonado-Colon, 1999).

## Teaching Initial Consonants

A somewhat easier approach to teaching initial consonants, speech-to-print phonics, was described in Chapter 3. See Building Literacy for more extensive examples of speech-to-print phonics: http://www. thomasgunning.org.

Phonics instruction typically begins with initial consonants. Being the first sound in a word, initial consonants are easier to hear. Initial consonants are typically the first element to appear in children's invented spelling. Students may pick up some knowledge of initial consonants through shared reading and through writing activities, but letter–sound relationships should also be taught explicitly to make sure that students have learned these important elements, to clarify any misconceptions that may have arisen, and to provide additional reinforcement. A phonics lesson starts with phonemic awareness to make sure students can perceive the sound of the element and proceeds to the visual level, where the children integrate sound and letter knowledge. A six-step lesson for teaching initial consonants is detailed in Lesson 4.1. It assumes that the students can segment a word into its separate sounds, have a concept of beginning sounds, and realize that sounds are represented by letters. These are skills that were explained in Chapter 3. The lesson is synthetic and analytic, so the consonant sound is presented both in isolation and in the context of a whole word. If possible, relate your instruction to a story, song, or rhyme or to an experience story that you have share-read. This whole-to-part approach helps students relate the phonics they are learning to real reading (Moustafa & Maldonado-Colon, 1999).

Although consonant sounds spoken in isolation are distorted, some youngsters do better when the target sound is presented explicitly.

If students are having difficulty perceiving initial *m,* ask questions that help them focus on the beginning sound. Pointing to a picture of the moon, ask, "Is this an 'oon'? No? What is it? What sound did I leave off?" Use this same procedure with other *m* words: *monkey, man, marker, milk.*

If students struggle with this approach to teaching initial consonants, try the speech-to-print approach on pp. 137–139.

**Analytic-synthetic introduction of initial consonant correspondence**

### Step 1. Phonemic awareness

Teach the letter–sound relationship in the initial position of words. In teaching the correspondence (letter–sound relationship) *m* = /m/, read a story such as *Papa, Please Get the Moon for Me* (Carle, 1987) that contains a number of *m* words. Call students' attention to the *m* words from the book: *moon, me, man.* Explain how the lips are pressed together to form /m/. Stressing the initial sound as you say each word, ask students to tell what is the same about the words: "mmmoon," "mmme," and "mmman." Lead students to see that all the words begin in the same way. Ask them to supply other words that begin like *moon*, *me*, and *man*. Give hints, if necessary—an animal that can climb trees (monkey), something that we drink (milk).

### Step 2. Letter–sound integration

Write the *m* words on the board, and ask what is the same about the way *moon*, *me*, and *man* are written. Lead students to see that the words all begin with the letter *m* and that the letter *m* stands for the sound /m/ heard at the beginning of *moon*. At this point, *moon* becomes a model word. This is a simple word that can be depicted and that contains the target letter and sound. When referring to the sound represented by *m*, say that it is /m/, the sound heard at the beginning of *moon*, so that students can hear the sound both in isolation and in the context of a word. You might ask if there is anyone in the class whose name begins like /m/ in *moon*. List the names of students whose names begin like /m/ in *moon*. Explain to students why you are using a capital letter for the names.

### Step 3. Guided practice

Provide immediate practice. Help students read food labels that contain /m/ words: *milk, mayonnaise, margarine, mustard, marshmallows*. Read a story together about monkeys or masks, or sing a song or read a rhyme that has a generous share of /m/ words. Try to choose some items in which students integrate knowledge of the correspondence with context. Compose sentences such as "I will drink a glass of milk" and "At the zoo we saw a monkey," and write them on the chalkboard. Read each sentence, stopping at the word beginning with /m/. Have students use context and their knowledge of the correspondence *m* = /m/ to predict the word.

### Step 4. Application

As share reading or on their own, have students read selections that contain /m/ words. Students might read the *m* pages in alphabet books.

### Step 5. Writing and spelling

If necessary, review the formation of the letter *m*. Dictate some easy *m* words (*me, man*) and have students spell them as best they can. Encourage students to use the letter *m* in their writing.

### Step 6. Assessment and reteaching

Note whether students are able to read at least the initial consonant of *m* words and are using *m* in their writing. Review and reteach as necessary. Throughout the school day, call attention to initial consonants that have been recently taught. As you prepare to write the word *Monday*, for instance, ask students to tell what sound *Monday* begins with and what letter makes that sound. Also label items in your class that begin with the letter *m*: *mirror, magnets*.

Continuants like /m/, /f/, and /s/ are less distorted because they are articulated with a continuous stream of breath.

Using context to verify decoding is known as cross-checking. The student checks to see whether the decoded word makes sense in the selection.

### ■ Using Children's Books to Reinforce Initial Consonants

A good children's book can be a powerful medium for presenting or providing practice with phonics. A book such as *Easy as Pie* (Folsom & Folsom, 1986) is excellent for integrating knowledge of initial consonants and context (see Figure 4.1). Common similes, except for the last word, are shown on the right-hand page, as is the letter of the missing word. The answer appears when the child turns the page. For instance, the *S* page contains the letter *S* and the words "Deep as the." Read the first part of the simile aloud, and tell the students that the last word begins with the letter *s*. Ask students to guess what they think the word is. Remind them that the word must begin with /s/, the sound heard at the beginning of *sun*. Write their responses on the board. If any word supplied does not begin with /s/, discuss why this could not be the right answer. Turn the page to uncover the word that completes the riddle, and let students read the answer. Discuss why the an-

**FIGURE 4.1**

***S* Pages from *Easy as Pie***

Deep as the    Sea

From *Easy as Pie* by Marcia Folsom and Michael Folsom, 1986, Boston: Houghton Mifflin. Copyright © 1986 by Marcia Folsom and Michael Folsom. Reprinted by permission of Marcia Folsom.

swer is correct. Emphasize that it makes sense in the phrase and begins with /s/, the same sound heard at the beginning of *sun*.

Another book that combines context and knowledge of beginning consonant correspondences is *The Alphabet Tale*, by Jan Garten (1964) (see Figure 4.2). Shown on the *S* page is a large red *S*, a seal's tail, and a riddle:

**FIGURE 4.2**

*S* **Pages from *The Alphabet Tale***

From *The Alphabet Tale* by J. Garten (1964). New York: Random House. © 1964 by Jan Garten and Muriel Batherman. Reprinted by permission of Jan Garten and Muriel Batherman.

His home is the Artic
Raw fish is his meal.
This is the tale of a whiskered . . .

The next page shows the rest of the seal and the word *Seal.* Listed in the Children's Reading List are some more titles that may be used to reinforce initial consonants.

## CHILDREN'S READING LIST — Recommended books for reinforcing initial consonants

Amery, H. (1997). *Usborne farmyard tales, alphabet book.* London: Usborne. Reinforces the target letter with an alliterative sentence and question.

Calmenson, S. (1993). *It begins with an A.* New York: Hyperion. Rhyming riddles challenge the reader to guess objects whose names begin with letters *A* to *Z.*

Cohen, N. (1993). *From apple to zipper.* New York: Macmillan. Rhyming text, with illustrations that form the letters they represent.

Ellwand, D. (1996). *Emma's elephant & other favorite animal friends.* New York: Dutton. In black-and-white photos and brief alliterative captions, children with animals are depicted.

Hindley, J. *Crazy ABC.* (1994). Cambridge, MA: Candlewick. Target letters are reinforced with zany alliterative sentences.

Hofbauer, M. (1993). *All the letters.* Bridgeport, CT: Greene Barke Press. Each letter is accompanied by an alliterative story.

Jonas, A. (1997). *Watch William walk.* New York: Greenwillow. The story of William walking with Wally and Wanda on the beach is told in drawings and words that begin only with *W.*

Joyce, S. (1999). *ABC animal riddles.* Columbus, NC: Peel Productions. Readers are asked to guess the identity of animals based on verbal and picture clues.

Laidlaw, K. (1996). *The amazing I spy ABC.* New York: Dial. Readers spy objects whose names begin with the target letter.

Moxley, S. (2001). *ABCD: An alphabet book of cats and dogs.* Boston: Little, Brown. Alliterative tale accompanies each letter.

---

When using alphabet books, be on the lookout for confusing presentations. In one book, the words *tiger, thin,* and *the* are used to demonstrate the sound usually represented by the letter *t.* However, *th* in *thin* represents a different sound than that heard at the beginning of *tiger,* and *th* in *the* represents the voiced counterpart of *th* in *thin.*

**ADAPTING INSTRUCTION for *ENGLISH LANGUAGE LEARNERS***

Before teaching elements that are not present in Spanish—*sh,* for instance—make sure that these elements have been introduced in the ESL class. For easily confused auditory items—*sh* and *ch,* for example—provide added auditory-discrimination exercises in which students tell whether pairs of easily confused words such as *choose-shoes, shine-shine* are the same or different. Also, use the items in sentence context or use real objects or pictures to illustrate them. When discussing *sheep,* for example, hold up a picture of sheep.

After an alphabet or other book has been discussed, place it in the class library so that students may "read" it. Encourage children to check out books for home use.

Be sure to make use of students' emerging knowledge of letter–sound relationships when reading big books. After reading Paul Galdone's (1975) *The Gingerbread Boy,* for instance, turn to the page on which the gingerbread boy meets the cow. Read the words *cow, can,* and *catch.* Discuss how the words sound alike and begin with the letter *c.* Encourage the use of context. Reread the story, stopping when you come to a word that begins with *c.* Encourage students to read the word. Using *cow* as a key word, remind students that the word should begin with /k/ as in *cow*. Also remind them of the context of the sentence to help them learn to integrate letter–sound relationships with context. To further reinforce the *c* = /k/ correspondence, have students draw a picture of something they can do and write a short piece about it. Individual stories could be the basis for a group story or booklet that tells about the talents and abilities of all class members.

### ■ Sorting

One activity that is especially useful in deepening students' understanding about phonics elements is sorting (Bear, 1995). Sorting forces children to analyze the elements in a word or picture and select critical features as they place the words or pictures in piles. Through sorting, students classify words and pictures on the basis of sound and spelling and construct an understanding of the spelling system. They also enjoy this active, hands-on, nonthreatening activity.

Students should sort only elements and words that they know. This allows them to construct basic understandings of the spelling system. Although they may be able to read *cat*, *hat*, and *bat*, they may not realize that the words all rhyme or that they follow a CVC (consonant-vowel-consonant) pattern. Sorting helps them come to these understandings.

Students' sorting activities are determined by their stage of spelling development. Students in the early alphabetic stage may sort pictures and, later, words according to their beginning sounds. In the consolidated alphabetic stage, students sort words according to whether they have long or short vowels, have an *e* marker, or have a double-vowel pattern, and then according to the specific long-vowel or other vowel pattern they illustrate. Words can also be sorted according to initial digraphs or consonant clusters or any other element that students need to study.

Here is how students in the early alphabetic stage might be taught to sort initial consonant sounds. The lesson is adapted from Bear (1995).

> **ADAPTING INSTRUCTION**
> **for *ENGLISH LANGUAGE LEARNERS***
> Native speakers of Spanish may have difficulty perceiving /b/, /v/, /k/, /j/, /z/, /sh/, /th/, and /ch/. You may need to spend additional time with auditory discrimination.

### LESSON 4.2  Sorting beginning consonant sounds

#### Step 1. Set up the sort

Set up two columns. At the top of each column, place an illustration of the sound to be sorted. If you plan to have students sort /s/ and /r/ words, use an illustration of the sun and an illustration of a ring. A pocket chart works well for this activity.

#### Step 2. Explain sorting

Tell students that you will be giving them cards that have pictures on them. Explain that they will be placing the cards under the picture of the sun if the words begin with /s/, the sound heard at the beginning of *sun*, or under the picture of the ring if the words begin with /r/, the sound heard at the beginning of *ring*.

> Some consonant letters pose special problems. One of these letters is *x*, which is a reverse digraph, except when it represents /z/, as in *xylophone*. It may represent either /ks/, as in *tax*, or /gz/, as in *example*.

### Step 3. Model the sorting procedure

Shuffle the cards. Tell the students, "Say the name of the picture. Listen carefully to see whether the name of the picture begins like /s/ as in *sun* or /r/ as in *ring*." Model the process with two or three cards: "This is a picture of a saw. *Saw* has a /s/ sound and begins like *sun*, so I will put it under *sun*. *Sun* and *saw* both begin with /s/."

### Step 4. Children sort the cards

Distribute the cards. Have the students take turns placing a card in the /s/ or /r/ column. When students place their cards, have them say the picture's name and the sound it begins with. Correct errors quickly and simply. For instance, if a student puts a picture of a rat in the /s/ column, say, "*Rat* begins with /r/ and goes under *ring*," or ask why *rat* was put there and discuss its correct placement. A sample sort can be found in Figure 4.3. Have students sort cards a second and third time to solidify their perception of beginning sounds.

### Step 5. Application

Have students find objects or pictures of objects whose names begin with /s/ or /r/. Proceed to other initial consonants, or sort known words that begin with /s/ or /r/.

Students might conduct sorts in pairs or small groups. A simple way to sort is to place a target word or illustration in the center of a table and then distribute cards, some of which contain the target element. Have students read or name the target element, and then have them take turns placing cards containing the target element. As students place cards, they should read the words or name the illustrations on

*Sorting is a powerful technique for helping students make discoveries about words.*

FIGURE 4.3

**A Sample Sort**

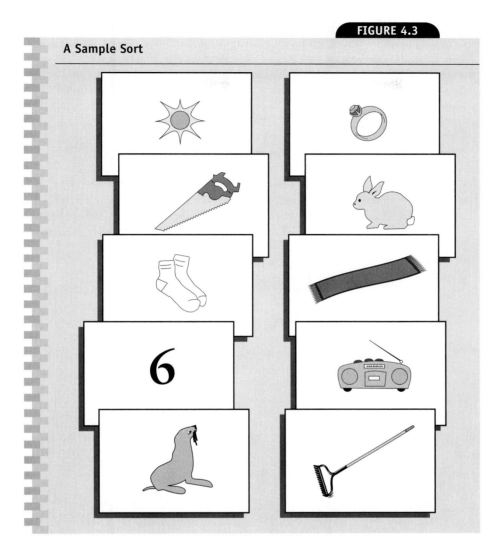

them (Temple, Nathan, Temple, & Burris, 1993). For illustrations that can be used for sorting, go to the Webbing into Literacy Web site. Although WIL was designed for preschool students, the illustrations and word cards can be used with any age student.

Sorts can be open or closed. In a closed sort, the teacher provides the basis for sorting the cards, as in Lesson 4.2. In an open sort, students decide the basis for sorting the cards.

Sometimes students sort words visually. For example, after one *at* word has been sorted, they simply put all the other *at* words under it without actually thinking about the sound that the words have in common. To overcome this practice, use a blind sort. Draw a word from the pile to be sorted and say it without showing it to the students. Then have them tell in which column it should be placed. After putting the word in the correct column, have a volunteer read it. For instance, picking up the word *rat*, you read it without showing it to students and they tell you whether it goes in the *cat*, *ran*, or *dad* column. A volunteer then reads all the words in that column (Johnston, 1999).

### REINFORCEMENT ACTIVITIES    Consonant letter–sound relationships

■ Have students encounter initial consonants they know in books.

■ Creating experience stories also affords students the opportunity to meet phonics elements in print. While reading the story with an individual or group, the teacher can call attention to any consonants that have already been introduced. The teacher might pause before a word that begins with a known consonant and have a student attempt to read it.

■ Play the game Going to Paris (Brewster, 1952). Players recite this:

I'm going to Paris.

I'm going to pack my bag with _____ .

The first player says an object whose name begins with the first letter of the alphabet. Subsequent players then say the names of all the objects mentioned by previous players and identify an object whose name begins with the next letter of the alphabet.

■ Play the game Alphabet It. In this counting-out game, one child recites the letters of the alphabet. As the child says each letter, she or he points to the other members of the class whose names begin with the letter being recited. Each child pointed to removes himself or herself from the game. The alphabet is recited until just one child is left. That child is "it" for the next round or next game.

■ Use software that helps students discover letter–sound relationships, for instance, *Dr. Peet's Talk/Writer* (Interest-Driven Learning) or *Write Out Loud* (Don Johnston). These word processing programs will say words that have been typed in. You might give students a list of three words that begin with *s* to type in and have them listen to hear what sound the letter *s* makes. However, it is not necessary to give students assignments. Just introduce them to the talking word processing program and let nature take its course. As they explore the program, they will make valuable discoveries about letter–sound relationships. Each program can also be used as a kind of sound dictionary. When students want to find out what a word says, all they have to do is type it in and the speech synthesizer will say it. A small number of words are distorted by the synthesizer, so students may have to make some minor adjustments in pronunciation. If the word does not make sense, even after adjustments, the student should ask for a teacher's help. *Dr.*

The first word that most children learn is their name. To take advantage of this natural learning, create a chart of children's first names. When studying words that begin with a certain sound, refer to names on the chart that also begin with that sound. Attach photos of the students to the chart so that students may learn to associate printed names and faces.

*Peet's Talk/Writer* also has an ABC Discovery module that introduces the alphabet.

- Use CD-ROM software such as *Letter Sounds* (Sunburst). The student matches, sorts, and manipulates consonants and composes tongue-twisters and songs based on initial sounds. *Curious George ABC Adventure* (Sunburst) reinforces letter names and letter sounds.

- As a review of initial consonant spelling–sound relationships, read the following jump-rope chant with students. Help students extend the chant through all the letters of the alphabet. Adapt the chant for boys by substituting *wife's* for *husband's*.

> A—my name is Alice,
> My husband's name is Andy,
> We live in Alabama,
> And we sell apples.

- Traditional rhymes can also be used to reinforce initial consonant sounds. Do a shared reading of the rhyme first. Stress the target consonant letter–sound correspondence as you read the selection. During subsequent shared readings of the selection, encourage the class to read the words beginning with the target letter.

> Deedle, deedle, dumpling, my son John,
> Went to bed with his stockings on;
> One shoe off, and one shoe on,
> Deedle, deedle, dumpling, my son John.

> Have students create their own alphabet books. After a letter–sound relationship has been presented, direct students to create a page showing the upper- and lowercase forms of the letter along with a key word and an illustration of the word. As students learn to read words beginning with the letter and sound, they may add them to the page.

> A good source of jump-rope chants and other rhymes is *A Rocket in My Pocket* (Withers, 1948), which is still available in paperback.

> For additional sources for rhymes, see Building Literacy: www.thomasgunning.org

## Teaching Final Consonants

Final consonants are handled in much the same way as initial consonants. Relate them to their initial counterparts. And do not neglect them. According to a classic research study by Gibson, Osser, and Pick (1963), final consonants are a significant aid in the decoding of printed words. You might teach final consonants as you teach the word patterns that use them. For instance, teach final /t/ before or as you are teaching the -*at* pattern and final /m/ before or as you are teaching the -*am* pattern. Be sure to develop phonemic awareness of final consonants. Use activities suggested in the lesson for initial consonants.

## Teaching Consonant Clusters

Clusters are more difficult to decode than single-consonant correspondences or digraph correspondences. Students who know all the single-consonant and digraph correspondences may still have difficulty with clusters (Gunning, 2002). Clusters, therefore, must be taught with care and with much reinforcement. You cannot assume that because a child knows *d* = /d/ and *r* = /r/, she will be able to

> When students misread a cluster—reading "fog" for *frog,* for instance—you might ask questions that lead them to see that they need to process two initial sounds rather than just one: What letter does the word *fog* begin with? What two letters does the word in the sentence begin with? What sound does *f* stand for? What sound does *r* stand for? What sounds do *f* and *r* make when said together? How would you say the word in the story?

handle *dr* = /dr/. Such clusters need to be taught as new elements. Many of the same activities that are used to reinforce single-consonant correspondences can be used. However, when introducing consonant clusters, build on what students already know. For instance, when presenting the cluster *br*, review *b* = /b/ and *r* = /r/ and have students build clusters by adding initial *b* to known words beginning with *r*. Students read *ring*, *rush*, and *rake*. Then, using a word-building approach, ask students what you would have to add to *ring* to make the word *bring*, to *rush* to make the word *brush*, and to *rake* to make the word *brake*. Lead them to see that *bring*, *brush*, and *brake* all begin with two letters that cluster together to make two sounds /br/. Because the phonemes in clusters are difficult to perceive, stress the separate sounds in the clusters. Also, conduct sorting exercises in which students sort words beginning with *b* and words beginning with *br*. This helps them to discover for themselves the difference between *b* and *br*.

## Troublesome Correspondences

The most difficult consonant letters are *c* and *g*. Both regularly represent two sounds: The letter *c* stands for /k/ and /s/, as in *cake* and *city;* the letter *g* represents /g/ and /j/, as in *go* and *giant*. The letter *c* represents /k/ far more often than it stands for /s/ (Gunning, 1975), and this is the sound students usually attach to it (Venezky, 1965); the letter *g* more often represents /g/. In teaching the consonant letters *c* and *g*, the more frequent sounds (*c* = /k/, *g* = /g/) should be presented first. The other sound represented by each letter (*c* = /s/, *g* = /j/) should be taught sometime later. At that point, it would also be helpful to teach the following generalizations:

- The letter *g* usually stands for /j/ when followed by *e*, *i*, or *y*, as in *gem*, *giant*, or *gym*. (There are a number of exceptions: *geese*, *get*, *girl*, *give*.)
- The letter *c* usually stands for /k/ when it is followed by *a*, *o*, or *u*, as in *cab*, *cob*, or *cub*.
- The letter *c* usually stands for /s/ when followed by *e*, *i*, or *y*, as in *cereal*, *circle*, or *cycle*.
- The letter *g* usually stands for /g/ when followed by *a*, *o*, or *u*, as in *gave*, *go*, or *gum*.

The *g* generalizations help explain the *gu* spelling of /g/ as in *guide* and *guilt*. Without the *u* following the *g*, there would be a tendency to pronounce those words with the /j/ sound (Venezky, 1965). Determining the sound of *c* and *g* at the end of a word is relatively easy. If a word ends in *e*, *c* represents /s/ and *g* stands for /j/ (*lace*, *page*). The letter *e* serves as a marker to indicate that *c* and *g* have their soft sounds.

When teaching the *c* and *g* generalizations, do so inductively. For instance, list examples of the *c* spelling of /k/ in one column and of /s/ in another. Have students read each word in the first column and note the sound that *c* represents and the vowel letter that follows *c*. Do the same with the second column. Then help students draw up generalizations based on their observations. Better yet, have students sort *c* = /k/ and *c* = /s/ words and discover the generalization for themselves.

**Variability strategy.** An alternative to presenting the *c* and *g* generalizations is to teach students to be prepared to deal with the variability of the spelling of certain sounds. Students need to learn that, in English, letters can often stand for more than one sound. After learning the two sounds for *c* and *g*, students should be taught to use the following **variability strategy** when they are unsure how to read a word that begins with *c* or *g*.

 **Applying the variability strategy to consonant correspondences**

1. Try the main pronunciation—the one the letter usually stands for.
2. If the main pronunciation gives a word that is not a real one or does not make sense in the sentence, try the other pronunciation.
3. If you still get a word that is not a real word or does not make sense in the sentence, ask for help.

Just as you post a chart to remind students of correct letter formation, display a chart showing all the major consonant correspondences and a key word for each. Students experiencing difficulty sounding out a word can refer to the chart. A child feeling puzzled when he pronounces *cider* as "kider" could look at the chart and note that *c* has two pronunciations: /k/ as in *cat* and /s/ as in *circle*. Since the /k/ pronunciation did not produce a word that made sense, the child should try the /s/ pronunciation. Table 4.1 could be used as a basis for constructing a consonant chart; a sample of such a chart is shown in Figure 4.4. Drawings, photos, or pictures may be used to illustrate each of the sounds. As new correspondences are learned, they can be added to the chart. The chart can also be used as a spelling aid.

## Teaching Vowel Correspondences

Vowels are taught in the same way as consonants. The main difference is that vowels can be spoken in isolation without distortion, so teaching vowels synthetically should not be confusing to students. Lesson 4.3 outlines how short *a* might be taught.

 **Vowel correspondence**

### Step 1. Phonemic awareness

Read a selection, such as *Cat Traps* (Coxe, 1996) or *The Cat Sat on the Mat* (Cameron, 1994), in which there are a number of short *a* words. Call student's attention to *a* words from the book: *cat, trap, sat*. Stressing the vowel sound as you say each word, ask students to tell what is the same about the words: "caaat," "traaap," and "saaat." Lead students to see that they all have an /a/ sound as in *cat*.

▪ The **variability strategy** is a simpler procedure than the application of rules. Rather than trying to remember a rule, all the student has to do is try the major pronunciation, and, if that pronunciation does not work out, try another.

▌Students need to see that the aim of phonics is to help them construct meaning from print. If they use phonics to decipher a word but they end up with a nonword, they should try again. Even when they construct a real word, they should cross-check it by seeing if it makes sense in the sentence they are reading.

▌Vowels can be taught in isolation or as part of patterns. In this lesson, they are taught in isolation. Teaching vowels in isolation is helpful for students who are still learning to detect individual sounds in words.

**FIGURE 4.4**

## Beginning Consonant Chart

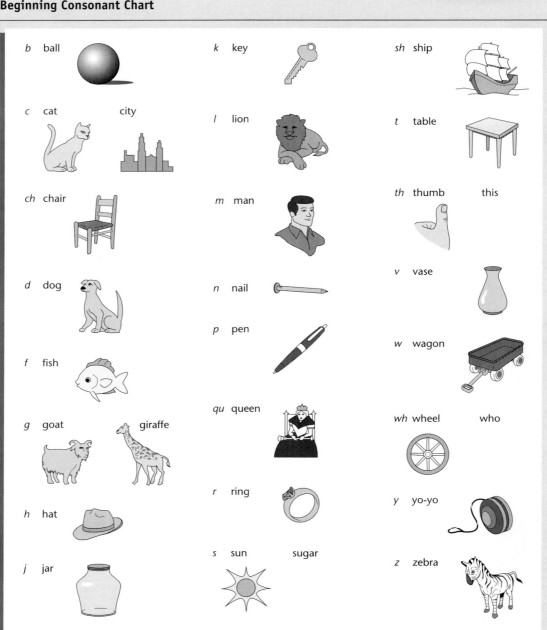

| | | | | | | | | |
|---|---|---|---|---|---|---|---|---|
| *b* | ball | | *k* | key | | *sh* | ship | |
| *c* | cat | city | *l* | lion | | *t* | table | |
| *ch* | chair | | *m* | man | | *th* | thumb | this |
| *d* | dog | | *n* | nail | | *v* | vase | |
| *f* | fish | | *p* | pen | | *w* | wagon | |
| *g* | goat | giraffe | *qu* | queen | | *wh* | wheel | who |
| *h* | hat | | *r* | ring | | *y* | yo-yo | |
| *j* | jar | | *s* | sun | sugar | *z* | zebra | |

**Step 2. Letter–sound integration**

Write the words *cat*, *trap*, and *sat* on the board, saying each word as you do so. Ask students whether they can see what is the same about the words. Show them that all three words have an *a*, which stands for the sound /a/ as pronounced in *cat*. Have students read the words. Discuss other words, such as *man*, *bag*, and *dad*, that have the sound /a/. Have students read the words chorally and individually.

**Step 3. Guided practice**

Share-read a story that contains a number of short *a* words. Pause before the short *a* words and invite students to read them. Also share-read songs, rhymes, announcements, and signs that contain short *a* words.

**Step 4. Application**

Have students read selections or create experience stories that contain short *a*.

**Step 5. Assessment and reteaching**

Note students' ability to read and write short *a* words. Review and extend the pattern.

> **ADAPTING INSTRUCTION for *STRUGGLING READERS and WRITERS***
> Struggling readers may have been through a number of programs and may have been taught a variety of decoding strategies, some of which may conflict with each other (Stahl, 1998). Focus on the teaching of a few strategies and meet with other professionals in the school to discuss and implement the use of a consistent set of strategies.

## Teaching the Word-Building Approach

One convenient, economical way of introducing vowels is in rimes or patterns: for example, *-at* in *hat*, *pat*, and *cat*, or *-et* in *bet*, *wet*, and *set*. Patterns can be presented in a number of ways. A word-building approach helps children note the onset and the rime in each word (Gunning, 1995). Students are presented with a rime and then add onsets to create words. Next, students are provided with onsets and add rimes. Because some students have difficulty with rimes (Bruck, 1992; Juel & Minden-Cupp, 2000), rimes are broken down into their individual sounds after being presented as wholes. After introducing the rime *-et* as a whole, the teacher would highlight its individual sounds: /e/ and /t/. This fosters phonemic awareness. In a study involving high-risk students in four first grades, only the two groups of students taught with an onset–rime approach were reading close to grade level by year's end (Juel & Minden-Cupp, 2000). The students who did the best were those whose teachers broke the rimes into their individual sounds. Students also did their best when given differentiated instruction in word analysis that met their needs. The more time that the at-risk students spent working at their level, the better their progress. This suggests that lessons provided to small groups of students who have approximately the same level of development in phonics is more effective than phonics instruction provided to the whole class. This benefits achieving readers as well, because they will not have to be subjected to instruction in skills that they have already mastered. Lesson 4.4 describes how the rime *-et* might be presented.

## Word-building pattern

### Step 1. Building words by adding onsets

To introduce the *-et* pattern, share-read a story or rhyme that contains *-et* words. Then write *et* on the board and ask the class what letter would have to be added to *et* to make the word *pet*, as in the story that you just read. (This reviews initial consonants and helps students see how words are formed.) As you add *p* to *et*, carefully enunciate the /p/ and the /et/ and then the whole word. Have several volunteers read the word. Then write *et* underneath *pet*, and ask the class what letter should be added to *et* to make the word *wet*. As you add *w* to *et*, carefully enunciate /w/ and /et/ and then the whole word. Have the word *wet* read by volunteers. The word *pet* is then read, and the two words are contrasted. Ask students how the two are different. Other high-frequency *-et* words are formed in the same way: *get, let, jet,* and *net*. After the words have been formed, have students tell what is the same about all the words. Have students note that all the words end in the letters *e* and *t*, which make the sounds heard in *et*. Then have them tell which letter makes the /e/ sound and which makes the /t/, or ending, sound in *et*. Calling attention to the individual sounds in *et* will help students discriminate between the *-et* and other short *e* patterns. It should also help students improve perception of individual sounds in words and so help improve their reading and spelling.

### Step 2. Building words by adding rimes to onsets

To make sure that students have a thorough grasp of both key parts of the word—the onset and the rime—present the onset and have students supply the rime. Write *p* on the board, and have students tell what sound it stands for. Then ask them to tell what should be added to *p* to make the word *pet*. After adding *-et* to *p*, say the word in parts—/p/ /e/ /t/—and then as a whole. Pointing to *p*, say the sound /p/. Pointing to *e* and *t*, say /e/ and then /t/. Running your hand under the whole word, say, "Pet." Show *wet, get, let, jet,* and *net* being formed in the same way. After all words have been formed, have students read them.

### Step 3. Providing mixed practice

Realizing that they are learning words that all end in the same way, students may focus on the initial letter and fail to take careful note of the rest of the word, the rime. After presenting a pattern, mix in words from previously presented patterns and have students read these. For example, after presenting the *-et* pattern, you might have students read the following words: *wet, when, pet, pen, net,* and *Ned* (assuming that *-en* and *-ed* have been previously taught). This gives students practice in processing all the letters in the words and also reviews patterns that have already been introduced.

### Step 4. Creating a model word

Create a model word. This should be a word that is easy and can be depicted. Construct a chart on which model words are printed and depicted with a photo or illustration. (A sample model words chart for short-vowel patterns is presented in Figure 4.5.) For the -*et* pattern, the word *net* might be used. Students can use the chart to help them decipher difficult words that incorporate patterns that have already been taught. Place the chart where all can see it. Explain to students that if they come across a word that ends in -*et* and forget how to say it, they can use their model words chart to help them figure it out. Explain that the model word *net* has a picture that shows the word. In case they forget how to say the model word, the picture will help them.

### Step 5. Guided practice

Under the teacher's direction, the class might read sentences or rhymes about a pet that got wet and was caught in a net, or they might create group or individual experience stories about pets they have or wish they had.

### Step 6. Application

Students read stories and/or create pieces using -*et* words. Two very easy books that might be used to reinforce the -*et* pattern are *Let's Get a Pet* (Greydanus, 1988) and *A Pet for Pat* (Snow, 1984). Also have students read words such as *vet* and *yet*, which incorporate the pattern but which were not presented. As students encounter words such as *letter*, *better*, and *settle*, encourage them to use the known *et* element in the word to help them decode the whole word.

### Step 7. Writing and spelling

If necessary, review the formation of the letters *e* and *t*. Dictate some easy but useful -*et* words (*get*, *let*, *wet*) and have students spell them. When dictating the words, stretch out their pronunciations (/g/ – /e/ – /t/) and encourage students to do the same so that they can better perceive the individual sounds. After students have attempted to spell the words, have them check their attempts against correct spellings placed on the board or overhead. Students should correct any misspellings. Encourage students to use -*et* words in their writing.

### Step 8. Extension

Students learn other short *e* patterns: -*en*, -*ep*, -*ell*, and so on.

### Step 9. Assessment and review

Note whether students are able to read words containing -*et*. Note in particular whether they are able to decode -*et* words that have not been taught. Note, too, whether students are spelling -*et* words in their writing.

**USING TECHNOLOGY**
*Simon Sounds It Out* (Don Johnston), an award-winning piece of software, pronounces and helps students build words by combining initial consonants (onsets) and word patterns (rimes). Featuring an electronic tutor, it provides especially effective practice for word building. Because it pronounces and shows parts of words, it also helps develop phonemic awareness.

A children's book that may be used to introduce the concept of building words is dePaola's (1973) *Andy: That's My Name*, in which Andy watches as older kids use his name to construct a number of words: *and, sand, handy, sandy,* and so on.

For a fuller discussion of word building, see Gunning (1995).

FIGURE 4.5

## Model Words

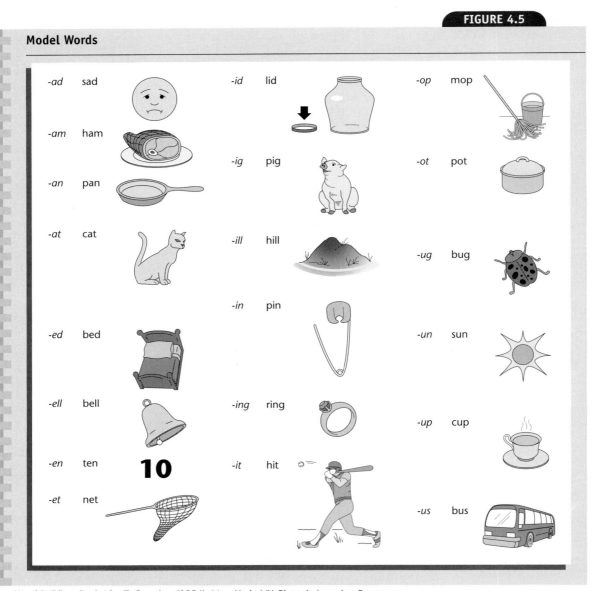

From *Word Building, Book A* by T. Gunning (1994). New York, NY: Phoenix Learning Resources.

### ■ Application through Reading

As students begin to learn decoding strategies that combine context and knowledge of letter–sound correspondences, it is important that they have opportunities to apply them to whole selections. If they read materials that contain elements they have been taught, they will learn the elements better and also be better at applying them to new words (Juel & Roper-Schneider, 1985). For instance, students who have been introduced to short *u* correspondences might read *Bugs* (McKissack & McKissack,

1988) and *Joshua James Likes Trucks* (Petrie, 1983), both of which are very easy to read; a somewhat more challenging text is *Buzz Said the Bee* (Lewison, 1992).

Books that might be used to reinforce vowel letter–sound relationships are listed in the following Children's Reading List.

## Books that reinforce vowel patterns
### Short-Vowel Patterns

*Short* a
Antee, N. (1985). *The good bad cat.* Grand Haven, MI: School Zone.
Cameron, A. (1994). *The cat sat on the mat.* Boston: Houghton Mifflin.
Carle, E. (1987). *Have you seen my cat?* New York: Scholastic.
Flanagan, A. K. (2000). *Cats: The sound of short a.* Elgin, IL: The Child's World.
Maccarone, G. (1995). *"What is THAT?" said the cat.* New York: Scholastic.
Wildsmith, B. (1982). *Cat on the mat.* New York: Oxford.

*Short* e
Flanagan, A. K. (2000). *Ben's pens: The sound of short e.* Elgin, IL: The Child's World.
Gregorich, B. (1984). *Nine men chase a hen.* Grand Haven, MI: School Zone.
Snow, P. (1984). *A pet for Pat.* Chicago: Children's Press.

*Short* i
Coxe, M. (1997). *Big egg.* New York: Random.
Greydanus, R. (1988). *Let's get a pet.* New York: Troll.
Meister, C. (1999). *When Tiny was tiny.* New York: Puffin.

*Short* o
Flanagan, A. K. (2000). *Hot pot: The sound of short o.* Elgin, IL: The Child's World.
McKissack, P. C. (1983). *Who is who?* Chicago: Children's Press.
Moncure, J. B. (1981). *No! no! Word Bird.* Elgin, IL: Child's World.

*Short* u
Capucilli, A. S. (1996). *Biscuit.* New York: HarperCollins.
Lewison, W. C. (1992). *Buzz said the bee.* New York: Scholastic.
McKissack, P., & McKissack, F. (1988). *Bugs.* Chicago: Children's Press.
Petrie, C. (1983). *Joshua James likes trucks.* Chicago: Children's Press.

*Review of short vowels*
Boegehold, B. D. (1990). *You are much too small.* New York: Bantam.
Kraus, R. (1971). *Leo, the late bloomer.* New York: Simon & Schuster.

### Long-Vowel Patterns

*Long* a
Cohen, C. L. (1998). *How many fish?* New York: HarperCollins.
Flanagan, A. K. (2000). *Play day: The sound of long a.* Elgin, IL: The Child's World.
Oppenheim, J. (1990). *Wake up, baby!* New York: Bantam.

Students who are unable to conserve or pay attention to two aspects of an object or a situation at the same time may have difficulty dealing with word patterns (Moustafa, 1995). Although they may know the words *hat* and *sat,* they may be unable to use their knowledge of these two words to read *bat* or *mat* because they fail to see the *at* pattern. These children may still be processing words sound by sound. As their cognitive skills mature, they should be able to grasp patterns.

Raffi. (1987). *Shake my sillies out.* New York: Crown.
Robart, R. (1986). *The cake that Mack ate.* Toronto: Kids Can Press.
Stadler, J. (1984). *Hooray for Snail!* New York: Harper.

*Long* e
Bonsall, C. (1974). *And I mean it, Stanley.* New York: Harper.
Shaw, N. (1986). *Sheep in a jeep.* Boston: Houghton Mifflin.
Ziefert, H. (1988). *Dark night, sleepy night.* New York: Puffin.
Ziefert, H. (1995). *The little red hen.* New York: Puffin.

*Long* i
Gelman, R. G. (1977). *More spaghetti I say.* New York: Scholastic.
Gordh, B. (1999). *Hop right on.* New York: Golden Books.
Hoff, S. (1988). *Mrs. Brice's mice.* New York: Harper.
Ziefert, H. (1984). *Sleepy dog.* New York: Random House.
Ziefert, H. (1987). *Jason's bus ride.* New York: Random House.

*Long* o
Armstrong, J. (1996). *The snowball.* New York: Random House.
Buller, J., & Schade, S. A. (1998). *Pig at play.* New York: Troll.
Cobb. A. *Wheels.* New York: Random House.
Hamsa, B. (1985). *Animal babies.* Chicago: Children's Press.
Kueffner, S. (1999) *Lucky duck.* Pleasantville, NY: Reader's Digest Children's
      Books.
McDermott, G. (1999). *Fox and the stork.* San Diego, CA: Harcourt.
Oppenheim, J. (1992). *The show-and-tell frog.* New York: Bantam.
Schade, S. (1992). *Toad on the road.* New York: Random House.

*Review of Long Vowels*
Matthias, C. (1983). *I love cats.* Chicago: Children's Press.
Parish, P. (1974). *Dinosaur time.* New York: Harper.
Phillips, J. (1986). *My new boy.* New York: Random House.
Ziefert, H. (1985). *A dozen dogs.* New York: Random House.

**r and Other Vowel Patterns**

r *Vowels*
Arnold, M. (1996). *Quick, quack, quick!* New York: Random House.
Hooks, W. H. (1992). *Feed me!* New York: Bantam.
Penner, R. (1991). *Dinosaur babies.* New York: Random House.
Wynne, P. (1986). *Hungry, hungry sharks.* New York: Random House.
Ziefert, H. (1997). *The magic porridge pot.* New York: Puffin.

/aw/ *Vowels*
Mann, P. Z. (1999). *Meet my monster.* Pleasantville, NY: Reader's Digest Children's
      Books.
Oppenheim, J. (1991). *The donkey's tale.* New York: Bantam.
Oppenheim, J. (1993). *"Uh-oh!" said the crow.* New York: Bantam.
Rylant, C. (1989). *Henry and Mudge get the cold shivers.* New York: Bradbury.

/ōō/ *Vowels*
Blocksma, M. (1992). *Yoo hoo, Moon!* New York: Bantam.
Rollings, S. (2000). *New shoes, red shoes.* New York: Orchard.
Silverman, M. (1991). *My tooth is loose.* New York: Viking.
Wiseman, B. (1959). *Morris the moose.* New York: Harper.
Ziefert, H. (1997). *The ugly duckling.* New York: Puffin.

/ŏŏ/ *Vowels*
Brenner, B. (1989). *Lion and lamb.* New York: Bantam.
Platt, K. (1965). *Big Max.* New York: Harper.

/ow/ *Vowels*
Lobel, A. (1975). *Owl at home.* New York: Harper.
Oppenheim, J. (1989). *"Not now!" said the cow.* New York: Bantam.
Siracusa, C. (1991). *Bingo, the best dog in the world.* New York: HarperCollins.

/oy/ *Vowels*
Marshall, J. (1990). *Fox be nimble.* New York: Puffin.
Witty, B. (1991). *Noises in the night.* Grand Haven, MI: School Zone.

*Review of* **r** *and Other Vowels*
Brenner, B. (1989). *Annie's pet.* New York: Bantam.
Hopkins, L. B. (1986). *Surprises.* New York: Harper.
Marshall, E. (1985). *Fox on wheels.* New York: Dutton.
Milton, J. (1985). *Dinosaur days.* New York: Random House.
Rylant, C. (1987). *Henry and Mudge: The first book.* New York: Bradbury.
Stambler, J. (1988). *Cat at bat.* New York: Dutton.

> **ADAPTING INSTRUCTION for *STRUGGLING READERS and WRITERS***
> Special needs youngsters are often given too much phonics. What they need is lots of opportunities to practice their skills by reading easy books. Instruction in phonics should be balanced with application.

### ■ Rhymes

Have students read nursery rhymes that contain the target pattern. A number of illustrated rhymes can be found at the Web site for Webbing into Literacy. For other sources of rhymes, see the Building Literacy Web site at http://www.thomas-gunning.org.

### ■ Word Wall

An excellent device to use for reinforcing both patterns and high-frequency words is a word wall. Words are placed on the wall in alphabetic order. About five new words are added each week (Cunningham & Allington, 1999). They are drawn from basals, trade books, experience stories, and real-world materials that students are reading. You might encourage students to suggest words for the wall from stories they have read or words that they would like to learn.

Kindergarten teachers might start their word wall by placing children's first names on it in alphabetical order. Placing the names in alphabetical order helps reinforce the alphabet (Campbell, 2001).

Before adding a word to the wall, discuss it with the children. Emphasize its spelling, pronunciation, and any distinguishing characteristics. Also talk over how it might relate to other words: for instance, it begins with the same sound, it rhymes,

*W*ords placed on the wall operate as a kind of dictionary and help students spell and read words.

or it is an action word. To reinforce beginning consonants, highlight the first letter of the words containing the consonant you wish to spotlight: the *p* in *pumpkin* and *pull.* To reinforce rimes, highlight the rime you are reinforcing: the *at* in *hat* and *cat.*

Because the words are on the wall, they can be used as a kind of dictionary. If students want to know how to spell *there* or *ball,* they can find it on the wall. Being on the wall, the words are readily available for quick review. Troublesome words can be reviewed on a daily basis.

After a pattern has been introduced, place the pattern words on the wall. However, place them on a separate part of the wall and arrange model words alphabetically by pattern. The *-ab* pattern would be placed first, followed by the *-ack* and *-ad* patterns, and so on. The model word should be placed first and should be accompanied by an illustration so that students can refer to the illustration if they forget how to read the model word. When students have difficulty with a pattern word and are unable to use a pronounceable word part to unlock the word's pronunciation, refer them to the word wall. Help them read the model word, and then use an analogy strategy to help them read the word they had difficulty with.

Review the words on the wall periodically, using the following or similar activities:

- Find as many animal names, color names, and number names as you can.
- Pantomime an action (sit, run) or use gestures to indicate an object or other item (pan, hat, cat, pen), and have students write the appropriate pattern word and then hold it up so that you can quickly check everyone's response. Have a volunteer read the word and point to it on the word wall. Before pantomiming the word, tell students what the model word of the pattern is—for example, *cat* or *pan.* To make the task a bit more challenging and to get students to analyze the ending letters of patterns, tell students that the word will be in one of two patterns—for example, the *-at* or the *-an* pattern.
- Sorting. Have students sort words by pattern. Students may sort a series of

short *a* pattern words into -*at*, -*am*, and -*an* patterns or might sort long *a* words according to their spellings: *a-e, -ay, -ai*.

■ Try "The Secret Word" (Cunningham & Allington, 1999). Select a word from a pattern, and jot it down on a sheet of paper, but do not reveal its identity. Have students number a paper from one to five. Give a series of five clues as to the identity of the word. After each clue, students should write down their guess. The object of the activity is to guess the word on the basis of the fewest clues. The clues might be as follows:

1. The secret word is in the -*at* pattern.
2. It has three letters.
3. It is an animal.
4. It can fly.
5. Into the cave flew the _____.

After supplying the five clues, show the secret word (*bat*) and discuss students' responses. See who guessed the secret word first.

**Making Words** is a hands-on manipulative activity in which students put letters together to create words. It provides excellent reinforcement for word building with patterns. Students assemble up to a dozen words, beginning with two-letter words and extending to five-letter or even longer ones (Cunningham & Cunningham, 1992). The last word that the students assemble contains all the letters they were given. For example, students are given the letters *a, d, n, s,* and *t* and are asked to do the following:

■ Use two letters to make *at*.
■ Add a letter to make *sat*.
■ Take away a letter to make *at*.
■ Change a letter to make *an*.
■ Add a letter to make *Dan*.
■ Change a letter to make *tan*.
■ Take away a letter to make *an*.
■ Add a letter to make *and*.
■ Add a letter to make *sand*.
■ Now break up your word and see what word you can make with all the letters (*stand*). Students might also sort the words that they formed.

### A making words lesson

**Step 1.**

Distribute the letters. You may have one child distribute an *a* to each student, a second child distribute a *t*, and so on. Lowercase letters are written on one side of the card and uppercase on the other. The uppercase letters are used for the spelling of names.

**Step 2.**

Give the directions for each word: "Use two letters to make *at*." Students form the word.

**Step 3.**

Have a volunteer assemble the correct response, the word *at*, on the chalkboard ledge (or pocket chart or letter holder). Have the volunteer read the word. Students should check and correct their responses.

**Step 4.**

Give the directions for the next word. Use the word in a sentence so that students hear it in context. If you have students who are struggling with phonological awareness and letter–sound relationships, slowly articulate each of the target words and encourage them to stretch out the sounds as they spell them with their letters. If a target word is a proper name, make note of that.

**Step 5.**

On the chalkboard ledge, line up in order enlarged versions of the words the students were asked to make. Have volunteers read each of the words. Also have volunteers help sort the words according to patterns or beginning or ending sounds. For instance, holding up the word *at*, the teacher might ask a student to come up to the ledge and find the words that rhyme with *at*.

> Scrabble letter holders can be used to hold students' letters, or letter holders can be constructed from cut-up file folders.

> One way to keep phonics functional is to analyze a text that students are about to read and note which phonics elements students would need to know in order to read the text. For instance, if the selection is about trains, you might present or review the *-ain* pattern.

To plan a Making Words lesson, decide which patterns you wish to reinforce and how many letters you wish students to assemble. The letters chosen must form the word, so you may want to select the final word right after you have chosen the pattern. As students grow more adept, they can be given more challenging patterns and asked to make longer words using a greater variety of patterns. You might also include two or more vowels so that students become involved in vowel substitution.

## SCOPE AND SEQUENCE

A well-planned program of phonics instruction features a flexible but carefully planned scope and sequence. Although vowels could be introduced first in a reading program, it is recommended that consonants be presented initially, as their sounds have fewer spelling options. The consonant sound /b/, for example, is spelled *b* most of the time. In addition, initial letters, which are usually consonants, yield better clues to the pronunciation of a word than do medial or final letters.

When teaching initial consonants, present consonants that are easiest to say and that appear with the highest frequency first. The sounds /s/, /m/, and /r/ are recommended for early presentation because they are easy to distinguish and are among the most frequently occurring sounds in the English language. After introducing about ten high-frequency initial consonants (*s, m, f, t, d, r, l, g* = /g/, *n, h*), introduce a vowel or two so that students will be able to form some words using the correspondences they have learned. Usually short *a* is introduced first. However, the two easiest vowels to hear and spell are long *e* (*he, me, we, see*) and long *o* (*no, so, go*) at the end of a word. Present them and then introduce some short *a* and short *i* patterns.

Table 4.6 is a phonics scope-and-sequence chart that shows the approximate grade levels where key skills are taught in today's reading programs. Skills taught in one grade are often retaught or reviewed in the next grade.

Correspondences within each level are listed in order of approximate frequency of occurrence. The levels are rough approximations and must be adjusted to suit the needs and abilities of your students and the structure of your specific program. Some advanced kindergartners might be taught grade one and even some of the grade two correspondences. On the other hand, a fourth-grader with a reading disability may have difficulty with short vowels and would need to work at that level.

Omitted from Table 4.6 are some correspondences that rarely occur (for example, *ge* or *z* = /zh/ in *beige* or *azure*). Because these elements are encountered infrequently, words containing them are best taught as the need arises, for example when they appear in a selection students are about to read. Also omitted from Table 4.6 is schwa, /ə/, the most frequently occurring vowel sound, often heard in unaccented syllables. It may be spelled with any vowel letter and is the sound heard in so*f*a, silent, d*i*vide, c*o*nnect, and circ*u*s. Knowledge of schwa is not much help in decoding words because identifying it entails being able to tell which syllable is accented. However, schwa should be learned when the dictionary pronunciation key is presented.

> Incorporate dialect differences in your planning. Although *egg* is often used as an example of a short *e* word, many people pronounce it as though it begins with a long *a* sound. If that's the way your students pronounce it, don't use it as an example of a short *e* word.

> **ADAPTING INSTRUCTION for *ENGLISH LANGUAGE LEARNERS*** Both Chinese- and Spanish-speaking youngsters have difficulty with long *e*. When working with these youngsters, start with long *o*.

## Major Word Patterns

If you use word building or another pattern approach, you can think of the scope and sequence in terms of word patterns. A listing of major word patterns is presented in Table 4.7. The sequence of presentation would be similar to the order in which the elements are listed: short-vowel patterns, followed by long-vowel patterns, followed by other vowel and *r*-vowel patterns. However, within each grouping, patterns are presented in alphabetical order. Do not present the patterns in alphabetical order. Start with the easiest and most useful patterns. When teaching short *a* patterns, begin with the -*at* pattern, for instance. When introducing patterns, do not present every word that fits the pattern. Present only words that students know, and present only words that they will be likely to meet in the near future. It's better for them to attain a good grasp of a few high-frequency pattern words rather than have an uncertain knowledge of a large number of pattern words. It also saves time to introduce just the important words. It is not necessary to teach every pattern. For instance, after five or six short -*a* patterns have been introduced, help students to generalize that all the patterns contain a short -*a* sound and help them apply this to short -*a* words from patterns that have not been intro-

**TABLE 4.6** Scope-and-sequence chart for phonics

| Level | Categories | Correspondence | Model Word | Correspondence | Model Word |
|-------|-----------|----------------|------------|----------------|------------|
| K–1 | Letter names, phonemic awareness, rhyming, segmentation, perception of initial consonants | | | | |
| K–1 | High-frequency initial consonants | s = /s/ | sea | r = /r/ | rug |
| | | f = /f/ | fish | l = /l/ | lamp |
| | | m = /m/ | men | g = /g/ | game |
| | | t = /t/ | toy | n = /n/ | nine |
| | | d = /d/ | dog | h = /h/ | hit |
| K–1 | Lower-frequency initial consonants and x | c = /k/ | can | c = /s/ | city |
| | | b = /b/ | boy | g = /j/ | gym |
| | | v = /v/ | vase | y = /y/ | yo-yo |
| | | j = /j/ | jacket | z = /z/ | zebra |
| | | p = /p/ | pot | x = /ks/ | box |
| | | w = /w/ | wagon | x = /gs/ | example |
| | | k = /k/ | kite | | |
| 1 | High-frequency initial consonant digraphs | ch = /ch/ | church | th = /th/ | thumb |
| | | sh = /sh/ | ship | wh = /wh/ | wheel |
| | | th = /th̲/ | this | | |
| K–1 | Short vowels | a = /a/ | hat | e = /e/ | net |
| | | i = /i/ | fish | u = /u/ | pup |
| | | o = /o/ | pot | | |
| 1–2 | Initial consonant clusters | st = /st/ | stop | fr = /fr/ | free |
| | | pl = /pl/ | play | fl = /fl/ | flood |
| | | pr = /pr/ | print | str = /str/ | street |
| | | gr = /gr/ | green | cr = /kr/ | cry |
| | | tr = /tr/ | tree | sm = /sm/ | small |
| | | cl = /kl/ | clean | sp = /sp/ | speak |
| | | br = /br/ | bring | bl = /bl/ | blur |
| | | dr = /dr/ | drive | | |
| 1–2 | Final consonant clusters | ld = /ld/ | cold | mp = /mp/ | lamp |
| | | lf = /lf/ | shelf | nd = /nd/ | hand |
| | | sk = /sk/ | mask | nt = /nt/ | ant |
| | | st = /st/ | best | nk = /ŋk/ | think |
| 2 | Less frequent digraphs and other consonant elements | ck = /k/ | lock | | |
| | | dge = /j/ | bridge | | |
| 1–2 | Long vowels: final e marker | a-e = /ā/ | save | e-e = /ē/ | these |
| | | i-e = /ī/ | five | u-e = /ū/ | use |
| | | o-e = /ō/ | hope | | |

| TABLE 4.6 | Scope-and-sequence chart for phonics *(continued)* | | | | |
|-----------|-----------|-----------|-----------|-----------|-----------|
| Level | Categories | Correspondence | Model Word | Correspondence | Model Word |
| 1–2 | Long vowels: digraphs | *ee* = /ē/ | green | *ow* = /ō/ | show |
| | | *ai/ay* = /ā/ | aim, play | *igh* = /ī/ | light |
| | | *oa* = /ō/ | boat | | |
| | | *ea* = /ē/ | bean | | |
| 1–2 | Other vowels | *ou/ow* = /ow/ | out, owl | *oo* = /o͝o/ | book |
| | | *oi/oy* = /oi/ | oil, toy | *oo* = /o͞o/ | tool |
| | | *au/aw* = /aw/ | author, paw | | |
| 1–2 | *r* vowels | *ar* = /ar/ | car | *are* = /air/ | care |
| | | *er* = /ər/ | her | *air* = /air/ | hair |
| | | *ir* = /ər/ | sir | *ear* = /i(ə)r/ | fear |
| | | *ur* = /ər/ | burn | *eer* = /i(ə)r/ | steer |
| | | *or* = /or/ | for | | |
| 2–3 | Consonants | *ti* = /sh/ | action | | |
| | | *ssi* = /sh/ | mission | | |
| | | *t, ti* = /ch/ | future, question | | |
| 2–3 | Consonant digraphs | *ch* = /k/ | choir | *kn* = /n/ | knee |
| | | *ch* = /sh/ | chef | *wr* = /r/ | wrap |
| | | *gh* = /g/ | ghost | *ph* = /f/ | photo |
| | Vowels | *y* = /ē/ | city | *o* = /aw/ | off |
| | | *y* = /ī/ | why | *al* = /aw/ | ball |
| | | *y* = /i/ | gym | *ew* = /ū/ | few |
| | | *a* = /o/ | father | | |
| | | *e* = /i/ | remain | | |

duced. Words from low-frequency patterns such as *-ab, -ag, -aft,* and *-ax* might be presented in this way.

## Teaching Vowel Generalizations

"When two vowels go walking, the first one does the talking." Recited by millions of students, this generalization is one of the best known of the vowel rules. It refers to the tendency for the first letter in a digraph to represent the long sound typically associated with that letter: For example, *ea* in *team* represents long *e*, and *ai* in *paid* represents long *a*. Although heavily criticized because, as expressed, it applies only about 50 percent of the time, it can be helpful (Gunning, 1975; Johnston, 2001).

About one word out of every five has a double vowel, or digraph; however, the generalization does not apply equally to each situation. For some spellings—

Familiar words are easier to decode. A student who has been taught the *-at* pattern may have little difficulty with the high-frequency words *cat, that,* and *sat* but may falter when encountering *chat, drat,* and *mat.*

TABLE 4.7    Major word patterns

## Short Vowels

| -ab | -ack | -ad | -ag | -am | -amp | -an | -and | -ang | -ank |
|---|---|---|---|---|---|---|---|---|---|
| cab | back | bad | bag | *ham | camp | an | and | bang | *bank |
| tab | jack | dad | rag | jam | damp | can | band | gang | sank |
| *crab | pack | had | tag | slam | *lamp | fan | *hand | hang | tank |
| | sack | mad | wag | swam | stamp | man | land | *rang | blank |
| | *tack | *sad | drag | | | *pan | sand | sang | thank |
| | black | glad | *flag | | | tan | stand | | |
| | crack | | | | | plan | | | |
| | stack | | | | | than | | | |

| -ap | -at | | -ed | -ell | -en | -end | -ent | -ess | -est |
|---|---|---|---|---|---|---|---|---|---|
| cap | at | | *bed | *bell | den | end | bent | guess | best |
| lap | bat | | fed | fell | hen | bend | dent | less | nest |
| *map | *cat | | led | tell | men | lend | rent | mess | pest |
| tap | fat | | red | well | pen | mend | sent | bless | rest |
| clap | hat | | shed | yell | *ten | *send | *tent | *dress | test |
| slap | pat | | sled | shell | then | tend | went | press | *vest |
| snap | rat | | | smell | when | spend | spent | | west |
| trap | sat | | | spell | | | | | chest |
| wrap | that | | | | | | | | guest |

| -et | -ead | -ick | -id | -ig | -ill | -im | -in | -ing | |
|---|---|---|---|---|---|---|---|---|---|
| bet | dead | kick | did | big | bill | dim | in | king | |
| get | head | lick | hid | dig | fill | him | fin | *ring | |
| jet | lead | pick | kid | *pig | *hill | skim | *pin | sing | |
| let | read | sick | *lid | wig | kill | slim | sin | wing | |
| met | *bread | click | rid | twig | pill | *swim | tin | bring | |
| *net | spread | *stick | skid | | will | | win | sting | |
| pet | thread | thick | slid | | chill | | chin | thing | |
| set | | trick | | | skill | | grin | | |
| wet | | quick | | | spill | | skin | | |
| | | | | | | | spin | | |
| | | | | | | | thin | | |
| | | | | | | | twin | | |

| -ink | -ip | -it | -ob | -ock | -op | -ot |
|---|---|---|---|---|---|---|
| link | dip | it | job | dock | cop | dot |
| pink | lip | bit | mob | *lock | hop | got |
| *sink | rip | fit | rob | rock | *mop | hot |
| wink | tip | *hit | sob | sock | pop | lot |
| blink | zip | kit | *knob | block | top | not |
| clink | chip | sit | | clock | chop | *pot |
| drink | flip | knit | | flock | drop | shot |
| stink | *ship | quit | | knock | shop | spot |
| think | skip | split | | | stop | |
| | trip | | | | | |
| | whip | | | | | |

**TABLE 4.7**  Major word patterns *(continued)*

## Short Vowels

| -ub | -uck | -ug | -um | -ump | -un | -unk | -us (s) | -ust | -ut |
|---|---|---|---|---|---|---|---|---|---|
| cub | *duck | bug | bum | bump | bun | bunk | *bus | bust | but |
| rub | luck | dug | hum | dump | fun | hunk | plus | dust | cut |
| sub | cluck | hug | yum | hump | gun | junk | us | just | hut |
| tub | stuck | mug | *drum | *jump | run | sunk | fuss | *must | *nut |
| *club | struck | *rug | plum | lump | *sun | shrunk | muss | rust | shut |
| scrub | truck | tug | | pump | spun | *skunk | | trust | |
| | | chug | | thump | | stunk | | | |
| | | | | stump | | | | | |

## Long Vowels

| -ace | -ade | -age | -ake | -ale | -ame | -ape | -ate | -ave | -ail |
|---|---|---|---|---|---|---|---|---|---|
| *face | fade | age | bake | pale | came | ape | ate | *cave | fail |
| race | made | *cage | *cake | sale | game | *cape | date | gave | jail |
| place | grade | page | lake | tale | *name | tape | *gate | save | mail |
| space | *shade | rage | make | *scale | same | scrape | hate | wave | *nail |
| | trade | stage | rake | | tame | grape | late | brave | pail |
| | | | take | | blame | shape | mate | | sail |
| | | | wake | | shame | | plate | | tail |
| | | | flake | | | | skate | | snail |
| | | | shake | | | | state | | trail |
| | | | snake | | | | | | |

| -ain | -ay | | -ea | -each | -eak | -eal | -eam | -ean | -eat |
|---|---|---|---|---|---|---|---|---|---|
| main | bay | | pea | each | *beak | deal | team | *bean | eat |
| pain | day | | sea | beach | leak | heal | *dream | lean | beat |
| rain | *hay | | *tea | *peach | peak | meal | scream | mean | neat |
| brain | lay | | flea | reach | weak | real | stream | clean | *seat |
| chain | may | | | teach | creak | *seal | | | cheat |
| grain | pay | | | bleach | sneak | squeal | | | treat |
| *train | say | | | | speak | steal | | | wheat |
| | way | | | | squeak | | | | |
| | gray | | | | | | | | |
| | play | | | | | | | | |

| -ee | -eed | -eel | -eep | -eet | | -ice | -ide | -ile | -ime |
|---|---|---|---|---|---|---|---|---|---|
| *bee | deed | feel | beep | *feet | | *mice | hide | mile | *dime |
| see | feed | heel | deep | meet | | nice | ride | pile | lime |
| free | *seed | kneel | *jeep | sheet | | rice | side | *smile | time |
| knee | weed | steel | keep | sleet | | slice | wide | while | chime |
| tree | bleed | *wheel | peep | sweet | | twice | *bride | | |
| | freed | | weep | | | | slide | | |
| | speed | | creep | | | | | | |
| | | | sleep | | | | | | |
| | | | steep | | | | | | |
| | | | sweep | | | | | | |

*continued*

**TABLE 4.7** Major word patterns *(continued)*

## Long Vowels

| -ine | -ite | -ive | -ie | -ind | -y | | -o, -oe | -oke | -ole |
|------|------|------|-----|------|-----|--|---------|------|------|
| fine | bite | dive | die | find | by | | go | joke | hole |
| line | *kite | *five | lie | kind | guy | | *no | poke | mole |
| mine | quite | hive | pie | *mind | my | | so | woke | *pole |
| *nine | white | live | *tie | blind | dry | | doe | broke | stole |
| pine | | drive | | | fly | | hoe | *smoke | whole |
| | | | | | *sky | | toe | spoke | |
| | | | | | try | | | | |
| | | | | | why | | | | |

| -one | -ope | -ose | -ote | -oad | -oat | -ow | -old | | u-e |
|------|------|------|------|------|------|-----|------|--|-----|
| bone | hope | hose | *note | load | boat | bow | old | | use |
| cone | nope | *nose | vote | *road | coat | low | cold | | fuse |
| *phone | *rope | rose | quote | toad | *goat | tow | fold | | *mule |
| shone | slope | chose | wrote | | float | blow | hold | | huge |
| | | close | | | | glow | *gold | | |
| | | those | | | | grow | sold | | |
| | | | | | | slow | told | | |
| | | | | | | *snow | | | |

## Other Vowels

| -all | -aw | -au | -oss | -ost | -ought | | -oil | -oy |
|------|-----|-----|------|------|--------|--|------|-----|
| *ball | caw | fault | boss | cost | ought | | *boil | *boy |
| call | jaw | *caught | loss | *lost | *bought | | soil | joy |
| fall | paw | taught | toss | frost | fought | | | toy |
| hall | *saw | | *cross | | brought | | | |
| wall | claw | | | | | | | |
| small | draw | | | | | | | |
| | straw | | | | | | | |

| -oud | -our | -out | -ound | -ow | -own | | -ood | -ook | -ould |
|------|------|------|-------|-----|------|--|------|------|-------|
| loud | our | out | bound | ow | down | | good | *book | *could |
| *cloud | *hour | *shout | found | bow | gown | | hood | cook | would |
| proud | sour | scout | hound | *cow | town | | *wood | hook | should |
| | flour | spout | mound | how | brown | | stood | look | |
| | | | pound | now | clown | | | took | |
| | | | *round | plow | *crown | | | shook | |
| | | | sound | | | | | | |
| | | | wound | | | | | | |
| | | | ground | | | | | | |

## *r* Vowels

| -air | -are | -ear, ere | -ar | -ard | -ark | -art | | -ear |
|------|------|-----------|-----|------|------|------|--|------|
| fair | care | *bear | *car | *card | bark | art | | *ear |
| *hair | hare | pear | far | guard | dark | part | | dear |
| pair | share | there | jar | hard | mark | *chart | | fear |

| **TABLE 4.7** | Major word patterns |

**r Vowels**

| chair | scare | where | star | | park | smart | hear |
|-------|-------|-------|------|--|------|-------|------|
|       | spare |       |      |  | *shark |     | year |
|       | *square |     |      |  | spark |      | clear |

| **-eer** | | **-or** | **ore** | **-orn** | **-ort** | | |
|----------|--|---------|---------|----------|----------|--|--|
| *deer    |  | *or     | more    | born     | *fort    |  |  |
| cheer    |  | for     | *sore   | *corn    | port     |  |  |
| steer    |  | nor     | tore    | torn     | sort     |  |  |
|          |  |         | wore    | worn     | short    |  |  |
|          |  |         |         |          | sport    |  |  |

*May be used as model words.

From *Assessing and Correcting Reading and Writing Difficulties* (2nd ed.) by T. Gunning, 2002. Boston: Allyn & Bacon. Reprinted by permission of Allyn & Bacon.

*ee*, for example—it applies nearly 100 percent of the time. The letters *ea*, however, represent at least four different sounds (as in *bean, bread, earth,* and *steak*). Moreover, the generalization does not apply to such vowel–letter combinations as *au, aw, oi, oy,* and *ou.*

This generalization about digraphs should not be taught as a blanket rule because it has too many exceptions. Instead, it should be broken down into a series of minigeneralizations in which the most useful and most consistent correspondences are emphasized. These minigeneralizations include the following:

*Instances where the double vowels usually represent a long sound.*

- The letters *ai* and *ay* usually represent long *a*, as in *way* and *wait*.
- The letters *ee* usually represent long *e*, as in *see* and *feet*.
- The letters *ey* usually represent long *e*, as in *key*.
- The letters *oa* usually represent long *o*, as in *boat* and *toad*.

*Instances where the double vowels regularly represent a long sound or another sound.*

- Except when followed by *r,* the letters *ea* usually stand for long *e* (*bean*) or short *e* (*bread*).
- The letters *ie* usually stand for long *e* (*piece*) or long *i* (*tie*).
- The letters *ow* usually stand for a long *o* sound (*snow*) or an /ow/ sound (*cow*).

The minigeneralizations could also be taught as patterns, such as *seat, heat, neat,* and *beat* or *boat, goat,* and *float*. Whichever way they are taught, the emphasis should be on providing ample opportunities to meet the double vowels in print. Providing exposure is the key to learning phonics. Generalizations and patterns draw attention to regularities in English spelling, but actually meeting the elements in print is the way students' decoding skills become automatic; they can then direct fuller attention to comprehension.

▌A number of vowel combinations are not used to spell long vowels:

*au* or *aw* = /aw/ *fault, saw*

*oi* or *oy* = /oy/ *toil, toy*

*oo* = /o͞o/ *moon*

*oo* = /o͝o/ *book*

*ou* or *ow* = /ow/ *pout, power*

▌One of the few generalizations that students make use of in their reading is the final *-e* generalization. When they reach the consolidated alphabetic stage of reading, students make use of final *e* as part of a larger pattern: *-age, -ate, -ive.*

▌The best way to "learn" generalizations is to have plenty of practice reading open and closed syllable words, final *e* words, and other words covered by generalizations.

Most vowel rules are not worth teaching because they have limited utility, have too many exceptions, or are too difficult to apply. However, the following generalizations are relatively useful (Gunning, 1975):

- *Closed syllable generalization.* A vowel is short when followed by a consonant: *wet, but–ter.* This is known as the closed syllable rule because it applies when a consonant "closes," or ends, a word or syllable.
- *Open syllable generalization.* A vowel is usually long when it is found at the end of a word or syllable: *so, mo–ment.* This generalization is known as the open syllable rule because the word or syllable ends with a vowel and so is not closed by a consonant.
- *Final* e *generalization.* A vowel is usually long when it is followed by a consonant and a final *e: pine, note.*

Vowel generalizations should be taught inductively. After experiencing many words that end in *e* preceded by a consonant, for example, students should conclude that words ending in a consonant plus *e* often have long vowels. Students might also discover this by sorting words that end in final *e* and words that don't.

The real payoff from learning generalizations comes when students group elements within a word in such a way that they automatically map out the correct pronunciation most of the time. For example, when processing the words *vocal, token,* and *hotel* so that the first syllable is noted as being open (*vo–cal, to–ken, ho–tel*) and the vowel is noted as being long, students are able to decode the words quickly and accurately. This is a result of many hours of actual reading. However, it is also a process that can be taught (Glass, 1976).

Because none of the vowel generalizations applies 100 percent of the time, students should be introduced to the variability principle. They need to learn that digraphs and single vowels can represent a variety of sounds. If they try one pronunciation and it is not a real word or does not make sense in context, then they must try another. A child who read "heevy" for *heavy* would have to try another pronunciation, because *heevy* is not a real word. A child who read "deed" for *dead* would need to check to see whether that pronunciation fits the context of the sentence in which the word was used. Although *deed* is a real word, it does not make sense in the sentence "Jill's cat was dead"; so the student would try another pronunciation. This strategy needs to be taught explicitly, and students must have plenty of opportunity for practice. To sound out a word, they should be taught the general steps outlined in the Student Strategy below.

 **Applying the variability strategy to vowel correspondences**

1. Sound out the word as best you can.
2. After sounding out the word, ask yourself, "Is this a real word?" If not, try sounding out the word again. (Applying the variability principle to a

word containing *ow*, a student might try the long-vowel pronunciation first. If that did not work out, he or she would try the /ow/ (*cow*) pronunciation. If there is a chart of spellings available, students can use it as a source of possible pronunciations.)

3.  Read the word in the sentence. Ask yourself, "Does this word make sense in the sentence?" If not, try sounding it out again.

4.  If you still cannot sound out a word so that it makes sense in the sentence, try context, skip it, or get help.

## Introducing Syllabic Analysis Early

Long words pose problems for students. Although students might know the words *car*, *pen*, and *her*, they have difficulty reading the word *carpenter*. Most multisyllabic words are composed of known word parts or patterns. After teaching several short-vowel patterns, present two-syllable words composed of those patterns. For instance, after students have studied the short -*a* and short -*i* patterns, present words such as *rabbit*, *napkin*, *distant*, and *instant*. When students encounter multisyllabic words, prompt them to use their knowledge of word parts to figure out the words. Also build words. After students have learned a word such as *swim*, have them make words that contain *swim*: *swims*, *swimming*, *swimmer* so they get used to reading words that contain suffixes.

## USING WORD ANALYSIS REFERENCES

From the very beginning, students should have references that they can use to help them read and spell unfamiliar words (Pinnell & Fountas, 1998). These references could include picture dictionaries, real dictionaries (for older students), illustrated charts of model words, lists of patterns and other words, a chart listing the steps in decoding a difficult word, and a talking word processor or talking electronic dictionary so that students could type in an unknown word and have it pronounced.

## USING AN INTEGRATED APPROACH

Although phonics, context clues, and vocabulary are treated as separate topics in this book, students make use of all three when they face an unknown word. In fact, they make use of their total language system. As noted earlier, when students decode words, four processors are at work: orthographic, phonological, meaning, and context (Adams, 1990; 1994). The processors work simultaneously and both receive information and send it to the other processors. Therefore, phonics instruction must be viewed as being part of a larger language process. Phonics is easier to apply when context clues are used, and, in turn, it makes those clues easier to use. Students who are adept decoders will be able to recognize more words

---

Because there is no way to predict on the basis of spelling whether *ow* will represent /ow/ (*cow*) or /ō/ (*snow*) or *oo* will represent a short (*book*) or long (*boot*) sound, you need to teach students to check whether the sounds they construct create a real word. If not, have them try the other major pronunciation of *ow* or *oo*. Model this process for your students.

Good evidence for the integration of context and phonics cues comes from reading sentences containing a word whose pronunciation depends on its meaning. Good readers can read the following sentences without difficulty: "The does have no antlers, but the bull does." "He wound the bandage around the wound" (McCracken, 1991, p. 91).

and so will have more context to use. Moreover, greater knowledge of the world, larger vocabularies, and better command of language increase students' ability to use phonics. If a student has a rich vocabulary, there is a better chance that the word he or she is decoding will be recognized by his or her meaning processor. Even if the word is not known, the student will have a better chance of deriving its meaning from context if most of the other words in the passage are known and if his or her background knowledge of the concepts in the passage is adequate.

To be most effective, therefore, phonics instruction should be presented in context and practiced and applied through extensive reading, which enables students to connect phonics instruction with its functioning as part of a total language system. Extensive reading also provides practice for phonics skills so that students' decoding becomes so effortless and automatic that they can devote full attention to comprehension, which is what reading is all about.

## DIALECT VARIATION

Note whether each row of words has the same pronunciation or a different pronunciation.

balm  bomb
merry  Mary  marry
pin  pen
root  route

In some dialects, each group of words has the same pronunciation. In other dialects, each word represents a different pronunciation. American English encompasses a variety of regional dialects. No one dialect is superior to another. However, if you teach a pronunciation that is different from that spoken by your students, it can be confusing. When teaching phonics, use the dialect that your students use. You might also give a brief lesson in dialects. If your dialect differs from that of your students, you might explain why this is so: because you came from a different part of the country, for instance. When you come to an element that you pronounce differently, explain that to students and let them pronounce the words in their own dialect. Some of the major dialect variations include the following:

/aw/ and /o/ Words such as *dog, frog,* and *hog* have an *aw* or short *o* pronunciation.
/ō͞o/ and /o͝o/ Words such as *room* and *roof* have either a long double-*o* pronunciation or a short double-*o* pronunciation.
/i/ and /e/ In some dialects, short *e* is pronounced as a short *i* so that *pen* and *pin* and *tin* and *ten* are homophones.
/e/ and /ā/ In some dialects words like *egg* and *beg* are pronounced with a long *a* instead of the more typical short *e*.

/o͞o/ and /ow/ In some dialects *route* rhymes with *boot;* in others it rhymes with *bout.*

## PHONICS AND SPELLING

Recent research suggests that children who are encouraged to write early and allowed to spell as best they can develop insights that carry over into their ability to read words (Burns & Richgels, 1989). Although invented spellings and spelling instruction can help children gain insights into alphabetic principles, a systematic program of teaching phonics is still necessary. Neither invented spellings nor regular spelling instruction provides all the skills necessary to decode printed words. Spelling is best seen as a useful adjunct to phonics instruction, especially in the beginning stages of reading, rather than as a major method of teaching students to crack the code.

> For a discussion of the research on phonics, see the National Reading Panel's report at http://www.Nationalreadingpanel.org.

## STRATEGY INSTRUCTION

The ultimate value of phonics instruction is that it provides students with the keys for unlocking the pronunciations of unknown words encountered in print. For instance, a child who has studied both the *-at* and the *-et* patterns but has difficulty with the words *flat* and *yet* needs strategies for decoding those words. In addition to context, there are two powerful decoding strategies that the student might use: pronounceable word part and analogy (Gunning, 1995).

To apply the pronounceable word part strategy, a student who is having difficulty with a word seeks out familiar parts of the word. You might prompt the student by pointing to *yet* and asking, "Is there any part of the word that you can say?" If the student fails to see a pronounceable word part, cover up all but that part of the word (*et*) and ask the student if she or he can read it. Once the student reads the pronounceable part, she or he adds the onset (*y*) and says the word *yet*. (This assumes that the student knows the *y* = /y/ correspondence.) In most instances, the student will be able to say the pronounceable word part and use it to decode the whole word.

If a student is unable to use the pronounceable word part strategy, try the analogy strategy. With the analogy strategy, the student compares an unknown word to a known one. For instance, the student might compare the unknown word *yet* to the known word *net*. The teacher prompts the strategy by asking, "Is the word like any word that you know?" If the student is unable to respond, the teacher writes the model word *net*, has the student read it, and then compares *yet* to *net*. Or the teacher might refer the child to a model words chart.

When students reconstruct a word using the pronounceable word part or analogy strategy, they must always make sure that the word they have constructed is a real word. They must also make sure it fits the context of the sentence. The pronounceable

> Stretching out the sounds as you say a word out loud ("sssuuunnn") and encouraging students to think of the sounds they hear helps students spell words and builds their knowledge of phonics. It helps even more if students also say the word out loud and stretch out the sounds.

> Do not ask students to "look for the little word in the big word." This may work sometimes but would result in a misleading pronunciation in a word like *mother*. Besides, there are many words that don't have "little words" in them.

> The pronounceable word part strategy takes advantage of students' natural tendency to group sounds into pronounceable parts.

word part strategy should be tried before the analogy strategy because it is easier to apply and is more direct. Although students may have to be prompted to use the strategies, they should ultimately apply the strategies on their own.

## Incorporating Phonics Strategies with Context

Pronounceable word part and analogy strategies should be integrated with the use of context clues. There are some situations in which context simply does not work. There are others in which neither pronounceable word part nor analogy will work. For instance, the pronounceable word part and analogy strategies would not work with *have* in the following sentence, but context clues probably would: "I have three pets." However, in the sentence "I like trains," context probably would not be of much help in decoding the word *trains*, but the pronounceable word part or analogy strategy would work if the student knows the *-ain* pattern or the word *rain*. Based on their studies and the studies of others, New Zealand researchers Chapman, Tunmer, and Prochnow (2001) concluded that in most instances, students will be more successful if they use the pronounceable word part strategy first: "Children . . . should be encouraged to look for familiar spelling patterns first and use context to confirm what unfamiliar words might be" (pp. 171–172).

 **Word recognition**

To cue the use of word recognition strategies, the student should ask one or more of the following questions when encountering an unknown word in print:

1. Is there any part of this word that I can say?
2. Is this word like any word I know?
3. What word would make sense here?

## Building Independence

When a student has difficulty with a printed word, you may be tempted to supply the word or give some unhelpful admonition, such as "You know that word. We had it yesterday." Size up the word. Think of the skills the student has, the nature of the word, and the context in which it appears. Then ask the question from the Student Strategy (change the "I" to "you") that will prompt the use of the cue that seems most likely to work. (Of course, if you feel the child has no chance of working out the word, supply two options by asking, "Would *pony* or *cow* fit here?" By giving students a choice of two words, one of which is the answer, you provide students with the opportunity to apply a skill and you also preserve their self-confidence.) Helping students apply decoding strategies provides them with a powerful tool that empowers them as readers. Encouraging them to work out words also affirms your faith in them and builds their confidence.

If a student is reading orally in a group situation, do not allow another student to correct her or him. This robs the student of her or his academic self-concept and also of the opportunity to apply strategies. If a student misreads a word and does not notice the error, do not immediately supply a correction or even stop the reading. Let the student continue to the end of the sentence or paragraph; there is a good chance that she or he will notice the misreading and correct it. If the student does correct the misreading, make sure that you affirm this behavior: "I like the way you went back and corrected your misreading. You must have seen that the word _____ didn't make sense in the sentence."

If the student does not self-correct a misreading, you have two choices. If the error is a minor one, such as *this* for *that* or *the* for *these*, which does not change the meaning of the sentence, ignore it. If the misreading does not fit the sense of the sentence, use a prompt that will help the student correct the misreading:

> If other prompts don't work and you believe the student can't decode a word, give the students a choice between two responses: "Is the word (incorrect response) or (correct response)?" This helps students think about what strategies might be used.

- If the misreading does not make sense, ask, "Does _____ make sense in that sentence?"
- If the misreading is not a real word, ask, "Does that sound right?"
- If the misreading makes sense but does not fit phonically, say, "*Dog* makes sense in the sentence, but the word in the sentence begins with a *w*. What letter does *dog* begin with? What word that begins with *w* would fit here?" (Clay, 1993b). (Prompt for a pronounceable word part or analogy if you think the student can work out the pronunciation of the word).

> Additional word analysis strategies can be found in Chapter 5.

Periodically, model the process of using strategies to figure out a word. Using a think-aloud, show how you go about seeking a pronounceable word part or using an analogy strategy.

Children also use combinations of strategies. Over time their use of strategies improves so that their ability to use strategies to decode an unfamiliar word or to spell a difficult word becomes faster and more accurate. Improvement is brought about by introducing and providing practice with more advanced strategies. But progress can also be obtained by fostering more effective use and more effective selection of existing strategies. As Ritttle-Johnson and Siegler (1999) explain,

> When a new strategy is discovered, it typically is used only occasionally at first. Many changes occur not through introduction of new strategies but instead through increasingly efficient execution of existing strategies, increasing use of the more accurate strategies, and more adaptive choice among strategies. (p. 335)

## ADAPTING BASAL READER INSTRUCTION

Today's basal reading programs introduce phonics early and at a fast pace. All of the programs published in 2000 or after introduce initial and final consonants at the kindergarten level, and most of the programs also present all the short vowels at that level. These are reviewed and reintroduced in grade one. In addition, the programs introduce most of the remaining major phonics elements in grade one. However, in one study of two suburban second-grade classes assessed early in the school year, all of the students had excellent knowledge of short-vowel patterns. Most had a good command of long-vowel patterns. However, at least a third of the students had difficulty with a number of other-vowel and *r*-vowel patterns (Gunning, 1999).

If your class is average or below and you are using a basal published in 2000 or later, you may need to provide extra practice and instruction. You may also have to adapt the program to fit the needs of your students. For below-average students, a realistic expectation is that they will master short-vowel patterns by the end of first grade and will also learn some long-vowel patterns, perhaps even mastering most of them. It would be better to provide them with a strong foundation in short-vowel and long-vowel patterns rather than trying to present all the major single-syllable patterns in one year.

One of the difficulties of deciding how much phonics to teach in first grade is that even fairly easy children's books contain a variety of patterns. For instance, note the vowel patterns in the following excerpt from a selection from a first-grade anthology (Cooper et al., 2001).

> John and I like to share
> Our toys, our food, and what we wear.

> We share a book.
> We share a bike.
> We share a game that we both like. (Hazen, 1998)

Assuming that students have been introduced only to short-vowel and long-vowel patterns, what might be done to prepare them to read this selection? One solution would be to analyze the selection and note phonics elements needed to read it that students have not yet been taught. Pick one or two elements that would appear most frequently in the selection and which would be most essential for an understanding of the text and present those. *Share* and *wear* might be taught as part of an *r*-pattern. This would be a useful choice because the words *bear* and *care* appear in the next selection in the anthology. The words *book*, *toys*, and *food* might be taught as words to be learned for the story. However, intensive instruction in the unfamiliar phonic elements /oy/, /o͞o/, and /o͝o/ could be presented at another time. Present all other words containing unknown elements as new words to be learned. You might also seek out reading material that is composed primarily of phonics elements that students have learned.

Although all of today's recently published major basals cover phonics in a systematic way, you may need to make some or all of the following adjustments to get the best results:

■ Use the word-building technique to present new patterns and to build on what students know. Have students blend onset and rimes and also each sound in the word. Today's programs blend onsets and rimes or blend each individual sound but fail to do both, which is what research and best practice advocate.

■ Arrange for mixed practice so that students analyze each element in patterns they are learning. Mix *-at* and *-am* patterns, for instance, so that students can't merely assume that each word has an *-at* pattern; they will have to analyze the whole word instead of just looking at the initial consonant.

- Some programs present one pattern at a time. Others present two or three. Adjust the rate of introduction to fit the pace at which your students are learning.
- Emphasize the independent use of strategies. Provide strategy instruction as suggested. Make use of prompts as needed. Gear prompts to students' level of development. Most programs recommend some but not all of the prompts suggested in this text. Introduce and reinforce all of the strategies presented in this text and the prompts that accompany them.
- Most of the programs move fairly rapidly. Provide students with extra reinforcement if they are falling behind. The basal series have numerous supplementary booklets for reinforcing phonics elements. Make use of these or select from the titles listed in the Children's Reading List on pp. 187–189.

> Stopping occasionally to decode a hard word or because the reading does not sound right to the reader does not mean that the reader lacks fluency. It means that the reader is monitoring for meaning, which is something that good readers do.

## Assessing Decodability

To assess the decodability of a text, list the elements needed to read it in order of difficulty: short vowels, long vowels, other vowels, *r*-vowels, and multisyllabic words as in Figure 4.6. Also list high-frequency words that are irregular. The decodability of the text is the highest point at which approximately 10 percent or more of the words fit into that category. If a selection has 10 percent long-vowel words but just a few words that are *r*-vowel, other vowel, or multisyllabic, then it is at the long-vowel level. Note in Figure 4.6 that the text has been assigned a short-vowel level because most of the words have short vowels. Most of the high-frequency words and some of the long-vowel, other vowel, and *r*-vowel words would be known by students who know short vowels. The teacher might want to introduce *learned*, *first*, and *pound* as story words.

### REINFORCEMENT ACTIVITIES    Phonics

- "Hinky Pinks," which is also known as "Stinky Pinky," can be used to reinforce both rhyming and a phonics element (initial or final consonants, consonant clusters, or word patterns). One person gives a definition, to which the partner responds with a two-word rhyme. For instance, the response to the definition "brown truck" is "tan van." To make the task somewhat easier, the teacher might supply the rime part of the word and have students add the consonant or cluster. Listed below are some examples. Others can be found in *Playing with Words* (Golick, 1987).

Large hog: _ ig _ ig
Unhappy boy: _ ad _ ad
Place for old pieces of cloth: _ ag _ag
Plane in the rain: _ et _ et
Bright place to sleep: _ ed _ ed

**FIGURE 4.6**

## Decodability Index

**Name** *Pet for Pat*　　　　　　　　**Author** *P. Snow*

### Short-Vowel Words

a (cat) *at, pat,'''' hat,' bat, that ('s)''*
e (pet) *pet,''''''''' bet, wet, get, let, ten, vet, set, yet*
i (pig) *will, with, this, stick, his,' trick*
o (pot) *not, stop*
u (cup) _____

### Long-Vowel Words

a (cake) *may, play*
e (seal) *we, see, he*
i (ride) *my*
o (goat) _____
u (use) _____

### Other Vowel Words

aw (ball, walk) *all*
oo (spoon, new) _____
oo (book) _____
ow (cow) *pound (s)'*
oy (boy) _____

### r-Vowel Words

ar (car) _____
air (chair) _____
ear (hear) _____
ir (sir) *learned, first*
or (store) *for'*

### Multisyllabic Words

Two syllables _____
Three syllables _____
Four or more syllables _____

### High-Frequency Words

(Words such as *of* or *the* whose spelling is unusual.)
*I, have,' a,'' of, you,' to, where,*
*the,'' your,''' has*

### Estimate of Decoding Skills Needed to Read the Text

____ **High-Frequency Word Level** (Text can be read through the use of pictures and knowledge of no more than 10 different high-frequency words.)

✔ **Short Vowel Level** (At least 10% of the words contain short vowels. At least 80% of the words contain short vowels or are high-frequency words.)

____ **Long Vowel Level** (At least 10% of the words contain long vowels. At least 80% of the words contain long vowels or short vowels or are high-frequency words.)

____ **Other Vowel Level** (At least 10% of the words contain other vowels. At least 80% of the words contain other vowels or long or short vowels or are high-frequency words.)

____ **R-Vowel Level** (At least 10% of the words contain R vowels. At least 80% of the words contain R vowels, long, short, or other vowels or are high-frequency words.)

____ **Multisyllabic Level** (At least 10% of the words have more than one syllable.)

- Have students create secret messages by substituting onsets in familiar words and then putting the newly formed words together to create a secret message (QuanSing, 1995). Besides being motivational, secret messages help students focus on the onsets and rimes of words and also foster sentence comprehension. Once students become familiar with the procedure, you can invite them to create secret messages as an individual or cooperative learning activity. Here is a sample secret message. (To make the exercise more challenging, you might put the target words in random order.)

Take *H* from *He* and put in *W*. *We*
Take *l* from *lot* and put in *g*. *got*
Take *p* from *pen* and put in *t*. *ten*
Take *st* from *stew* and put in *n*. *new*
Take *l* from *looks* and put in *b*. *books*
Secret message: *We got ten new books.*

- Encourage students to create mnemonic letters that incorporate a drawing suggesting the sound each letter usually represents. For example, the circle in the letter *d* might be drawn to look like a doughnut. Students might want to work in small groups on this project.

- In the morning message, use words that contain the phonics elements taught recently.

- Integrate phonics with other subject areas. After *c* = /k/ has been introduced, you might read about cows or corn, or the class might follow a printed recipe for carrot cake.

- Have students create a consonant chart and a vowel chart and add new elements as they are being taught. The charts should contain a drawing of a key word, the key word spelled out, and other spellings of the sound being studied. The entry for *f* might show an *f*, a drawing of a *fish*, and the key word *fish*. Later, when the *ph* spelling of /f/ is studied, this additional element would be added to the chart.

- Students can create dictionaries that contain new phonics elements. After *ch* has been introduced, have them make a *ch* page and list *ch* words they know.

- Dramatize elements. A student picks an onset from a grab bag and matches it to a rime placed on the board. The group reads the word and acts it out. Focusing on the rime *-op*, they say "hop" and hop as an *h* is added, pantomime mopping when an *m* is added, and so on (McMaster, 1998).

- Display real-world materials that contain the phonics element you are working on. If working on *ch*, for example, bring in a box of Cheerios, chocolate chip cookies, and a menu that features cheeseburgers or chicken. Help students read the items, and encourage them to bring in some of their own.

## DECODABLE TEXTS

Ardith Cole (1998) noticed that some of her first-graders who had apparently done well in the first half of first grade began to struggle in the second half. In fact, their progress came to a grinding halt. Heidi Mesmer (1999) observed a similar phenomenon. Both discovered a mismatch between their students and the materials they were reading. Their students did well with the highly predictable texts in which most of the words could be predicted by using illustrations as cues or with the help of repeated, highly predictable language. As students encountered more complex text, they floundered. Cole and Mesmer came to a similar conclusion. Text should be chosen that provides support to students.

Decodable texts are selections that contain phonics elements that have been taught. Figure 4.7 shows a page from a well-written decodable text. Note that except for the familiar "once upon a time" and a few high-frequency words, all of the words can be decoded by the application of short-vowel patterns.

No text is totally decodable. High-frequency words such as *is*, *are*, and *the* need to be included, as do content words such as *angry* and *animal* if the story is about an *angry animal*. Two factors have to be considered in order to determine the decodability of a text: the skills that the student has learned and the skills demanded

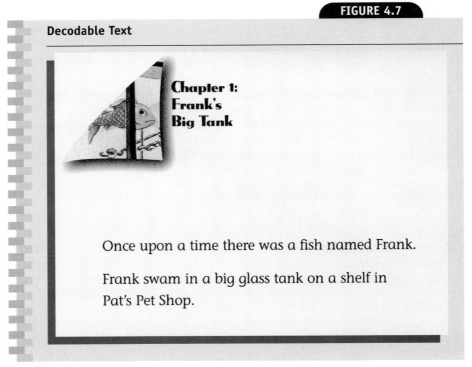

**FIGURE 4.7**

**Decodable Text**

**Chapter 1: Frank's Big Tank**

Once upon a time there was a fish named Frank.

Frank swam in a big glass tank on a shelf in Pat's Pet Shop.

From *Frank the Fish Gets His Wish* by Laura Appleton-Smith, 1998. Lyme, NH: Flyleaf Publishing. Copyright © Laura Appleton-smith. Reprinted by permission of Laura Appleton-Smith.

by the text. Texas (Texas State Board of Education, 2000) requires that first-grade texts be at least 80 percent decodable. In Texas, the state purchases approved texts and then distributes them free to public schools. Texas will not approve or purchase series that do not have first-grade texts that are at least 80 percent decodable. Other states also require decodable texts. As a result, all of the early reading texts in today's basal reading programs are at least 80 percent decodable.

Some materials emphasize high-frequency words. Most of the predictable books are composed primarily of high-frequency words. However, as these books become more complex, they become less predictable. If students have not learned basic decoding skills, they will have difficulty coping with them. This is what happened to Cametera, the student that Mesmer (1999) was working with. Realizing that Cametera was falling behind the other students because she lacked adequate decoding skills, Mesmer began teaching her key patterns. The patterns she taught were those that were emphasized in the books that Cametera would be reading. Cametera did well with the patterns when they were introduced but failed to use them when she met them in text. Reflecting on her instruction, Mesmer realized that there was a mismatch between instruction and materials. Because the texts were not decodable, they contained a variety of patterns. Trying to prepare Cametera to read the texts, Mesmer was covering too many patterns too fast. Not having had enough practice to really learn the patterns, Cametera regressed to using picture and language clues. Hesitating to use decodable texts because so many of them sounded like tongue twisters, Mesmer found a series of texts that progressed at a reasonable pace and used fairly natural language. With the support of these texts, Cametera began making encouraging progress. Her rate of using decoding skills doubled and her use of picture clues lessened. Her spelling also improved. These more readily decodable texts had become an effective support for her.

## Transitional Nature of Decodable Texts

Decodable texts are transitional. As students progress in phonics, there is less need for the support of decodable texts. The texts can be written in a more natural fashion and include easy children's books such as the *Little Bear* or *Frog and Toad* series. One well-known reading program (Houghton Mifflin) phases out decodable texts written specifically for the program halfway through the first-year program and switches over to selections from easy children's books that contain many of the patterns that have been taught.

As explained in Chapter 1, there are four processors at work when students read: orthographic, phonological, meaning, and context. The processors operate simultaneously. Rich context speeds and makes easier the use of phonics. For most students, a word in context is easier to read than a word in a list. In their attempt to provide students with decodable text, authors have sometimes included words that incorporate the phonic element that has been taught but the words are difficult or unusual and the language lacks a natural flow. Because one processor has been overemphasized and the others neglected, the reading is made more difficult. For instance, in their attempt to include as many decodable words as possible, authors might include unfamiliar words such as *vat* and *drat* while reinforcing the -*at* pat-

Texas requires that texts in the early part of basal reader programs be at least 80 percent decodable. Some other states also have decodability standards. Setting a high arbitrary level of decodability can result in tongue twisting language. Texts need to be written in such a way that they are decodable but the language is natural. Books listed on pp. 187–189 are decodable but have a natural flow.

**USING TECHNOLOGY**
Texas Reading Initiative
**http://www.tea.state.tx.us/reading/products/products.html**
Refer to *Guidelines for Examining Phonics & Word Recognition Programs* for an excellent explanation of phonics instruction and useful checklist for assessing programs.

To assess the decodability of a text, use the Decodability Index on p. 208.

tern. Because of the way students process written language, familiar -*at* pattern words are easier to decode than unfamiliar ones.

Because the inclusion of high-frequency words makes for more natural sounding text, and because text that is partly predictable is easier to read, and because students should have the opportunity to apply decoding skills, the best texts are those that have a balanced mix of decodable elements, high-frequency words, and predictability. The focus should match students' stage of development. For students in the pre-alphabetic and very early alphabetic stage, highly predictable text works best. As students move into the alphabetic stage, they need decodable text that will allow them to apply what they have learned. Over time, an increasing number of high-frequency words should be introduced so that the text has a more natural sound and more complex topics can be covered. Most of the texts contained in the Children's Reading List, pp. 187–189, incorporate a balanced blend of decodability and predictability.

## TEACHING PHONICS TO ENGLISH LANGUAGE LEARNERS

In teaching English language learners to read, determine the extent of their literacy in their first language and build upon that. Also be aware of the similarities and differences between the two languages so that you can provide explanations or extra help where it is needed. Here are some comparisons between Spanish and English and some adjustments that might be made in an English phonics program for Spanish speakers.

Spanish has a simpler phonology and orthography than English. For one thing it has fewer speech sounds. In addition, there is a near one-to-one correspondence between Spanish sounds and the letters that represent them. However, Spanish has more multisyllabic words than English does.

There are significant differences between consonant sounds in English and Spanish (see Table 4.8). The following consonant sounds are not present in Spanish: /j/ /v/, /sh/, and /ng/. In addition, some consonant sounds that are the same in initial position in English and Spanish do not occur in final position in Spanish: final /b/ (*cab*), /f/ (*if*), /g/ (*bag*), and /ch/ (*match*). Just as in English, many Spanish words have clusters. There are *l* clusters (*blusa*, *playa*) and *r* clusters (*fryoles*, *gratia*) but no *s* clusters in Spanish (*stop*, *spot*).

### Vowels

Most English reading programs start with short vowels. However, Spanish has no short *a* (*hat*), short *i* (*hit*), short *u* (*cut*), short *oo* (*book*), or schwa (*banana*) vowels (see Table 4.9). Most *r*-vowels will also be unfamiliar to Spanish speakers. The sound /r/ has a different pronunciation in Spanish. However, the *ar* (*cart, carne*) and *or* (*horn, horno*) have similar pronunciations in Spanish and English. The *r*-sounds in *sir, fear, hair,* and *were* will be unfamiliar to Spanish speakers. Both English and Spanish have the /oy/ (*boy, soy*) and /ow/ (*cow*) sound but /ow/ is spelled *au* in Spanish

**TABLE 4.8** Comparison of English and Spanish consonants and their spellings

| Phoneme | English | Spanish |
|---------|---------|---------|
| b | b ball | b, v bebé, vaca |
| d | d dog | d dentista |
| f | f fish | f familia |
| g | g goat | g gallina |
| h | h hat | j jardín |
| j | j jar | does not occur in Spanish |
| k | c, k cat key | c, k, qu caimán, kilo, qué |
| l | l lion | l lobo |
| m | m man | m mucho |
| n | n nail | n no |
| ñ | like ni in onion | ñ niña |
| p | p pen | p papá |
| r | r ring | r rojo |
| rr | does not occur in English | rr perro |
| s | s sun | s, z seis, zapatos |
| t | t table | t taxi |
| v | v vest | does not occur in Spanish |
| w | w, qu wagon quiz | u, hu cuarto, huerta |
| y | y yo-yo | y, i yo, fiambre |
| z | z zebra | does not occur in Spanish |
| ch | ch chair | ch chapeo |
| sh | sh shoe | does not occur in Spanish |
| th | th thin | does not occur in some Spanish dialects |
| th | <u>th</u> that | does not occur in some Spanish dialects |
| ng | ng ring | does not occur in Spanish |
| zh | age garage | does not occur in Spanish |

(*causa*). Because of differences in the sound systems of the two languages, Spanish speakers may experience some of the following confusions:

final /b/ pronounced as /p/: *cab* becomes *cap*

/j/ pronounced as /y/: *jet* becomes *yet*

/ng/ pronounced as /n/: *thing* becomes *thin*

/ch/ pronounced as /sh/: *chin* becomes *shin*

/v/ pronounced as /b/: *vote* becomes *boat*

/y/ pronounced as /j/: *yes* becomes *jes*

*s* clusters pronounced with an *e*: *speak* becomes *espeak*

/a/ pronounced as /e/: *bat* becomes *bet*

/i/ pronounced as /ē/: *hit* becomes *heat*

/ē/ pronounced as /i/: *heal* becomes *hill*

| TABLE 4.9 | Comparison of English and Spanish vowels and their spellings | |
|---|---|---|
| **Phoneme** | **English** | **Spanish** |
| a | a cat | does not occur in Spanish |
| e | e bed | e es |
| i | i fish | does not occur in Spanish |
| o | o mop | a gato |
| u | u cup | does not occur in Spanish |
| ā | a-e, ai, ay rake | ei, ey rey, seis |
| ē | ee, e, ea, e-e wheel | i, y misa, y |
| ī | i-e, igh, ie, –y nine | ai, ay baile, haya |
| ō | o-e, o, ow, oa nose | o oso |
| ū | u-e, –u cube | yu ayuda |
| o͞o | oo, ew, ou, ui school | u uno |
| o͝o | oo, ou, u book | does not occur in Spanish |
| aw | aw, au saw | does not occur in Spanish |
| ow | ow, ou cow | au causa |
| oy | oi, oy boy | oi, oy estoi, soy |
| schwa | a, e, i, o, u banana | does not occur in Spanish |
| ar | ar car | ar carpa |
| or | or, oor, our four | or hora |
| air | air, are, ere chair | does not occur in Spanish |
| eer | ear, eer deer | does not occur in Spanish |
| ier | ire fire | does not occur in Spanish |

/u/ pronounced as /o/: *hut* becomes *hot*
/o͝o/ pronounced as /o͞o/: *look* becomes *Luke*

When learning English phonics, students will need exercises helping them to perceive sounds not present in Spanish. When presenting a new phonics element, that might be confusing, spend extra time introducing the sound of the element. Have students complete oral exercises such as the following, in which they discriminate between easily confused elements:

Students tell which word correctly completes the spoken sentence:

Maria is wearing her new (choose, shoes).
The explorers sailed away on a large (chip, ship).
Little Bo Peep lost her (cheap, sheep).
Which book did you (choose, shoes) to read?
You may not (chew, shoe) gum in class.

You might enlist the help of the ESL or bilingual specialist to help students perceive unfamiliar speech sounds. However, focus on the purpose of phonics instruction. The purpose of instruction in phonics is to provide students with a tool for decoding difficult words. It isn't necessary that they be able to pronounce the words without any trace of an accent. Don't turn phonics lessons into speech lessons.

| TABLE 4.10 | Phonics elements with the same sounds in Spanish and English but different spellings | |
|---|---|---|
| **Phoneme** | **English Spelling** | **Spanish Spelling** |
| ē | e: me (i-spaghetti) | i: mi |
| o | o: top (a-father) | a: gato |
| ā | a-e, ai, ay rake, rain, ray (ei, ey-reign, they) | ei, ey rey, seis |
| ī | i-e, igh, ie, nine, high, tie | ai, ay baile, haya |
| ow | ou, ow out, owl | au causa |

## Teaching Students Who Are Literate in Spanish

When teaching students who are literate in Spanish to read in English, explain to them that they already know much of the phonics that they will meet in English (Thonis, 1983). You might create a chart showing them skills in Spanish that will transfer to English.

Unfortunately, some of the sounds that are the same in both languages have different spellings. For instance, long *e* is spelled with an *i* in Spanish as in *si*, and long *a* is typically spelled with an *ei* or *ey* as in *rey*, *seis*. (See Table 4.10 for a listing of divergent spellings.) In addition, Spanish does not have a final silent *e* that marks vowels as being long. Spanish readers seeing the word *came* might read it as *cahmay*. Miscues such as this tell you that the student is applying Spanish phonics to English spelling and so needs instruction that will help him learn English phonics. When introducing elements in which there are possible confusions, explain the potentially confusing part.

> Long *o* is a good starting point for teaching phonics to Spanish-speaking students because it is spelled the same in both languages.

 ## HIGH-FREQUENCY WORDS

Close your book and on a separate piece of paper spell the word *once*. As you write the word, try to be aware of the processes you are using. Did your lips move? As you wrote the word, did you sound it out? A small number of words, such as *of* and *once*, and, to a lesser extent, *were* and *some*, are said to be irregular. Their spellings don't do a good job of representing their sounds. Because these words are irregular, at one time it was thought that the best way to learn them was to memorize them visually. They were put on cards and studied. Because it is believed that they were memorized visually, they became known as **sight words**. However, more recent research indicates that even irregular words are learned phonologically. That's why when you wrote the word *once*, chances are you said the word, at least subvocally, and then said the sounds of the word as you spelled each sound. There is also an element of visual memory involved. Otherwise, you may have spelled *once* as *wuns*.

A list of **high-frequency words** is presented in Table 4.11. Note that these are all common words. Ironically, the words that appear most frequently tend to have the most irregular spellings, mainly because they are some of the oldest words in the language. Over the years, English evolved so that, in many instances, spellings no longer do a very good job of representing pronunciations.

> ■ A **sight word** is one that is recognized immediately. However, the term *sight words* also refers to words that occur with high frequency and words that are learned through visual memorization. Only a small number of words can be learned through visual memory. The vast majority of words are learned through phonics.
>
> ■ **High-frequency words** are words such as *the, of,* and *them* that appear in printed material with a high rate of occurrence.

| TABLE 4.11 | High-frequency words |

| | | | | |
|---|---|---|---|---|
| 1. the | 41. which | 81. made | 121. also | 161. name |
| 2. of | 42. their | 82. over | 122. around | 162. should |
| 3. and | 43. said | 83. did | 123. another | 163. home |
| 4. a | 44. if | 84. down | 124. came | 164. give |
| 5. to | 45. will | 85. way | 125. three | 165. air |
| 6. in | 46. do | 86. only | 126. high | 166. line |
| 7. is | 47. each | 87. may | 127. come | 167. mother |
| 8. you | 48. about | 88. find | 128. work | 168. set |
| 9. that | 49. how | 89. use | 129. must | 169. world |
| 10. it | 50. up | 90. water | 130. part | 170. own |
| 11. he | 51. out | 91. little | 131. because | 171. under |
| 12. for | 52. then | 92. long | 132. does | 172. last |
| 13. was | 53. them | 93. very | 133. even | 173. read |
| 14. on | 54. she | 94. after | 134. place | 174. never |
| 15. are | 55. many | 95. word | 135. old | 175. am |
| 16. as | 56. some | 96. called | 136. well | 176. us |
| 17. with | 57. so | 97. just | 137. such | 177. left |
| 18. his | 58. these | 98. new | 138. here | 178. end |
| 19. they | 59. would | 99. where | 139. take | 179. along |
| 20. at | 60. other | 100. most | 140. why | 180. while |
| 21. be | 61. into | 101. know | 141. things | 181. sound |
| 22. this | 62. has | 102. get | 142. great | 182. house |
| 23. from | 63. more | 103. through | 143. help | 183. might |
| 24. I | 64. two | 104. back | 144. put | 184. next |
| 25. have | 65. her | 105. much | 145. years | 185. below |
| 26. not | 66. like | 106. good | 146. different | 186. saw |
| 27. or | 67. him | 107. before | 147. number | 187. something |
| 28. by | 68. time | 108. go | 148. away | 188. thought |
| 29. one | 69. see | 109. man | 149. again | 189. both |
| 30. had | 70. no | 110. our | 150. off | 190. few |
| 31. but | 71. could | 111. want | 151. went | 191. those |
| 32. what | 72. make | 112. sat | 152. tell | 192. school |
| 33. all | 73. than | 113. me | 153. men | 193. show |
| 34. were | 74. first | 114. day | 154. say | 194. always |
| 35. when | 75. been | 115. too | 155. small | 195. until |
| 36. we | 76. its | 116. any | 156. every | 196. large |
| 37. there | 77. who | 117. same | 157. found | 197. often |
| 38. can | 78. now | 118. right | 158. still | 198. together |
| 39. an | 79. people | 119. look | 159. big | 199. ask |
| 40. your | 80. my | 120. think | 160. between | 200. write |

Adapted from *The Educator's Word Frequency Scale* by S. M. Zeno, S. H. Ivens, R. T. Millard, & R. Duvvuri, 1995. Brewster, NY: Touchstone Applied Science Associates.

Table 4.11 gives 200 high-frequency words in order of their frequency of appearance. The list is drawn from a compilation of words that appear in books and other materials read by school children (Zeno, Ivens, Millard, & Duvvuri, 1995). These 200 words would make up about 60 percent of the words in continuous text. For example, the most frequently occurring word, *the*, would appear about 2 percent of the time.

Many students will pick up a number of high-frequency words through reading signs and other print to which they are exposed in the class and through shared reading of big books and other materials. However, direct teaching is also necessary. When teaching high-frequency words, limit the number being taught to three or four. Choose words that students will soon be meeting in print. If they are about to read Dr. Seuss's *The Cat in the Hat Comes Back* (Geisel, 1961), you might present *this*, *off*, *done*, and *know*, irregular words that figure prominently in the story. Select words that are different in appearance. Presenting *put* and *but* or *where*, *when*, and *were* together is asking for trouble, as students are almost sure to confuse them.

When teaching high-frequency words, take full advantage of phonic regularities, such as initial and final consonant correspondences. Also, seek out commonalties of words. For instance, when teaching *at* as a high-frequency word, also teach *that* and show how the two are related; have students note that *that* contains the pronounceable word part *at*. Except for dramatically irregular words like *of* and *one*, help students match up spellings and sounds. For *were*, help students see that *w* represents /w/ and *ere* represents /er/ as in *her*. For the word *some*, match *s* with /s/, note that *o* is a very unusual way of spelling /u/, and match *m* with /m/. Encourage students to spell out the words and provide opportunities for them to meet the words in many contexts so they form a visual image of the words in addition to making phonological connections. As students are learning exception words such as *know* or *sure*, they also need to be taught specific distinguishing features of these words.

Because high-frequency words are such a prominent part of just about everything that students read, it is important that they learn to recognize them rapidly. The idea behind rapid recognition of words is that the human mind has only so much mental-processing ability and time. If students get caught up trying to sound out words, they lose the memory of what they are attempting to read. They need automaticity, the ability to process words effortlessly and automatically (Laberge & Samuels, 1974). Students who are able to recognize words rapidly have ample attention and mental energy left to comprehend what they are reading. Ultimately, because of lots of practice, most of the words that skilled readers meet in print, although learned through phonics, are processed as rapid recognition words. Only when they meet strange names or unfamiliar words do they resort to decoding words.

## Teaching High-Frequency Words

When presenting high-frequency words, emphasize activities that reflect this purpose. Use phonics to help students accurately decode words—accuracy must come

Knowing how to spell and/or sound out a word partially or fully helps students learn and remember new words (Ehri, 1991), but time spent discussing known definitions may be wasted (Kibby, 1989). However, hearing and seeing function words such as *the* and *are* is helpful.

▌Two factors are involved in rapid recognition of words: accuracy and automaticity (Samuels, 1994). To reach an effective level of accuracy, students must actively process words and process virtually every letter. Students need varying amounts of time to reach a high level of accuracy. Once they have reached an acceptable level of accuracy, they seem to gain automaticity at similar rates (Samuels, 1994). Children who seem to take longer to become fluent readers may not have achieved accuracy.

first. As Samuels (1994) notes, accuracy precedes automaticity, or rapid recognition. Use of knowledge of patterns and individual correspondences facilitates accurate recognition. Once accuracy has been achieved, stress rapid recognition.

As you gradually introduce added phonics skills, include high-frequency words as part of your instruction. For instance, when teaching the consonant cluster *bl*, use the high-frequency words *black* and *blue* as examples. When studying short *a*, present the high-frequency words *am*, *an*, and *at*. Being able to relate the printed versions of these words with their sounds gives students another way to process them, which aids memory and speed of processing. Use the steps listed in Lesson 4.6 as a framework for presenting high-frequency words.

## High-frequency words

### Step 1. Develop understanding of the words

This step is only necessary if students do not have an adequate understanding of the words being presented. Since high-frequency words are among the most common in the language, they will be in the listening vocabularies of the majority of students. However, some high-frequency words may be unknown to English Language Learners.

### Step 2. Present printed words in isolation

▌There are actually few words in which phonics cannot be used at least partially. These include such irregular words as *one, once,* and *of.*

Write each word to be learned on the chalkboard, or present each one on a large card. Although students may not be able to read the words, they may know parts of them. Build on any part they know. This will make the task of learning the word easier, as students will be faced with learning only a portion of the word rather than the whole word; it also helps them connect new knowledge with old knowledge. If students know only initial consonant correspondences, build on that knowledge: Emphasize the *y* = /y/ in *you* and the *f* = /f/ in *for*. If they know initial and final consonants, talk about the *c* = /k/ and *n* = /n/ in *can*. If they know word patterns, make use of those: Help them use their knowledge of *-an* to read *man* and their knowledge of *-op* to read *stop*. Present these elements as ways of perceiving and remembering sight words, but do not turn the sight word lesson into a phonics lesson. For words that are highly irregular, such as *of*, *one*, and *once*, simply stress their spellings. Do not attempt to discuss any phonics elements.

After all the words have been introduced, have students read them chorally and individually. Distribute cards containing the words so that each student has a set. If long cards are used, the reverse side might contain the word used in a sentence.

### Step 3. Present printed words in context

On the chalkboard, story paper, or overhead transparency, present the high-frequency words in context. Underline the target words so that they stand out.

Take care to use each word in the same sense in which students will most likely see it. For instance, if the high-frequency word *water* is going to be a verb in an upcoming story, show it as a verb. In composing sample sentences, except for the target high-frequency words, use words already taught so that students can concentrate their efforts on the new ones. Actually, using high-frequency words that have already been taught is a good way to review them. Read the sentences to the students, and then have them read in unison as you sweep your hand under the words. Later, individual volunteers can read the sentences.

### Step 4. Practice

Provide ample practice for high-frequency words. Practice could be in the form of maze worksheets on which students choose from three words the one that correctly completes the sentence:

```
          take
I am new years old.
          five
```

Or it could be a brief story, a game, or a piece of computer software such as *Richard Scarry's Busytown* (Paramount Interactive) or *Bailey's Schoolhouse* (Edmark), in which a few high-frequency words are featured.

### Step 5. Application

Have students create experience stories or read easy stories that contain target high-frequency words. Experience stories naturally contain a high proportion of sight words. Easy readers also provide an opportunity for students to meet sight words in context. In one study, students who read easy books learned more sight words than those who used a basal series (Bridge, Winograd, & Haley, 1983). They also expressed more positive feelings about reading, and, because their books were written about a variety of topics, they had an opportunity to learn more about their world.

### Step 6. Assessment and review

Observe students as they read to see how well they do when they encounter high-frequency words.

> **USING TECHNOLOGY**
> Talking CD-ROM books that highlight the words that are being read are a good way to build up students' rapid recognition of high-frequency words, especially if the student reads the story several times. It is crucial that students read along as the words are being highlighted. To test themselves, students might turn down the sound and see if they can read the words as they are being highlighted.

There is some disagreement about how expert readers recognize words. Ehri (1994) theorizes that they are recognized holistically because the word's letters and pronunciation have become bonded through repeated encounters, thus providing an access route which leads instantaneously from the word's graphic representation to the word's pronunciation. Gough and Hillinger (1980) believe that readers process words phonologically, but the processing is so rapid that recognition appears to be instantaneous.

## Using Children's Books to Build a High-Frequency Vocabulary

Several types of children's books can be used to build a high-frequency vocabulary, including predictable books, caption books, and label books. Predictable books are those that follow a set pattern, making it easy for the child to predict what the sentences are going to say. Caption books feature a single sentence per page that describes or relates to the illustration in much the same way that a caption goes with a photo. Label books, as their name suggests, depict a number of ob-

It's better for novice readers to read a variety of books than to read a few books over and over. Students may have memorized these books and so are not getting adequate practice applying phonics skills and meeting high-frequency words. Although in the beginning stages students might memorize a few books, once they start grasping basic phonics they should be putting these skills to use (Hiebert et al., 1998).

jects, actions, or people and provide printed labels for them. These kinds of books may be read over and over again.

There are literally thousands of children's books that can be used to foster instant recognition of words. However, it is important that the books be on the right level. Students should know most of the words, so that their focus is on moving just-introduced or barely known words to the category of words that are well known and rapidly recognized. Although it is helpful for students to build fluency by rereading the same book or story, it is also important that they read many different books to see the same words in a variety of contexts.

However, it is not enough just to read the books. Many predictable books are, in fact, so predictable that students are actually "reading" the pictures; in a pattern book, students may simply have memorized the pattern and so are not actually processing the words. Therefore, it is important to follow the procedure outlined by Bridge, Winograd, and Haley (1983) in Lesson 4.7.

 **Using predictable books to build a high-frequency vocabulary**

**Step 1.**

Select a book that students will enjoy and that contains words that you want to reinforce. Obtain a big book version so that students can follow along as you read.

**Step 2.**

Preview the text, read it to students, and discuss it. Point to each word as you read it.

**Step 3.**

Reread the text. Invite students to read the repeated portions or other easy parts.

**Step 4.**

After several rereadings, copy the text onto chart paper or cover the illustrations in the big book. With the pictures eliminated, students can concentrate on reading the words. Have students read the pictureless version, with your help.

**ADAPTING INSTRUCTION for *STRUGGLING READERS and WRITERS***

Poor readers may require extra practice learning high-frequency words. Good readers apparently learn four times as many new words as poor readers (Adams & Higgins, 1985).

**Step 5.**

Duplicate the story, and cut the duplicated versions into sentence strips. Have students match the individual sentence strips to those in the chart version. Also have students reassemble the story, sentence by sentence. Sentences can be cut up into individual words as well. Have students match the individual words with those in the chart story. Also have students reconstruct individual sentences by putting the cut-up words in the right order.

Presented in Appendix A are children's books that can be used to reinforce high-frequency words. Select books from the Picture, Caption/Frame, and Easy High-Frequency (Primer 1) levels. All the books at these levels are brief and well illustrated. They increase in difficulty from those that require a minimum of reading to those that contain three lines of text on a page. In addition to the children's books listed in Appendix A, there are several series of books designed to reinforce sight words. These include the following:

*Reading Corners*. San Diego, CA: Dominie Press. This series reinforces a number of basic patterns: I like _____; I have _____; I do _____. Consisting of just eight to twelve pages of text, these books are very easy.

*Read More Books*. San Diego, CA: Dominie Press. This series reinforces a number of basic sentence patterns. The text is brief and explicitly illustrated with color photos and so is very easy to read.

*Seedlings*. Columbus, OH: Seedling Publications. This series features sixteen-page booklets in which each page contains one line of text accompanied by an illustration. Vocabulary is varied.

## Using Word Banks

A word bank is a collection of known words and consists primarily of high-frequency words. As students learn new words, these are added to their word banks. Students might also include words that they are working on or want to learn. A good source of words would be the high-frequency words in the books they are reading. After reading *Cat on the Mat* (Wildsmith, 1982), students might add *cat, on, the,* and *sat* to their word banks. Word banks should be limited to about one hundred words. At that point, the bank is too extensive to handle and students' decoding skills should

**INVOLVING PARENTS**

Parents or grandparents can provide struggling readers and writers with the additional practice they need. One grandfather, following the advice of his grandson's teacher, taught his grandson a store of 100 high-frequency words. Although the child was still far behind, the grandfather stopped helping his grandson because he didn't know what else he could do. A little teacher time spent showing the grandfather what he might do would have had invaluable payoff.

*R*eading stories is an excellent way to reinforce phonics and high-frequency words.

have developed to a point where word banks have lost their usefulness (Graves, Juel, & Graves, 2001).

So that the words in the banks are recognized automatically, students might work with them for brief periods each day. Working in pairs, students can quiz each other on words from their word banks. Using word-bank cards, they might make a list of things they can do. They can sort words by placing color words in one pile, action words in another, and animal words in a third. They can search out opposites or write stories about individual words. For concrete nouns or some action words, students might draw an illustration of the word on the reverse side of the paper or card. They might then quiz themselves by attempting to read the word, turning the card or paper over to see if they got it right. Creating sentences with words from their banks is another possible activity.

Using items from the word banks is also one way of introducing or reinforcing phonics elements. After learning *see*, *so*, and *say*, students might be taught that *s* represents /s/. After learning *cat*, *hat*, and *sat*, they might be introduced to the *-at* pattern.

After students have accumulated a number of words in their word banks, they can keep them in alphabetical order by first letter. This will reinforce the use of the alphabet and also help them locate words. In time, the word bank becomes a kind of dictionary as well as a source of motivation: Word banks that are growing signal to the children that they are learning.

## ▦ BUILDING FLUENCY

In the beginning stages of learning to read, students may read in slow, halting fashion. This is understandable since students are still learning the code. However, if it persists, comprehension will suffer. Students will expend so much effort decoding that they won't be able to devote mental energy to understanding what they read. Students need to become fluent as well as accurate readers. Although often equated with smoothness of oral reading, **fluency** has been defined as "freedom from word identification problems that might hinder comprehension in silent reading or the expression of ideas in oral reading; **automaticity**" (Harris & Hodges, 1995, p. 85). Fluency has two components: **accuracy** and automaticity. Students are accurate readers if they can recognize the words. They have automaticity if they recognize the words rapidly. Students can be accurate but slow decoders. One way of judging fluency is by noting students' rate of silent reading and their comprehension. If they can read at a reasonable pace, then they probably are able to recognize the words rapidly. If they can answer questions about what they read, their word recognition is probably accurate. Another way of assessing fluency is through having students read a selection orally. If they misread a number of words, this indicates that accuracy is a problem. It also may be an indication that the material is beyond their instructional level. If they read word by word and seem to need to sound out an excessive number of words, then automaticity is an issue.

■ **Fluency** is freedom from word identification problems that might hinder comprehension in silent reading or the expression of ideas in oral reading.

■ **Automaticity** refers to tasks that can be performed without attention or conscious effort.

■ **Accuracy** means being able to pronounce or sound out a word and also knowing the word's meaning.

Comprehension is also an element in fluency. Students' phrasing and expressiveness should be noted. Does their reading indicate an understanding of what they are reading? Understanding what one reads is important for proper expression. Of course, it is essential that students be given material that is on the appropriate level. Given material that is too difficult, even the best readers become dysfluent.

Accuracy and speed of reading have to be balanced. An overemphasis on accuracy will lead to a decrease in reading speed. Do not insist on 100 percent accuracy (Samuels, 1994). An overemphasis on oral reading will decrease reading speed. Students will also get the wrong idea about reading. They will begin to see reading as an oral performance activity in which they are expected to pronounce each word correctly. This could carry over into students' silent reading and so hinder comprehension. When students read orally, their purpose should be to convey the meaning of the passage rather than to render accurate pronunciation of each word.

Less fluent readers comprehend less. In a study of oral fluency among fourth-grade readers, the more fluent readers had better comprehension (Pinnell et al., 1995). Although they had 94 percent accuracy, the least fluent readers read much more slowly. Their average reading speed was just 65 words per minute. Fluent readers in fourth grade read between 126 and 162 words a minute.

The foundation for fluency is to build solid word analysis skills (Wolf & Katzir-Cohen, 2001) and to monitor for meaning. Beginning readers need to check themselves as they read by asking: Do the words that I am reading match the letters? Do the words make sense? Monitoring links the use of decoding and context (New Standards Primary Literacy Committee, 1999).

In addition to prompting students to monitor for meaning, activities that foster rapid recognition of high-frequency words will foster fluency, as will wide reading of books at the students' independent level. This reading need not be oral. In fact, silent reading provides more realistic practice. At all levels, silent reading is recommended for building fluency. As they read books in which nearly all the words are known, students' ability to recognize the words faster should increase. Like any other complex behavior, reading requires substantial practice before it becomes automatic and seemingly effortless. If students persist in reading in a labored, halting fashion, the material is probably too difficult. Try material that is easy, and gradually move up to more difficult selections. Students, especially if they are younger, might also be encouraged to read the same selections a second, a third, or even a fourth time.

The ability to read orally with expression is, in part, a public speaking skill. Its goal is to convey meaning to others rather than to construct meaning. Oral reading should be preceded by silent reading. Readers need to construct a good understanding of the text so they can then read it orally in such a way as to covey their interpretation of the text. If you wish to promote oral reading skills, use drama and poetry to provide practice. Students don't mind reading a script over and over again if they are going to dramatize it. Students are also motivated to read accurately and expressively if they are reading to others. Having older children read to young children—first-graders reading to kindergartners, fourth-graders reading to second-graders—provides students with a reason to read a selection over and over again.

Fluency is sometimes equated with phrasing, smoothness, and expressiveness as well as rate, accuracy, and automaticity (Worthy & Broadus, 2001).

Except when working with very beginning readers, the initial reading of a selection should almost always be silent. While discussing a selection read silently, students might read orally a favorite part, dramatize dialogue, or read a passage out loud to provide support for a point they are making.

**ADAPTING INSTRUCTION for *ENGLISH LANGUAGE LEARNERS***
Reading along with a taped version of a story fosters fluency, as does simply reading the story several times. Taped versions, however, are especially helpful for students whose reading speed is extremely slow and for students who are still learning English (Blum et al., 1995; Dowhower, 1987).

When students are asked to read orally, they should have a chance to read silently first and should be asked to read in such a way as to convey what the author meant. Students will then have to think about and emphasize the meaning of what they read. Model the process frequently.

## Choral Reading

Unrehearsed oral reading in which students take turns reading (round robin) can be painful for struggling readers, who are embarrassed by their mistakes, and good readers, who are bored by slow, choppy reading.

Choral reading of selections also fosters fluency (McMaster, 1998). Choral reading involves two or more people but can take many forms. In unison reading, the whole group reads together. In refrain reading, the leader reads most of the text and the group reads the refrain. In antiphonal reading, two or more groups alternate. The boys may read one portion, the girls another. Or one side of the room might read a portion and the other side read the other portion. Or one child or group reads a couplet or line and the next child reads the next line or couplet (Bromley, 1998). One group might read designated lines in a loud voice, the second group in a soft voice. Variations are endless.

*Refrain:*
Tom, Tom, the Piper's Son

*Leader:*
Now Tom with his pipe made such a noise,
That he pleased all the girls and boys;
And they stopped to hear him play,

Antiphonal
Baa, Baa, Black Sheep

*Group 1:* Baa, Baa, black sheep,
Have you any wool?

*Group 2:* Yes, sir, yes, sir,
Three bags full.

*Child 1:* One for the money
*Child 2:* Two for the show
*Child 3:* Three to get ready
*Child 4:* And four to go

Twinkle, Twinkle, Little Star

Twinkle, twinkle, little star,
How I wonder what you are!
Up above the world so high,
Like a diamond in the sky.

**USING TECHNOLOGY**

eThemes

Resources for choral reading are found at **http://emints.more. net/ethemes/ resources/S00000298. html.**

Choral reading can be a whole-class or small-group activity. Choral reading is an excellent way to foster fluency and expression in reading. In a choral reading lesson, you might emphasize any of a number of oral reading skills: reading with expression, interpreting punctuation, phrasing of words, varying speed of reading. Poems, speeches, and tales with repeated parts lend themselves to choral reading. Choral reading lends itself to repeated reading as the class rereads in order to improve timing or expression or smoothness. It is a nonthreatening way for English language learners and struggling readers to practice their skills.

Because oral reading is used to measure fluency, there is a tendency to overemphasize oral reading as a way of fostering fluency. However, silent and oral reading are different tasks. Oral reading focuses the reader's attention on pronouncing words correctly. Silent reading stresses constructing meaning, which is the essence of reading. Silent reading also provides students the opportunity to work out troublesome words on their own without feeling rushed or embarrassed because people are listening to them struggle.

| TABLE 4.12 | Reading rate in words per minute | |
|---|---|---|
| Instructional Reading Level | Oral Reading | Silent Reading |
| Grade 1 | 55 | 55 |
| Grade 2 | 85 | 85 |
| Grade 3 | 115 | 130 |
| Grade 4 | 135 | 155 |

Adapted from Powell (1980); cited in Lipson and Wixson (1997) and Harris and Sipay (1990).

Silent reading is faster and more efficient. Readers can skip unnecessary words or sections. Beyond second grade, silent reading speed should exceed oral reading (see Table 4.12). If students are reading at a very slow pace, try to determine why and take corrective action. If the material is too difficult—if they miss more than five words out of one hundred—obtain materials on the appropriate level. If they are having difficulty decoding words, work on decoding skills. If they have mastered decoding skills but are reading in a slow or labored fashion, work on fluency. They may also be very anxious readers who feel they have to read each word carefully.

## Modelled Techniques for Building Fluency

A first step in building fluency is to model the process. As you read orally, you are modeling the process of smooth, expressive reading. As you read orally to students, explain the techniques that you use: how you read in phrases, how you use your voice to express the author's meaning, how you read at a pace that listeners can keep up with but that isn't too fast.

Reading along with a taped or CD-ROM version of a selection can build oral fluency. Paired reading, which is also known as Duolog Reading (Topping, 1998), can be effective in building oral fluency. The teacher, a parent, or a child who is a more proficient reader teams up with a student. The student chooses the book to be read. The book selected is one that would be a little too difficult for the student to read on his own. After a brief discussion of the title and cover illustration, the helper and student simultaneously read the book out loud. During this dual reading, the helper adjusts her reading rate so it matches that of the student. When the student feels that he can read a portion of the text on his own, he signals the helper by raising his left hand. When he wants the helper to resume reading with him, he raises his right hand. The helper automatically provides assistance when the student stumbles over a word or is unable to read the word within five seconds (Topping, 1987; 1989). As an alternative to paired reading, the teacher, parent, or tutor may take turns reading the selection. At first, the teacher might do most

Because they have students read scripts aloud, *Tales and Plays* (Rigby) and *Primary Reader's Theatre* (Curriculum Associates) provide opportunities for oral reading that have genuine purpose.

of the reading. The student would read any words that he could. As the student becomes more proficient, he can read larger segments. All of these techniques provide a model of phrasing and expression that students might then incorporate into their silent reading.

## Repeated Readings

A popular technique for fostering fluency is through repeated reading (Samuels, 1979). Repeated reading helps students achieve accuracy and rapid recognition of high-frequency words. In one study, slow-reading second-graders doubled their reading speed after just seven weeks of repeated reading training (Dowhower, 1987). In another study, students enjoyed the fluency exercises so much that after the experiments were concluded, they asked for additional repeated reading sessions (Rashotte & Torgesen, 1985).

Rereadings are effective because students meet high-frequency words over and over, and these become part of their automatic recognition vocabulary (Dowhower, 1987). However, this means that selections chosen should be on the same approximate level and should be on the students' instructional level. Lesson 4.8 lists suggested steps for a repeated reading lesson.

 **Repeated readings**

**LESSON 4.8**

### Step 1. Introducing repeated readings

Explain the reasons behind repeated readings. Discuss how we get better when we practice. Explain to students that they will be practicing by reading the same story over and over. Tell students that this will help them read faster and better.

### Step 2. Selecting a passage

Select or have the students choose short, interesting selections of approximately 100 words. They or you might choose books, such as *Brown Bear, Brown Bear, What Do You See?* (Martin, 1967) or *Are You My Mother?* (Eastman, 1960), that are rhythmic and fun to read. Make sure that books are on the students' instructional level.

### Step 3. Obtaining an initial timing

Obtain a baseline reading and accuracy rate. Have students read a selection orally. Time the reading and record the number of words read correctly. If students take more than two minutes to read the selection and make more than five errors out of 100 words (not counting missed endings), the selection is too hard. If students make only one or two errors and read the selection at 85 words per minute or faster, the selection is too easy. If students can read 100 words a minute or close to it, repeated reading is probably a waste of instructional time (Dowhower, 1987). They would be better off with self-selected reading.

### Step 4. Rereading

Go over the students' miscues with them. Help them read these words correctly. Also help them with phrasing problems or any other difficulties they may have had. Then direct them to reread the selection until they feel they can read it faster and more smoothly. Practice can take one of three forms: (1) reading the selection to oneself; (2) listening to an audiotape or viewing the selection on a CD-ROM while reading the selection silently and then reading the selection without the aid of the tape or CD; (3) reading the selection to a partner. If students' reading speed is very slow, below 50 words per minute, they will do better reading along with a person or taped or CD version (Dowhower, 1987). After they reach speeds of 60 words per minute, they can practice without the tape or CD. Initially, students with very low reading rates will need lots of practice to reach 80 words per minute. But as the reading rate increases, they won't need as many practice readings. Once they get used to the procedure, four or five rereadings should provide optimal returns for time spent. Additional rereadings would provide diminishing returns.

### Step 5. Evaluating the reading

Students read the selections to you or to a partner. The number of word recognition errors and reading speed are recorded. Students are informed of their progress. A chart might be constructed to show the degree of improvement. The goal is to have students read at least 80 words per minute. Students should practice until they reach that standard. Errors in word recognition should also decrease. However, do not insist upon perfect word recognition. Setting a standard of 100 percent accuracy leads students to conclude that reading is a word-pronouncing rather than a meaning-constructing activity. It also slows the reading rate. Afraid of making a mistake, students will read at a slow-but-sure pace (Samuels, 1988).

### ■ Variations on Rereading

Instead of working with a teacher, students may work in pairs. However, explain and model the procedure first. One student reads while the other charts her progress. Then they switch roles. Show students how to time the reading and count errors. To make the charting easier, have students check one-hundred-word samples only. Students might read a selection that contains more than one hundred words but only one hundred words are used for charting reading rate. Students may hurry through a selection to obtain a fast time. Explain to students that they should read at a normal rate. On occasion have students read a song or a poem instead of the usual reading selections. Because of their rhythm, narrative poems and songs lend themselves to a rapid reading.

## Recorded-Book Method

To build students' ability to recognize words automatically and to improve their phrasing, have them read along as a selection is read. You or an aide can read selections to students, or you can have them read along with taped stories. Because taped stories are read at the pace of normal speech, this may be too rapid for the listener to match printed and spoken words. When a student reads along with a tape, the pace should be at about the same rate as the student can read orally or slightly faster. If the pace is too rapid, the student may not be able to keep up and may become frustrated (Carbo, 1997). In deciding which books to record, select those that are interesting and that students will be able to understand when they hear them read aloud. When recording selections, read with expression but read slowly enough so that students can follow along. Pace your reading at about 80 to 100 words per minute. Also obtain a tape recorder that has a speed regulator. Have students set the speed at a comfortable pace (Shany & Biemiller, 1995). As you encounter words or expressions that might be unfamiliar to students, pause before and after reading them so that students will have time to process them (Carbo, Dunn, & Dunn, 1986).

Recordings should be brief. Record from five to ten minutes of text on each side of a tape. Obtain short stories and brief articles that lend themselves to being recorded. Begin the recording by announcing title and author. Provide an overview of the selection to give students an orientation to the selection. Also provide a purpose for listening. Signal when it is time to turn a page and announce when the reading has been completed (Carbo, Dunn, & Dunn, 1986).

Encourage students to read along with the taped selection several times, until they judge that they can read it on their own. When they feel ready to read on their own, students should try reading the selection without the tape and note difficult parts. They should then listen to the tape once more and reread the text to practice parts that proved to be difficult. Students can work alone or with partners. If working with partners, they can read to each other after practicing with the tape.

### ■ CD-ROM Books

In some ways, CD-ROM selections work better than tapes. Some have a feature that highlights the portion being read, so that makes following along easier. When attempting to read the selections on their own, students can turn off the read-aloud feature. However, they can have read aloud any words that pose problems.

### ■ CD-ROM Fluency Read-Alongs

Many reading software programs, such as *Reading Blasters* (Davidson) have a feature that allows students to read stories out loud and then hear the read-aloud. After students have heard a story read and read along with it, they can then record their reading of it and compare their reading with that of the professional reader. Students can practice reading a small segment and move on to the next segment once they have mastered it. They can have as many practice read-alouds as they want and can read along with the correct version as many times as they want. This could be especially helpful for English language learners who are struggling with correct pronunciation and expression.

## Alternate Reading

In alternate reading, the teacher (parent or tutor) and the student take turns reading the selection. Initially, the teacher reads most of the selection. The student reads any words or phrases that she can. For some students this might be a few high-frequency and short-vowel words or a repeated sentence. As the student improves, she reads larger portions. The teacher reads the first page, and the student reads the second page. Or the teacher might read the difficult parts, and the pupil reads the easy parts. The teacher also provides whatever help the student needs. If the student encounters a difficult word, the teacher tells the student the word or provides prompts that help the student figure out the word.

## Increasing the Amount of Reading

Fluency is most effectively fostered by increasing the amount of reading that students do. In one study, second-graders engaged in partner and echo reading of the basal text and silent reading in school and at home of self-selected books. Although the program was only a year long, students gained nearly two years (Stahl, Heubach, & Crammond, 1997). The students who gained the most were reading at least on a preprimer level. Apparently, students need some foundational reading skill before they can profit from fluency instruction (Kuhn & Stahl, 2000).

## Series Books

Series books are especially effective for developing fluency. Because they have the same characters and often the same setting, series books are easier to read. If they like the first book they read in a series, chances are students will be motivated to read the other books in the series. Often students will read all the books in a 20-book series. Because the reading is easy and highly motivating, this fosters automaticity of word recognition and speed of processing, which are key components in fluency. For kindergartners and first-graders, Clifford, Curious George, and Arthur are popular series. For students in grades 2 to 4, Kids of Polk Street, Nate the Great, Cam Jansen, and Magic Tree House are popular.

## Phrasing of Text

Fluency is more than just accuracy and speed in reading; it also includes proper phrasing. Word-by-word reading is frequently caused by giving students material that is too difficult so that they literally have to figure out just about every word. It also can be caused by a lack of automaticity. Students have to stop and decode a large proportion of words because they don't recognize them immediately. Word-by-word reading should fade out as students improve their decoding skills and as their skills become automatic. If word-by-word reading persists even though word recognition is adequate and automatic, model reading orally in logical phrases and have students read selections in which phrases are marked so that they have practice reading in meaningful chunks.

## SYLLABIC ANALYSIS

Fortunately, many of the most frequently used words in English have just one syllable. The Harris-Jacobson list of words (Harris & Jacobson, 1982) that appears in at least half of basal readers has no multisyllabic words on the preprimer level. On the primer level, however, 15 percent are polysyllabic; on the first-grade level, the figure rises to more than 25 percent. By second grade, more than 30 percent are multisyllabic; by fourth grade, the figure is more than 60 percent. The implications are clear. Students have to know early on how to deal with multisyllabic words. That need grows rapidly as students progress to higher levels. **Syllabication,** or structural analysis as it is sometimes called, may be introduced informally in the latter half of first grade and should be taught formally in second grade and beyond.

Syllabic analysis is deceptively difficult. Surprisingly, several students, in one study of thirty-seven second-graders who were proficient readers and could easily read *let* and *her*, read *letter* as *later*, *weeding* as *wedding*, *cabbage* as *cab bag*, and *ribbon* as *rib bahn*, the last two errors being nonwords (Gunning, 2001). In 20 percent of the multisyllabic words, students omitted at least one syllable. An analysis of students' errors has a number of implications for instruction. These include:

- Students should be taught and prompted to process all the syllables in a word.
- Students need to be taught to see patterns in words. Students who can read *let* and *her* but read *letter* as *later* are not seeing the familiar *et* pattern.
- Students need to be flexible in their decoding of words. If one pronunciation doesn't work out, they should be prepared to try another. This ties in with reading for meaning. Pronouncing *even* as *ev-en*, the student should note that this is not a word and so should try a long pronunciation: *e-ven*.
- Students should integrate context and syllabic analysis. A number of students read *wedding* for *weeding* in the sentence: "Amy was weeding her garden," which indicates failure to use context. A number of other students read the sentence as "Amy was watering her garden," which suggests that although they used context they failed to process the whole word.
- Students need to be reminded to use the orthographic aspects of phonics. Many students had difficulty with words containing final *e* markers and digraphs. Students did not make use of the final *e* marker that indicates a soft *g* in *cabbage* or the digraph *ai* in *contain* that indicates a long *a*. When presenting syllable patterns, it may be helpful to review the single-syllable elements that make up those patterns.

■ **Syllabication** is the division of words into syllables. In reading, words are broken down into syllables phonemically, according to their sound (*gen e rous, butt er*), rather than orthographically, according to the rules governing end-of-line word division (*gen er ous, but ter*).

**ADAPTING INSTRUCTION for *STRUGGLING READERS and WRITERS***
Some students have difficulty decoding multisyllabic words even though they are able to decode single-syllable words. These students may not realize that they can apply their single-syllable skills to the decoding of multisyllabic words. Having them seek out known parts in multisyllabic words helps them make use of what they know.

- Students should also be taught that sometimes an element in a multisyllabic word is not read in the same way as when it appears in a single-syllable word. For instance, many students read the *car* in *carrots* as though it were the word *car*. Students also need to know that often the pronunciation of an element changes when it is in a multisyllabic word. Because of reduced stress, the *on* in *ribbon* has a schwa rather than a short-*o* pronunciation. Many students pronounced it as though it had a short-*o* pronunciation and ended up with the nonword *ribbahn*. Students need to be flexible in their pronunciation of the syllables in mulitsyllabic words and should also be using context as an aid.

- Elements such as *tion* and *ture* as in *mention* and *future*, which occur only in multisyllabic words, need a careful introduction, frequent review, and a great deal of practice.

## Generalization Approach to Teaching Syllabic Analysis

Sort the following words. You can have a question mark category for words that don't seem to fit a pattern.

| | | | |
|---|---|---|---|
| spider | super | magnet | clever |
| secret | flavor | bitter | custom |
| rabbit | hotel | tiger | over |
| supper | music | fever | elbow |
| pepper | pupil | wagon | future |

How did you sort the words? One way of sorting them would be by sounds. All the words with long vowels are in one column; all the words with short vowels are in a second column. You can also sort them by sound and spelling. Notice that the words that end in a consonant seem to be short and those that end in a vowel seem to be long. You might also note that the long vowels were followed by one consonant and short vowels were followed by two consonants. However, there were two exception words: *wagon* and *clever*. Sorting is a way of helping students make discoveries about words. Through sorts of this type students discover one of the most sweeping generalizations in phonics: the open and closed vowel syllables rule, which states that syllables that end in a vowel are generally long and those that end in a consonant are short.

The two approaches to teaching syllabication are generalization and pattern. Sorting is an excellent device to help students discover or reinforce their knowledge of generalizations or patterns in syllabication.

In the generalization approach, students learn general rules for dividing words into syllables. The generalizations listed below seem to be particularly useful (Gunning, 1975). These should be presented in the following order, which reflects both their frequency of occurrence and approximate order of difficulty:

1. *Easy affixes: -ing, -er, -ly.* Most prefixes and suffixes form separate syllables: *un-safe, re-build, help-ful, quick-ly.* Except for *s* as a plural marker, affixes

Although students formulate a generalization, the emphasis is on using patterns or model words rather than generalizations to read multisyllabic words.

Students often confuse open and closed syllables. They tend to read open syllables such as those occurring in *even* and *noticed* as closed syllables: *ev-en, not-iced.*

Putting words into syllables can be a challenging task because it's sometimes difficult to tell where one syllable ends and another begins. Even the experts disagree. If you look up the word *vocational,* for instance, you will see that Merriam-Webster dictionaries divide it into syllables in one way and Thorndike-Barnhart dictionaries syllabicate it in another way.

generally are composed of a vowel and consonant(s). Thus, they are syllables in themselves: *play-ing, re-play.*

2. *Compound words.* The words that make up a compound word usually form separate syllables: *sun-set, night-fall.*

3. *Two consonants between two vowels.* When two consonants appear between two vowels, the word generally divides between them: *win-ter, con-cept.* The place of division is often an indication of the pronunciation of the vowel. The *i* in *winter,* the *o* in the first syllable of *concept,* and the *e* in the second syllable of *concept* are short. Note that all three vowels are in closed syllables—that is, syllables that end in consonants: *win, con, cept.* Closed syllables often contain a short vowel. (The *e* in winter is not short because it is followed by *r.*) Note, too, that digraphs are not split: *broth-er, with-er.*

4. *One consonant between two vowels.* When one consonant appears between two vowels, it often becomes a part of the syllable on the right: *ma-jor, e-vil.* When the single consonant moves to the right, the syllable to the left is said to be open because it ends in a vowel. If a syllable ends in a vowel, the vowel is generally long. In a number of exceptions, however, the consonant becomes a part of the syllable on the left: *sev-en, wag-on.*

5. *le.* The letters *le* at the end of a word are usually combined with a preceding consonant to create a separate syllable: *cra-dle, ma-ple.*

6. *Two vowels together.* A limited number of words split between two vowels: *i-de-a, di-al.*

It is important to keep in mind that syllabication is designed to help students decode an unfamiliar word by separating it into its syllabic parts and then recombining the parts into a whole. It is not necessary for students to divide the word exactly right, which is a highly technical process. All that matters is whether students are able to arrive at the approximate pronunciation.

As with other skills and strategies that involve sounds in words, instruction in syllabication begins on an auditory level. Students must be able to hear the syllables before they can be expected to break a word into syllabic parts and reconstruct it. Lesson 4.9 presents the steps in teaching syllabication using the generalization approach.

 **Syllabication using the generalization approach**

### Step 1. Auditory perception of syllables

Explain to students that words have parts called syllables. Say a group of words or student's names and clap for each syllable: *be-cause, chil-dren, help-er, pic-ture.* Once students catch on to the idea, have them join in. Also have students assemble into groups according to the number of syllables in their names. Three-syllable names such as *Samantha* might pose problems because the second syllable is accented and the first shortened so that it might not be counted as a syllable (Educate the Children, 2001). Also use picture sorting to reinforce the concept of auditory syllables. Students might sort packs of animal cards according to number of syllables.

### Step 2.  Perception of printed syllables

Present one- and two-syllable words that contrast with each other so that students get a sense of printed syllables:

| a | fast | be | win | some |
|---|---|---|---|---|
| ago | faster | being | window | sometime |

Have students read the one-syllable word and then the two-syllable word with which it contrasts. Emphasize that the top word has one syllable and the bottom word has two syllables.

### Step 3.  Perception of syllable generalization

Once students have a sense of what syllables are, present words that illustrate a syllable generalization. The following words illustrate the affix *-ing* generalization:

| do | call | play | see | sing |
|---|---|---|---|---|
| doing | calling | playing | seeing | singing |

Have students read the words and contrast them. Lead them to see that the words on the top have one syllable and those on the bottom have two. Read each word on the bottom, and encourage the class to clap as they hear the separate syllables in each one. Lead students to see that *-ing* at the end of a word forms a separate syllable. In ensuing lessons, cover other affixes and broaden the generalization.

### Step 4.  Guided practice

Have the class read rhymes, poems, signs, and short pieces and sing songs that contain words incorporating the generalization that has been taught. Have students complete exercises in which they use both context and syllabication clues to choose the word that correctly completes a sentence, for example:

> Did you (call, calling) me up?
> I hear a bird (sing, singing).
> I cannot (see, seeing) you from here.
> We are (play, playing) a new game.

### Step 5.  Application

Have students read stories and articles that contain multisyllabic words. Encourage them to apply the generalization(s) they have learned.

Have students sort multi-syllabic words. This enables them to discover generalizations and patterns. Words to be sorted should be words they can read.

**Step 6. Assessment and reteaching**

Provide assistance and additional feedback if students experience difficulty using the syllabication generalization.

## Pattern Approach to Teaching Syllabic Analysis

Knowing syllabic generalizations is one thing; applying them is quite another. Research (Gunning, 1975) and experience suggest that many students apparently do not apply syllabic generalizations. When faced with unfamiliar, multisyllabic words, they attempt to search out pronounceable elements or simply skip the words. These students might fare better with an approach that presents syllables in patterns (Cunningham, 1978).

In a pattern approach, students examine a number of words that contain a syllable that has a high frequency. For example, dozens of words that begin with a consonant and are followed by a long *o* could be presented in pattern form. The advantage of this approach is that students learn to recognize pronounceable units in multisyllabic words and also to apply the open-syllable generalization in a specific situation. The pattern could be introduced with a one-syllable word contrasted with multisyllabic words to make it easier for students to grasp, for example:

so
soda
total
local
vocal
motel
hotel
notice

The steps to follow in teaching a syllabication lesson using the pattern approach are presented in Lesson 4.10. Schwa *a*, as in *above*, a high-frequency pattern, is introduced.

 **Syllabication using the pattern approach**

**Step 1. Introducing the schwa *a* pattern**

Write the word *go* on the board, and have students read it. Then write *ago* under it, and have students read it. Contrast *go* and *ago* by pointing to the sound that each syllable makes. To help students perceive the separate syllables in *ago*, write them in contrasting colors or underline them. Then have students read *ago*. Present the words *away*, *alone*, *awake*, and *asleep* in the same way. As students read the separate syllables in each word, point to each one. Note similarities among the words.

### Step 2. Formulating a generalization and selecting a model word

Lead students to see that *a* at the beginning of a word often has the schwa sound /uh/. Since schwa, according to most systems of categorizing speech sounds, occurs only in multisyllabic words, provide students with a multisyllabic model word for the *a* spelling of schwa. Tell students that *ago* is the model word for this pattern. If they forget the pattern or have difficulty with a schwa *a*, they can use the model word to help them. If you have a model words chart, add *ago* to it. If you do not have a model words chart, you may wish to start one.

### Step 3. Guided practice

For guided practice, have students read a second set of schwa *a* words: *around, along, alive, across, about.* Also have students search out schwa *a* words in a reading selection so they can see this pattern in context. Have students complete exercises similar to the following:

Make words by putting together two of the three syllables in each row. Write the words on the lines.

| | | |
|---|---|---|
| sleep | a | read |
| a | go | play |
| head | a | next |
| over | a | round |
| a | long | lamp |

Underline the word that fits the sense of the sentence better.

Toads and frogs look (*alike, away*).

Do you know how to tell them (*alive, apart*)?

Toads like to live in gardens that are (*alive, alone*) with bugs.

Toads eat an (*amazing, awakening*) number of bugs.

A toad can flick its tongue so fast that a bug would have a hard time getting (*awake, away*). (Gunning, 1994)

### Step 4. Application

Have students read selections—stories, informational pieces, and/or real-world materials—that contain schwa *a* words.

### Step 5. Assessment and review

Note students' ability to read multisyllabic words that follow the pattern introduced. Also note what they do when they encounter multisyllabic words. Are they able to use strategies to decode the words? Review and reteach as necessary.

---

Why might students who can read elements in single-syllable words have difficulty with those same elements in multisyllabic words? The students may have difficulty locating the known element in a polysyllabic word. For instance, *par* is a single-syllable word that appears as an element in *partial, parcel,* and *particle* but has a different identity in *parade* and *paradise.* As Shefelbine (1990) notes, "Identifying patterns of syllables requires more developed and complex knowledge of letter and spelling patterns than the knowledge needed for reading single syllable words" (p. 225).

---

When students decode polysyllabic words, do not insist upon exact syllable division. All that should be expected is that the student break polysyllabic words into smaller units so that she or he can pronounce each one and then put the units back together again to form a whole word.

> Students need not be able to pronounce every syllable. Often, if they find a key syllable or two that they can pronounce, they can use this to reconstruct the whole word.

### ■ Additional Practice Activities for Multisyllabic Words

- Have students read or sing song lyrics in which the separate syllables of multisyllabic words are indicated.
- Make available books in which difficult words are put into syllables and phonetically respelled.
- Write words on the board, syllable by syllable. After writing the first syllable, have students read it and guess what the word might be. Then write the second syllable. Have them read the first syllable again and combine it with the second syllable. Continue until the whole word has been written.
- Encourage students to bring in multisyllabic words that they have noticed in their reading and which they were able to pronounce. They might write their words on the board and have the other students read them.
- When introducing new words that have more than one syllable, write the words on the board and encourage students to read them. Provide help as needed.
- Use software, such as *Word Parts* (Sunburst), that challenges students to build words by combining syllables and use multisyllabic words to compose poems, riddles, and stories.
- To help students differentiate between open and closed syllables, have them read contrasting word pairs (*super, supper; biter, bitter*) or complete sentences by selecting one of two contrasting words: Although the dog looked mean, it was not a (*biter, bitter*). We had chicken and mashed potatoes for (*super, supper*).

## Multisyllabic Patterns

In approximate order of difficulty, the major multisyllabic patterns are:

- Easy affixes: *play-ing, quick-ly*
- Compound words: *base-ball, any-one*
- Closed-syllable words: *rab-bit, let-ter*
- Open-syllable words: *ba-by, ti-ny*
- *e* marker words: *es-cape, do-nate*
- Vowel digraph words: *a-gree, sea-son*
- Other patterns: *cir-cle, sir-loin*

Major syllable patterns and example words for the patterns are presented in Table 4.13.

> Instead of, or along with, the traditional strategy for decoding multisyllabic words presented on the previous page, students might use the prounceable word part or analogy strategy.

## Combining the Generalization and Pattern Approaches

Although the pattern approach is highly effective and builds on what students know, students sometimes are unable to see patterns in words. In these instances,

**TABLE 4.13**  Common syllable patterns

### Compound-Word Pattern

| some | day | out | sun |
|---|---|---|---|
| someone | daylight | outside | sunup |
| sometime | daytime | outdoor | sundown |
| something | daybreak | outline | sunfish |
| somehow | daydream | outgrow | sunlight |
| somewhere | | outfield | sunbeam |

### Schwa *a* Pattern

| a | a |
|---|---|
| ago | around |
| away | along |
| alone | alive |
| awake | apart |
| among | across |
| asleep | about |

### High-Frequency Patterns

| en | o | er |
|---|---|---|
| pen | go | her |
| open | ago | under |
| happen | over | ever |
| enter | broken | never |
| twenty | spoken | other |
| plenty | frozen | farmer |
| **ar** | **at** | **it** |
| car | mat | sit |
| garden | matter | sitter |
| sharpen | batter | bitter |
| farmer | chatter | kitten |
| marker | clatter | kitchen |
| partner | scatter | pitcher |
| **in** | **is(s)** | **un** |
| win | miss | under |
| winter | mister | until |
| window | mistake | hunter |
| dinner | sister | thunder |
| finish | whisper | hundred |
| **be** | **re** | **or** |
| became | remind | order |
| beside | report | morning |
| below | reward | corner |
| begin | refuse | forty |
| belong | receive | before |

| a | y = /ē/ | ey | ble |
|---|---|---|---|
| pay | sunny | turkey | able |
| paper | funny | monkey | table |
| baby | dusty | money | cable |
| famous | shady | honey | bubble |
| favorite | | | mumble |
| **i** | **ur** | **um** | |
| tie | fur | sum | |
| tiger | furry | summer | |
| spider | hurry | number | |
| tiny | turkey | pumpkin | |
| title | turtle | stumble | |
| Friday | purple | trumpet | |
| **ic(k)** | **et** | **et** | **im** |
| pick | let | ticket | swim |
| picnic | letter | pocket | swimmer |
| attic | better | rocket | chimney |
| nickel | lettuce | bucket | limit |
| pickle | settle | magnet | improve |
| chicken | metal | jacket | simple |

### Short-Vowel Patterns

| ab | ad | ag |
|---|---|---|
| cab | sad | bag |
| cabin | saddle | baggy |
| cabbage | paddle | dragon |
| rabbit | shadow | wagon |
| habit | ladder | magazine |
| absent | address | magnet |
| **an** | **ap** | |
| can | nap | |
| candy | napkin | |
| handy | happy | |
| handle | happen | |
| giant | captain | |
| distant | chapter | |
| **ent** | **el** | |
| went | yell | |
| event | yellow | |
| prevent | elbow | |
| cement | elephant | |
| invent | jelly | |
| experiment | welcome | |

*continued*

**TABLE 4.13** Common syllable patterns *(continued)*

| ep | es(s) | ev | ub | uc(k) | ud |
|---|---|---|---|---|---|
| pep | less | seven | rub | luck | mud |
| pepper | lesson | several | rubber | lucky | buddy |
| peppermint | address | never | bubble | bucket | study |
| September | success | clever | stubborn | chuckle | puddle |
| shepherd | yesterday | every | subject | success | huddle |
| separate | restaurant | level | public | product | sudden |

| ea | ea | | uf | ug | up |
|---|---|---|---|---|---|
| sweat | treasure | | stuff | bug | pup |
| sweater | measure | | stuffy | buggy | puppy |
| weather | pleasure | | muffin | ugly | supper |
| feather | pleasant | | suffer | suggest | upper |
| leather | threaten | | buffalo | struggle | puppet |
| meadow | wealthy | | | | |

| id | ig | il | us | ut | uz |
|---|---|---|---|---|---|
| rid | wig | pill | muss | but | fuzz |
| riddle | wiggle | pillow | mustard | button | fuzzy |
| middle | giggle | silver | muscle | butter | puzzle |
| hidden | signal | silly | custom | clutter | muzzle |
| midnight | figure | building | customer | flutter | buzzer |
| | | | discuss | gutter | buzzard |

**Long-Vowel Patterns**

| ob | oc | od | ade | ail/ale |
|---|---|---|---|---|
| rob | doc | cod | parade | detail |
| robber | doctor | body | invade | female |
| problem | pocket | model | lemonade | airmail |
| probably | chocolate | modern | centigrade | trailer |
| hobby | rocket | product | | |
| gobble | hockey | somebody | | |

| ol | om | on | ain | ate |
|---|---|---|---|---|
| doll | mom | monster | obtain | hesitate |
| dollar | momma | monument | explain | hibernate |
| volcano | comma | honest | complain | appreciate |
| follow | common | honor | | |
| holiday | comment | concrete | | |
| jolly | promise | responsible | | |

| ea | ea | ee | e |
|---|---|---|---|
| sea | eat | bee | equal |
| season | eaten | see | secret |
| reason | beaten | beetle | fever |
| beaver | repeat | needle | female |
| eagle | leader | indeed | even |
| easily | reader | succeed | |

| op | ot | age |
|---|---|---|
| shop | rot | cabbage |
| shopper | rotten | bandage |
| chopper | gotten | damage |
| popular | bottom | message |
| opposite | bottle | baggage |
| copy | robot | garbage |

| ide | ire | ize | ise | ive |
|---|---|---|---|---|
| side | tire | prize | wise | drive |
| beside | entire | realize | surprise | arrive |
| divide | require | recognize | exercise | alive |
| decide | admire | memorize | advise | survive |
| provide | umpire | apologize | disguise | beehive |

**TABLE 4.13**     Common syllable patterns *(continued)*

| ope | one | u | ture | ou | ou | ow |
|-----|-----|---|------|-----|-----|-----|
| hope | phone | use | future | round | mountain | power |
| antelope | telephone | music | nature | around | fountain | tower |
| envelope | microphone | human | adventure | about | surround | flower |
| telescope | xylophone | museum | creature | announce | compound | allow |
| | | | | amount | thousand | allowance |

**Other Vowel Patterns**

| al | au | au | aw | oo | ove | u |
|----|----|----|----|----|-----|---|
| also | cause | caution | draw | too | prove | Sue |
| always | saucer | faucet | awful | bamboo | proven | super |
| already | author | sausage | awesome | shampoo | improve | student |
| altogether | August | daughter | drawing | cartoon | approve | studio |
| although | autumn | auditorium | crawling | raccoon | remove | truly |
| walrus | audience | | strawberry | balloon | movements | tuna |

| oi | oy | tion | tion | sion | y = /ī/ |
|----|----|------|------|------|---------|
| point | joy | action | question | conclusion | try |
| poison | enjoy | addition | mention | confusion | reply |
| disappointment | destroy | station | suggestion | occasion | supply |
| noisy | royal | invention | exhaustion | explosion | deny |
| avoid | loyal | information | indigestion | persuasion | magnify |
| moisture | voyage | | | | |

From *Assessing and Correcting Reading and Writing Difficulties* (2nd ed.) by T. Gunning, 2002. Boston: Allyn & Bacon. Reprinted by permission of Allyn & Bacon.

they should try applying generalizations. In his research, Shefelbine (1990) found that instruction in open (*mo-*, *ta-*, *fi-*) and closed (*-at*, *-em*, *-in*) syllables and affixes (*un-*, *pre-*, *-less*, *-ful*) was especially helpful. After teaching a number of open-syllable patterns, you might have students construct a generalization about the pattern, such as, "Syllables that end in a vowel are often long (*ta ble*). After teaching a number of closed-syllable patterns, you might have students construct a generalization about the pattern, such as, "Syllables that end in a consonant are often short (*hap py*)."

To apply generalizations, students should identify the first syllable by locating the first vowel and note whether the syllable is open (followed by one consonant or digraph) or closed (followed by two or more consonants). Students should say the first syllable and then proceed in this same way, syllable by syllable. After they have pronounced all the syllables, they should attempt to say the word, making any adjustments necessary. Prompt students as needed. If students misread an open syllable as a closed one, for instance, reading *no-tice* as *not-ice*, ask them to tell where the vowel is so they can see that the vowel should be ending the syllable and should be long (Shefelbine & Newman, 2000). Often vowel sounds are reduced when they appear in multisyllabic words, as in *educate*, where the *u* has a schwa pronunciation. Explain to students that they should not just pronounce syllables but should change pronunciations if they have to so they can "read the real word" (Shefelbine & Newman, 2000).

Whether you teach using generalizations, patterns, or, as this book recommends, a combination of approaches, students must have a plan of attack or strategy when facing an unfamiliar multisyllabic word. Students can use the steps in the following traditional Student Strategy on their own.

### Attacking multisyllabic words

1. See whether the word has any prefixes or suffixes. If so, pronounce the prefix, then the suffix, and then the remaining part(s) of the word. If the word has no prefix or suffix, start with the beginning of the word and divide it into syllables (as explained on previous pages). Say each syllable.

2. Put the syllables together. If the word does not sound like a real word, try other pronunciations until you get a real word.

3. See if the word makes sense in the sentence in which it appears. If it does not, try other pronunciations.

4. If nothing works, use a dictionary or ask the teacher.

**ADAPTING INSTRUCTION for STRUGGLING READERS and WRITERS**

Struggling readers often fail to process all the letters in a word and so misread it. To help students match all the sounds and letters in a word, try this activity. Say a word (*snack*), stretching out its sounds as you do so: "sssnnnaaakkk." Have students repeat the word and *explain* how many sounds they hear. Show a card that has the word written on it. Match up the sounds and their spellings. Have students tell why there are five letters but only four sounds. Have students find another word with the same vowel sound, spell the word from dictation, and meet it in their reading (Gaskins et al., 1996–1997).

## Using the Pronounceable Word Part and Analogy Strategies

The pronounceable word part and analogy strategies recommended for decoding single-syllable words may also be used to decode multisyllabic words. For instance, if students are having difficulty with the word *silver*, they might look for a pronounceable word part such as *il* and add /s/ to make *sil*. They would then say *er*, add /v/ to make *ver* and reconstruct the whole word. In many instances, saying a part of the word—the *sil* in *silver*, for example—is enough of a clue to enable students to say the whole word. If the pronounceable word part strategy does not work, they may use an analogy or compare/contrast strategy, in which students employ common words to help them sound out the syllables in a multisyllabic word that is in their listening but not their reading vocabulary. For instance, faced with the word *thunder*, the student works it out by making a series of comparisons. The first syllable is *thun*, which is similar to the known word *sun*, and the second syllable is *der*, which is similar to the known word *her*. Putting them together, the student synthesizes the word *thunder*.

As students read increasingly complex materials and meet a higher proportion of polysyllabic words, their ability to perceive the visual forms of syllables should develop naturally. As with phonics skills, the best way to practice dealing with polysyllabic words is through a combination of instruction and wide reading.

# HELP FOR STRUGGLING READERS AND WRITERS

Struggling readers and writers do best when given a systematic program in word analysis skills (Foorman et al., 1998). Although most students will grasp word analysis skills regardless of the approach used to teach them, at-risk learners need direct, clear instruction (Snow, Burns, & Griffin, 1998). For students who are struggling, this text recommends word building, with one important adaptation. When presenting a pattern, emphasize the components of the pattern. As explained in the sample lesson, say the parts of a pattern word. When adding *p* to *et* to form *pet*, say, "When I add /p/ to /et/, I get the word *pet*." Then point out each letter and the sound it represents. Pointing to *p* say /p/, pointing to *e* say /e/, pointing to *t* say /t/. Then say the word as a whole. Later, after adding *et* to *p* to form *pet*, again say the word in parts and then as a whole. Pointing to *p*, say the sound /p/. Pointing to *e*, say the sound /e/. Pointing to /t/, say the sound /t/. Then say the word as a whole. Have students say the word in parts and as a whole. Saying the individual sounds in a word helps the students to note all the sounds in the word and the letters that represent them. It also fosters phonemic awareness, which develops slowly in many struggling readers. In addition, some struggling readers may find it easier to deal with individual sounds.

Also, use spelling to reinforce phonics. Dictating and having students spell pattern words helps them to focus on the individual sounds and letters in the pattern words and provides another avenue of learning. Most important of all, encourage students to read widely. Struggling readers often need much more practice than do achieving readers. Reading books on their level that apply patterns they have been taught is the best possible practice.

For syllabic analysis, use the pattern approach. One advantage of this approach is that it reviews basic phonics as new elements are being introduced. For instance, when introducing the *aw* multisyllabic pattern, the teacher automatically reviews the *aw* element, as in *law*. This is helpful to struggling readers, who often have gaps in their skills. Shefelbine (1990) found that 15 to 20 percent of the students in the fourth- and eighth-grade classes that he tested had difficulty with multisyllabic words, and some students were still experiencing problems with single-syllable phonics, especially vowel elements.

A variety of word lists for practice with both single-syllable words and multisyllabic words can be found at **http://www. resourceroom.net/ OGLists/wordlists.asp.**

**INVOLVING PARENTS**

Parents might want to know what to do if their children ask for help with a word. Having them simply tell their children unknown words is the safest, least frustrating approach (Topping, 1989). But in some situations, you may want to have them encourage their children in the use of specific strategies.

# ESSENTIAL STANDARDS

### Kindergarten
See Essential Standards at end of Chapter 3.

### Grade one
*Students will*

- continue to develop phonemic awareness, especially segmentation and blending skills, as they learn phonics skills.

- learn consonant, consonant digraph, and consonant cluster correspo
  short vowels, long vowels, other vowels, *r* vowels, and vowel patter
- use their knowledge of consonants, consonant digraphs, clusters, sł
  els, long vowels, other vowels, *r* vowels, and vowel patterns to dec
- recognize high-frequency, irregular words, such as *of*, *was*, and ⌐
- use pronounceable word part, analogy, picture clue, and contextual clue su⌐
  gies to decode words.
- read words with inflectional endings such as *-s, -ed, -ing.*
- integrate the use of contextual and word analysis strategies.
- begin to read both regularly and irregularly spelled words automatically.
- begin to use common word patterns to read multisyllabic words.
- read with accuracy, fluency, and expression at about fifty to sixty words per minute.

### Grade two
*Students will*

- learn advanced and less frequent consonant digraph and consonant cluster correspondences and advanced and less frequent short vowels, long vowels, other vowels, *r* vowels, and vowel patterns.
- use their knowledge of consonants, consonant digraphs, consonant clusters, short vowels, long vowels, *r* vowels, other vowels, and vowel patterns to decode words.
- use high-frequency syllabication patterns such as affixes and compound words and common word patterns to decode words.
- use pronounceable word part, analogy, and contextual strategies to decode words.
- integrate the use of contextual and word analysis strategies.
- read with accuracy, fluency, and expression at about sixty to seventy words per minute.

### Grades three and four
*Students will*

- use a full range of phonics skills to decode words.
- use a full range of syllabic analysis skills and patterns to decode words.
- use pronounceable word part, analogy, and contextual strategies to decode words.
- integrate the use of contextual and word analysis strategies.
- read with accuracy, fluency, and expression at an appropriate rate (see Table 4.9).

## ACTION PLAN

1. Assess students' knowledge of word analysis skills and strategies.
2. Construct or adapt a program for development of word analysis skills and strategies based upon students' needs.
3. Introduce needed phonics and syllabication skills and strategies in functional fashion.
4. Provide ample practice and application opportunities.
5. Develop fluency through modeling, instruction, wide reading, and rereading.
6. Plan a systematic program. However, provide on-the-spot instruction when the need arises.
7. For English language learners, plan a program that takes into consideration word analysis knowledge that they already possess in their native language and areas that might pose problems.
8. Monitor students' progress and make necessary adjustments.

## ASSESSMENT

Assessment should be ongoing. Through observation, note whether students are learning the skills and strategies they have been taught. Watch to see what they do when they come across an unfamiliar word. Do they attempt to apply pronounceable word part, analogy, or context strategies? When they read, what phonics elements are they able to handle? What phonics elements pose problems for them? In addition to observation, you might use the Beginning Consonant Correspondences survey to assess knowledge of initial consonants, the Word Pattern Survey to assess students' knowledge of major phonics patterns, and the Syllable Survey in Appendix B to get a sense of students' ability to handle multisyllabic words. Chapter 2 contains additional assessment suggestions, including using a running record.

## SUMMARY

1. The ultimate goal of phonics is to enable students to become independent readers. Functional practice and extensive reading are recommended to help them reach that goal.
2. Words can be read in a number of ways: predicting, decoding, analogizing, or retrieving as sight words. How a word is read depends, in part, on the stage that the reader is in: prephonemic, early alphabetic, full alphabetic, or consolidated alphabetic. Instruction should be geared to students' stage.
3. The two main approaches to teaching phonics

are analytic (whole word, implicit) and synthetic (sound by sound, explicit). Today, almost all approaches use a systematic, explicit approach. This book recommends combining both through a pattern, or word-building, approach. Phonics can also be presented whole part or part whole.

4. Consonants are generally taught before vowels because their sounds have fewer spellings and because they are more useful in helping students sound out unfamiliar words.

5. Consonant elements to be taught include single consonants, digraphs, and clusters. Vowel elements include short- and long-vowel correspondences, other vowels, *r* vowels, and schwa. Phonics generalizations have limited usefulness.

6. Along with phonics, students should use semantic and syntactic clues and their general knowledge to decode words. Along with context clues, students should be taught how to use two powerful word identification strategies: pronounceable word part and analogy.

7. As children invent spellings, they make important discoveries about their language's writing system. Invented spellings can also give the teacher insight into a child's grasp of the writing system.

8. High-frequency words are frequently appearing words. These include some words such as *want* and *once* that have irregular spellings. Although irregular, these words are learned through phonological and spelling connections. Because they occur so frequently, students should be given extra practice with them so that they can be recognized rapidly.

9. Fluency is "freedom from word identification problems that might hinder comprehension in silent reading or the expression of ideas in oral reading." Fluency is fostered by providing a solid foundation in word analysis skills and numerous opportunities to read materials on the appropriate level of challenge.

10. In syllabication, words are broken up into parts primarily based on sound patterns. Syllabication may be taught through generalizations or patterns or some combination of the two.

11. All basal programs use decodable text in the early stages of reading. Decodable text is written in such a way that it contains a high percentage of words that students can read by using the word analysis skills and strategies that they have been taught.

## EXTENDING AND APPLYING

1. Read over the pronunciation key of a dictionary. Notice the spellings given for the consonant sounds and the vowel sounds. Check each of the sounds. Are there any that are not in your dialect? The following words have at least two pronunciations: *dog* ("dawg" or "dog"), *roof* ("roof" or "roof"), *route* ("root" or "rowt"). How do you pronounce them?

2. Examine the word analysis component of a basal series. What is its approach to teaching phonics and syllabic analysis? Are the lessons and activities functional and contextual? Is adequate practice provided? What is your overall evaluation of the word analysis program in this series?

3. Using the word-building (pattern) approach described in this chapter, plan a lesson in which a phonics or a syllabic analysis element is introduced. State your objectives and describe each of the steps of the lesson. List the titles of children's books or other materials that might be used to reinforce or apply the element taught. Teach the lesson and evaluate its effectiveness.

4. Working with a small group of elementary students, note which strategies they use when they encounter difficult words. Providing the necessary instruction and prompts, encourage them to use the pronounceable word part, analogy, and context strategies.

## DEVELOPING A PROFESSIONAL PORTFOLIO

Document your knowledge of and ability to teach word analysis skills. Include a sample word analysis lesson that you have taught and your reflection on it. Keep a record of any inservice sessions or workshop sessions on word analysis that you have attended.

## DEVELOPING A RESOURCE FILE

Maintain a list of books that you might use to provide students with opportunities to apply their word analysis skills. Seek out books that have a natural sound to them. Using the Decodability Index in Figure 4.6 on p. 208, analyze the skills needed to read the books. Keep a list, too, of helpful Web sites and software.

# 5

# Building Vocabulary

*F*or each of the following statements, put a check under "Agree" or "Disagree" to show how you feel. Discuss your responses with classmates before you read the chapter.

|  | *Agree* | *Disagree* |
|---|---|---|
| **1** Vocabulary words should be taught only when students have a need to learn them. | _____ | _____ |
| **2** All or most of the difficult words in a selection should be taught before the selection is read. | _____ | _____ |
| **3** Building vocabulary leads to improved comprehension. | _____ | _____ |
| **4** The best way to build vocabulary is to study a set number of words each week. | _____ | _____ |
| **5** Using context is the easiest way to get the meaning of an unfamiliar word. | _____ | _____ |
| **6** The best way to learn about roots, prefixes, and suffixes is to have a lot of experience with these word parts. | _____ | _____ |
| **7** Using the dictionary as a strategy to get the meanings of unfamiliar words is inefficient. | _____ | _____ |

## USING WHAT YOU KNOW

*C*hapter 4 explained techniques for teaching children how to decode words that were in their listening vocabularies but which they might not recognize when they saw them in print. This chapter is also concerned with reading words. However, the focus in this chapter is on dealing with words whose meanings are unknown. In preparation for reading this chapter, explore your knowledge of this topic.

How many words would you estimate are in your vocabulary? Where and how did you learn them? Have you ever read a book or taken a course designed to increase your vocabulary? If so, how well did the book or the course work? What strategies do you use when you encounter an unknown word? How would you go about teaching vocabulary to an elementary or middle school class?

# THE NEED FOR VOCABULARY INSTRUCTION

Estimates of the number of words known by average first-graders vary widely from 2,500 to 24,000. However, 5,000 to 6,000 seems a reasonable figure.

Read the following paragraph, which is excerpted from Beverly Cleary's *Ramona Quimby, Age 8* (1981), a book typically read in grade three. What challenges does the passage present for the typical third-grader?

> Rainy Sunday afternoons in November were always dismal, but Ramona felt this Sunday was the most dismal of all. She pressed her nose against the living-room window, watching the ceaseless rain pelting down as bare black branches clawed at the electric wires in front of the house. Even lunch, leftovers Mrs. Quimby had wanted to clear out of the refrigerator, had been dreary, with her parents, who seemed tired or discouraged or both, having little to say and Beezus mysteriously moody. Ramona longed for sunshine, sidewalks dry enough for roller skating, a smiling happy family. (p. 33)

Although meant for third-graders, the vocabulary is surprisingly advanced. Students might have difficulty with *dismal, ceaseless, pelting,* and *longed*. In the initial stages of reading, virtually all the words are known by readers. They are in the readers' listening vocabularies. But as students advance into higher-level texts, vocabulary becomes more challenging. To be proficient readers and writers, students must build their vocabularies and learn strategies for coping with difficult words. As students progress through the grades a key element in their growth as readers and writers is vocabulary development.

# STAGES OF WORD KNOWLEDGE

Knowing a word's meaning is not an either/or proposition. Graves (1987) posited six tasks in word knowledge:

*Task 1: Learning to read known words.* Learning to read known words involves sounding out words that students understand but do not recognize in print. It includes learning a sight vocabulary and using phonics and syllabication to sound out words.

*Task 2: Learning new meanings for known words.* Even a cursory examination of a dictionary reveals that most words have more than one meaning. A large part of expanding a student's vocabulary is adding new shades of meaning to words partly known.

*Task 3: Learning new words that represent known concepts.* Because the concept is already known, this really is little more than learning a new label.

*Task 4: Learning new words that represent new concepts.* As Graves (1987) observed, "Learning new words that represent new concepts is the most difficult word-learning task students face" (p. 169).

*Task 5: Clarifying and enriching the meanings of known words.* Although this task is accomplished when students meet known words in diverse contexts, Graves felt that more systematic, more direct involvement is called for. Teachers have to help students forge connections among known words and provide a variety of enrichment exercises to ensure greater depth of understanding.

*Task 6: Moving words from receptive to expressive vocabulary.* It is necessary to teach words in such a way that they appear in students' speaking and writing vocabularies. The ultimate test is whether students actually use newly learned words correctly. As Nagy and Scott (2000) comment, "Knowing a word means being able to do things with it. . . . Knowing a word is more like being able to use a tool than it is like being able to state a fact" (p. 273).

As can be seen from the six tasks just described, word knowledge is often a question of degree. The person who uses a CD burner on a regular basis has a better knowledge of the words *CD burner* than does one who has simply seen the device advertised. Instruction needs to be devoted to refining as well as to introducing vocabulary and concepts.

> It is difficult to say when a word is learned. Some concrete words may be learned instantaneously; others may be learned slowly, after repeated encounters. In time, words take on a greater depth of meaning as they conjure up more associations.

## SEVEN PRINCIPLES OF DEVELOPING VOCABULARY

Developing vocabulary is not simply a matter of listing ten or twenty words and their definitions on the board each Monday morning and administering a vocabulary quiz every Friday. In a sense, it is a part of living. Children learn their initial 5,000 to 6,000 words by interacting with parents and peers, gradually learning labels for the people, objects, and ideas in their environment. As children grow and have additional experiences, their vocabularies continue to develop. They learn *pitcher, batter, shortstop,* and *home run* by playing or watching softball or baseball. They learn *gear shift, brake cable, kick stand,* and *reflector* when they begin riding a bicycle.

### Building Experiential Background

The first and most effective step that a teacher can take to build vocabulary is to provide students with a variety of rich experiences. These experiences might involve taking children to an apple orchard, supermarket, zoo, museum, or office. Working on projects, conducting experiments, handling artifacts, and other hands-on activities also build a background of experience.

Not all activities can be direct. Viewing computer simulations and demonstrations, films, videotapes, filmstrips, and special TV shows helps build experience, as do discussing, listening, and reading. The key is to make the activity as concrete as possible.

### ■ Talking Over Experiences

Although experiences form the foundation of vocabulary, they are not enough; labels or series of labels must be attached to them. A presurvey and postsurvey of visitors to a large zoo found that people did not know much more about the animals after leaving the park than they did before they arrived. Apparently, simply looking at the animals was not enough; visitors needed words to define their experiences. This is especially true for young children.

### ■ Learning Concepts versus Learning Labels

■ A **label** is simply a name for a concept. Students may use labels without really understanding the meanings behind the labels.

For maximum benefit, it is important that experiences be discussed. It is also important to distinguish between learning **labels** and building concepts. For example, the words *petrol* and *lorry* would probably be unfamiliar to American students preparing to read a story set in England. The students would readily understand them if the teacher explained that to the British *petrol* means "gasoline" and *lorry* means "truck." Since the concepts of gasoline and truck are already known, it would simply be a matter of learning two new labels. If the word *fossil* appeared in the selection, however, and the students had no idea what a fossil was, the concept would have to be developed. To provide a concrete experience, the teacher might borrow a fossil from the science department and show it to the class while explaining what it is and relating it to the children's experiences. Building the **concept** of a fossil would take quite a bit more teaching than would learning the labels *petrol* and *lorry*.

■ A **concept** is a general idea, an abstraction derived from particular experiences with a phenomenon. In our rush to cover content, we may not take the time necessary to develop concepts thoroughly; thus students may simply learn empty labels for complex concepts such as *democracy* or *gravity*.

Over time, our expanding background of experience allows us to attach richer meaning to words. For example, *love*, *truth*, *justice*, and *freedom* mean more to us at age twenty than they did at age ten, and even more as we approach thirty or forty. In many instances, when dealing with abstract terms, students know the forms of words but not the concepts behind them. A child may have heard and seen the word *independence* many times but have no real idea of what it means. The child may not even realize that as she or he grows and develops, her or his own independence is gradually being gained. The student must learn the concept behind the label; otherwise, the word will be literally meaningless.

## Relating Vocabulary to Background

The second principle of vocabulary development is relating vocabulary to students' background. It is essential to relate new words to experiences that students may have had. To teach the word *compliment*, the teacher might mention some nice things that were said that were complimentary. Working in pairs, students might compose compliments for each other.

Gipe (1980) devised a background-relating technique in which students are asked to respond to new words that require some sort of personal judgment or observation. For example, after studying the word *beacon*, students might be asked, "Where have you seen a beacon that is a warning sign?" (p. 400). In a similar vein, Beck and McKeown (1983) asked students to "Tell about someone you might want to eavesdrop on," or "Describe the most melodious sound you can think of" (p. 624). Carr (1983) required students to note a personal clue for each new word. It could be an experience, object, or person. One student associated a local creek with *murky*; another related *numbed* to how one's hands feel when shoveling snow.

## Building Relationships

The third principle of developing vocabulary is showing how new words are related to each other. For example, students may be about to read a selection on autobiographies and biographies that includes the unfamiliar words *accomplishment*, *obstacles*, and *nonfiction*, as well as *autobiography* and *biography*. Instead of simply presenting these words separately, demonstrate how they are related to each other. Discuss how autobiography and biography are two similar types of nonfiction, and they often describe the subject's accomplishments and some of the obstacles that he or she had to overcome.

Other techniques for establishing relationships include noting synonyms and antonyms, classifying words, and completing graphic organizers. These techniques are covered later in this chapter.

## Developing Depth of Meaning

The fourth vocabulary-building principle is developing depth of meaning. The most frequent method of teaching new words is to define them. Definitions, however, may provide only a superficial level of knowledge (Nagy, 1988). They may be adequate when new labels are being learned for familiar concepts, but they are not sufficient for new concepts. Definitions also may fail to indicate how a word should be used. The following sentences were created by students who had only definitional knowledge. Obviously, they had some understanding of the words, but it was inadequate.

> The *vague* windshield needed cleaning.
> At noon we *receded* to camp for lunch.

It takes time to learn a word well enough to use it appropriately in a sentence. Instead of having students write sentences using newly learned words, have them complete sentences stems, which prompt them to use the word appropriately and in a sentence which shows that they know the meaning of the word: The farmers had to irrigate their fields because _____. In order to complete the sentence, students will have to know what *irrigate* means and why farmers might have to irrigate their fields. (Beck, McKeown, & Kucan, 2002).

Words may have subtle shades of meanings that dictionary definitions may not quite capture. Most students have difficulty composing sentences using new words when their knowledge of the words is based solely on definitions (McKeown, 1993). Placing words in context (Gipe, 1980) seems to work better, as it illustrates use of words and thereby helps to define them. However, in order for vocabulary development to aid in the comprehension of a selection, both the definition and the context should reflect the way the word is used in the selection the students are about to read.

Obviously, word knowledge is a necessary part of comprehension. Ideas couched in unfamiliar terms will not be understood. However, preteaching difficult vocabulary has not always resulted in improved comprehension. In their review of the

When concerned about comprehension, choose a few key terms for intensive teaching. The words should be taught so well that pupils don't have to pause when they encounter them.

research on teaching vocabulary, Stahl and Fairbanks (1986) found that methods that provided only definitional information about each word to be learned did not produce a significant effect on comprehension; nor did methods that gave only one or two exposures to meaningful information about each word. For vocabulary instruction to have an impact on comprehension, students must acquire knowledge of new words that is both accurate and enriched (Beck, McKeown, & Omanson, 1987). Experiencing a newly learned word in several contexts broadens and deepens understanding of it. For instance, the contexts *persistent detective*, *persistent salesperson*, *persistent pain*, and *persistent rain* provide a more expanded sense of the word *persistent* than might be conveyed by a dictionary or glossary definition.

## Presenting Several Exposures

Although students may derive only a vague idea of a word's meaning after a single exposure, additional incidental exposures help clarify the meaning. Over a period of time, many words are acquired in this way.

Frequency of exposure is the fifth principle of vocabulary building. Beck, McKeown, and Omanson (1987) suggested that students meet new words at least ten times; however, Stahl and Fairbanks (1986) found that as few as two exposures were effective. It also helps if words appear in different contexts so that students experience their shades of meaning. Frequent exposure or repetition of vocabulary is essential to comprehension because of limitations of attention and memory. Third-graders reading a selection about the brain that uses the new words *lobe* and *hemisphere* may not recall the words if the teacher has discussed them only once. Although the students may have understood the meanings of the words at the time of the original discussion, when they meet them in print they are vague about their definitions and must try to recall what they mean. Because they give so much attention to trying to remember the meanings of the new words, they lose the gist of the fairly complex passage. Preteaching the vocabulary did not improve their comprehension because their reading was interrupted when they failed to recall the words' meanings immediately or their knowledge of the words was too vague.

Vocabulary knowledge is the most important predictor of reading comprehension (Davis, 1968; Thorndike, 1973).

Even if the students do recognize the words, their recognition may be slower because they have seen the words only once before. Slowness in accessing the meanings of words from one's mental dictionary can hinder comprehension (Samuels, 1994). This discouraging situation does have a positive side. Although limited exposure may not help immediate comprehension, the long-term payoff is that students should gain some knowledge of words even from just a single, brief encounter. Perhaps it is enough to move the word from the I-never-saw-it stage to the I've-heard-of-it plateau. Added encounters may bring added knowledge until the word moves to the I-know-it stage.

## Creating an Interest in Words

A useful resource for word play activities is *Wordworks: Exploring Language Play* by Bonnie von Hoff Johnson. Golden, CO: Fulcrum Publishing.

Generating interest in words can have a significant impact upon vocabulary development. In their experimental program, Beck and McKeown (1983) awarded the title of "Word Wizard" to any student who noted an example of a taught word outside of class and reported it to the group. Children virtually swamped their teachers with instances of seeing, hearing, or using the words as they worked toward gaining points on the Word Wizard Chart. On some days, every child in the class came in with a Word Wizard contribution. Teachers also reported that the children would occasionally cause a minor disruption—for example, at an assembly when a speaker used one of the taught words and the entire class buzzed with recognition (p. 625).

## Teaching Students How to Learn New Words

The seventh and last principle of vocabulary development is promoting independent word-learning skills. Teaching vocabulary thoroughly enough to make a difference takes time. If carefully taught, only about 400 words a year can be introduced (Beck, McKeown, & Omanson, 1987). However, students have to learn thousands of words, so teachers also have to show them how to use such tools of vocabulary acquisition as context clues, morphemic analysis, and dictionary skills. Vocabulary instruction must move beyond the teaching of words directly as a primary activity. Because students derive the meanings of many words incidentally, without instruction, another possible role of instruction is to enhance the strategies readers use when they do learn words incidentally. Directly teaching such strategies holds the promise of helping children become better independent word learners (Kameenui, Dixon, & Carnine, 1987).

# TECHNIQUES FOR TEACHING WORDS

Dozens of techniques are available for introducing and reinforcing new vocabulary. Those discussed here follow all or some of the seven principles presented above.

## Graphic Organizers

**Graphic organizers** are semantic maps, pictorial maps, webs, and other devices that allow students to view and construct relationships among words. Because they are visual displays, they allow students to picture and remember word relationships.

■ A **graphic organizer** is a diagram used to show the interrelationship among words or ideas.

### ■ Semantic Maps

Suppose that your students are about to read an informational piece on snakes that introduces a number of new concepts and words. For example, it states that snakes are reptiles, a concept that you believe will be new to the class. You have scheduled an article about alligators and crocodiles for future reading. Wouldn't it be efficient if you could clarify students' concept of snakes and also prepare them to relate it to the upcoming article? There is a device for getting a sense of what your students know about snakes, helping them organize their knowledge, and preparing them for related concepts: semantic mapping, or, simply, mapping.

A **semantic map** is a device for organizing information graphically according to categories. It can be used for concepts, vocabulary, topics, and background. It may also be used as a study device to track the plot and character development of a

■ A **semantic map** is a graphic organizer that uses lines and circles to organize information according to categories.

*W*ebs are useful for developing and organizing concepts.

*Inspiration* (Inspiration Software) or similar software can be used to create graphic organizers.

story or as a prewriting exercise. Mapping may be presented in a variety of ways but is generally introduced through the following steps (Heimlich & Pittelman, 1986; Johnson & Pearson, 1984):

1. *Introduce the concept, term, or topic to be mapped.* Write the key word for it on the chalkboard, overhead transparency, or chart paper.
2. *Brainstorm.* Ask students to tell what other words come to mind when they think of the key word. Encourage them to volunteer as many words as they can. This may be done orally, or students may write their lists and share them. If the new words that you plan to teach are not suggested, present them and discuss them.
3. *Group the words by category, discussing why certain words go together.* Encourage students to supply category names.
4. *Create the class map, putting it on a large sheet of paper so that the class can refer to it and add to it.*
5. *Once the map has been finished, discuss it.* Encourage students to add items to already established categories or to suggest new categories.
6. *Extend the map.* As students discover, through further reading, additional new words related to the topic or key word, add these to the chart.

Lesson 5.1 shows, in abbreviated form, how a map on *snakes* was produced by a class of third-graders.

---

### LESSON 5.1 — Semantic mapping

**Step 1.**

The teacher writes the word *snakes* on the board and asks the class to tell what words come to mind when they think of snakes.

**Step 2.**

Students suggest the following words, which are written on the chalkboard: *poisonous, rattlesnakes, nonpoisonous, garter snakes, sneaky, king snakes, dangerous, frightening, deserts, rocky places,* and *forests*. No one mentions *reptiles*, which is a key word in the article students are about to read. The teacher says that he would like to add that word and asks students if they know what a reptile is. One student says reptiles are cold-blooded. This word is also added to the list.

**Step 3.**

Words are grouped, and category names are elicited. Students have difficulty with the task, so the teacher helps. He points to the words *forests* and *deserts* and asks what these tell about snakes. The class decides that they tell where snakes live. The teacher then asks the class to find another word that tells where snakes live. Other words are categorized in this same way, and category labels are composed. The map in Figure 5.1 is created.

### Step 4.

Students discuss the map. Two of them think of other kinds of snakes—water moccasins and boa constrictors—which are added. During the discussion, the teacher clarifies concepts that seem fuzzy and clears up misconceptions. One student, for instance, thinks that all snakes are poisonous.

### Step 5.

Students read to find out more information about snakes. They refer to the map, which is displayed in the front of the room, to help them with vocabulary and concepts. After reading and discussing the selection, students are invited to add words or concepts they learned. The following are added: *dry, smooth skin; scales; vertebrae;* and *flexible jaws.*

### Step 6.

A few weeks later, the class reads a selection about helpful snakes. The map is reviewed before reading the story and then expanded to include new concepts and vocabulary.

> Actively involving students aids both their understanding of concepts and retention. In one project in which maps were used to help portray complex concepts, students failed to show improvement. Analysis revealed that the instructors were doing much of the mapmaking. Having minimal involvement in the process, students received minimal benefit (Santa, 1989).

After students have grasped the idea of mapping, they can take a greater share of responsibility for creating maps. The sequence listed below gradually gives children ownership of the technique (Johnson & Pearson, 1984).

1. Students cooperatively create a map under the teacher's direction.
2. Students begin assuming some responsibility for creating maps. After a series of items has been grouped, they might suggest a category name.
3. Students are given partially completed maps and asked to finish them. They can work in groups or individually.
4. The teacher supplies the class with a list of vocabulary words. Working in groups, students use the list to create maps.
5. Working in groups or individually, students create their own maps.

### ■ Pictorial Maps and Webs

Pictorial and mixed pictorial–verbal maps work as well as, and sometimes better than, purely verbal maps. A **pictorial map** uses pictures along with words. For some words or concepts, teachers may want to use a more directed approach to constructing semantic maps. After introducing the topic of the planet Mars, the teacher might discuss the characteristics in a **web,** which is a simplified map. A web does not have a hierarchical organization, and it is especially useful for displaying concrete concepts (Marzano & Marzano, 1988). A web is displayed in Figure 5.2

> ■ A **pictorial map** uses drawings, with or without labels, to show interrelationships among words or concepts.

> ■ A **web** is another name for a semantic map, especially a simplified one.

FIGURE 5.1

**Semantic Map on Snakes**

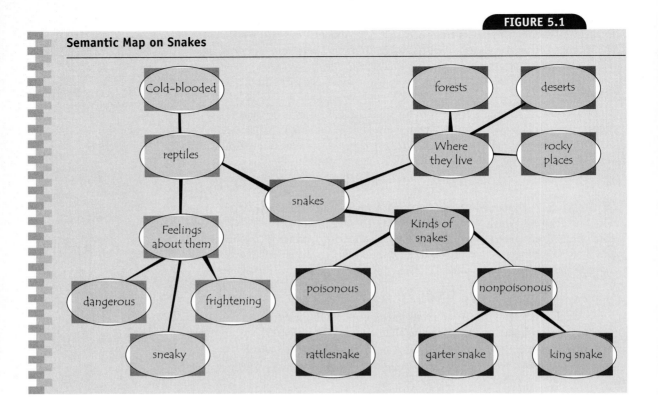

FIGURE 5.2

**Web for Mars**

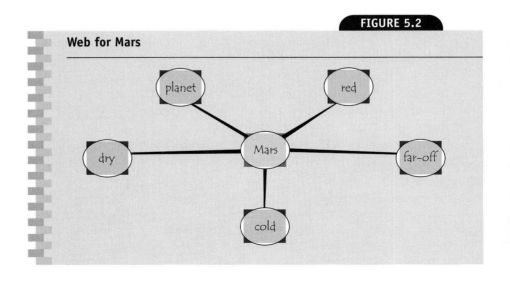

### ■ Semantic Feature Analysis

**Semantic feature analysis** uses a grid to compare words that fall in a single category. For example, it could be used to compare different mammals, means of transportation, tools, sports, and so on. In constructing a semantic feature analysis, complete the steps outlined in Lesson 5.2, which are adapted from Johnson and Pearson (1984).

■ A **semantic feature analysis** is a graphic organizer that uses a grid to compare a series of words or other items on a number of characteristics.

## LESSON 5.2    Semantic feature analysis

**Step 1.**

Announce the topic, and ask students to give examples. In preparation for reading a story about boats, ask students to name different kinds of boats.

**Step 2.**

List the boats in the grid's left-hand column.

**Step 3.**

Ask students to suggest characteristics or features that boats have. List these in a row above the grid.

**Step 4.**

Look over the grid to see if it is complete. Have students add other boats or their qualities. At this point, you might suggest additional kinds of boats or added features of boats.

**Step 5.**

Complete the grid with the class. Put a plus or minus in each square to indicate whether a particular kind of boat usually has the quality or characteristic being considered. If unsure, put a question mark in the square. Encourage students to discuss items about which they may have a question—for example, whether hydrofoils sail above or through the water. As students become proficient with grids, they may complete them independently.

**Step 6.**

Discuss the grid. Help students get an overview of how boats are alike as well as of how specific types differ.

**Step 7.**

Extend the grid. As students acquire more information, they may want to add other kinds of boats and characteristics.

Eventually, students should compose their own grids. Through actively creating categories of qualities and comparing items on the basis of a number of features, students sharpen their sense of the meaning of each word and establish relationships among them. A sample of a completed grid is shown in Figure 5.3.

### ■ Venn Diagram

■ A **Venn diagram** is a graphic organizer that uses overlapping circles to show relationships between words or other items.

Somewhat similar in intent to the semantic feature analysis grid is the **Venn diagram** (Nagy, 1988), in which two or three concepts or subjects are compared. The main characteristics of each are placed in overlapping circles. Those traits that are shared are entered in the overlapping area, and individual traits are entered in the portions that do not overlap. In discussing crocodiles and alligators, the teacher might encourage students to list the major characteristics of each, noting which belong only to the alligator and which belong only to the crocodile. A Venn diagram like that in Figure 5.4 could then be constructed. After they grasp the concept, students should be encouraged to construct their own diagrams. Because this activity requires active comparing and contrasting, it aids both understanding and memory.

## Dramatizing

Although direct experience is the best teacher of vocabulary, it is not possible to provide it for all the words that have to be learned. Dramatization can be a reasonable substitute. Putting words in the context of simple skits adds interest and reality.

Dramatizations can be excerpted from a book or created by teachers or students. They need not be elaborate; a simple skit will do in most instances. Here is one dramatizing the word *irate*.

**FIGURE 5.3**

### Semantic Feature Analysis

| BOATS | On water | Under water | Above water | Paddles, oars | Sails | Engines |
|---|---|---|---|---|---|---|
| Canoe | + | − | − | + | − | − |
| Rowboat | + | − | − | + | − | − |
| Motorboat | + | − | − | ? | − | + |
| Sailboat | + | − | − | ? | + | ? |
| Submarine | − | + | − | − | − | + |
| Hydrofoil | − | − | + | − | − | + |
| Hovercraft | − | − | + | − | − | + |

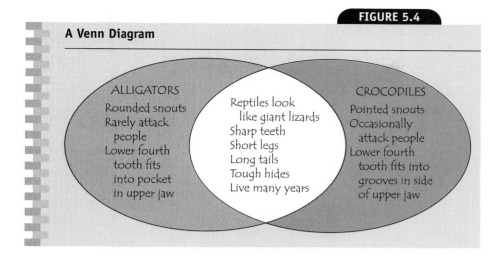

**FIGURE 5.4**

**A Venn Diagram**

ALLIGATORS
Rounded snouts
Rarely attack
people
Lower fourth
tooth fits
into pocket
in upper jaw

Reptiles look
like giant lizards
Sharp teeth
Short legs
Long tails
Tough hides
Live many years

CROCODILES
Pointed snouts
Occasionally
attack people
Lower fourth
tooth fits into
grooves in side
of upper jaw

*Student 1:* Hey, Brian, what's wrong? You seem really mad.

*Student 2:* Someone's eaten my lunch. They must have known my dad packed my favorite sandwich, peanut butter and banana with raisins. I'm boiling inside. I'm really irate.

*Student 1:* I'd be irate, too, if someone took my lunch. But before you blow your lid, calm down. Maybe you misplaced it. Say, isn't that your dad coming down the hall? And what's that in his hand? It looks like a lunch bag.

Another way of dramatizing words is to use a hinting strategy (Jiganti & Tindall, 1986). After a series of new words has been introduced and discussed, the teacher distributes to individuals or pairs of students cards on each of which is one of the new words. Each student or pair creates a series of sentences that contain hints to the identity of the target word. Hints for *exaggerate* can be found in the following paragraph:

I like being around Fred, but he tends to stretch the truth a little. The other day he caught a fairly large fish. But to hear him tell it, it sounded like a whale. When Fred catches five fish, he pretends that he really caught twenty. And when it's a little chilly, Fred says it's the coldest day of the year. I like Fred, but I wish he'd stick a little closer to the facts.

The new words are written on the chalkboard. Students read their hints, and the class then tries to figure out which of the new words they describe.

## Enjoying Words

In school, words are used to instruct, correct, and direct. They should also be used to have fun, as one of the functions of language is to create enjoyment. Recite appropriate puns, limericks, and jokes to the children, and encourage them to share

**USING TECHNOLOGY**
Funbrain.com features a variety of intriguing activities, including several word games.
**http://www.funbrain.com/vocab/index.html**

their favorites. Include word-play collections, such as those listed in the following Children's Reading List, in the classroom library.

## CHILDREN'S READING LIST  Word play

Agee, J. (1998). *Who ordered the jumbo shrimp and other oxymorons.* New York: HarperCollins. Features humorous illustrations.

Cerf, B. (1960). *Bennett Cerf's book of riddles.* New York: Random House. This collection features a variety of easy-to-read riddles.

Christopher, M. (1996). *Baseball jokes and riddles.* Boston: Little, Brown. Presents more than fifty jokes and riddles.

Clark, E. C. (1991). *I never saw a purple cow and other nonsense rhymes.* Boston: Little, Brown. The collector has illustrated her collection of more than 120 nonsense rhymes about animals.

Hall, K., & Eisenberg, L. (1998). *Puppy riddles.* New York: Dial. Presents a series of forty-two easy-to-read puppy riddles.

Heller, R. (1991). *A cache of jewels and other collective nouns.* New York: Grosset & Dunlap. Rhyming text and illustrations introduce a variety of collective nouns, such as a "drift of swans" and a "clutch of eggs." See also *Many Luscious Lollipops* (adjectives) and *Up, Up, and Away* (adverbs).

Kitchen, B. (1990). *Gorilla/chinchilla and other animal rhymes.* New York: Dial. Rhymed text describes a variety of animals whose names rhyme but who have very different habits and appearances.

Mathews, J., & Robinson, F. (1993). *Oh, how waffle! Riddles you can eat.* Morton Grove, IL: Whitman, 1993. Features riddles related to food.

Meddaugh, S. (1992). *Martha speaks.* Boston: Houghton Mifflin. Problems arise when Martha, the family dog, learns to speak after eating alphabet soup.

Rattigan, J. (1994). *Truman's aunt farm.* Boston: Houghton Mifflin. When Truman sends in the coupon for an ant farm, a birthday present from his Aunt Fran, he gets more than he bargains for when aunts instead of ants show up.

Rosen, M. (1995). *Walking the bridge of your nose, wordplay poems and rhymes.* New York: Kingfisher. Features a variety of poems and rhymes that play with words.

Terban, M. (1992). *Funny you should ask: How to make up jokes and riddles with wordplay.* Boston: Houghton Mifflin.

Terban, M. (1999). *Too hot to hoot: Funny palindrome riddles.* Boston: Houghton Mifflin.

### ■ Crossword Puzzles

Crossword puzzles are excellent for reinforcing students' vocabulary. When creating them, also use previously introduced words. Puzzles are more valuable if they re-

*T*hrough playing Scrabble and other word games, students develop an interest in words.

volve around a theme—such as farm implements, the parts of the eye, or words that describe moods, for example. For younger readers, start out with limited puzzles that have only five to ten words and expand them as students gain in proficiency. *Worksheet Magic Plus* (Teacher Support Software) or a similar piece of software can be used to create crossword puzzle grids. Crossword and other puzzles can also be created at Web sites such as Puzzlemaker at http://puzzlemaker.school.discovery.com/. All you have to do is supply the words and definitions. Crossword puzzles and word games frequently appear in the following periodicals: *Chickadee Magazine, Child Life, Children's Digest, Cobblestone, Cricket, Highlights for Children, Humpty Dumpty's Magazine, Lady Bug, My Friend, National Geographic World, Ranger Rick, Wee Wisdom,* and Web sites such as those listed in Surfing the Net with Kids: Crossword Puzzles at http://www.surfnetkids. com/crossword.htm.

> **USING TECHNOLOGY**
> Puzzlemaker creates several different kinds of puzzles including crossword and word search. All you need are the words and definitions (for crossword puzzles).

### ■ Riddles

Riddles are inherently interesting to youngsters, and they provide an enjoyable context for developing vocabulary. They can be used to expand knowledge of homonyms, multiple meanings, figurative versus literal language, and intonation as a determiner of word meaning (Tyson & Mountain, 1982). Homonyms can be presented through riddles such as the following:

> Why is Sunday the strongest day?
> Because the other days are weak days. (p.171)

Multiple meanings might be reinforced through riddles of the following type:

> Why couldn't anyone play cards on the boat?
> Because the captain was standing on the deck. (p. 171)

*Exemplary Teaching*

### Developing Vocabulary and Confidence

*B*orrowing from Sylvia Ashton-Warner, Mrs. Warren, a resource room teacher at P. S. 94 in the Bronx, New York, invites her remedial readers each day to choose a word that they would like to learn. A second-grader chose *discrimination*; a third-grader asked to learn *suede*. The words chosen were as varied as the children.

Warren's students are operating well below grade level. Having a history of failure, they feel discouraged, frustrated, and incompetent. Learning long words builds their confidence and their self-esteem. As they learn words such as *discombobulate*, *spectacular*, and *advise*, they begin to see themselves as competent learners.

As Warren explains, "You have to prove to these children that they can learn. Telling them is not enough. You have to get them to be successful at something. The words convince them they're smart." Learning new words also builds an interest that snowballs. "If you can get children to love words, for whatever reason, you've got it made," Warren comments (Rimer, 1990, p. B5).

The students draw their words from many sources. Some come from their reading, others from discussions or television. A favorite source is a 365-new-words-a-year calendar. Students record their words on three-by-five index cards and keep them in a file box. The growing number of cards becomes a testament to their success in building their vocabularies and their overall competence as learners.

---

Riddles containing figurative language can be used to provide practice with common figures of speech:

> Why were the mice afraid to be out in the storm?
> Because it was raining cats and dogs. (p. 172)

Some of the riddle books listed in the Children's Reading List might be used to implement these suggestions. Also, plan activities in which riddles and puzzles are not tied to a lesson, so that students can experience them just for the fun of it.

## Word of the Day

**BUILDING LANGUAGE**
Students enjoy the challenge of learning long words. Actually, long words are easier to learn because their length makes them more distinctive.

A good way to begin the day is with a new word. The word might tie in with the day, the time of year, or some special local or national event. Or choose a word related to a topic the students are studying. Select interesting, useful words. Write the word on the chalkboard, or put it on a special bulletin board. Read or write the context in which the word is used. Have students try to guess the meaning of the word. Provide a history of the word, and discuss why it's an important word. Encourage students to collect examples of the word's use. Working alone or in pairs, older students might present their own words of the day.

## Labeling

Labeling provides greater depth of meaning to words by offering at least secondhand experience and, in some instances, helps illustrate relationships. The parts of plants, the human body, an airplane, and many other items lend themselves to labeling. For instance, when students are about to read a true-life adventure about a pilot whose life was endangered when the flaps and ailerons froze, present a labeled diagram showing these and other airplane parts, such as fuselage, landing gear, aileron, stabilator, fin, rudder, and trim tab. A sample of such a labeled drawing is presented in Figure 5.5. Discuss each part and its function. Relate the parts to each other and show how they work together to make the plane fly. Ask students to picture the parts in operation during takeoff, level flight, turns, and landing. After the story has been read, give them drawings of a plane. Have them label the parts. Better yet, let them label their own drawings of a plane.

## Feature Comparison

Through questions that contain two newly learned words, students can compare major meanings (Beck & McKeown, 1983). For example, ask such questions as "Could a virtuoso be a rival?" and "Could a philanthropist be a miser?" (p. 624). Answering correctly is not the crucial point of this kind of activity. What is important is that students have the opportunity to discuss their responses so as to clarify their reasoning processes and their grasp of the meanings of the words.

## Using Word-Building Reference Books

Dictionaries give definitions, illustrative sentences, and sometimes drawings of words. However, this is often not enough, especially for words that apply to concepts that

> Labeling helps students visualize words. Information may be coded in words or images (Sadowski & Paivio, 1994), and if it can be coded into both, memory is enhanced.

**USING TECHNOLOGY**

*The Way Things Work* (Dorling Kindersley), a CD-ROM program, uses explanations, labeled illustrations, and animations to show how dozens of technical devices work. Excellent for building background and vocabulary.

**FIGURE 5.5**

Labeled Drawing of an Airplane

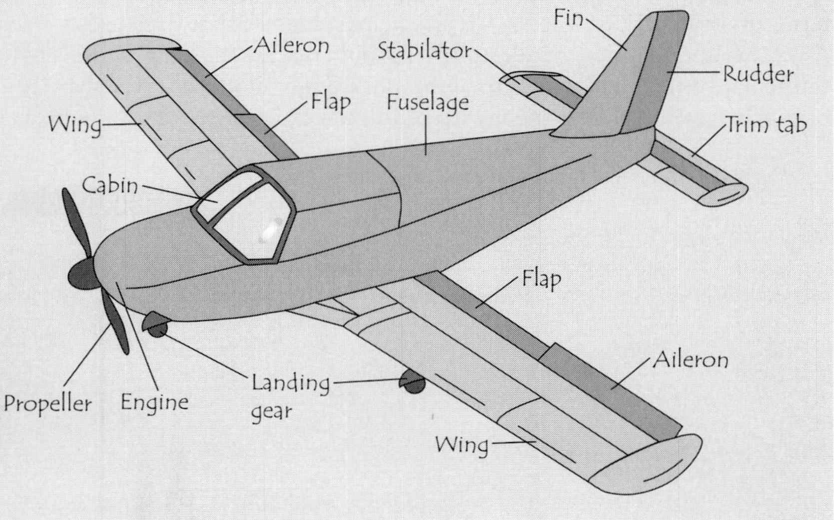

are unknown or vague. For example, a dictionary definition of *laser* is not sufficient for a student who is reading a selection that assumes knowledge of both the operation and the uses of lasers. In contrast, an encyclopedia entry on lasers explains how they work, what their major uses are, and how they were invented. Encourage the use of the encyclopedia so that students eventually refer to it or other suitable references independently to clarify difficult words.

## Predicting Vocabulary Words

The main purpose of studying vocabulary words before reading a selection is to improve comprehension. Two techniques that relate new vocabulary to the selection to be read are the predict-o-gram, which works only with fictional pieces, and possible sentences, which works best with informational text.

### ■ Predict-O-Gram

In a predict-o-gram, students organize vocabulary in terms of the story grammar of a selection (Blachowicz, 1977). Students predict which words would be used to describe the setting, the characters, the story problem, the plot, or the resolution. Here's how the technique works: First, the teacher selects key words from the story. The words are written on the board and discussed to make sure students have some grasp of the meanings of the words. Students are then asked to predict which words the author would use to tell about the main parts of a story: the setting, the characters, the story problem, the plot, the resolution. The teacher asks the class to predict which words might fit in each part of the story grammar: "Which words tell about the setting? Which tell about the characters?" and so on. Once all the words have been placed, students might predict what the story is about. A completed predict-o-gram based on *Make Way for Ducklings* (McCloskey, 1941) is presented in Figure 5.6.

The predict-o-gram forces students to think about new vocabulary words in terms of a story that is to be read. It also helps students relate the words to each other. After the story has been read, students should discuss their predictions in terms of the actual content and structure of the story. They should also revise their predict-o-grams, which provides them with additional experience with the new words.

**FIGURE 5.6**

**Predict-o-gram for *Make Way for Ducklings***

| Setting | Characters | Story Problem | Plot | Resolution |
|---------|-----------|---------------|------|------------|
| Boston | Mr. and Mrs. Mallard | nest | hatched | Michael |
| Public Garden | Michael | pond | responsibility | police |
| Charles River | | island | | |
| | | ducklings | | |
| | | eggs | | |

■ **Possible Sentences**

Possible sentences is a technique by which students use new vocabulary words to predict sentences that might appear in the selection to be read. Possible sentences has five steps (Moore & Moore, 1986):

1. *List key vocabulary.* The teacher analyzes the selection to be read and selects two or three concepts that are the most important. Vocabulary words from the selection that are essential to understanding those concepts are chosen. These words are listed on the board, pronounced by the teacher, and briefly discussed with the class.

2. *Elicit sentences.* Students use the words listed to compose sentences. They must use at least two words in each sentence and create sentences they feel might occur in the selection. It is suggested that the teacher model the creation of a sample sentence and the thinking processes involved. Students' sentences are written on the board even if not correct. Words may be used more than once. This step ends when all the words have been used in sentences or after a specified time.

3. *Read to verify sentences.* Students read the text to verify the accuracy of their possible sentences.

4. *Evaluate sentences.* After reading the selection, students evaluate their sentences. They discuss each sentence in terms of whether or not it could appear in the selection. Sentences are modified as needed.

5. *Create new sentences.* Students use the words to create new sentences. These sentences are also discussed and checked for accuracy of usage.

The value of the possible sentences technique is that, in addition to being motivational, it helps students use informational text to refine their knowledge of new words. Because students write the words, it also helps them put new words into their active vocabularies. Putting new words in sentences is difficult, so the teacher should provide whatever guidance is necessary.

## Word Sorts

Word sorts is a useful activity when dealing with groups of related words. Sorting forces students to think about each word and to see similarities and differences among words. Students might sort the following words: *melancholy, weary, tired, sorrowful, exhausted, glad, contented, cheerful, delighted, unhappy, gloomy, overworked, dejected.* The sort could be open, which means that students would decide on categories, or it could be closed. In a closed sort, the teacher decides the categories: happy, sad, tired. After sorting the words, students would discuss why they sorted them the way they did.

## Wide Reading

The most productive method for building vocabulary—wide reading—requires no special planning or extra effort (Nagy & Herman, 1987). Research (Herman, Anderson, Pearson, & Nagy, 1987) indicates that average students have between a one in twenty and a one in five chance of learning an unfamiliar word they meet in context. Those who read for twenty-five minutes a day at the rate of 200 words per minute for 200 days of the year will encounter a million words (Nagy & Herman, 1987). About 15,000 to 30,000 of these words will be unfamiliar. Given just a one in twenty chance of learning an unfamiliar word from context, students should pick up between 750 and 1,500 new words. Of course, if they read more, they have even greater opportunity for vocabulary growth. If they read 2 million rather than 1 million words a year, they theoretically would double the number of new words they learn.

Many of today's informational books for young people contain glossaries or phonetic spellings of difficult words and provide definitions in context. Some also contain labeled diagrams of technical terms. Note how the following excerpt from a reader-friendly informational book entitled *Fish that Play Tricks* (Souza, 1998) provides both phonetic respelling and contextual definitions:

> The grouper is only one of more than 20,000 different species (SPEE-sheez), or kinds, of fish that live in waters around the world. All fish are cold-blooded, meaning they cannot make themselves much warmer than the temperature around them. Like you, fish are vertebrates (VUHR-tuh-brits), or animals with skeletons inside their bodies. The skeletons of some fish, such as sharks and rays, are made of cartilage, a flexible tissue. (p. 4)

In addition to encouraging wide reading of varied materials, teachers can also provide students with strategies for using context clues, morphemic analysis, and the dictionary to decipher unknown words. Sternberg (1987) found that average adults trained to use context clues were able to decipher seven times as many words as those who spent the same amount of time memorizing words and definitions. If elementary school students are taught to use such clues with greater efficiency, it should boost their vocabulary development as well. For instance, students reading the book *Fish that Play Tricks*, from which the excerpt above was taken, would benefit if they were helped to discover that many of the terms in the book are explained in context, and the explanatory context often begins with the word *or.* Modeling the use of context clues and guided practice should also prove to be helpful.

Some books that are especially effective at building vocabulary are listed below.

**CHILDREN'S READING LIST   Building vocabulary**

DuTemple, L. A. (1998). *Moose*. Minneapolis: Lerner.

Gibbons, G. (1990). *Weather words and what they mean*. New York: Holiday House.

Parson, A. (1997). *Electricity*. Chicago: World Book.

Souza, D. M. (1998). *Fish that play tricks*. Minneapolis: Carolrhoda.

Tarsky, S. (1997). *The busy building book*. New York: Putnam.

# Reading to Students

Read-aloud books are better sources of new words for students in the early grades than are the books they read silently. Up until about grade three or four, the books that students read are composed primarily of known words. At these levels teachers frequently read books to students that would be too hard for them to read on their own. Therefore, carefully chosen read-alouds can be effective for building word knowledge. Whereas it is best to introduce words beforehand when students are reading on their own, it is better to discuss vocabulary words after a selection has been read aloud to students. If words are needed for an understanding of a selection, then they can be explained briefly as the selection is being read. That way students can immediately use their knowledge of the new words to comprehend the selection.

Beck and McKeown (2001) devised an approach in which a portion of the read-aloud was devoted to developing vocabulary. From each book two to four words were selected. Words were selected that were probably unknown to students but which labeled concepts or experiences that would be familiar. These included words such as *reluctant, immense, miserable*, and *searched*. The words were presented in the context of the story, discussed, and later used by students. After reading *A Pocket for Corduroy* (Freeman, 1978) to students, the teacher stated, "In the story, Lisa was reluctant to leave the laundromat without Corduroy. *Reluctant* means you are not sure you want to do something. Say the word for me" (Beck, McKeown, & Kucan, 2002, p. 51). Students say the word so that they gain a phonological representation of it. The teacher then gives examples of *reluctant*, such as foods that they might be reluctant to eat or amusement park rides that they might be reluctant to go on. Students are then asked to tell about some things that they might be reluctant to do. "Tell about something that you might be reluctant to do. Try to use *reluctant* when you tell about it. You could start by saying something like "I would be reluctant to _____." (p. 51).

Notice how the teacher provided a prompt to help student formulate a sentence using *reluctant*. This would be especially helpful to English language learners. Note, too, the steps in the presentation:

- Presenting the word in story context.
- Providing an understandable definition of the word.
- Providing examples of the use of the word in other contexts, so that the word generalizes. Otherwise, students might form the impression that *reluctant* means "to leave something behind that you don't want to leave behind" as in "leaving the laundromat without Corduroy."
- Having children relate the word to their own lives. They did this by talking about things that they were reluctant to do. They might also make a list of things that they are reluctant to do or write about a time when they felt reluctant.
- The word is reviewed. The word is related to other words that are being introduced and to other words that students have learned. For instance, students might discuss how *reluctant* and *eager* are opposites. As occasions arise, the

teacher uses newly taught words. She might say that she is reluctant to go out-side because it is cold and rainy or is reluctant to take down the Thanksgiving decorations because they look so nice. She might also read aloud *The Reluctant Dragon* (Grahame, 1966).

- Students are encouraged to use the word in their speaking and writing and also to note examples of hearing or seeing the words. As Dale and O'Rourke (1971) explain, learning a new word is serendipitous. Newly learned words have a way of cropping up in our reading and listening.

Some books are better than others for developing vocabulary. The frequency with which a new word appears in the text, whether the word is illustrated, and the helpfulness of the context in which the word appears are factors that pro-mote the learning of a new word (Elley, 1989). Having students retell the story in which the word appears also seems to foster vocabulary growth. Words are used with more precision and in more elaborated fashion during students' second and third retellings (Leung, 1992).

To be more effective at building vocabulary, the story being read to students should be within their listening comprehension. If the words are too abstract for the students' level, gains may be minimal. In one study in which a fairly diffi-cult text was read to students aged eight to ten, only the best readers made signifi-cant gains (Nicholson & Whyte, 1992). An inspection of the target words in the text suggested that they may have been too far above the level of the average and below-average readers. The study also suggested that while bright students might pick up words from a single reading, average and below-average students may re-quire multiple encounters with the words.

## Speaking and Writing

Expository text seems to lead to more word learning. Expository texts typically define words, provide examples, and sometimes, include illustrations. Expository texts also elicit more interaction from par-ents and teachers (Schickedanz, 1999).

The ultimate aim of vocabulary development is to have students use new words in their speaking and writing. In-depth study of words and multiple exposures will help students attain sufficient understanding of words and how they are used so they will be able to employ them in their speech and writing. Students should be en-couraged to use new words in the classroom so that they become comfortable with them and so feel confident in using them in other situations. Students should also be encouraged to use new words in their written reports and presentations. As part of preparing students for a writing assignment, teachers might highlight words that lend themselves to inclusion in the written pieces.

## Developing the Vocabulary of English Language Learners

English language learners know fewer English words than their native speaking peers, and they also possess fewer meanings for these words (Verhallen & Schoonen, 1993). Ironically, English Language Learners rely more on their vocabulary knowl-edge than do native speakers of English when reading. Intensive instruction in vo-cabulary can make a difference. After two years of systematic instruction, English language learners closed the gap in vocabulary and comprehension that existed between their performance and that of native speakers by about 50% (McLaughlin et al., 2000). Taking part in a similar program that lasted for four years, language minority elementary school students in Holland made gains of one or two years beyond that made by a control group (Appel & Vermeer, 1996, as cited in McLaughlin et al., 2000). There were also encouraging gains in reading comprehension. The researchers concluded that language minority students can catch up to native speakers in vocabulary knowledge if they receive targeted vocabulary instruction for about four hours a week throughout the school year and if the instruction is carried out for all eight grades of elementary and middle school.

Knowing how words are stored in bilingual students' minds will help you plan ways to develop their vocabularies. Unfortunately, there is no agreement on how words are stored. Some experts believe that the words are stored separately. Words learned in Spanish are not stored in the same place as words stored in English so that *amigo* and *friend* do not share a storage location. Others believe that there is a single store so that *amigo* and *friend* are stored in the same location. A third possibility is that the L2 words are linked to the L1 words. When the student hears *friend*, she thinks first of the equivalent in her language: *amigo*. The fourth theory is that there are overlapping stores. Some words are linked; some are not. The most reasonable theory seems to be that there is overlap between the two stores (Cook, 2001). With some words, students might have to access the meaning in their native language first. With others they can access the meaning without going through a translation process. For young students, it is easier for them to learn a word through translation than it is through an explanation, definition, or even illustration. A young Spanish-speaking student will learn the word *cat* faster if you say it means "el gato" than she will if you show her a picture of a cat or point to a cat (Durgunoglu & Oney, 2000).

To promote full understanding, provide translations of new vocabulary words. If you are unable to translate the words, enlist the services of an older student, a parent, or a bilingual teacher. You might post key vocabulary words in both languages in a prominent spot. Also explore cognates. Some cognates have identical spellings, such as as *color* (KOH-lor) and *chocolate* (choh-koh-LAH-teh) but, as you can see, do not have the same pronunciations. Others have similar spellings: *calendario, excelente, lista*. Still others have spellings that are similar but might not be similar enough to be recognized: *carro (car), crema (cream), difícil (difficult)*.

Spanish-speaking students may know some advanced English words without realizing it. For instance, the word *luna (moon)* would be known by very young Spanish-speaking children. However, *lunar*, as in *lunar landing*, is an advanced word for native speakers of English. Spanish developed from Latin. *Luna*, for instance, is a Latin word. Although English has thousands of words that it borrowed from Latin, English developed primarily from Anglo-Saxon. Our most basic words are derived from Anglo-Saxon. Words derived from Latin tend to be more advanced words. They are a more advanced way of expressing common concepts encapsulated by our most basic words. Although Spanish-speaking students have to learn most common English words from scratch, they have a running start on learning many of the more advanced words because a large proportion of these words are derived from Latin. Explain to Spanish-speaking students that they know some of the harder words in English. You might use *lunar* as an example. This will affirm the value of the students' first language but will also provide them with a most valuable tool for learning English. Make use of this principle when introducing new vocabulary. For instance, when introducing *annual*, ask Spanish-speaking students to tell you the word for *year (año)*. Help them to see that the word *annual* is related to *año*. Follow a similar approach for words like *arbor (árbol-tree), ascend (ascensor), grand (grande-big), primary (primero-first), rapidly (rapidamente-quickly), tardy (tarde-late)*.

Not having had the same opportunity to learn English as native speakers have, English language learners understandably have a more limited store of English words. Experts agree that this is their main stumbling block on the road to literacy in English. They need a long-term, well-planned program of vocabulary development, which builds on their growing knowledge of English and their command of another language. In many instances, vocabulary development for them will simply consist of learning the English label for a familiar concept. In other instances, they might be able to use cognates to help them develop their English vocabulary.

## A PLANNED PROGRAM

■ A **planned program** is one in which a certain amount of time is set aside each week for vocabulary instruction. Vocabulary may be preselected from materials students are about to read or from words they may need to understand content-area concepts.

Although young people apparently learn an amazing number of words incidentally, a **planned program** of vocabulary development is highly advisable. Research from as far back as the 1930s (Gray & Holmes, 1938, cited in Curtis, 1987) suggested that direct teaching is more effective than a program that relies solely on incidental learning. A more recent review of a number of research studies confirmed these results (Petty, Herold, & Stoll, 1968).

Based on their extensive investigations, Beck, McKeown, and Omanson (1987) opted for a program that includes both direct teaching and incidental learning of words and also differentiates among words. Words especially important to the curriculum are given "rich instruction." These words are chosen from basals, content-area texts, or trade books that are to be read by students and are selected on the basis of their importance in understanding the text, frequency of appearance in students' reading, and general usefulness. Rich instruction goes beyond simple definition to include discussion, application, and further activities. Words selected for rich instruction might be presented five to ten times or more. Less important words are simply defined and used in context. This process introduces words that become more familiar as students meet them in new contexts. Any remaining new words are left to incidental learning. Perhaps the most important feature of this program is that words are taught within the context of reading, as opposed to being presented in isolated lists.

Another important component of a planned vocabulary program is motivation. Students will try harder and presumably do better if they encounter intriguing words in interesting stories and if they can relate learning vocabulary to their personal lives. As Sternberg (1987) commented, "In most of one's life, one learns because one wants to or because one truly has to, or both" (p. 96).

## A Balanced Blend

Vocabulary instruction should be a balanced blend of the planned and the incidental. The **incidental approach** capitalizes on students' immediate need to know words. It gives the program spontaneity and vitality. A planned approach ensures that vocabulary instruction is given the attention it deserves. Important words and techniques for learning words are taught systematically and in depth. Combining these two types of approaches should provide the best possible program.

 ## TEACHING SPECIAL FEATURES OF WORDS

Many words have special characteristics that have to be learned if the words are to be understood fully. Among such important features are homophones, homographs, figurative language, multiple meanings, connotation, and denotation.

### Homophones

**Homophones** are words that are pronounced the same but differ in spelling and meaning and often have different origins as well: for example, *cheap* and *cheep* or *knew*, *gnu*, and *new*. In reality, homophones are more of a problem for spelling than for reading because context usually clarifies their meaning. In some instances, however, it is important to note spelling to interpret the meaning of a sentence correctly—for example:

> He complements his wife.
> The shed is dun.
> To avoid being tackled, you must feint.

To build awareness of homophones, discuss riddles. Write a riddle on the chalkboard, and have students identify the word that has a homophone—for example, "What is black and white and read all over?" (the newspaper). Students might enjoy reading Fred Gwynne's books on homophones, such as *The King Who Rained* (1970), *Chocolate Moose for Dinner* (1988a), and *A Little Pigeon Toad* (1988b), or one of Peggy Parrish's *Amelia Bedelia* books. Additional riddles may be found in the books listed in the Children's Reading List, Word Play (pp. 260).

### Homographs

**Homographs** are words that have the same spelling but different meanings and possibly different pronunciations—for example, *palm* (part of the hand or a tree) and *bat* (a club or a mammal). They make spelling easier but reading more difficult. For instance, on seeing the word *page*, the reader must use context to decide whether the word means "a piece of paper" or "someone who attends a knight or runs errands for lawmakers." Homographs may share a single pronunciation or have different pronunciations. Homographs such as the following, which have two distinct pronunciations, can be particularly troublesome for students: *bass, bow, desert, dove, lead, minute, sewer,* and *sow.*

**■ Incidental learning** occurs when vocabulary words are studied as they occur in the natural course of reading and writing. A balanced vocabulary program is both incidental and planned.

> **ADAPTING INSTRUCTION for *ENGLISH LANGUAGE LEARNERS***
> Television, radio, lessons, lectures, discussions, and conversations are rich sources of new words. Set aside a few minutes each day to discuss new words that your pupils have heard. This could be especially helpful to students still learning English. They may have questions about pronunciation and shades of meaning.

■ The combining form *phon* means "sound," so **homophones** are words that have the same sound but differ in meaning and often have different origins. They may or may not have the same spelling: *be, bee; him, hymn.*

To convey the concept of homophones, you might have students translate sentences similar to the following that have been written in homophones: Aye gnu Gym wood bee hear. Dew ewe no hymn?

■ *Graph* is a combining form meaning "written element," so **homographs** are two or more words that have the same spelling but different meanings and different word origins. Homographs may have the same or different pronunciations: *bark* (dog), *bark* (tree); *bow* (ribbon), *bow* (front of a boat).

ADAPTING INSTRUCTION
for *ENGLISH LANGUAGE LEARNERS*
Self Study Quizzes for ESL Students offers a variety of self-checking quizzes on common words, idioms, homonyms, and slang expressions. It also includes games and crossword puzzles. Although designed for ESL students, it could be used with native speakers of English: http://www. aitech.ac.jp/~iteslj/ quizzes/ lb/ho1.html.

■ An **idiomatic expression** is one that is peculiar to a language and cannot be understood from the individual words making up the expression: for example, *call up* a friend.

Elementary school pupils may not realize that figures of speech can be found in the dictionary, usually under the key word in the phrase. For instance, the expressions "big heart," "take to heart," and "with all one's heart" would be found under *heart*.

When learning words having multiple meanings, students learn concrete and functional meanings first (The dog barked at me) followed by more abstract meanings (The coach barked out instructions for the team) (Asch & Nerlove, 1967).

As students learn that a word may have two, three, or even more entirely separate meanings, stress the importance of matching meaning with context. Students may also need to learn an entirely new meaning, and perhaps a pronunciation, for a word that looks familiar. Reading the sentence "The neighbors had a terrible row," students will see that neither of the familiar meanings "paddle a boat" or "in a line" fits this sense of *row*. They must learn from context, a dictionary, or another source that the word's third meaning is "a noisy fight or quarrel." They will also need to learn that *row* in this context is pronounced /rau/.

## Figurative Language

Young students tend to interpret language literally and may have difficulty with figurative language. This is especially true for children who have a profound hearing loss and those whose native language is not English. It is important to make them aware that language is not always to be taken literally. As they grow in their ability to handle figurative expressions, they should be led to appreciate phrases that are especially apt and colorful. The *Amelia Bedelia* books, in which Amelia takes language very literally, can serve as a good introduction. Children might also keep a dictionary of **idiomatic** and figurative **expressions**. Some books of idioms are listed in the following Children's Reading List.

 **Figurative language**

Arnold, T. (2001). *More parts.* New York: Dial.

Christopher, M. (1996). *Baseball jokes and riddles.* Boston: Little, Brown.

Rosen, M. (1995). *Walking the bridge of your nose: Wordplay poems and rhymes.* Las Vegas, NV: Kingfisher.

Terban, M. (1990). *Punching the clock: Funny action idioms.* Boston: Clarion.

Terban, M. (1993). *It figures! Fun figures of speech.* New York: Scholastic.

Terban, M. (1998). *Scholastic dictionary of idioms.* New York: Scholastic.

## Multiple Meanings

One study found that 72 percent of the words that appear frequently in elementary school materials have more than one meaning (Johnson, Moe, & Baumann, 1983). When teaching new meanings for old words, stress the fact that words may have a number of different meanings and that the context is the final determinant of meaning. Some words with apparently multiple meanings are actually homographs. For instance, *bark* means "a noise made by a dog," "the covering of a tree," and "a type of sailing ship." These are really three different words and have separate dictionary entries. Other examples for which there are diverse meanings associated with one word are *elevator* ("platform that moves people up and down," "place for storing grain," "part of airplane") and *magazine* ("periodical" and "building where arms and/or ammunition are stored"). Provide exercises that highlight the new meaning of an old word by asking questions specific to a definition: "What does a plane's elevator do? Why would a fort have a magazine?"

 # LEARNING HOW TO LEARN WORDS

A key objective for a vocabulary-building program is to teach students how to learn words on their own. Three major skills for learning the meanings of unknown words are morphemic analysis, contextual clues, and dictionary usage.

## Morphemic Analysis

One of the most powerful word-attack skills is **morphemic analysis.** Morphemic analysis is the ability to determine a word's meaning through examination of its prefix, root, and/or suffix. A **morpheme** is the smallest unit of meaning. It may be a word, a prefix, a suffix, or a root. The word *believe* has a single morpheme; however, *unbelievable* has three: *un-believ(e)-able. Telegraph* has two morphemes: *tele-graph.* Whereas syllabic analysis involves chunks of sounds, morphemic analysis is concerned with chunks of meaning.

Instruction must be generative and conceptual rather than mechanical and isolated. For example, students can use their knowledge of the familiar word *microscope* to figure out what *micro* means and to apply that knowledge to *microsecond, microwave, micrometer,* and *microbe.* By considering known words, they can generate a concept of *micro* and apply it to unknown words, which, in turn, enriches that concept (Dale & O'Rourke, 1971). The key to teaching morphemic analysis is to help students note prefixes, suffixes, and roots and discover their meanings. It is also essential that elements having a high transfer value be taught and that students be trained in transferring knowledge (Dale & O'Rourke, 1971).

### ■ Compound Words

One way of generating or creating new words is to put two words together. In this way, the English language has been enriched with thousands of **compound words** and is growing richer by the day. For novice readers, however, compounds often pose a problem. For example, even though students may have no difficulty reading *out* and *doors* when they see the words separately, they may give up when they come to *outdoors* because it looks long and difficult. Reassure them that they can read most compounds if they break them down into their component parts. Except for words like *necklace,* components generally retain their single-word pronunciations.

Help students see that the separate words in a compound often give a clue to the long word's meaning, so that *sunburn* means a burn from the sun and *birdhouse* means a house where a bird lives. There are exceptions, of course, such as *shortstop* and *hangup.*

### ■ Prefixes

In general, **prefixes** are easier to learn than suffixes (Dale & O'Rourke, 1964, cited in O'Rourke, 1974). According to Graves and Hammond (1980), there are relatively few prefixes, and they tend to have constant, concrete meanings and rel-

---

■ **Morphemic analysis** is the examination of a word in order to locate and derive the meanings of the morphemes.

■ A **morpheme** is the smallest unit of meaning. The word *nervously* has three morphemes: *nerv(e)-ous-ly.*

Based on their research, White, Power, and White (1989) estimated that average fourth-graders double their ability to use morphemic analysis after just ten hours of instruction.

**ADAPTING INSTRUCTION for *STRUGGLING READERS and WRITERS***
Learning-disabled students' knowledge of morphemic elements is especially poor. However, given systematic instruction, they make encouraging gains (Henry, 1990).

■ **Compound words** actually come in three forms: solid, hyphenated, and open. That is, the compound may be written as one word (*sunup*), a hyphenated word (*good-bye*), or as two words (*home run*). Most compounds provide clues to the word's meaning (*backdoor, fireplace, sundown, sidewalk*) but some do not (*otherwise, shortstop*).

■ A **prefix** is an affix placed at the beginning of a word or root in order to form a new word: for example, *prepay.*

atively consistent spellings. When learning prefixes and other morphemic elements, students should have the opportunity to observe each one in a number of words so that they have a solid basis for constructing an understanding of the element. Lesson 5.3 describes how the prefix *pre-* might be taught.

## LESSON 5.3    Prefixes

### Step 1.  Construct the meaning of the prefix

Place the following words on the board:

> pregame    prepay    preview    pretest    predawn

■ The most frequently occurring prefixes include: *un-, re-, in-, im-, ir-, il-, dis-, en-, em-, non-, in-, im-* (meaning "into"), *over-, mis-, sub-, pre-, inter-, fore-, de-, trans-, super-, semi-, anti-, mid-, under-* (White, Sowell, Yanagihara, 1989).

Discuss the meanings of these words and the places where students may have seen them. Note in particular how *pre-* changes the meaning of the word it precedes. Encourage students to construct a definition of *pre-*. Lead students to see that *pre-* is a prefix. Discuss, too, the purpose and value of knowing prefixes. Explain to students how knowing the meanings of prefixes will help them figure out unknown words. Show them how you would syllabicate words that contain prefixes, and how you would use knowledge of prefixes to sound out the words and determine their meanings.

### Step 2.  Guided practice

Have students complete practice exercises similar to the following:

> Fill in the blanks with these words containing prefixes: *preview, pregame, prepay, predawn, pretest.*

■ Prefixes are most useful when they contribute to the meaning of a word and can be added to other words. The prefix *un-* is both productive and easy to detect (*unafraid, unable, unhappy*), but the prefix *con* in *condition* is unproductive and difficult to detect (McArthur, 1992).

> To make sure they had enough money to buy the food, the party's planners asked everyone to _____.
>
> The _____ show starts thirty minutes before the kickoff.
>
> The _____ of the movie made it seem more exciting than it really was.
>
> Everyone got low marks on the spelling _____ because they had not been taught the words yet.
>
> In the _____ quiet, only the far-off barking of a dog could be heard.

### Step 3.  Application

Have students read selections that contain the prefix *pre-* and note its use in real-world materials.

### Step 4.  Extension

Present the prefix *post-*, and contrast it with *pre-*. Since *post-* is an opposite, this will help clarify the meaning of *pre-*.

### Step 5.  Assessment and reteaching

■ An **affix** is a morphemic element added to the beginning or ending of a word or root in order to add to the meaning of the word or change its function. Prefixes and suffixes are affixes: for example, *prepayment*.

Through observation, note whether students are able to use their knowledge of **affixes** to help them pronounce and figure out the meanings of unfamiliar words. Review common affixes from time to time. Discuss affixes that appear in selections that students are reading.

**Scope-and-Sequence Chart.** Since some prefixes appear in reading materials as early as second grade, this seems to be the appropriate level at which to initiate instruction. A scope-and-sequence chart based on an analysis of current reading programs is presented in Table 5.1. At each level, elements from earlier grades should be reviewed. Additional suffixes that students encounter in their reading should also be introduced.

### ■ Suffixes

The two kinds of **suffixes** are derivational and inflectional. **Derivational suffixes** change the part of speech of a word or change the function of a word in some way. Common derivational suffixes are presented in Table 5.2. **Inflectional suffixes** mark grammatical items and appear early. In fact, *-s*, *-ed*, and *-ing* occur in the easiest materials and are taught in first grade; *-er*, *–est*, *-ly* are introduced in most basals by second grade.

For the most part, students are already using inflectional suffixes widely in their oral language by the time they meet them in their reading. They simply have to become used to translating the letters into sounds. If they are reading for meaning and using syntactic as well as semantic cues, translating the letters into sounds should happen almost automatically. For example, children's grammatical sense will tell them that a /z/ sound is used in the italicized word in the following sentence: The two *boys* were fighting. Also, it is not necessary to teach students that *s* represents /z/ at the end of some words: *friends*, *cars*, and so on. The sound is automatically translated. In the same way, students automatically pronounce the *-ed* correctly in the following words, even though three different pronunciations are represented: *called*, *planted*, and *jumped*. Exercises designed to have children identify which pronunciation each *-ed* represents—/d/, /id/, or /t/—are time wasters.

Suffixes are taught in the same way as prefixes. As can be seen from Tables 5.1 and 5.2, the definitions of prefixes and suffixes are sometimes vague. Although only one or two definitions are given in the tables, in reality, some affixes have four or five. To give students a sense of the meaning of each affix, provide experience with several examples. Experience is a better teacher than mere definition.

### ■ Root Words

As students move through the grades, knowledge of morphemic elements be-

---

■ A **suffix** is an affix added to the end of a word or a root in order to form a new word: for example, *helpless*.

■ A **derivational suffix** produces new words by forming derived words or words whose meanings have been added to: *happiness*, *penniless*.

■ An **inflectional suffix** changes the inflected ending of a word by adding an ending such as *s* or *ed* that shows number or tense: *girls*, *helped*.

❚ Suffixes, especially those that appear often, are worth teaching because they help students add words to their meaning vocabularies. The most frequently occurring derivational suffixes include: *-er*, *-tion (-ion)*, *-ible (-able)*, *-al (-ial)*, *-y*, *-ness*, *-ity (-ty)*, *-ment*, *-ic*, *-ous (-ious)*, *-en*, *-ive*, *-ful*, *-less* (White, Sowell, & Yanagihara, 1989).

| **TABLE 5.1** | Scope-and-sequence chart for common prefixes |
| --- | --- |

| Grade | Prefix | Meaning | Example |
| --- | --- | --- | --- |
| 2–3 | un- | not | unhappy |
| | un- | opposite | undo |
| | under- | under | underground |
| 3–4 | dis- | not | dishonest |
| | dis- | opposite | disappear |
| | re- | again | reappear |
| | re- | back | replace |
| | im- | not | impossible |
| | in- | not | invisible |
| | pre- | before | pregame |
| | sub- | under | submarine |

| TABLE 5.2 | Scope-and-sequence chart for common derivational suffixes | | |
|---|---|---|---|
| **Grade** | **Suffix** | **Meaning** | **Example** |
| 1–2 | -en | made of | wooden |
| | -er | one who | painter |
| | -or | one who | actor |
| 2–3 | -able | is; can be | comfortable |
| | -ible | is; can be | visible |
| | -ful | full of; having | joyful |
| | -ness | having | sadness |
| | -(t)ion | act of | construction |
| | -y | being; having | dirty |
| 3–4 | -al | having | magical |
| | -ance | state of | allowance |
| | -ence | state of; quality of | patience |
| | -ify | make | magnify |
| | -less | without | fearless |
| | -ment | state of | advertisement |
| | -ous | having | curious |

comes more important for handling increasingly complex reading material. As the reading becomes more abstract and therefore more difficult in every subject area, the number of words made up of **roots** and affixes becomes greater. Science, for instance, often uses Greek and Latin words and compounds (O'Rourke, 1974). As with prefixes and suffixes, roots that should be taught are those that appear with high frequency, transfer to other words, and are on the appropriate level of difficulty. For example, the root *cil (council)*, meaning "call," should probably not be taught because it is difficult to distinguish in a word. Roots such as *graph (autograph)*, and *phon (telephone)* are easy to spot and appear in words likely to be read by elementary school students. Roots that are good candidates for inclusion in a literacy program are shown in Table 5.3. The sequence is based on O'Rourke's research (1974) and an analysis of the roots found in current reading programs.

■ The **root** of a word is the part of the word that is left after all the affixes have been removed. A root is also defined as the source of present-day words. The Latin verb *decidere* is the root of the English verb *decide* (McArthur, 1992). The words *base, combining form, root,* and *stem* are sometimes used interchangeably but actually have different meanings. To keep matters simple, this text uses the word *root*.

**Teaching root words.**   Teach root words inductively, and take advantage of every opportunity to develop students' knowledge of them. For example, if students wonder what a thermal wind is, discuss known words such as *thermos, thermostat,* and *thermometer.* Lead them to see that in all three words, *therm* has to do with heat; thus, thermal winds are warm winds. Choose elements to be taught from students' reading. If students read about dinosaurs, use the opportunity to introduce *tri, saurus, pod, ornitho,* and other roots. This often helps students use the name to identify the distinguishing characteristics of the creature. For example, *triceratops* uses three word parts to

| TABLE 5.3 | Scope-and-sequence chart for common roots | | |
|---|---|---|---|
| **Grade** | **Root** | **Meaning** | **Example** |
| 3 | graph | writing | autograph |
| | tele | distance | telescope |
| 4 | port | carry | import |
| | saur | lizard | dinosaur |
| | phon | sound | telephone |
| | vid, vis | see | visible |

describe a dinosaur that has three horns, two of which are over the eyes: *tri*, "three"; *cerat*, "horn"; and *ops*, "eyes." Two of the parts also transfer to a number of other words: *tri* to *triangle*, *tripod*, etc., and *op* to *optical*, *optician*, *optometrist*, etc.

Scope-and-sequence charts for affixes and roots have been provided to give you a sense of when certain ones are usually presented. The real determinants, however, are the needs of the students and the demands of their reading tasks.

### ■ Morphemic Analysis for English Language Learners

Just as in English, Spanish has roots, prefixes, and suffixes. In fact, Spanish has more affixes than English does because Spanish nouns and adjectives have endings that show agreement in gender and number. However, there are many similarities between Spanish and English. A number of elements are identical in both languages or altered slightly. For instance, the prefixes *re-* and *sub-* are the same in both languages; so are the suffixes *-able* and *-ion*. The suffix *-tion* is slightly different in Spanish. It is spelled *cion* in Spanish but may also be spelled *-sion* or *-xion*. If students know prefixes, suffixes, and roots in Spanish, they can transfer some of this knowledge to English.

> Included among the list of roots are combining forms. A combining form is a base designed to combine with another combining form (*tri* + *pod*) or a word (*tri* + *angle*). Combining forms differ from affixes because two combining forms can be put together to make a word but two affixes cannot. Although combining forms are not roots, they are included in with the roots because in most texts that is where they are presented (McArthur, 1992).

---

### REINFORCEMENT ACTIVITIES  Morphemic analysis

■ Provide students with several long words composed of a number of morphemic units, for example:

| | | | |
|---|---|---|---|
| unbelievable | improperly | unimaginable | disagreeable |
| prehistoric | photographer | disagreeable | misjudgment |
| irregularly | unfavorable | uncomfortable | oceanographer |

Have them determine the morphemic boundaries and try to figure out what the words mean based on analysis of the units. Good sources of other words to analyze are the texts that students are encountering in class.

■ Ask students to create webs of roots and affixes in which the element is displayed in several words (Tompkins & Yaden, 1986). A web of the root *loc* might look like Figure 5.7.

■ Students can incorporate roots and affixes into their everyday lives by constructing personal experiences. Have them tell or write about times when they were helpful, helpless, careful, and careless.

■ Using root words, prefixes, and suffixes, let students create words that label a new creature, invention, or discovery. For example, a *quintocycle* would be a cycle with five wheels. A *monovideopod* would be a single walking eye.

■ Ask students to bring in examples of roots and affixes from periodicals, children's books, textbooks, signs, and labels or from spoken language. For example, a child who has recently been on an airplane may have noted the word *preboard*. Let the class determine the word's root and/or affix and discuss the word's meaning.

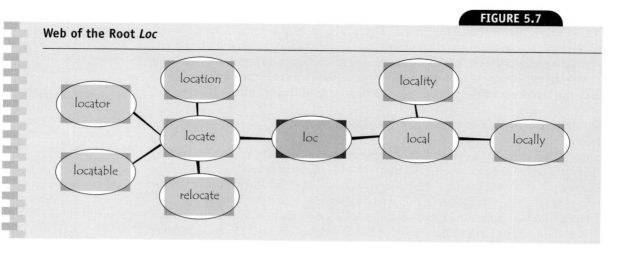

**FIGURE 5.7**

**Web of the Root *Loc***

## Contextual Analysis

Imagine that you are a fourth-grader who has never seen or heard the word *salutations*. What does the following passage indicate about its meaning?

> "Salutations!" repeated the voice.
> "What are they, and where are you?" screamed Wilbur. "Please, please, tell me where you are. And what are salutations?"
> "Salutations are greetings," said the voice. "When I say 'salutations' it's just my fancy way of saying hello or good morning." (White, 1952, p. 35)

Not only does E. B. White define the word *salutations* in context in *Charlotte's Web*, but also he implies that its use is somewhat pompous. Of course, not all difficult words are explained with such care; in fact, in many instances, **contextual analysis** is not at all helpful (Schatz & Baldwin, 1986). Context determines the particular meaning of a word, but it may not reveal it (Deighton, 1959).

An informal survey of difficult words in children's periodicals, textbooks, and trade books indicates that definitions or usable **context clues** are supplied about one-third of the time (Gunning, 1990). The helpfulness of contexts varies from those that provide no useful clues to those that supply explicit definitions or explanations. School texts, since their purpose is to instruct, generally provide explicit clues. Trade books vary in the helpfulness of the clues they provide. Informational children's books often provide helpful clues for key terms but not for the general vocabulary. However, it is estimated that the average reader is able to use context successfully only between 5 and 20 percent of the time (Jenkins, Matlock, & Slocum, 1989; Nagy, Anderson, & Herman, 1987). Even when context clues are fairly obvious, students may fail to take advantage of them. Fortunately, children do become more proficient at using context clues as they progress through the grades. They also do significantly better with practice. Simply directing students to use context to get the meaning of an unfamiliar word is not effective.

---

Even when contextual clues are as rich as they are in this excerpt from *Charlotte's Web,* some students still may not pick up the meaning of *salutations.* After the story has been read, write *salutations* and other words that had rich contextual clues on the board and ask the class what the words meant. This will give you a rough idea as to how well students were using context.

■ **Contextual analysis** is an attempt to derive the meaning of a word by examining the context in which the unknown word appears.

■ **Context clues** are bits of information in the surrounding text that might be used to derive the meaning of an unknown word.

has to be accompanied by practice and feedback to let them know whether their contextual guesses are correct (Carnine, Kameenui, & Coyle, 1984).

## ■ Processing Context Clues

Instruction in the use of context clues should make explicit the thinking processes involved. Sternberg and Powell (1983) postulated a three-step cognitive process in using context clues:

1. *Selective encoding.* Students separate relevant from irrelevant information, choosing only information that will help them construct a meaning for an unfamiliar word.
2. *Selective combination.* Students combine clues into a tentative definition.
3. *Selective comparison.* Students use their background of experience to help figure out the meaning of a word.

Here is how the three steps would be put to use to figure out the meaning of *dismal* in this passage from Cleary's (1981) *Ramona Quimby, Age 8:*

> Rainy Sunday afternoons in November were always dismal, but Ramona felt this Sunday was the most dismal of all. She pressed her nose against the living-room window, watching the ceaseless rain pelting down as bare black branches clawed at the electric wires in front of the house. Even lunch, leftovers Mrs. Quimby had wanted to clear out of the refrigerator, had been dreary, with her parents, who seemed tired or discouraged or both, having little to say and Beezus mysteriously moody. Ramona longed for sunshine, sidewalks dry enough for roller skating, a smiling happy family. (p. 33)

**1.** *Selective encoding.* What information in the sentence containing the unknown word will help me figure out what this word means? Is there any information in earlier sentences that will help? Is there any information in later sentences that will help?

Helpful clues include the falling rain, Ramona's obvious boredom, the moods of the other family members, and the fact that Ramona longed for sunshine, sidewalks dry enough for roller skating, and a smiling happy family.

**2.** *Selective combination.* When I think about all the information given about this unknown word, what does the word seem to mean?

When readers put all the clues together, they can see that the scene that is being described is a gloomy or unhappy one.

**3.** *Selective comparison.* What do I know that will help me figure out the meaning of this word?

Using past experience, students can think about days in which it was raining and they couldn't go out and everyone seemed crabby. This will help them confirm the fact that *dismal* means "gloomy" or "unhappy." Once readers have used context to construct a tentative meaning for the unknown word, they should try substituting the tentative meaning for the word. If the meaning does not fit the sense of the sentence, they should revise their substitution, use the dictionary, or get help.

Context clues should be used to complement phonics strategies and help students predict the pronunciations of words that are in their listening vocabularies but not in their reading vocabularies. However, context clues in this section are designed to help students derive the meanings of words that are not in the students' listening or reading vocabularies.

Oral context is probably more helpful than written context. As Beck, McKeown, and Kucan (2002) explain, "Written context lacks many of the features of oral language that support learning new words, such as intonation, body language, and shared physical surroundings. As such, the text is a far less effective vehicle for learning new words than oral language" (p. 3).

## ■ Types of Context Clues

Listed in the following paragraphs in approximate order of difficulty are eight main types of context clues. They have been drawn from a variety of materials that elementary or middle school students might read.

**1.** *Explicit explanation or definition.* The easiest clue to use is a definition in context. For instance, the following passage from *The Wright Brothers at Kitty Hawk* (Sobol, 1961) gives a detailed, conceptual explanation of warping:

> "Why the wings are twisting!" exclaimed Bill Tate.
>
> "We call it warping," said Orville. "See the wings on the side? Their ends are turned upward and forward."
>
> "And the wings on the left side are pulled downwards and rearward," said Bill Tate.
>
> Orville let go of the rope. "Now, in front—"
>
> "Hold on," said Bill Tate. "I'm not sure I understand what I saw."
>
> "The warping is our idea for keeping the glider level," said Orville. Carefully he explained how it changed the way the wind pushed against the wings. (p. 24)

Explicit definitions are usually more concise, as in this excerpt from *Brown Bears* (Stone, 1998): "Brownies are omnivores (AHM-nih-vorz). Omnivores eat both plants and animals" (p. 14).

**2.** *Appositives.* Definitions are sometimes supplied in the form of appositives immediately after the difficult word: "On a clear summer morning, a pod, or group, of close to fifty dusky dolphins moves toward deeper water" (Souza, 1998, p. 27).

**3.** *Synonyms.* Finding a synonym sometimes takes some searching. It often appears in a sentence after the one that used the target word. In the following passage from *Little House on the Prairie* (Wilder, 1941), the synonym for *ague* is given in a preceding sentence: "Next day he had a little chill and a little fever. Ma blamed the watermelon. But next she had a chill and a little fever. So they did not know what could have caused their fever 'n' ague" (p. 198).

**4.** *Function indicators.* Sometimes context provides clues to meaning because it gives the purpose or function of the difficult word (Sternberg, 1987). In the following sentence, the reader gets an excellent clue to the meaning of *derrick* in a sentence that indicates what a derrick does: "The derrick lifted the glider into the sky" (Sobol, 1961, p. 27).

**5.** *Examples.* The example—lions—in the following passage would give the reader a sense of the meaning of *predators:* "Only 5 percent of cheetah cubs live to become adults. The remainder die from disease, starvation, or attacks from other predators, such as lions" (Thompson, 1998, p. 7).

**6.** *Comparison–contrast.* By contrasting the unknown word *foreigners* with the known word *nationals* in the following passage, readers can gain an understanding of the unknown word: "Halmoni walked Yunni over to the long line that said 'Foreigners.' The line moved slowly as the officer checked each passport. Halmoni got to stand in the fast-moving line that said 'Nationals.' Yunni looked like all the Koreans in the nationals line, but she had to stand in the foreigners line" (Choi, 2001, p. 146). Students must be able to reason that the word *foreign-*

*ers* is the opposite of *nationals*, however. Being able to use this content clue assumes that the students know the meaning of *nationals*.

**7.** *Experience.* A main clue to the meaning of an unfamiliar word is students' background of experience. In the following passage, readers can use their own experience of being cut or injured together with imagining what it might be like to undergo the experience that is described; this will enable them to make an informed guess as to what the unfamiliar word *excruciating* means: "Suddenly, the hedge clippers caught a branch, and my left middle finger was pulled into the blades. I felt an excruciating pain. The tip of my finger was hanging by a thread" (Rolfer, 1990, p. 25).

### ■ Presenting Context Clues

Use of context should permeate the reading program from its very beginning. When emerging readers use phonics skills to try to decode words that are in their listening but not in their reading vocabulary, they should use context as well, both as an aid to sounding out and as a check to make sure they have decoded the words correctly. Context clues presented in this chapter are designed to help readers derive the meanings of unknown words—words that are not in the students' listening vocabularies. Although one hopes that over the years the use of context will become automatic, context clues should be taught explicitly. Using a direct teaching model, the teacher should explain what the clues are, why it is important to use context, and how they can be applied. Modeling use of clues, guided practice, and application are important elements in the process. Lesson 5.4 describes how context clues might be presented.

> ▌As your class studies context clues, encourage students to be alert to especially good clues that they encounter in their reading and bring these into class. Set aside a few minutes each day for a discussion of context clues, with one student reading the clue and the rest of the class attempting to use the clue to derive the meaning of the word.

### Context clues

#### Step 1. Explain context

Demonstrate the usefulness of context clues. Select five or six difficult words from a book the class is reading and show how context could be used to derive their meanings.

#### Step 2. Demonstrate Sternberg and Powell's (1983) three-step process

This can be done by asking the following questions:

> What information in the selection will help me figure out what the unknown word means? (selective encoding)
>
> When I put together all the information about the unknown word, what does the word seem to mean? (selective combination)
>
> What do I know that will help me figure out the meaning of this word? (selective comparison)

#### Step 3. Try out the tentative meaning of the unknown word

Show students how they should try out the tentative meaning of the unknown word by substituting the meaning for the word and reading the sentence to see whether the substitution fits. Explain that if the tentative meaning does not fit the sense of the sentence, they should revise it.

### Step 4. Model the process

Model the process of using context with a variety of words. Explain the thinking processes that you go through as you attempt to figure out their meanings and then try out these tentative meanings. Show, for example, how you might use examples as clues, use a comparison, search out synonyms, look for appositives, use your background of experience, or try a combination of strategies. Show, too, how you would use context and experience to construct a tentative meaning for the unknown word and then try out the meaning by substituting it in the sentence.

### Step 5. Guided practice

Have students use context clues to figure out unfamiliar words in selected passages that provide substantial clues. Do one or two cooperatively. Then have students try their hands. Discuss the meanings of the unfamiliar words and the types of clues they used.

### Step 6. Application

Encourage students to try using context clues in selections that they read. After the reading, talk over the meanings that they derived and the strategies they used. Ask how they went about determining what the unknown word meant, what clues they used, and how they decided on their definition of the unknown word.

### Step 7. Assessment and review

Note how often and how well students apply context clues on their own. From time to time, check on their use of context. Provide additional instruction as needed.

---

**USING TECHNOLOGY**

Vocabulary Drill for Kids presents words in context. Students select from three options the one they think is the correct response: **http://www. edu4kids.com/lang1/.**

---

Review context clues periodically. Whenever a selection is discussed, talk over passages that contained especially effective context clues so as to remind students to use context clues and also to refine students' usage of them.

---

### ■ Subsequent Lessons in the Use of Context Clues

In a series of lessons, present other major context clues, emphasizing the thinking processes involved in using each one. After introducing all the types of clues appropriate for students' level, review them. However, instruction should be focused on using context clues effectively rather than on identification of types of clues. Draw sample sentences from children's periodicals, trade books, content-area texts, and the Internet, so that students can see that the skills have relevance and that context clues will help them analyze words. Most important, encourage students to get in the habit of using context to figure out the meanings of unfamiliar words. Instead of merely suggesting that they use clues, model the process from time to time to remind them about it. Also, encourage them to use the dictionary as a means of checking definitions derived by using context clues.

Also integrate the use of context with morphemic and syllabic analysis. Note how morphemic analysis and context clues might be used to derive the meanings of *microbats* and *megabats*.

Bats are the masters of the ultrasonic world. They are divided into two groups, the microbats and the megabats. Most microbats are insect eaters. All microbats rely on ultrasound to guide them when they fly and to help them find food and communicate with each other. The large, fruiteating megabats can make ultrasounds, too, but they do not use them when flying or searching for food. (Arnold, 2001)

## Dictionary Usage

Context, especially when combined with phonics and morphemic and syllabic analysis, is a powerful word-attack strategy, but some words defy even these four strategies. When all else fails, it is time for the student to consult the world's greatest expert on words, the dictionary. Although students might not use a real dictionary in first and second grades, preparation begins early. In first grade and, in some cases, kindergarten, students compile word books and picture dictionaries. They also learn alphabetical order, a prerequisite skill for locating words, and phonics, which is necessary for using the pronunciation key.

### ■ Using Predictionaries

Most students are not able to use dictionaries until the third grade. However, predictionaries, which can be used by first- and second-graders, have been compiled by several publishers. **Predictionaries** are books in which limited numbers of words are defined through illustrations. A more advanced predictory, which is usually called the first dictionary, uses sentences and pictures to define words but does not supply syllabications or pronunciation. Predictionaries are available on CD-ROM; the advantage of this format is that the selected words are pronounced orally and their definitions spoken. Predictionaries are a useful tool but must be used with care. Because they can include only a limited number of words, students may find that many words they want to look up are not there. Locating entry words may also be fairly time-consuming, unless electronic dictionaries are used.

### ■ Using Glossaries

Glossaries are included in the anthologies of major reading programs and content-area texts. In some programs, glossaries can be found as early as first grade. Easier to use than dictionaries because they have only a limited number of words and definitions, glossaries are a useful tool and a good preparation for the dictionary.

### ■ Using Dictionaries

By third grade, students with average reading achievement are ready to use real dictionaries. They should, of course, use beginning dictionaries that are simplified so that the definitions are readable. For reading, students must have three major skills: locating the target word, finding the proper definition, and learning the pronunciation. For writing, determining correct spelling and usage is also important.

**Locating the words to be looked up.** The first thing that students must realize is that words are arranged in alphabetical order—*a* to *z*—by first letter and then by second letter, and, if necessary, by third letter, and so on. From the begin-

---

▌ Emphasize the need to comprehend a passage in order to be able to use context. Often the general sense of the passage will provide a clue as to the meaning of a word. However, students won't be able to use the overall sense of the passage if they don't comprehend it (Beck, McKeown, Kucan, 2002). Ask students what's going on in the passage or what the passage says and then discuss what the target word might mean.

■ A **predictory** is an easy dictionary that has fewer entries than a regular dictionary, simplifies definitions, but does not contain a pronunciation key.

**USING TECHNOLOGY**

*My First Incredible Amazing Dictionary* (Dorling Kindersley) is an excellent example of a talking predictory.

▌ Model the use of the dictionary by letting students see how you use the dictionary to look up an unfamiliar word, check the spelling or pronunciation of a word, or use its style guide section to get information on a question of style.

> Do not make dictionary use so tiresome that students acquire genuine dislike of this tool. Looking up all one's vocabulary words is just the type of assignment that gives the dictionary a bad name. Make sure that tasks that students are required to do are not too complex. Asking students to use new words in sentences after looking them up is difficult. It often takes a number of experiences with a word before a student acquires enough feeling for it to use it in a sentence.

**ADAPTING INSTRUCTION for *ENGLISH LANGUAGE LEARNERS***

For ELLs, a translation dictionary that contains English and their first language could be an invaluable aid. Students might use one of the many language translators found on the Web, such as Web-a-dex Language Translator: http://www.web-a-dex.com/translate.htm.

ning, train students to use guide words so that they do not adopt the time-wasting habit of simply thumbing through the *s*s or the *w*s page by page until they find the appropriate location. Explain that not all letters encompass the same number of words; for example, *c* words take up many more pages than *x*, *y*, and *z* words put together. Describe how the dictionary can be divided in such a way that each of the following groups of letters covers approximately one fourth of all the words: *a–d*, *e–l*, *m–r*, and *s–z*. Even after they have mastered alphabetical order, students may be confused as they search for some entry words. Entry words often exclude inflected forms. A student looking up *rallies* or *exporter*, for example, will have to look under *rally* or *export*.

**Locating and understanding meanings.**   Definitions are not the only way words are explained. Many dictionaries also include synonyms, illustrations, and phrases or sentences in which the word is used. Some give a word history for selected words and explain how words that are synonyms differ in meaning. For instance, *Webster's New World Dictionary* supplies a definition for *kiosk*, gives a history of the term, and includes a photo of a kiosk. For the word *model*, it presents a brief explanatory paragraph that contrasts *model* and *pattern*.

Demonstrate the various ways a dictionary explains words. Direct students to look up words that are accompanied by illustrations. Discuss the definition, illustration, synonym, and example, if given, for each one. Words likely to have illustrations include the following (this will vary from dictionary to dictionary): *manatee*, *lattice*, *isobar*, *ibex*, *hoe*, *heart*, and *funnel*. Choose examples that are at the appropriate level for your students and that would be helpful for them to know.

Once students have a good grasp of how to locate words and how to use the several kinds of defining and explanatory information, have them look up words. Choose words that students have a genuine need to know, such as hard words from a content-area text or children's book that they are reading. In the beginning, stress words that have just one or two meanings, like *edifice*, *egret*, or *cellist*.

As students grow in skill in using the dictionary, tell them that some words may have many meanings. Have them look up the following words and count the number of meanings given: *ace*, *bit*, *bowl*, *comb*, and *free*. Emphasize that context can help them choose the correct meaning for a word that has several definitions. Have them practice finding the correct meaning for each of several words that have just two or three distinct meanings:

> Because I moved the camera, the photo was a bit *fuzzy*.
> The blanket was warm and *fuzzy*.
> The explorers packed up their *gear* and left.
> Use second *gear* when going up a steep hill.

**Homographs.**   Have students note how homographs are handled in their dictionaries. Usually, they are listed as separate entries and numbered, as in Figure 5.8. For practice, students can use context to help them determine which definition is correct in sentences such as the following:

**FIGURE 5.8**

### Homographs in a Dictionary

**bay**[1] (bā), a part of a sea or lake extending into the land. A bay is usually smaller than a gulf and larger than a cove. *noun*.

**bay**[2] (bā), **1** a long, deep barking, especially by a large dog: *We heard the distant bay of the hounds.* **2** to bark with long, deep sounds: *Dogs sometimes bay at the moon.* 1 *noun*, 2 *verb*.

**bay**[3] (bā), **1** reddish-brown. **2** a reddish-brown horse with black mane and tail. 1 *adjective*, 2 *noun*.

*Scott, Foresman Beginning Dictionary* (p. 51) by E. L. Thorndike & C. L. Barnhart, 1988, Glenview, IL: Scott, Foresman and Company. Copyright © 1988 by Scott, Foresman & Company. Reprinted by permission of Scott, Foresman and Company.

The doctor gave me medicine for my *sty.*
The king signed the paper and put his *seal* on it.
We landed on a small sandy *key.*

**Constructing the correct pronunciation.**   While reading a historical selection, one young girl pronounced the word *plagues* as /plā-jiz/. From context, she had a sense of what the word meant and so mispronouncing it did not interfere with her comprehension. Students do not have to be able to pronounce a word accurately to understand its meaning. Most of us have had the experience of discovering that for years we have been mispronouncing a word we see in print. Even so, being aware of the correct pronunciation means that students can make connections between the word they see in print and the word when spoken. For example, if they have read the word *quiche* but have no idea how to pronounce it, they will not recognize it as being the same word they saw in print when they hear it spoken. Not knowing how to pronounce a word also means that they will not be able to use it in speech. On the other hand, knowing how to pronounce a word is another aid to remembering it.

After students have acquired some skill in locating words and deriving appropriate meanings, introduce the concept of phonetic respellings. Display and discuss the pronunciation key contained in the dictionary your class is using. To avoid confusion, have all students use the same dictionary series, if possible, because different publishers use different keys. Help students discover what they already know about the key. Almost all the phonetic respellings of consonants will be familiar, except for, perhaps, *ng* in words like *sung*, which is signified by /ŋ/ in some systems. Short vowels, indicated by *a, e, i, o* (sometimes symbolized as /ä/), and *u*, will also be familiar. Inform the students that long vowels are indicated by a symbol known as a macron, as in /gōt/. Explain that the macron is a diacritical mark and that such marks are used to show pronunciation.

Show how diacritical marks are used to indicate the pronunciation of *r* vowels. Other symbols that may have to be explained to students are the pronuncia-

> Build your pupils' skill in using dictionary phonetic respellings to get the correct pronunciations along with the meanings of unknown words. Just as it's easier to remember a person's name if you can pronounce it, so, too, it's easier to remember a new word if you can say it correctly.

> Merriam-Webster presents a number of vocabulary-building exercises. The site also provides pronunciations for words: **http:// www.m-w.com/.**

tions of short and long double *o*, schwa, the vowel sounds heard in *paw*, *toy*, and *out*, and short *o* (in Merriam-Webster).

After providing an overview of the pronunciation key, concentrate on its segments so that students acquire a working knowledge of the system. In order of difficulty, these segments might include consonants and short vowels, long vowels, *r* vowels, short and long double *o*, other vowels, and schwa. After introducing each segment, have students read words using the elements discussed. Encourage the active use of the pronunciation key.

Once students have mastered phonetic respelling, introduce the concept of accent. One way to do this would be to say a series of words whose meaning changes according to whether the first or second syllable is accented: *record, present, desert, minute, object*. As you say the words, stress the accented syllable. Have students listen to hear which syllable is said with more stress. After the class decides which syllable is stressed, write the words on the board and put in the accent marks while explaining what they mean. Discuss how the change in stress changes the pronunciation, meaning, or use of each word. To provide guided practice, select unknown words from materials students are about to read and have students reconstruct their pronunciation. Discuss these reconstructions, and provide ample opportunity for independent application. Later, introduce the concept of secondary stress.

**Electronic dictionaries.**   Electronic dictionaries are far easier to use than book versions. Words are easier to look up. All the student need do is to type in the target word. Some electronic dictionaries accept misspelled words so that students looking up the spelling of a word can find it even if they can't spell it accurately. Speaking dictionaries also pronounce the word being looked up and read the definition, so students don't have to be able to use the pronunciation key before they can use the dictionary. Electronic dictionaries are also motivational: They're more fun to use than a traditional dictionary. Electronic dictionaries come in CD-ROM and handheld versions or are available on the Web. Handheld versions have the advantage of being small and portable. And some of the simpler models are not much more expensive than book versions.

■ **The Dictionary as a Tool**

Many school dictionaries include generous instructions for use, along with practice exercises. Use these selectively. Avoid isolated drill on dictionary skills. Concentrate on building dictionary skills through functional use—that is, show students how to use the dictionary, and encourage them to incorporate it as a tool for understanding language. For instance, when they have questions about word meaning, pronunciation, spelling, or usage, encourage them to seek help in the dictionary.

One word of caution is in order: For word recognition, the dictionary should generally be used as a last resort. Looking up a word while reading a story interrupts the flow of the story and disturbs comprehension. Students should try context, phonics, and morphemic or syllabic analysis before going to the dictionary. Moreover, unless the word is crucial to understanding the story, they should wait until they have read the selection to look up the word. The dictionary is also a good check on definitions derived from context clues. After reading a story in

**USING TECHNOLOGY**

Kids Click
**http://sunsite. berkeley.edu/ KidsClick!/**
Click on Dictionaries. Has links to online dictionaries that range from regular to rhyming.

**USING TECHNOLOGY**

If possible, acquire a CD-ROM or other electronic dictionary. The advantages of an electronic dictionary are that it locates the word faster and is motivational. An electronic dictionary may also read the word and its definition. This is a help for students whose reading skills are limited.

which they used context clues, students should check their educated guesses against the dictionary's definitions.

## REINFORCEMENT ACTIVITIES  Dictionary usage

- Have students find out how the following words should be pronounced: *psalm, ptomaine, crepes, depot,* and *czar.*

- Have students use the dictionary to find out what the following sports are and tell which one(s) they might enjoy: *quoits, cricket, boccie, curling, biathlon, rugby,* and *billiards.*

- Ask students to determine from whose names the following words were created: *Braille, xylophone, silhouette,* and *gardenia.*

- Have students use the dictionary to determine which of the following are animals:

  | | | |
  |---|---|---|
  | oryx | peccary | marten |
  | okapi | parka | manatee |
  | ocarina | parabola | marmoset |
  | oboe | pagoda | marquee |

- To give students guided practice in looking up words, have them answer questions similar to the following:

  Are all *nocturnal* animals dangerous?

  Would a *yurt* taste good?

  Would a *filigree* make a good pet?

  Have you ever been *reticent*?

  Could you use the word *bayou* to say good-bye to a friend?

- An excellent activity for helping students understand how the dictionary works is the dictionary builder at Word Central (Wordcentral.com). Students build a word by providing a definition, a part of speech, a history of the word, a sample sentence, and, if they wish, personal information. They can also have the word included in the site's listing of student-built words. Sample entries include such words as *enticon* (fabricated word) and *puffenglooper* (person who is never on task but always has a joke to tell).

> **USING TECHNOLOGY**
> Handheld electronic dictionaries are available from Franklin Learning Resources, One Franklin Plaza, Burlington, NJ, 08016-4907, 800-266-5626.

## SUPPLYING CORRECTIVE FEEDBACK

A student is reading and is suddenly stopped cold by an unknown word. What should the teacher do? If the student does not self-correct and the error is not substantive —the student says *this* for *that*—you may choose to do nothing. Sometimes an error is substantive and disturbs the sense of the sentence, but it is obvious that the student will not be able to work out the word using phonics, syllabication, context, or morphemic analysis. In such a case, you might supply the word as one of two options so the student is involved in the process: "Would *chat* or *champ* fit here?" If there is a chance that the student can use strategies to decode the word, pause briefly—about five seconds or so—to provide an opportunity for the student to work out the word (Harris & Sipay, 1990). If the student fails to work out the word but might be able to with a little help, try a **corrective cues hierarchy** (McCoy & Pany, 1986).

## Applying a Corrective Cues Hierarchy

The following corrective cues hierarchy is adapted from McCoy and Pany (1986):

For words in the students' listening but not reading vocabulary

- *Strategy 1.* Seeking out a pronounceable word part and using it to reconstruct a word is often the simplest, most direct strategy and, in most instances, should be attempted first. When encountering an unknown word, the student should ask, "Is there any part of this word that I can say?" If that does not work, the student should try an analogy strategy, asking, "Is this word like any word I know?" If the word is a multisyllabic one, the student might need to reconstruct the word part by part. Once the word has been reconstructed, the student should verify the reconstruction by checking whether the word is real and fits the context of the sentence.

- *Strategy 2.* If the student is unable to use the pronounceable word part or analogy strategy to work out the pronunciation of the difficult word rapidly, encourage the use of context. The student should say "blank" for the unknown word and read to the end of the sentence and ask, "What would make sense here?"

For words not in the students' listening or reading vocabulary

- *Strategy 1.* The student should use context clues designed to help derive the meaning of an unknown word. The student should determine what information in the sentence containing the unknown word—and additional sentences, if necessary—helps her to figure out the word. The student should think about all the information given and about what she knows that might help in determining the meaning of the word. The student should then check to make sure that a real word has been constructed and that the word fits the context of the sentence.

- *Strategy 2.* If the meaning of the word is unknown and context does not help, the student should use morphemic analysis. The student should look for parts of the word whose meaning she knows and use those to construct the meaning of the word. The student should then reread the sentence, substituting the constructed word to see whether it fits the sense of the sentence. If neither contextual analysis nor morphemic analysis works, students should use a glossary or the dictionary.

### Margin notes

■ A **corrective cues hierarchy** is a series of corrective feedback statements arranged in order of utility and ease of application.

■ As students are taught how to use word recognition strategies, they should also be taught when to apply them so that they can make the choice as to whether to try context, phonics, syllabic analysis, or morphemic analysis first. The corrective cues hierarchy depends on the nature of the word to be identified and the student's background and ability to apply strategies.

■ The six major word-attack skills are phonics, sight words, syllabication (covered in Chapter 4), morphemic analysis, context clues, and dictionary use. Each was presented separately, but they are applied in an integrated fashion. Context is used to act as a check on the results of the student's attempt to use one of the other strategies. If a word the student has reconstructed does not make sense, or if the definition selected from the dictionary does not quite fit the sense of the passage, this is a signal for the student to try again.

Although the strategies are presented here in consecutive order, they may be applied in tandem. For instance, a student may use both morphemic analysis and context to derive the meaning of a word or may use context and pronounceable word parts or phonics and syllabication to reconstruct the pronunciation of a word.

## Using Prompts

When students are having difficulty with a word, use a prompt to encourage the use of word analysis. Listed below are suggested prompting questions that you might ask students in order to cue the use of a particular strategy. Some of the prompts have been adapted from the highly successful early intervention program Reading Recovery.

- *Pronounceable word part.* Is there any part of the word that you can say?
- *Analogy.* Is the word like any that you know?
- *Context.* What would make sense here? What would fit? Say "blank" for the word, and read to the end of the sentence. Then ask yourself, "What word would make sense here?"
- *Syllabic analysis.* How would you say the first syllable? The second syllable? The next syllable? What does the word seem to be?
- *Morphemic analysis.* Is there any part of the word that you know?
- *Dictionary or glossary usage.* Would the dictionary or glossary help?
- *Affirmation.* I like the way you used context (or another strategy) to help you figure out that word.
- *Probing.* What could you do to help you figure out that word?

The probing prompt encourages the students to reflect on their knowledge of strategies and to select the most appropriate one.

## Using Think-Alouds

To assess students' use of word analysis skills and to provide guidance in their use, conduct a **think-aloud** (Harmon, 1998). In a think-aloud, students stop when they come to a difficult word and then give a description of what is going on in their minds as they try to figure out the word. Instead of providing direct instruction, the teacher offers neutral prompts that encourage students to explain their thinking: "Can you tell me what you are thinking? Can you tell me more?" Once you know what strategies students are using, you can then use the think-aloud as an instructional tool. You might use such prompts as: "Can you find clues to the word's meaning in other sentences or other parts of the article? What might help you to get the word's meaning? Would the glossary help?"

Guidance provided in a think-aloud is designed to help students apply and integrate strategies. It also helps build students' confidence in the use of word analysis strategies and helps build their sense of competence. If individual think-alouds are too time-consuming, group think-alouds might be used instead. That way students learn from each other.

■ **Think-alouds** are procedures in which students are asked to describe the processes they are using as they engage in reading or another cognitive activity.

## HELP FOR STRUGGLING READERS AND WRITERS

As struggling readers and writers make their way through the grades, they may master phonics only to find that they are having difficulty in reading because their background knowledge and vocabularies are limited. Having struggled with reading, poor readers generally read less and so meet and learn fewer new words and acquire less background information. With these students, it is essential to build background and related vocabulary. Spend more time building essential concepts and vocabulary before they read a selection. Also spend time after the selection has been read clarifying and deepening concepts. Try to help students see how new concepts are related to concepts they already know.

Encourage students to read widely, but be sure that they have lots of materials on their level. Also seek out reader-friendly informational books, such as books from the *Early Bird Nature Books* series, that do a particularly good job of building background and vocabulary.

Struggling readers often have poor concepts of themselves as learners. To build their self-concepts and vocabulary, plan a program of vocabulary development that introduces challenging words to them. They will appreciate learning "big" words. Also provide instruction in morphemics, context clues, and dictionary skills to help them to become independent word learners. A handheld speaking electronic dictionary can be a big help for struggling readers and writers. It allows them to obtain the pronunciation of words in their listening but not their reading vocabularies and it also allows them to obtain the meanings of words not in their listening vocabularies. And it helps them with their spelling.

## ESSENTIAL STANDARDS

### Kindergarten
- Students will expand their vocabularies.

### First grade
*Students will*
- expand their vocabularies.
- use context to derive the pronunciation of words that are in their listening vocabularies but that are unknown in print.
- identify simple homophones.
- identify the meanings of simple words that have multiple meanings.
- use picture dictionaries and predictionaries and simplified glossaries to derive the meanings or pronunciations of words.
- use simple morphemic analysis to help them read printed words. They will be able to use such elements as -*s*, -*ed*, and -*ing*.

## Second grade

*Students will*

- use context to derive the pronunciation of words that are in their listening vocabularies but that are unknown in print.
- expand their vocabularies.
- use picture dictionaries and predictionaries and simplified glossaries to derive the meanings or pronunciations of words.
- use simple morphemic analysis to help them read printed words. They will be able to use such elements as *-ly*, *-en*, and, *-er*; and simple prefixes such as *over-* and *un-*.
- use knowledge of simple homophones, synonyms, and antonyms to determine the meanings of words.
- identify the meanings of simple words that have multiple meanings.

## Third and fourth grades

*Students will*

- use context to derive the meanings of unknown words.
- use knowledge of homophones, homographs, synonyms, antonyms, and idioms to determine the meanings of words.
- use knowledge of word origins and derivations to determine the meanings of words.
- expand their vocabularies.
- use dictionaries, including electronic ones, and glossaries to derive the meanings and pronunciations of words.
- use morphemic analysis to derive the meanings of words. At each level, they will be able to use increasingly sophisticated morphemic elements.
- identify the meanings of words that have multiple meanings.

## ASSESSMENT

Through observation, note whether students are learning the skills and strategies they have been taught. Watch to see what they do when they come across an unfamiliar word. Do they attempt to use context? Do they attempt to apply morphemic analysis strategies? Do they have a working knowledge of morphemic elements that have been introduced? When all else fails, do they use the dictionary or glossary as an aid? Do they know when to use which strategy? Are they able to integrate strategies? To enhance your observation, take advantage of selections that contain words that lend themselves to a particular strategy and see how well students do. For instance, if the selection has especially rich context clues, see whether students were able to make use of the clues. You might question them orally or have them write down what they think the target words meant or do both. Having them write down meanings gives you an indicator of everyone's performance.

## ACTION PLAN

1. Assess students' word knowledge.
2. Construct or adapt a program for vocabulary development based upon students' needs.
3. Gear instruction to the students' level of knowledge. Words that convey new concepts will need a greater degree of teaching than words that are simply labels for known concepts.
4. Develop a depth of meaning of a core of essential words rather than trying to cover a wide range of words.
5. Use graphic organizers, wide reading, games, sorting, self-collection of words, and other activities to provide practice and application.
6. Introduce morphemic analysis, contextual clues, and dictionary usage in functional fashion. Integrate use of skills.
7. Provide ample practice and application opportunities.
8. Help students to develop an interest in words.
9. Help English language learners recognize and take advantage of cognates. Be aware that ELL have many concepts developed in their native language and may only be lacking English labels for the concepts.
10. Monitor students' progress and make necessary adjustments.

Discussing responses gives you the opportunity to ask probing questions so that you can determine how they applied their strategies.

Also, note the quality of students' word knowledge. Is their vocabulary adequate for the materials they must read and the concepts they must learn? Are they acquiring new words at an adequate rate? Do they have an interest in words? Standardized tests often have a vocabulary section. If so, use these results as a possible indicator of the students' word knowledge. Note, however, whether the test required students to read the words or whether the words and definitions were read to students. Poor readers' vocabularies are underestimated if they have to read the vocabulary words. See Chapter 2 for limitations of standardized test results.

## SUMMARY

1. Average first-graders know between 5,000 and 6,000 words and learn about 3,000 new ones each year. By the end of high school, students generally know more than 40,000 words. Having rich experiences and talking about them are important factors in learning new words. Also important are relating vocabulary to background, building relationships, developing depth of meaning, presenting numerous exposures, creating an interest in words, and promoting transfer. A variety of activities, such as graphic organizers and playing word games, can be used to develop word knowledge. The most powerful word learning activity is wide reading.

2. A planned program of vocabulary development is advisable. Words chosen for intensive instruction should be key words that will be encountered again and again. Techniques that help students

remember new words include organizing the words to show relationships, elaboration, and the key word approach.

3. A carefully planned program of vocabulary devel-opment should include provision for teaching students how to learn words on their own through the use of morphemic analysis, contextual analysis, and the dictionary.

## EXTENDING AND APPLYING

1. Try using graphic devices, such as semantic feature analysis, a Venn diagram, or a semantic map, to organize words that you are studying or in which you are interested. Which of these devices works best for you? Why?
2. Plan a program of vocabulary development. Include a description of the class, your objectives, the source of words, the activities that you will use to reinforce words, and the techniques you will use. Also tell how you will evaluate the program.
3. Choose four to six words from a chapter in a children's book. Then, using the steps detailed in this chapter, create a vocabulary lesson. Teach the lesson to a group of students, and critique it. What worked well? What might be changed?
4. Investigate one of the vocabulary-building Web sites mentioned or one that you have discovered. How might you use this site?
5. Using procedures explained in this chapter, create a semantic map with an elementary school class. Evaluate the map's effectiveness. In what ways did it help students? Did the activity engage their attention?

## DEVELOPING A PROFESSIONAL PORTFOLIO

Teach and record a morphemic analysis lesson. Select elements that appear in students' texts and that have a high degree of utility. Summarize the lesson and reflect on its effectiveness.

## DEVELOPING A RESOURCE FILE

Keep a list of children's books and Web sites that do a particulary good job of developing vocabulary. Also collect riddles, jokes, and games that make learning words fun.

# 6

# Comprehension: Theory and Strategies

*F*or each of the following statements related to the chapter you are about to read, put a check under "Agree" or "Disagree" to show how you feel. Discuss your responses with classmates before you read the chapter.

|  |  | *Agree* | *Disagree* |
|---|---|---|---|
| **1** | Reading comprehension is understanding the author's meaning. | _____ | _____ |
| **2** | The less one knows about a topic, the more one will learn by reading about it. | _____ | _____ |
| **3** | Comprehension is a social activity. | _____ | _____ |
| **4** | Knowledge of words is the most important ingredient in comprehension. | _____ | _____ |
| **5** | As students read, they should be aware of whether they are comprehending. | _____ | _____ |
| **6** | Before learning to draw inferences, the reader must master comprehension of literal details. | _____ | _____ |
| **7** | In comprehension instruction, the teacher should focus on the processes students use rather than on whether they obtain the right answers. | _____ | _____ |

## USING WHAT YOU KNOW

*I*n a sense, all the previous chapters have provided a foundation for this one, which is about comprehension. This chapter begins with a discussion of the nature of comprehension and goes on to describe the strategies used to obtain meaning from reading, with suggestions for teaching them. Comprehension is very much a matter of bringing your knowledge to the task. What do you know about comprehension? What strategies do you use as you try to understand what you read? What do you do when your comprehension goes astray? What tips for comprehension might you share with a younger reader?

## THE PROCESS OF COMPREHENDING

Comprehension is the main purpose of reading. In fact, without it, there is no reading, since reading is the process of constructing meaning from print. Comprehension is a constructive, interactive process involving three factors—the reader, the text, and the context in which the text is read. For comprehension to improve, the interaction among all three factors must be taken into consideration. Readers vary in the amount and type of prior knowledge they possess, the strategies they use, their attitudes toward reading, and their work habits. Texts vary in genre, theme or topic, style, difficulty level, and appeal. The context includes when, where, and why a text is being read. Is it being read at home in preparation for a test the next day? Is it an antidote description printed on the can of a pesticide being read by a frantic parent whose child has sprayed himself with the substance? Or is it a novel being read for pleasure in an easy chair on a sunny day? Although the bulk of this chapter will discuss comprehension strategies, the use of these strategies will be affected by reader, text, and context factors.

### Schema Theory

To gain some insight into the process of comprehension, read the following paragraph, which has been divided into a series of sentences. Stop after reading each sentence and ask yourself: "What did the sentence say? How did I go about comprehending it? What does this paragraph seem to be about?"

> A hoatzin has a clever way of escaping from its enemies.
> It generally builds its home in a branch that extends over a swamp or stream.
> If an enemy approaches, the hoatzin plunges into the water below.
> Once the coast is clear, it uses its fingerlike claws to climb back up the tree.
> Hoatzin are born with claws on their wings but lose the claws as they get older.

To make sense of the selection, you would have to rely heavily on the knowledge you bring to the text. One definition of comprehension is that it is the process of building a connection between what we know and what we do not know, or the new and the old (Searfoss & Readence, 1994). It is currently theorized that our knowledge is packaged into units known as schemata. A **schema** is the organized knowledge that one has about people, places, things, and events (Rumelhart, 1984). A schema may be very broad and general (for example, a schema for animals) or it may be fairly narrow (for example, a schema for Siamese cats).

◼ A **schema** is a unit of organized knowledge. (The plural of *schema* is *schemata.*)

In R. C. Anderson's (1984) view, comprehension primarily involves activating or constructing a schema that accounts for the elements in a text, similar to constructing an outline of a script. For example, a script outline for buying and selling includes the following categories, which are known as slots: buyer, seller, merchandise, money, and bargaining (Rumelhart, 1980). Comprehending a story involves filling these slots with particular examples or instances. As a student reads about a character in a story who is purchasing a bicycle, her or his buyer schema is activated. The student fills in the buyer and seller slots with the characters' names. The bicycle is placed in the merchandise slot. The story says that the buyer got a good deal, so that is placed in the bargaining slot. The story may not say how the character paid for the bike—cash, check, charge card, or an IOU—but the reader may infer that it was with cash because in her or his buyer schema, goods are purchased with cash. A schema thus provides a framework for comprehending a story and making inferences that flesh it out. A schema also aids retention, as students use it to organize their reconstruction of the events.

In constructing the meaning of the selection on the hoatzin, you used various processes to activate the appropriate schema and fill the slots. In reading the first sentence, assuming that you did not know what a hoatzin is, you may have made a reasoned prediction that it was some kind of animal. The information in the first sentence was probably enough to activate your animal-survival-from-enemies schema. The slots might include type of animal, enemies, ability to flee, and ability to fight; guided by your schema, you may have been on the lookout for information to fill the slots. Integrating or summarizing the first three sentences made it possible for you to place "plunges into the water" into the ability to flee slot. You also did quite a bit of inferencing. When you read about the wings in the last sentence, you probably inferred that the hoatzin is a bird, even though it dives into the water. Thus you were able to fill in the type of animal slot. You probably also inferred that the hoatzin's enemies could not reach it in the water. You may have inferred, too, that the creature is not fierce, since it seems to prefer fleeing to fighting. These inferences enabled you to fill in the enemies and ability to fight slots. As you can probably see, comprehending the selection about the hoatzin was not so much a question of getting meaning from the text as it was bringing meaning to it or constructing meaning by transacting with the text.

Not only do readers have schemata for ideas and events, but also they have schemata for text structures, which help them organize information. For instance, a selection might have a main idea and details organization. A reader who realizes this can use the structure of the text to organize the information in his or her memory.

Although activating schemata is essential in reading, reading is more complex than simply filling slots. As they transact with text, proficient, active readers are constantly relating what they are reading to other experiences they have had, other information in the text they have read, and texts previously read. Their interest in the text plays a powerful role in the web of linkages that they construct (Hartman, 1994). A student captivated by the idea that a bird has claws on its wings might relate this text to passages that he or she has read or a TV show about unusual animals.

## Situation Models

Comprehension can also be thought of as the construction of a mental or **situation model.** Comprehension requires that readers create a mental model or representation of textual information and its interpretation (van den Broek & Kremer,

**USING TECHNOLOGY**
Because comprehension is dependent on what we know, one way to foster comprehension is to build background. Hundreds of sites that students might use to learn about a vast array of topics can be found in Polly, J. A. (2002). *The Internet Kids & Family Yellow Pages.* New York: McGraw-Hill.

■ A **situation model,** also known as a mental model, views comprehension as a "process of building and maintaining a model of situations and events described in text" (McNamara, Miller, & Bransford, 1991, p. 491). Schema theory describes how familiar situations are understood. Situation model theory describes how new situations are comprehended.

Activating schemata is part of a situation model. As Zwaan and Graesser (1998) noted, "To construct situation models, readers must integrate information from the text with prior knowledge" (p. 197).

Making inferences about consequences is more difficult than inferring causes. Making inferences about consequences, because it entails predicting future events, requires a deliberate approach, one that makes use of specific strategies (Graesser & Bertus, 1998).

Based on a situation model, you could take at least three steps to improve comprehension: build background, give students material on the appropriate level, and teach strategies, such as generating questions as they read, that would help them make connections.

Following directions is an example of a situation model of reading. It requires that students go beyond merely remembering information. They must also put the information to use.

2000). In expository text, the mental model reflects the organization of the content. The situation model for a science article would include a representation or mental sketch of the physical parts of the system, the steps in the system's process, relationships among the parts of the system and the steps in its operation, and the ways in which people might use the system.

As they read, adept readers ask themselves "why" questions about processes. They want to know why an event occurred or why the author decided to include a certain piece of information in the text. In reading about the formations on the ceilings of underground caves, the reader might wonder why crystals form on the cave's ceilings. The cause, which is often answered in the next sentence, is then connected to the effect. Causal connections are made in rapid-fire fashion. These causal connections are the glue that holds the information together. They provide a bridge from one sentence or thought to the next (Graesser & Bertus, 1998). The process is especially fast when the reader's expectation of the cause is confirmed. However, if the topic of the text is unfamiliar and the reader has little background knowledge to bring to it, making causal connections is more difficult. Making connections is also impeded if the reader is not committed to active comprehension. Situation models emphasize the active, constructivist nature of comprehension and the importance of prior knowledge.

## Role of Reasoning

Reasoning is a key component in comprehension. Students may be called upon to infer character traits, judge a solution, analyze a situation, compare settings, draw conclusions, form concepts, apply a principle, or evaluate the credibility of information. Reasoning and background knowledge interact. Comprehension relies heavily on the reader's ability to use background knowledge to make inferences. Students who have a richer background and can make more connections between what they know and what they are reading have better comprehension and retention.

## Role of Attention

Attention is also a factor in comprehension. Constructing meaning is hindered if the student is not reading actively and purposely: "Successful comprehension depends in part on readers' ability to allocate their limited attention efficiently and effectively to the most relevant pieces of information within the text and within memory" (van den Broek & Kremer, 2000, p. 7).

## Developmental Nature of Comprehension

As children's background knowledge increases and their reasoning ability matures, their ability to comprehend improves. Until they reach the stage of concrete operations, children might have difficulty with tales in which things are not what they seem. They take their reading very literally. For instance, one second-grader had a great deal of difficulty with a trickster tale in which a fox disguised itself as a tree to make a meal of the hens. Despite the fact that the story described the tree's feet and teeth, she believed that it was still a tree. Between the ages of five and seven, children tend to think in one dimension (Donovan & Smolkin, 2002). By age eight or so, children are able to think in more than one dimension and so can learn comprehension strategies more readily. Young children also experience difficulty with metacognitive tasks. They have difficulty explaining their cognitive processes and also have difficulty planning cognitive strategies. Comprehension instruction for young children should be explicit and concrete and in keeping with where they are developmentally. This does not mean that they should not be taught comprehension skills; what it does mean is that the skills need to be taught on their level of understanding. In discussions, it is important to probe to see how students are understanding what they read and to build on their understanding. Open-ended questions work best at revealing children's thinking: What is happening here? What is the author telling us? Is there anything that is puzzling you? Also ask questions that guide children's thinking as they read. What is different about this tree? Do you know any trees that have feet and teeth? Why do you think this tree has feet and teeth?

## COMPREHENSION STRATEGIES

Before you began reading this chapter, what did you do? Did you read the title? Did you ask yourself what you know about comprehension? As you read, did you question what the author was saying? Did you try to relate information in the text to your experience? Did you reread sections because you didn't quite understand what the author was saying or you were momentarily distracted? If you did any of these things, you were using reading strategies.

To help you understand strategies, think about the processes you use as you read. Because we are experienced readers, our strategies have become relatively automatic. Stop your reading from time to time and think about the processes you are using to comprehend what you are reading. Do this especially when you are reading difficult material. Strategies tend to become more conscious when the material is difficult because we have to take deliberate steps to comprehend it. One group of highly effective staff developers and classroom teachers tried out each strategy on their own reading before teaching it. They discovered that their comprehension as well as their understanding of strategies and ability to teach them to students improved.

> We test the strategies on our reading. We became more conscious of our own thinking processes as readers. We realized that we could concentrate simultaneously on the text and our ways of thinking about it. What seems most extraordinary, however, was that by thinking about our own thinking—by being metacognitive (literally, to think about one's thinking)—we could actually deepen and enhance our comprehension of the text. (Keene & Zimmermann, 1997, p. 21)

According to a schema–situational model of comprehension, the reader plays a very active role in constructing an understanding of text. One way the active reader

■ A **strategy** is a deliberate, planned activity or procedure designed to achieve a certain goal.

constructs meaning is by using **strategies.** Strategies are deliberate, planned procedures designed to help us reach a goal. Comprehension strategies include preparing, organizing, elaborating, rehearsing, and monitoring. There are also affective strategies (Weinstein & Mayer, 1986), in which motivation and interest play a role in the construction of meaning.

Preparational strategies are processes that readers use, such as surveying a text and predicting what it will be about, to prepare themselves to construct meaning. Using organizational strategies, readers construct relationships among ideas in the text, specifically between the main idea and supporting details. Paraphrasing, summarizing, clustering related words, noting and using the structure of a text, and creating semantic maps are also ways of organizing.

Elaborating involves building associations between information being read and prior knowledge or integrating them by manipulating or transforming information. Elaboration strategies include drawing inferences, creating analogies, visualizing, and evaluating, or reading critically. (Evaluating is discussed in Chapter 7.)

■ **Rehearsing** is studying or repeating something so as to remember it.

**Rehearsing** involves taking basic steps to remember material. Outlining, taking notes, underlining, testing oneself, and rereading are rehearsal strategies. Elaborating or organizing and rehearsing are often used in combination to learn complex material.

■ **Monitoring** is being aware of or checking one's cognitive processes. In reading comprehension, the reader monitors his understanding of the text.

**Monitoring** consists of being aware of one's comprehension and regulating it. Monitoring strategies include setting goals for reading, adjusting reading speed to difficulty of material, checking comprehension, and taking corrective steps when comprehension fails. (Some preparational strategies are actually a special set of monitoring strategies that are employed prior to reading.) See Table 6.1 for a listing of comprehension strategies.

## Preparational Strategies

In this text, strategies are presented according to cognitive or affective processes involved.

Preparational strategies include previewing, activating prior knowledge about a topic before reading, and predicting what a piece is about or what will happen in a story. Setting purposes and goals are also in this category.

### ■ Activating Prior Knowledge

Because comprehension involves relating the unknown to the known, it is important that students become aware of what they know about a subject. The teacher

**TABLE 6.1** Major comprehension strategies

| Preparational Strategies | Organizational Strategies | Elaboration Strategies | Metacognitive Strategies |
|---|---|---|---|
| Previewing | Comprehending the main idea | Making inferences | Regulating |
| Activating prior knowledge | Determining important details | Imaging | Checking |
| Setting purpose and goals | Organizing details | Generating questions | Repairing |
| Predicting | Sequencing | Evaluating (critical reading) | |
| | Following directions | | |
| | Summarizing | | |

should model the process. In preparation for reading an article about computers, the teacher should show the class how she previews and asks herself what she already knows about the subject and then decides what she would like to find out.

Before students read a selection, the teacher activates students' **prior knowledge** through questioning. This works best when both subject knowledge and personal knowledge are activated. For instance, before reading a story about poisonous snakes, the teacher asks students to tell what they know about poisonous snakes and also relate any personal knowledge they have about snakes. In one study, students who activated both subject knowledge (school-type knowledge) and personal knowledge prior to reading were better able to apply their knowledge and also had a more positive attitude (Spires & Donley, 1998). In time, students should be led to activate both subject and personal knowledge on their own, because much of their reading will be done without benefit of preparatory discussion or teacher assistance.

### ■ Setting Purpose and Goals

Although the teacher often sets the **purpose** for reading a piece by giving students a question to answer, students must be able to set their own purpose. This could fit in with activating prior knowledge. As readers activate knowledge about computers, they may wonder how the machines work, which could be a purpose for reading. Readers also have to decide their overall **goal** for reading—for pleasure, to gain information, or to study for a test—as each goal requires a different style of reading. Again, these are processes that the teacher should model and discuss. However, students should gradually take responsibility for setting purposes and goals.

### ■ Previewing

A strategy that helps readers set a purpose for reading is **previewing.** In previewing, also known as surveying, students read the title, headings, introduction, and summary and look at illustrations to get an overview of the selection. This preview orients them to the piece so that they have some sense of what it will be about. It can function as a kind of blueprint for constructing a mental model of the text and also activates readers' schemata. As readers preview, they ask themselves what they know about the subject. Previewing is often used with predicting: Information gathered from previewing can be used to make predictions.

### ■ Predicting

Powerful, but relatively easy to use, predicting activates readers' schemata because predictions are made on the basis of prior knowledge. Predicting also gives readers a purpose for reading and turns reading into an active search to see whether a prediction is correct. This strategy can and should be taught even before children can read on their own. Before reading a storybook aloud, the teacher should read its title, show the students one or more illustrations, and have them predict what they think the story might be about or what they think will happen. Consensus is not necessary. Each student should feel free to make her or his own prediction. However, the teacher might ask students to justify their predictions; for example, for a prediction for Zion's (1956) *Harry the Dirty Dog*, the teacher might ask, "What makes you think that Harry will be given a bath?"

**■ Prior knowledge** is the background information that a reader brings to the text.

> **ADAPTING INSTRUCTION**
> **for *STRUGGLING READERS***
> **and *WRITERS***
> Stress that the goal of reading is to construct meaning. Poor readers may be more concerned with pronouncing words correctly than with making meaning. If students realize that the goal of reading is comprehension, they are more likely to be "actively involved in achieving this goal by monitoring their effectiveness toward it" (Westby, 1999, p. 154).

**■** The **purpose** for reading is the question that the reader wants to answer or the information the reader is seeking. The **goal** for reading is the outcome the reader is seeking: to gain information, to prepare for a test, to learn how to put a toy together, to relax, etc.

**■ Previewing** can also be applied during reading. A reader may complete a section and then activate prior knowledge and make predictions for the upcoming selection.

For setting up predictions, Nessel (1987) suggested two questions that could be asked at the beginning or at crucial points in the story:

1. What do you think will happen? (e.g., What do you think *X* will do? How do you think this problem will be resolved?)

2. Why do you think so? (What have you experienced and what did you read in the story that leads you to make that prediction?) (p. 604)

The first question elicits the prediction; the second asks students to explain it to ensure that it is thoughtful and plausible. Students also must learn to be flexible so that they can alter a prediction if it proves to be off the mark.

In addition to teaching students what kinds of questions to ask, the teacher should show them the best sources of predictions: title, illustrations, introductory note, and first paragraph. Gradually, students can create their own predictions as they read. Predicting becomes an excellent device for enhancing comprehension when students are reading independently—ideally, it will become automatic. Predicting should also be a lifelong strategy. As they move into higher grades, students should use predicting as part of a study technique as well as for other sustained reading.

Part of being an effective user of strategies is knowing when and where to use a particular strategy. Making predictions requires prior knowledge. Students beginning to read about a topic for which they have little background information will have difficulty making reasonable predictions and so should use another strategy.

## Organizational Strategies

Organizational strategies are at the heart of constructing meaning. In contrast to preparational strategies, they are employed during reading as well as after reading. As students read, they form a situation model. Organizational strategies involve selecting important details and building relationships among them. For reading, this entails identifying the main idea of a passage and its supporting details and summarizing.

### ■ Comprehending the Main Idea

Deriving the main idea is at the core of constructing meaning from text, as it provides a framework for organizing, understanding, and remembering the essential details. Without it, students wander aimlessly among details. Being able to identify or compose main ideas is essential for summarizing, note taking, and outlining. (Although suggestions for teaching comprehension of main ideas and important details are presented separately in this chapter for the sake of clarity, these should be taught together.)

The **main idea** has been defined in a variety of ways (Cunningham & Moore, 1986). In this book, the main idea will be defined as a summary statement that includes the other details in a paragraph or longer piece; it is what all the sentences are about. Despite the importance of main ideas, little is known about how elementary school students generate them.

---

**USING TECHNOLOGY**

Technology can foster active reading. In *Alex's Scribbles* **http://www.scribbles. com.au/max/book-main.html,** Max, the koala, has a series of adventures. To continue each story, the reader must point and click in response to a question. This site also lends itself to writing. Alex, the coauthor, and Max invite readers to e-mail them.

---

■ The **main idea** is the overall meaning or gist of a passage. It is what the passage is all about, a summary statement of its meaning.

Adept readers tend to use either a whole-to-part strategy, in which they draft or hypothesize the whole and confirm it by reading the parts, or a part-to-whole strategy, in which they note important parts, construct relationships among them, and compose a main idea statement (Afflerbach, 1990; Afflerbach & Johnston, 1986). The whole-to-part strategy fits best with a schema theory of comprehension; the part-to-whole strategy exemplifies the construction of a situation model.

Because of its complexity and importance, main idea comprehension has to be taught step by step. Instruction should include presenting underlying processes, one of which is classifying.

**Classifying.**   Determining the main idea is partly a classification skill. The main idea statement is a category label for all or most of the details in the piece. The best way to convey the concept of a main idea and to provide instruction in its underlying cognitive process is to have students classify a series of objects or words (Baumann, 1986; Johnson & Kress, 1965; Williams, 1986b).

To demonstrate classifying to younger students, bring in a variety of objects and indicate how they might be sorted. For example, display an apple, orange, pear, banana, and book, and ask students to tell which go together. Discuss why the book does not belong. Put the objects in a box. Tell students you want to label the box so that you know what is in it and ask them what word you might use. Students can name other objects that might be put in the box, with a discussion of why they belong there. Follow a similar procedure with tools, toys, and other objects.

Once students have grasped the idea of classifying objects, have them classify words. First, give them lists of words that include labels. Model how you would go about choosing the category label. Tell students that you are looking for a word that tells about all the others. Read a series of related words that have been written on the board: *cats, fish, pets, dogs.* Model how you would choose *pets* as the label because it includes the other three words. After working through several sample series of words, have students complete exercises similar to the following. The exercise contains words that are easy enough for first-graders. For older students, select more challenging items.

| | | | |
|---|---|---|---|
| ball | toys | blocks | doll |
| oak | trees | maple | pine |
| fruit | apple | peach | banana |

To vary the activity, include an item in the series that does not belong (*train, bus, car, ball*) and have students identify it. Also, list a series of related items (*three, nine, four, two*) and let students supply a category label.

After students are able to categorize words with ease, have them categorize groups of sentences by identifying the one that tells about all the others. Call this the main idea sentence. To construct exercises of this type, locate brief paragraphs that have an explicitly stated main idea. Write the sentences in list form, and have students point out which sentence tells about all the others. Groups of sentences similar to the following can be used:

The car door locks were frozen.

Small children refused to venture from their warm homes.

It was the coldest day that anyone could remember.

The temperature was twenty below zero.

The lake was frozen solid.

Model the process of choosing the most inclusive sentence, thinking aloud as you choose it. Let students see that the process involves checking each sentence to determine which one includes all the others and then examining the other sentences to make sure that each one can be included under the main sentence. In your explanation, you might use the analogy of a roof. Explain that the main idea sentence is like a roof. The other sentences contain details that hold up the roof. They are like the walls that support a roof. As part of the process, explain how pointing out the inclusive sentence will help them find main ideas in their reading. After students have acquired a concept of an inclusive sentence, have students complete a series of similar exercises under your guidance.

Although well-formed paragraphs might be used for initial instruction in main ideas, students should apply their strategies to informational trade books and texts. Authors do not begin each paragraph with a main idea. Often, the main idea is implied, and some paragraphs simply provide an introduction or additional information and lack a clear-cut main idea.

**Recognizing topic sentences.** Once students have a sense of what a main idea is, begin working with brief paragraphs that contain an explicitly stated main idea, a sentence that tells about all the others. Explain that the main idea sentence is called a topic sentence because it contains the topic of the paragraph. It is often the first sentence of a paragraph, but may be last or in the middle. Move the topic sentence in a sample paragraph around to show students how it could make sense in a number of positions. Also point out how the details in a paragraph support the main idea.

Provide students with guided practice in locating topic sentences and supporting details in paragraphs. Locating supporting details is like proving a problem in math: If the details do not support the sentence chosen as the topic sentence, the student has probably not located the real topic sentence. Take practice paragraphs from children's periodicals, books, and textbooks. At first, select paragraphs in which the main idea sentence comes first, as this is the easiest organizational pattern to understand. Students have more difficulty with paragraphs in which the topic sentence occurs last (Kimmel & MacGinitie, 1984). Also choose paragraphs that are interesting and well written. Students will then enjoy the activity more and will pick up incidental information. Using real books and periodicals also demonstrates that this is a practical activity, one students can use in their everyday reading. It also makes the practice more realistic because students will be working with the kinds of material they actually read rather than with paragraphs contrived for teaching the main idea. The following is an example of a paragraph that might be used:

The largest members of the cat family are truly large. They range in size from about 6 feet to 12 feet long, measured from the tips of their noses to the tips of their tails. They weigh from 50 to 500 pounds, and are 22 to 44 inches tall at the shoulder. (Thompson, 1998, p. 26)

Presenting paragraphs that contain topic sentences makes sense in the beginning stages of instruction as it simplifies identifying the main idea, but you must emphasize that not all paragraphs contain topic sentences. In fact, most do not. Baumann and Serra (1984) found that only 44 percent of the paragraphs in elementary social studies textbooks had explicitly stated main ideas, and only 27 percent of the main ideas occurred in the opening sentence.

Even when the main idea is explicitly stated and is in the opening sentence, readers must still infer that the first sentence tells what the rest of the paragraph is about. Young readers and poor readers tend to select the first sentence as the topic sentence almost automatically (Gold & Fleisher, 1986). To prevent this, ask them to check by specifying the supporting details in this paragraph and to see whether all the other sentences support the first one (Duffelmeyer, 1985). If that is the case, the first sentence is the topic sentence. If not, the students should search for a sentence that does serve that function.

## ■ Selecting or Constructing the Main Idea

Most passages do not have an explicitly stated main idea, so it must be constructed. Students might use the following steps to select a stated main idea or construct a main idea if it is not stated:

1. Use the heading, title, or first sentence to make a hypothesis (careful guess) as to what the main idea is.
2. Read each sentence and see whether it supports the hypothesis. If not, revise the hypothesis.
3. If you can't make a hypothesis as to what the main idea is, see what all or most of the sentences have in common or are talking about.
4. Select a sentence or make a sentence that tells what all the sentences are about. (Post these steps or an adaptation of them.)

One problem that students have in recognizing or generating main ideas is a tendency to focus on a narrow statement of a single detail instead of on a broad statement that includes all the essential information in a paragraph (Williams, 1986a). As students work with paragraphs, you might use a series of prompts to help them identify what the paragraph is about. Start off by asking them what the general topic of the paragraph is, and then ask them to identify the specific topic and check whether all the details support it. For instance, using the following simple paragraph about robots, you might ask, "What is the general topic of the paragraph? What is the specific topic? What does the paragraph tell us about robots?"

> Robots help us in many ways. Robots work in factories. They help put cars and TVs together. In some offices, robots deliver the mail. And in some hospitals, robots bring food to sick people. A new kind of robot can mow lawns. And some day there may even be robots that can take out the trash and take the dog for a walk.

If students provide the correct specific topic, ask them to verify their response. The class should go over each sentence to determine whether it tells how robots help out. If, on the other hand, students supply a supporting detail rather than a statement of the specific topic, the teacher would have the class examine the detail to see if it encompassed all the other details in the paragraph. Lesson 6.1 presents suggestions for teaching the main idea.

## LESSON 6.1 Determining the main idea and its supporting details

### Step 1. Introducing the strategy

Explain what main ideas and supporting details are and why it is important to locate and understand them in reading. Give a clear definition of what a main idea is—it tells what the paragraph or section is all about. Provide examples of main ideas.

### Step 2. Modeling the process

Show how you would go about determining a main idea and its supporting details. Starting off with well-constructed paragraphs, demonstrate the hypothesis strategy, because this is the strategy most frequently used by adept readers. Show students how you would use a title, heading, graphic clues, and the apparent topic sentence to predict the main idea. Then confirm or revise your hypothesis as you read and see whether the details support your hypothesized main idea. (Even if the main idea is directly stated, it is still necessary to use a hypothesis or other strategy because readers cannot be sure that the sentence is indeed a topic sentence until they read the rest of the paragraph.)

In subsequent lessons that tackle implied main idea paragraphs that have no titles or headings that could be clues to the main idea, you may have to use a part-to-whole strategy. Note the details in such a paragraph and then construct a main idea statement after seeing how the details are related or what they have in common. A part-to-whole strategy is best taught after students have a firm grasp of the hypothesis-confirmation strategy. Model the process with a variety of paragraphs.

### Step 3. Guided practice

Have students derive main ideas from brief, well-constructed paragraphs. If possible, choose paragraphs that cover familiar topics, as it is easier to construct main ideas when the content and vocabulary are known. Students face a double burden when they must grapple with difficult concepts and vocabulary while trying to construct a main idea. Although shorter paragraphs should be used in the beginning stages, have students gradually apply this skill to longer pieces, such as selections from content-area textbooks.

### Step 4. Independent practice and application

Have students derive main ideas and supporting details in children's books, textbooks, periodicals, and other materials that they read on their own. From well-written, well-organized science or social studies textbooks or children's books, choose sections that convey an overall main idea or theme and develop

---

Comprehension instruction requires scaffolding. Teachers provide examples, modeling, explicit instruction, prompts, and discussions in helping students learn strategies (Dole, Duffy, Roehler, & Pearson, 1991). In time, the scaffolding is reduced and the students apply the strategies independently.

---

Noting main ideas in longer sections is the ultimate payoff. This helps pupils better understand and remember information. Today's content-area texts make plentiful use of heads and subheads, which announce main ideas or can be used to construct them.

it in several paragraphs. At first, choose pieces that have an explicitly stated main idea. Show students how you would use a hypothesis strategy to derive the main idea. Using a selection similar to that illustrated in Figure 6.1, demonstrate how you would use the heading "'Eggs-traordinary' Eggs!," the subheadings, and the illustrations to guess what the main idea of the section is. Lead students to see that the main idea seems to be stated in the heading and that the main idea of each paragraph is found in the first or first two sentences.

### Step 5.  Assessment and reteaching

Observe students as they obtain main ideas from a variety of passages in texts and trade books. Note how well they can do the following:

_____ Identify the main idea and supporting details in a brief, well-constructed paragraph in which the main idea is directly stated in the first sentence.

_____ Identify the main idea and supporting details in a brief, well-constructed paragraph in which the main idea is directly stated in the middle or end of the paragraph.

_____ Infer the main idea in a well-constructed paragraph in which the main idea is not directly stated.

_____ Identify or infer the main idea in general reading.

Based on the results of your assessment, review and reteach.

> ▎If students fail to construct a main idea during their first pass through the text, show them how to skim through the passage and note related words, ideas, or concepts. Have them create a main idea statement that tells what all the sentences are about. As an alternative, show students how to use the draft-and-revise strategy. That is, they use their initial reading to construct a main idea statement and then check the validity of their statement by rereading the passage.

### Constructing the main idea

In a discussion with students, create a series of steps that they might use to locate or construct the main idea. Make a poster containing the steps and put it in a prominent place so students can refer to it while reading. (Use the steps listed on p. 305 or an adaptation of them.)

**Extending the ability to construct the main idea**.   Take advantage of discussions of selections that students have read and other naturally occurring opportunities to apply and extend the skill of constructing main ideas. Note how important details are related to the main idea of a selection. Also apply the concept to writing. Have students create and develop topic sentences on nonfiction subjects of their own choosing.

Graphic displays can help students identify the topic sentence and its supporting details. Use a simplified semantic map, which is sometimes called a spider web when the supporting details are equal, as shown in Figure 6.2. Use a linear

> ▎As with other strategies, this one follows a gradual release of responsibility. As students grow in skill, they gradually take responsibility for their own learning.

**FIGURE 6.1**

**Main Ideas in a Science Text**

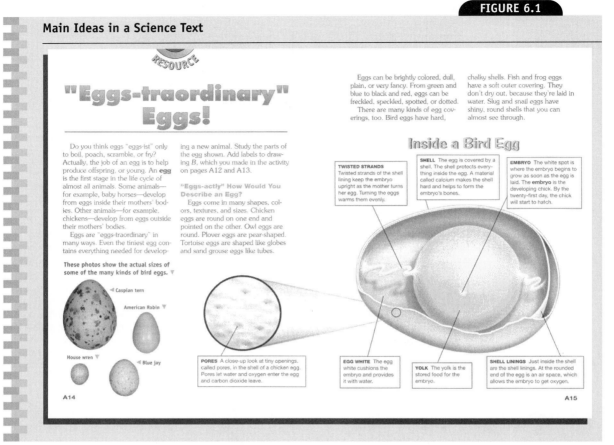

From *Science Discovery Works Grade 3* by Carolyn Sumners, et al. © by Silver Burdett Ginn, Simon & Schuster Education Group. Used by permission.

display like that in Figure 6.3 when the piece has a sequential order, that is, when the ideas are listed in order of occurrence.

Main idea instruction is more appropriate for nonfiction than for fiction. Fiction has a theme rather than a main idea. Identifying a theme can be subtler and more complex than noting a main idea. Most children's fiction also has a central problem that gives coherence to the story (Moldofsky, 1983).

■ **Reviewing the Strategy**

Learning a strategy may take a month or more. In subsequent lessons, review and extend the strategy. To review the strategy, ask the following kinds of questions:

- ■ What strategy are we learning to use? (main idea)
- ■ How does this strategy help us? (Helps us understand and remember what we read. Helps us organize important details.)

FIGURE 6.2

**Spider Web for Main Idea and Equal Supporting Details**

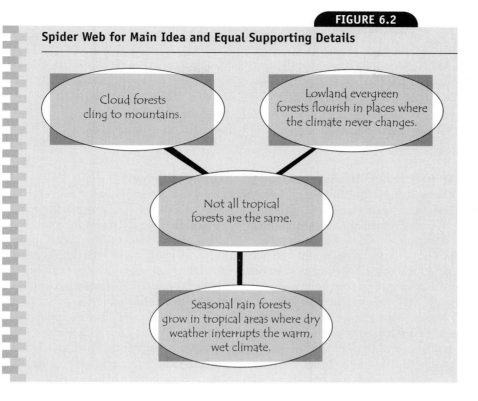

- When do we use this strategy? (with nonfiction)
- How do we use this strategy? (Review the steps presented on p. 305.) Also ask students to tell about instances when they used the strategy on their own (Scott, 1998).

FIGURE 6.3

**Main Ideas and Details in Sequential Display**

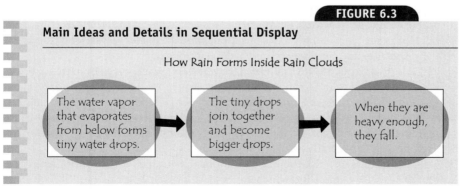

Text from *Weather Words,* by G. Gibbons, 1990, New York: Holiday House.

REINFORCEMENT
ACTIVITIES    **Main idea construction**

- Cut out newspaper headlines and titles of articles, and have students match them with the articles.
- Have students classify lists of items.
- When discussing selections that students have read, include questions that require them to identify and/or construct a main idea.

### ■ Determining the Relative Importance of Information

The ability to determine what is important in a selection is a key factor in comprehension as it keeps readers from drowning in a sea of details or having to cull out trivial information. Determining main ideas and the relative importance of information should be taught together. Determination of what is important in a selection is often dependent on the derivation of the main idea. Once they know the main idea, readers are in a better position to identify the relative importance of information and to construct a situation model of the text. For instance, once they know that the main idea of an article is how to use a video camera, they can assume that the steps in the process will be the important details. Readers have to ask themselves which details support or explain a selection's main idea or, if the article is especially rich in details, which are the most important. If an article cites twenty capabilities of lasers, readers might decide which five are most essential.

Adept readers will use textual clues to help determine which details are most important. A carefully written text might state which details are essential. Or the reader might note those details that are discussed first and given the most print. Minor details might be signaled by words such as *also*, as in the sentence "Laser readers are also used to check out books in many libraries and to check times in many competitive sports."

Expert readers also use text structure, relational terms, and repetition of words or concepts to determine importance. Relational terms and expressions such as "most important of all" and "three main causes" help readers determine important ideas. A repeated word or concept is an especially useful clue. The structure of the piece also gives clues as to which details are most essential (Afflerbach & Johnston, 1986). With a problem–solution organization, an adept reader will seek out the problem and solution and ignore extraneous descriptions or examples.

In addition to using textual clues, readers can use their schemata or background knowledge to determine what is important. A student who raises tropical fish would seek out certain kinds of information when reading about a new species, such as a description of the species, its habits, and where it is found. The purpose for reading is also a factor. A student who is contemplating buying a new tropical fish will realize that details on cost and care are significant.

Expert readers also use their beliefs about the author's intention to determine which details are essential and which are not (Afflerbach & Johnston, 1986). Expert readers are able to step back from the text and consider the author's purpose. If, for instance, the author is trying to establish that a certain point is true, the reader will seek out the details or examples the author provides as proof of the contention. Lesson 6.2 includes some steps that might be used to help students determine important information.

## LESSON 6.2  Determining important details

### Step 1. Introduction of strategy

Explain what is meant by "important details" and why being able to identify them is an essential skill. Display and discuss several short selections that contain both important and unimportant information, and help students discriminate between the two.

### Step 2. Model the process

Determine important information in a sample paragraph. Show how you would use contextual clues: topic sentences, placement of ideas, and graphic aids. In another session, demonstrate how you might use knowledge of the topic or your purpose for reading.

### Step 3. Guided practice

Provide guidance as students determine important information in a selection. Start with well-structured texts that supply plenty of clues and gradually work up to selections from their basal readers, content-area textbooks, library books, or periodicals. Ask students to justify their choice of important details, because this skill is somewhat subjective.

### Step 4. Application

Have students note important ideas in materials that they read independently. The more experience students have with varied reading materials and the broader and deeper their knowledge base, the better prepared they will be to determine the relative importance of information. Set purposes that lead students to grasp essential information. Ask questions that focus on important information. By asking such questions, you will be modeling the kinds of questions that students should be asking themselves before they read and as they read.

### Step 5. Assessment and reteaching

During discussions of selections that have been read, ask questions that require selecting important details. Take note of students' performance. Ask the kinds of questions that provide insight into students' reasoning processes. Supply on-the-spot help if students need it. Also, plan reteaching lessons if needed.

### ■ Reviewing the Strategy

In subsequent lessons, review and extend the strategy. To review the strategy, ask the following kinds of questions:

- What strategy are we learning to use? (Understanding important ideas.)
- How does this strategy help us? (Helps us understand and remember important details. Keeps us from getting lost in too many details.)
- When do we use this strategy? (with nonfiction)
- How do we use this strategy?
    1. Use the title, heading, and first sentence to make a hypothesis (careful guess) about what the main idea will be.
    2. Read the selection to see whether you have chosen the right main idea. If not, change it.
    3. Choose the most important details. These will be details that support the main idea. The author might signal the most important details by using phrases such as "most important of all" (Scott, 1998). (Post these steps or your adaptation of them.)

### REINFORCEMENT ACTIVITIES  Determining importance of information

- Have students predict the important ideas in a selection they are about to read.
- After they have read a selection, ask students to tell which ideas are most important.
- Encourage students to write newspaper stories. In most newspaper stories, the important information is provided in the first paragraph.

To provide practice with the sequence of steps in a process, you might encourage students to read such books as *Howling Hurricanes* (Richards, 2002) or *Recycle! A Handbook for Kids* (Gibbons, 1992).

**Sequencing.**    Because some details have to be comprehended and then remembered in a certain order, readers must organize them sequentially. These include historical or biographical events, steps in a process, and directions. Because the extra step of noting the sequence is involved, organizing sequential details often poses special problems, especially for younger readers. To introduce sequence, have students tell about some simple sequential activities in which they engage, such as washing dishes, playing a favorite game, or assembling a puzzle. Discuss the order of the activities, and place them on the chalkboard using cue words such as *first, second, next, then, before, last,* and *after.*

Place lists of other events on the chalkboard, and ask students to put them in order. Start with a series of three or four events for younger students and work up to six or seven items for more advanced readers. Encourage students to use their sense of the situation or the process to put the events in order. Show how cue words help indicate sequence.

After students have become adept at this activity, let them apply their skill to stories and articles. To help them become aware of the sequence of a story, have them map out the main events, showing how the story progresses to its climax and the resolution of a problem. Help students create causal links between events in a story, as this aids retention (McNamara, Miller, & Bransford, 1991).

For biographies and historical accounts, show students how to use dates to keep events in order. Show students books like *The Ancient Greeks* (Shuter, 1997) and *Leonardo da Vinci* (Malam, 1998), in which the authors use time lines or chronologies to help readers keep track of key events. When time lines have not been included in a selection, encourage students to create them to help keep a sequence of events in order. As students read about the steps in a process (e.g., a caterpillar becoming a butterfly), have them note the sequence and visualize it if possible. Show them how they might use a graphic organizer to display a process or chain of events. Figure 6.4 presents a chain map showing how radar works.

**USING TECHNOLOGY**
HyperHistory Online presents a variety of time lines for famous people and key events.
**http://www. hyperhistory.com/ online_n2/ History_n2/a.html**

**Following directions.**    Following directions is a natural outgrowth of sequencing. As students read directions, remind them to make use of cue words such as *first*, *next*, and *last*. Also introduce words such as *list*, *match*, and *underline*, which are frequently found in directions and with which young children often have difficulty (Boehm, 1971). Students can create mental models of directions by visually depicting the process, using an accompanying diagram or other illustration, or describing the steps. If possible, have students carry out the procedures outlined in the directions.

After techniques for understanding directions have been taught, students should be made responsible for reading and following directions. They should read the directions once to get an overview, and then a second time to find out exactly what they are to do. Encourage them to study any samples that are given; however, these samples should be examined after the directions are read, not before. Some students skip the directions and look only at the sample, and some do not even bother looking at the sample. They simply plunge ahead or ask the teacher what to do. If students ask what they are supposed to do, tell them to read the directions carefully. If they still fail to understand, have them tell you what they think they are to do, and then redirect their thinking as necessary.

Being able to comprehend and follow directions is more important than ever. Many items that we purchase come unassembled. And many appliances have to be programmed. Downloading a file from the Internet or using a new program requires being able to follow sophisticated directions.

Use printed directions for some classroom routines—for example, how to operate the computer or the tape recorder. Also, use directions that accompany real-world materials. Students might follow sets of printed directions for assembling a simple toy or using a new piece of software. Have them note how studying the illustration is an important part of following the directions.

Use writing to support reading. Encourage students to write a series of directions for a favorite game or other activity. Have students work in pairs. The partners can check the clarity of each other's directions by trying them out and seeing whether they can follow them.

**FIGURE 6.4**

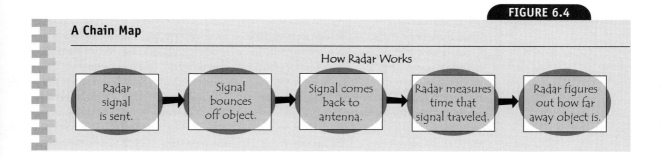

**A Chain Map**

How Radar Works

Radar signal is sent. → Signal bounces off object. → Signal comes back to antenna. → Radar measures time that signal traveled. → Radar figures out how far away object is.

**Following directions**

Students can use these steps to follow directions:

■ Read the directions to get an overview.
■ Look at any pictures or diagrams that go along with the directions.
■ Make sure all parts have been included.
■ Get all necessary tools and materials or ingredients.
■ Read and follow each step. Use any pictures or diagrams as an aid.
  (Post these steps or your adaptation of them.)

Other activities that provide natural practice in following directions are planting seeds, caring for classroom animals or plants, using a computer program, finding a site on the Web, and following recipes. The best thing about real-life exercises is that they are self-checking. A computer program that is not used correctly will flash an error message, recipes incorrectly followed result in inedible food, and devices improperly constructed do not work.

### ■ Summarizing

What is the most effective comprehension strategy of all? When five experts in learning examined the research on comprehension in order to discover which strategies seemed to have the greatest payoff and were the most solidly grounded in research, they listed summarization first (Pressley, Johnson, Symons, McGoldrick, & Kurita, 1989). Summarization, which builds on the organizational strategy of determining main ideas and supporting details, improves comprehension and increases retention. It is also a metacognitive means of monitoring, through which students can evaluate their understanding of a passage that they have just read. If a student has not comprehended a selection, she or he is almost certain to have difficulty summarizing it. Summarizing also helps students understand the structure of text. In writing a summary, students are brought face-to-face with the organization of a piece of writing. This should help them detect the underlying structure of the text, which is a key to understanding text and writing effective summaries (Touchstone Applied Science Associates, 1997).

Summarizing is a complex skill that takes years to develop. Even college students may have difficulty summarizing. Young children realize that a summary is a retelling of material; however, they have difficulty determining what points should be included in a summary. The view of young students seems to be egocentric: They choose details that are personally interesting rather than selecting details that seem important from the author's point of view. Young students also have difficulty with the procedures necessary to summarize (Hidi & Anderson, 1986). They delete information but do not combine or condense details; they also tend to use a copy strategy. Students record details word for word in their summaries. Once they learn to put information into their own words, they begin combining and condensing.

**Introducing summarizing.** Summaries need not be written. All of us make oral summaries of movie and book plots, events, conversations, and so on. Because writing summaries can be difficult (Brown & Day, 1983; Hare & Borchardt, 1984), teachers should first develop students' ability to summarize orally.

Retelling is a natural way to lead into summarizing. Young children tend to recount every incident in a story and give every detail about a topic. Help them structure their retellings so as to emphasize major events and main ideas. Ask questions like these: "What were the two most important things that the main character did? What were the three main things that happened in the story? What are the main things you learned about robots? What are the main ways in which robots are used?" (See Chapter 7 for a fuller discussion of retelling.)

*S*tudents should be taught strategies for reading to follow directions.

From kindergarten on, teachers can model the process of summarizing by providing summaries of selections read, especially nonfiction, and of discussions and directions. As students get into content-area material, they can be directed to pay special attention to chapter summaries. Although they may not be capable of writing well-formed summaries until the upper elementary or middle school grades, they can begin learning the skill in ways appropriate to their level of development from their very first years of school. With younger and less able students, emphasize including the most important information in a summary. As students become proficient in extracting the most essential information, teach techniques for condensing information.

Certain activities can build summarizing or its underlying skills. Encourage students to use titles, illustrations, topic sentences, headings, and other textual clues. In K. K. Taylor's (1986) study, many students failed to use the title and topic sentence when composing their summaries, although both contained the main idea of the selection. Teach students how to read expository text. Ineffectual summarizers read such works as though they are fiction and so fail to note textual cues that could help them create better summaries (Taylor, 1986). Have students compose oral summaries of stories, articles, and class discussions. Also compose group summaries.

To create a group summary, read an informational article aloud and ask students what the most important points are. After listing the points on the board, have the class summarize them. Group summaries provide preparation for the creation of independent summaries (Moore, Moore, Cunningham, & Cunningham, 1986).

Summarizing can be an excellent device for checking comprehension. Encourage students to stop after reading key sections of expository text and mentally summarize the materials. Once they have some ability to identify relevant details, make

■ Present summarizing as a tool that students can use to share information and better comprehend and remember what they read (Touchstone Applied Science Associates, 1997). When teaching and applying summarization, use students' content-area texts so they can see how summarizing can be a learning aid.

■ Organizational strategies are effective. Whether it be creating main ideas, making semantic maps, or summarizing, just about any attempt to organize information results in better understanding and recall.

To help students structure their summaries of fictional pieces, you might use story grammar, which is explained in the next chapter.

Being able to determine relative importance of information is essential for summarizing. However, in addition to sifting out the important ideas, the summarizer must also synthesize those ideas into a coherent whole, which makes summarizing a difficult, complex skill (Dole, Duffy, Roehler, & Pearson, 1991).

■ **Elaboration** refers to additional processing of text by the reader which may result in improved comprehension and recall. Elaboration involves building connections between one's background knowledge and the text or integrating these two sources through manipulating or transforming information.

use of structural cues, and identify and construct main ideas, they are ready for a more formal type of instruction in summarizing.

**Presenting summarizing skills.** When teaching summarizing, begin with shorter, easier text. Texts that are shorter and easier to comprehend are easier to summarize. Also, start off with narrative text, which is easier than expository text to summarize (Hidi & Anderson, 1986). Focus on the content rather than the form of the summaries. After students become accustomed to summarizing essential details, stress the need for well-formed, polished summaries. Because many students have great difficulty determining which details are important, have them list important details. Discuss these lists before they compose their summaries. Also have students create semantic maps before writing summaries. In addition to helping students select important information, such maps may help them detect important relationships among key ideas. In one study students who constructed maps before summarizing used a greater number of cohesive ties than those who did not (Ruddell & Boyle, 1989).

## Elaboration Strategies

**Elaboration** is a generative activity in which the reader constructs connections between information from text and prior knowledge. Like organizational strategies, elaboration strategies are employed during reading but may also be put into operation after reading. The reader generates inferences, images, questions, judgments, and other elaborations. A powerful strategy, elaboration increased comprehension by 50 percent in a number of studies (Linden & Wittrock, 1981).

### ■ Making Inferences

Although children have the cognitive ability to draw inferences, some do not do so spontaneously. A probable cause of this deficiency is a lack of background information about the topic or the failure to process information in the text that would foster drawing inferences. Or students may not realize that inferences are necessary. They might believe that only literal comprehension is called for (Westby, 1999). Two approaches enhance the ability to make inferences: building background and teaching specific strategies for making inferences. However, sustained instruction is required. When students were taught processes for making inferences, no significant change was noted until after four weeks of teaching. The effects were long-lasting, and, as a side benefit, literal comprehension improved (Dewitz, Carr, & Patberg, 1987).

There are two kinds of inferences: schema-based and text-based (Winne, Graham, & Prock, 1993). Schema-based inferences depend on prior knowledge. For instance, reading the sentence "They rode into the sunset," inferring that it was late in the day and the riders were heading west is schema-based. The reader uses her or his schema for the position of the sun to infer approximate time and direction. Schema-based inferences allow the reader to elaborate on the text by adding information that has been implied by the author. A text-based inference is one that requires putting together two or more pieces of information from the text. Reading that peanuts have more food energy than sugar and that a pound of peanut butter has more protein than thirty-two eggs but more fat than ice cream, the reader might put all this information together to infer that peanuts are nutritious but fattening.

Making inferences is the most important elaboration strategy. Much of the information in a piece, especially fiction, is implied. Authors show and dramatize rather than tell. Instead of directly stating that a main character is a liar, the author dramatizes situations in which the character lies. This is true even in the simplest of stories. For instance, in the third paragraph of *The Tale of Peter Rabbit*, Beatrix Potter (1908) wrote:

> "Now, my dears," said old Mrs. Rabbit one morning, "you may go into the field or down the lane, but don't go into Mr. McGregor's garden. Your Father had an accident there. He was put in a pie by Mrs. McGregor."

The reader must infer that Father was killed by Mr. McGregor and that Mr. McGregor will harm any rabbits that he catches in his garden. The reader might also infer that the reason Mr. McGregor does not like rabbits is that they eat the vegetables in his garden. None of this is stated, so the reader must use his schema for rabbits and gardens, together with his comprehension of the story, to produce a series of inferences. In a sense, the author erects the story's framework, and the reader must construct the full meaning by filling in the missing parts.

Activating prior knowledge helps students make inferences. For instance, if the teacher discusses the fact that rabbits anger gardeners by nibbling their vegetables before the students read *The Tale of Peter Rabbit*, they will be much more likely to draw appropriate inferences from the passage previously cited. Asking questions that require students to make inferences also helps. It increases both their ability and their inclination to make inferences (Hansen, 1981).

Although above-average students make more inferences than average ones (Carr, 1983), below-average readers can be taught the skill. Hansen and Pearson (1982) combined activation of prior knowledge, direct instruction in an inference-making strategy, posing of inferential questions, and predicting to create a series of lessons in which poor readers improved to such an extent that their inferential comprehension became equal to that of good readers. Here is how Hansen and Pearson's prior knowledge–prediction strategy works:

1. The teacher reads the story and analyzes it for two or three important ideas.

2. For each important idea, the teacher creates a previous-experience question that elicits from students any similar experiences that they may have had. This is a have-you-ever question (Pearson, 1985).

3. For each previous-experience question, an accompanying prediction question is created. This is a what-do-you-think-will-happen question.

4. Students read the selection to check their predictions.

5. Students discuss their predictions. Inferential questions, especially those related to the key ideas, are discussed.

---

To make inferences, students must have access to the information necessary to make the inference. If students can't recall the information or can't recall enough of it, they won't be able to make an inference. Adequate literal comprehension is a second prerequisite for inferential comprehension. Also important is being able to implement inference-making procedures such as combining several pieces of text information or combining text information and prior knowledge (Winne, Graham, & Prock, 1993).

Students should only be given text that they can decode with a fair degree of accuracy (95 percent) and at a reasonable speed (85 words per minute). If these conditions are not met, students might expend so much energy decoding text that they have little or no cognitive energy left for comprehension because they have expended all their cognitive resources on lower-level processes (Sinatra, Brown, & Reynolds, 2002).

The following important ideas, previous-experience questions, and prediction questions were used in the study (Pearson, 1985, Appendix B):

*Important idea number 1:* Even adults can be afraid of things.

*Previous-experience question:* Tell something an adult you know is afraid of.

*Prediction question:* In the story, Cousin Alma is afraid of something even though she is an adult. What do you think it is?

*Important idea number 2:* People sometimes act more bravely than they feel.

*Previous-experience question:* Tell about how you acted some time when you were afraid and tried not to show it.

*Prediction question:* How do you think that Fats, the boy in the story, will act when he is afraid and tries not to show it?

*Important idea number 3:* Our experience sometimes convinces us that we are capable of doing things we thought we couldn't do.

*Previous-experience question:* Tell about a time that you were able to do something you thought you couldn't do.

*Prediction question:* In the story, what do you think Cousin Alma is able to do that she thought she couldn't do?

An important element of the technique is the discussion, with students' responses acting as a catalyst. One student's answer reminds others of similar experiences that they have had but do not think apply. For example, a girl mentioning that her uncle is afraid of snakes might trigger in another student the memory that his grandfather is afraid of dogs, even small ones. The teacher also emphasizes that students should compare their real-life experiences with events in the story.

Together with having background activated and being asked inferential questions, students should be taught a strategy for making inferences. Gordon (1985) mapped out a five-step process, which is outlined in Lesson 6.3.

> **ADAPTING INSTRUCTION for *STRUGGLING READERS and WRITERS***
>
> As Hansen and Pearson (1982) noted, poor readers are typically asked literal questions, so their inferential skills are underdeveloped. If carefully taught, lower-achieving readers can make inferences.

## LESSON 6.3  Making inferences

### Step 1. Explaining the skill

The teacher explains what the skill is, why it is important, and when and how it is used. This explanation might be illustrated with examples.

### Step 2. Modeling the process

While modeling the process of making inferences with a brief piece of text written on the chalkboard, the teacher reveals her or his thinking processes: "It says here that Jim thought Fred would make a great center when he first saw him walk into the classroom. The center is usually the tallest person on a basketball team, so I inferred that Fred is tall." The teacher also models the process with several other selections, so students see that inferences can be drawn from a variety of materials.

### Step 3.  Sharing the task

Students are asked to take part in the inferencing process. The teacher asks an inferential question about a brief sample paragraph or excerpt and then answers it. The students supply supporting evidence for the inference from the selection itself and from their background knowledge. The reasoning processes involved in making the inference are discussed. The teacher stresses the need to substantiate inferences with details from the story.

### Step 4.  Reversing the process

The teacher asks an inferential question and the students supply the inference. The teacher provides the evidence. As an alternative, the teacher might supply the evidence and have the students draw an inference based on it. Either way, a discussion of reasoning processes follows.

### Step 5.  Integrating the process

The teacher just asks the inferential question. The students both make the inference and supply the evidence. As a final step, students might create their own inferential questions and then supply the answers and evidence. Basically, the procedure turns responsibility for the strategy over to students.

### Step 6.  Application

The students apply the process to texts and trade books.

### Step 7.  Assessment

Observe students as they make inferences in texts and trade books. Note how well they can do the following:

_____  Make an inference based on two or more pieces of information in the text.

_____  Make an inference based on information in the text and their own background knowledge.

_____  Find support for an inference.

_____  Make increasingly sophisticated inferences.

### ■  Reviewing the Strategy

In subsequent lessons, review and extend the strategy. To review the strategy, ask the following kinds of questions:

- ■ What strategy are we learning to use? (making inferences)
- ■ How does this strategy help us? (Helps us to read between the lines, to fill in details that the author has hinted at but which she has not directly stated.)
- ■ When do we use this strategy? (When we have to put together two or more pieces of information in a story. When the author has hinted at but not directly stated information.)

Although making inferences is more difficult than literal comprehension, it isn't necessary that students master literal comprehension before they are instructed in making inferences. Both can and should be taught simultaneously.

*S*tudents learn to locate evidence for inferences they have made.

- How do we use this strategy?
   1. As you read, think, "What is the author suggesting here?"
   2. Put together pieces of information from the story or put together information from the story with what you know.
   3. Make an inference or come to a conclusion.

**Using QAR.**   Some students are text-bound and may not realize that answers to some questions require putting together several pieces of information from the reading or using their background of experience plus that information to draw inferences. Teachers frequently hear students lament that the answer is not in the book; those students do not know how to construct the answer from prior knowledge and textual content (Carr, Dewitz, & Patberg, 1989). Such readers may benefit from using QAR (question–answer relationship), in which questions are described as having the following four levels, based on where the answers are found (International Reading Association, 1988):

1. *Right there.* The answer is found within a single sentence in the text.
2. *Putting it together.* The answer is found in several sentences in the text.
3. *On my own.* The answer is in the student's background of knowledge.
4. *Writer and me.* A combination of information from the text and the reader's background is required to answer the question.

In a series of studies, Raphael (1984) observed that students' comprehension improved when they were introduced to the concept of QAR and given extensive training in locating the source of the answer. Initially, they worked with sentences and very short paragraphs, but they progressed to 400-word selections. Raphael (1986) recommended starting with two categories of answers: "in the book" and "in my head." This would be especially helpful when working with elementary students. "In the book" includes answers that are "right there" or require "putting it together." "In my head" items are "on my own" and "writer and me" answers. Based on Raphael's (1986) suggestions, QAR might be presented in the manner described in Lesson 6.4.

As Alvermann and Phelps (1994) explain, the QAR progression is oversimplified. Readers do not begin by comprehending information that is right there, then move on to putting it together, and end up with on-my-own or writer-and-me responses. These processes operate simultaneously and interact with each other. However, QAR is a useful way of viewing the process of question answering.

## Presenting QAR

**LESSON 6.4**

### Step 1. Introducing the concept of QAR

Introduce the concept by writing on the board a paragraph similar to the following:

> Andy let the first pitch go by. It was too low. The second pitch was too high. But the third toss was letter high. Andy lined it over the left fielder's outstretched glove.

Ask a series of literal questions: "Which pitch did Andy hit? Where did the ball go? Why didn't Andy swing at the first pitch? The second pitch?" Lead students to see that the answers to these questions are "in the book."

Next, ask a series of questions that depend on the readers' background: "What game was Andy playing? What do you think Andy did after he hit the ball? Do you think he scored a run? Why or why not?" Show students that the answers to these questions depend on their knowledge of baseball. Discuss the fact that these answers are "in my head."

### Step 2. Extending the concept of QAR

After students have mastered the concept of "in the book" and "in my head," extend the in-the-book category to include both "right there" and "putting it together." Once students have a solid working knowledge of these, expand the in-my-head category to include both "on my own" and "writer and me." The major difference between these two is whether the student has to read the text for the question to make sense. For instance, the question "Do you think Andy's hit was a home run?" requires knowledge of baseball and information from the story. The question "How do you feel when you get a hit?" involves only experience in hitting a baseball.

### Step 3. Providing practice

Provide ample opportunity for guided and independent practice. Also refine and extend students' awareness of sources for answers and methods for constructing responses.

> To provide practice with making inferences at all levels, have students infer character traits based on the character's actions, because authors typically let a character's actions show what kind of a person the character is. In addition, even kindergartners make inferences about people based on their actions.

One version of QAR is known as Everybody Read To (ERT) (Cunningham & Allington, 2003). ERT is an attempt to help students respond to both literal and inferential questions. When students are reading for literal comprehension, they are given the instruction: "Everybody read to find out . . ." when they are reading for inferential comprehension, they are given the instruction: "Everybody read to figure out . . . ." Through modeling and guided practice students are taught how to locate specific answers to literal questions and also to use the text and background knowledge to figure out answers to inferential questions. ERT was also created to provide a substitute for round robin reading. In round robin reading, a practice that is generally frowned upon, students take turns reading orally. Using ERT students read silently but are provided with opportunities to read passages orally that support their answers.

ERT works especially well when students are reading dense or difficult text. The text is divided up into segments. Students reading a story about the origins of basketball are asked to read to the end of the page (or section) to find out why the game was called basketball. Students are then asked to read the next section to figure out why basketball became so popular so fast (the selection does not directly state this but it can be inferred). One student answers the question. Other students locate and read passages that show where the answer is located, if the question is literal, or which provide support for the answer, if the question is inferential. Dividing the task up allows for more students to participate. ERT works well because it helps students focus on short segments of text, gives them specific purposes for reading, and also highlights the importance of going back to the text to find support for answers. ERT should not be used all the time. Students would grow tired of it and they need to have the experience of reading and making predictions and reading for broader purposes. However, ERT would be especially effective for helping poor readers.

**Difficulties in making inferences.**   Some students' responses to inference questions are too specific. In addition to knowing that they can use both text and background knowledge as sources of information, students need to learn to gather all the information that is pertinent (McCormick, 1992). They need to base their inferences on several pieces of textual or background information. Some students choose the wrong information on which to base their inferences, and others do not use the text at all. They overrely on prior knowledge or do not recall or use sufficient pertinent text to make valid inferences (McCormick, 1992). This is especially true of poor readers.

**Applying the skill.**   Comprehension relies heavily on the reader's ability to use background knowledge to make inferences. Inferencing is a cognitive skill that can be used in all areas of learning. Have students apply it in class discussions and when reading in the content areas. Emphasize the need to go beyond facts and details in order to make inferences.

### ■ Imaging

Although readers rely heavily on verbal abilities to comprehend text, they also use imaging. According to a **dual coding** theory of cognitive processing, information can be coded verbally or nonverbally. The word *robot* for instance, can be encoded verbally. It can also be encoded visually as a mental picture of a robot. Because it can be encoded as a word or mental picture, it can be retrieved from memory either verbally or visually, so it is twice as memorable. In one research study, participants who encoded words visually remembered twice as many words as those who encoded the words just verbally (Schnorr & Atkinson, 1969).

**Imaging** is relatively easy to teach. In one study, students' comprehension increased after just thirty minutes of instruction (Gambrell & Bales, 1986). The in-

---

Students who are good decoders but poor comprehenders have problems with all kinds of comprehension, but have the most difficulty making inferences (Oakhill & Yuill, 1996).

■ **Dual coding** is the concept that text can be processed verbally and nonverbally. Nonverbal coding focuses on imaging.

■ **Imaging** refers to creating sensory representations of items in text.

One way of enhancing imaging is to read high-imagery selections to children and ask them to try to picture the main character, a setting, or a scene. Possibilities include Burton's (1942) *The Little House,* Williams's (1926) *The Velveteen Rabbit,* and Byars's (1970) *Summer of the Swans.*

## *Exemplary Teaching*

### *Using Imaging*

*C*reating images is a powerful strategy for enhancing both comprehension and memory of text. Maria (1990) encouraged fourth-graders to construct images to foster their understanding of a social studies passage that described an Iroquois village. Maria started the lesson by having students study a detailed drawing of an Iroquois village. After shutting their eyes and visualizing the scene, students discussed what they had seen. Their images varied.

Students were then directed to close their eyes as Maria described a scene laden with sensory images and asked image-evoking questions:

> You are at an Iroquois village in New York State about the year 1650. It is winter. Feel how cold you are. Feel the snow crunch under your feet. The wind is blowing. You can hear it and feel it right through your clothes. See yourself walk through the gate into the village. See the tall fence all around the village. . . . (p. 198)

After discussing what they saw, heard, and felt, the students read a passage in their social studies textbook about life in an Iroquois longhouse. After each paragraph, they stopped and created images of what they had read and discussed the images. In the discussion, Maria asked questions that focused on the important details so that when students later created images on their own, they, too, would focus on these elements. The images that students created demonstrated that their comprehension was indeed enriched. Best of all, many of the students who responded were those who usually had little to say in class discussions.

crease was not large, but it was significant. When teaching students to create images, start with single sentences and then move on to short paragraphs and, later, longer pieces. Have students read the sentence or paragraph first, and then ask them to form a picture of it.

Creating images serves three functions: fostering understanding, retaining information, and monitoring for meaning. If students are unable to form an image, or if it is incomplete or inaccurate, encourage them to reread the section and then add to the picture in their minds or create a new one. As a comprehension strategy, imaging can help students who are having difficulty understanding a high-imagery passage. For example, it might be effective for comprehending the following highly visual description:

> A comet is like a dirty snowcone. A comet has three parts: a head, coma, and tail. The head is made of ice, gases, and particles of rocks. The heads of most comets are only a few kilometers wide. As a comet nears the sun, gases escape from the head. A large, fuzzy, ball-shaped cloud is formed. This ball-shaped cloud is the coma. The tail is present only when the coma is heated by the sun. The tail is made of fine dust and gas. A comet's tail always points away from the sun. The tail can be millions of kilometers long. (Hackett, Moyer, & Adams, 1989, p. 108)

Imaging can also be used as a pictorial summary. After reading a paragraph similar to the one about comets, students can review what they have read by trying to picture a comet and all its parts. A next step might be to draw a comet based on

▌Make sure that strategy instruction matches the text. When teaching imaging, for instance, make sure that the text is one in which there are many opportunities for imaging.

**ADAPTING INSTRUCTION for *ENGLISH LANGUAGE LEARNERS***
Have students draw pictures of concepts or topics rather than use words to describe or talk about them. This works especially well with students who are still learning English or other students who might have difficulty expressing their ideas through words alone.

their visual summary. They might then compare their drawing with an illustration in the text or an encyclopedia and also with the text itself to make sure that they have included all the major components.

Like other elaboration strategies, imaging should be taught directly. The teacher should explain and model the strategy; discuss when, where, and under what conditions it might be used; and provide guided practice and application. From time to time, the teacher should review the strategy and encourage students to apply it.

Questions that ask students to create visual images should become a natural part of postreading discussions. Auditory and kinesthetic or tactile imaging should also be fostered. Students might be asked to tell how the hurricane in the story sounded, or what the velvet seats in the limousine they read about felt like. In discussing images that children have formed, remind them that each of us makes our own individual picture in our mind. Ask a variety of students to tell what pictures they formed.

Whether used with fiction or nonfiction, imaging should follow these guidelines (Fredericks, 1986):

- Students create images based on their backgrounds. Images will differ.
- Teachers should not alter students' images but might suggest that students reread a selection and then decide whether they want to change their images.
- Students should be given sufficient time to form images.
- Teachers should encourage students to elaborate on or expand their images through careful questioning: "What did the truck look like? Was it old or new? What model was it? What color? Did it have any special features?"

## ■ Question Generation

Accustomed to answering questions posed by teachers and texts, students enjoy composing questions of their own. In addition to being a novel and interesting activity, **question generation** is also an effective strategy for fostering comprehension. It transforms the reader from passive observer to active participant. It also encourages the reader to set purposes for reading and to note important segments of text so that questions can be asked about them and possible answers considered. Creating questions also fosters active awareness of the comprehension process. Students who create questions are likely to be more aware of whether they are understanding the text and are more likely to take corrective action if their comprehension is inadequate (Andre & Anderson, 1978–1979).

**ReQuest.** One of the simplest and most effective devices for getting children to create questions is **ReQuest,** or reciprocal questioning (Manzo, 1969; Manzo & Manzo, 1993). Although originally designed for one-on-one instruction of remedial pupils, ReQuest has been adapted for use with groups of students and whole classes. In ReQuest, the teacher and students take turns asking questions. ReQuest can be implemented by following the steps outlined in Lesson 6.5.

---

### Margin notes

Dramatizing fosters the creation of images. When called on to act out a scene in a play, readers can be asked to picture the scene and speaker and try to imagine how the words were spoken. To build imaging ability, students might act the part of a character in a selection the class has read and invite the other class members to guess who the character is. Characters could be historical figures (McMaster, 1998).

■ **Question generation** is a powerful strategy. Through creating questions, students' comprehension jumped from the fiftieth percentile to the sixty-sixth percentile and in some instances from the fiftieth to the eighty-sixth percentile (Rosenshine, Meister, & Chapman, 1996).

The aim for strategy instruction is to have it become automatic. As students become more proficient in the application of a strategy, make them responsible for its use (Sinatra, Brown, & Reynolds, 2002).

■ **ReQuest** is a procedure in which the teacher and student(s) take turns asking and answering questions.

## LESSON 6.5  ReQuest procedure

**Step 1.** Choose a text that is on the students' level but is fairly dense so that it is possible to ask a number of questions about it.

**Step 2.** Explain the ReQuest procedure to students. Tell them that they will be using a teaching technique that will help them better understand what they read. Explain that in ReQuest, they get a chance to be the teacher because they and you take turns asking questions.

**Step 3.** Survey the text. Read the title, examine any illustrations that are part of the introduction, and discuss what the selection might be about.

**Step 4.** Direct students to read the first significant segment of text. This could be the first sentence or the first paragraph but should not be any longer than a paragraph. Explain that as they read, they are to think up questions to ask you. Students can make up as many questions as they wish. Tell them to ask the kinds of questions that a teacher might ask (Manzo & Manzo, 1993). Model how they might go about composing questions. Read the segment with the students.

**Step 5.** Students ask their questions. The teacher's book is placed face down. However, students may refer to their texts. If necessary, questions are restated or clarified. Answers can be checked by referring back to the text.

**Step 6.** After student questions have been asked, ask your questions. Pupils' books are face down. You might model higher-level questioning by asking for responses that require integrating several details in the text. If difficult concepts or vocabulary words are encountered, they should be discussed.

**Step 7.** Go to the next sentence or paragraph. The questioning proceeds until enough information has been gathered to set a purpose for reading the remainder of the text. This could be in the form of a prediction: "What do you think the rest of the article will be about?" Manzo and Manzo (1993) recommended that the questioning be concluded as soon as a logical purpose can be set but no longer than ten minutes after beginning.

**Step 8.** After the rest of the selection has been read silently, the purpose question and any related questions are discussed.

Students enjoy reversing roles and asking questions. Initially, they may ask lower-level questions but with coaching and modeling will soon ask higher-level ones. ReQuest is especially effective with lower-achieving readers.

Other elaboration strategies include applying information that has been obtained from reading, creating analogies to explain it, and evaluating text (covered in Chapter 7). A general operating principle of elaboration is that the more readers do with or to text, the better they will understand and retain it.

## Monitoring

As you were reading this chapter, did you reread a section because you didn't quite understand it? Did you go back and reread any sentences? Did you have an awareness of whether or not the text was making sense? Did you decide to use a particular strategy such as summarizing or questioning or imaging? If so, you were engaged in metacognition. Summarizing, inferring, creating images, predicting, and other strategies are valuable tools for enhancing comprehension. Knowing how to use them is not enough, however; it is also essential to know when and where to use them. For example, visualizing works best with materials that are concrete and lend themselves to being pictured in the imagination (Prawat, 1989). Predictions work best when the reader has a good background of knowledge about the topic. Knowing when and where to use these and other strategies is part of monitoring, which is also known as **metacognition,** or metacognitive awareness.

■ **Metacognition** or metacognitive awareness means being conscious of one's mental processes.

Monitoring also means recognizing what one does and does not know, which is a valuable asset in reading. If a reader mouths the words of a passage without comprehending their meaning and does not recognize his or her lack of comprehension, the reader will not reread the passage or take other steps to understand it; the reader is not even aware that there is a problem. "Metacognitive awareness is the ability to reflect on one's own cognitive processes, to be aware of one's own activities while reading, solving problems, and so on" (Baker & Brown, 1984, p. 353). A key feature of metacognitive awareness is knowing what one is expected to be able to do as a result of reading a selection. All of the other activities are examined in light of the desired outcome. Students will read a book one way if they are reading it as part of voluntary reading, another way if they are to evaluate it, and still another way if they are taking a test on it. Their criteria for success will depend on their specific goal for reading the text. A critical factor is the level of comprehension that students demand. Proficient readers generally demand a higher level of comprehension than do struggling readers.

The four major aspects of metacognition in reading are knowing oneself as a learner, regulating, checking, and repairing (Baker & Brown, 1984; McNeil, 1987).

### ■ Knowing Oneself as a Learner

The student is aware of what he or she knows, his or her reading abilities, what is easy and what is hard, what he or she likes and dislikes. The student is able to activate his or her prior knowledge in preparation for reading a selection:

I know that Theodore Roosevelt was a president a long time ago. Was it during the late 1800s or early 1900s? I'm not sure. I remember reading a story about how he was weak as a child and had bad eyesight. I'll read about him in the encyclopedia. I'll try *World Book* instead of *Encyclopedia Britannica*. *Encyclopedia Britannica* is too hard, but I can handle *World Book*.

## ■ Regulating

In **regulating,** the student knows what to read and how to read it and is able to put that knowledge to use. The student is aware of the structure of the text and how this might be used to aid comprehension. The student also understands the criterial task for what he or she will be expected to do as a result of reading this selection: retelling, writing a story, taking a test. He or she surveys the material, gets a sense of organization, sets a purpose, and then chooses and implements an effective strategy:

> Wow! This is a long article about Roosevelt. But I don't have to read all of it. I just need information about his boyhood. These headings will tell me which section I should read. Here's one that says "Early Life." I'll read it to find out what his childhood was like. After I read it, I'll make notes on the important points.

■ **Regulating** is a metacognitive process in which the reader guides his reading processes.

## ■ Checking

The student is able to evaluate his or her performance. He or she is aware when comprehension suffers because an unknown term is interfering with meaning or an idea is confusing. Checking also involves noting whether the focus is on important, relevant information and engaging in self-questioning to determine whether goals are being achieved (Baker & Brown, 1984):

> The part about Roosevelt's great grandparents isn't important. I'll skim over it. I wonder what *puny* and *asthma* mean. I've heard of asthma, but I don't know what it is. This is confusing, too. It says, "He studied under tutors." What does that mean? Let's see if I have all this straight. Roosevelt's family was wealthy. He was sickly, but then he worked out in the gym until he became strong. He liked studying nature and he was determined. I don't know about his early schooling, though, and I ought to know what *asthma* and *puny* mean.

## ■ Repairing

In **repairing,** the student takes corrective action when comprehension falters. He or she is not only aware that there is a problem in understanding the text but does something about it:

■ **Repairing** refers to taking steps to correct faulty comprehension.

> I'll look up *asthma*, *puny*, and *tutor* in the dictionary. Okay, I see that *tutor* means "a private teacher." Oh, yeah, it's like when my brother Bill had trouble with math and Mom got him a private teacher. Did Roosevelt have trouble in school? Is that why he had tutors? I'm still confused about his early schooling. I think I'll ask the teacher about it.

Failure to comprehend might be caused by a problem at any level of reading (Collins & Smith, 1980):

- Words may be unknown or may be known but used in an unfamiliar way.
- Concepts are unknown.
- Punctuation is misread.
- Words or phrases are given the wrong emphasis.
- Paragraph organization is difficult to follow.
- Pronouns and antecedent relationships are confused. Relationships among ideas are unclear.
- Relationships among paragraphs and sections are not established.
- The reader becomes lost in details. Key ideas are misinterpreted.
- The reader has inadequate prior knowledge, or a conflict exists between that knowledge and the text.

Repair strategies (Baker & Brown, 1984; Harris & Sipay, 1990) include the following:

- Rereading the sentence or paragraph may clear up a confusing point or provide context for a difficult word.
- Reading to the end of the page or section might provide clarification.
- Having failed to grasp the gist of a section, the student might reread the preceding section.
- If there are specific details that a student cannot remember, she or he should skim back through the material to find them.
- The text may be difficult or require closer reading, so the student may have to slow down, adjusting his or her rate of reading.
- Consulting a map, diagram, photo, chart, or illustration may provide clarification of a puzzling passage.
- Using a glossary or dictionary will provide meaning for an unknown word.
- Consulting an encyclopedia or similar reference may clarify a confusing concept.

Figure 6.5 shows a series of questions that students might ask themselves if they encounter difficulties as they read. The questions provide prompts for the major repair strategies and should be posted in a prominent spot in the classroom.

**Lookbacks.**  Students may not realize that they can look back at a text when they cannot recall a specific bit of information or do not understand a passage (Garner, Hare, Alexander, Haynes & Winograd, 1984). If students' overall comprehension of a passage is faulty, they will need to reread the entire

**FIGURE 6.5**

**Repair Strategies**

**What to Do When I Don't Understand**

What is keeping me from understanding?

Should I read the sentence or paragraph again?

Will looking at maps, charts, photos, or drawings help?

Should I look up key words?

Should I keep on reading and see whether my problem is cleared up?

Should I slow down?

Should I ask for help?

passage. If, however, they have simply forgotten or misunderstood a detail, they may use the lookback strategy, skimming back over the text and locating the portion that contains the information they need.

To present the strategy, the teacher should explain why it is needed: It is not possible to remember everything (Garner, MacCready, & Wagoner, 1984). Therefore, it is often necessary to go back over a story. The teacher should then model the strategy by showing what he or she does when unable to respond to a question. The teacher should demonstrate how he or she skims through an article to find pertinent information and then uses that information to answer a difficult question. Guided practice and application opportunities should be provided. When students are unable to respond to questions during class discussions or on study sheets or similar projects, remind them to use **lookbacks**. As they learn how to use lookbacks, students should discover when and where to use them. Lookbacks, for instance, are useful only when the information needed to answer the question is present in the text.

### ■ Instruction in Metacognitive Strategies

For most students, metacognitive awareness develops automatically over time; however, instruction is also helpful (Anthony, Pearson, & Raphael, 1989). In fact, it should be a part of every reading strategy lesson.

During each part of the lesson, the teacher should make explicit the cognitive processes involved. In the early stages, for instance, the teacher might model how he or she recalls prior knowledge, sets a purpose, decides on a reading strategy, executes the strategy, monitors for meaning, organizes information, takes corrective action when necessary, and applies knowledge gained from reading. Later, the teacher should discuss these elements with students, asking them what they know about a topic, how they plan to read a selection, and what they might do if they do not understand what they are reading. The ultimate aim is to have metacognitive processes become automatic. In the past, teachers have not made their thinking processes explicit. The teaching of reading now follows the novice–expert or master craftsperson–apprentice model. The student learns from the teacher's modeling and guidance as she or he progresses from novice reader and writer to expert.

One way of reminding students of metacognitive strategies is to make a list of those that have been introduced and place them in a prominent spot in the classroom. A sample list of metacognitive strategies appears in Figure 6.6. This list can be used with fiction or nonfiction. You may want to adapt the list so that it fits the needs of your class. You may also want to have two lists: one for fiction and one for nonfiction.

To reinforce the use of metacognition, ask process, as well as product, questions. Product questions get at the content of a story. You might ask who the main character is, what problem he had in the story, and how he felt. A process question attempts to uncover how a student arrived at an answer. After a student responds that the main character was angry, ask, "How do you know that?" Other process questions are "How did you figure out that word? How did you find the answer? What did you do when you realized that you had forgotten some main facts?"

> ■ **Lookback** is a strategy that involves skimming back over a selection that has already been read in order to obtain information that was missed, forgotten, or misunderstood.

> ❚ Although teachers agree that strategies are important, they may not spend enough time teaching them. In one study, the teachers assessed and provided practice opportunities for students to use strategies but spent little time teaching students how to use strategies (Pressley, Wharton-McDonald, Mistretta-Hampston, & Echevarria, 1998).

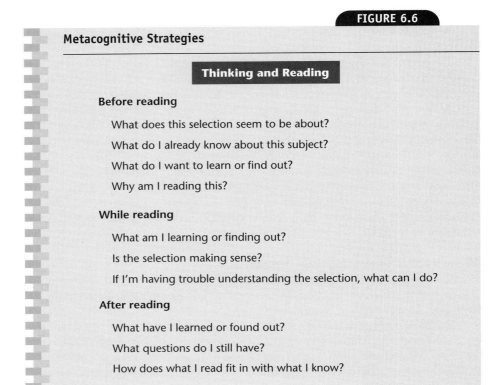

FIGURE 6.6

**Metacognitive Strategies**

**Thinking and Reading**

**Before reading**

What does this selection seem to be about?

What do I already know about this subject?

What do I want to learn or find out?

Why am I reading this?

**While reading**

What am I learning or finding out?

Is the selection making sense?

If I'm having trouble understanding the selection, what can I do?

**After reading**

What have I learned or found out?

What questions do I still have?

How does what I read fit in with what I know?

Metacognitive awareness has to be built into virtually all reading instruction; "any attempt to comprehend must involve comprehension monitoring" (Baker & Brown, 1984, p. 385). This monitoring need not be on a conscious level. The skilled reader operates on automatic pilot until some sort of triggering event signals that comprehension is not taking place. At that point, the reader slows down, focuses on the problem, and decides how to deal with it (Baker & Brown, 1984).

### ■ Click and Clunk

To reinforce monitoring for meaning, use the click and clunk analogy. Clicks and clunks are compared to driving a car. When everything is going smoothly, the car is clicking along. When the car hits a pothole, there is a clunk. Clicks are portions of the text that are easy to understand. Clunks are problem portions. When students hit clunks, which are generally hard words or confusing sentences, they attempt to clarify them. Strategies for dealing with clunks might be listed on a chart or bookmark. If students are unable to resolve a clunk, they can place a sticky note next to the confusing element and get help later (Vaughn, Klinger, & Schumm, n. d.).

As might be expected, younger readers and poorer readers are less aware of the purpose of reading and the most effective reading strategies. They may see reading primarily as a decoding task and fail to search for meaning. They may not notice when the text fails to make sense (Bransford, Stein, Shelton, & Owings, 1981). In other words, they don't know when they don't know. Therefore, metacognitive skills have to be taught early. Children should be informed early in their schooling that the purpose of reading is to construct meaning and not just to sound out words.

In addition to scheduling lessons devoted to teaching monitoring and fix-up strategies, be alert for opportunities to do on-the-spot teaching or reinforcement. When a student is reading orally and makes an error, do not immediately correct her or him. Give the student the opportunity to monitor her or his own reading and apply a fix-up strategy. In fact, if the miscue makes sense in the sentence, you might ignore it. If it changes the meaning of the sentence and the student does not correct it, ask questions like these: "Did that sentence make sense? What might you do to read the sentence correctly?" If the student cannot make the correction after a reasonable effort, supply the correct word by asking, "Would (unknown word) fit here?" or "Does it look like (unknown word)?" However, it is important that students be given a chance to correct their errors. To develop monitoring and fix-up strategies, students need ample opportunity to apply them. They also need an environment in which they are not afraid to make mistakes.

To promote monitoring and use of repair strategies during silent reading, review monitoring and repair strategies from time to time. During times when it is not possible for students to get help with comprehension difficulties, have them make a note of problems they encounter. A sticky note might be put under the word or passage that poses a problem. As part of every postreading discussion, talk over any difficulties that students may have had while reading the text. Also make sure that the text is not too difficult for students. They will have difficulty monitoring for meaning if they are unable to construct a coherent situation model of the text (Paris, Wasik, & Turner, 1991).

To understand metacognition and to try to become aware of the strategies that you use when reading becomes difficult and comprehension breaks down, what repair strategies do you use?

## ■ Making Connections

Students who have a richer background and can make more connections between what they know and what they are reading have better comprehension and retention. For instance, students reading about germs might relate it to a time when they had strep throat and took medicine to get rid of the strep germs. Comprehension can be thought of as a network of ideas connected largely by causal–logical relationships. Good readers use higher-level thought processes to establish relationships and store information in network form so that the concept of germs has a number of connections in the students' schemata.

One way of helping students, especially below-level readers, improve their comprehension is to use causal questioning. In causal questioning, students are asked why and how questions to help them make inferences. These questions can be asked during discussions or can be added to the text at locations where comprehension

> **ADAPTING INSTRUCTION**
> **for *STRUGGLING READERS***
> ***and WRITERS***
> Good readers have good monitoring skills and poor readers don't. Poor readers are less likely to detect lapses in comprehension and, when they do detect them, are less able to repair them. However, when instructed, poor readers can and do learn to become effective monitors (Palincsar et al.,1993).

> Because metacognition is a developmental process, young students are less adept than older readers. However, developmentally appropriate instruction in metacognitive processes is effective.

> In addition to being taught how to use strategies, students should learn why, where, and when to use them so as to acquire cognitive command of them.

Strategy instruction works best when students evidence a need for a strategy, when the strategy taught is applied to a selection, when the teacher repeatedly models and explains the strategy, when the students have many opportunities to use the strategy, and when assessment is based on comprehension of the text and the use of the strategy (Duffy, 2002). The key element is the teacher's ability to adapt instruction to students' understanding and to provide a depth of instruction.

Culturally diverse youngsters do especially well in cooperative learning situations.

is likely to falter. This might be at points where important cause–effect relationships are being established (van den Broek & Kremer, 2000).

## Special Comprehension Strategies for Bilingual Readers

For bilingual students, reading and comprehending in their weaker or nondominant language is more difficult. One of the major obstacles is vocabulary. If they have recently learned to speak English, chances are they will encounter a greater number of unknown words than will their same-age English-speaking counterparts. Fortunately, successful bilingual readers do use a repertoire of strategies to aid themselves. For one thing, they seem to be more metacognitively aware. Apparently, the process of learning a second language has provided them with insights into language on an abstract level, as an object of study. They are more likely to notice problems in word recognition or comprehension. While using the same kinds of strategies (predicting, inferencing, monitoring, etc.) as their monolingual counterparts, they also use additional strategies: translating from one language to another and transferring information learned in one language to another.

Achieving bilingual readers see similarities between their native language and their new language. They use their native language as a source of help by activating prior knowledge in both languages and by translating when encountering a difficult passage, especially when they are in the earlier stages of learning English. Transferring, translating, and reflecting on text in their native or stronger language has the potential for improving comprehension (Jiménez, 1997).

## SOCIAL-CONSTRUCTIVIST NATURE OF COMPREHENSION

According to Vygotsky (1978), learning is a social process. Directions and explanations provided by a more knowledgeable other are internalized by the learner and become part of his or her thinking. In similar fashion, when teacher and students or just students gather in groups and discuss a selection, they help each other construct meaning. Comprehension is still an individual task. Participants discuss their personal understandings of the text, but as they engage in an interchange of ideas, they may modify their understandings as they perceive the selection from other perspectives. This is especially true in their reading of literature, where understandings are enriched and broadened by discussion with others. However, even when reading informational texts, understandings are deepened and clarified through discussion. If the discussion includes processes of reading in which students explain how they comprehended a particular passage or what they did when a passage was confusing, understanding of reading processes is enhanced (Kucan & Beck, 1996).

The degree to which comprehension is fostered depends on the quality of the thinking and the ideas exchanged. The talk must be accountable (New Standards Primary Literacy Committee, 1999). It must go beyond mere opinion. Students must be prepared to back up a judgment about a literary piece by using passages from the text, for instance. For a conclusion drawn from a passage in a social studies text, they must cite supporting details. In this way, students learn to draw evidence from text, check facts, and reason with information. Teachers play a key role in modeling accountable talk and in shaping discussions so that student talk becomes accountable.

## Reciprocal Teaching

As a form of social–constructivist learning and cognitive apprenticeship in which students gradually learn key comprehension strategies by imitating and working along with the teacher, **reciprocal teaching** introduces group discussion techniques created to improve understanding and retention of the main points of a selection. Reciprocal teaching also has built-in monitoring devices that enable students to check their understanding of what they are reading and to take steps to improve their comprehension if it is found wanting.

In a reciprocal teaching situation, the group reads a story and then discusses it. Members of the group take turns leading the discussion. They use four tried-and-true techniques for building comprehension and for monitoring for meaning—predicting, question generating, clarifying, and summarizing (Palincsar & Brown, 1986):

**1.** *Predicting.* Students predict what information a section of text will present based on what they have read in a prior section. If they are just starting a selection, their prediction is based on illustrations, headings, or an introductory paragraph. They must activate their background knowledge to guess what the author is going to say next. Predicting makes them active readers and gives them a purpose for reading.

**2.** *Question generating.* Students must seek out the kinds of information in a text that provide a basis for well-formed questions. Not being able to formulate a question may be a sign that they have failed to understand the significant points in the text and so must reread or take other corrective action.

**3.** *Clarifying.* Students note words, concepts, expressions, or other items that hinder comprehension, and they ask for explanations during discussion.

**4.** *Summarizing.* The discussion leader, with or without the help of the group, retells the selection, highlighting the main points. This retelling reviews and integrates the information and is also a monitoring device. Inability to paraphrase is a sign that comprehension is poor and rereading is in order (A. L. Brown, 1985). Summarizing also becomes a springboard for making predictions about the content of the next section.

> **BUILDING LANGUAGE**
> Model accountable talk by showing how you use facts and details or passages from a selection to back up your judgments. Use probes and prompts to coach students as they do the same. Discuss the difference between opinions that have no backing and those that are supported by facts or incidents.

■ **Reciprocal teaching** is a form of cooperative learning in which students learn to use four key reading strategies in order to achieve improved comprehension: predicting, questioning, summarizing, and clarifying.

Reciprocal teaching is based on four highly regarded learning principles: expert scaffolding, cooperative learning, guided learning, and Vygotsky's zone of proximal development.

In addition to fostering monitoring for meaning, the strategy known as clarifying introduces students to the idea that students can help each other (Rosenshine & Meister, 1994).

Using direct instruction, the teacher introduces reciprocal teaching over approximately a week's time but may take longer if necessary. Lesson 6.6 outlines the teacher's role in reciprocal teaching.

## LESSON 6.6 Reciprocal teaching

### Step 1. Introduce reciprocal teaching

Ask students whether they have ever wanted to switch places with the teacher. Tell them that they will be using a new method to help them read with better understanding and that each student will have a chance to lead a discussion of a story that the class has read. Outline for the students the four parts of the method: predicting what will happen; making up questions; clarifying, or clearing up details that are hard to understand; and summarizing.

### Step 2. Explain the four basic parts

(a) Explain that predicting helps readers think what a story might be about and that it gives them a purpose for reading. Students will want to see whether their predictions are correct, so they will read with greater interest and understanding. Model the process, and give students a chance to try it out.

(b) Explain to students that asking questions will help them read with better understanding. Model the process by reading a selection and constructing questions. Emphasize the need to ask questions about the important parts of the selection, and provide guided practice in constructing some questions.

(c) Explain what clarifying is. Tell students that it is important to notice words or ideas that make it hard to understand a selection. Explain that clarifying hard parts of a selection will help them get more meaning out of what they are reading. Have them locate which words, sentences, or ideas in a sample selection need clarifying. Explain that what is clear to one person may not be clear to another.

(d) Explain why summarizing is an important skill. Tell students that summarizing a paragraph helps them concentrate on important points while reading. Demonstrate creating a summary for a model paragraph. Explain that if students summarize, they will better understand what they read and remember it longer.

Depending on students' age, ability, and previous experience with the strategies, the teacher might introduce the strategies all at once, one a day, or even one a week. It is not expected that students will become proficient in their use or even fully understand them at this point. That will come when the strategies are applied in a reciprocal teaching lesson. At first, the teacher plays a major role in the application of reciprocal teaching, modeling the four strategies, making corrections, and providing guidance when necessary. Gradually, the students take more responsibility for leading discussions and applying the strategies.

> Some students may have difficulty composing questions. Supply these students with model questions. As they begin to catch onto the process, provide prompts or partial questions until they are able to create questions on their own.

The following is a sample reciprocal teaching lesson based on the reading of a selection about Daisy Low, the founder of the Girl Scouts of America.

(Lead-in question)

*Carmen (student discussion leader):* My question is, how did Daisy Low help people and animals?

*Paula:* She fed stray cats and dogs.

*Frank:* She got clothes for needy children.

(Clarification request)

*Charles:* I think we should clarify *needy*.

*Ann:* I think needy children need stuff, like clothes and maybe food.

*Teacher:* What would be another word for *needy*?

*James: Poor.* I think *poor* means the same thing as *needy*.

*Teacher:* Good answer. *Poor* and *needy* mean just about the same thing. I have another question. Why did Daisy put a blanket on the cow?

*Paula:* She was afraid it would get cold.

*James:* I think that should be clarified. Do cows get cold?

*Teacher:* Does anybody know? Did any of you ever live on a farm? How can we find out?

*Paula:* We could look in the encyclopedia.

*John:* My grandfather raised cows. He's visiting us. I could ask him.

*Teacher:* That's a great idea. You ask him and report back to us. Maybe your grandfather could come in and talk to the class about life on a farm. By the way, Carmen, do you feel that your question has been answered?

*I*n reciprocal teaching, students learn key strategies by imitating and working along with the teacher.

*Carmen:* I think the story tells about some more things that Daisy Low did to help people. Can anyone tell me what they were?

*Ann:* Yes, she started a children's group called Helping Hands.

*Frank:* And the first sentence says that she was the founder of the Girl Scouts in America.

*Teacher:* Those are good answers. Can you summarize this section of the story, Carmen?

(Summary)

*Carmen:* The paragraph tells about Daisy Low.

*Teacher:* That's right, Carmen. The paragraph tells us about Daisy Low. In a summary, you give the main idea and main details. What does the paragraph tell us about Daisy Low?

*Carmen:* She helped animals and children who were in need.

(Prediction)

*Teacher:* Very good, Carmen. What do you predict will happen next?

*Carmen:* I think the story will tell how Daisy Low started the Girl Scouts.

*Teacher:* Does anyone have a different prediction? Okay. Let's read the next section to see how our prediction works out. Who would like to be the leader for this section?

> Reciprocal teaching can be used with nonreaders, the major difference being that the teacher reads the selection to the students. The process can also be adapted to a peer-tutoring situation in which a good reader is trained in the strategies and works with a poor reader (Palincsar & Brown, 1986).

During the session, the teacher provides guidance where needed and also models the four strategies. The teacher provides prompts and probes and models strategies as necessary. For instance, creating questions is difficult for many students. The teacher might show how she or he would go about creating a question, supply question words—*who, what, why, when, where,* and *how*—or use prompts to help students reformulate awkward questions. Ultimately, students should be able to apply the comprehension and strategy lessons they have learned. Research suggests that this does happen: Students who were trained in the use of the strategies were apparently able to apply them to their social studies and science reading; their rankings in content-area evaluations shot up from the twentieth to the fiftieth percentile (A. L. Brown, 1985).

An entire class can use reciprocal teaching if it is adapted in the following two ways. First, students use the headings to make two predictions about the content of the text they are about to read. Second, after reading a segment, they write two questions and a summary, as well as list any items that require clarification. The predictions, summaries, and clarification requests are discussed after the selection has been read. Even with these whole group adaptations, comprehension improved 20 percent after using the approach for just one month (Palincsar & Brown, 1986).

Why is reciprocal teaching so powerful? Reciprocal teaching leads students to a deeper processing of text. It may also change the way students read. It focuses their attention on trying to make sense of what they read, instead of just decoding words (Rosenshine & Meister, 1994).

# INTEGRATION OF STRATEGIES

For the sake of clarity, the major comprehension strategies presented in this chapter have been discussed in isolation. However, it should be emphasized that reading is a holistic act. Often, several interacting strategies are being applied simultaneously. As Pressley, Borkowski, Forrest-Pressley, Gaskins, and Wiley (1993) explained,

> Strategies are rarely used in isolation. Rather, they are integrated into higher-order sequences that accomplish complex cognitive goals. For example, good reading may begin with previewing, activation of prior knowledge about the topic of a to-be-read text, and self-questioning about what might be presented in the text. These prereading activities are then followed by careful reading, reviewing, and rereading as necessary. General strategies (e.g., self-testing) are used to monitor whether subgoals have been accomplished, prompting the reader to move on when it is appropriate to do so or motivating reprocessing when subgoals have not been met. That is, good strategy users evaluate whether the strategies they are using are producing progress toward goals they have set for themselves. (p. 9)

Learning to use a strategy is a long process. Although researchers may get positive results after twenty lessons on predicting or summarizing, it may actually take students many months to master a particular strategy (Pressley, 1994). In addition, strategies learned at one level may have to be refined when used at higher levels with more complex materials.

Some theorists see reading as a holistic attempt to construct meaning rather than a problem-solving attempt to apply specific strategies (Kucan & Beck, 1996). This text views reading as a combination of the two: strategies, once learned, are ultimately applied in a holistic, integrated fashion.

**USING TECHNOLOGY**

Cool Sites for Kids presents dozens of sites on a variety of topics. These sites are good for applying comprehension strategies and are recommended by the American Library Association.
**http://www.ala.org/ alsc/children_links. html**

# IMPORTANCE OF AFFECTIVE FACTORS

Motivation is a key factor in strategy use. If students believe that the strategies they possess can help improve their performance, they are more inclined to use them. Believing that they have sufficient competency to complete the task motivates students to put forth the necessary effort (Pressley, Borkowski, Forrest-Pressley, Gaskins, & Wiley, 1990, 1993; Gaskins, 1998). As part of your program, be sure to call attention to students' successes. For instance, after students have done a good job comprehending a selection, discuss the strategies that they used. But also set aside time to help them with any difficulties that they are having. Overcoming difficulties is also motivational.

Being attentive, active, and reflective are key factors in strategy use. Provide students with a rationale for being attentive: the more attentive you are, the more you learn and remember. Attentiveness is enhanced by applying strategies covered here—surveying, predicting, inferring, and monitoring—all of which require active student involvement. Students are also more motivated and more involved when they are consulted and given choices and when they have the opportunity to collaborate with classmates. Reflection is also important. Taking time to think about what we have read improves comprehension and retention. Provide students with questions that require careful thinking about what they have read. And provide time for them to reflect (Gaskins, 1998).

## HELP FOR STRUGGLING READERS AND WRITERS

When explicitly taught strategies, poor readers typically do as well as average or even better-than-average readers. However, it is essential that struggling readers be given materials on their level. They should know at least 95 percent of the words and have 75 percent comprehension of materials used for instructional purposes. If given materials on a higher level than that, the material is so overwhelming that they are unable to apply strategies (Kletzien, 1991).

Intensive, step-by-step, explicit instruction is also part of the package. At the Benchmark School, which is a special school for disabled readers, students are taught one strategy at a time, with each strategy being taught for nearly two months. During that time, students have frequent reviews and use the strategy on a daily basis. A chart is displayed reviewing the steps of the strategy, and students discuss when, where, and how to use the strategy.

Strategy instruction is also made an integral part of the reading lesson. Along with building background and introducing new vocabulary, the teacher introduces or reviews a strategy that students are expected to use in their reading. After reading, the students discuss the selection and also talk over ways in which they used the strategy in their reading.

After a strategy has been thoroughly learned, a new strategy is introduced. The new strategy is related to the old, and students are shown how to use both together. Another key to success is to apply strategies to a variety of materials and especially to the content areas, so that it generalizes (Gaskins, 1998). Two strategies that are especially helpful for struggling readers are self-questioning and summarizing. In addition to helping students become more active, they also serve as a self-check on understanding. If students can't summarize or answer questions that they have posed, this is a sign that they haven't understood what they have read and should lead to a rereading, using illustrations, or some other fix-up strategy.

## ESSENTIAL STANDARDS

*Students will*
- prepare for reading by previewing, activating prior knowledge, and setting a purpose for reading.
- seek out main ideas and essential details as they read and summarize by retelling a selection.
- make inferences, create images, generate questions, and make judgments about their reading.

- make connections between what they have read and their own experiences.
- monitor their reading to see that it makes sense and use basic fix-up strategies, such as using illustrations and rereading, if it doesn't.
- compare selections that they have read.
- follow increasingly complex written directions.
- apply information that they have gained through reading.

## ASSESSMENT

Assessment should be ongoing. Through observation, note the strategies students use before, during, and after reading. Note in particular what they do when they are stumped by a passage. During discussions, note the overall quality of their comprehension and the kinds of strategies they seem to be using. Occasionally, ask them how they were able to comprehend a difficult passage. Ask them to describe the strategies they used. For older students, you might ask them to submit a

### ACTION PLAN

1. Use comprehension test and quiz results, observations of students as they discuss selections, think-alouds, and samples of written responses to assess students' comprehension. Plan a program accordingly.
2. Use modeling, think-alouds, explanation, and explicit, direct instruction of strategies with lots of opportunities for practice, review, and application. It might take weeks or even months for students to master a strategy.
3. Before students read selections, provide activities that help them to activate prior knowledge, set purpose and goals, preview the selection and predict based on their previews
4. Teach and provide practice with strategies such as comprehending the main idea, determining important details, organizing details, and summarizing. Help students organize information.
5. Teach and provide practice with strategies, such as inferring, imaging, generating questions, and evaluating, that help students make connections between what they have read and their prior knowledge.

6. Provide instruction and activities that help students to become aware of their comprehension and to take corrective action when comprehension is inadequate.
7. Use approaches such as reciprocal teaching that make use of discussion and working together to construct meaning.
8. Model how you would integrate strategies. Also model how you go about selecting which strategies to use. Provide practice and application opportunities.
9. Adapt instruction for English language learners by spending added time building background and vocabulary. Also use culturally-relevant materials and draw on the students' background knowledge and strong metacognitive skills. Focus on the content of student responses rather than the way they express their answers.
10. Provide extra instruction for struggling readers. Make sure struggling readers are given materials on their level.
11. Monitor students' progress and revise the program as needed.

web of a selection or a written summary. Also, from time to time, have students mark confusing passages. Analyze the passages and discuss students' difficulties to get a sense of the kinds of things that are hindering their comprehension. Also note how students do with different types of texts being read for different purposes. How well do students do when reading on a literal level? How well do they read when they have to organize, infer, or evaluate information?

## SUMMARY

1. Comprehending involves activating a schema, which is an organized package or network of information. Comprehension can also be viewed as a process of constructing situation models. While processing text, the reader continually reconstructs or updates the situation model.
2. Major types of comprehension strategies include preparational, organizational, elaboration, and monitoring. Preparational strategies are activities in which a reader engages just before reading a selection. Organizational strategies involve selecting the most important details in a piece and constructing relationships among them. Elaboration strategies involve constructing relationships

between prior knowledge and knowledge obtained from print. Monitoring strategies include being aware of oneself as a learner and of the learning task, regulating and planning comprehension activities, monitoring one's comprehension, and repairing it when it is faulty.
3. Reciprocal teaching is a well-researched technique that integrates predicting, question generating, clarifying, and summarizing.
4. Integrating strategies and establishing an environment conducive to learning foster comprehension. Students' motivation, willingness to pay attention, active involvement, and reflection also have an impact on comprehension.

## EXTENDING AND APPLYING

1. In your own reading, try out for at least a week one of the strategies introduced in this chapter. Note its effectiveness. Did you encounter any difficulties implementing it?
2. To gain insight into the comprehension process, do a think-aloud with a partner as you read a challenging selection. What processes and strategies did you use? What difficulties, if any, did you experience? How did you cope with these difficulties?
3. Plan a direct instruction lesson for teaching one of the comprehension strategies. If possible, teach it and evaluate its effectiveness.
4. Obtain information about a student's use of comprehension strategies. Ask the student what she or

he does to prepare for reading. Then ask what the student does if she or he is reading a selection and discovers that she or he does not understand it.
5. Introduce ReQuest or the reciprocal teaching approach to a group of elementary school students or try it out with a group of classmates. What seem to be the advantages and disadvantages of the approach? (If you choose to try out reciprocal teaching, be aware that it will take some time. This is a complex technique with many parts but is highly effective and so worth the effort.)

## DEVELOPING A PROFESSIONAL PORTFOLIO

Videotape a lesson in which you teach a comprehension strategy to a group of students. Describe the lesson and reflect on its effectiveness. Explain what you did in subsequent lessons to help students apply the strategy. Document progress that students you taught made in comprehension. Documentation might include completed graphic organizers, written summaries, or pre- and post-test results.

## DEVELOPING A RESOURCE FILE

Keep a list of activities and techniques that foster comprehension. Also keep a list of books, periodicals, and Web sites that are especially effective for fostering comprehension strategies: books that lend themselves to imaging, books that lend themselves to creating questions, etc. Collect brief articles from periodicals, children's books, or other soures that might be used to provide practice with inferring, visualizing, or other strategies.

# 7

# Comprehension: Text Structures and Teaching Procedures

$F$or each of the following statements related to the chapter you are about to read, put a check under "Agree" or "Disagree" to show how you feel. Discuss your responses with classmates before you read the chapter.

|  | Agree | Disagree |
|---|---|---|
| **1** The structure of a piece of writing influences its level of difficulty. | _____ | _____ |
| **2** Talking about the structure of a story ruins the fun of reading it. | _____ | _____ |
| **3** How you ask a question is more important than what you ask. | _____ | _____ |
| **4** Struggling learners should be asked a greater proportion of lower-level questions. | _____ | _____ |
| **5** Students should play the most important role in class discussions. | _____ | _____ |
| **6** Structured reading lessons usually work better than unstructured ones. | _____ | _____ |
| **7** Critical (evaluative) reading skills have never been more important or more neglected. | _____ | _____ |

## USING WHAT YOU KNOW

$T$he emphasis in Chapter 6 was on learners and the strategies they might use to construct meaning. Of course, strategies have to be integrated with text, which has an effect on the types of strategies that can be applied. This chapter emphasizes the role of text, both narrative and expository, in comprehension. However, a number of teaching procedures are also explored, such as the use of questions and techniques for asking them, reading lessons, and the cloze procedure, which consists of supplying missing words. This chapter also includes a section on critical (evaluative) reading.

What do you already know about text structure? How might that knowledge improve your comprehension? What kinds of questions might foster comprehension? How should questions be asked? Think back on lessons that were used to introduce reading selections when you were in elementary school. What procedures did the teacher use? What aspects of those procedures worked best?

## NATURE OF THE TEXT

A text has both content and organization. Students are prepared for the content when the teacher activates schema or builds background; however, they also have to interact with the structure. Therefore, they develop another schema for organizational patterns. Knowledge of structure provides a blueprint for constructing a situational model of a story or informational piece. As students read, text is transformed into ideas or details known as propositions. **Propositions** are combined, deleted, and integrated so that a macrostructure is formed. The **macrostructure** is a running summary of the text. The propositions are organized according to their relative importance or hierarchy. A general statement would be toward the top of the hierarchy. Details are lower. A reader who is able to detect the main idea of a text and its supporting details will better understand and retain information in the text than will a reader who fails to use the text's organization. Likewise, a reader who has a good sense of story structure can use the structure of a story as a framework for remembering it (Gordon, 1989).

■ A **proposition** is a statement of information. "Janice hit the ball" is a proposition; "Janice hit the red ball" is two propositions because it contains two pieces of information: Janice hit the ball. The ball is red.

■ **Macrostructure** is the overall organization of a selection. It refers to the main idea or overall meaning of the selection. Microstructure refers to the details of a selection.

### Narrative Text and Story Schema

Having heard a variety of stories over a period of years, children as young as four develop a schema for them—that is, an internal representation or sense of story. This sense of story continues to grow, and students use it to guide them through a tale, remember the selection, and write stories of their own. They "use a sort of structural outline of the major story categories in their minds to make predictions and hypotheses about forthcoming information" (Fitzgerald, 1989, p. 19). To put it another way, the reader uses structure to construct a situation model of the story.

Various **story grammars,** or schemes, are available for analyzing a story into its parts. Although each may use different terminology, they all tend to concentrate on setting, characters, and plot. Plot is divided into the story problem and/or the main character's goal, the principal episodes, and the resolution of the problem. In most story grammars, characters are included in the setting; however, as setting is a literary word that has long been used to indicate only time and place, it is used in that sense in this book. Different types of stories have different types of structures, and, as students progress through the grades, both stories and structures become more complex. Goals and motivations of major characters become more important. Settings may be exotic and include mood as well as time and place.

■ A **story grammar** is a series of rules designed to show how the parts of a story are interrelated.

Narratives progress primarily in terms of the main character's goals. The reader comprehends the story in terms of the main character's attempts to resolve a problem or conflict. For instance, readers comprehend *The Barn* (Avi, 1994) in terms of Ben's goal of building a barn so that his father will be inspired to recover.

Narratives differ in their overall orientation. Some are action oriented. Mystery novels, such as the *Cam Jansen* or *Nate the Great* series, tend to fall in this category. They stress actions. Others emphasize characters' consciousness and explore thoughts and feelings and motivations. *Ramona Forever* (Cleary, 1984) and *Charlotte's Web* (White, 1952) delve into the characters' emotions. In action-oriented narratives, the tale is composed of a series of episodes arranged in the order in which they happened. Little space is devoted to the psychological states of the main characters. The story is usually told from the perspective of a third-person narrator (Westby, 1999). More complex are stories that embody the consciousness of the characters. These are often told from the perspectives of several characters and are more complex because they require an understanding of human motivation. This involves understanding the actions of others in terms of their goals and plans (Bruce, 1980). Most books combine action and consciousness but emphasize one or the other.

What can be done to build a sense of story? The most effective strategy is to read aloud to students from a variety of materials, from prekindergarten right through high school. Most children gain a sense of story simply from this exposure, but it is also helpful to highlight major structural elements. This can be done by discussing the story's setting, characters, plot, and main problem. Story structure can be used to guide discussions through questions such as the following (Sadow, 1982):

When and where does the story take place?
Who are the characters?
What problem does the main character face?
What does the main character do about the problem? Or what happens to the main character as a result of the problem?
How is the problem resolved?

These questions will help students create an understanding of action-oriented narratives. However, to promote understanding of consciousness-oriented narratives, it is necessary to ask questions about motives and feelings: Why did Marty lie to his parents? How do you think he felt about it? How would you feel if you lied to your parents? Consciousness-oriented narratives have a double level: the level of action and the level of thought and emotion. The student must be prepared to grasp both levels.

Asking what, how, and why questions fosters understanding. What questions generally assess literal understanding; why and how questions help the reader integrate aspects of the story and create causal or other relationships. Why questions also foster making inferences (Tabasso & Magliano, 1996).

Discussions should also include an opportunity for students to construct personal responses. The structure is the skeleton of a story. The reader's response is the heart of the piece.

Another technique for reinforcing story structure is having students fill out generic guide sheets. Students reading significantly below grade level found that guide sheets and maps based on story structure helped them better understand the selections they read (Cunningham & Foster, 1978; Idol & Croll, 1985). In their review of the research, Davis and McPherson (1989) concluded that **story maps** are effective because they require students to read actively to complete the maps and also require self-monitoring.

Bartlett (1932), a British psychologist, asked subjects to read and retell an Indian folk tale, which contained an unfamiliar structure. In the retelling, aspects of the tale were changed so that the reconstructed tale was more like that of a traditional English tale. Bartlett concluded that we tend to reinterpret tales in terms of our own experience.

**ADAPTING INSTRUCTION for *ENGLISH LANGUAGE LEARNERS***
Some ESL students and also some native-speaking students may come from cultures that have different norms for storytelling. In some cultures, children only listen to stories. They don't tell them until they are teenagers (Westby, 1999).

■ **Story maps** provide an overview of a story: characters, setting, problem, plot, and ending.

A generic story map based on McGee and Tompkins's (1981) simplified version of Thorndyke's (1977) story grammar is presented in Figure 7.1. As students meet increasingly complex stories, other elements can be added—for example, theme, conflict, and multiple episodes. Maps can be filled in by students working alone or in small groups, with each student having a different part to work on. They can also be used in the prereading portion of the lesson. The teacher might give students a partially completed map and ask them to finish it after reading.

### ■ Retelling

One of the best devices for developing both comprehension and awareness of text structure has been around since the dawn of speech but is seldom used in classrooms—**retelling.** It has proved to be effective in improving comprehension and providing a sense of text structure for average learners and learning-disabled students (Koskinen, Gambrell, Kapinus, & Heathington, 1988; Rose, Cundick, & Higbee, 1983); it also develops language skills. According to research by Morrow (1985), children who retell stories use syntactically more complex sentences, gain

■ **Retelling** is the process of telling a story that one has read or heard. Retelling is used to check comprehension or gain insight into a student's reading processes.

---

FIGURE 7.1

**A Generic Story Map**

| | |
|---|---|
| **Setting** | Where does the story take place? |
| | When does the story take place? |
| | _____ |
| | _____ |
| **Characters** | Who are the main people in the story? |
| | _____ |
| | _____ |
| **Problem** | What problems does the main character face? |
| | _____ |
| | _____ |
| **Goal** | What is the main character's goal? |
| | What is he or she trying to do? |
| | _____ |
| | _____ |
| **Plot** | What are the main things that happened in the story? |
| | _____ |
| | _____ |
| **Outcome** | How was the story problem resolved? |
| | _____ |
| | _____ |

a greater sense of story structure, and evidence better comprehension than those who simply draw pictures of the stories that are read to them. Combining questions with retelling enhances the effectiveness of the technique. This was especially true in Morrow's study when the questions prompted students whose retelling was flagging or helped students elaborate. Kindergarten students who retold stories and answered questions did better than those who only retold stories or only answered questions. They also seemed to grow in confidence and were better at story-sequencing tasks.

Although all of us engage in retellings everyday, retelling is more complex than it might first seem. Retelling begins with meaning. If the children fail to grasp the meaning of a selection, they will not be able to retell it. In a successful retelling, students must not only comprehend the story, they must also understand the components of a story, be able to analyze the story, have the language required to retell the story, and have the cognitive tools to retell the selection in sequence (Benson & Cummins, 2000). There are children who have formed a detailed representation of a story but lack the skill to relate that representation to others. Some students have difficulty with retellings because they have had few opportunities to hear and discuss stories. English language learners may be able to construct representations in their home language but might not have sufficient grasp of English to retell stories.

### ■ Developmental Retelling

Developmental retelling is a way of improving students' comprehension of selections as well as their language and cognitive skills by building prerequisite skills and fostering retelling skills that match students' level of development (Benson & Cummins, 2000). Major developmental levels consist of pretelling, guided retelling, story map retelling, and written retelling.

For more information on developmental retelling, see *The power of retelling: Developmental steps for building comprehension.* (Benson & Cummins, 2000).

### ■ Pretelling

At the pretelling level students learn to explain everyday tasks, such as making a sandwich, taking a pet for a walk, playing a game, catching a baseball, covering a book, or using a new computer program. To retell, the child must be able to think backwards to reconstruct the steps of a task and then think forwards to put the steps in order. The best activities are those that can be conducted within the classroom. Students can take part in the activity and then identify the steps in the activity. As with other strategies, model the process. In demonstrating the steps in making a paper bag puppet, for instance, show each step while explaining what you are doing. Then in reconstructing the steps, hold up the puppet and show and explain what was done first, what was done second, and so forth. Then model putting the steps in order by writing them on the chalkboard or chart paper. Emphasize the use of the sequence signaling words *first, second, third,* and *last.* After more modeling, invite students to share in pretellings. When ready, students pretell with partners and then alone.

When students are able to retell the key steps in an activity, introduce guided retelling. Since guided retelling requires familiarity with story structure, read

Props such as puppets or felt board figures are a visual reminder of main characters and help shy children, who tend to forget themselves and assume the identities of the puppets. Other visual aids include drawing a series of pictures of the main episodes in the tale and using these as a way of structuring the story.

A retelling has several advantages over the question–answer discussion format. A retelling is more holistic. It avoids the fragmentation of questions and answers about specific parts of a story. A retelling helps students assimilate the concept of story structure (Morrow, 1985).

**ADAPTING INSTRUCTION for *ENGLISH LANGUAGE LEARNERS***

Because they are still learning English, retelling a story will be more difficult for ELL students but could be a valuable tool for developing language. Model the process and provide prompts. Also, start with simple stories and work up to more complex ones.

**USING TECHNOLOGY**

Students might use wordless videos to retell stories. Videos can be motivating for reluctant writers. *Max the Mouse* stories (Society for Visual Literacy) are brief, one-episode wordless stories that lend themselves to this. Students who have basic writing skills might retell their stories in writing.

aloud and discuss books that have a strong story structure. Books with a clearly delineated plot should be introduced first, followed by books in which the setting is key, followed by books with characters that stand out. Continue to read aloud and discuss books until students have acquired a strong sense of story structure. At that point, introduce guided retelling.

### ■ Guided Retelling

In guided retelling, students are aided first by illustrations and then by artifacts. Read selections aloud and show how you use the illustrations to help you retell the story. Select pieces that have illustrations that do a particularly good job of depicting a story. Once students catch on to the idea of using illustrations to retell a story, invite them to join in as you retell with illustrations. Then have them engage in illustration-supported retellings. Encourage students to use only the illustrations when retelling. In fact, it's probably best if you use correction tape or some other means of covering up the words. Once students have caught on to retelling with illustrations, have them use props. Props can be puppets; artifacts such as a ball, a bat, a glove, and a baseball cap for a baseball story; or illustrations. However, the props do not convey every element in the selection the way pictures do in an illustration-aided retelling. Props might consist of four or five pictures or artifacts that represent highlights of the selection. Felt boards or pocket charts might be used to hold the props.

After mastering retelling with props, students use story maps or graphic organizers to aid in their retellings. Graphic organizers help students pick out key elements and note relationships among elements, The graphic organizer might be a story map as in Figure 7.1, a time line as in Figure 7.2, an enumeration-description as in Figure 7.3, or another type of graphic organizer. The type of graphic organizer will depend on the type of selection being retold and the purpose for retelling. Graphic organizers also provide good preparation for written retellings. At each stage, model the process of retelling but gradually turn the process over to students. Provide prompting, guiding, and reviewing as needed.

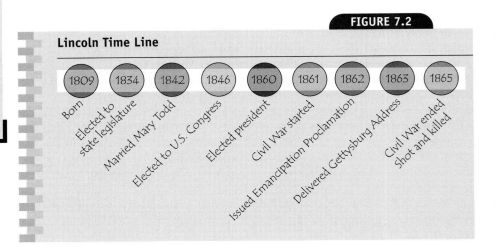

**FIGURE 7.2**

Lincoln Time Line

1809 — Born
1834 — Elected to state legislature
1842 — Married Mary Todd
1846 — Elected to U.S. Congress
1860 — Elected president
1861 — Civil War started
1862 — Issued Emancipation Proclamation
1863 — Delivered Gettysburg Address
1865 — Civil War ended Shot and killed

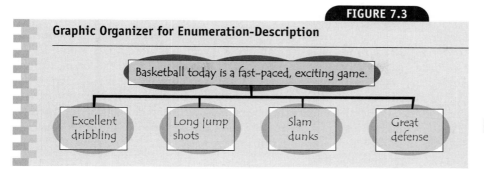

FIGURE 7.3

**Graphic Organizer for Enumeration-Description**

Basketball today is a fast-paced, exciting game.

- Excellent dribbling
- Long jump shots
- Slam dunks
- Great defense

### ■ Writing Stories

Story structure can also be used as a framework for composing stories. Laura Pessah, a staff developer at P.S. 148 in New York City, introduced students to the fact that picture books have different patterns of development (Calkins & Harwayne, 1991). Students discovered that some are a series of snapshots; others are circular, as the ending returns to the beginning; still others embody contrasts. Studying these structures gave students ideas about how they might organize picture books they were creating. However, students should be encouraged to follow the dictates of their own imaginations. As Calkins and Harwayne noted, too strict an adherence to structure could limit individual visions. Fitzgerald (1989) cautioned, "Strict adherence to a particular story structure could have a detrimental effect, resulting in formulaic stories" (p. 20).

Fostering the comprehension of narratives requires being aware of the students' level of knowledge of narratives. To assess student's understanding of narrative schema, ask them to retell a familiar story or to compose a story based on a wordless picture book. Also note students' understanding of a story that they have read. Ask questions that probe the students' understanding of a story: How did Yvonne feel at the end of the game? Why do you think she felt that way? What might she do to make up for her error? Students with poorly developed story schema will compose or retell stories as a string of unrelated episodes or will have difficulty composing or retelling a coherent story. Younger students and struggling learners will also have difficulty inferring goals, motivation, emotions, and characteristics. The ability to grasp what characters think, feel, and believe undergoes a fuller development between the ages of nine and eleven, as does the ability to view situations through the perspective of more than one character (Westby, 1999).

Narrative structures are easier to understand for a number of reasons. Children acquire familiarity with narratives before coming to school. Narratives incorporate one or several sequences of events. A sequence of events is a more familiar system of organizing knowledge than are main idea—details or other more abstract structures. Narrative structures are similar to oral language (Graesser, Golding, & Long, 1991).

*W*riting stories helps students develop a greater awareness of narrative structure.

# Expository Text

Generally speaking, stories are easier to read than science articles, how-to features, and descriptions of historical events (Graesser, Golding, & Long, 1991). Children's schema for **expository text** develops later than that for narration. Expository text has a greater variety of organizational patterns, and, typically, young students have limited experience hearing and reading it. Narrative text is linear; there is generally an initiating event and a series of following episodes which lead to a climax or high point, a resolution of the story problem, and the ending. Because of its structure and linear quality, narrative text is generally more predictable than expository text.

Narrative and expository texts are also based on different ways of thinking. We think in narrative fashion and logical–scientific style. Narrative texts are based on the more straightforward style of thinking, whereas expository text is based on the more complex logical–scientific style (Bruner, 1986). If children are presented with narrative text only, they tend to focus on linear thinking (Trussell-Cullen, 1994). A mix of narrative and expository text is needed to promote a full range of thinking and comprehension skills.

One key to comprehension of expository text is understanding the **text's structure**—that is, the way the author has organized her or his ideas. The author may develop an idea by listing a series of reasons, describing a location, supplying causes, or using some other technique. Often, content dictates structure. In science texts, students expect to see both descriptive passages that tell, for example, what a nerve cell is or what an anteater looks like and explanatory paragraphs that tell how a nerve cell passes on impulses or how an anteater obtains food.

Knowledge of structure has a three-way payoff. It focuses attention on individual ideas, it provides a clearer view of the relationship among ideas, and it is a framework to aid retention of information (Slater & Graves, 1989). The reader can use text structure to organize information from the text and build a situation model.

## ■ Types of Expository Text Structure

Listed below are some of the most important types of text structure (Armbruster & Anderson, 1981; Meyer & Rice, 1984):

**1.** *Enumeration–description.* This type of structure is a listing of details about a subject without any cause–effect or time relationship among them. Included in this category are structures that describe, give examples, and define concepts. It uses no specific signal words except in pieces that provide examples, where *for example* and *for instance* may be used as signals.

**2.** *Time sequence.* This type of structure is similar to enumeration; however, time order is specified. Signal words include the following:

| | | |
|---|---|---|
| after | first | and then |
| today | next | finally |
| afterward | second | earlier |
| tomorrow | then | dates |
| before | third | later |

---

■ **Expository text** is writing that is designed to explain or provide information.

■ **Text structure** is the way a piece of writing is organized: main idea–details, comparison–contrast, problem–solution, etc.

**ADAPTING INSTRUCTION for *ENGLISH LANGUAGE LEARNERS***
Students who are still learning English can transfer their ability to use text structure in their native language to the ability to use it in English. However, students must be proficient readers in their native language and proficient in reading English (Hague, 1989). A lack of proficiency in English "short circuits" the transfer process.

**3.** *Explanation–process.* An explanation tells how something works, such as how coal is formed, how a diesel engine works, or how a bill becomes law. Sequence may be involved, but steps in a process rather than time order are stressed. An explanation structure may include some of the same signal words as those found in a time-sequence structure.

**4.** *Comparison–contrast.* This type of structure presents differences and/or similarities. Signal words and terms include the following:

| although | similar | on the one hand |
| but | different | on the other hand |
| however | different from | |

**5.** *Problem–solution.* A statement of a problem is followed by a possible solution or series of solutions. Signal words are *problem* and *solution.*

**6.** *Cause–effect.* An effect is presented along with a single cause or a series of causes. Signal words and terms include the following:

| because | therefore | thus |
| cause | since | for this reason |
| effect | as a result | consequently |

When reading, students need to activate two kinds of schema: prior knowledge and text structure. The content of a text cannot be separated from the way that content is expressed. Teachers are "well advised to model for students how to figure out what the author's general framework or structure is and allow students to practice finding it on their own" (Pearson & Camperell, 1994, p. 463).

### ■ Teaching Expository Text Structure

One way to teach expository text structure is simply to have students read a variety of expository materials. This may include periodicals, trade books, content-area textbooks, recipes, sets of directions, and other real-world materials. Teachers should also read expository prose aloud to students, beginning in kindergarten.

Before preparing students to read an expository piece, examine it for content and structure. Usually, the two will go together. Purpose questions and discussion questions should also reflect both features. For example, a brief biography of Abraham Lincoln may highlight the main events of his life and use a time-sequence structure. You might instruct students to note these events and their dates to help keep them in order.

Direct instruction in the recognition of text patterns is also helpful. Text patterns should be introduced one at a time. Start off with well-organized, single paragraphs that reflect the structure being taught. Signal words used in that structure should be presented. To provide practice in the recognition of signal words, use a cut-up paragraph or article and have students re-create the piece by using signal words and the sense of the piece as guides. For instance, students might use dates to help them rearrange a chronologically organized piece. Or they might use the signal words *first*, *second*, *next*, and *last* to arrange sentences or paragraphs explaining a step-by-step process.

To foster awareness of paragraph organization, one teacher divides a bulletin board into six segments, one for each type of paragraph organization. Students are encouraged to bring in examples of different types of paragraphs. Before the teacher places the sample, she reads it aloud, and the class discusses in which category it should be placed (Devine, 1986).

Although cause–effect structure aids comprehension, it is one that elementary school students may be less familiar with (Richgels, McGee, & Slaton, 1989).

Gradually, work up to longer selections. Whole articles and chapters often use several text structures, and students should be aware of that. However, in many cases, a particular structure dominates.

**Using graphic organizers.**   As a postreading activity, students might fill in a time line, as in Figure 7.2, to capitalize on both content and structure. Or they may use a graphic organizer, in which concepts are written in circles, rectangles, or triangles, and interrelationships are shown with lines and arrows. Generally, the more important ideas are shown at the top of the display and subordinate concepts are shown at the bottom. The organizers can be constructed to reflect a variety of patterns (Sinatra, Stahl-Gemeke, & Berg, 1984; Sinatra, Stahl-Gemeke, & Morgan, 1986). After reading a selection, students complete an appropriate graphic organizer and, in so doing, organize the major concepts in a text and discover its underlying structural pattern. Graphic organizers for two major types of text structures, enumeration–description and time sequence, are presented in Figures 7.3 and 7.4.

**Using questions to make connections.**   Identifying the structure of a text is only a first step. The reader must then make two kinds of connections: internal (how ideas in the text are related to each other) and external (how text ideas are related to the reader's background) (Muth, 1987). The right kinds of questions can help students detect relationships among ideas in a text. For instance, if the text has a cause–effect relationship, you can ask questions that highlight that relationship. Your questions can seek out causes or effects. Questions can also help the students relate ideas in the text to their own backgrounds. Here are some questions (adapted from Muth, 1987) that might be asked to help students who have read a piece about the process of rusting make internal connections:

What causes rusting?
What are some effects of rusting?
Under what conditions does rusting take place fastest? Why?

These questions focus on external connections:

What kinds of things rust in your house? Why?
In what areas of the house do things rust? Why?

**FIGURE 7.4**

**Graphic Organizer for Time Sequence**

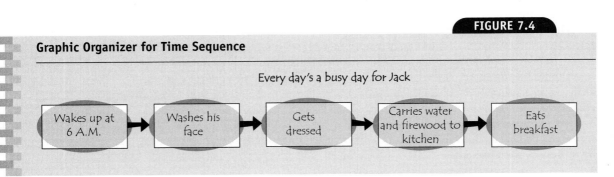

Every day's a busy day for Jack

Wakes up at 6 A.M. → Washes his face → Gets dressed → Carries water and firewood to kitchen → Eats breakfast

What can be done to prevent rusting? Why would these preventive steps work?

Note that all these questions require students to establish internal or external cause–effect relationships. Questions can also be posed that facilitate establishing relationships in comparison–contrast, problem–solution, or other kinds of patterns. Once students have grasped the concept, have them create their own connection questions.

**Writing for organization.**  Another way to teach expository text structure is to encourage students to compose pieces that employ comparison–contrast and other types of structures. After reading a text that has an explanation–process structure, students might write an explanation of a process they find intriguing. Over time, they should have the opportunity to practice with all the major types of structures.

Students might also use photos or drawings to help them grasp a selection's organizational pattern. For time sequence, they might sequentially arrange photos of a vacation trip they have taken with their family. For explanation–process, they might create a series of drawings showing how to plant tomato seeds. They might use a series of photos to compare or contrast two vehicles, two countries, or two animals. After arranging the graphics, students can add a title, headings, and captions.

##  THE ROLE OF QUESTIONS IN COMPREHENSION

Questions play a central role in facilitating comprehension. They can be used to develop concepts, build background, clarify reasoning processes, and even lead students to higher levels of thinking. In one study, second-graders became more adept at making inferences simply by being asked inferential questions (Hansen & Pearson, 1980).

Questions foster understanding and retention. When questions are asked about information in text, that information is remembered longer. Asking higher-level questions is especially helpful. Questioning that demands integrating information in a text "will promote deeper processing, and therefore more learning and better remembering than questions that require recall of specific facts only" (Sundbye, 1987, p. 85). As Wixson (1983) put it, "What you ask about is what children learn" (p. 287). If you ask questions about trivial facts, then those facts are what children will focus on and remember. The questions we ask shape students' comprehension and also their concept of what is important in a text.

### Planning Questions

Because of their importance, questions need to be planned carefully. They should be used to establish the main elements in a story or the main concepts in a nonfiction selection (Beck, Omanson, & McKeown, 1982). Poor readers benefit from questions that elicit the basic elements in a selection (Medley, 1977). Once the basic plot of a story or the main facts in an article are established, students can be led to

To help students incorporate structure in their writing, use frames in which students fill in the blanks with details or planning sheets which lead students step-by-step through the writing of a well-organized piece. Both of these are covered in detail in Chapter 10.

When asked inferential questions during the reading of a story, third-graders generated inferences and included this information in a later retelling. The inferences they generated became a part of their memory for the story (Sundbye, 1987). Through questioning, they had constructed an elaborate version of the tale.

Asking "Why?" can increase retention of information (Menke & Pressley, 1994). One group of students was given paragraphs about animals and told to study the information in the paragraph. A second group was given the same paragraphs but was instructed to ask "Why?" after each piece of information. The group that asked why remembered significantly more.

a deeper understanding of the material. It is important to ask questions that help children see relationships among ideas, relate new information to their background of experience, and modify their schema. Students must also have opportunities to respond in a personal way to literary pieces—to judge the material and apply the information they gather to their own lives.

## Placement of Questions

The placement of questions has an impact upon their effect. Questions asked before reading help readers activate schema and set a purpose (Harris & Sipay, 1990). They guide readers into the text and tell them what information to seek. Questions that are asked after reading help readers organize and summarize the text. Questions asked during reading help readers process text. During-reading questions are especially prevalent in the primary grades. Teachers may stop the reading of a selection halfway through or even at the end of each page and pose questions. Such questioning can clarify any confusing elements in text just read and prepare students to read the upcoming segment.

## Types of Questions

One way of looking at questions is to examine the kinds of thinking processes involved in asking and answering them. An arrangement of skills from least demanding to those that require the highest mental powers is known as a **taxonomy.** The following taxonomy or levels of questions is based on Weinstein and Mayer's (1986) system, which has also been used to classify the comprehension strategies described in this text. However, the first level, comprehending, is drawn from Bloom's (1957) taxonomy.

■ A **taxonomy** is a classification of objectives, types of questions, or other items.

*Comprehending.* Students understand prose on a literal level. They can recite five facts stated in a selection, name the main characters, and indicate dates and places. This level also includes having students put information in their own words.

*Organizing.* Students select important details from the selection and construct relationships among them. This involves identifying or constructing main ideas, classifying, noting sequence, and summarizing.

One of the simplest taxonomies is that which describes comprehension in terms of the reader's interaction with the text: literal, interpretive, and applied. Literal comprehension entails comprehending the basic meaning of the text. Interpretive comprehension entails making inferences by putting together several pieces of information or combining information from the text with the reader's knowledge. In applied comprehension, the reader makes use of ideas found in the text.

*Elaborating.* Elaborating entails making connections between information from the text and prior knowledge and includes a wide range of activities: making inferences, creating images and analogies, and evaluating or judging.

*Monitoring.* Monitoring involves being aware of cognitive processes. It entails knowing whether a selection makes sense and knowing what steps might be taken to repair comprehension.

Listed below are examples of each type of question. They are drawn from *Supergiants: The Biggest Dinosaurs* (Lessem, 1997).

*Comprehending*

Which of the dinosaurs was the biggest? When was the biggest dinosaur discovered? Which of the dinosaurs was the longest?

*Organizing*

In what ways were the biggest dinosaurs alike? In what ways were they different?

*Elaborating*

How do you know that Professor Rodolfo is determined and hard-working? In your mind, picture Argentinosaurus. What does Argentinosaurus look like? What is the area where Argentinosaurus lives like? What sounds do you hear?

*Monitoring*

Did you find any confusing parts? Did you run into any words that you couldn't read or whose meanings you didn't know? If so, what did you do? Can you summarize each dinosaur's main characteristics? If you forget some important details, what might you do?

> **ADAPTING INSTRUCTION for *STRUGGLING READERS and WRITERS***
> There is a tendency to give struggling readers mostly lower-level questions. Be sure to include some higher-level questions, but provide scaffolding and prompts as necessary.

## Using Wait Time

One way of extending responses is to make use of **wait time.** Teachers often expect an immediate answer and, when none is forthcoming, call on another student. Waiting five seconds results in longer, more elaborative responses, higher-level thought processes, and fewer no-responses and I-don't-knows. Teachers who use wait time become more proficient at helping students clarify and expand their responses (Dillon, 1983; Gambrell, 1980). It would be difficult to find a better instructional use of five seconds of silence.

Silence after an answer is given also helps. Used to rapid-fire responding, teachers tend to call on another pupil the second the respondent stops talking. Often, however, students have more to say if given a few moments to catch their mental breath. Dillon (1983) suggested waiting from three to five seconds when a student pauses, seems to be unable to continue, or seems to be finished speaking. Often the student will resume talking and may even supply the most thoughtful part of the response at that point. Such postresponse wait time must be a genuine grace period. Maintain eye contact and do not turn away. Failing to maintain eye contact and turning away are cues that your attention is being diverted and will shut down any additional response that the student is about to make (Christenbury & Kelly, 1983).

> ■ **Wait time** is a period of silence between asking a question and repeating or rephrasing the question, calling on another student, or making some sort of comment.

> Wait time requires practice and patience; you will have to make a conscious effort to implement it. Try counting to five thousand by thousands after asking a question or after a student has halted an initial response. Ask a colleague to evaluate your beginning attempts.

## Classroom Atmosphere

Even more important than using wait time or asking thought-provoking questions is establishing the right classroom atmosphere. The spirit of inquiry and exploration should be obvious. The teacher must be warm and accepting, so students will feel free to speculate, go out on an intellectual limb, or take an unpopular stand without being criticized. Criticism by teachers or classmates actually leads to lowered performance. Less emphasis should be placed on the rightness or wrongness of an answer and more on the reasons supporting the response.

Questions should be democratic, with everyone's contribution valued. That means calling on slower students as often as brighter ones and giving introverts as

> Teacher's guides may include an excessive number of questions. If so, ask only the most relevant ones. Note the major concepts or ideas that you want students to take away from their reading and then restrict questions to the ones that lead to those learnings.

Searfoss and Readence (1994) caution against asking questions that are too diffuse. A question such as: "What is the main idea of the selection?" is so general that it fails to provide the kind of structure that helps prompt a response. Rather than asking a single general question, it would be better to ask several questions that are more specific and provide better support.

much opportunity to respond as extroverts. Ironically, research suggests that not only are bright students asked more questions than are slow students but also they are given more prompts (Brophy & Good, 1970). All too often, the teacher calls on another student as soon as a slower learner begins to falter. Thus, the ones who would profit the most from prompting receive the least.

## Techniques for Asking Questions

Discussions should be considered opportunities to expand students' background and enhance their verbal and thinking skills. All too often, however, discussions become oral quizzes with a focus on correct answers; emphasis should instead be on helping the child. If a student is unable to provide an answer, it may be the fault of the question—rephrase it, or ask an easier one (Pearson & Johnson, 1978). Some students, because of shyness or because they come from an environment that does not prepare them for the types of questions asked in school, have difficulty answering higher-level questions (Heath, 1991). They may know the answers but must be prompted to help shape their responses. Questioning procedures that make effective use of prompts are described below.

### ■ FELS

A useful, research-based technique for using questions to evoke higher-level thinking processes was devised by Taba (1965). Known by the acronym FELS, it consists of asking questions and using prompts and probes that are focusing, extending, lifting, and substantiating.

Hyman (1978) describes a technique similar to FELS as being the plateaus approach. Using this technique, the questioner asks at least three questions on one level of cognition, thereby establishing a plateau, before asking a higher-level question and moving to a higher plateau.

Focusing questions, as the name implies, direct the student's attention to a particular topic—for example, the peculiar behavior of Sam, a character in a story. The teacher asks literal questions designed to help students describe that behavior.

Extending questions are designed to elicit clarification and elaboration. By extending the student's thoughts on the same level, they might seek additional information about a character or event and clear up points of confusion. Extending is important because it prepares students for the next step and also provides slower students with an opportunity to become involved.

Lifting is the crucial stage. Through questioning or other means, the teacher lifts the discussion to a higher level. Through focusing and extending, the teacher has established that Sam refused to go into the reptile house on the class trip to the zoo, would not get out of the car when the family stopped for a picnic in the woods, and has not visited his friend Joe since Joe obtained a pet snake. The teacher asks, "What do all these actions tell us about Sam?" Now, instead of just giving factual responses, students are asked to draw the conclusion that Sam is afraid of snakes.

Substantiating questions ask students what evidence they found or what standards or criteria they used to draw a conclusion, make a judgment, or prove a point—for example, the evidence that Sam is afraid of snakes.

The following example shows how FELS might be used to build higher-level comprehension. The questions are based on a selection about Andrea, a knowledgeable backpacker who is trekking through the forest.

### Focusing

*Teacher:* Where was Andrea?

*Student:* Forest.

*Teacher:* What did she watch out for?

*Student:* Snakes.

*Teacher:* What was she wearing?

*Student:* Shirt and jeans.

### Extending

*Teacher:* What else did she watch out for besides snakes?

*Student:* I don't know.

*Teacher:* Let's look back over the story.

*Student:* Oh, I see. She was watching out for poison ivy.

*Teacher:* What kind of shirt was she wearing?

*Student:* Old.

*Teacher:* What kind of sleeves did it have?

*Student:* Long.

### Lifting

*Teacher:* We usually judge people by their actions. Think over Andrea's actions. What do they tell us about her? What kind of person does she seem to be?

*Student:* Careful.

### Substantiating

*Teacher:* Which actions led you to believe that Andrea is careful?

*Student:* She watched out for snakes and poison ivy. She wore a shirt with long sleeves so she wouldn't get poison ivy or insect bites.

Taba (1965) cautioned that FELS should be used with care. Frequent shifting from level to level may produce a lack of sustained achievement at any level and result in a return to a more basic level. It is also important for teachers to encourage students to reason out and substantiate their answers. If teachers do the students' thinking for them, the strategy is ineffective. Timing and pacing are also important. The teacher has to know, for example, when to proceed to a higher level. Moving to lifting before building a solid understanding of the selection through focusing and extending hinders students' progress. It is also important that the FELS procedure be individualized, as some students require more time on a level than others (Taba, 1965).

> All too often, our responses to questions correctly answered are a lukewarm "That's right" or "Uh-huh." Try using a stronger response such as "You're absolutely right!" or "That's a very thoughtful observation!" (Hyman, 1978).

### ■ Responsive Elaboration

Despite use of a carefully constructed questioning procedure such as FELS, students' thought processes sometimes go astray. They may have misinterpreted instructions or may be misapplying a strategy. A procedure that works well in these

■ **Responsive elaboration** is a process of asking a student to tell why an idea or concept is true or why something works the way it does.

instances is **responsive elaboration** (Duffy & Roehler, 1987). Responsive elaboration is not an introduction to or a new explanation of a strategy or skill but an elaboration. It is responsive because it is based on students' answers, which are used as guides to students' thought processes.

To use responsive elaboration, teachers listen to answers to determine how students arrived at those responses. Instead of asking, "Is this answer right or wrong?" they ask, "What thought processes led the student to this response?" And, if the answer is wrong, "How can those thought processes be redirected?" Instead of calling on another student, telling where the answer might be found, or giving obvious hints, teachers ask questions or make statements that help put students' thinking back on the right track. The key to using responsive elaboration is asking yourself two questions: "What has gone wrong with the student's thinking?" and "What can I ask or state that would guide the student's thinking to the right thought processes and correct answer?"

The following is a scripted example of how a teacher might use responsive elaboration with a student who has inferred a main idea that is too narrow in scope:

*Student (giving incorrect main idea):* Getting new words from Indians.

*Teacher:* Well, let's test it. Is the first sentence talking about new words from the Indians?

*Student:* Yes.

*Teacher:* Is the next?

*Student:* Yes.

*Teacher:* How about the next?

*Student:* No.

*Teacher:* No. It says that Indians also learned new words from the settlers, right? Can you fit that into your main idea?

*Student:* The Indians taught the settlers words and the settlers taught the Indians words.

*Teacher:* Good. You see, you have to think about all the ideas in the paragraph to decide on the main idea. (Duffy & Roehler, 1987, p. 517)

### ■ Other Probes and Prompts

In addition to the probes and prompts recommended in FELS and responsive elaboration, there are several additional ones that can be used to foster students' thinking. If students' answers are too brief, use an elaboration probe: "Would you please tell me more?" If a response is unclear, you might use a restating–crystallizing probe. In this probe, you restate what you believe the student said and then ask whether your restatement is correct: "You seem to be saying that Gopher should have told someone about his problem. Is that right?" The purpose of a restating-crystallizing probe is to help the speaker clarify her or his thoughts. It can also be used to keep the speaker on track if she or he has gotten off the subject (Hyman, 1978).

# FRAMEWORKS FOR FOSTERING COMPREHENSION

Asking the right kinds of questions, building background, activating schema, learning to use strategies, and monitoring one's cognitive processes are all essential elements in fostering comprehension. Systematic but unified approaches that incorporate all these elements are required so that building background and vocabulary and prereading and postreading questions are all related to the selection's major concepts and the students' needs. Three such frameworks are guided reading, the directed reading activity, and the directed reading–thinking activity.

## Guided Reading

**Guided reading** is a framework within which the teacher supplies whatever assistance or guidance students need in order for them to read a selection successfully (Fountas & Pinnell, 1996; Fountas & Pinnell, 2001). Guided reading is used with individuals or groups who are on approximately the same level of reading development. Selections are provided that match the students' level of development. Students should know most but not all of the words (at least 95 percent). Selections should contain some challenge so that students could apply strategies but should not contain so many new words or unfamiliar concepts as to be overwhelming. "The ultimate goal in guided reading is to help children learn how to use independent reading strategies successfully" (Fountas & Pinnell, 1996, p. 2). This includes both word recognition and comprehension strategies. Students read silently and, as they progress in skill, they read increasingly more difficult selections or whole books.

■ **Guided reading** is an instructional framework within which the teacher supplies whatever help or guidance students need to read a story successfully.

Guided reading can be initiated as soon as students have a firm sense of what reading is, know some initial consonant correspondences, and have learned some high-frequency words. Students are able to take part in guided reading when they can read the kinds of books listed in the Caption/Frame level in Appendix A.

The amount of guidance provided varies depending on students' abilities and the complexity of the selection to be read. For beginning readers, the guidance might consist of going through the text page by page and discussing the selection and highlighting unfamiliar expressions, unknown concepts, and difficult words. For more advanced readers, guidance may consist of a brief preview. Lesson 7.1 shows what a thorough introduction to a selection might look like. Because the teacher figuratively walks the students through the selection page by page and pictures are used to provide an overview of the selection, this type of heavily guided lesson is sometimes called a text or picture walk.

▌See Chapter 9 for suggestions for managing guided reading and providing the rest of the class with useful activities while you are working with groups.

 **Text walk for beginning readers**

### Step 1. Analyzing the text

Analyze the text. Note concepts, background information, words, or language structures that pose difficulties for the students with whom the selection will

For more information about the text walk technique, see the article "Introducing a New Storybook to Young Readers" by Marie Clay in *The Reading Teacher, 45,* 1992, 264–272.

be used. Note, too, word analysis and comprehension strategies needed to read the text. In the book *Up the Ladder, Down the Slide* (Everitt, 1998), readers would need to know what things you might do if you go to the park and have a picnic. The expressions "Sun peeks out" and "Blow a kiss" might be unfamiliar to some students. Students might also have difficulty decoding words such as *spread, peeks, shout, ladder, slide,* and *share.*

**Step 2. Introducing the title and topic**

Introduce the title to the students, *Up the Ladder, Down the Slide.* Point to each word as you read the title. Ask students to tell where the children are. Invite them to predict what might happen in the story.

**Step 3. Highlighting the story**

Walk the students through the first twenty-four pages of the story page by page or picture by picture so that they get an overview of the tale. Knowing the gist of the selection and being familiar with the format, the students will be better able to use contextual and other clues to achieve a successful reading. As you walk the students through the story, preview words, concepts, and language structures that you think students might have difficulty understanding. Paraphrase key portions of the text that contain difficult items. Then help the students point out these items. For instance, after paraphrasing the second page, in which the unfamiliar word *spread* is used, ask students to point to the word *spread.* On the next page, discuss the expression, "Sun peeks out." Then have students point to the word *peeks.* After paraphrasing the following page, have students point to the word *shout.* Go through the rest of the book in this same fashion. Stop three or four pages from the end and have students predict what the rest of the story will tell. Then have students read the book on their own to see what the rest of the story tells.

**Step 4. Reading of the story**

Encourage the students to read the story on their own, but provide guidance and support as needed. Generally, stories are read silently first. However, selected portions might be read aloud during the discussion to back up or clarify responses or dramatize a portion of the text.

As you walk students through the selection, summarize what is happening and highlight elements that might be difficult. "The children are going to the park to play. Now the sun peeks out. What does that mean? Can you find *peeks*?"

**Step 5. Discussing the story**

Discuss the story. Start with the student's purpose for reading, which was to find out what the rest of the story told. Discuss with students what the children did at the park. You might have them read aloud passages that tell what the children did. As children read selected portions aloud, note whether the selection seems to be on the appropriate level and also analyze the students' performance to see what strategies they are using and which strategies they might need to work on.

**Step 6. Skill/strategy instruction**

Begin instruction by affirming students' efforts. Praise the students for their use of strategies: "I like the way you used the meaning of the story to help you read *with.*" Call attention to strategies that might need introducing or refining: "You read this word," (pointing to *fold*) "as *hold*. The word *hold* makes sense in the story. But what letter does *hold* begin with? What letter does this word begin with? What word that begins with *f* might make sense here?"

### Step 7. Rereading

Encourage the students to dramatize the story. Each student might read one or two pages and pantomime the actions described.

### Step 8. Extension

Students might draw pictures that show what they like to do at the park or playground and write captions for their pictures.

How do you get started with guided reading? Start off with reading aloud, shared reading, and other group activities. Also, introduce independent reading. As students are reading independently or working in centers, administer an abbreviated informal reading inventory if you don't know the students' reading levels. To save time, use only the oral selections. Based on inventory results and other data that you have, form groups. You may wish to start with just one small group and gradually form additional groups.

## Directed Reading Activity

As students acquire a basic reading vocabulary, shift to techniques, such as the directed reading activity, that require more input from them. The **directed reading activity** (DRA) is probably the most widely used and the most highly respected instructional procedure used in reading and is a form of guided reading. A flexible procedure, the DRA is the basis for a number of teaching techniques, including guided reading, the directed reading–thinking activity, and the instructional framework. The traditional DRA has five steps: preparation or readiness, silent reading, discussion and skill development, rereading, and follow-up. Today's DRA also incorporates schema theory, metacognition, and text analysis (Adoption Guidelines Project, 1990) and may also include strategy review (Gaskins, 1998).

■ **Directed reading activity** is a traditional five-step lesson plan designed to assist students in the reading of a selection.

### ■ Steps in a Directed Reading Activity

An updated DRA proceeds as follows.

**Preparation.**   Through discussion, demonstration, use of audiovisual aids, and/or simulations, students are given guidance in the following areas:

- *Experiential background or concepts.* Experiential gaps that impede understanding of the selection's major concepts are filled in. If students are about to read a piece about solar power but have no experience with the subject, the teacher might demonstrate the workings of a solar toy. Concepts or ideas crucial to understanding the selection are also developed. Batteries would be an important concept in this instance; however, in the discussion, students might indicate that they know that batteries are necessary to make certain devices run, but they do not know why. The battery's use as a device for storing energy would then be discussed.

- *Critical vocabulary.* Vocabulary necessary for understanding the selection is presented. For a factual article about Australia's animals, the words *kangaroos, marsupials,* and *herbivores* are presented. Care is taken to show how these words are related to each other.

- *Reading strategies.* Students have to know how a selection is to be read. Most selections require a mix of preparational, organizational, and elaboration strategies. However, some strategies work better than others with certain kinds of materials. An editorial, for example, requires evaluation. A fictional story might require students to visualize the setting. At times, the format might be unfamiliar. For example, before tackling a play, students should be given tips on techniques for reading stage directions and dialogue. Because teaching a strategy is time consuming, it would be best if the needed strategy were taught beforehand and then briefly reviewed during the preparatory discussion.

- *Purpose for reading.* Whether set by the teacher or the class, the purpose for reading usually embraces the overall significance of the selection. It may grow out of the preparatory discussion. Students discussing hearing-ear dogs might want to find out how they are chosen, and that would become the purpose for reading. On other occasions, the teacher might set the reading purpose.

- *Interest.* Last but not least, the teacher tries to create interest in the selection. To do this in a piece about an explorer lost in a jungle, the teacher might read the portion of the selection that describes the dangers the explorer faced.

For the purpose of clarity, the elements in the preparation step have been described separately, but in actual practice they are merged. For instance, background concepts and the vocabulary used to label them are presented at the same time. The purpose for reading flows from the overall discussion, and throughout the discussion, the teacher tries to create an interest in the selection. Reading strategies might become a part of the purpose: "Read the story straight through, but read it carefully, to find out how the Great Brain solved the mystery" (reading purpose); "Look for clues as you read the story and try to figure out what they mean" (reading strategy).

**Silent reading**.    The first reading is usually silent. Silent reading is preferred because reading is a meaning-obtaining process rather than a speech activity. What a student understands is more important than how the selection's words are pronounced. During silent reading, a student might reread a difficult portion of text, get help from an illustration, use context, look up a word in the glossary, or take other steps to foster comprehension. Normally, none of these steps would be taken during an oral reading (Hammond, 2001). During the silent reading, the teacher should be alert to any problems that students might be hav-

> The directed reading activity is the model for basal reader lessons and the foundation for the informal reading inventory.

ing. If the class is listless, the piece may be too difficult or too boring. If it is humorous and no one is chuckling, perhaps the humor is too sophisticated or too childish. Finger pointing and lip movement are signs that individuals are having difficulty with the selection. The teacher should also be available to give assistance as needed, making note of who requested help and what kinds of help were supplied. Those students can then be scheduled for added instruction or practice in those areas. Reading speed should also be noted. Very fast reading with good comprehension might be a sign that materials are too easy. Very slow reading might be a sign that they are too difficult.

During the silent reading, students should monitor their comprehension to check whether they adequately understand what they are reading and, if necessary, take appropriate steps to correct the difficulties. The teacher should note these monitoring and repair strategies. In some classrooms, steps for attacking unfamiliar words or repairing comprehension failure are posted in prominent spots.

**Discussion.** The discussion complements the purpose for reading. Students read a selection for a specific purpose; the discussion begins with the purpose question. If the students read about how hearing-ear dogs are trained, the purpose question is "How are hearing-ear dogs trained?" During the discussion, concepts are clarified and expanded, background is built, and relationships between known and unknown, new and old are reinforced.

Difficulties applying comprehension and word-attack strategies are corrected spontaneously, if possible. The teacher also evaluates students' performance, noting whether they were able to consider evidence carefully and draw conclusions and noting weaknesses in concepts, comprehension, word attack, and application. Any difficulties noted provide direction not only for immediate help for those that can be resolved on the spot, but also for future lessons for those that require more work. Although the discussion is partly evaluative, it should not be regarded as an oral quiz. Its main purpose is to build understanding, not test it. Questioning techniques, such as probes, prompts, FELS, and wait time should be used. Part of the discussion might also be devoted to asking students to describe their use of strategies, with a focus on the strategy being emphasized.

**Rereading.** In most lessons, rereading blends in naturally with the discussion. It may be done to correct misinformation, to obtain additional data, to enhance appreciation or deepen understanding, and to give students opportunities for purposeful oral reading. During the discussion of hearing-ear dogs, students might indicate that they believe the dogs are easy to train (a mistaken notion). Students can then be directed to locate and read aloud passages that describe how long training takes. If students disagree as to what main character traits such dogs should possess, they can be asked to locate and read orally passages that support their assertions.

On occasion, rereading may be an entirely separate step. For instance, students might dramatize a story that has a substantial amount of dialogue or reread a selection to gain a deeper appreciation of the author's style. A separate reading is generally undertaken for a new purpose, although it may be for a purpose that grows out

The directed reading activity is probably the most widely used instructional technique. A flexible procedure, the DRA is the basis for a number of teaching techniques, including guided reading, the directed reading–thinking activity, and the instructional framework.

of the discussion. Rereading is not a necessary step. Some selections are not worth reading a second time, or students might grasp the essence in the first reading.

In the rereading stage, oral reading should not be overemphasized. Unless a selection is being dramatized, it is generally a poor practice to have students reread an entire selection orally. Oral rereading should be for specific purposes: to clarify a point, to listen to a humorous passage or enjoy an especially vivid description, and to substantiate a conclusion or an answer to a question.

**Follow-up.** Follow-up or extension activities offer opportunities to work on comprehension or word-attack weaknesses evidenced during the discussion phase, to provide additional practice, to extend concepts introduced in the selection, or to apply skills and strategies. These activities may involve any or all of the language arts or creative arts. Students might read a selection on the same topic or by the same author, draw illustrations for the selection, hold a panel discussion on a controversial idea, create an advertisement for the text, or write a letter to the author. The possibilities are virtually limitless, but the follow-up should grow out of the selection and should encompass worthwhile language or creative arts activities. As with rereading, it is not necessary to have follow-up or extension activities for every reading. In fact, follow-up activities should be conducted sparingly. "Extending every book (brief books that can be read in a single sitting) through art, writing, or drama is impractical and could interfere with time needed to read widely" (Fountas & Pinnell, 1996, p. 3).

*D*uring a directed or guided reading activity discussion, students may be asked to go back to the text to find support for a statement.

### ■ Preparing a Directed Reading Activity

Creating a DRA starts with an analysis of the selection to be read. After reading the selection, the teacher decides what she or he wants the students to learn from it. Content analysis of fiction may result in statements about plot, theme, character, setting, or author's style. For nonfiction, the statements concern the main principles, ideas, concepts, rules, or whatever the children are expected to learn. After analyzing the selection, the teacher chooses two or three ideas or story elements that she or he feels are most important. The piece may be saturated with important concepts; however, more than two or three cannot be handled in any depth at one time and could diffuse the focus of the activity. Even if an accompanying teacher's guide lists important concepts or provides key story events, the teacher should still complete a content analysis. That way, the teacher, not the textbook author, decides what is important for the class to learn. For example, for a piece entitled "Dream

Cars for the 2000s," the teacher composes the following major learnings. These will provide the focus for prereading and postreading activities and strategies for prereading, during reading, and postreading.

The T-2008 will be easier to care for, repair, and guide.
The T-2008 will be safer and more flexible.
The Express will be faster.

After selecting these major ideas, the teacher lists vocabulary necessary to understand them. If the list contains a dozen terms, the teacher knows that is too many to attempt to cover. As a rule of thumb, no more than five or six vocabulary words should be chosen. An excessive number of difficult words may be a sign that the selection is too difficult.

The teacher selects the words that will be difficult for the students. From the list of difficult words, those most essential to an understanding of the selection are chosen. For example, the following words are chosen as most essential to understanding the three learnings listed for the dream cars selection and as being ones that students are likely to find difficult: *turbine engine, protective devices, sensors, communicate,* and *satellites.* Examining these words gives the teacher a sense of what prior knowledge or schema the passage requires. A mental assessment of the students helps the teacher decide whether additional background has to be built. For example, poor urban children whose families do not own a car may have very limited experience with cars and so would require more background than middle-class children whose families own one or two cars.

Once the major understandings and difficult vocabulary words have been chosen, the teacher looks over the selection to decide what major cognitive and reading strategies are necessary to understand it. For the dream cars selection, visualizing and using illustrations would be helpful strategies. Comprehension should be improved if students visualize the futuristic vehicles and their major capabilities and characteristics. In addition, the photos illustrating the cars being described should help students understand the text.

Building background and vocabulary, activating schema, piquing interest, setting purposes, and giving guidance in reading and cognitive strategies are all done in the preparatory segment of the lesson. Generally, this takes the form of a discussion. Key vocabulary words are written on the board. When discussing each word, the teacher points to it on the board so that students become familiar with it in print. Lesson 7.2 presents a sample DRA for "Dream Cars for the 2000s."

▌The DRA in Lesson 7.2 is just one of many possible lessons. Another teacher might choose to stress different understandings and would tailor discussion and other activities to match her or his teaching style and the abilities, backgrounds, and interests of the students. The teacher might also choose different purposes for rereading or elect not to have any follow-up.

 **A sample DRA**

### Step 1. Preparation

(During the discussion, the teacher introduces vocabulary words and concepts that might be difficult for students. These are italicized. As the teacher mentions the words, she or he points to each, which has already been written on the board.)

To start the discussion, the teacher asks, "What is your favorite car? What do you like best about that car? If you were a designer of cars for the future, what kind of a dream car would you build? What kind of an engine would you put in it? A *turbine engine?* Why or why not? (Explain that a turbine engine is used on jets.) How many passengers would your car hold? What kind of *protective devices* would it have? *Protective devices* are things like air bags and seat belts that help keep passengers safe in case of a crash. Would you have any *devices* that would help you *communicate?* What do we do when we *communicate?* Would your car make use of *satellites?* What are *satellites*, and how might they help car drivers in the future? What kind of *sensors* might the car have? What do *sensors* do? (Although judged to be difficult for students, the key words *module* and *guidance system* are not introduced because it is felt that they are adequately explained in the selection.) Now that we have talked over some of the parts of a future car, put all your ideas together, close your eyes, and picture your dream car and its main parts. (Students are given a few minutes to picture their dream cars.) What do your dream cars look like? (Students discuss possible dream cars.) Read 'Dream Cars for the 2000s.' Find out what two of tomorrow's dream cars, the T-2008 and the Express, are like. As you read, use the imaging strategy that we have been studying. (Teacher briefly goes over the steps of the strategy, which are posted in the front of the room.) Try to picture in your mind what the car or car part looks like or what's happening in the car. Also look at the pictures of the T-2008 and Express. They will help you to understand the selection."

### Step 2.  Silent reading

During silent reading, the teacher looks around to get a sense of the students' reactions to the story. Their silence suggests that they are intrigued. She notes that most of them are glancing at the photos as they read. One student raises his hand and asks for help with the word *ambulance.* The teacher suggests that he look for pronounceable word parts and put them together; when he is unable to do so or use an analogy or contextual strategy successfully, she asks whether the word *ambulance* or *animal* would fit the sense of the selection. Another student has difficulty with *anniversary*, a third with *efficiently*, and a fourth with *kilometers.* The teacher makes a note to work with polysyllabic words in the future.

### Step 3.  Discussion

The teacher begins the discussion with the purpose question "What are the T-2008 and Express like?" Additional questions flow from the students' responses; however, the teacher keeps in mind the three major understandings that she wants students to learn and will make sure that they are explored: "Why might a variety of people buy the T-2008? What could an owner who needed more passenger room do? How many passengers will the T-2008 hold?" There is some disagreement, and the teacher asks the class to go back over the story to find a passage that will answer the question. Then she asks, "How will the T-2008 use a satellite link?" The class seems confused. Satellite link is an important concept. The teacher decides that it is worth some in-depth teaching. She directs the class to go back over the part that tells about it. She reminds students to try to picture in their minds how the satellite link operates and suggests that after rereading the section, they make a drawing showing how it works. The drawings are discussed, demonstrating students' improved understanding. The teacher asks further questions: "How will the driver and the car use the satellite link? Why will the T-2008 be hard to steal? Why do you think there will be fewer accidents with a T-2008? In case of an accident, would the passengers be safer than if they were in a regular car? What is the Express like? Which car do you like better? How do these cars compare with your dream car?"

"What strategies did you use to help you read the story? How did the pictures help? How did imaging help? Which parts of the selection did you image? What did your image look like? Did it have sounds? What were the sounds like?"

### Step 4. Rereading

During the discussion, the teacher notes that the students had difficulty scanning through the selection to find facts that would justify their responses. The next day, she reviews the skill of scanning. She models the process and explains why it is important and when it is used. She gives the class a series of questions whose answers are numerals, alerting them to this fact so they know to look for numerals rather than words. The questions are "What does T-2008 stand for? How fast does the Express go? When will cars like the Express be seen?"

The teacher also reviews methods for attacking multisyllabic words and stresses the importance of both syllabication and context. Students scan to find the words *information, ambulance, notified, location, kilometers,* and *anniversary,* which are examined in context. Students use both syllabication and context clues to figure them out. As a review of vocabulary, students create and then discuss semantic maps for words they learned in "Dream Cars for the 2000s."

### Step 5. Follow-up

Some students design their own dream cars and create ads for them. Others read books about transportation in the future or other books about cars. Still others elect to read about satellites. A few write to auto manufacturers to obtain information about the newest experimental cars. One group checks the Internet for information about experimental cars. They look under the heading "Concept Cars." The class also makes plans to visit the auto show.

### ■ DRA for Fiction

The sample DRA in Lesson 7.2 was written for informational text. A lesson for a piece of fiction would incorporate the same features; however, it might use a **story elements map** instead of a list of main concepts as the framework. Created by Beck,

■ A **story elements map** lists the key components of a story: theme, problem, plot, and needed concepts. One way of creating a story elements map is to begin by noting the problem or the conflict. Then list the major events leading up to the resolution. At that point, use that information to compose the story's theme or moral. You might also list the key characters and also identify and list any vocabulary or concepts needed to understand the key elements of the story. Then create questions that focus on the central elements of the story.

Omanson, and McKeown (1982), story elements maps result in better questions and improved comprehension. Basically the teacher asks him- or herself, "What is the core of this story?" and then gears questions for students to it. To reach the core, the teacher decides what the starting point of the story is and then lists "the major events and ideas that constitute the plot or gist of the story, being sure to include implied ideas that are part of the story though not part of the text, and the links between events and ideas that unify the story" (Beck, Omanson, & McKeown, 1982, p. 479). A sample story elements map is presented in Figure 7.5.

A story elements map provides a sense of the most important elements in a story, allowing the teacher to gear preparatory and postreading activities to understanding those elements. Preliminary questions lead up to the story; postreading questions enhance understanding of its main elements. Questions about style and questions that lead to appreciation of the author's craft are asked after the reader has a grasp of the essentials. However, some provision should be made for eliciting a personal response.

## Directed Reading–Thinking Activity

■ **Directed reading–thinking activity (DR–TA)** is an adaptation of the directed reading activity in which readers use preview and prediction strategies to set their own purposes for reading.

The DRA is primarily a teacher-directed lesson. The **DR–TA (directed reading–thinking activity)** has been designed to help students begin to take responsibility for their own learning. Although based on the DRA, the DR–TA puts the ball in the students' court. The teacher leads them to establish their own purposes for reading, to decide when these purposes have been fulfilled, and to attack unfamiliar words independently. The DR–TA works best when students have background knowledge to bring to the selection and can attack difficult words in-

**FIGURE 7.5**

**A Story Elements Map**

**Title:** *Leo the Late Bloomer*
**Author:** Robert Kraus
**Theme:** Some people take longer than others to develop.
**Problem:** Leo can't do the things that others his age can do.
**Plot:** Leo can't do anything right.
Leo's mom says he is a late bloomer.
Leo's father watches for signs of blooming but nothing happens.
Leo's mother tells the father to stop watching, but nothing happens.
At last, Leo can do things.
**Ending:** Leo says, "I made it."

**Needed Concepts or Ideas:** *Bloom* means "to grow and develop." Late bloomers are people who take longer to develop.

dependently. If students are lacking in background or have weak word analysis skills, then the DRA is a better choice.

Stauffer (1970), the creator of the DR–TA, based the approach on our penchant for predicting and hypothesizing. By nature, we have an innate tendency to look ahead. We are also decision-making creatures who need opportunities as well as the freedom to make decisions. Building on these propensities, Stauffer structured a predict–read strategy that has the following facets:

- *Setting purposes.* Students have to know how to ask questions about text they are about to read.

- *Obtaining information.* Students have to know how to sift through reading material to get the information they need to answer a question.

- *Keeping goals in mind.* Students must be able to work within the constraints of their goals, noting information that fits in with these goals and not being led astray by information that does not.

- *Keeping personal feelings in bounds.* Students have to be able to suspend personal judgments when reading a piece that contains ideas with which they might not agree, at least until they have finished the piece and have a good grasp of what the author is trying to say.

- *Considering options.* Students must be able to consider a number of choices as they make their predictions and also be flexible enough to change or refine a prediction in the light of new information.

Like the DRA, the DR–TA has five steps, as outlined in Lesson 7.3. The major difference is that students are given a more active role in the DR–TA (Stauffer, 1969).

## LESSON 7.3  A DR–TA

### Step 1.  Preparation

Students are led to create their own purposes for reading. The title of the selection, headings and subheads, illustrations, and/or the beginning paragraph are used to stimulate predictions about the content of the selection. The aim is not to have students guess what happens in the story but to make reasonable predictions based on the information available and their background knowledge. Students make initial predictions based on the title. It is better to use the title as the initial basis for a prediction rather than an illustration because good titles generally suggest the overall story problem or theme, whereas the cover illustration typically depicts a single event. In addition, discussing the title provides an opportunity for students to play close attention to and interpret a key language element. It also conveys the idea that carefully considering a title is a good way to prepare for the reading of a selection. After making predictions based on the title, students then examine the cover illustration or first illustration for the story. On the basis of an examination of the illustration—if there is one—they amplify or revise their predictions. They might then read the

**BUILDING LANGUAGE**

Encourage students to explain why they are making predictions. Prompt them to give a full explanation.

One problem with using the DR–TA is that developing students' background knowledge and vocabulary prior to reading a selection might be neglected (Tierney, Readence, & Dishner, 1995). To build background, spend additional time with the predicting phase. While discussing the title and illustrations and other elements needed to make predictions, build essential background and vocabulary. One indicator that students may not have adequate background is difficulty in making reasonable predictions.

story introduction or first paragraph and once again amplify or revise predications. In preparation for reading *Mrs. Brown Went to Town* (Yee, 1996), a picture book about animals who take over a farm when the owner is injured, the teacher might have the students read the title and predict what the book might be about. They might infer that the phrase "went to town" suggests that Mrs. Brown lives in the country, perhaps on a farm. They might predict why she is going to town or what might happen when she gets there or what is happening back home while she is in town. The teacher then invites children to examine the first illustration, which shows animals dancing as Mrs. Brown bikes to town. Students might predict that the animals look very happy that Mrs. Brown is going to town and might get into trouble. Or maybe they are planning a party or some surprise for her. After discussing what the illustration shows about the animals, the teacher might then have students read the first paragraph, which states that everything changed when Mrs. Brown went to town. Students are then invited to put together information from the title and illustration with information from the first paragraph to revise their predictions and to predict what changed. The teacher asks students to justify their predictions to convey the idea that predictions should be logical and should have some basis in the evidence. She might ask them why they made a particular prediction: "What led you to make that prediction?" Sometimes students have a perfectly logical rationale of what at first seems an implausible prediction. If a prediction turns out to be implausible, listen closely to the students' rationale. This will give you clues for guiding their thinking. Students might have misinterpreted the title or the illustration. Use probes that guide students to a more accurate reading of the title or more careful examination of the illustration's details. You might ask such questions as, "Does your prediction fit in with what the title says or the picture shows? How might you change your prediction so that it better fits in with what the title says and the picture shows?" Affirm the students' efforts but use probes and prompts to redirect their thinking.

Predictions should be written on the board. Because the DR–TA is an active process, all students are encouraged to make a prediction or at least to indicate a preference for one of the predictions made by others. The teacher reads the predictions aloud and asks students to raise their hands to show which one they think is most likely. One way of introducing potentially difficult vocabulary is to have the students predict what words the author might use to tell the story. The teacher can add key words to the students' list (Benson & Cummins, 2000).

### Step 2. Silent reading

Students read silently until they are able to evaluate their predictions; this might entail reading a single page, several pages, or a whole chapter. Students are encouraged to modify their initial predictions if they find information that runs counter to them.

### Step 3. Discussion

This stage is almost identical to Step 3 of the DR–TA, except that it begins with the consideration of the class's predictions. After reading *Mrs. Brown*

*Went to Town*, students evaluate their predictions. The teacher might ask them to tell how they did with their predications and how they might have revised their predictions as they read and why they changed their predictions, if necessary. Focus is on the logic and reasonableness of the predictions rather than accuracy. Additional questions flowing from the sense of the selection are then asked: "Why do you think Mrs. Brown moved into the barn? Do you think she was angry with the animals? Why or why not?" During the discussion, students offer proof of the adequacy of their predictions or clarify disputed points by reading passages orally. As in the DRA, the teacher develops comprehension, background, and concepts as the need arises and the opportunity presents itself. If a selection is being read in parts, the discussion also leads students into making further predictions, as the teacher asks, "What do you think will happen next?" If students do not respond to prediction-making questions, the questions should be rephrased or altered. The teacher might also read a few paragraphs aloud to stimulate predictions. As in Step 1, predictions are written on the board and students select the ones they believe are best or most probable.

### Step 4. Rereading

This is the same as Step 4 of the DRA (see p. 367).

### Step 5. Followup

This is the same as Step 5 of the DRA (see p. 367).

The DR–TA should be used with both fiction and nonfiction. If students apply the strategies of surveying, predicting, sifting, and verifying to fiction only, they may not develop the ability to transfer these to nonfiction. In time, the strategies practiced in the DR–TA should become automatic.

## Modified Cloze

Cloze is an activity in which students supply missing words in a sentence or paragraph. Cloze is a good device for building comprehension at the sentence level and getting students to use context. Traditional **cloze** exercises are not recommended until students are in fourth grade and/or have achieved a fourth-grade reading level. However, modified cloze activities can be introduced as early as kindergarten.

### ■ Oral Cloze

Very young students can complete cloze exercises orally. The teacher reads a story, hesitates before a word that students have a good chance of supplying because of its predictability, and asks them to tell what word comes next. For example, when reading *The Little House* (Burton, 1942) aloud, the teacher would pause upon reaching the italicized words:

> Once upon a time there was a Little House way out in the *country*. She was a pretty Little *House* and she was strong and well built. The men who built her so well said,

■ **Cloze** is a procedure in which the reader demonstrates comprehension by supplying missing words. Cloze is short for "closure," which is the tendency to fill in missing or incomplete information.

"This Little House shall never be sold for gold or *silver* and she will live to see our great-great-grandchildren's great-great-grandchildren living in *her.*" (p. 1)

Oral cloze is greeted enthusiastically by students and occasions lively discussion of alternatives (Blachowicz, 1977). It also introduces children to predicting.

### ■ Word Masking

As children begin to acquire some reading skills, word masking is used. A nursery rhyme, poem, or story is shared with students. Students follow along as the teacher reads the selection in a big book. During the second reading, some of the words are covered over. When the teacher gets to one of them, he or she pauses and the children predict what it might be. After they respond, the word is uncovered, and students are asked whether they were correct (Hornsby, Sukarna, & Parry, 1986).

### ■ Multiple Choice Cloze

In modified cloze, each blank is accompanied by answer choices so that students do not have to supply the word; they simply identify the best of three or four possible choices. This is a format employed by a number of commercial workbooks and some tests. Although they provide valuable practice, these exercises shift the focus from predicting a word to considering which alternative is best. The task is changed from being one of constructing meaning to recognizing meaning, a subtle but significant alteration. However, modified cloze can be good preparation for completing classic cloze exercises.

## CRITICAL READING

Today's students are barraged with an overwhelming number of sophisticated, slick television and print ads. Even the youngest readers encounter slanted writing, illogical arguments, and persuasive techniques of all types. In addition, the Internet is becoming a major source of information. Virtually anyone can put information on the Internet. Unlike in book and periodical publishing, there need not be any editors or reviewers to check the accuracy or fairness of the information. Many of the sites and services provided on the Internet are sponsored by commercial enterprises, so the information may be biased. The ability to evaluate what one hears and reads has never been more important.

When reading critically, children judge what they read. This judgment is not a mere opinion but an evaluation based on either internal or external standards. In the process of learning to evaluate what they read, students deal critically with words, statements, and whole selections.

To encourage **critical reading,** the teacher must create a spirit of inquiry. Students must feel free to challenge statements, support controversial ideas, offer divergent viewpoints, and venture statements that conflict with the majority view. When they see that their own ideas are accepted, they are better able to accept the ideas

---

■ **Critical reading** refers to a type of reading in which the reader evaluates or judges the accuracy and truthfulness of the content.

**ADAPTING INSTRUCTION for *STRUGGLING READERS and WRITERS***

The typical sequence for handling the reading of content-area texts is read-listen-discuss. Students read a chapter, perhaps for homework, which the teacher then explains. After the explanation, the class discusses the text. A more effective sequence might be listen-read-discuss, in which the teacher gives a five- to fifteen-minute explanation of the material, directs the students to read it, and then has the class discuss it. Because the explanation precedes the reading of the text, the students are better prepared to read it.

*T*oday's students should be taught how to read advertisements critically.

of others. The program, of course, must be balanced. The idea is not to turn students into mistrustful young cynics but to create judicious thinkers.

##  USING CONTENT-AREA TEXTBOOKS

In many classrooms, the whole class usually reads the same textbook, generally one designed for the average student. In the average class, however, such a book will be too difficult for approximately one child out of four or more. Also, some children will be able to use a more challenging book. Some provision has to be made for these varying reading abilities, especially for students reading significantly below the level of the textbook.

If the text is too difficult, obtain an easier one or supplement the book with easy-to-read children's books, discussions, audio-visual aids, and simulations.

### Applying Literacy Skills to the Content Areas

Content-area texts require reading to learn, which is a step beyond reading to comprehend. The skills and strategies that students learned in language arts classes form a foundation for reading in the content areas, especially if students have read a high proportion of informational text. However, students needed to be guided as they apply these skills and strategies to content-area texts. The first principle of content-area reading instruction is to help students build conceptual understanding. Building conceptual understanding requires that the teacher decides what major concepts she wishes her students to learn and then designs learning activities that will help students construct those concepts. For instance, as a result of studying mountain, river, desert, and other communities, the teacher might want students to understand that the kinds of communities in which people live have an effect on their way of life. Activities need to be designed that lead to this understanding. Simply answering factual end-of-chapter questions will lead to shallow understanding. Through careful reading, discussions, and questions that help students see the big picture, a conceptual understanding can be formulated.

It is also important that students make connections. Concepts are stored in networks. Students can understand and retain new information better if they relate it to already existing schemata. For instance, if students have a well-developed schema for the effect of geography on communities, they can understand why many sites were built near major rivers and why people might move from one part of the country to another. Questions and activities that involve students in making comparisons, connecting bits of information, and drawing conclusions help students construct a conceptual understanding.

Techniques such as the directed reading activity, the directed reading-thinking activities, and reciprocal teaching work well with content-area texts. One adaptation that might be made is to have students read in short segments. Because content-area texts are relatively dense with information, this helps students to comprehend one topic before going on to the next one. Summarizing and creating graphic organizers also help students organize and retain information.

## CHILDREN'S BOOKS IN THE CONTENT AREAS

In addition to or instead of using content-area textbooks, you might use children's books written on the topic being studied. Excellent sources of brief, heavily illustrated, easy-to-read children's books are the Harper's Trophy series and Random House's *Step into Reading* series, which feature a variety of lively, easy-to-read books on dinosaurs, whales, dolphins, sharks, and historical figures. Books in the *Picture Biography* series by Adler (Holiday House), which are written on a third-grade level and are brief and heavily illustrated, or the *First-Start Biography* series (Troll), written on a second-grade level, portray a number of famous Americans and the times in which they lived. Other easy-to-read informational books include the following:

*Biographies from American History.* Upper Battle River, MN: Globe Fearon. Thirty historical biographies written on a second-grade level. Subjects range from Susan B. Anthony to Frank Lloyd Wright.

*Colonial Leaders, Revolutionary War Leaders, Famous Figures of the Civil War Era.* New York: Chelsea House. Fifty historical biographies written on a grade three to four level.

*Rookie Read-About Science.* Chicago: Children's Press. Easy readers that cover a wide range of topics, including seasons, weather, the five senses, mammals, and plants. Written on a first- and second-grade level.

Appendix A lists a number of easy-to-read books that cover content-area topics.

**USING TECHNOLOGY**
An excellent software series that explores a variety of science topics is the *Magic School Bus* (Scholastic).

A good source of current high-quality materials in social studies is the annual listing of "Notable Children's Trade Books in the Field of Social Studies," which is published in the April/May issue of *Social Education* and can also be found online (http://www. ncss.org/resources/notable/ home.html). A list of excellent science books is published each year in the March issue of *Science and Children*.

**USING TECHNOLOGY**
*Making Multicultural Connections through Trade Books* offers many resources for using multicultural books: **http://www.mcps. k12.md.us/ curriculum/socialstd/ MBDBooks_Begin.html**

| **TABLE 7.1** Science and social studies periodicals | | |
|---|---|---|
| **Periodical** | **Appropriate Grades** | **Content** |
| *Chickadee* | K–4 | General science |
| *Child Life* | 1–4 | General interest, with focus on health |
| *Children's Digest* | 1–6 | General interest, with emphasis on health |
| *Children's Playmate* | 1–6 | General interest and health topics |
| *National Geographic World* | 3–6 | General interest, with emphasis on nature and ecology |
| *Odyssey* | 3–8 | Emphasis on astronomy and space |
| *Ranger Rick* | 1–6 | Wildlife and ecology |
| *Scholastic News* | K–6 | Social studies, science, and other topics of interest to children |
| *U\*S\* Kids* | 1–5 | Children in other lands |
| *Your Big Backyard* | K–2 | Nature |
| *Weekly Reader* | K–6 | Social studies, science, and other topics of interest to children |

## Using Periodicals

Living in such a fast-changing world, keeping up to date means reading periodicals as well as books. Periodicals are especially important in social studies because they usually present current events; Table 7.1 shows some examples. Table 7.1 also lists periodicals that explore science and social studies topics.

## KWL PLUS: A TECHNIQUE FOR BEFORE, DURING, AND AFTER READING

A lesson designed to give students an active role in reading content-area text and relate what they know to new information is **KWL Plus:** Know, Want to know, and Learn. According to Ogle (1989), KWL evolved as she and a number of classroom teachers searched for a way to "build active personal reading of expository text" (p. 206).

The before-reading stage of KWL consists of four steps: brainstorming, categorizing, anticipating or predicting, and questioning. Brainstorming begins when the teacher asks the class what they know about a topic. If they are about to read a selection about camels, for example, the teacher asks what they know about camels. Responses are written on the board and discussed. If a disagreement occurs or students seem puzzled by a statement, this cognitive conflict can be used to create a what-we-want-to-know question. The group brainstorming activates prior knowledge so that students become more aware of what they know. The students would then write about their personal knowledge of camels in the first column of a KWL worksheet.

Next, in a step similar to semantic mapping, students categorize their prior knowledge. The process of categorization is modeled. Brainstormed items already

> Online magazines include: *Dragonfly,* which features a number of intriguing activities: **http://miavx1.acs. muohio.edu/~dragonfly/.** *Consumer Reports for Kids,* which features articles on school lunches, clothing, toys, and other areas of interest to young consumers: **http://www. zillion.org.**

> ■ **KWL Plus** (Know, Want to know, and Learn) is a technique designed to help readers build and organize background and seek out and reflect on key elements in a reading selection.

The categorizing and anticipating categories steps in KWL are frequently skipped and can be considered optional.

KWL is excellent preparation for writing a report. If details are classified, each group could be written as a separate paragraph.

written on the board are placed in appropriate categories. Students then label the items in the "what we know" column with letters that indicate category names as shown in Figure 7.6: H = habitat, C = characteristics, and F = food. Students also anticipate what categories of information the author will provide. This helps them both anticipate the content of the text and organize the information as they read it. The process of anticipating categories is modeled. The teacher might ask, for example, what kinds of information an author might provide about camels. Students then write these items at the bottom of the KWL worksheet.

In the third step, questions are created. As a group, the class discusses what they want to know about camels. Questions are written on the chalkboard. Each student then records in the second column of the worksheet her or his personal questions.

With these questions in mind, the class reads the text. After reading, students discuss what they learned and the teacher writes their responses on the chalk-

**FIGURE 7.6**

## KWL Plus

Name: _____  Topic: ___Army ants___  Date: _____

| What we know | What we want to find out | What we learned | What we still want to know |
|---|---|---|---|
| H  Live in the jungle | How large a group do army ants form? | Tens of thousands form a group. | Do army ants harm people? |
| C  Are fierce | Why are there so many army ants in a group? | The queen lays 100,000 to 300,000 eggs at a time. | What are larvae and pupae? |
| H  Live in the ground | Why do the ants form armies? | Form armies to get food for larvae and pupae | |
| F  Eat plants | What do army ants eat? | Kill other insects and small animals and take them back to their home | |
| C  Work together | | Live in the ground or in trees in the jungles of South America | |
| F  Eat insects | | | |

### Categories of information we expect to see

Habitat _____    Society _____
Food _____    Travel _____
Characteristics _____    Appearance _____

board. Information is organized, misconceptions are clarified, and emerging concepts are developed more fully. After the discussion, students enter what they learned personally in the third column. In light of this information, they cross out any misconceptions that were written in the first column. They may find that they still have questions about the topic, so a fourth column—with the heading "what we still want to know"—could be added to the worksheet. You might also discuss with the class how they might go about finding the answers to the questions they still have. A completed KWL worksheet is presented in Figure 7.6. Ogle (1989) presents a fuller description of KWL, including a sample lesson.

## WRITING TO LEARN

Writing is also a powerful way to promote learning in the content area. Writing is a way of learning as well as a method of communication. Zinsser (1988), a professional writer and teacher of writing, observed,

> We write to find out what we know and want to say. I thought of how often as a writer I had made clear to myself some subject I had previously known nothing about by just putting one sentence after another—by reasoning my way in sequential steps to its meaning. (pp. viii–ix)

In her study of first-grade classrooms, Duke (2000) found that very little time was devoted to informational topics, and the classroom libraries contained a very small number of informational books.

Students' writing in the content areas often consists of simply retelling information. One solution is to have them conduct firsthand investigations and report the results. They might undertake activities such as the following:

- Writing observations about a natural phenomenon (for example, changes in plants that are being grown from seed)
- Describing birds that visit a bird feeder, changes in a tree from season to season, or changes in a puppy or kitten as it develops over a period of months
- Summarizing and interpreting the results of a classroom poll
- Interviewing older family members about life when they were growing up

A writing activity that can be used in any content-area class is having students explain a process to someone who has no knowledge of it. Processes include finding the area of a rectangle, how magnets work, how the president is elected, and how to find a particular state on a map. Students might also use graphics to help explain a process. Where appropriate, the explanation might be oral, instead of written.

Other kinds of writing-to-learn activities include the following (Noyce & Christie, 1989):

- Writing letters to convey personal reactions or request information on a topic
- Writing scripts to dramatize key events in history
- Writing historical fiction

- Writing a children's book on an interesting social studies or science topic
- Writing an illustrated glossary of key terms
- Creating captions for photos of a scientific experiment
- Creating a puzzle for key terms

Supplying appropriate models of writing is important. Students' writing closely follows the model provided by the teacher (Harper, 1997). Of course, models can be limiting if followed too closely. Once students have grasped the basics of a certain type of writing, they should be encouraged to explore for themselves.

Reports lend themselves to cooperative learning. If students are studying countries in South America, for instance, the following steps might be followed:

- The class decides what kind of information they would like to find out about the countries. These are written on the board in the form of questions: How large is the country and how many people does it have? What is the country's climate? What natural resources does the country have? What kind of a government does the country have?
- Using Brazil as her topic, the teacher models the writing of a report. Students then choose other countries in South America that they would like to investigate.
- Students are grouped according to the country they are investigating. Students in each group then decide which questions they will answer. Members of the group, however, help one another by sharing information they have found which falls under another member's topic. Members of the group also inform each other of their findings so that each member of a group learns the answers to all the questions posed by the group. Each group is responsible for completing a chapter of a booklet composed of the work of all the groups.
- Once each member of a group has finished his or her section, the group holds revising and editing sessions and also conferences with the teacher.
- When the editing has been completed, the group word processes and illustrates its chapter with a map and drawings. The finished book is entitled *Countries of South America* and includes a chapter for each country studied.
- The class, with the teacher's assistance, provides an introduction for the booklet, a table of contents, title page, map of South America, and glossary.

> ■ A **learning log** is a type of journal in which students record and reflect upon concepts that they are studying.

## Learning Logs

One easy device that combines personal reaction with exploration of content is the **learning log.** It consists of a notebook that is

> ❙ The major advantage of learning logs is that they provide students with the opportunity to reflect on their learning and raise questions about concepts that puzzle them and issues that are of concern.

> . . . informal, tentative, first draft, and brief, usually consisting of no more than ten minutes of focused free writing. The teacher poses questions and situations or sets themes that invite students to observe, speculate, list, chart, web, brainstorm, role-play, ask questions, activate prior knowledge, collaborate, correspond, summarize, predict, or shift to a new perspective: in short, to participate in their own learning. (Atwell, 1990, p. xvii)

The class can discuss their learning logs, or the teacher can collect them and respond to them in writing. Following is a learning log from a third-grader who drew up a summary based on the teacher's reading of *Squirrels* (Wildsmith, 1988):

> Squirrels nests are called dreys. Squirrels tails are used for leaps, a parachute, change directions, swim, balance, blanket. Sometimes squirrels steal eggs. (Thompson, 1990, p. 48)

The main purpose of logs is to have students examine and express what they are learning, not to air personal matters (Atwell, 1990). Logs can also be used to ask questions. Calkins (1986) suggested that before viewing a film or reading a selection, students might record the questions they have about that topic. Later, they can evaluate how well their questions were answered. On other occasions students might record what they know about a topic before reading a selection or undertaking a unit of study.

Whether students pose a question, jot down a reaction, or create a semantic map, the writing stimulus should help them think as scientists, historians, or mathematicians and think about what they are learning. At times, they can draft free responses in their learning logs; at other times, the teacher might want to provide prompts. Log-writing prompts for a unit on weather might include the following, only one of which would be provided for any one session:

- What do I know about weather forecasting?
- What questions do I have about weather?
- What is the worst kind of storm? Why?
- What kind of weather do I like best? Least? Why?
- How does weather affect my life?
- What kinds of people might be most affected by the weather?
- What causes fog?
- What are some of the ways in which people who are not scientists predict the weather?

Prompts that foster reflection, manipulation of information, evaluation, and relating information to one's personal life also foster higher-level thinking skills.

Students can also write prelearning and postlearning entries in their logs. Before studying snakes, they might write what they know about snakes and then share their knowledge with a partner. Talking to a partner helps them to elicit more information. Students then read the selection and make journal entries indicating what they know now. Prelearning and postlearning entries help students become more metacognitive, more aware of what they know and are learning (Santa, 1994).

## I-CHARTS

I-Charts, which can be used by individuals, small groups, or the whole class, can also help students prepare reports (Hoffman, 1992). After selecting a topic, the

**FIGURE 7.7**

## I-Chart

| | Guiding Questions | | | | | |
|---|---|---|---|---|---|---|
| **Topic** Penguins | What are penguins like? | How many different kinds are there? | What do penguins eat? | Where do penguins live? | **Other Interesting Facts** | **New Questions** |
| **What We Know** | Penguins are birds that walk funny. | | fish | South Pole | Slide on their stomachs | Do penguins have enemies? |
| *The New Book of Knowledge,* Vol. 15, Grolier Incorporated, 2001. | Have webbed feet. | 17 kinds of penguins | fish | Antarctic Continent and Antarctic Islands | | How do chicks learn to swim? |
| *World Book Encyclopedia,* Vol 15, World Book, 2000. | Have rolls of fat to keep them warm. | | | Southern half of world in areas touched by cold water | Have rookeries of 1,000,000 | How do chicks learn to get food? |
| *Looking at Penguins,* Dorothy Hinshaw Patent, New York: Holiday House, 1993. | Bodies are shaped like torpedoes; have powerful flippers; breathe air. | Smallest is blue penguin; largest is emperor. | krill, squid, and fish | | Rockhoppers hop on both feet. | Leopard seals, killer whales, and pollution kill penguins. |
| **Summary** | Penguins are birds that are built like torpedoes and have strong flippers and webbed feet so they can swim fast. Rolls of fat keep them warm. | There are 17 kinds of penguins. Smallest is blue penguin; largest is emperor. | Eat fish, krill, and squid | Live on Antarctic Continent and islands; live only in southern part of world in areas touched by cold water. | Penguins gather in large groups to lay and hatch eggs. Penguins have funny ways of moving. | Found out that seals, killer whales, and pollution kill penguins. Find out how chicks learn to swim and get food. |

*Sources* (vertical label on left)

teacher creates a series of three or four key questions to which students will seek answers. (Once students become familiar with I-Charts, they might create their own questions.) The topic and questions are listed at the top of a large chart, as shown in Figure 7.7. Once the questions are written, students talk about what they already know or believe about the topic and list known information and beliefs on the chart. Students' information and beliefs are recorded, even if inaccurate. Students then discuss possible sources of answers to their questions, such as books, articles, Web sites, and CD-ROM databases, and list these on the chart. Students consult the sources and list their findings in the appropriate blocks. Information that seems important but does not address the original questions is listed under "Other Interesting Facts." New questions that arise from students' reading are listed under "New Questions." This provides students with the opportunity to seek answers to questions not posed by the teacher. Information about each question is summarized and recorded. As students summarize information, they must reconcile conflicting data and revise any misconceptions they have. The summaries can be used as a basis for a written or an oral report. Unanswered questions in the "New Questions" column can be researched by individuals or small groups. A major purpose of I-Charts is to foster critical thinking.

*W*hen using a Web site, students should evaluate the accuracy and fairness of information.

## USING THE INTERNET TO OBTAIN INFORMATION

A number of search engines and directories have been specially designed for student use. Sites have been inspected by librarians or other professionals to make sure that they are appropriate for students. Some of the most widely used include:

- *AOL NetFind Kids Only:* Contains links to sites that are safe for students.
- *Ask Jeeves for Kids:* Uses questions rather than keywords to conduct a search. The reader types in a question, and the engine responds by listing the writer's question and/or similar questions and sites that provide possible answers to the questions.
  http://www.ajkids.com/

Ivy's Search Engine Resources for Kids
**http://www.ivyjoy.com/ rayne/kidssearch.html**
Contains an extensive listing of general and specialized search engines for children as well as recommended Web sites.

- *CyberDewey:* Internet sites organized using Dewey Decimal Classification codes. http://ivory.lm.com/~mundie/CyberDewey/CyberDewey.html
- *KidsClick!* Web search for kids by librarians. Lists about 5,000 Web sites. Gives estimated readabilities of sites. http://sunsite.berkeley.edu/KidsClick!/
- *Yahooligans!* Launched in 1996 and designed for young people from seven to twelve, Yahooligans is the oldest major directory for students. http://www.yahooligans.com/

## HELP FOR STRUGGLING READERS AND WRITERS

Achieving readers often pick up strategies on their own. Struggling readers and writers have a greater need for structure and explicit instruction. They also need to have materials on the appropriate level of difficulty. In an experiment with a class of thirty-two students in an elementary school that was part of a public housing project, Mosenthal (1990) noted that all thirty-two youngsters received whole class instruction and read from a text that was on grade level, even though some children were reading below grade level. Selecting the seven lowest-achieving students,

### ACTION PLAN

1. Gear instruction to students' level of cognitive development. With skills such as retelling, begin with supported retelling and gradually lead students to independent retelling.
2. Guide students in the use of text structure to help them comprehend narrative and expository selections.
3. Create a classroom atmosphere that values inquiry and discussion but in which the students feel safe to venture opinions and conjectures.
4. Ask questions on a variety of levels. Use wait time, prompts, and probes to build students' confidence and comprehension. Use QAR and ERT as needed.
5. Use frameworks such as text walk, guided reading, DRA, and DR–TA to foster comprehension. Adapt techniques to the needs of the students. Use a DRA or guided reading for

students who need maximum structure and DR–TA or KWL for those who need less structure.
6. Incorporate activities and ask questions that lead students to evaluate what they read.
7. Guide students as they apply skills to the content areas. Make sure that texts are on the appropriate level of challenge or steps have been taken to make them accessible to students.
8. Use journals, logs, reports, and other forms of writing to foster learning.
9. Use children's books and children's periodicals to extend students' knowledge of content topics and as a means for providing struggling readers with appropriate level materials.
10. Monitor students' progress and make adjustments as called for.

Mosenthal and the children's teacher, who was highly experienced, obtained materials on a second-grade level and provided the children with supplementary comprehension instruction that consisted of directed reading–thinking activities and written retellings. Retellings were chosen because they offered insights into the children's changing ability to comprehend narrative text.

Over a period of three months, the students' retellings improved dramatically. They became more complete and began to reflect the most important elements in the tales that had been read. Although instruction and practice were undoubtedly essential factors in the children's improvement, setting may have been even more important than the quality of instruction. As the children's teacher noted, "I know at times in the beginning that they (the students in the reading and writing group) were elated that they were part of a small group. I think the stories helped. They were stories they could read and they could enjoy" (Mosenthal, 1990, p. 282). Although reluctant to write at first, the children's attitudes changed because they were praised for their efforts. Over time, they also felt better about themselves. As their teacher remarked, "They saw improvement and I think they felt better about what they were doing" (Mosenthal, 1990, p. 283).

As the researchers noted, improved learning environment interacted with direct instruction in reading and writing. Being given materials they could read; tasks they could perform; and a positive, can-do atmosphere, students were able to make the most of instruction.

## ESSENTIAL STANDARDS

*Students will*

- use their knowledge of story grammar to help them understand narratives.
- recognize cause and effect and other relationships.
- grow in their ability to use retelling procedures to build and demonstrate comprehension.
- begin to use expository text structures to foster comprehension of informational text.
- use writing as a learning aid.
- use text features such as headings, maps, charts, and graphs to foster understanding.

## ASSESSMENT

Through observation and discussion and oral or written retellings, note students' ability to use story grammar and knowledge of text structure to foster comprehension. Using these same assessment techniques, note students' ability to think, read, and write critically. Use techniques such as responsive elaboration to both assess and guide students' thinking and processing of text. Through assessment, obtain information that you can then use to improve instruction. See Chapter 2 for additional information on assessing comprehension.

## SUMMARY

1. Through hearing stories, reading, and writing, children develop a schema for narrative tales.
2. Generally, expository works are harder to read than narratives. Major types of text structures are enumeration–description, time sequence, explanation–process, problem–solution, comparison–contrast, and cause–effect.
3. Questions play a vital role in facilitating comprehension. A taxonomy is a useful guide for constructing questions on a variety of thinking levels and for judging questions that have already been created. Establishing an accepting atmosphere enhances students' responses.
4. Guided reading and the DRA (directed reading activity) are highly useful frameworks for conducting reading lessons. The DR–TA (directed reading–thinking activity) gives students more responsibility for their learning.
5. Cloze is valuable for building comprehension because it forces students to read for meaning, use context, and make predictions.
6. An affective as well as a cognitive skill, critical reading involves willingness to suspend judgment, consider another point of view, and think carefully about what one reads. Thoughtful reading and discussion also promote critical thinking.
7. The total class setting has an impact on comprehension. Students do better when materials are on the proper level of difficulty, when assignments seem doable, and when there is a positive can-do atmosphere.
8. Content-area textbooks, which account for most of the teaching and learning of subject matter, pose special problems because they are more complex than narrative materials and may contain a high proportion of difficult concepts and technical vocabulary. In addition, they require reading to learn, which is a step beyond reading to comprehend. Children's books, periodicals, and Web sites enliven content-area instruction and can be used instead of or along with content-area texts. Use of graphics, writing to learn, and techniques such as KWL foster learning in the content areas.

## EXTENDING AND APPLYING

1. Examine a lesson from a basal series that is no more than three or four years old. Examine the questions for three selections, and classify them according to Weinstein and Mayer's taxonomy. What percentage are on a comprehension level? Organizing level? Elaboration level? Monitoring level?
2. Plan a DRA or similar guided reading lesson for a chapter of a children's book, a short story, an informational piece, or information from a Web site. Teach the lesson and evaluate its effectiveness.
3. Create and teach a cloze or KWL lesson. Evaluate its effectiveness.
4. Try out the FELS system for asking questions with a class. Also use wait time, and create an accepting atmosphere. Do this for a week. Have a colleague observe your performance and give you objective feedback.

## DEVELOPING A PROFESSIONAL PORTFOLIO

Look over the comprehension standards issued by the state or district where you are teaching or plan to teach. Also look at the tests or other devices used to assess comprehension. How well are the two aligned? In your portfolio, note any work you have done or plan to do so that your instructional program in comprehension is aligned with state or district standards and the assessment measures.

## DEVELOPING A RESOURCE FILE

Maintain a file of different types of text structures so that these can be used to illustrate ways in which ideas can be presented. Collect articles, trade book, and Web sites that cover key content-area concepts. Seek out sources that provide especially clear information.

8

# Reading Literature

*F*or each of the following statements related to the chapter you are about to read, put a check under "Agree" or "Disagree" to show how you feel. Discuss your responses with classmates before you read the chapter.

|  | *Agree* | *Disagree* |
|---|---|---|
| **1** A literature program for the elementary school should emphasize the classics. |  | ✓ |
| **2** Students should have some say in choosing the literature they read. |  | ✓ |
| **3** It does not really matter what children read just as long as they read something. | ✓ |  |
| **4** Setting aside a period each day for voluntary reading is an excellent use of time. | ✓ |  |

## USING WHAT YOU KNOW

*H*ow do you go about reading a piece of literature? Do you read it in the same way that you read a popular novel? If your approach is different, how is it different? When reading literature, students use many of the same processes that they use when reading more mundane materials; word-attack and comprehension strategies and skills are necessary. However, reading literature involves going beyond mere comprehension. The focus is on appreciation, enjoyment, and reader response. This chapter explores ideas for building understanding and appreciation of folklore, myths, poems, plays, and novels and ends with suggestions for promoting voluntary reading.

What are your favorite kinds of literature? What experiences have you had that created a love of literature? What experiences have you had that may have created negative feelings about literature? How might literature be taught so that students learn to understand and appreciate it without losing the fun of reading it? What might be done to make students lifelong readers of high-quality novels, poetry, plays, and biographies?

## EXPERIENCING LITERATURE

Literature has an aesthetic force: It evokes a deep personal response (this is the basis of reader response). Literature is also seen as a force for enlightenment: We respond to its universal themes and so come to understand ourselves and others better.

■ **Reader response theory** is a view of reading in which the reader plays a central role in constructing the meaning of a text. The meaning is not found in the text or the reader but is found in the relationship or transaction between the two.

■ **Aesthetic reading** refers to experiencing emotions evoked by a piece of writing.

■ **Efferent reading** means reading to comprehend the information conveyed by a piece of writing.

From a strictly reading point of view, literature makes more demands than does popular fiction. On the language level, literature has a distinctive richness. There may be more figures of speech, more allusions, a more varied vocabulary, and a distinctive style. The text is less explicit. The author makes greater use of symbols and portrays characters in more subtle fashion. There also may be several layers of meaning, so that a second or third reading reveals deeper insights. The world created in a work of literature is more complex than that created in popular fiction (Chall, Bissex, Conard, & Harris-Sharples, 1996). A work of literature makes heavier demands on the reader's life experiences and requires careful reading and reflection. A work of literature cannot be presented in the same way as a work of popular fiction. *Amber Brown Goes Fourth* (Danziger, 1995) does not require the same attention as *Charlotte's Web* (White, 1952), although both contribute to a third- or fourth-grader's overall development.

According to **reader response theory,** the reader plays a central role in constructing the meaning of a text. The meaning is not found in the reader or in the text but in a transaction between reader and text. This transaction is especially noticeable when literature is being read. Reading literature involves a dimension beyond reading ordinary material. If read properly, a classic tale draws out a feeling of wholeness or oneness, a carefully drawn character or situation evokes a feeling of recognition, and a poem that speaks to the heart engenders a feeling of tranquility. Louise Rosenblatt (1978) called this the **aesthetic** response: "In aesthetic reading, the reader's attention is centered directly on what he is living through during his relationship with that particular text" (p. 25).

In contrast to aesthetic reading is **efferent reading,** in which the reader's attention is directed to "concepts to be refined, ideas to be tested, actions to be performed after the reading" (Rosenblatt, 1978, p. 24). In efferent reading, the reader "carries away" meaning. In aesthetic reading, the reader is carried away by feelings evoked by the text. Text can be read efferently or aesthetically, depending on the reader's stance. As Rosenblatt (1991) explained, "We read for information, but we are conscious of emotions about it and feel pleasure when the words we call up arouse vivid images and are rhythmic to the inner ear" (p. 445).

Rosenblatt cautioned that it is important to have a clear sense of purpose when asking children to read a particular piece. The purpose should fit in with the nature of the piece and the objective for presenting it. By its nature, for instance, poetry generally demands an aesthetic reading. But if the focus of the reading is on literal comprehension, then the experience will be efferent. The reading is aesthetic if the focus is on experiencing the poem or story and savoring the sounds, sights, and emotions that the words conjure up.

Reading aesthetically results in a deeper level of involvement for students (Cox & Many, 1992). As they read aesthetically, children tend to picture the story in their minds. They imagine scenes, actions, and characters. As they become more deeply involved, they may enter the world that they have constructed and try to understand events and characters "in terms of how people in their world would act in similar circumstances" (Cox & Many, 1992, p. 30). Aesthetic readers also extend and hypothesize. They might wonder what happens to the characters after the story is over and imagine possible scenarios or create alternative endings. Students might also identify with a particular character and wonder how they might act if they were that character and experienced the story events.

How might students' responses be fostered? The research suggests several possibilities. Students might be allowed to choose the form of their response: It could be a poem, a story, a letter, a journal entry, or, simply, an oral reaction. It is important that students be encouraged to make connections with their personal lives and other texts that they have read. Children also need time to respond, with ample opportunity to share and discuss. As Cox and Many (1992) commented, "A lot of groping goes on during this talking and again seems necessary to provide for quick flashes of personal understanding that come suddenly and quickly during informal, open discussions" (p. 32). Individual response is at the heart of reading literature.

How does one go about eliciting reader response? Probst (1988) described the following general steps:

**1.** *Creating a reader response environment.* Establish a setting in which students feel free to respond and each response is valued so that students are free of worry about rightness or wrongness.

**2.** *Preparing to read the literary piece.* Preparation for reading a literary piece is basically the same as that for reading any text: A DRA framework might be used. In the preparatory stage, a schema is activated, new concepts and vocabulary words are taught, interest in reading the selection is engendered, and a purpose is set. The purpose generally is open-ended, to evoke a response. As an alternative, the teacher might read aloud and discuss the first portion, especially if it is a chapter book or novel.

**3.** *Reading the literary piece.* The work is read silently by students. However, if it is a poem, you may elect to read it aloud, as the sound of poetry is essential to its impact.

**4.** *Small-group discussion.* The literary piece is discussed by groups consisting of four or five students. In small groups, each student has a better opportunity to express her or his response to the piece and compare it with that of others. Discussion is essential because it leads to deeper exploration of a piece.

To foster a fuller discussion, students might be asked to take a few moments to jot down their responses before they discuss them. Writing facilitates careful consideration. Questions that might be used to evoke a response include the following, some of which were suggested by Probst (1988). Select from the questions. Four or five questions should be sufficient to evoke a full discussion.

- Which part of the selection stands out in your mind the most?
- Picture a part of the piece in your mind. Which part did you picture? Why?
- Was there anything in the selection that bothered you?
- Was there anything in it that surprised you?

To promote aesthetic reading, "teachers should recognize, support, and further encourage signs that the reader's focus of attention is on the lived-through experience of the literary evocation. . . . [T]he signs of the aesthetic response may include: picturing and imagining while reading or viewing; imagining themselves in a character's place or in story events; questioning or hypothesizing about a story; making associations with other stories and their own life experiences; and mentioning feelings evoked" (Cox & Many, 1992, pp. 32–33).

Huck (1989) stated, "Most of what children learn in school is concerned with knowing; literature is concerned with feeling" (p. 254).

Readers who make aesthetic responses enjoy a richer experience and produce more elaborated written responses. When elementary school students write from an aesthetic stance, the students' responses are more fully developed and more likely to show connections between the text and their lives. Efferent responses are more likely to consist of a barebones retelling of the tale and a brief evaluation of literary elements (Many, 1990, 1991).

Students need assistance in holding discussions. Set ground rules, and have a group role-play the process.

This is a menu of questions. Choose ones that are most appropriate for your circumstances, but do not attempt to ask them all.

Rosenblatt (1991) comments: "Textbooks and teachers' questions too often hurry students away from the lived-through experience. After the reading, the experience should be recaptured, reflected on. It can be the subject of further aesthetic activities— drawing, dancing, miming, talking, writing, role-playing, or oral interpretation. It can be discussed and analyzed efferently. Or it can yield information. But first, if it is indeed to be literature for these students, it must be experienced" (p. 447).

- What main feeling did it stir up?
- What is the best line or paragraph in the piece?
- Does this selection make you think of anything that has happened in your life?
- As you read, did your feelings change? If so, how?
- Does this piece remind you of anything else that you have read?
- If the author were here, what would you say to her or him?
- What questions would you ask?
- If you were the editor, what changes might you suggest that the author make?
- What do you think the writer was trying to say?
- What special words, expressions, or writing devices did the author use? Which of these did you like best? Least?
- If you were grading the author, what mark would you give her or him? Why? What comments might you write on the author's paper?

**5.** *Class discussion.* After the small groups have discussed the piece for about ten minutes, extend the discussion to the whole class. The discussion should center on the responses, beginning with those made in the small groups. Ask each group, "How did your group respond to the piece? In what way were responses the same? Is there anything about the work that we can agree on? How were the responses different? Did your response change as your group discussed the piece? If so, how?"

Throughout the discussion, you, as the teacher, must remain neutral and not intervene with your interpretation. Students have to be empowered to construct their own interpretations, and they need opportunities to develop their interpretive skills. Lesson 8.1 shows how a reader response lesson might be presented using the poem "The Land of Counterpane" (Stevenson, 1885).

## Reader response

### Step 1. Preparing to read the literary piece

Ask students to tell what they do when they aren't feeling well and have to spend the day in bed. Explain that the author of the poem they are about to read, Robert Louis Stevenson, was a sickly child and often spent time in bed. Also explain that *counterpane* is an old-fashioned word for *bedspread*.

### Step 2. Reading the literary piece

Have students read "The Land of Counterpane" or listen as you read it. Their purpose should be to see what feelings, thoughts, or pictures the poem brings to mind.

*The Land of Counterpane*

When I was sick and lay a-bed,
I had two pillows at my head,
And all my toys beside me lay
To keep me happy all the day.
And sometimes for an hour or so
I watched my leaden soldiers go,
With different uniforms and drills,
Among the bed-clothes, through the hills;
And sometimes sent my ships in fleets
All up and down among the sheets;
Or brought my trees and houses out,
And planted cities all about.
I am the giant great and still
That sits upon the pillow-hill,
And sees before him, dale and plain,
The pleasant land of counterpane.

## Step 3. Responding to the piece

Have students write a brief response to each of the following questions, using their thoughts and feelings:

- What feelings, thoughts, or pictures come to mind as you read the poem?
- After reading the poem, what stands out most in your mind?
- Was there anything in the poem that bothered you or surprised you?
- Does the poem remind you of anything that has ever happened to you?
- Have you ever had a day like the boy had?

## Step 4. Small-group discussion

Students talk over their responses in groups of four or five. Each question should be discussed. Students will have been taught previously to accept everyone's responses, but they can ask for explanations. Each group should have a discussion leader and a spokesperson. The leader keeps the discussion moving and on track. The spokesperson sums up the group's reactions.

## Step 5. Whole-class discussion

Have the whole class discuss the responses. Being careful not to inject your own interpretation, guide the discussion to obtain a full range of responses, thereby making it possible for students to hear them all. You can first take a quick survey of reactions by calling on the spokespeople for each group. Probe and develop those responses by calling on other members of the class. Encourage students to justify their responses by reading phrases or lines from the poem. As the opportunity presents itself, discuss how the language of the poem helps create feelings, images, and thoughts. Also talk about the mental pictures the poem evokes. Students might want to discuss mental pictures they have formed of the boy.

> Refrain from asking "Why?" after a reader has described his response. "Why?" implies that the youngster must justify his reaction to a piece. It tends to make him defensive. Instead of asking why, request that the student "tell me more about how you're thinking" (McClure & Kristo, 1994, p. xvi).

> Choose works that touch students' lives and to which they identify and respond. The "Land of Counterpane" would probably work best with third-graders.

> In her study of elementary school children's reading stance, Cox noted that the children had a variety of ways of responding aesthetically (Cox & Zarillo, 1993). They talked about their favorite part, discussed what pictures the selection brought to mind, or made connections between the piece and their own lives or between another piece that they had read.

> Notice how the questions are geared to the readers' feelings or affective responses. Instead of asking typical comprehension questions, such as, "What did the boy do?" the questions ask the students to tell about what they pictured or felt as they read or to tell what impact the poem had upon them.

**Step 6. Extension**

Have students read other poems by Robert Louis Stevenson. Many of his poems for children can be found in his classic collection, *A Child's Garden of Verses.*

## Using Journals to Elicit Responses

■ A **response journal** is a notebook in which students write down their feelings or reactions to a selection they have read. They may also jot down questions that they have about the selection.

**Response journals,** or literary logs, can also be used to evoke responses to literature. After reading a chapter in a novel, students might write their thoughts and reactions in a literary log. These responses could be open-ended or could be the result of a prompt. Parsons (1990) suggested the following types of questions, some of which have been altered slightly:

■ What surprised you about the section that you read today? How does it affect what might happen next in the story?

■ As you read today, what feelings did you have; for example, did you feel anger, surprise, fear, or disappointment? Why do you think you felt that way?

■ Was there anything in the story that puzzled you?

■ What characters and happenings in the story reminded you of people and events in your own life? How are they similar, and how do they differ?

▌One problem with using literary logs or journals is that students may fall into a rut. When this happens, provide creative prompts that invite students to see selections in new ways. Also, share entries from your journal so that you can model "new ways of thinking about literature" (Temple, Martinez, Yokota, & Naylor, 1998, p. 463).

Two other response prompts that might be used are "What if . . . " and "If I were in the story . . . " In the "What if . . . " response, readers speculate what might have happened if a character had taken a different course of action or if a key event in the story had been different. In the "If I were in the story . . . " response, readers tell what they would have done if they had been a part of the story's action (Raphael & Boyd, 1997).

Generally, students would be provided with just one or two prompts but should feel free to respond to other concerns or situations. Gradually, the prompts should be faded so that students can come up with their own concerns. Responses in the logs become the basis for the next day's discussion of the selection read. In supplying prompts for literary journals, Meyers (1988) took a different tack. She supplied students with a list of twenty questions, similar to those listed above and earlier in this chapter. They were free to choose two or three questions from the list.

▌Although students should be given choices in their written responses to literature, assigned writing can sometimes lead students to investigate themes and issues that they might not have considered (Lehr & Thompson, 2000). In one study of literature discussions, students were asked to write a letter from the main character's eyes. The assignment gave the students the opportunity to role-play, see life through a character's perspective, and problem solve.

Two other kinds of journals include the literary and the dialogue journal. In the literary journal, the student assumes the role of one of the characters in a selection and writes as though he or she were that character. A student assuming the role of Henry in *Henry, and Mudge, the First Book* (Rylant, 1990) might tell how he felt when he got Mudge as a pet. In dialogue journals, students write to the teacher and the teacher responds, or pairs of students might write to each other.

Dialogue journals help the teacher keep close contact with her students and also extend their understanding of selections. The journal writing should be a genuine exchange between teacher and student and not simply a means for checking on students' reading. If viewed as a checking device, journals may lose their vitality. In a study by Bagge-Rynerson (1994), responses showed more life after the teacher modeled the kinds of responses that might be written and also made her responses to the journal entries more personal and more affirming.

## Using Literature Discussion Groups to Elicit Responses

One effective technique for fostering a genuine response to literature is to form a literature discussion group, an interpretative community that shares a text much as a group of adults might do. This sharing can be both formal and informal. It can take place in whole-class discussions, small groups, or between partners.

Discussion groups, which are also known as literature circles, literature study groups, conversational discussion groups, and book clubs, are an attempt to improve upon the quiz-type formats that are typical of many traditional discussions. In traditional discussions, the teacher's questions follow an IRE (Initiate, Respond, Evaluate) format, in which the teacher initiates a question, the student responds, and the teacher evaluates the response. Literature discussion groups allow students to describe responses, compare impressions, contrast interpretations, and, in general, engage in the same type of talk that we might have with peers when we talk about books that we have read. The discussions, which have been termed "grand conversations," feature a natural give-and-take and a freedom to offer one's interpretation with the expectation that it will be respected (Eeds & Wells, 1989). In preparation for meeting with their discussion group, students read the selection and might jot down a response in a log or journal. The ultimate intent of literature discussion groups is to lead students to engage in higher-level talk, not just more talk.

Students find literature discussion groups to be valuable in fostering deeper comprehension of material that they have read (Alvermann et al., 1996). However, groups need to be carefully prepared and monitored. Proficient discussion groups are especially effective at staying on task and sticking with a topic long enough to

> Responses need not be written. Young children may respond by drawing their favorite character, favorite part of the story, funniest or scariest event, and so on. The drawings become a basis for response-oriented discussions.

> Questions designed to elicit a genuine response from a reader are much like those that might occur in a conversation between two adults discussing a book. Thus a conversation about *Aunt Flossie's Hats (and Crab Cakes Later)* (Howard, 1991) might go something like this: "Aunt Flossie reminds me of my Aunt Sarah. My Aunt Sarah loves to talk about the old days."

*D*uring a discussion of a literary work, emphasis is placed on eliciting an aesthetic response.

When working with a group of youngsters discussing a literary piece, the most difficult part of initiating reader response might be refraining from taking over. "The real work of adults in the group is to LISTEN, LISTEN, LISTEN. The children are working at creating meaning for themselves. By listening carefully, our own reflections can be carefully phrased to stimulate higher levels of thinking or at least more informed reflections" (Borders & Naylor, 1993, p. 27).

Only about one teacher out of every three uses peer discussions on a regular basis. It takes time for students to learn how to conduct discussions. Almasi, O'Flahavan, and Arya (2001) found that it takes at least five meetings before students learn to function together.

develop it fairly fully (Almasi, O'Flahavan, & Arya, 2001). They are effective at making connections between the current topic and points made earlier in the discussion or in previous discussions. The teacher's role is crucial. Although the teacher needs to provide direction, especially in the early stages, it is important that the teacher gradually turn over responsibility to students. Students need to learn how to manage group processes. If the teacher becomes the one who provides directives for staying on task, the students will not take ownership of the procedure. Deprived of the opportunity to think through problems, students fail to learn how to conduct discussions. Through scaffolded instruction, the teacher must lead students to recognize when procedural problems arise and to resolve them. However, over time, the teacher must assign this responsibility to students. As Almasi, O'Flahavan, and Arya (2001) noted, "By failing to give students the opportunity to monitor their own discussion, teachers may hinder students' ability to operate in the group independent of the teacher" (p. 118).

### ■ Book Club

In Book Club, a carefully researched form of discussion group, the following procedures are used (McMahon, 1997):

- *Books are selected.* The class might read the same book or choose from a selection of three or four books related to a common theme. Books could be on different levels of difficulty to accommodate varying levels in a typical class.

- *Students are organized in groups of four or five.* Small groups foster more interaction and individual participation. Groups should be balanced on the basis of factors, such as interests, communication skills, and leadership. All the leaders shouldn't be in the same group.

- *Procedures are explained.* Students are given explicit instruction about the nature of a literate or grand conversation, providing opportunities for all members of the group to participate, and about how to encourage others to participate. Sample discussions are modeled. Basic rules for conducting the discussion should also be set:

  Sit in a circle so that everyone can see each other.
  Only one person talks at a time.
  Listen to each other.
  Stay on the topic. (McGee, 1995, p. 113)

- *Students are taught how to respond to their reading.* After reading a segment of text, students complete a response log. This response might be triggered by a teacher prompt: "How did Jennifer react to the witch's offer? If you had been Jennifer, what would you have done?" Responses might also be unprompted. Students can simply write their reaction to what they read. Responses might be in the form of a sentence or a paragraph, but they could also be diagrams of plots or a web of character interactions or a drawing of the main character.

- *Book Club discussions are held.* The teacher might start the discussion by asking students to share their responses, or the teacher might ask a general question, such as "What was the most important thing that happened in Chapter 5?" or "Was there anything in Chapter 5 that puzzled or surprised you?" It's important to create the kind of atmosphere and ask the kinds of questions that motivate students to respond to books in a thoughtful but relaxed way, much the same way that you might respond if you were sitting with a group of friends discussing a favorite book.

Literature discussion groups meet for about twenty minutes. Discussions might be student led, teacher led, or a combination of the two (Temple, Martinez, Yokota, & Naylor, 1998). Students feel freer to express themselves when the teacher isn't present, but the teacher can provide expert assistance. Even if the discussion is student led, in the beginning the teacher should be there to assist the group in getting started and might model the literary kinds of questions that students are learning to ask. The teacher should also monitor the group to make sure they are on task and everyone is participating. From time to time, the teacher might drop in to model higher-level questioning or to perk up a flagging group.

### ■ Literature Circles as Cooperative Learning Groups

A second kind of literature discussion group, known as literature circles, incorporates the principles of cooperative learning to provide more structure (Bjorklund, Handler, Mitten, & Stockwell, 1998). The circles are composed of five or six students who have chosen to read the same book. Students choose from six books the three that they would most like to read. Books could cover the same theme or topic, be in the same genre, or have the same author. They might all be biographies, or they might all have survival in the wilderness as a theme, for instance. The books should represent a range of interests and difficulty levels so that students have a genuine choice and there are books that are appropriate for average, below-average, and above-average readers.

The books are presented. The teacher provides an overview of each one, and students are invited to examine the books. Students are invited to look over the books to see whether they are interesting and whether they are on the right level of challenge. Students are urged to read two or three pages at scattered intervals in order to judge the difficulty level of the book. Students then list their top three choices.

Based on the students' choices, the teacher forms four or five groups. The teacher tries to get a mix of students in each group so that a number of perspectives are represented and a number of personalities are included. The teacher also tries to match below-average readers with books that they can handle.

Once the groups have been formed, roles are assigned by the teacher or the group decides who will fulfill which role. Key roles are the discussion leader, summarizer, literary reporter, illustrator, word chief, and connector. The discussion leader develops questions for the group and leads the discussion. The summarizer summarizes the selection. The literary reporter locates passages that stand out because they are funny, sad, contain key incidents, or feature memorable language.

> **ADAPTING INSTRUCTION for *STRUGGLING READERS and WRITERS***
> Although similar to Book Clubs, literature circles provide students with choice and also can be organized according to cooperative learning principles, with each student having a well-defined role. Because students have a choice of materials, struggling readers can select books that are closer to their level. Struggling ELL students and many members of minority groups do better in cooperative learning groups.

> If there are more roles than students, some students may fulfill more than one role, or roles may be combined.

The reporter can read the passages out loud, ask the group to read them silently and discuss them, or, with other members of the group, dramatize them. An illustrator illustrates a key part of the selection with a drawing or graphic organizer. The word chief locates difficult words or expressions from the selection, looks them up in the dictionary, and writes down their definitions. At the circle meeting, the word chief points out and discusses the words with the group. The connector finds links between the book and other books the group has read or with real events, problems, or situations. The connector describes the connection and discusses it with the group. Although each student has a certain role to fulfill in the circle, any student may bring up a question for discussion, a passage that stands out, a confusing word, a vivid figure of speech, or a possible connection.

The roles reflect the kinds of things that students should be doing as they read a text. They should be creating questions in their minds, making connections, visualizing, summarizing, noting key passages, coping with difficult words and confusing passages, and appreciating expressive language and literary techniques. Students switch roles periodically so that each student has the opportunity to carry out each of the roles.

To help students fulfill their roles, they are given job sheets. A sample job sheet for a discussion leader is shown in Figure 8.1. Each of the jobs is also modeled and discussed. The class, as a whole, also practices each of the jobs by apply-

**BUILDING LANGUAGE**

Introduce concepts and words such as *theme, moral, point of view, realistic characters,* and *suspense* that enable children to judge and talk about literary selections. From time to time, join in the groups' discussions. Provide prompts that help the students engage in thoughtful discussions.

**FIGURE 8.1**

### Discussion Leader Job Sheet

The discussion leader's job is to ask a series of questions about the part of the book that your group will be discussing. Ask questions that will make the other students in your group think carefully about what they read and walk in the shoes of the main characters. Some possible questions are:

How do you feel about this part of the story?

Was there anything that bothered or surprised you?

What would you have done if you had been the main character?

What do you think will happen in the next part of the story?

Write your questions on the lines below.

1. _____

2. _____

3. _____

4. _____

Adapted from Daniels, H. (1994). *Literature Circles, Voice and Choice in the Student-Centered Classroom.* York, ME: Stenhouse

ing it to a brief, relatively easy selection. Creation of questions is given special attention. Questions that lead to in-depth sharing of responses are stressed. Discussions are modeled. The teacher might do this by training a group and then having them demonstrate before the class. Students are given two or three weeks to complete a book. After a group has been formed, the group meets and sets up a schedule for how much reading they will do each evening. A written schedule is created and pasted to the inside cover of the response journal. If students are doing some or all of their work in school, they meet every other day. Days they don't meet are used to complete their reading and tasks.

The teacher visits each group and in the early stages might model asking questions or responding to a selection. As students become more adept, the teacher takes on the role of participant.

Whole-class sessions are held each day so that groups can share with each other. This is also a good time to present minilessons or perhaps read aloud a selection that pertains to the theme or topic of the books being read.

After the books have been completely read and discussed, students meet in groups according to the roles they fulfilled. All the discussion leaders meet, as do all the summarizers, connectors, illustrators, word chiefs, and literary reporters. In these groups, students give an overview of the book they read and their opinion of the book. They also discuss the books they read from the point of view of their roles. In this way, all of the students become acquainted with the books read in other groups.

Each group also makes a brief presentation of its book. This might be in the form of an ad, a skit based on the book, a panel discussion, an interview of the main character, or a dramatization of a key passage. Literature circles can also be organized in a less structured way so that students meet to discuss their reading but don't have specific roles. However, teachers who have used this structured approach find that in time, students automatically carry out the various roles as they read.

## TYPES OF LITERATURE

### Folklore

A good place to start the study of literature is with folklore, which includes folktales, myths, rituals, superstitions, songs, and jokes. **Folklore** follows an oral tradition. As M. A. Taylor (1990) put it, "The tales of the tongue are a good introduction to the tales of the pen." Having stood the test of time, folklore has universal appeal.

Every culture has produced its own **folktales.** Students can investigate those drawn from the culture of their ancestors. African American students might look into one of Aardema's works, such as *Why Mosquitoes Buzz in People's Ears: A West African Folk Tale* (1975), or one of Harold Courlander's collections of African folktales. Closer to home is Virginia Hamilton's (1985) *The People Could Fly: American*

*Black Folktales.* Latino students might enjoy one of Alma Flor Ada's tales. Other outstanding sources of materials about diverse cultures are *Kaleidoscope: A Multicultural Booklist for Grades K–8* (Yokota, 2001), *Multicultural Literature for Children and Young Adults* (Kruse & Horning, 1997), and *Multicultural Teaching* (Tiedt & Tiedt, 2002). To provide follow-up after students have read and discussed a piece of folklore, use the following reinforcement activities.

---

**REINFORCEMENT ACTIVITIES** **Folktales**

- Because folktales were meant to be told orally, have a volunteer retell a tale. Students can pretend to be members of the storyteller's family or village. They can decide when and where the tale was told and how the listeners might have reacted. Have a storytelling festival, with students retelling a tale that they located on their own.
- Have older students create a semantic map of major types of folktales and their elements.
- Encourage students to ask parents and grandparents to retell favorite folktales they remember hearing. If possible, parents or grandparents might tell the stories to the class.
- Students can retell folktales through puppet shows and other dramatizations. Older students might put on shows for primary-grade students.
- Point out allusions to folktales as these occur in newspapers, magazines, or books. Discuss, for instance, terms such as *cried wolf* and *Cinderella team.*
- Above all, acquire collections of folktales for the classroom library so that students may have easy access to them. Also, continue to read folktales aloud to the class.

---

> To find varied versions of folktales, consult *The Storyteller's Sourcebook: A Subject, Title, and Motif-Index to Folklore Collections for Children* (McDonald, 1982).

> Reactions to poetry are very personal. One student's favorite could be another student's least liked. For example, in Terry's (1974) study of preferences, one student had a special feeling for Edwin Hoey's "Foul Shot" because it reminded him of something that happened in a game in which he had played. A second student, however, disliked the poem because she had difficulty making shots.

**USING TECHNOLOGY**

Children's poetry is published on the Poetry Gallery.
http://www.
kidlit@mgfx.com

## Poetry

Students like poetry that has humor and a narrative element and that rhymes. Include both light verse and more thoughtful pieces. Before reading a poem to the class, practice it so that your reading is strong and dramatic. Briefly discuss vocabulary words or concepts that might interfere with students' understanding or enjoyment. Give students a purpose for listening, such as creating images in their minds, awaiting a surprise ending, or hearing unusual words.

You might emphasize questions that evoke a personal response: "What about the poem stands out most in your mind? What pictures came to mind as you listened? Which line do you like best? How does the poem make you feel? Is there anything in the poem that you do not like? Is there anything in it that surprises you?" Better yet, invite students to ask questions about anything in the poem that may have confused them. Gear discussions toward personal responses and interpretations. The emphasis should be "upon delight rather than dissection" (Sloan, 1984, p. 86).

 **Poetry**

Ciardi, J. (1962). *You read to me, I'll read to you.* New York: HarperCollins. Features thirty-five lighthearted poems.

Greenfield, E. (1991). *Night on neighborhood street.* New York: Dial. A collection of seventeen poems that focuses on life in an African American neighborhood.

Hopkins, L. B. (Ed.) (1986). *Surprises.* New York: Harper. Thirty-eight easy-to-read poems on a variety of subjects ranging from pets to flying.

Hopkins, L. B. (Ed.). (2001). *My America: A poetry atlas of the United States.* Fifty-one poems celebrate different sections of the United States.

Hudson, W. (1993). *Pass it on: African-American poetry for children.* New York: Scholastic. An illustrated collection of poetry by such African American poets as Langston Hughes, Nikki Giovanni, Eloise Greenfield, and Lucille Clifton.

Hughes, L. (1993). *The dream keeper and other poems.* New York: Knopf. A collection of sixty-six poems selected by the author for young readers, including lyrical poems and songs, many of which explore the African American tradition.

Kennedy, X. J., & Kennedy, D. M. (1999). *Knock at a star: A child's introduction to poetry.* Boston: Little, Brown. A Horn Book review praises it as one of the best introductions to poetry around.

Kushkin, K. (1992). *Soap soup and other verses.* New York: HarperCollins. Features a variety of easy-to-read poems.

Prelutsky, J. (1997). *The beauty of the beast.* New York: Knopf. Features a variety of poems about ants, cats, birds, dogs, fish, sharks, lizards, toads, and other creatures. Science tie-in: study of animals.

## REINFORCEMENT ACTIVITIES — Poetry appreciation

- Set aside time for students to talk about their favorite poems in small groups. Groups can be arranged by topic or author.

- Students can give dramatic readings of their favorite poems. These can be simply animated recitations or more elaborate events with background music and costumes.

- Arrange for choral readings for poems that lend themselves to it.

- Encourage pairs of students to read poems. Use poems that lend themselves to being read in two parts.

- Tie poetry in with the study of content-area subjects. For instance, students can read "Arithmetic" (Sandburg) in connection with the study of math. While studying insects, read poems about bugs. In *The Beauty of the Beast*, Jack Prelutsky (1997) includes a number of poems about insects.

For additional ideas for poetry activities, see Bauer, C. F. (1995). *The poetry break.* New York: H. W. Wilson.

**USING TECHNOLOGY**

Making Multicultural Connections through Trade Books offers many resources for using multicultural books. Provides an extensive listing of multicultural books and suggestions for content and technology connections. **http://www.mcps.k12.md.us/curriculum/socialstd/MBD/Books_Begin.html**

Poetry Workshops **http://teacher.scholastic.com/writewit/poetry/index.htm** Poetry workshops for student poets are presented by Jack Prelutsky (grades 1–4), Karla Kushkin (grades 4–8), and Jean Marzollo (grades 2–5). Writing tips are so specific that every student should be able to write a poem.

Giggle Poetry: Poetry Class **http://www.gigglepoetry.com/poetryclass.cfm** Poet Bruce Lasky has more than a dozen suggestions for writing poems.

Yahooligan School Bell: Language Arts: Poetry **http://www.yahooligans.com/School_Bell/Language_Arts/Poetry/** Links to a wide variety of sites.

## Chapter Books and Novels

In a literature-based program, chapter books or novels are often set aside as a separate unit of study. Before embarking on a chapter book or novel, students should receive some guidance to build background essential for understanding the text. Their interest in the book should also be piqued. Place particular emphasis on understanding the first chapter. If students, especially the poorer readers, have a thorough understanding of the first chapter, they will have a solid foundation for comprehending the rest of the text. It will also build their confidence in their ability to read the rest of the book (Ford, 1994).

Generally, students are asked to read a chapter or more each day. Questions to be considered during reading can be provided, or students might make predictions and read to evaluate them. Students might also keep a response journal for their reading. Responses might be open-ended, with students jotting down their general reactions to the segment being read, or students might react to response questions posed by the teacher.

After a segment has been read, it is discussed. Students might also do some rereading to clarify confusing points or might dramatize exciting parts. A cumulative plot outline or story map could be constructed to keep track of the main events. If the story involves a long journey, the characters' progress might be charted on a map. Extension activities can be undertaken once the book has been completed. The novel might be presented within the framework of an extended directed reading activity or directed reading–thinking activity, or it might be discussed as a grand conversation in a literature discussion group. Emphasis is on building appreciation and evoking a response; skills are secondary.

Both content and form should be discussed. Design questions to help students understand what is happening in the story and to see how the setting, plot, characters, theme, point of view, and author's style work together. However, take care that you do not overanalyze a piece or ask too many questions at any one time. Balance analysis with eliciting personal responses. Response should precede analysis and general discussion. Once the reader has responded, she or he is in a better position to analyze the piece. Part of the analysis might involve discovering what elements in the piece caused the student to respond (see the earlier section on reader response for some possible prompts).

### ■ Story Element Activities

Several activities help students gain a deeper understanding and appreciation of the story elements.

**Character analysis.**    A number of devices can be used to analyze characters in a story. One such device is an opinion–proof, in which readers write an opinion about a character and cite proof to back it up. The proof could be the character's actions or comments made about the person by other characters or the author (Santa, 1988). Figure 8.2 presents an opinion–proof for Chibi from *Crow Boy* (Yashima, 1955).

---

Through prompts, teachers can lead students to practice a variety of literacy and comprehension strategies. Prompts might ask students to predict what will happen next or make inferences about a character based on the character's actions, for instance. Or prompts might ask students to create character webs or note examples of figurative language.

**USING TECHNOLOGY**

Some selections on CD-ROM allow the reader to choose different perspectives when reading a story. On the CD-ROM *The Princess and the Pea* (Softkey, 1996), the reader can read the story from the perspective of the princess, the prince, or a third character—a lion (Westby, 1999).

**FIGURE 8.2**

### Opinion–Proof for Chibi from *Crow Boy*

| Opinion | Proof |
|---|---|
| Chibi knew the ways of nature. | He could hold insects in his hand.<br>He knew where wild grapes and wild potatoes grew.<br>He knew about flowers.<br>He could imitate the voices of crows. |

Compare–contrast or semantic feature analysis charts might also be constructed to highlight characters' relationships or traits. A semantic feature analysis (SFA) chart of the characters in *Charlotte's Web* (White, 1952) is shown in Figure 8.3.

On a simplified level, a semantic map can be created for the main character. The character's name is written in the center circle, with his or her major attributes written in surrounding circles. Figure 8.4 is a semantic map for Ramona in *Ramona Quimby, Age 8* (Cleary, 1981).

**Plot analysis.**   Understanding the structure of a story aids comprehension and gives students a framework for composing their own stories. A plot chart shows the story problem, the main actions or events leading up to the climax, the climax,

> Remember that the goal in reading a book is to have students understand, enjoy, and appreciate it. Do not assign so many activities that the life is squeezed out of the book. Some teachers report spending a month or more with a novel. For most books, two weeks should be adequate.

**FIGURE 8.3**

### SFA Chart for *Charlotte's Web*

|  | Animal | Person | Young | Old | Foolish | Wise | Kind | Selfish | Lonely | Afraid |
|---|---|---|---|---|---|---|---|---|---|---|
| Fern | − | + | + | − | − | ? | + | − | − | − |
| Wilbur | + | − | + | − | + | − | ? | − | + | + |
| Charlotte | + | − | − | + | − | + | + | − | − | − |
| Talking sheep | + | − | − | + | − | + | ? | − | − | − |
| Templeton | + | − | − | + | − | ? | − | + | − | − |
| Mr. Arable | − | + | − | + | − | + | + | − | − | − |

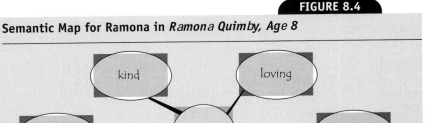

FIGURE 8.4

**Semantic Map for Ramona in *Ramona Quimby, Age 8***

the resolution of the problem, and the ending. It could be a series of rectangles, a diagram, or a picture. Figure 8.5 provides an example of a plot chart.

Students might also draw the major events of a story or put the events on a time line. Acting out key scenes or putting on a puppet show would highlight the action. To help them choose the most exciting parts of the story, have students pretend that they are making a movie of the book and must decide which scenes to depict in a preview of coming attractions and which scene to show on a poster advertising the movie.

Most books lend themselves to a variety of follow-up activities. Plan activities such as the following to deepen students' understanding and appreciation of the book and to promote the development of language arts skills.

**REINFORCEMENT ACTIVITIES**    **Chapter books and novels**

- Read a sequel or another book by the same author or a book that develops the same theme or can be contrasted with the book just completed.
- Dramatize portions of the book.
- Create a print or TV ad for the book.
- Create a dust cover for the book, complete with blurbs that highlight the story and that tell about the author.
- View a movie based on the book, and then compare the two.
- Create a montage, diorama, or other piece of art related to the book.
- Write a review of the book for the school newspaper.
- Have a Characters' Day during which students dress up and act the parts of characters in the book.

FIGURE 8.5

**Illustrated Plot Chart for *Crow Boy***

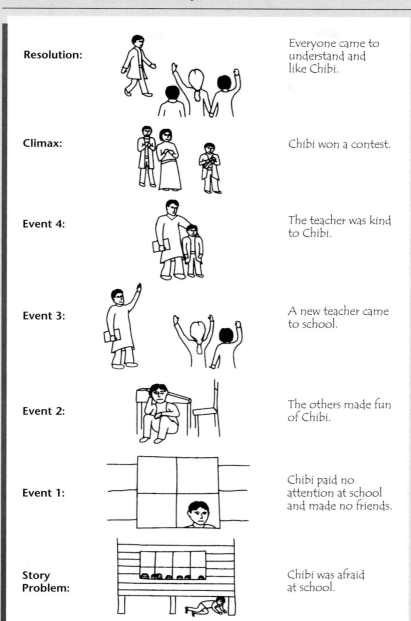

**Resolution:** Everyone came to understand and like Chibi.

**Climax:** Chibi won a contest.

**Event 4:** The teacher was kind to Chibi.

**Event 3:** A new teacher came to school.

**Event 2:** The others made fun of Chibi.

**Event 1:** Chibi paid no attention at school and made no friends.

**Story Problem:** Chibi was afraid at school.

Acting out plays provides a legitimate opportunity for students to read orally. Give them ample time to rehearse their parts, however. A drama could be presented as a radio play. Sound effects and background music might be used, but no costumes would be required. If students videotape the play, other classes might enjoy their efforts.

**USING TECHNOLOGY**

Storytelling, Drama, Creative Dramatics, Puppetry & Readers Theater for Children & Young Adults has a long list of resources for drama.
**http://falcon.jmu.edu/~ramseyil/drama.htm**

- Arrange for a panel discussion of the book. The panel might be composed of the book's characters.
- Describe books on the school's or class's homepage. Include links to the author's site, if there is one.

## Drama

Plays are a welcome change of pace but require some special reading skills. Although designed to be acted out or at least read orally, plays should first be read silently so that students get the gist of the work. Students need to be taught to read stage directions so that they can picture the setting. They also require practice in reading dialogue, which does not contain the familiar transitions and descriptive passages of their usual reading. If possible, students should see plays put on by local professional or amateur groups to give them firsthand experience with theater.

Plays are found in many basal readers. Scripts from TV shows and movies are often included in children's magazines. The magazine *Plays* is, of course, an excellent source.

The following Children's Reading List identifies a number of anthologies of children's plays.

 **Drama**

Barchers, S. I. (1993). *Reader's theatre for beginning readers.* Englewood, CO: Teachers Ideas Press.

Blau, T. (2000). *The best of reader's theatre.* Bellevue, WA: One From the Heart Publications.

Braun, W. & Braun, C. (2000). *A reader's theatre treasury of stories.* Winnipeg, Manitoba, CAN: Portage & Main Press.

McBride-Smith, B. (2001). *Tell it together: Foolproof scripts for story theatre.* Little Rock, AR: August House.

Tripp, V. (1995). *Five plays for boys and girls to perform.* Middletown, WI: Pleasant Company. Features a play for each of the main characters in the popular *American Girls Collection*.

### ■ Dramatizations

To dramatize a story, actors must understand the action and must think carefully about the characters they are portraying. Instead of passive comprehension, readers as actors must put themselves into the piece. They must make the characters come alive by giving them voice, expression, and motivation. This requires that readers think carefully and creatively about what they have read.

**Story theater.** In **story theater,** readers pantomime a selection—a folktale, a realistic story, or a poem—while a narrator reads it aloud. Their actions need not be limited to those performed by human characters. For example, the sun, the wind, trees swaying in the breeze, and a babbling brook can all be pantomimed. The teacher will probably have to help students organize the production, at least in the beginning. As students become familiar with the technique, they should be able to work out production details for themselves. Working out the details encourages cooperative learning and also involves all the language arts.

■ **Story theater** is a form of dramatization in which participants pantomime a selection while a narrator reads it aloud.

**Reader's theater.** In **reader's theater,** participants dramatize a selection by reading it aloud. A whole selection or just one portion of it can be dramatized. Pieces having a generous amount of dialogue work best. A narrator reads the portions not spoken by characters. Parts are not memorized but are read from the text. Even though they do not have to memorize their parts, readers should spend time developing their interpretation of the dialogue and rehearsing. A reader's theater production might be implemented in the following way (Pike, Compain, & Mumper, 1994):

■ **Reader's theater** is a form of dramatization in which the participants read aloud a selection as though it were a play.

**1.** *Select or write the script.* In starting out, it might be helpful to use scripts that have already been prepared for reader's theater. Scripts can also be written by the class, but this takes more time and effort. They should include extensive dialogue, be interesting to your students, and be on the appropriate level of difficulty. The script should have from three to eight participants. Composing a script could be a fruitful cooperative learning project. However, students would need some guidance.

**2.** *Assign parts.* The parts can be either assigned by the teacher or decided upon by students.

▌Prepared scripts are available from Reader's Theater Script Service (P.O. Box 178333, San Diego, CA 92117). *Spotlight on Reader's Theater* (Phoenix Learning Resources, 2349 Chaffee Drive, St. Louis, MO 63146) features a series of twenty-seven plays organized around nine themes. Designed to integrate social studies and language arts, most of the plays focus on famous people or multicultural topics. Speaking parts vary in difficulty so that even poor readers will be able to participate.

*O*ne way of interpreting literature is by dramatizing it.

Introduce students to a variety of types of reading: short stories, novels, biographies, poems, plays, and informational pieces. Students may have a favored genre or may exclude informational text from their reading. They need to experience a full range of literary types.

According to the National Assessment of Educational Progress reading assessment results, students who are given time to read books of their own choosing in school have higher reading scores than those who don't (Donahue, Voekl, Campbell, & Mazzeo, 1999).

**3.** *Rehearse the script.* Although the scripts are read aloud, they should be rehearsed. Before students rehearse the scripts, they should have read and discussed the selection. As a group, students should decide how each part is to be read. Focus should be on interpreting the character's mood and feelings. Should a character sound angry, sad, or frightened? How are these emotions to be portrayed? Students then rehearse individually and as a group.

**4.** *Plan a performance.* Students decide where they want to stage their performance. Although no props are needed, they may want to place their scripts in colorful folders. They may use stools if they are available, or they may stand.

**Other dramatic activities.**   Students might also like to try improvisation, role-playing, and use of puppets. Role-playing works well with all ages but seems to work best with younger children, whereas improvisation seems to suit older children better. Using improvisation, students spontaneously dramatize a story or situation. Improvisation might be used to portray a character in a tale or extend a story. It might also be used to dramatize a concept in science or social studies.

## Nonfiction

### ■ Biographies

Although biographies generally rank poorly when students are asked to tell what types of books they like best, the lives of interesting and relevant subjects are often runaway favorites. Biographies of sports heroes and singing stars are among some of the most heavily circulated books in the children's departments of libraries.

When properly motivated, students show an intense, long-lasting interest in historical figures. In one elementary school, students were involved in reading and writing biographies for as long as three months. One fourth-grader, who was completing an intensive study of Benjamin Franklin, commented,

> I started writing this book in March and here I am still writing it. And believe me this is no piece of cake. I have to write it over and over to get it right. It's taking me a long time, but it's worth it. (Zarnowski, 1990, p. 18)

The key to motivating children to become interested in biography is to choose the right subject. Above all, the subject should have led an interesting life and should be someone that the students can relate to and care about.

## VOLUNTARY READING

The key to improved reading achievement is very simple: Encourage students to read ten minutes a day on their own. According to carefully conducted research, these extra ten minutes result in significant improvements in reading (Fielding, Wilson, & Anderson, 1986). Unfortunately, a nationally administered questionnaire revealed that fewer than half the nation's fourth-graders read for fun every day, and 13 percent never or hardly ever read for fun on their own time (Mullis, Campbell,

& Farstrup, 1993). Responding to the Motivation to Read Profile (Gambrell, Codling, & Palmer, 1996), 17 percent of the students reported that they would rather clean their rooms than read, 10 percent said that people who read are boring, and 14 percent stated that they would spend little time reading when they grew up.

What can be done to motivate children to read? First of all, demonstrate that reading is both personally fulfilling and fun, and put children in contact with books that they will enjoy. Attractive classroom libraries attract readers. In a large-scale study of children's reading, the classroom library was the major source of books for most of the children. Children also like to choose their books and they like to talk about them with other students and the teacher. Students frequently selected a book to read because a friend or a teacher had recommended it (Gambrell, Codling, & Palmer, 1996).

## Determining Interests and Attitudes

A good starting point for creating a voluntary reading program is to determine students' reading interests and their attitudes toward reading. Close observation of your students yields useful information about these areas—you probably have a good sense of who likes to read and who does not. Through observation, classroom discussions, and conversations with individual children, you probably also know who likes sports, who prefers mysteries, and who is interested in animals. An easy way to obtain an overview of the kinds of books your students might enjoy reading voluntarily is to duplicate several pages at their grade level from the catalog of a distributor of paperbacks or children's library books. Ask students to circle the ones that interest them. One experienced librarian recommended indirect questioning when exploring children's interests:

> The best way to learn what any child likes to read is to ask, but a direct question may not elicit clear information. A bit of probing may be necessary. What does he do with leisure time? What are his favorite television programs? The last good book he read? (Halstead, 1988, p. 35)

## The Classroom Library

Once you have a sense of what your class might like to read, start building a classroom library and involve students in the process. Propinquity is a primary principle in promoting voluntary reading. When books are close by and easy to check out, students will read more. The goal is to build a community of readers (Fielding, Wilson, & Anderson, 1986). If students feel they have a stake in the classroom library, they will be more highly motivated to read.

Invite students, their parents, and the community at large to contribute books to your classroom library. You might also be able to obtain some volumes from the school librarian and other local librarians. Students, as they get older, find paperbacks especially appealing. Paperbacks are also cheaper to buy and to replace if lost or damaged.

---

Children like to read about characters who are their own age or who are facing problems that are similar to theirs (Harris & Sipay, 1990). Humor is also enjoyed by children of all ages (Greenlaw, 1983). Animals and make-believe are ranked high by primary-grade students; middle-grade students, on the other hand, have a distinct preference for mystery, adventure, and sports.

Surveys and questionnaires might be used to complement data from observations. Two copyright-free, useful surveys of reading attitudes are the Motivation to Read Profile (MRP) (Gambrell, Codling, & Palmer, 1996) and the Elementary Reading Attitude Survey (ERAS) (McKenna & Kerr, 1990).

Many libraries make special provision for teachers and will loan one hundred or more books.

**USING TECHNOLOGY**

For information on the latest and best-selling children's books, consult the Web sites of online book stores, such as the ones listed below:

Amazon.com
**http://www.amazon.com/**

Barnes and Noble
**http://www.bn.com/**

### ■ Obtaining Books on a Variety of Levels

Students need reading material they can handle. Students are most likely to read on their own when they have books or periodicals that are interesting and when they feel competent enough to read the materials (Gambrell, Codling, & Palmer, 1996). Although students will read books that are beyond their level if they have a special interest in the subject, a steady diet of such books can be discouraging. Students are more likely to read a book all the way through if it is on their level. One study found that both good and poor readers chose books on the same level; however, a higher percentage of good readers finished their books (Anderson, Higgins, & Wurster, 1985). If the less able readers had selected books closer to their ability, perhaps they would have completed them.

### ■ Setting Up the Classroom Library

Make the classroom library as appealing as possible. Display books with their covers showing. You might also have special displays of books on high-interest topics. Update the collection periodically—at least once a month, add new titles to keep children interested.

One of the essentials that students learn from a classroom library is how to choose books. In informal research, P. Wilson (1992) noted that many students have difficulty selecting books during classroom visits to the library. They do not seem to know how to browse. Browsers are very selective about the books they read. They typically look through five books before choosing one and may later decide not to read the books that they have chosen. Having a classroom library with sufficient books to provide children with a genuine choice is important. Another way to promote wise selection among your students is to obtain books that children are genuinely interested in.

*S*tudents should have time during the day when they can read books of their own choosing.

### ■ Managing the Classroom Library

P. Wilson (1992) suggested that the teacher involve the poorest readers in helping with the management of the classroom collection. By helping display, advertise, and keep track of the collection, poor readers become familiar with its contents.

Involve students in setting up checkout procedures and rules. Keep the rules simple; if they are complicated and punitive, they will discourage borrowing (P. Wilson, 1986). Inevitably, some books will be lost or damaged. Consider this part of the cost of "doing business." Do not charge late fines or fees for lost or damaged books; these could be a genuine hardship for poor children. Instead, have a talk with students about being more responsible. If it is not a hardship, students could contribute replacement books, which do not necessarily have to have the same titles as the lost books. Put students in charge of keeping track of books; they can handle checking in, checking out, and putting books away.

## Setting Aside Time for Voluntary Reading

When provided with time for recreational reading, students learn that reading is important. Initially, the time set aside for voluntary reading may be only five minutes (Fader, 1977), but it can be lengthened gradually up to twenty or thirty minutes. Some classrooms, and even entire schools, adopt a program known as SSR. Although SSR originally stood for **Sustained Silent Reading,** it should probably be changed to Self-Selected Reading. Research suggests (Manning & Manning, 1984; Wilson, 1992) that students get more out of their reading and read more when they can share with their peers. Students should be allowed to discuss books in small groups, read with a buddy, dramatize the reading of a book in a small group, view a CD-ROM version of a book or listen to a taped version, or silently read a book in the traditional way. Adapted rules for SSR are listed below:

1. Each student is involved in reading.
2. The teacher reads or holds conferences or discussions with students.
3. Books to be read should be chosen before the session starts. (Students should choose two or three books, in case the original selection does not work out.)
4. A timer is used.
5. Absolutely no book reports are required. However students should keep a record of books read.

Young children may require special provisions during SSR. Kaissen (1987) observed that SSR works well with first-graders if several books are available to them, including those that have been read to them previously. In addition, books on the easiest levels and taped books should be available (see Appendix A). Kindergartners showed a preference for books that had been read to them that morning or earlier in the week (Gutkin, 1990).

## Modeling the Process of Selecting and Discussing Books

Some students have little experience choosing or discussing books. From time to time, tell them how you happened to select a book that you are reading. Discuss how you got a sense of its contents by examining the cover, finding out who the author is, reading the blurb on the jacket, glancing through the book, and reading selected parts. For younger students, you might also post the book selection suggestions noted in Figure 8.6.

At the end of each SSR seesion, briefly discuss with students the books or other materials they have been reading. To help students who have difficulty sharing, model the

■ **Sustained Silent Reading** (SSR) is a period in which all the students and the teacher in a class or everyone in a whole school read materials of their own choosing.

We want children to read the best that has been written. However, students must be allowed to choose what they wish to read. Once students experience the joy of reading, then, through skillful guidance, they might be led to experience high-quality literature.

**FIGURE 8.6**

**Choosing Boooks**

■ Does the book look interesting?

■ Is the book about as hard as other books I have read?

■ Can I read most of the words?

■ Can I understand what the book is saying?

**ADAPTING INSTRUCTION for *STRUGGLING READERS and WRITERS***

Some struggling readers select books that are too difficult because they want to read the same books that their friends are reading, even though these books may be well beyond their capability. Have available in your classroom library books that are interesting but easy. From time to time, highlight these books and allow everyone to read them so they don't become stigmatized as being "baby books."

A major benefit of sharing is that students recommend books to each other. Students are more likely to read a book when it is recommended by a friend than when it is suggested by a parent, teacher, or librarian (Gallo, 1985).

An effective reinforcer for voluntary reading is to have students keep a record of their reading. This might be a simple list, a wheel, or a graph showing number of books read, number of pages read, or number of minutes spent reading. Since students differ in reading speed, and number of words on a page varies, the fairest measurement might be number of minutes spent reading rather than number of pages read.

process by talking about a book that you are reading. Also ask about their books so that they realize that in a community of readers, people share their reading.

## Activities for Motivating Voluntary Reading

To motivate voluntary reading, be enthusiastic, accepting, and flexible. Present reading as an interesting, vital activity. Include a wide range of material from comics to classics. Do not present books as vitamins, saying, "Read them. They're good for you." Share reading with students in the same way that you might share with friends. By doing so, you are accepting students as serious readers. Above all, be a reader yourself. Some activities for motivating voluntary reading follow:

■ *Match books with interests.* Make casual, personal recommendations. For a Gary Soto fan, you might say, "Joe, I know you enjoy Gary Soto's books. The school library has a new book by him. I read it, and it's very interesting."

■ *Use the indirect approach.* Choose a book that would be appropriate for your students and that you would enjoy reading. Carry the book to class with you. Mention that it is interesting to read. Tell students that they can borrow it when you're finished. Or you may just want to carry the book around and see how many inquiries you get.

■ *Pique students' interest.* Read a portion of a book and stop at a cliff-hanging moment; then tell students that they can read the rest themselves if they want to find out what happened.

■ *Use videotapes to preview books.* Show a portion of a videotape of a book that has been made into a movie; then encourage students to find out what happened by reading the book. (First, be sure that the book is available to students.)

■ *Substitute voluntary reading for workbook or other seatwork assignments.* The Center for the Study of Reading (1990) made the following statement: "Independent, silent reading can fulfill many of the same functions as workbook activities—it permits students to practice what they are learning, and it keeps the rest of the class occupied while you meet with a small group of students" (p. 5).

## HELP FOR STRUGGLING READERS AND WRITERS

Because they are reading below grade level, struggling readers may experience difficulty handling literary selections. If they are not reading too far below the level of the selection, providing them with additional help with difficult vocabulary and concepts might make it possible for them to read the text successfully. Reading all or part of the selection to them or obtaining an audiotape or CD-ROM version of the text is another possibility. However, one reason struggling readers are behind is because they typically read less. They should also be given quality selections on their reading level so they have the experience of reading on their own. This is easier to do if you use an approach that features self-selection.

For voluntary reading, make sure you have a variety of high-interest materials on levels that would be appropriate for your struggling readers. Because some students would rather clean their rooms than read, have available intriguing, highly motivating materials: joke and riddle books; sports biographies and animal books that are heavily illustrated but have limited text; high-interest periodicals, such as *Chickadees*; books on CD-ROM; and books that incorporate activities, such as a book on magnets that is accompanied by magnets.

 ## ESSENTIAL STANDARDS

### Kindergarten
*Students will*

- listen and respond to a variety of classic and current literary works.
- identify characters, setting, and important plot events.
- listen, speak, and read to gain knowledge of their own culture, the culture of others, and the common elements of cultures.
- listen to one or two books read aloud at school and one or two books read at home or in an after-school care program.
- "read" alone, with a partner, or with an adult two to four familiar books a day.

### First and second grades
*Students will*

- listen to or read and understand and appreciate a variety of types of literary selections.
- describe key elements in a selection, such as characters, setting, story problem, and plot.
- respond to literary selections in writing, art, movement, or drama, and in discussion groups.
- compare and contrast different versions of the same tale and works by different authors and connect ideas and themes across texts.
- identify and appreciate literary techniques, such as rhythm, rhyme, alliteration, and imaginative use of language.
- learn basic literary techniques such as using dialog and action to develop characters.
- recite, read aloud with expression, or dramatize poems, stories, and plays.
- listen, speak, and read to gain knowledge of his or her own culture, the culture of others, and the common elements of cultures.
- read and enjoy a variety of books and periodicals.
- read to acquire information that is important to them.

**INVOLVING PARENTS**

Richgels and Wold (1998) involved parents of first-graders in their children's reading by sending home "Three for the Road" backpacks. Each backpack contained three books, three sock puppets that students could use to talk about their reading, a response book, markers and pencils, a letter to parents, and suggestions for using the backpack. Parents and their children were invited to compose a response.

**USING TECHNOLOGY**

Authors and Illustrators on the Web lists author sites. **http://www.acs. ucalgary.ca/~dkbrown/ authors.html8-666a** HarperCollins also provides links to its authors as do some of the other publishers. **http://www. harperchildrens.com/ index.htm**

To help children build personal libraries, use books as awards for winners of food drives, writing competitions, and other school contests.

■ read two to four short books or other texts such as poems or songs each day alone or with assistance or read one or two brief chapter books each day.

### Third and fourth grades
*Students will*

■ understand and appreciate a variety of types of literary selections.

■ respond to literary selections in writing, art, movement, or drama, and in discussion groups.

■ support responses and conclusions by referring back to the text.

■ determine the underlying theme in a selection and connect ideas and themes across texts.

■ learn advanced literary techniques, such as using metaphors, similes, and symbols.

■ use a set of increasingly sophisticated standards to evaluate literary works.

■ read and discuss to gain knowledge of their own culture, the culture of others, and the common elements of cultures.

■ read and enjoy a variety of books and periodicals.

■ read to acquire information that is important to them.

■ read the equivalent of thirty chapter books a year (third-graders) or the equivalent of twenty-five full-length books (fourth-graders). (Some standards have been adapted from the Texas, California, and New Standards.)

 ## ASSESSMENT

Based on your observations and students' written and oral responses, assess whether they appreciate and respond on a personal and aesthetic level to works of literature. Through their responses, also determine whether or not they are becoming knowledgeable about techniques used in creating literature and whether they are acquiring standards for judging literary selections. As far as reading for enjoyment

 ### ACTION PLAN

1. Use a reader response approach to literature. Through focusing on personal response, foster in students enjoyment of and appreciation for literature.
2. Introduce students to a variety of genres and authors.
3. Use class discussions, literature discussion groups, journals, dramatizations, and art to foster responses to literature.

4. Involve students in the establishment and management of a classroom library. Encourage students to read widely and frequently. Encourage them to share their responses to reading with friends, classmates, and family.
5. Obtain materials on a variety of levels and topics so that all students have a choice of appealing but readable materials.

and personal satisfaction, note whether students choose to read books on their own and talk about books. Note whether they have a favorite book or a favorite author. Look over students' reading logs and journals to see how much students are reading, what they are reading, and how they are responding to their reading. You might also use the Motivation to Read Profile (Gambrell, Codling, & Palmer, 1996) or the Elementary Reading Attitude Survey (McKenna & Kerr, 1990) to obtain additional information about students' reading attitudes and habits.

## SUMMARY

1. Until recently, reading was looked upon as primarily being a skills subject. Today, the emphasis is definitely on reading quality material.
2. Reading literature involves fostering appreciation and enjoyment as well as understanding. The teacher's stance becomes an aesthetic one. Focus is on eliciting a personal response and valuing students' interpretations.
3. Students should read a variety of types of literature: folklore, poetry, novels, plays, and biography.

4. Just ten minutes a day of voluntary reading results in significant gains in reading achievement. To promote voluntary reading, demonstrate that it is enjoyable and personally fulfilling.
5. For struggling readers, make adaptations so that they have access to literary selections that the class is reading. To foster voluntary reading, provide for students' interests and reading levels. Have available joke, riddle, and other appealing but easy-to-read books.

## EXTENDING AND APPLYING

1. Read at least three current anthologies of children's poetry. Which poems did you like best? Which do you think would appeal to your students?
2. With a group of classmates, start a literature discussion group in which you discuss children's books.
3. Create a lesson in which you introduce a poem, play, or other literary piece. In your lesson, stress

appreciation, enjoyment, and personal response. Teach the lesson and evaluate it.
4. Try out one of the suggestions listed in this chapter or an idea of your own for increasing voluntary reading. Implement the idea and evaluate its effectiveness.

## DEVELOPING A PROFESSIONAL PORTFOLIO

Document your ability to develop an understanding and appreciation of literary works by composing a written description of a literature unit. If possible, illustrate the description with photos of students in discussion groups or photos of presentations. Also include samples of students' literature logs, dialogue journals, or other responses to literature.

## DEVELOPING A RESOURCE FILE

1. Keep a card or computer database file of high-quality chapter books and novels that you feel would appeal to students you are teaching or plan to teach. Include bibliographic information, summaries of the selections, some questions you might ask about the work, and some ideas for extension activities.
2. Keep a file of activities that might be used to motivate students to read.

9

# Approaches to
# Teaching Reading

*F*or each of the following statements related to the chapter you are about to read, put a check under "Agree" or "Disagree" to show how you feel. Discuss your responses with classmates before you read the chapter.

|   |  | *Agree* | *Disagree* |
|---|---|---|---|
| **1** | A structured approach to reading is most effective. | _____ | _____ |
| **2** | Extensive reading of children's books should be a part of every elementary school reading program. | _____ | _____ |
| **3** | Teacher and method are equally important. | _____ | _____ |
| **4** | A writing approach to reading works best with young children. | _____ | _____ |
| **5** | An individualized reading program would be hard to manage. | _____ | _____ |
| **6** | A commercial reading program, such as a basal, is best for new teachers because it shows them step by step how to teach reading. | _____ | _____ |
| **7** | Teachers should combine the best parts of each reading approach. | _____ | _____ |
| **8** | Teachers should be free to choose the approach to reading that they feel works best. | _____ | _____ |

## USING WHAT YOU KNOW

*T*here are really just two main ways of learning to read: by reading and by writing, or some combination of the two. The approach that uses writing is known as language experience. Reading approaches use textbooks (including basal anthologies and linguistic reading series) and children's books. Children's books are used in the individualized and literature-based approaches. Of course, these approaches can also be combined in various ways. Teachers who use basals often supplement their programs with language-experience stories and children's books.

Which of these approaches are you familiar with? What are the characteristics of the approaches? What are their advantages? Their disadvantages?

##  CHANGING APPROACHES TO TEACHING READING

Until recently, reading was considered a skills subject. It did not really matter what students read. Today, content is paramount, the idea being that students' minds and lives will be greatly enriched if they read the best that has been written.

In a little more than a decade, there have been two dramatic changes in reading instruction. Up until the mid-1980s, most of the nation's children were taught through basal readers. However, a holistic movement espousing the use of children's books to teach reading took hold. There was a switch from basals to children's literature and from structured teaching to a more naturalistic approach to literacy. Now, after more than a decade in which skills were downplayed in many areas, there is a movement to teach a balanced approach in which skills instruction and reading of good literature are integrated. Basal readers have also made a comeback. They are more skills oriented than ever. However, they also advocate use of high-quality literary selections and feature extensive libraries of children's literature.

Regardless of whether they are holistic or balanced, effective approaches incorporate the basic principles of teaching literacy that have been emphasized throughout this book:

- Children become readers and writers by reading and writing.
- Reading programs should include a rich variety of interesting, appropriate material and should stress a great deal of reading and writing.
- Strategies should be presented that promote independence in word recognition and comprehension.
- Reading programs should be language based. Provision should be made for developing speaking and listening as well as reading and writing skills.
- Because reading fosters writing development and writing fosters reading development, literacy programs should develop both.
- Provision should be made for individual differences. Because students differ in terms of interests, abilities, learning rate, experiential background, and culture, the approach used should take into consideration the needs of all students.
- Students' progress should be monitored, and provision should be made for helping students fully develop their potential.

This chapter examines the major approaches to teaching reading and writing. Each approach has its strengths and weaknesses. Suggestions are made for adapting each of the approaches to take advantage of its strengths and compensate for its weaknesses. For instance, suggestions are made for making the basal approach more holistic. Thus, if it has been mandated that you use a basal but you prefer a holistic approach, you can adapt your instruction to make the program more holistic and still keep within the guidelines of the school or school district that employs you.

■ A **basal reading program** is a comprehensive program of teaching reading that includes readers or anthologies that gradually increase in difficulty, teacher's manuals, workbooks, and assessment measures.

##  BASAL APPROACH

How were you taught to read? Chances are you were taught through a **basal reading program.** Basal readers are the main approach to teaching reading in the United States. A complex package based on a relatively simple concept, the basal program includes a series of readers, or anthologies, and supplementary materials that gradually increase in difficulty and act as stepping stones along a path that begins with emergent literacy and extends through sixth-grade reading. Accompanying teacher's manuals provide guidance so that the classroom teacher can lead students upward.

Basal readers have changed from the time when you were in elementary school. Costing 100 million dollars or more to produce, today's basals are created by only the largest of the educational publishers. Whereas there were more than a dozen basals just a few decades ago, today there are only five. But the most dramatic change in basals is not the consolidation that has taken place in the industry, but the change in the way word-analysis skills are presented. For most of the twentieth century, the major basals advocated an analytic approach in which letter sounds were never isolated and there was heavy reliance on the use of the initial consonant of a word and context. Selections were chosen on the basis of topic or literary quality, so they didn't reinforce the phonics elements that had been taught. Today, all of the basals use a systematic approach to phonics in which students are taught to say individual sounds and blend them, and they apply skills in selections that incorporate the elements that have been presented.

During the 1980s and 1990s, basal readers lost some of their popularity. Many teachers began using children's books rather than basals. Basal reader publishers reacted swiftly and decisively. Today's basals feature the best in children's literature and also contain extensive libraries of trade books. Basal readers are once again being used to teach reading in more than 90 percent of America's elementary school classrooms. However, many teachers complement the use of basals with trade books.

Today's basals place greater emphasis on providing for all students. Basals of the 1990s emphasized quality literature and whole-class teaching. For struggling readers these more difficult selections were an obstacle (Hoffman et al., 1998). Today's basals have made specific provision for below-average, average, and above-average achievers. Basals have also became more language based. Today's basals generally include writing and spelling along with reading and are known as literacy, rather than reading, series.

In fact, basal systems offer an embarrassment of riches. In addition to anthologies, related workbooks, and detailed teacher's manuals packed with teaching suggestions, basals offer big books, supplementary libraries of the best in children's books, read-aloud books, a wide array of games and manipulatives, audiotapes, computer software, videodiscs, inservice programs, posters, charts, supplementary spelling and language books, a wide variety of unit and end-of-book tests, placement tests, observation guides, portfolio systems, Web sites, and more.

▌Producing a basal program is a three-year undertaking involving fifteen to twenty program authors, consultants, editors, writers, teacher advisors, student advisors, designers, artists, and publishers' representatives and consultants (Singleton, 1997).

▌The latest basals, which are in a cycle of almost constant revision, attempt to implement recent research and feature the most popular children's authors. They include high-quality literature, elaborate illustrations, and up-to-date teaching strategies.

*T*oday's basals feature anthologies containing a rich variety of children's literature.

Clearly, today's basals are bigger and better than ever. But the real question is "Are today's basals good enough?" Considering all that is known about reading and writing, have basal publishers composed the kinds of programs that will help students reach their fullest potential? Have the basals done an effective job implementing research and promising practices? The answer is yes and no. Basals have many advantages, but they also have some shortcomings.

## Advantages of Basals

Basals offer teachers a convenient package of materials, techniques, and assessment devices, as well as a plan for orchestrating the various components of a total literacy program. In their anthologies, which, for the most part, gradually increase in difficulty, basals offer students a steady progression from emergent literacy through a sixth-grade reading level. They also offer varied reading selections, an abundance of practice material, carefully planned units and lessons, and a wealth of follow-up and enrichment activities.

## Disadvantages of Basals

Despite a major overhaul, basals are still driven by the same engine. The core of the basal program is the trio of anthology, workbook, and manual. Although the contents of the anthology are much improved, its function remains the same—to provide a base of materials for all students to move through. However, students have diverse interests and abilities and progress at different rates. Although basal selections are meant to be of high quality, they will not all be of interest to all students. The sports biography that delights one child is a total bore to another. A second shortcoming has to do with the way basal readers are assembled: They are anthologies and often contain excerpts from whole books. For example, the fourth-grade reader from a typical series contains "The Diary of Leigh Botts," a delightful tale of a budding young writer that is excerpted from Beverly Cleary's 1983 Newbury Award winner, *Dear Mr. Henshaw.* If reading the excerpt is worthwhile, reading the whole book should be even better.

There is also the question of pacing and time spent with a selection. Students often move through basals in lockstep fashion. Part of the problem is the nature of the teacher's guides; they offer too much of a good thing. Stories and even poems are overtaught. There are too many questions asked before a selection is read, too many asked after the piece has been read, and too many follow-up activities. A class might spend three to five days on a thousand-word story. To be fair, the guides do present activities as choices. Teachers can choose those that they wish to undertake and omit the others. Teachers may even be provided a choice of ways of presenting a story: interactively with the teacher modeling strategies, independently with the teacher providing a minimum of assistance, or with support, which means that students follow along as the teacher reads the story. All in all, the typical basal lesson has many fine suggestions, but the ideas are "canned," that is, created by someone in an editorial office far from the classroom. Designed to be all things to all

> Although basals may offer excerpts of selections, the manuals in basal series feature bibliographies of whole texts so that children might read the entire works on their own. Each series also offers supplementary libraries of whole texts.

**USING TECHNOLOGY**

Information about the major basal series is available on the following sites:

Harcourt School Publishers
**http://www.hbschool.com/**

Houghton Mifflin
**http://www.eduplace.com/**

Macmillan/McGraw-Hill
**http://www.mmhschool.com/teach/reading/index.html**

Open Court
**http://www.sra-4kids.com/**

Scott Foresman
**http://www.sfreading.com**

teachers, the activities are not designed for a specific class of students having specific needs and interests.

Perhaps the biggest disadvantage of basals is the organizational pattern they suggest. Basal reading series have core selections in anthologies and also supplementary reading in libraries of leveled readers. The core basal selections are presented to the whole class. The selections will generally be appropriate for average students but may lack sufficient challenge for the best readers and will be too hard for as many as the one student out of four in the typical classroom who is reading below grade level. Suggestions are made for adapting instruction for all learners. This may mean reading selections to the poorest readers or providing them with audio versions of the selection so that they can read along. Only two of the basal systems (Harcourt & Houghton Mifflin) offer an alternative selection for struggling readers, which is related to the theme in the core selection but is easier to read. However, all of the series have sets of books on three levels—easy, average, and challenging—so that struggling readers will be reading on their level at least some of the time. Even so, this means that for series that fail to provide alternative core selections, struggling readers will be given fewer opportunities to read at their level.

> Currently, most basals recommend that all students experience the same selection, but that steps be taken to provide extra help for those students who might find the selection to be too difficult, perhaps even reading it to them. Guided reading is also recommended. In guided reading, students are instructed in small groups and read materials on their level.

## Adapting Basals

Despite the criticisms voiced here and elsewhere, there is nothing intrinsically wrong with basals. Over the years, thousands of teachers have successfully used basals to teach millions of children. However, in keeping with today's research and promising practices, basals should be adapted in the following ways.

Although basal manuals have been criticized as being too didactic (K. S. Goodman, 1994), the fault may be with the professionals who them. Manuals and, in fact, the entire basal program should be viewed as a resource. The manual is a treasure chest of ideas, and the anthologies are good, representative collections of children's literature. As professionals, we should feel free to use those selections that seem appropriate and to use the manual as a resource rather than a guide. Select only those suggestions and activities that seem appropriate and effective. Other adaptations that might be made to make basals more effective include the following:

> Four of the five basals offer teachers a variety of instructional choices. However, one basal, Open Court, is scripted. It tells teachers what to say and offers a tightly structured sequence of teaching activities. Although novice teachers might welcome the guidance, veteran teachers may desire more flexibility, despite the good results that this series often obtains.

- *Emphasize real writing and real reading.* Basal activities in which children write a letter to a storybook character or reread a story to practice reading in phrases or to reinforce new vocabulary words are exercises (Edelsky, 1994). They do not constitute reading and writing for real purposes. Where feasible, students should write letters that get mailed and respond openly to stories and poems. They should also be involved in setting their own purposes for reading and writing.
- *Workbooks should be used judiciously.* They play both management and instructional roles. Students can work in them independently while the teacher meets with a small group or individual children. Workbooks can also provide students with additional practice and yield information that the teacher can use to assess children's progress (Adoption Guidelines Project, 1990). If a work-

> Reading easy books independently provides students with much needed practice. "Clocking up reading mileage on easy materials is one of the most important aspects of independent reading" (Learning Media, 1991, p. 76).

book exercise fails to measure up, it should be skipped. The teacher should provide alternative activities, such as having the students read children's books or work in learning centers.

■ *Emphasize wide reading of a variety of materials.* No matter how well the basal has been put together, students need to read a broader range of fiction and nonfiction materials, including books, magazines, newspapers, sets of directions, brochures, ads, menus, schedules, and other real-world materials. Make use of the extensive libraries of children's books offered by basal publishers to supplement the basal materials; excellent suggestions for additional reading are also provided in basal manuals.

■ *Focus on a few key skills or strategies.* Teach and use these in context. Today's basal readers offer instruction in a wide variety of skills or strategies. In trying to cover so many areas, they typically spread themselves too thin and so fail to present crucial skills in sufficient depth. It may take twenty lessons or more before students are able to draw inferences or infer main ideas, but a basal might present just two or three lessons.

■ *Provide opportunities for struggling readers to read appropriate-level material every day.* Make use of the supplementary programs or leveled libraries designed for struggling readers.

■ *Gradually take control of your program.* Decide what your philosophy of teaching literacy is. List the objectives that you feel are important, aligning them, of course, with the standards set by your school and school district. If possible, work with other professionals to create a literacy program that makes sense for your situation. Consider basals as only one source of materials and teaching ideas. Basals are neither a method nor an approach to teaching reading. They are simply a carefully crafted set of materials. The core of the reading program is the teacher. It is the teacher who should decide how and when to use basals and whether to choose alternative materials.

## Phonic–Linguistic Basals

■ A **linguistic patterns** approach is a way of teaching reading that emphasizes the regularities of the language by presenting regularly spelled patterns first. It also presents patterns by comparing and contrasting words that have minimal differences so that students can see how they differ (*pat–pan*). Although linguistic programs aren't used by many classroom teachers, they are frequently employed by remedial specialists. Today's major basals also use a pattern approach in their beginning levels.

Several minor basals, such as *Reading Mastery* (also known as *Distar*) (SRA) and *Merrill Linguistic Readers* (SRA), have been written specifically to reinforce phonic elements or **linguistic patterns.** These series feature tightly controlled vocabulary and are used primarily in programs for struggling readers. As a result of the tightly controlled vocabulary, the selections are highly contrived and stilted. Because the selections are contrived, it is difficult for students to use context clues.

## Selecting a Basal

Selecting a basal is a major decision. Ideally, the selection should be made by a committee that includes teachers, students, parents, administrators, and the school's reading/language arts specialist. The first order of business should be listing the schools' or district's literacy goals and then examining materials in light of those goals. One of the best ways to assess a set of materials is to try it out before making a final decision.

## Minibook Series

A number of beginning-reading programs consist of kits of minibooks that gradually grow in difficulty. The kits ease children into reading and move them from emergent to fluent reading. Books at the emergent stage are designed so that students can enjoy books before they can actually read them. Illustrations help children predict what the text might say. The text itself is brief, often consisting of a single sentence that contains a repetitive phrase. Each page of the book might contain the same repeated phrase. The books are read through shared reading, and eventually students can, with the help of illustrations, read the books on their own. At this point, students are primarily "reading" pictures rather than text. The intent is to emphasize reading for enjoyment and meaning. Of course, they are also picking up concepts about print.

After students have enjoyed a number of books and shown an interest in reading print, text-reading strategies are introduced. Difficulty and length of text are carefully controlled so that students gradually grow into reading. As students gain in skill, they move into more challenging stages. Some of the best-known kits include *Story Box* (The Wright Group), *Sunshine Series* (The Wright Group), and *Literacy 2000* (Rigby). One drawback of these kits is that they fail to reinforce decoding patterns. A series that provides reinforcement for phonics patterns without resorting to tongue-twisting tales is *Ready Readers* (Modern Curriculum Press). Minibook kits enjoy widespead use, especially in grade one, and are often used as supplements to a basal or other approach. In fact, all of the basal series have available supplementary kits of easy-to-read booklets. However, supplementary booklets in today's basals feature decodable texts at the early levels.

## LITERATURE-BASED APPROACH

More and more teachers are using literature as the core of their programs. Today's basal anthologies feature high-quality selections drawn from children's literature. Increasingly, basals are including children's books in their entirety as an integral part of the package or a recommended component. Although there is some overlap between a basal program and a literature-based approach, the term **literature-based approach** is used here to describe programs in which teachers use sets of children's books as a basis for providing instruction in literacy. A major advantage of this approach is that teachers, independently or in committees, choose the books they wish to use with their students so the reading material can be tailored to students' interests and needs.

A literature-based program may be organized in a variety of ways. Three popular models of organizing literature instruction include core literature, text sets, and thematic units.

■ The **literature-based approach** is a way of teaching reading in which literary selections are the major instructional materials.

## Core Literature

■ **Core literature** is a piece
of literature selected to be
read and analyzed by the
whole class. In a core book
approach, students read the
same book.

**Core literature** is literature that has been selected for a careful, intensive reading. Core selections are often read by the whole class, but may be read by selected groups. Core literature pieces might include such children's classics as *The Little House* (Burton, 1942), *Aesop's Fables*, or more recent works, such as *The Keeping Quilt* (Rev.) (Polacco, 2001) or *Days of the Ducklings* (McMillan, 2001).

In addition to providing students with a rich foundation in the best of children's literature, the use of core selections also builds community (Ford, 1994). It gives students a common experience, thereby providing the class with common ground for conversations about selections and also a point of reference for comparing and contrasting a number of selections. The use of core literature should help boost the self-esteem of the poorer readers, who are often given less mature or less significant reading material. As Cox and Zarillo (1993) noted, in the core book model, "no child is denied access to the best of children's literature" (p. 109).

## Exemplary Teaching

### Literature-Based Instruction

*C*oming to a second-grade classroom composed primarily of poor children, many of whom were reading on a beginning reading level, researcher James Baumann set up a balanced literature-based program that was based on three principles: reading of high-quality children's books, explicit instruction in skills and strategies, and engaging in a significant amount of reading and writing each day.

The program was implemented through a series of routines that included reading aloud to students; intensive instruction in skills and strategies; providing students opportunities to read and discuss; high-quality literature selections; providing time for self-selected, independent reading; and conducting writer's workshops. In addition, Baumann related reading and writing, used a variety of grouping patterns so that individual needs were met, and conducted a study buddies program with the fifth-grade class next door. In the study buddies program, half of Baumann's class went next door to meet their study buddies. The other half stayed where they were, and the study buddies came to them. During the thirty-minute sessions, the second-graders worked on reading and writing with the help of their study buddies.

Baumann made use of a wide variety of techniques, including reading aloud, shared reading, choral reading, direct instruction, functional phonics lessons, and directed reading activities. Although explicit instruction was stressed, it was conducted within the context of real reading or writing. Baumann also used an 80–20 rule in which 80 percent of the time was spent reading and 20 percent was spent in skills/strategy instruction.

Working closely with parents, Baumann kept them informed about their children's progress and the work that the class was doing. In notes sent home and in formal and informal conferences, parents were given suggestions for supporting their children's work. To foster reading at home, Baumann invited the children to take turns taking home Read-With-Lion and Molly, the Read-With-Me Monkey. Both stuffed animals had a pocket to hold a book and a parent card describing techniques that the parents might use to share the book with the child.

Assessment was conducted through observation, interviews, and examination of samples of the children's work. An abbreviated informal reading inventory was also administered. Based on inventory results, children gained an average of two years. More importantly, they became avid readers. As Baumann commented, "They read up a storm" (Baumann & Duffy, 1997; Baumann & Ivey, 1997).

However, there are some obvious problems with the core literature approach. Children are diverse in interests and abilities. What is exciting to one child may be boring to another. An easy read for one child may be an overwhelming task for another. Careful selection of core books with universal appeal should take care of the interest factor. It is difficult, for instance, to imagine any child not being intrigued by the Frog and Toad books. Selections can also be presented in such a way as to be accessible to all. Suggestions for presenting texts to students of varying abilities can be found in Chapter 12.

## Text Sets

**Text sets** are related books. Reading text sets fosters the making of connections. When connections are made, the reading of all related texts is enriched (Harste, Short, & Burke, 1988). In addition to deepening readers' background, text sets broaden readers' framework for thinking about literature. Having read two or more related books, they can compare and contrast them. Discussions are also enlivened because students have more to talk about. If students read books on the same topic, understanding can be developed in greater depth.

■ A **text set** is a series of related books. Because the books are related, reading and comparing them deepens the reader's understanding of the theme or topic of the text set.

## Thematic Units

Another model of literature-based instruction is the **unit,** which has a theme or other unifying element. Its unifying element may be the study of a particular author, a genre—mystery or picture books, for example—or a theme. Themes might include such diverse topics as heroes, distant places, sports and hobbies, animals, teddy bears, friendship, plants, or pets. A unit's theme may involve only the language arts, or it may cut across the curriculum and include social studies, science, math, and the visual and performing arts.

■ A **unit** is a way of organizing instruction around a central idea, topic, or focus.

Thematic organization has a number of advantages, the principal one being that it helps students make connections among reading, writing, listening, speaking, and viewing activities and among different pieces of literature. If there is integration with other subjects, even broader and more numerous connections can be constructed. However, Routman (1991) cautioned that before the language arts are integrated with content-area subjects, they should first be integrated with each other.

Routman (1991) also warned that some thematic units lack depth and "are nothing more than suggested activities clustered around a central focus or topic" (p. 277). In her judgment, this is correlation rather than integration. In order for true integration to occur, there must be some overall concepts or understandings that the unit develops, with activities designed to support those concepts or understandings. For instance, a unit may revolve around famous people, with students reading and writing about such people, but the unit would not be truly integrated unless the reading and related activities developed a genuine theme or core idea. "Famous people" is a topic rather than a theme because it does not express a unifying idea. Some unifying ideas include "Successful people have had to overcome obstacles on their way to success" or "Successful people have many characteristics in common." An excellent way to integrate such a unit is to create broad questions to be answered by students: "What are the secrets of success?" or "What are successful people like?" Ideally, these are questions that students have had a hand in creating. As part of the unit's activities, students read about successful people, then interview and write about them in order to integrate information from the unit and answer broad questions. They might also look at successful people in science, social studies, and the arts. The suggested procedure for creating and implementing a thematic unit follows:

**1.** *Select a topic or theme that you wish to explore.* When deciding upon a theme, select one that encompasses concepts that are an important part of the curriculum and that will facilitate the development of essential language arts goals. The theme should be significant and interesting to students. It might be a unit on transportation entitled "The World Is Getting Smaller," which has as its theme, "Today's Transportation Has Changed the World." Or it might be a unit on the impact of traditions or the value of pets or the meaning of friendship.

**2.** *Involve students in the planning.* Determine through a modified KWL or similar technique what they know about the topic and what they would like to learn. For instance, having decided on the theme "Trucks help us in many ways," place the word *trucks* on the board and ask students what comes to mind when they think of trucks. List and discuss their responses. You might then ask them what they would like to learn about trucks and list these items.

**3.** *State the overall ideas that you wish the unit to emphasize.* Include questions that your students might have about the topic (Routman, 1991). Your unit might focus on three overall or big ideas: the many different kinds of trucks, the many jobs that trucks do, and the people who drive trucks. Also, compose a list of language arts objectives. What literary appreciations and comprehension, study, and writing or other skills/strategies will the unit develop? These objectives should tie in with the unit's big ideas. They should help students understand the variety of trucks and the kinds of jobs that trucks do and the skills of the people who drive them. Included in the list of skill/strategy objectives are reading skills, such as comparing and contrasting, using graphics, summarizing, and writing skills, such as expository writing, that students need in order to explore the unit's themes and complete unit activities. Because the unit is interdisciplinary, objectives are listed for each content area.

**4.** *Decide on the reading materials and activities that will be included in the unit.* Using a semantic map or web, show how you might integrate each of the language arts. Show, too, how you might integrate science, social studies, and other areas. Each activity should advance the theme or the major ideas of the unit. Activities should also promote skill/strategy development in the language arts and other areas. For instance, in the unit, students working in small groups will select the kind of truck they would like to explore and create a children's book telling about the truck.

**5.** *List and gather resources, including materials to be read, centers to be set up, audiovisual aids, and guest speakers or resource personnel.* Be sure to work closely with the school media specialist to obtain materials. *Big Rigs: Giants of the Highway* (Robbins,

---

For a unit on trees, the major understandings that teacher Elaine Weiner wanted to emphasize were "We cannot live on earth without trees" and "Trees provide shade, beauty, paper, homes for animals, and more" (Routman, 1991, p. 278).

---

As you plan a unit, focus on the theme rather than activities. Given the unit's theme and major concepts, ask: "What activities will best help students acquire an understanding of the unit's theme and major concepts?" (Lipson, Valencia, Wixson, & Peters, 1993).

---

A core book, a text set, or books chosen by a literature discussion group could also be the focus of a unit. The unit would then consist of the reading of the core book, text set, or literature discussion book(s), and the completion of related activities.

2002), *Fire Trucks* (Stille, 2002), and the award winning *How Many Trucks Can a Tow Truck Tow?* (Pomerantz, 1987) are a few of the possible books on trucks that might be read. Materials chosen will vary in difficulty so that all students might have materials on an appropriate level of challenge.

**6.** *Plan a unit opener that will set the stage for the unit.* It could be the showing of a film or video, a reading of a poem or the first chapter of one of the books, or it might be a simulation. Students might pretend that they are driving across country in a big rig.

**7.** *Evaluate.* Evaluation should be broad-based and keyed into the objectives that you have set for your students or that they have set for themselves in collaboration with you. It should include the unit's major concepts or understandings as well as skills and strategies that were emphasized. For example, if the ability to visualize was emphasized, it needs to be assessed. If you emphasized the ability to write an expository piece, that might be assessed through holistic evaluation of students' booklets. As part of the evaluation, you must decide whether students learned the concepts and skills or strategies listed in the objectives. If not, reteaching is in order. In addition, you should evaluate the unit itself and determine what might be done to improve the unit. You might eliminate activities or materials that proved boring or ineffective and revise other elements as necessary.

## Choosing Materials

One of the most important tasks in structuring a literature-based program is choosing the books. If the program is to be schoolwide or districtwide, teachers at each grade level should meet and decide which books might be offered at each grade level. Quality and appeal of the materials must be considered. Teachers also have to think about students' reading abilities, with easy, average, and challenging books provided for each grade. All genres should be included: novels, short stories, poems, plays, myths, and well-written informational books. And, of course, students should have a voice in the selection of books to be read.

## Advantages and Disadvantages of a Literature-Based Approach

The primary advantage of a literature-based approach is that books can be chosen to meet students' needs and interests. The major disadvantage of a literature-based program is that fine literature may be misused, by being made simply a means for developing reading skills rather than a basis for fostering personal response and an aesthetic sense. A second major disadvantage is that

Units may encompass a single area, such as language arts or social studies, or they may be integrated and cut across subject matter areas. Integrated units apply the language arts to one or more content areas. The focus is on a theme, problem, or central question. Curriculum lines are dropped, and all activities are devoted to that topic.

**USING TECHNOLOGY**

Children's Literature: Electronic Journals & Book Reviews contains a variety of sources for reviews of children's books.
http://www.acs.ucalgary.ca/~dkbrown/journals.html

*I*n a literature-based approach, students read whole books by well-known authors.

**USING TECHNOLOGY**
Children's Publishers on the Internet lists a variety of sites maintained by publishers of children's books. Some of the sites also include free teaching guides and other instructional resources.
**http://www.acs. ucalgary.ca/~dkbrown/ publish.html**

the books chosen may not be equally appealing to all students and some books may be too difficult for struggling readers.

## Adapting a Literature-Based Approach

In a literature-based approach, selections can be read in one of three ways: whole class, small group, or individually. Whole-class reading creates a sense of community and builds a common background of knowledge but neglects individual differences in reading ability and interest. Working in small groups does not build a sense of larger community but can allow for better provision for individual differences. Individualized reading, which is described in the next section, provides for individual differences and fosters self-selection but may be inefficient. If you do use whole-class reading, use it on a limited basis and complement it with small groups or an individualized approach and self-selection.

 **INDIVIDUALIZED READING–READING WORKSHOP**

■ **Individualized reading– reading workshop** is a system of teaching reading in which students select their own reading material, read at their own pace, and are instructed in individual conferences and whole-class or small-group lessons.

The **individualized reading–reading workshop** approach is designed to create readers who can and do read. Each child chooses her or his own reading material and has periodic conferences with the teacher to discuss it. The most popular form of individualized reading is known as **reading workshop.** Reading workshop is similar to writing workshop, but the focus is on reading. Reading workshop has three major components: preparation time, self-selected reading and responding, and student sharing (Atwell, 1987; Cooper, 1997; Reutzel & Cooter, 1991).

■ **Reading workshop** is a form of individualized reading in which students choose their own books and have individual or group conferences but may meet in groups to discuss books or work on projects. There may also be whole-class or small-group lessons.

## Preparation Time

Reading workshop begins with preparation time, which includes a state-of-the-class conference and a minilesson. The state-of-the-class conference is a housekeeping procedure and can be as brief as a minute or two. During this time, the schedule for the workshop is set, as students note what they will be doing. In the minilesson, the teacher presents a skill/strategy lesson based on a need evidenced by the whole class. It could be a lesson on making inferences, predicting, using context clues, deciphering multisyllabic words, or interpreting metaphors. Or it could be a lesson on selecting a book, finding more time to read, or how to share a book with a partner (Calkins, 2001). The minilesson might be drawn from the basal reader or literature resource book or might be created by the teacher (Cooper, 1997). It should be presented within the framework of a story or article that students have read or listened to, and it should be applicable to the reading that they will do that day. The minilesson should last approximately ten minutes, but could be longer.

■ Pinnell and Fountas (2002) recommend that guided reading be a part of reading workshop for students in grades three and beyond.

Although brief, minilessons should be memorable and effective. Calkins (2001) has found a five-part lesson to be effective. The parts are connection, teaching, active involvement, link, and follow-up. The connection explains why a particular strategy or topic was chosen. For instance, the teacher might say, "When I'm reading a book about a new topic, I use the pictures to help me. Yesterday, I was reading about robots. I don't know much about robots, but the illustrations really helped." The teaching is the actual instruction. The teacher shows specifically how the illustrations and diagrams added to his understanding of robots and clarified some ideas that weren't clear. Active involvement means that at least for a few minutes, students try out the strategy or a portion of it. The teacher gives students a handout that describes several unusual animals but contains no illustrations. The teacher then gives students the same handout with illustrations. The students briefly discuss how the second handout helped them better understand the selection. The link connects the strategy with a story that the students are about to read. Students are reading informational books of their own choosing. The teacher suggests to students that they use the illustrations to help them better understand the topics they are reading about. In a follow-up, students are asked to tell or demonstrate how they applied the strategy. During the sharing, the teacher asks students to tell how illustrations helped them better understand the articles they read.

> Minilessons may not allow sufficient time for instruction in complex skills. When introducing a skill, especially a complex one, you may need to extend the lesson. Shorter lessons might suffice when you are reviewing a skill.

## Self-Selected Reading and Responding

At the heart of the workshop is the time when students read self-selected books, respond to their reading, or engage in group or individual conferences. Self-selected reading may last approximately thirty minutes or longer. If time is available, this period can be extended. If children have difficulty reading alone for that period of time, a portion of the period might be set aside for reading with a partner or in a small group. Because students will be reading their self-selected books independently, they should be encouraged to use appropriate strategies. Before reading, they should survey, predict, and set a purpose for reading. As they read, they should use summarizing, inferencing, and imaging strategies—if appropriate—and should monitor for meaning. As they read, students can use sticky notes to indicate a difficult word or puzzling passage. Or, as suggested by Atwell (1987), they can record difficult words and the page numbers of puzzling passages on a bookmark. A full bookmark could be a sign that a book is too difficult. After reading, students should evaluate their original prediction and judge whether they can retell the selection and relate it to their own experiences.

Response time may last from fifteen to thirty minutes or longer. During response time, students may meet in a literature discussion group to discuss their reading, write in their journals, work on an extension activity, plan a reader's theater or other type of presentation, work at one of the classroom's centers, continue to read, or attend a conference. During response time, hold individual and/or group conferences. If time allows, circulate around the room, giving help and guidance as needed. Visiting literature circles should be a priority.

## Conferences

Just as in writing workshop, conferences are a key part of reading workshop. Both individual and group conferences are recommended, each having distinct advantages.

In the original version of individualized reading, teachers held individual conferences with students. In reading workshop, teachers hold group as well as individual conferences.

## BUILDING LANGUAGE

In conferences, ask open-ended questions, such as "Tell me about your book. What do you like best about it?" Use wait time to help students develop their responses more fully. Model the use of literary language as you ask such questions as, "How did the author build suspense in the story? How did she develop the characters? How did she make them seem real?"

## ASSESSING STUDENTS' PROGRESS

After holding a conference, be sure to summarize it. Include date, selection read, and student's reaction to the text. Does she enjoy it? Is she able to respond to it? Can she cope with the book? Is it too difficult or too easy? Does she select books wisely? Did you note any needs? If so, how will these be provided for? What are her plans for the future? Will she engage in an extension or enrichment activity? Will she read another book?

### ■ Individual Conferences

Although time consuming, the individual conference allows each student to have the teacher's full attention and direct guidance and instruction for at least a brief period. It builds a warm relationship between teacher and student and provides the teacher with valuable insights into each child and her or his needs. While individual conferences are being held, other students are engaged in silent reading. No interruption of the conference is allowed, and those involved in silent reading are not to be disturbed.

An individual conference begins with some questions designed to put the student at ease and to get a general sense of the student's understanding of the book. Through questioning, the teacher also attempts to elicit the child's personal response to the text and encourages the child to relate the text to her or his own life. The teacher poses questions to clear up difficulties and to build comprehension—and concepts, if necessary—and reviews difficult vocabulary. In addition, the teacher assesses how well the student understood the book, whether she or he enjoyed it, and whether she or he is able to apply the strategies and skills that have been taught. The teacher notes any needs the student has and may provide spontaneous instruction or give help later. To prepare for individual conferences, students choose a favorite part of the book to read to the teacher and also give a personal assessment of the book, telling why they did or did not like it or what they learned from it. Students also bring words, ideas, or items they want clarified or questions that they have about the text. In addition, students may be asked to complete a generic response sheet or a specific response sheet geared to the book they have read. Figures 9.1 and 9.2 present generic response forms that include items designed to elicit a personal response from students. To avoid having students do an excessive amount of writing, you might focus on just a few of the personal response questions or have students respond to the questions orally rather than in writing.

Another way that students can prepare for an individual conference is to keep track of their reading in journals. Students note the date and title and author of the book and their personal response to the piece, answering questions such as these: How does the selection make me feel? What will I most remember about it? Was there anything in it that bothered me (Gage, 1990)? Did it remind me of a person or event in my life? Do I have any questions about the piece (Parsons, 1990)? For an informational book, students answer such questions as these: Which details did I find most interesting? How might I use the information? What questions do I still have about the topic? Questions should not be so time consuming or arduous that children avoid reading so they will not have to answer them. As an alternative, you might have students keep a dialogue journal as described later in this chapter. And younger children may respond to a book by drawing a picture. Whatever form the response takes, it should be geared to the maturity level of the child and the nature of the text.

Students should keep a record of all books that they read. While helping the teacher keep track of students' reading, such records are also motivational. Students get a sense of accomplishment from seeing their list grow. A simple record such as that in Figure 9.3 would suffice.

FIGURE 9.1

**Response Sheet for Fiction**

Name: _____    Date: _____

Title of book: _____    Publisher: _____

Author: _____    Date of publication: _____

Plot

       Problem: _____

                     _____

Main happenings: _____

                     _____

       Climax: _____

                     _____

       Outcome: _____

Answer any three of the following questions:

1. What did you like best about the book?

    _____

    _____

2. Is there anything in the book that you would like to change? If so, what? Also tell why you would like to make changes.

    _____

    _____

3. Is there anything in the book that puzzled you or bothered you?

    _____

    _____

4. Would you like to be friends with any of the characters in the book? Why or why not?

    _____

    _____

5. If other students your age asked whether you thought they might like to read this book, what would you tell them?

    _____

    _____

Individual conferences can last anywhere from five to ten minutes. At least one individual or group conference should be held for each student each week. Not every book needs a conference. A student who is reading two or three books a week should decide on one book to talk about. On the other hand, if the student is a slow reader, a conference may be held when she or he is halfway through the

FIGURE 9.2

**Response Sheet for Informational Books**

Name: _____     Date: _____

Title of book: _____     Publisher: _____

Author: _____     Date of publication: _____

Topic of book: _____

Main things I learned: _____
_____
_____
_____

Most interesting thing I learned: _____
_____

Questions I still have about the topic: _____
_____
_____
_____

Recommendation to others: _____
_____
_____

Teachers might hold conferences during silent reading and during response time.

book. Conferences should be scheduled. A simple way to do this is to have students who are ready for conferences list their names on the chalkboard. The teacher can then fill in the times for the conferences.

After the conference is over, the teacher should make brief notes in the student's folder, including date, title of book read, assessment of student's understanding and satisfaction with the book, strategies or skills introduced or reinforced, student's present and future needs, and student's future plans. A sample conference report form is presented in Figure 9.4.

### ■ Group Conferences

USING TECHNOLOGY
Field Guides provide suggestion for introducing and discussing children's books in a workshop setting. **http://fieldguides. heinemann.com**

Group conferences are an efficient use of time and can be used along with or instead of individual conferences. The teacher has the opportunity to work with five or six students rather than just one. Conferences can be held to discuss books by the same author, those with a common theme, or those in the same genre. Group conferences work best when students have read the same book. If several copies of a book are available, they can be given to interested students, who then confer.

A group conference includes three types of questions: an opening question to get the discussion started, following questions to keep the discussion moving, and process questions to "help the children focus on particular elements of the text" (Hornsby, Sukarna, & Parry, 1986, p. 62). Process questions focus on comprehending and appreciating a piece and are similar to those asked in the discussion and reread-

**FIGURE 9.3**

## A Reading Log

Name: _____

Title of book: _____

Author: _____

Publisher: _____

Date of publication: _____

Number of pages: _____

Subject: _____

Date started: _____

Date completed: _____

Recommendations to others: _____

_____

_____

_____

ing portions of a DRA. They are often related to reading strategies and might ask students to summarize a passage, compare characters, predict events, clarify difficult terms, or locate proof for an inference. Students should also have the opportunity to respond personally to the text. Process and response questions might be

**FIGURE 9.4**

## An Individualized Reading Conference Report

Name: *Althea S.*                    Date: *10/19*

Title: *Owl at Home*                Author: *Arnold Lobel*

| | |
|---|---|
| Understanding of text and personal response: | *Discussion of Ch. 1 of text: Saw humor in story. Remembered time when furnace broke and apartment was cold but became cozy again.* |
| Oral reading: | *Fairly smooth. Good interpretation. Some difficulty reading dialogue. 97% accuracy.* |
| Needs: | *Read behav for behave. Needs to integrate context and phonics.* |
| Future plans: | *Plans to finish book by end of week. Will join Arnold Lobel Literature Circle and compare Owl books with Frog and Toad books. Will share funniest incident with whole class.* |

interwoven. The teacher should lead the discussion, although students eventually may take on that role. Just as in individual conferences, the teacher evaluates students' performance, notes needs, and plans future activities based on those needs. Along with or instead of a group conference, students might take part in a literature discussion group.

## Using Dialogue Journals

■ **A dialogue journal** is a journal in which the students react to or make observations about their reading or other topic and the teacher responds by writing in the journal.

You might try **dialogue journals** as an alternative to conferences or along with conferences. After Nancy Atwell (1987) instituted self-selection and time to read in her classroom, her students read an average of thirty-five books. She commented, "Last year's average of thirty-five books per student grew as much from students' power to choose as from the time I made for them to read. I heard again and again from students of every ability that freedom of choice had turned them into readers" (p. 161). Although providing students with time to read and freedom to choose started them reading, Atwell was not satisfied. She realized that response was needed to allow students to reflect on their reading and deepen their understanding and appreciation. Because individual conferences were so brief, they did not lend themselves to an in-depth discussion of the text. To provide the framework for response, Atwell used dialogue journals to initiate an exchange with the students.

Having the opportunity to write about their reading gave students time to reflect and led to deeper insights. With the give and take of dialogue, they were led to develop their thoughts and reconsider interpretations.

In addition to providing students with an opportunity to respond, dialogue journals yield insight into students' growth as readers. Thus, they offer the teacher a rich source of ideas for teaching lessons. Although, at first, the dialogue was between teacher and individual students, Atwell discovered students passing notes about poems they had read. She extended an invitation for students to dialogue with a partner, and students began exchanging their responses. Because responding to each student's journal on a daily basis could be overwhelming, you might want to have one-fifth of the class turn in their journals each day. That way you respond each day to just a few students, but you see each student's journal once a week.

**BUILDING LANGUAGE**
You can ask students to expand on responses in dialogue journals, perhaps asking a student who said that he liked *Officer Buckle and Gloria* because it was funny to tell what made it funny or to tell what the funniest part was.

❚ One of the primary advantages of dialogue journals is that teachers can model and scaffold more mature expression (Atwell, 1987). Through thoughtful comments and careful questioning, they can elicit lengthier, more elaborated responses and they can direct students to look at essential aspects of the texts being discussed. Closed questions such as, "Which character did you like best?" would tend to elicit a limited response. However, open questions such as "The story sounds interesting. Tell me about it" would tend to bring forth a fuller response.

## Student Sharing

During the student-sharing portion of reading workshop, which should last from ten to twenty minutes, students share their reading with the entire class. They might give the highlights of a book they especially enjoyed, read an exciting passage, share a poem, make a recommendation, enact a reader's theater performance, or share in some other way. "Sharing time advertises and promotes the excitement of literacy learning and helps to promote the class as a community of readers" (Cooper, 1997, p. 491). As an alternative to whole-class sharing, the teacher might arrange for small-group sharing with four or so students in each group. The teacher can then visit with the groups as a participant or observer (Cooper, 1997).

## Organizing the Program

The classroom must be organized carefully. Just as in a library, it should have an inviting browsing area where students can choose books and settle down comfortably to read. Routines should be established for selecting books, keeping track of books circulated, taking part in conferences, and completing independent activities. The nature of the activity should determine the types of rules and routines. Because they are expected to follow these procedures, students should have a role in formulating them. The teacher might describe the situation and have students suggest ways to make it work.

The following basic conditions must be managed: (1) the teacher must be able to hold individual or group conferences with students that are free from interruptions; (2) students must be able to work on their own without disturbing others; and (3) students must be responsible for choosing books on their own and reading them. Some commonsense rules and routines might include the following:

- *Book selection.* The number of students choosing books at one time is limited to five; students may select two to five books at one time; students may make one exchange. Some students, especially those who are struggling with their reading, may waste a great deal of time choosing books. Instead of having students select books during reading workshop, you might have students gather books to be read from the school or classroom library prior to reading. Younger students might gather four or five books that they intend to read. Older students might gather two or three. These can be kept in book boxes or accordion folders or oversized envelopes along with students' reading logs and conference sheets and any other reading aids, such as a model words chart (Calkins, 2001).
- *Circulation.* Students are responsible for the books they check out; a card, sign-out sheet, or computerized system is used to keep track of books; students are in charge of the circulation system; books may be taken home.
- *Conference time.* No one may interrupt the teacher during conferences; students must come prepared to conferences; students (or the teacher) must arrange for periodic conferences.

## Advantages and Disadvantages of Reading Workshop

Self-selection, moving at one's own pace, using group processes, and relating reading and writing are the major advantages of reading workshop. Disadvantages include potential neglect of skills and the possibility that the teacher might spread himself too thin in an attempt to meet with a va-

An approach that features self-selected reading requires a large collection of materials. As a rule of thumb, there should be at least three times as many books as children in the class, with more books being added over time. School and local libraries might loan a classroom collection, children might bring in books from home, or the community might be asked to contribute. Old basals can be a part of the collection.

*During* reading workshop, students might share their response journals with a partner.

A main reason that teachers found individualized reading unmanageable in the past was the demand that conferences made on their time. However, with group conferences and the experience gained by holding writing conferences, this should no longer be a major hindrance.

**ADAPTING INSTRUCTION for *STRUGGLING READERS and WRITERS***
Because students select their own books and read at their own pace, individualized reading–reading workshop works extremely well with students reading below grade. No longer are they stigmatized by being put in the low group or forced to read material that is too difficult for them.

■ **Language experience** is an approach to teaching reading in which students dictate a story based on an experience they have had. The dictated story is written down by a teacher or aide and used to instruct the students in reading.

When initiating the language-experience approach, start with group stories so that the class becomes familiar with procedures. As students share experiences and learn about each other, this also builds a sense of community.

riety of groups and individuals and respond to students' journal entries. Also, reading workshop might be unsuitable for students who have a difficult time working independently or whose skills are so limited that there are few books they can read on their own.

## Adapting Reading Workshop

Reading workshop can be used instead of a basal series or along with it. For instance, you might use a basal three days and reading workshop two days. Or you might use a basal for a part of the day and reading workshop for a portion. Use whole-class instruction as appropriate. For instance, teach book selection and strategies needed by all students to the whole class. Use small-group instruction for those children who evidence a specific need for additional help. Obtain multiple copies of selected titles, just as you might do for a literature-based approach, and periodically invite students to choose one of the titles and read it as part of a small group–guided reading lesson. Use efficient management techniques, and do not overextend yourself. If you use reading workshop with younger students whose writing skills are still rather limited, gradually lead them into the use of dialogue journals. They might begin by drawing pictures in response to selections read.

## LANGUAGE-EXPERIENCE APPROACH

As noted in Chapter 3, the **language–experience approach** is very personal. Children's experiences expressed in their own language and written down by the teacher or an aide become their reading material. Because both the language and the experience are familiar, this method presents fewer difficulties for children who are learning to read. It also integrates thinking, listening, speaking, reading, and writing. Through discussion, the teacher can lead students to organize and reflect on their experiences. If time order is garbled, the teacher can ask, "What happened first? What happened next?" If details are scant, the teacher can request the children to tell more or can ask open-ended questions, such as "How do you think the dinosaur tracks got there? What do the tracks tell us about dinosaurs?" Through comments that show an interest in the children and the topic, the teacher affirms them and encourages them to elaborate.

Whereas the teacher should affirm, support, encourage, and scaffold, she or he needs to be careful not to take over. The teacher should draw language from the children—not put words in their mouths. When recording students' stories, it is important to write their exact words. Rephrasing what they have dictated shows a lack of acceptance for the language used. In addition, if the story is expressed in words that the child does not normally use, the child may have difficulty reading it. For instance, if the child dictates, "I been over my grandma's house," and the teacher rewords it as "I have been to my grandma's house," the child might stumble over the unfamiliar syntax. As Cunningham and Allington (1999) have observed,

If language experience is being used with an individual child to help the child understand what reading and writing are and that the child can write and read what he or she can say, then the child's exact words must be written down. To do anything else will hopelessly confuse the child about the very things you are trying to clarify by using individual language experience. (p. 92)

However, when a group story is being written, the situation is somewhat different. The story and the way it is written reflect the language structures that the group typically uses. To record a nonstandard structure might confuse some members of the group and result in criticism for the child who volunteered the structure. Displaying group stories containing nonstandard structures might also result in protests from parents and administrators (Cunningham & Allington, 1999).

The language-experience approach can be used with individuals or groups. Lesson 9.1 describes the steps for a group activity that extends over three days.

 **Group language-experience chart**

**Day 1**

**Step 1. Building experiential background for the story**

The students have an experience that they share as a group and that they can write about. It might be a field trip, the acquisition of a pet for the classroom, the baking of bread, or similar experience.

**Step 2. Discussing the experience**

Students reflect on their experience and talk about it. During the discussion, the teacher helps them organize the experience. In discussing a visit to the circus, the teacher might ask them to tell what they liked best so that they do not get lost in details. If they baked bread, the teacher would pose questions in such a way that the children would list in order the steps involved.

**Step 3. Dictating the story**

The children dictate the story. The teacher writes it on large lined paper, an overhead transparency, or on the chalkboard or might even type it on a computer that has an attachment to magnify the input and project it on a screen. The teacher reads aloud what she or he is writing so that children can see the spoken words being written. The teacher reads each sentence to make sure it is what the child who volunteered the sentence wanted to say. The teacher sweeps her or his hand under the print being read so that students can see where each word begins and ends and that reading is done from left to right. For students just learning to read, each sentence is written on a separate line, when possible.

If, as part of composing an experience story, students talk about a field trip, planting a tree, or another experience, this provides the teacher with the opportunity to help them think about the experience and clarify and extend their understanding of it (Reutzel & Cooter, 1991).

### Step 4. Reviewing the story

After the whole story has been written, the teacher reads it aloud once more. Children listen to see that the story says what they want it to say. They are invited to make changes.

### Step 5. Reading of story by teacher and students

The teacher reads the story, running her or his hand under each word as it is read. The children read along with the teacher.

### Step 6. Reading of familiar parts by students

Volunteers are asked to read sentences or words that they know. The teacher notes those children who are learning words and phrases and those who are just getting a sense of what reading is all about.

### Day 2
### Step 1. Rereading of story

The story is reread by the teacher, who points to each word as it is read. The children read along. The story might then be read in unison by the teacher and students. The teacher continues to point to each word. Volunteers might be able to read some familiar words or phrases.

### Step 2. Matching of story parts

The teacher has duplicated the story and cut it into strips. The teacher points to a line in the master story, and students find the duplicated strip that matches it. Individual words might also be matched. A volunteer reads the strip, with the teacher helping out as necessary.

For students who can go beyond matching, the teacher plans activities that involve reading, asking questions such as the following: Which strip tells where we went? Which strip tells what we saw? Students identify and read the strips. On a still more advanced level, students assemble the strips in correct order. This works best with stories that have no more than four or five sentences.

Individual sentences can also be cut up into words that students assemble into sentences. This can be done as a pocket chart activity. The scrambled words are displayed, and volunteers read each one. Then a volunteer reads the word that should come first, puts it in its place, and reads it once more. A second volunteer reads the word that should come next and places it after the first word. The teacher reads the two words that have been correctly placed or calls on a volunteer to do so. This continues until the sentence has been assembled correctly. Once the entire strip has been assembled, the teacher or a volunteer reads it. The class listens to see whether the sentence has been put together correctly. Once students agree that it has, they read it in unison. This technique works best with short sentences.

### Day 3
### Step 1. Rereading of story

A copy of the story is distributed to each student. The story is discussed and read in unison.

> **Step 2. Identification of familiar words**
>
> Students underline words that they know. Known words are placed in word banks or otherwise saved for further study and used in other activities (see sections on high-frequency words and phonics in Chapter 4).

## Personalizing Group Stories

One way to personalize group language-experience stories is to identify the name of each contributor. After a volunteer has supplied a sentence, the teacher writes the student's name and the sentence, as shown in Figure 9.5. When the story is reread, each student can read the sentence that she or he contributed originally. Seeing their names in print gives students a sense of ownership of the product. It also helps them remember the sentences that they supplied.

## An Individual Approach

Individual language-experience stories are similar to group stories, except that they are more personalized. (Figure 3.2 in Chapter 3 is an individual language-experience story about a trip to an apple orchard.) Just as in the group approach, the child dictates a story and the teacher, an aide, or a volunteer writes it down and uses it as the basis for teaching reading. Often, an individual language-experience story starts out as a drawing. The child then dictates a story that tells about the drawing. A photo can also be used to illustrate a story or as a stimulus for dictating one.

When dictating a language-experience story, a child may bring up experiences that are highly personal or that reveal private family matters. Affirm the child's feelings, but suggest a more appropriate way for the child to relate the experience. "I'm pleased that you trusted me enough to share that with me, but I think maybe you should tell your mom or dad about it." If the child uses language that is unsuitable for the classroom, have her or him use more appropriate language: "Can you think of another way to say it?" (Tierney, Readence, & Dishner, 1995). Maintaining the child's dignity and self-concept is of primary importance. Handle delicate situations with sensitivity and careful professional judgment.

> If your students are creating individual language-experience stories, it's helpful if you have an aide or volunteers to assist with dictation. First explain the process to your helpers and let them observe you until they feel they can undertake the procedure on their own.

## The Language-Experience Approach and ELL Students

Because it uses a child's own language and can draw on aspects of the child's culture, the language–experience approach can be especially helpful for ELLs. However, even a bilingual child who has learned enough English to read a little may have difficulty with idiomatic expressions, many syntactical structures, and, of course, some words.

**FIGURE 9.5**

### Personalized Group-Experience Story

*OUR PETS*

*Billy said, "I have a dog.*
*My dog's name is Ralph."*
*Amy said, "I have a cat.*
*My cat's name is Sam."*
*Julio said, "My pets are goldfish.*
*They don't have names.*
*They just swim and swim."*

Because language experience is based on students' individual backgrounds, it allows each student to share her culture, experience, and mode of self-expression. It has the power to promote understanding and community among students whose backgrounds may differ.

■ A **dialect** is a variety of a language that may differ somewhat in pronunciation, grammar, and vocabulary.

How to handle dialect is a controversial issue. Shuy (1973) made the point that it is developmentally inappropriate to introduce another dialect to a young child. The child would be confused and wouldn't pick up the second dialect. As students grow older, they may choose to use other dialects to be able to communicate more effectively with diverse groups. This does not mean that they will surrender their home dialect.

Teachers often wonder whether they should edit an ELL's dictation if it contains unconventional or nonstandard items. As with native speakers of English, the best advice is to accept the child's language and show that it is valued. If the teacher edits it, it becomes the teacher's language, not the child's. This is especially true when children are in the initial stages of learning to read. In general, students' words should be written exactly as they are dictated; however, even if mispronounced, they should be spelled correctly, for example:

*Dictation:* I happy. My dog do'an be sick.
*Written:* I happy. My dog don't be sick.

As children grow in language, they will have opportunities to develop fuller knowledge of verbs, contractions, and pronunciation. The teacher might work on these patterns at appropriate times or consult with the ESL teacher if the child is taking part in such a program. However, focus at this point should be on introducing reading in English. Because the child is demonstrating a basic grasp of English, waiting for further refinement is an unnecessary delay.

## Variant Dialects

Some students may speak a **dialect** that is somewhat different from that typically expected by the school. It is important to accept that language: It will be confusing if the children say one thing and you write another, and constant correction will turn them off. At this point, children are rapidly acquiring vocabulary and developing their understanding of increasingly complex constructions. The last thing a teacher wants to do is to cut off the flow of language and risk interfering with their development. Introducing a standard dialect and correcting variant English should not be a part of early reading instruction.

## The Language-Experience Approach in the Content Areas

Science and social studies topics are often covered in the primary grades without books. Group-experience stories can be used to summarize main concepts or events. After studying mammals, for example, the teacher can discuss the main ideas and have the class dictate an experience story that highlights them. Duplicated copies of the stories can be distributed and collected into a science booklet; students can then illustrate their booklets.

If textbooks are used and are too difficult for some students, discussions, projects, filmstrips, and experiments can be used to present the subject matter. Language-experience stories can be used to summarize key topics so that students have a text—their own—to read.

## Other Uses for the Language-Experience Approach

The language-experience approach does not have to be confined to narratives or summaries of content-area textbooks. Thank-you notes to a visiting author, a letter to a classmate who is hospitalized, an invitation to a guest speaker, recipes, a set of directions for the computer, class rules, charts, lists, captions, diaries, booklets, plays, and similar items are suitable for the language-experience approach. When possible, the pieces should be written for real purposes.

Shared writing is another way in which the language-experience approach might be used. Shared writing is a cooperative venture involving teacher and students. In a regular language-experience story, the teacher records students' exact words. In shared writing, the teacher draws from the children the substance of what they want to say but may rephrase it (Cunningham & Allington, 1999). For instance, at the end of the day, the teacher may ask the students what they learned that day. Summarizing the contributions of many children, the teacher records the day's highlights. In doing so, the teacher is modeling how spoken language is transformed into written language.

> Group language-experience stories can be used beyond the beginning or early reading level to demonstrate writing techniques. One way of showing students how to write a letter to the editor, a persuasive essay, or a story is to arrange for the class to compose these items as group experience stories.

## Advantages and Disadvantages of the Language–Experience Approach

The language-experience approach is most frequently used as a supplement to other programs and is especially useful in the beginning stages of learning to read. The major advantage of the approach is that it builds on children's language and experience. A major disadvantage of using it as the sole approach to teaching reading is that the child's reading will be limited to his or her own experiences.

> See the discussion of language experience in Chapter 3.

## Adapting the Language-Experience Approach

Because it neglects published reading materials and because it limits children's reading experiences, language experience should not be the sole approach to reading instruction. However, it makes an excellent supplement to any of the other approaches presented in this chapter, especially at the emergent and early stages of reading.

# WHOLE LANGUAGE

Described as a philosophy of learning rather than a teaching approach, **whole language** incorporates a naturalistic, organic view of literacy learning. The basic premise is that children learn to read and write in much the same way that they learn to speak. Oral language is learned by being used for real purposes, not by completing artificial practice exercises that present it piecemeal—work on adjectives today, nouns tomorrow, verbs the day after. Because theorists see reading and writing as a part of the whole, they reason that they should be learned in the same way oral language is learned—through use and for real purposes. The basic belief underlying whole language is acquisition of all aspects of language, including reading and writing, "through use not exercise" (Altwerger, Edelsky, & Flores, 1987, p. 149).

> ■ **Whole language** has been described as a grassroots movement. It's a movement that classroom teachers across the land embraced and pushed forward. To help each other apply a whole language approach, a number of vigorous support groups sprang up. These include national networks, such as TAWL (Teachers Applying Whole Language).

In whole language classes, students take responsibility for their own learning. As Crafton (1991) explains, "When learners of any age initiate their own learning, the intent and purpose of the experience are clear. With self-initiation comes a greater degree of ownership, involvement, and commitment to the activity" (p. 16).

Whole-to-part learning, an important element in a holistic approach, is a form of instruction in which students experience the skill or strategy to be learned in the context of reading a selection or other activity, then focus on the skill or strategy, and apply or encounter the skill or strategy in a new reading selection or other context.

**USING TECHNOLGY**

Whole Language Umbrella provides an overview of whole language and links to related organizations. **http://webserv.edu. yorku.ca/~WLU/home. html**

Because whole language is not a prescribed program or method, its implementation varies from setting to setting and is expected to evolve and change as more is learned about how literacy is acquired. Basically, it embodies the following principles.

First, reading is best learned through actual use. Students learn by reading whole stories, articles, and real-world materials. Because of the richness of these materials, children are able to use their sense of language and the three cueing systems of semantics, syntax, and letter–sound relationships to grow in reading.

In a whole language classroom, students read and write for real purposes. There are no letters written to aunts who do not exist, thanking them for gifts that were not sent, just so that students can practice the format of the friendly letter. They write letters to real people for real reasons and mail them. Nor are children given isolated skill exercises such as circling words that contain short *a*. Instead, they read a story that has short *a* words.

According to the whole language philosophy, literacy is a social undertaking best learned in the context of a group. Therefore, in whole language classrooms, one sees writing workshops, group conferences, peer editing, and other examples of cooperative learning.

## GUIDED READING

Guided reading is a way of organizing reading instruction that uses grouping. In guided reading, students are grouped and instructed according to their level of development (Fountas & Pinnell, 1996, 2001). The groups meet on a daily basis for ten to thirty minutes or more. The teacher may organize as many groups as she believes are necessary, but the more groups assembled, the less time there is for each one. As a practical matter, three or four groups are the most that can be handled efficiently. Grouping, however, is flexible. When appropriate, students are moved into other groups.

What does the rest of the class do while the teacher is working with guided reading groups? While the teacher is working with guided reading groups, students can engage in a number of independent activities. These activities should provide students with the opportunity to apply and extend their skills. One of the best activities for developing reading skills is, of course, to read. Students can

- read independently in the reading corner.
- read with a buddy.
- read along with an audiotape or CD-ROM.
- read charts and stories posted around the room.
- meet with a literature circle.
- meet with a cooperative learning group.
- work on a piece of writing.

## *Exemplary Teaching*

### *Guided Reading*

$A$fter whole-group shared reading and writing, students in Pat Loden's first-grade class assemble for guided reading. Loden has five groups of four to five students in each group. Students are grouped according to their levels and needs. While Loden is meeting with a group, other students read independently for twenty minutes. They can reread books that they read during guided reading or select new books. A record is kept of books read, and they respond to at least one book each week. After twenty minutes of silent reading, students engage in journal writing. After completing journal writing, they work in learning centers. They work in three centers. Centers include an Internet pen-pal center, a science center, a literacy center, a poetry center, a writing center, a letter and word work center, and a read-the-room center. Each center contains directions for completing the activity. Students also make a note of the work that they have completed at the center.

Meanwhile, Loden conducts her guided reading lessons. Each lesson begins with a minilesson designed to teach a skill related to the reading of today's text. Children read the text silently. While they read silently, Loden has each of the children in the group read a passage orally to her. After students finish reading the selection, they discuss it. Loden then signals another group to come to the guided reading table (Morrow & Ashbury, 2001).

■ research a project in the library or on the Internet.

■ work on a carefully chosen Web site that fosters literacy.

■ work at one of the classroom learning centers.

## Learning Centers

Learning centers can provide practice for skills, provide enrichment, or allow students to explore interests. Many of the reinforcement activities suggested throughout this text can be made into learning centers. For instance, a number of sorting activities are suggested. Word-analysis centers can be set up that include sorting activities. The nature of the centers should be dictated by learning outcomes. What do you want students to know or be able to do as a result of using the centers? Centers offer an almost infinite number of possibilities. However, most classrooms feature a reading center or book corner in which students choose and read books or periodicals; a listening center in which students listen to taped stories or CD-ROMs; an Internet center in which students engage in Web-related activities; a writing center in which students compose messages, poems, or stories; a word-work center that might feature riddles, word games, or sorting activities; and a drama center that might feature books or scripts and puppets that can be used to dramatize selections or compose scripts. There might also be math, science, art, and social studies centers. For younger students, there might be a pretend play or role-playing center.

Connect the centers to the curriculum. The centers should extend skills and themes students are currently working on. Each center should have an objective.

▌ To join a group discussing whole language, you can sign up with the listserv: **TAWL@Listserv.Arizona. Edu**

▌ Not Another Inservice offers a host of suggestions for learning centers: **http://www.geocities. com/Wellesley/ Atrium/1783/ NotAnotherInservice. html.**

Where possible, centers should contain puzzles, magnets, word games, magazines, and manipulatives that are naturally appealing to children but which allow them to make discoveries on their own. The best centers are those that contain materials and activities that children would want to work on even if they weren't assigned to do so (Cuningham & Allington, 2003).

Basal readers have suggestions for literacy center activities that reinforce the skills and themes students are studying.

If your curriculum is standards based, you might want to note the standard that it addresses. This prevents having centers that are fun and interesting but don't really further any educational objective. Also have a means for tracking student's performance at the centers. As a result of working at a center, students might record the title of a book and the number of pages they read or they might produce a piece of writing or note a story that they dramatized. Also have students discuss with the class the kinds of things they are doing at the centers. This helps keep the work at the centers related to the overall objectives of the classroom. Components of a learning center include title, activities, directions, materials, and assessment. See Figure 9.6 for a description of the activities in two typical centers.

Involve students in the creation of learning centers. Change the content of the centers frequently to keep them interesting. Although the nature of the center might stay the same, change the activities and materials periodically. Assess the centers. Which ones seem most popular? Which ones seem to result in the most learning?

## FIGURE 9.6

### Two Sample Centers

| Type | Objective | Sequence of Activities |
|---|---|---|
| Listening post | Building fluency | 1. Students listen to a brief taped play.<br>2. Students read along with the taped play. Each student reads his part.<br>3. Students listen to the taped play again.<br>4. Students dramatize the play once more. |
| CD-ROM center | Building understanding | 1. Students examine the title and illustration on the first frame and predict what the story might be about.<br>2. Students read the story silently.<br>3. Students discuss the story in light of their predictions.<br>4. Students take turns reading their favorite part to each other.<br>5. Students fill out a response form, supplying their name, the title of the story, and a summarizing sentence that tells what the story is about. |

Adapted from Ford, 1994.

*In* this learning center, students listen to a taped story.

Where possible, provide choices. Students might practice a phonics skill by reading a selection along with a CD-ROM, or they might complete a crossword puzzle or a sorting activity. The objective is the same in each case, but the means for getting there varies.

The Internet is an excellent resource for centers. Familiar Tales at Familiar tales.com, for instance, offers a range of interactive alphabet-recognition, letter-formation, and word-creation activities for students in kindergarten through second grade. All the teacher need do is provide directions for logging on, select activities, and assess student's performance.

Education Place provides a variety of links that could be used in learning centers. Click onto Houghton Mifflin Reading to access links. Other basal reader publishers have similar resources. Education Place: **http://www. educationplace.com.**

### ■ Managing Centers

To manage the task, a magnetic schedule board or pocket chart is set up. On the board, list the possible activities, as in Figure 9.7.

Depending on the length of time students will be working independently, they may complete two or three activities. In Figure 9.7, students have each been assigned three activities. Students may be required to complete certain activities, or you might give them choices. Some teachers post a schedule so that students know exactly what they are to do. This allows staggering of visits to centers so that the centers don't become too crowded.

## Advantages and Disadvantages of Guided Reading

A key advantage of guided reading is that students are instructed on their level and are given the support and instruction they need. The approach works especially well

**FIGURE 9.7**

**Pocket Chart Schedule of Learning Centers**

|  | **Wednesday** | **November 15** |  |
|---|---|---|---|
| Edna, Ashley, Kayla, Michael, Dylan | ABC | 🎧 | ✏️ |
| Luis, Juan, Alyssa, William | 💻 | ✏️ | 📖 |
| Jacob, Aaron, Maria, Marisol | 🎧 | 📖 | ABC |
| Rachel, Edith, Latasha, Carlos | 📖 | 💻 | 🎧 |
| Raymond, Nicole, Michael, Angel | ✏️ | ABC | 💻 |

**BUILDING LANGUAGE**

A pocket chart center is versatile because it allows manipulation of small or large cards in a variety of ways. To practice sequencing and retelling a story, students might put in order a series of scrambled sentences. Or students might match sentences with pictures that illustrate them. Or they might put scrambled words in order. Pocket charts can also be used to sort words or pictures.

if the grouping is flexible and students not meeting in groups are provided with worthwhile activities. However, unless carefully planned, learning centers can deteriorate into busywork.

## AN INTEGRATED APPROACH

A large-scale comparison of approaches to teaching reading in the 1960s came up with no clear winner (Bond & Dykstra, 1967, 1997). All of the approaches evaluated were effective in some cases. However, some children experienced difficulty with each one. The study suggested that the teacher is more important than the method and that a method successful in one situation may not be successful in all. Combinations of approaches were recommended. Adding language experience to a basal program seemed to strengthen the program. A word-attack element also seemed to be an important component, a conclusion that was reached repeatedly in a number of studies and research reviews (Adams, 1990; Anderson, Hiebert, Scott, & Wilkinson, 1985; Chall, 1967, 1983a; Dykstra, 1974; Snow, Burns, & Griffin, 1998).

Another interpretation of the research strongly suggests that what is really most effective is using the best features of all approaches. Draw from holistic literature-based approaches the emphasis on functional–contextual instruction, the use of children's literature, and integration of language arts. From basal programs, adopt some of the structure built into the skills/strategies components. From individualized approaches, take the emphasis on self-selection of students' reading material.

From the language-experience approach, adopt the practice of using writing to build and extend literacy skills.

Above all else, use your professional judgment. This book presents a core of essential skills and strategies in word recognition, comprehension, reading in the content areas, and study skills. Use this core of skills as a foundation when implementing your literacy program, regardless of which approach or approaches you use. If a skill or strategy is omitted or neglected, then add it or strengthen it. For instance, not all basals recommend the use of pronounceable word parts or analogy strategies. If you are using a basal and these elements are missing, add them.

## HELP FOR STRUGGLING READERS AND WRITERS

No one of the approaches described is necessarily best for struggling readers and writers. A program, such as reading workshop, that implements self-selected reading would be less likely to stigmatize poor readers because students would be able to choose materials on their level. A basal program would offer the structure that struggling readers and writers need. However, it would be imperative that poor readers be given materials on the appropriate level of challenge, perhaps in a guided reading format. A literature-based program would work well, too, as long as students were given the skills instruction they needed and books on the appropriate level. The language-experience approach works well with struggling readers because it is based on their language. When obtaining suitable reading material is a problem

### ACTION PLAN

1. Become acquainted with the major approaches to reading.
2. Whatever approach you use, incorporate principles of effective literacy instruction. Make sure that students are reading on their levels, are reading widely, and are being taught skills in a functional fashion and that progress is being monitored.
3. If students don't learn with one approach, try to find out why this is so and make adjustments. If the approach fails to work despite your best efforts, try another approach. Also match approaches to students' needs. Most students will learn regardless of what approach you use. But some students will only be successful when certain approaches are used. That is why it is necessary for you to have command of several approaches. If you are in a situation where an approach is mandated, make modifications so that the program is as effective as it can be.
4. Set up learning centers that are appealing to students but provide them with opportunities to apply skills independently.
5. Monitor the effectiveness of your program and make adjustments as necessary.

because the struggling reader is older but is reading on a very low level, language-experience stories can be used as the students' reading material.

If you are using a twenty-first-century basal, take advantage of the materials and techniques suggested for use with students who are struggling. If you are using an older basal and it seems too difficult for your struggling readers, provide books that the students can handle successfully. Working with students who were struggling with literary selections, Cole (1998) used books from easy-to-read series, including *Step into Reading* (Random House), *Puffin Easy-to-Read* (Penguin), *All Aboard Reading* (Grossett & Dunlap), and *Bank Street Ready to Read* (Bantam). Books from these and other easy-to-read series can be found in Appendix A.

Regardless of approach used, it would be most helpful if struggling readers and writers were given extra instruction, perhaps in a small group. Literacy programs for struggling readers are discussed in Chapter 11.

## SUMMARY

1. There are a number of approaches to teaching reading. Approaches that use a textbook to teach reading include basal and linguistic. The literature-based approach and reading workshop use children's books, as does whole language, which is more a philosophy than a method. Language experience uses writing to teach reading. Each approach has advantages and disadvantages and may be combined with other approaches and/or adapted.

2. Guided reading is a way of grouping and instructing students according to their needs. Whole language is a holistic, functional philosophy for teaching literacy.

3. According to research, no one approach to teaching reading yields consistently superior results. A combination is probably best. Teachers should use their professional judgment and know-how to adapt programs to fit the needs of their students.

4. Struggling readers need materials on their level and may benefit from additional instruction.

## EXTENDING AND APPLYING

1. Examine your philosophy of teaching literacy. Make a list of your beliefs and your teaching practices. Also note the approach to reading that best fits in with your philosophy of teaching reading. Do your practices fit in with your beliefs? If not, what might you do to align the two?

2. Examine a current basal series. Look at a particular level and assess the interest of the selections, the kinds of strategies and teaching suggestions presented in the manual, and the usefulness of the workbook exercises. Summarize your findings.

3. Plan a series of language-experience lessons, either for an individual or for a group of students, in which an experience story is written and used to present or reinforce appropriate literacy understandings or skills and strategies. Evaluate the effectiveness of your lessons.

4. Adapt a lesson in a basal reader to fit the needs of a group of students you are teaching. Teach the lesson and assess its appropriateness. In what ways was the manual a helpful resource? What adaptations did you have to make?

## DEVELOPING A PROFESSIONAL PORTFOLIO

If possible, videotape the adapted basal reader lesson described in Item 4 above. Place the videotape and/or a typed copy of the plan for the lesson in your portfolio. Summarize the plan and note adaptations you made to the lesson as described in the basal reader manual. Explain why adaptations were made and reflect on the effectiveness of the lesson.

## DEVELOPING A RESOURCE FILE

Prepare conference cards or database entries for three children's books that you might use to teach reading. Include bibliographic information, a summary of the selection, a series of questions that you might ask about the book, and a description of some possible extension activities. Keep a list of possible learning centers that you might set up in your classroom.

# 10

# Writing and Reading

## ANTICIPATION GUIDE

*F*or each of the following statements related to the chapter you are about to read, put a check under "Agree" or "Disagree" to show how you feel. Discuss your responses with classmates before you read the chapter.

|  |  | *Agree* | *Disagree* |
|---|---|---|---|
| **1** | Reading and writing are two sides of the same coin. | _____ | _____ |
| **2** | New writers should write short pieces to keep their mistakes to a minimum. | _____ | _____ |
| **3** | Students should be allowed to choose their own topics. | _____ | _____ |
| **4** | Completing endings for unfinished stories written by others is good practice for budding fiction writers. | _____ | _____ |
| **5** | The most time-consuming part of the writing process is revising. | _____ | _____ |
| **6** | Teachers should mark all uncorrected errors after a piece has been edited by a student. | _____ | _____ |
| **7** | Emphasis in a writing program for elementary school students should be on content rather than form. | _____ | _____ |

## USING WHAT YOU KNOW

*W*riting and reading are related processes that are mutually supportive. Reading improves writing and vice versa. The last two decades have witnessed a revolution in writing instruction, which today is based on the processes that expert student and professional writers use as they compose pieces.

What is your writing process? What steps do you take before you begin writing? What elements do you consider when you choose a topic? How do you plan your writing? How do you go about revising and editing your writing? How are your reading and writing related? What impact does your reading have on your writing? What impact does writing have on your reading?

##  THE ROOTS OF WRITING

Children discover pictures and words in storybooks that are read aloud to them. They draw pictures of mommy and daddy and their house. They scribble for the fun of it. In time, these scribbles become invested with meaning. Ultimately, children discover that not only can they draw pictures of people and objects but also they can represent people and objects with words. Many children make this crucial discovery about writing before they reach kindergarten; for other kindergartners, the concept is still emerging.

It is important to determine where children are on the writing continuum to know how best to help them. Writing development generally follows the stages listed in Figure 10.1. However, it should be noted that children can and do move back

**FIGURE 10.1**

### Developmental Stages/Scoring Guidelines

#### Stage 1: The Emerging Writer

- Little or no topic development, organization, and/or detail.
- Little awareness of audience or writing task.
- Errors in surface features prevent the reader from understanding the writer's message.

#### Stage 2: The Developing Writer

- Topic beginning to be developed. Response contains the beginning of an organization plan.
- Simple word choice and sentence patterns.
- Limited awareness of audience and/or task.
- Errors in surface features interfere with communication.

#### Stage 3: The Focusing Writer

- Topic clear even though development is incomplete. Plan apparent although ideas are loosely organized.
- Sense of audience and/or task.
- Minimal variety of vocabulary and sentence patterns.
- Errors in surface features interrupt the flow of communication.

#### Stage 4: The Experimenting Writer

- Topic clear and developed (development may be uneven). Clear plan with beginning, middle, and end (beginning and/or ending may be clumsy).

- Written for an audience.
- Experiments with language and sentence patterns. Word combinations and word choice may be novel.
- Errors in surface features may interrupt the flow of communication.

#### Stage 5: The Engaging Writer

- Topic well developed. Clear beginning, middle, and end. Organization sustains the writer's purpose.
- Engages the reader.
- Effective use of varied language and sentence patterns.
- Errors in surface features do not interfere with meaning.

#### Stage 6: The Extending Writer

- Topic fully elaborated with rich details. Organization sustains the writer's purpose and moves the reader through the piece.
- Engages and sustains the reader's interest.
- Creative and novel use of language and effective use of varied sentence patterns.
- Errors in surface features do not interfere with meaning.

From Georgia Department of Education, *Developmental Stages/Scoring Guidlines for Writing,* Atlanta, GA: 2000.

and forth between stages and that the stages overlap. In addition, students may be in one stage for narrative writing and another for expository.

Although the description of the stages of writing may not indicate it, all acts of writing are not the same. Writing a poem or essay relies on more complex processes than writing a friendly letter. Processes also develop and change with age and experience. Novice writers use a knowledge-telling process in which writing is similar to telling a story orally or providing an oral explanation. It requires "no greater amount of planning or goal setting than ordinary conversation" (Bereiter & Scardamalia, 1982, p. 9). Novice writers use a what-next strategy in which they write from one sentence to the next without having an overall plan for the whole piece (Dahl & Farnan, 1998). The sentence currently being written provides a springboard for the next sentence.

Gradually, writers acquire a knowledge-tranforming ability in which they alter their thoughts as they write. As they compose, their writing affects their thinking, and their thinking affects their writing. Instead of merely summarizing thoughts, writers are reconsidering and drawing conclusions, which are reflected in their writing. Thus, as students progress, some of the writing activities provided should go beyond having them merely list or summarize and should ask them to compare, contrast, conclude, and evaluate.

## GUIDED WRITING

Just as reading instruction should be geared to the students' level of reading development, writing instruction should be geared to students' level of writing development. Although some skills can be taught to the whole class, students' specific needs can be more directly targeted if students are members of small groups. To estimate where students are in their writing development, examine sample pieces of their writing, using Figure 10.1 as a guide. The teacher meets with one or two groups each day and conducts a writing process or strategy lesson. Grouped by their level of development, students are given instruction geared to their stage. For the emergent writer, the focus of instruction might be on drawing to illustrate a recent field trip and then writing about the drawing. For the experimenting writer, the focus of instruction might be on using examples or details to develop a topic (Davis, Jackson, & Johnson, 2000). As part of guided writing, students need to be taught specific strategies for reading and writing. Teaching students writing strategies has four steps:

1. Identifying a strategy worth teaching.
2. Introducing the strategy by modeling it.
3. Helping students try the strategy out with teacher guidance.
4. Helping students work toward independent mastery of the strategy through repeated practice and reinforcement. (Collins, 1998, p.65)

To identify a strategy that needs teaching, examine students' writing. You might also discuss their writing with them. Note areas that are posing problems or that they are having difficulty with. Choose a strategy such as adding interesting examples that would seem to be of most benefit to them in terms of their level of development. The strategy can be introduced to a whole class, to a guided writing group, or to an individual. After the strategy has been introduced, students should have ample opportunity to apply it. As you work with students, help them adapt the strategy so that it becomes a part of their writing repertoire. Provide opportunities for students to use the strategy in a number of situations so that they attain independent mastery of it. Guided strategic writing is presented within the framework of a process writing approach.

## THE PROCESS APPROACH TO WRITING

■ The **writing process** is an approach to teaching writing that is based on the way students and professionals write.

In the **writing process approach,** writing instruction is based on writing processes that professional writers and students actually use. From the research of D. H. Graves (1983), Emig (1971), and others, a series of steps has been described that attempts to explain how writers write. The steps are prewriting, composing, revising, editing, and publishing. However, these steps are not linear. They are recursive. Writers may engage in prewriting activities after composing and may be revising while composing. Although some children enjoy writing, others see it as a chore and as little more than an exercise undertaken for the teacher. Once students see that they have stories to tell, that their unique observations of life have value, writing will take on a new meaning for them.

Writing is not a linear process. We don't plan and then write and then revise. As we write, we plan and revise.

### Prewriting

Easily the most important step, prewriting encompasses all necessary preparation for writing, including topic selection, researching the topic, and gathering information.

The writing process approach needs to be applied flexibly. Writing a friendly letter, for instance, would require a bare minimum of planning and doesn't usually involve revising and editing. A letter to the editor, however, might require very careful planning, revising, and editing.

#### ■ Topic Selection

Topic selection is the hallmark of the process approach. In the past, students were supplied with topics and story starters. The intent was to help, but the result was writing that was wooden, contrived, and lacking in substance and feeling because the topics were ones in which the students had no interest. Letting students choose their own topics is one of the keys to good writing because there is a greater chance that students will invest more of themselves in a piece that means something to them. When seven-year-olds were allowed to choose their topics, they wrote four times as much as a peer group that was assigned subjects (D. H. Graves, 1975).

It isn't necessary for students to have a piece blocked out in their minds before they begin writing. In a way, writing is an exploration. Writers may not be sure what they want to say until they've said it.

D. H. Graves (1982) recounted the story of a teacher who left Graves's weekly workshop filled with enthusiasm for the process approach but returned to the next session angry and discouraged. The problem? Hearing that they were to choose their own topics, the students demanded that the teacher supply them with suitable subjects. They felt that it was bad enough they had been asked to write; having to decide on their own subject matter was adding insult to injury. According to Graves, these students were unable to choose topics because they had never been taught how to do so. In previous years, well-meaning teachers had always provided them with topics. There was an implicit message in this: These students had nothing worth writing about and thus had to be fed a diet of story starters, topic sentences, finish-the-story exercises, and other canned activities. Undoubtedly, some of these topics were quite creative. However, the best writing is about something that matters to the writer—a question that the writer wants to answer, a discovery or adventure that the writer wants to share, or a humorous episode that the writer wants to recount.

Murray (1989) suggested that teaching writing is mainly a matter of helping students discover what they have to say and how to say it. The teacher should model the process of selecting a topic and begin by discussing what he or she has done, seen, or knows that he or she would like to tell others. The teacher then jots down three or four topics on the chalkboard. They might be similar to the following:

I saw a real whale close up.
I saw the tallest building in the world.
I saw the longest baseball game ever played.

As the class listens, the teacher goes through the process of choosing a topic. The teacher rejects the first two because many people have seen whales and the tallest building, but only a handful of fans watched the longest game ever played. Most important, that is the topic that holds the greatest interest for the teacher.

Once the teacher has demonstrated the process, he or she asks the class to **brainstorm** topics and then lists them on the board. This helps others discover subjects of interest. After a discussion, each student lists three or four tentative topics and, later, chooses one to develop. In group discussions and one-on-one conversations or conferences with the teacher, children discover additional topics. With the teacher's questioning as a stimulus, they find subjects in which they have expertise, that they would like to explore, and that they would like to share.

Knowing that they will be writing nearly every day and so must have many subjects to write about, students search for topics continuously. They find them on television, in their reading, in their other classes, in their homes, in writing notebooks, and in outside activities. They can keep lists of topics in their folders or in special notebooks or journals (Calkins & Harwayne, 1991; Calkins, 1994). Students might also keep a list of questions. Questions to be answered are an excellent source of topics. They might have personal questions, questions about sports or hobbies, or questions about a topic they are studying or an interesting fact that they heard (Spandel, 2001).

Journals are a favorite repository for writers' observations and ideas. In their writing journals, students can list topic ideas, outline observations they have made, or explore ideas. They can also record passages from their reading that were especially memorable or that contained distinctive language. Students might also use their journals to test out writing techniques or experiment with story ideas. Journals keep ideas germinating until they are ready to flower. When students keep writing journals or notebooks, prewriting might consist primarily of selecting an anecdote or question from the notebook to explore or elaborate.

Canned topics have been repackaged as writing prompts. Pressured to prepare students for upcoming competency tests, teachers require students to write to test-type prompts. While it is important to prepare students for tests, practice should not be excessive. Students' abilities are best developed through a balanced program of writing instruction.

■ **Brainstorming** is a process in which members of a group attempt to accomplish a task by submitting ideas and writing spontaneously.

Over time, journal writing can deteriorate. Routman (2000) suggests that journal writing can become more worthwhile if teachers encourage students to "write for several days on a topic they care very much about and if they teach students how to write with detail and voice" (p. 235).

An excellent repository of topics is the idea folder. Idea folders hold newspaper clippings, notes, or magazine articles that could become stories. For example, intriguing newspaper articles about flying snakes or the return of monarch butterflies can be stored for future reference.

For younger writers, planning and composing or writing are very similar operations. Young writers' composing duplicates their planning notes.

Distressed that a number of her students typically produced brief paragraphs almost totally devoid of detail, J. L. Olson (1987) encouraged them to draw a picture of their subjects. After discussing the drawings with her, the students then wrote. The improvement was dramatic; the resulting pieces were rich in detail. Drawing helped students retrieve details about their subjects.

With students, establish guidelines for journals. If you plan to read the journals, make that known to students so that the journals do not become private diaries. Reading students' writing journals has several advantages. It makes the journals part of the writing program and encourages students to make entries. It also provides you with the opportunity to gain insight into students' thoughts about writing and to respond. Students could highlight any items that they would like you to focus on, and they can mark as private or fold over a page containing any item that they do not want you to see. Journals are not graded, and corrections are not made, because doing so will shut off the flow of ideas. However, you should write a response.

One of the shortcomings of journals is that they can, over time, become a diary of mundane events. Encourage students to take a broader look at the world and also to dig beneath the surface. The student's journal entry "I struck out three times in the Little League game" might draw the following responses from the teacher: "What happened because you struck out? How did you feel? Why do you think you struck out? What might you do about it? Could this be the start of a story?" You might also encourage students to write for several days on a topic they care about (Routman, 2000). From time to time, model the process of composing journal entries. Show students how you develop topics or try out new techniques in your journal.

Time expended on collecting and selecting topics is time well spent. Children discover that they have stories to tell. Their writing becomes better and less time-consuming to produce. In one study, as children learned to choose and limit topics, fewer drafts were required (D. H. Graves, 1983).

### ■ Planning

Research and preparation are also essential parts of prewriting. For older students, preparation might take the form of discussing, brainstorming, creating semantic maps or webs, reading, viewing films or filmstrips, or devising a plot outline or general outline. For younger students, it could be discussing topics or drawing a picture. Drawing is especially useful, as it provides a frame of reference. Drawing also helps older students who have difficulty expressing themselves verbally.

A particularly effective prewriting strategy is to have students brainstorm words that they think they might use to develop their topics. Brainstorming is a free-flowing, spontaneous activity. All ideas should be accepted and recorded but not critiqued. Everyone should contribute. After brainstorming, ideas generated can be discussed, elaborated on, and clarified. Related ideas can also be introduced.

Brainstorming helps students note details to include in their pieces (Bereiter & Scardamalia, 1982). D'Arcy (1989) recommended several different kinds of brainstorming. The simplest form involves writing down names—of birds, famous people, or mystery places, for example. Students jot down the results of their brainstorming rather than simply think aloud. This gives them a written record of their associations as well as concrete proof of the power of brainstorming to draw out items. Students then share their lists with partners, which may result in additional items. At this point, students might circle the name of a bird, famous person, or place that they know the most about and brainstorm that item. Later, they brainstorm questions about the item they have chosen: Where do bald eagles live? What kinds of nests do they have? Are they in danger of becoming extinct? What do they eat? How fast do they fly? The questions can be the basis for exploring and writing pieces about the topic.

Memories, feelings, images, and scenes can also be brainstormed. For instance, students might go down their lists of items and note the one that drew the strongest feelings or created the sharpest image. Words to describe the feelings or details that describe the image could be brainstormed and listed.

Clustering and freewriting are versions of brainstorming. **Clustering** is a kind of mapping in which students jot down the associations evoked by a word. Lines and circles are used to show relationships. In **freewriting,** students write freely for approximately ten minutes on an assigned or self-selected topic, about a real event or an imagined one. The idea is to have children catch the flow of their thoughts and feelings by writing nonstop. Ideas or themes generated can then become the basis for more focused work. In some instances, freewriting might be an end in itself—an exercise that promotes spontaneity in writing.

To help students flesh out their writing and determine what kinds of details they might include, model how you might brainstorm possible questions that the readers of your article might have. For instance, if students plan to write about flying snakes, they might brainstorm questions such as:

How do the snakes fly?
Where do they live?
Are they poisonous?
How big are they?
What do they eat?
Why do they fly out of trees?

Orally sharing ideas is another form of preparing for writing. Discussing helps students "order their thoughts and generate many more ideas and angles for writing" (Muschla, 1993, p. 37). This technique is especially effective when students work in pairs. After students have generated ideas through brainstorming, clustering, or some other method, have them talk over their ideas with their partners. The listener should summarize what the speaker has said, ask the speaker to clarify any parts that are not clear, and answer questions that the speaker might have, thereby helping the speaker shape and clarify his ideas.

Role-playing can be an effective way to draw out ideas (Muschla, 1993). Students can role-play fictional or real-life events, including historical happenings or events that they have personally experienced. Role-playing can also help students elaborate on and clarify what they want to say. For instance, if students are about to write a letter to a classmate who has moved away, they might divide up into pairs and role-play the writer of the letter and the intended receiver. Students might role-play situations that they intend to write about: persuading the town to fix up the park or requesting that the local health department get rid of rats in the neighborhood. Students might also role-play the landing of astronauts on the moon, the Pilgrims' arrival or other historical occasions. Or they could role-play a

■ **Clustering** is a form of brainstorming.

■ **Freewriting** is a form of writing in which participants write for a brief period of time on an assigned or self-selected topic without prior planning and without stopping. Freewriting can be used as a warm-up activity or a way of freeing up the participant's writing ability. One danger of freewriting is that students might get the mistaken idea that writing is an unplanned, spontaneous activity.

Little League coach giving her team a pep talk, the principal confronting two students who have been arguing, or a zookeeper answering questions about the newly acquired giraffe.

Actually beginning to write is another way of getting started. "Writing is generative. The hardest line to write is the first one" (Spandel, 2001, p. 135). Often, after writers get that first sentence down, the ideas begin to flow.

## Composing

■ **Composing** is that part of the writing process in which the writer creates a piece.

**Composing** is the act of writing a piece. The idea is for the writer to put her or his thoughts down on paper without concern for neatness, spelling, or the mechanics. A writer who is concerned about spelling is taking valuable time away from the more important job of creating. Reassure students that they will have time later to revise and edit. Model how you go about composing a piece. As you compose your piece, explain what is going on in your mind so that students can gain insight into the process.

Experienced writers generally have far more information than they can use, and discard much of it either before or after it is put on the page. However, elementary school students often do not seem to have enough to say. According to Scardamalia and Bereiter (1986), "For young writers finding enough content is frequently a problem and they cannot imagine discarding anything that would fit" (p. 785).

Finding enough to say may be essentially a problem of access (Scardamalia & Bereiter, 1986). Younger students are used to oral conversations in which the responses of the listener act as cues for retrieving knowledge. When the speaker fails to supply enough information, the listener's blank look or questions ferret out more talk:

> Written speech is more abstract than oral speech. . . . It is speech without an interlocutor. This creates a situation completely foreign to the conversation the child is accustomed to. In written speech, those to whom the speech is directed are either absent or out of contact with the writer. Written speech is speech with a white sheet of paper, with an imaginary or conceptualized interlocutor. Still, like oral speech, it is a conversational situation. Written speech requires a dual abstraction from the child. (Vygotsky, 1987, pp. 202–203)

This need to supply the missing listener when writing explains, perhaps, why prewriting activities are so important and why postdrafting conferences are so helpful in evoking a full written response from younger students. Scardamalia, Bereiter, and Goelman (1982) found that just encouraging young writers, who claimed to have written everything they knew, doubled their output. What the children had apparently done was extract their top-level memories, which are the main ideas, the generalities. They had not mined the lower-level memories, the examples, details, and explanations, that give body to the general ideas. With encouragement, they proceeded to do so.

Instruction for novice writers might begin with narrative writing. Narrative writing is easier and more natural for young writers than is expository writing. They

---

Composing is difficult because writing is decontextualized, so the writer must compose the whole message without the prompts supplied in conversation, must also create a context so the message is understandable, and must compose for an unseen audience. Prewriting activities and conferences help supply some of the support that is provided in conversation but not composition.

---

**BUILDING LANGUAGE**

Before students can write stories, they must become acquainted with the language of stories. Reading to them and discussing stories will help, as will using story books as models for their writing. After reading *A Dinosaur Named after Me* (Most, 1991), children might imitate the author's style as they write about their favorite dinosaur.

are used to hearing and reading stories. Narratives by beginning writers might only be a sentence or two long (New Standards Primary Literacy Committee, 1999). Later, in about grade two, young writers use a technique known as chaining in which one event is linked to another but there is no central focus. In another early form of narrative, students write "bed to bed" stories in which they simply recount the day's happenings. In the dialogue narrative, which is another form of early writing, the story is told through conversations between two people: The boy said, "I am scared." Then the girl said, "Why are you scared?" The boy said, "I am afraid that dog will bite me." Then the girl said, " I don't think that dog will bite you." In the event narrative, a third form of early writing, young writers simply recount one event after another with no attempt to show connections. By about third grade, students are able to write simple narratives that have a central focus.

A number of techniques foster the development of narrative writing. Shared reading can be used to present models of narrative writing. One easy type of writing is to use the structure of a piece but substitute one's own ideas or words. For instance, using the structure of *Brown Bear, Brown Bear, What Do You See?* (Martin, 1983), students might write a story entitled "Gray Owl, Gray Owl, What Do You Spy?"

After students have acquired some experience writing narratives, wordless picture books, such as the *Carl* series, might be used to encourage young students to create a story that goes along with the illustrations. Also, have students use toys, puppets, a felt board, or other props to create a story (Education Department of Western Australia, 1994). This helps them to structure their stories.

For older students, cut out a series of pictures and have students sequence the pictures and create a story to accompany the pictures. This could be a whole-group or small-group activity. Students might also create a storyboard. A storyboard is a series of drawings used by creators of ads, TV shows, and movies to show the plot of their work. The storyboard might show the main scenes, actions, or events.

For novice writers, the mechanical production of letters and words may take an extraordinary amount of effort. Place less emphasis on handwriting and mechanics so students can focus on content and style.

Students need to know that their first writing is a draft and that the focus should be on getting thoughts down. There is plenty of time for revising and correcting later.

Beginnings are often the most difficult part of a piece to create. If students are blocked by an inability to create an interesting beginning, advise them to write down the best beginning they can think of and then return to it after they have com-

> Because much of the writing students will be asked to do in life and in content-area subjects will be expository, the program should include a balance of narrative and expository writing. One way of achieving this balance is to include writing in all areas of the curriculum.

> Composing is an uneven process. We sometimes can't get our ideas down fast enough. At other times, we labor to get a few words down so the paper won't look so blank.

*C*omposing a first draft is a key element in the writing process.

■ A **draft** is the writer's first copy and is not intended to be a finished product.

pleted their first **draft.** This same principle applies to other aspects of composing. If students cannot remember a fact, a name, or how to spell a word, they can leave a blank or insert a question mark and come back later. Nothing should interrupt the forward flow of the composing process.

Some students freeze at the sight of a blank piece of paper. Discuss some possible opening sentences. If nothing else works, suggest to the students that they just start writing. Their first sentence might simply be a statement that they are having difficulty getting started. As they continue to write, it is very likely that other thoughts will kick in.

▌Composing requires focus, discipline, and time. Make the writing period as long as possible, and if your schedule permits, allow students whose writing is flowing to continue for a longer stretch of time.

### ■ Focusing on Audience

Although we make lists or diary entries strictly for ourselves, most of our writing is geared toward an audience. A sense of audience helps shape our writing. As we write, we consider the backgrounds and interests of our readers. We try to think of ways of making our writing appealing as well as informative. Young writers typically lack a sense of audience and may assume that the readers already know whatever the writers know. A first step in writing is to define whom one is writing for. To help young students write for a particular audience, help them ponder the following questions (Learning Media, 1991):

What is my topic?
Why am I writing this piece?
Who will read my piece?
What might they already know about the topic?
What do they need to know?

▌Once students gain a sense of audience, their writing becomes more restricted. They begin to worry whether their peers will approve of their writing.

The answers to these questions should help sharpen students' focus and provide them with a plan for gathering information. As they look over what they need to know and what they want to tell their audience, students can begin collecting information from books, family members, Web sites, computer databases, or experts. They might then use semantic webs or other diagrams to help them organize their information. Again, audience comes into play as students ask themselves, "How can I present this information so that my audience will understand it?" Teacher modeling, minilessons, and conferences with teacher and peers might be used to help students organize their material.

To help students gain a sense of audience, have them share what they have written. Students should focus on communicating with others rather than writing to meet a certain standard of performance or earn a certain grade. As they get feedback, they can clarify confusing details or add examples if that is what their audience seemed to need. The teacher can model sharing by reading pieces she has written and inviting students to respond.

■ **Revising** is that part of the writing process in which the author reconsiders and alters what she has written.

## Revising

For many students, revising means making mechanical corrections—putting in missing periods and capital letters and checking suspicious spellings. Actually, **revising** goes to the heart of the piece and could involve adding or deleting material, changing the sequence, getting a better lead, adding details, or substituting more vivid words for overused expressions. Revising means rethinking a work and can, in fact, lead to a total reworking of the piece. Revision may be aided by a peer conference or a conference with the teacher.

### ■ Modeling the Revision Process

One way of conveying the concept of revision is for the teacher to model the process. The teacher puts an original draft that he or she has written on the chalkboard or overhead. She or he poses pertinent questions such as: "Does this piece say what I want it to say? Have I fully explained what I want to say? Is it clear? Is it interesting? Is it well organized?" The teacher can then show how to add details, clarify a confusing passage, or switch sentences around. The teacher might also model some highly productive revising routines. Essential routines include rewriting for clarity, rewriting beginnings and endings to give them more impact, substituting more vivid or more appropriate words, rearranging sentences or paragraphs, and adding additional examples or details.

Another helpful approach is to use samples of published pieces and students' writing to demonstrate effective writing. When working on improving leads, for instance, show students a variety of pieces in which writers have composed especially effective openings. Also encourage students to note particularly creative leads in their reading. Do the same with endings and also middles. Summarize by looking at pieces that do all three well.

To dramatize the power of good leads, share a piece that has an especially good opening but omit the opening. Instead have students select from three leads the one they think the author wrote. Do the same with conclusions.

Over a series of lessons, the teacher shows students how to make revisions, as indicated by the kinds of writing challenges that students are meeting. One group might be grappling with lead sentences, whereas another group might not be fully developing ideas. In time, students can demonstrate to their peers how they successfully revised a piece. Having professional writers such as children's authors and newspaper reporters visit the class to demonstrate how they revise will emphasize the importance of revision and the fact that virtually everyone who writes must do it.

Have students practice revising by revising someone else's paper. The paper could be one that you have composed for this purpose or it could be from a published source or one that was done by a student in a former class. The author, of course, should be anonymous. Start with papers that obviously need revising but aren't so hopelessly bad that they would overwhelm students. Revise some of the papers as a group exercise. Allow students to add or delete details or examples so they aren't just rewording the piece. After students have caught on to the idea of revising, have them work in pairs and then individually. When working in pairs, they should discuss the reasons for any changes they made. As they work individually, they revise their own writing. However, after revising a paper, they might then confer with a partner.

Show students how you read and reread a draft and decide what changes need to be made. With the class, devise a revision checklist. A key question to ask is: Does it sound right? Students should develop an "ear" for good writing.

Instruction should also include the mechanical techniques of revision. Students can cross out, cut and paste, and use carets to insert to their hearts' content. Long insertions may be indicated with an asterisk and placed on a separate sheet of paper. Students should be encouraged to revise as much as they feel they have to. To remind students of the kinds of things they should be doing when they revise, you might develop a revision checklist. Figure 10.2 presents a sample checklist.

> If students are using word processing programs, show them the mechanics of making revisions: how to check spelling, how to replace and delete items, how to use the thesaurus. Demonstrate how they might make major changes by adding ideas or shifting sentences or whole paragraphs around.

Students have five areas of concern in writing: spelling, motor aesthetic (handwriting and appearance), convention, topic information, and revision (Graves, 1983). Although they operate in all five areas from the very first stages of writing, early emphasis is on the lower-level processes: spelling, motor aesthetic, and convention. New writers find it most difficult to revise content. However, what the teacher stresses in class also has an effect on what the child emphasizes. Given good teaching, children will put aside undue concern about spelling, handwriting, and appearance and concentrate on improving content and expression. Spelling, handwriting, and conventions must be taught, but in perspective. Mechanical issues usually recede into the background by the time a child is seven years old or so, but if overemphasized, they could "last a lifetime" (D. H. Graves, 1983, p. 237). From an early concern with spelling and handwriting, children can be led to add information to their pieces and, later, to making more complex revisions such as reordering sentences or clarifying confusing points. One of the last revision skills to develop is the ability—and willingness—to delete material that should be left out.

> Revising takes objectivity. To distance themselves from their writing, professional writers usually let a piece sit for at least twenty-four hours and then take a good, hard look at it.

Conferences help children move beyond mechanical revisions. "Revisions that children make as a result of the conference can be at a much higher level than those made when the child is working and reading alone" (D. H. Graves, 1983, p. 153). This is an excellent manifestation of Vygotsky's (1987) concept of zone of proximal development, which states that with the support of adults, children can operate on a higher level and, ultimately, perform higher-level tasks on their own. In other words, what students ask for help with now they will be able to do on their own in the future.

As with other cognitive activities, younger students are less likely to monitor their writing. For example, they may fail to consider the background or interests of their intended audience (Maimon & Nodine, 1979). Through skillful questioning in conferences, the teacher can help students see their writing from the point of view of the audience. This helps them figure out what they want to say and how to say it so others will understand. The teacher provides an executive structure to help students revise effectively (Scardamalia & Bereiter, 1986). In time, students internalize such a structure, allowing them to monitor their writing just as they learn with experience and instruction to monitor their reading.

> Revising should not be neglected, but there is some danger in overemphasizing it. Although all pieces should be reread carefully, they may not have to be revised or may require only minor changes. This is especially true if the writer is experienced and has prepared carefully before writing. Knowing when to revise and when not to revise is an important skill.

During the revision process, focus on one element. Revision is more effective when the focus is on just one element at a time—the lead, details, word choices, or concluding sentence (Spandel, 2001).

### FIGURE 10.2

**A Sample Revision Checklist**

_____ Does the piece say what I want it to say?

_____ Will the audience understand it?

_____ Is it interesting?

_____ What might I do to make it more interesting?

_____ Did I give enough details or examples?

_____ Does it sound right?

# Editing

In the **editing** stage, students check carefully for mechanical errors, adding commas and question marks and correcting misspelled words. Ideally, all mechanical errors should be corrected. Realistically, the teacher should stress certain major elements. For some students, correcting all errors could be a very discouraging process. The degree of editing depends on students' maturity and proficiency.

Editing can begin as early as kindergarten, with children checking to make sure they put names, dates, and page numbers on their pieces (Calkins, 1986). As new skills are acquired, the items to be checked increase to include spelling, punctuation, capitalization, and so on.

Just as with revision, editing should be modeled. Children should also have access to its tools: pencils, a dictionary, easy style guides, and editing checklists. Such checklists help support students' evolving executive function and encourage them to focus on the conventions of writing, which require looking at writing objectively and abstractly. Such a checklist should be geared to the students' expertise and experience; a sample is presented in Figure 10.3. Peer editing can also be employed. However, this is just an additional check. The authors should realize that, ultimately, it is their own responsibility to correct errors.

When deciding which editing skills to introduce, examine students' current writing and see what is most needed. Sometimes, the nature of the writing will dictate the skill. If students are writing pieces in which they will be talking about titles of books, introduce italicizing and underlining. After you have taught a skill, have students add it to their editing checklists. Also display a brief explanation or example of the skill's use on the bulletin board, as shown in Figure 10.4, so that students have a reminder of it (Muschla, 1993).

As a final editing check, the teacher should examine the piece before approving it for copying onto good paper or typing. The teacher might decide to note all errors for an advanced student and focus on only one or two areas for a less advanced

**FIGURE 10.3**

### A Sample Editing Checklist

\_\_\_\_ Is my story clear? Will readers be able to understand it?

\_\_\_\_ Did I write in complete sentences?

\_\_\_\_ Did I capitalize the first word of every sentence?

\_\_\_\_ Did I capitalize the names of people, cities, towns, and other places?

\_\_\_\_ Did I end each sentence with a period, question mark, or exclamation point?

\_\_\_\_ Did I spell all the words correctly?

■ **Editing** is that part of the writing process in which the author searches for spelling, typographical, and other mechanical errors.

**USING TECHNOLOGY**
With talking word processing programs, students can listen as the program recites their pieces. Hearing their pieces read, they are better able to note dropped *ing*s and *ed*s, omitted words, and awkward expressions.

Collect children's books and periodicals that provide good models for writing. For instance, when introducing a question-and-answer format, use *What Food Is This?* (Hausher, 1994), *Ask Me Anything about Dinosaurs* (Phillips, 1997), or similar question-and-answer texts as models.

**FIGURE 10.4**

### Editing Reminder

*Underline the titles of books, magazines, newspapers, and movies:*
*The Paper Chase, My Friend Rabbit, Your Big Backyard.*
*(If you are using a word processor, italicize instead of underlining. Underlining is used to tell whoever is printing the piece to use italics.)*

■ **Publishing** is that part of the writing process in which the author makes her writing public.

■ **Author's chair** is the practice of having a student author share her work with the rest of the class.

■ A **conference** is a conversation between teacher and student(s) or among students designed to foster the development of one or more aspects of the writing process.

student. If the piece is to be published, however, all errors should be corrected. The corrections should be handled in such a way that the child is not deprived of pride in his product. Making such corrections must be recognized for the lower-level, mechanical skill that it is.

The writing process has been described step by step to make it more understandable; however, in reality, many steps may be operating at the same time, and the steps are not necessarily executed in order. For example, writers mentally plan and revise and edit as they compose (Scardamalia & Bereiter, 1986).

## Publishing

As Emig (1971) noted in her landmark study, students all too often write for an audience of one—the teacher—which limits their style. Students tend to write in a way they think will be most appealing to the teacher and so never gain a true sense of audience. In the writing process approach, the emphasis is on writing for real purposes and real audiences and on going public with the works. Poems are collected in anthologies. Stories are bound in books, which are placed in the library. Essays and reports are shared and placed on classroom and school bulletin boards or on the class or school Web site. Scripts are dramatized. Essays and stories are entered in contests and printed in class and school publications or submitted to Web sites and children's magazines that print young people's works. Other ways of **publishing** include creating charts, posters, ads, brochures, announcements, sets of directions, book reviews, and video- or audiotapes.

To emphasize the importance of the writer, the teacher might arrange to have a student share his or her writing orally through use of the **author's chair.** Seated in this special chair, the author reads her or his piece to the class and invites comments. Special assemblies are also held to honor authors. Professional writers are invited to share with the other writers in the class. With publication and celebration, children put their hearts into their writing.

## Conferences

Wanting to improve her writing, Lucy McCormick Calkins (1986) wrote to Donald Murray, a well-known writing teacher, and asked if he could help her. Murray agreed to hold **conferences** with her once a month. For two years, Calkins made the five-hour round trip from Connecticut to the University of New Hampshire each month for a fifteen-minute conference, which was primarily a conversation about her writing. Was the drive worth it? According to Calkins, yes: "He taught me I had something to say" (p. 124).

If a conference does not show writers that they have something to say, it fails to achieve its purpose. Through encouraging, careful questioning and responding, the teacher tells the writer, "You have a story to tell!" A conference is an affirmation. A belief in young people is the only unbreakable rule for conducting conferences. If we have a fundamental faith that everyone has a story to tell, we do not supply topics. Students must search within themselves and their experiences for subjects to write about. If we start directing and shaping, we are taking over the topic. Written under our direction, the piece may actually sound better, but it will be our piece—we will have stolen it from the student. Through careful questioning and responding, help students discover their stories and techniques for telling them. According to Turbill (1982), the teacher "is advised to develop the art of questioning; instead of telling what to do, [the teacher] uses questions to move the child to find answers" (p. 35).

### Conference Questions

In a typical conference, three types of questions are asked: opening, following, and process. They are nonjudgmental and are intended to evoke an open and honest response. Opening questions might take one of the following forms: "How is it going? How is your piece coming? What are you working on today?" The student's response provides clues for following questions, which are asked to find out more about how the child's writing is progressing. Process questions such as "What will you do next?" prompt students to make plans or take action. However, do not be so concerned about asking questions that you forget to listen. Calkins (1986) cautioned, "Our first job in a conference, then, is to be a person, not just a teacher. It is to enjoy, to care, and to respond" (p. 119).

Sometimes, a human response is all that is necessary. At other times, the teacher reflects the child's line of thinking but gently nudges the child forward. The student might say, for example, "I'm not sure how to describe my dog. My dog isn't a purebred." The teacher reflects that concern by saying, "You're not sure how to describe your dog because he is just an ordinary dog?" The repetition is an expression of interest that encourages the child to elaborate and continue the flow. If that does not work, more directed responses might include such questions as "You say your dog isn't a purebred, but is there anything special about him? What does your dog look like? Can you think of anything about the way your dog acts or looks that might set him apart from other dogs?" Care must be taken that questions are not too directed, or there may be the danger that the teacher is taking over the writing. The purpose of the questioning is to have writers explore ways in which they might develop their work.

If a piece is confusing, the teacher might say, "I liked the way you talked about the funny things your dog did, but I don't understand how you taught him to roll over." The child will then tell how she or he taught the dog to roll over and most likely realize that this is an element to be included in the piece.

If a child has not developed a piece adequately, the teacher might say, "You said your dog was always getting into trouble. Can you

In helping young writers, teachers tend to stress content, which is as it should be. However, some attention has to be paid to form, especially when children are exploring new modes, such as a first attempt to write an informational piece or a mystery.

*S*tudents plan a class newspaper in which they will publish their writing.

tell me what kind of trouble he gets into?" Often, the response will be an oral rehearsal for what to write in the next draft. "They tell me what they are going to write in the next draft, and they hear their own voices telling me. I listen and they learn" (Murray, 1979, p. 16).

Through our questioning, we come to an understanding of the writer. Using this understanding, we are better able to supply the guidance that will best help the writer develop. We ask ourselves, "Of all that I could say to this student, what will help her most?" (Calkins, 1994). Questions are geared to the nature and needs of the student. Table 10.1 presents some common writing difficulties that students encounter and teacher prompts that might be used to help them focus on these difficulties. At times, students will reject the teacher's hints or suggestions, preferring to take a piece in a different direction. That is their prerogative. After each conference, note the student's writing strengths, needs, plans, and other pertinent information. A sample writing conference summary sheet is shown in Figure 10.5.

### ■ Peer Conferences

Conferences with peers can also be very helpful. Group discussions in which students weigh alternatives lead students to plan on a deeper level and weigh suggestions (Bereiter & Scardamalia, 1982).

Effective peer conferencing is a learned behavior. Discuss the ingredients of a successful conference and then model and supervise the process. In addition to being effective and producing improved writing, conferences must be humane and should build a sense of community and respect. Some general principles of conferencing include the following:

- Students should learn to listen carefully.
- Students should lead off with a positive comment about the piece.
- Students should make concrete suggestions.
- Suggestions should be put in positive terms.

**TABLE 10.1** Teacher prompts for common writing difficulties

| Writing Difficulty | Teacher Prompts |
| --- | --- |
| Topic is too broad or lacks focus | What is your purpose in writing this? What's the most important or most interesting idea here? How might you develop that? |
| Piece lacks details or examples | I like your piece about _____. But I don't know very much about _____. Can you tell more about it? |
| Needs a beginning sentence | How might you start this off? What might you say to pull your reader into this story? |
| Inadequate conclusion or lack of ending | How might you sum up what you've said? What thought or idea do you want your reader to take away from this? |
| Lack of coherence or unity | What is your main purpose here? Do all your ideas fit? Are your ideas in the best order? |

Adapted from *Writing Workshop Survival Kit* by G. R. Muschla, 1993, West Nyack, NY: The Center for Applied Research in Education.

FIGURE 10.5

## Writing Conference Summary

| Name | Date | Topic | Strengths | Needs | Plans |
|------|------|-------|-----------|-------|-------|
| Angel | 11/15 | Football game | Exciting opening. | Key part not clear. | Tell how he caught pass. |
| Amy | 11/15 | Pet rabbit | Interesting subject. | Not developed enough. | Give examples of pet's tricks. |
| James | | Little sister | | | |
| Keisha | | Making friends | | | |
| Maria | | Dream vacation | | | |
| Marsha | | Recycling trash | | | |
| Robert | | Letter to sports star | | | |
| Stephanie | | New bicycle | | | |

Highly effective teachers carefully instruct students in the art of conducting successful writing and reading conferences. They might even have a group of students from a previous year model a conference. They also continue to monitor conferences so that they can lend their expertise to making sure that conferences are as productive as they can be (Wharton-McDonald, 2001). Working with a student, model a peer conference and show how suggestions can be used to make revisions.

### ■ Authors' Circle

One form of peer conference is the **authors' circle.** When students have pieces they wish to share, they gather at an authors' table and read their works to each other. The teacher may also join the circle. The only requirement is that everyone in the circle have a work he or she wishes to read (Harste, Short, & Burke, 1988).

The authors' circle is designed for rough drafts rather than edited pieces. By seeking and listening to the reactions of others, students can determine whether

■ An **authors' circle** is a form of peer conferencing in which students meet to discuss their drafts and obtain suggestions for possible revision.

their works need clarification and which parts might have to be revised. Both authors and listeners benefit from the circle. Harste, Short, and Burke (1988) commented:

> As they shared their stories with others through informal interactions and authors' circles, the children shifted from taking the perspective of an author to taking the perspective of reader and critic. These shifts occurred as they read their pieces aloud and listened to the comments other authors made about their stories. As children became aware of their audience, they were able to see their writing in a different light. (p. 32)

The ultimate purpose of conferences is to help writers internalize the process so that they ask themselves such things as: "How is my writing going? What will I do next? How do I like what I have written? Is there anything I would like to change?"

##  WRITING WORKSHOP

Just as students learn to read by reading, they learn to write by writing. The **writing workshop** is a way of providing students with the opportunity to try out newly introduced strategies under the teacher's guidance (Collins, 1998). Through individual or small-group conferences, the teacher can help students adapt and implement strategies that were taught in whole-class or guided writing sessions. Writing workshop consists of the following elements: minilessons, guided writing, writing time, conferences, and sharing. If possible, the workshop should be held every day.

### Minilesson

Minilessons are generally presented to the whole group. The purpose of the **minilesson** is to present a needed writing skill or concept. The minilesson lasts for only about ten minutes, so the skill should be one that is fairly easy to understand. The skill could be capitalizing titles, selecting topics, using correct letter form, or any one of a dozen fairly easy-to-teach skills. Minlessons can also be used to explain workshop procedures.

### Guided Writing/Strategic Writing

During guided writing, students are taught writing strategies in small groups according to their stage of writing development. To teach a writing strategy, provide examples of the target strategy as it appears in selections that students are reading and also in pieces written by their peers and you. Just as in other sample lessons, discuss the strategy and how it will help their writing. Model the use of the strategy, showing, for instance, how you might write an interesting lead. Provide guided practice and have students apply the skill by using it in their own writing. Revision and evaluation should focus on the element introduced. The skill should be reviewed and reintroduced in conferences and follow-up lessons until it becomes virtually automatic. Lesson 10.1 shows a sample strategic writing lesson. Notice that this lesson is more extensive than a minilesson and may take ten to twenty minutes to teach.

## LESSON 10.1 Writing strategy: Adding specific details

**Step 1.** Show a paragraph, such as the following, that calls out for elaboration. Do not use a student's paragraph, as this will embarrass the writer.

> The Strange Day
> I turned on the radio. The announcer said to stay inside. She said that the streets were very dangerous. My father said that the announcement was a joke. But it wasn't.

Invite students to read the paragraph. Ask students whether they have questions that they might like to have answered. Write students' questions on the board. Discuss the author's failure to include needed details.

**Step 2.** Show the students how you can make the piece come alive by adding details. Add needed details and compare the revised paragraph with the original.

> The Strange Day
> On my way to my place at the breakfast table, I switched on the radio. My favorite song was being played. Suddenly, the music stopped. "We have an important news flash for our listeners," the announcer said. "A monkey stole keys from the zoo keeper and opened all the cages. The streets are now full of dangerous, wild animals. The elephants have already smashed five cars. Stay in your homes. If you spot any wild animals, call the police immediately. But do not let the animals into your home."
>
> "Hey, Mom and Dad," I shouted. "Come quick. There's trouble in the streets." When I told them what I had heard, they started laughing. Dad pointed to the calendar. "Don't you remember what day this is? It's April first. It's April Fool's Day. Somebody is playing a trick on the town."
>
> Dad was still laughing when he headed out the door for work. But he wasn't laughing seconds later when he rushed back inside and slammed the door shut. "Call 911!" he shouted. "There's a tiger sitting on the roof of my car."

### Step 3. Guided practice

Provide one or two practice paragraphs that are lacking in details. Working with students, add needed details.

**Step 4. Application**

Encourage students to flesh out their stories by adding needed details. During the ensuing workshop session, provide any needed assistance.

**Step 5. Extension**

As a follow-up, have volunteers show how they added details to their stories. In subsequent lessons, discuss the many ways in which writing can be elaborated.

**Step 6. Assessment and review**

In conferences and while looking over various drafts of students' writing, evaluate whether they are fully developing their pieces. Provide additional instruction as needed.

## Writing Strategies

There are dozens of writing strategies. Listed below are the ones that seem most essential for students. The strategies are listed in approximate order of difficulty. However, some strategies are taught at every level. For instance, writing an interesting lead would be a concern throughout the lower grades but would be a more complex undertaking in grade four than it would be in grade one.

### ■ Expository Writing

- Writing clear, complete sentences.
- Writing a lead or beginning sentence. The lead or beginning sentence often gives the main idea of a piece and should grab the reader's interest and entice her or him to read the piece.
- Developing informational pieces. Informational pieces can be developed with details, including facts, opinions, examples, and descriptions. Failure to develop a topic is a major flaw in students' writing.
- Writing an effective ending. An effective ending should provide a summary of the piece and or restate the main point of the piece in such a way that it has an impact on the reader.
- Using precise, varied, and vivid words, using substitutes for *said* or *good*, for instance.
- Using a thesaurus to help achieve a varied vocabulary.
- Gathering appropriate and sufficient information for a piece. Writers do their best work when they are overflowing with information and can't wait to put it down on paper.
- Using figurative language, including similes.
- Using advanced writing devices such as alliteration.
- Using varied sentence patterns.
- Combining short sentences into longer ones.

**USING TECHNOLOGY**

Real Kids, Real Adventures is an informative site for young writers that features author information, writing guidelines and hints, and book reviews.
**http://www.realkids. com/club.shtml**

Biography Maker provides step-by-step directions for composing biographies.
**http://www.bham. wednet.edu/bio/ biomak2.htm**

**http://www. web4school.com** lists a number of sites that assist students with their writing.

- Writing in a variety of forms: poems, stories, plays, letters, advertisements, announcements, expository pieces, newspaper articles.
- Writing for a variety of purposes and audiences.
- Providing transitions so that one thought leads into another and the writing flows.

### Narrative or Fictional Writing

- Writing a story that has a well-developed beginning, middle, and end.
- Developing believable characters by using description, action, and dialogue.
- Creating a setting.
- Developing an interesting plot.
- Creating an interesting ending, including surprise endings.
- Writing dialogue that sounds natural.
- Creating a title that makes the reader want to read the piece.
- Building suspense.

> "Time is an important element in writing workshop. If students are going to become deeply invested in their writing . . . and if they are going to let their ideas grow and gather momentum, if they are going to draft and revise, sharing their texts with one another as they write, they need the luxury of time" (Calkins, 1994, p. 186).

## Writing Time

Writing time, which is the core of the workshop, lasts for thirty minutes or longer. During that time, students work on their individual pieces, have peer or teacher conferences, meet in small groups to discuss their writing, or meet in their guided writing groups. Before beginning this portion of the lesson, you may want to check with students to see what their plans are for this period.

*Students should have specific plans for each day's writing workshop.*

As students write, hold one or two guided writing sessions. As time allows, circulate in the classroom and supply on-the-spot help or encouragement as needed. You might show one student how to use the spell checker, applaud another who has just finished a piece, encourage a third who is searching for just the right ending, and discuss topic possibilities with a student who cannot seem to decide what to write about. You might also have scheduled conferences with several students or sit in on a peer conference that students have convened.

In peer conferences, students can meet in pairs or in small groups of four or five. In these conferences, one or more students may read their drafts and seek the comments and suggestions of the others.

### Group Sharing

At appropriate times, such as the end of the day, students gather for group sharing. Volunteers read their pieces. The atmosphere is positive, and other students listen attentively and tell the author what they like about the piece. They also ask questions, make suggestions, and might inquire about the author's future plans for writing. Through large-group sharing, a sense of community is built. Student writers are shown appreciation by their audience. They also have the opportunity to hear what their peers are writing about, what techniques their peers are using, and what struggles they are having.

## Management of the Writing Workshop

Active and multifaceted, the writing workshop requires careful management. The room should be well organized. Professional writers have offices, studies, or at least desks at which to work. They also have access to the tools of writing. The classroom should be set up as a writer's workshop. Younger students need an assortment of soft lead pencils, crayons, magic markers, and sheets of unlined paper. Older students can get by with pencil and paper but should have some choices, too. At times, they might feel the need to write on a yellow legal pad or with a pink magic marker. You should have a round table or two for group meetings, a word processing or editing corner, and a reference corner that contains a dictionary, style guide, and other references. Staplers, paper, and writing instruments of various kinds should be placed in the supply corner. Writing folders or portfolios should be arranged alphabetically in cartons. Involve students in helping with housekeeping chores. They can take turns seeing that materials are put away and that writing folders are in order.

Before starting the workshop, explain the setup of the room and show where supplies and materials are located. With the class, develop a series of rules and routines. Before students engage in peer conferences or small sharing groups, discuss and model these activities.

Be aware of students' productivity. Students should have specific plans for each day's workshop: revise a piece, confer with the teacher, obtain additional information about a topic, start a new piece. Make sure that peer conferences are devoted to writing and not last night's TV programs.

Writing is a social as well as a cognitive act. Writers are influenced by the teacher's expectations and by the expectations of peers. Students try to figure out what the teacher wants and write accordingly. Writers also want approval from their peers. They may hesitate to include certain details or write on certain topics if they fear their classmates will criticize them (Dahl & Farnan, 1998).

It is important to note the social dynamics of peer group conferences. Lensmire (1994) found teasing in the peer groups in his third-grade classroom. And he found that students who were not socially accepted in general were mistreated in the peer conference group. Lensmire suggested that students work toward a common goal, such as investigating a particular genre. With a common goal to guide them, it was hoped that the focus would be on working toward the goal rather than on peer relationships. He also recommended more teacher guidance in the workshop setting. Getting feedback from students on the impact of peer and teacher conferences and other aspects of the workshop on their development as writers would also be helpful (Dahl & Farnan, 1998).

Note students who do more conferencing than writing, those who never seem to confer, and those who have been on the same piece for weeks. You might keep a record of students' activities in a daily log. A sample daily log, adapted from Muschla (1993), is presented in Figure 10.6.

As you circulate in the room, note students' strengths and weaknesses. During the guided writing or sharing period, call attention to the positive things that you saw: Mary Lou's colorful use of language, Fred's title, Jamie's interesting topic. Needs

**FIGURE 10.6**

### Daily Log: Student's Plans for Writing Workshop

| Name | Topic | M | T | W | Th | F |
|------|-------|---|---|---|----|---|
| Angel | Football game | D-1, TC | RE | | | |
| Amy | Pet rabbit | E, TC | PE | | | |
| James | Little sister | AC | R, TC | | | |
| Keisha | Making friends | AC | M | | | |
| Maria | Dream vacation | TC, D-2 | E | | | |
| Marsha | Recycling trash | M | P, S | | | |
| Robert | Letter to sports star | AC | R | | | |
| Stephanie | New bicycle | R | D-3, TC | | | |

Key

| | | | | | | | |
|---|---|---|---|---|---|---|---|
| P: | Planning | E: | Editing | M: | Making final copy | TC: | Teacher conference |
| D: | Drafting | PE: | Peer editing | RE: | Researching | AC: | Author's circle |
| R: | Revising | PUB: | Publishing | PC: | Peer conference | S: | Sharing |

that you note might be the basis for a future mini- or guided writing lesson or a brief, on-the-spot, one-on-one lesson or—if several students display a common need—a small-group lesson.

Most of all, serious writing demands time. Even professionals need a warm-up period to get into their writing. Once the thoughts begin to flow on paper, however, writers have to keep on writing. If possible, at least thirty minutes to an hour a day, three to five days a week, should be set aside for writing.

## INTERPERSONAL WRITING

■ **Interpersonal writing** is writing that is exchanged and responded to by two participants over a period of time.

A highly motivating method for eliciting writing from students is **interpersonal writing,** which is a written dialogue or conversation. It can be conducted between teacher and student, two students, student and pen pal, or student and grandparent or other adult. Interpersonal writing most often takes the form of dialogue journals but can be embodied in letters, notes, e-mail, or written conversations.

■ **Written conversation** is a type of writing in which teacher and student or two students carry on a conversation by writing a series of notes to each other.

In a **written conversation,** two students or a student and a teacher converse by writing to each other. Either party may initiate the conversation, which may be conducted at a table or other convenient spot and include the teacher and one or more students. The teacher might start with a statement or a question such as, "How is your new puppy?" The student responds, and then the teacher replies. As one student is responding, the teacher can initiate a written conversation with a second student, and then a third.

Written conversations provide practice in both reading and writing. The teacher's writing is geared to the student's reading level. If the student's reading level is very limited, the teacher can read her letter to the student. If a student's writing ability is so rudimentary that the teacher cannot understand it, the student is asked to read it.

Duffy (1994) used written conversation with primary-grade students. When visiting a writing group, she would jot down an initiating sentence in each of their journals. As they wrote responses, Duffy would visit another group and then return to the first group to reply to their responses. Prompted by the teacher's writing, typical student responses might produce up to one hundred words. Written conversations have also been used with older learning-disabled children. Both reading and writing fluency increased (Rhodes & Dudley-Marling, 1988).

The use of interpersonal writing does raise several issues. Students' privacy must be respected. Teacher responses need to be genuine, caring, and sensitive. If health or safety concerns are raised because of information revealed by students, consult with the school principal regarding your legal and ethical responsibilities.

## JOURNALS AND PERSONAL NARRATIVES

Two kinds of writing predominate in the early grades: journals and personal narratives (Wharton-McDonald, 2001). Journals have a number of purposes but are most often used to record personal experiences or personal reflections. A first-grader might record an account of a T-ball game or a trip to the vet with his sick dog. However, journals can take the form of a dialogue in which the teacher or another student responds to a journal entry. Journals might also be used to record science observations or responses to literature. Journal entries might be open-ended or prompted or a combination. Since they are typically a daily activity, journals run the risk of becoming humdrum and routine. Using imaginative prompts, discussing journal entries, and modeling the writing of imaginative or exciting journal entries can improve the quality and creativity of journal writing.

Journals seem to be most effective when they are used not just as a device to foster fluency in writing but are also viewed as a tool of communication. For instance, journals are used to record observations in science, to communicate with other members of the class, to record ideas for writing, or to inform parents about school activities. An especially beneficial outcome of journals is what they reveal about students' learning. By examining students' journals teachers are able to identify skills and concepts that were being mastered as well as some that needed additional instruction and reinforcement.

The second most popular form of writing in the early grades is the personal narrative. In fact, if left to their own devices, children will write personal narratives to the exclusion of other kinds of writing (Hagerty, Hiebert, & Owens, 1989). Although it is important to give children choice in their writing, they need to be encouraged to try many different kinds of writing.

## IMPROVING EXPOSITORY WRITING

Although some students seem to have a natural bent for narrative and others prefer composing expository text, all students should become acquainted with all major structures, learning how each is written and developed. Part of that instruction simply involves having children read widely in order to acquire a rich background of comparison–contrast, problem–solution, and other expository and narrative structures. However, instruction should also include explaining each structure, modeling the writing of it, and having students compose similar structures.

Expository writing needs special attention. Students' early writing is primarily narrative, so that as students progress through the primary grades, there is a growing gap between narrative and expository writing. Whereas students can write fairly complex narrative structures in third grade, their expository writing typically contains a simple listing of the main idea and supporting details (Langer, 1986).

In a program known as **cognitive strategy instruction in writing,** Raphael, Englert, and Kirschner (1989) combined instruction in text structure and writing strategies to improve students' composing skills. Based on tryouts and experiments that spanned a number of years, these researchers devised strategies that help students make use of text structure to both understand and produce expository prose. In addition to instruction, scaffolding is provided through the use of a series of guides that students might use to plan, compose, and revise their pieces. These guides are dubbed "think sheets" and correspond to the major types of text organization; there are sheets for narrative pieces, compare–contrast structures, explanation, and other text forms. The think sheets are designed to be "concrete reminders of appropriate strategies to use and of the times when particular strategies might be relevant" (Raphael & Englert, 1990, p. 242).

The first think sheet (shown in Figure 10.7) prompts students to plan their writing by noting their audience and reason for writing and to list details that might

> To foster expository writing, read informational pieces aloud so that students get a feel for the language of expository prose.

> **ADAPTING INSTRUCTION for *STRUGGLING READERS and WRITERS***
> **Cognitive strategy instruction in writing** is an approach to writing that emphasizes instruction in writing process and text structure and uses planning sheets as a scaffolding device. It has been especially useful for students with learning disabilities.

FIGURE 10.7

**Planning Think Sheet**

Author's Name: _____ Date: _____

Topic: _Echolocation_ _____

**Who: Who am I writing for?**
_The kids in my group._ _____

**Why: Why am I writing this?**
_Our group is making a book on dolphins._ _____

**What: What is being explained?**
_How dolphins find objects._ _____

**What are the steps?**

First, _Dolphin sends out clicks._ _____
_____

Next, _Clicks bounce off object._ _____
_____

Third, _Clicks return to dolphin._ _____
_____

Then, _Dolphin senses how long it took click to return._ _____
_____

Finally, _Dolphin can tell how far away object is._ _____
_____

Adapted from *Cognitive Strategy Instruction in Writing Project* by C. S. Englert, T. E. Raphael, & L. M. Anderson, 1989, East Lansing, MI: Institute for Research on Teaching.

be included in the piece. Students might also be asked to group ideas or show how they might be organized: steps in a process, comparison–contrast, or problem–solution, for instance. Having shown which ideas they will include and how they will organize their writing, students must then consider an interesting beginning and suitable closing. These can be created as students compose a rough draft, or they can be noted at the bottom of the planning think sheet.

After composing their pieces, students use a self-edit think sheet (shown in Figure 10.8) to assess their pieces. This think sheet prompts them through the first stage of the revising process and asks them to note whether the paper is clear, interesting, and well organized. Because the think sheet will be used by a peer editor to examine the first draft, the student also notes changes that she or he plans to make or questions for the editor. The peer editor uses the sheet to make rec-

**FIGURE 10.8**

## Self-Edit Think Sheet

Author's Name: _____    Date: _____

First, reread my paper. Then answer the following:

What do I like best about my paper?  Gives a good explanation

Why?   Has all the steps

What parts are not clear?

Why not?

Did I . . .

| | | | |
|---|---|---|---|
| 1. Tell what was being explained? | (Yes) | Sort of | No |
| 2. Make the steps clear? | (Yes) | Sort of | No |
| 3. Use keywords to make it clear? | (Yes) | Sort of | No |
| 4. Make it interesting to my reader? | Yes | (Sort of) | No |

What parts do I want to change?
 Make a more interesting beginning

What questions do I have for my editor?
 Is the explanation clear?
 Is the ending OK?

Adapted from *Cognitive Strategy Instruction in Writing Project* by C. S. Englert, T. E. Raphael, & L. M. Anderson, 1989, East Lansing, MI: Institute for Research on Teaching.

ommendations for changes. The editor lists changes that might be made and can also offer suggestions for making the paper more interesting.

After a conference with the peer editor, the student lists the editor's suggestions, decides which ones to use, lists ways of making the paper more interesting, completes a revision think sheet (as shown in Figure 10.9), and then revises the paper.

In real writing, some of the subprocesses presented separately are combined and some may be skipped. Others, such as revision, may be repeated several times. However, it is recommended that students go through all the steps of the process and use the suggested think sheets. Later, as students no longer need scaffolding to use appropriate writing strategies, they may adapt the process. Like other forms of scaffolding, think sheets are intended to be used only until students are able to use the strategies without being prompted to do so. Having incorporated the strategies prompted by the think sheets, the students will no longer need the think sheets.

FIGURE 10.9

**Revision Think Sheet**

Suggestions from My Editor

List all the suggestions your editor has given you:

X  1. _Use a question as a beginning sentence._

X  2. _Use more key words._

X  3. _Write a good closing._

   4. _____

Put an X next to all the suggestions you would like to use in revising your paper. Also think of ideas of your own that might make your paper clearer or more interesting. Read your paper once more, and ask yourself:

Is my beginning interesting? Will it make people want to read my paper?  Not exactly

Are the steps in my explanation clear?  Yes

Did I write down all the steps?  Yes

Are the steps in the right order?  Yes

Do I have a good closing sentence?  No

**Returning to My Draft**

On your draft, make all the changes you think will help your paper. Use ideas from the list above, those from your self-edit think sheet, and any other ideas you may have for your paper. When you are ready, you can write your revised copy.

Adapted from *Cognitive Strategy Instruction in Writing Project* by C. S. Englert, T. E. Raphael, & L. M. Anderson, 1989, East Lansing, MI: Institute for Research on Teaching.

## ASSESSING AND IMPROVING WRITING: THE KEY TRAITS APPROACH

Improving writing requires having a concept of what good writing is, being able to explain to and show students the traits of good writing, and having an assessment system that enables students and teachers to judge whether a piece of writing contains those characteristics. The last part of the piece is devising a plan for teaching students how to revise their writing so as to strengthen key characteristics (Spandel, 2001). In a sense, it's creating a rubric that students can use to plan their writing, assess their writing, and revise their writing. The teacher can use this same rubric, or perhaps a more elaborated form, to plan in-

Classroom teachers at all levels are invited to join the Profiles Network. Details are available at http://www.misd. net. Type in "Profiles Network" under Search.

## *Exemplary Teaching*

### The Profiles Network

*T*he Profiles Network is an organization of teachers who ask students in K through twelfth grade to write to a common prompt. They seek out the best pieces and then analyze these pieces to extract attributes of effective writing. This helps teachers better understand the writing process, and it also provides them with a basis for instruction. Using feedback from their analysis and model pieces, they instruct their students.

Implementing the Profiles approach, teachers in Hamtramck, Michigan, had their students write to the prompt "What I do best." Teachers met and analyzed their papers in order to determine what kinds of things students could do well in their writing and what kinds of things they had difficulty with. On the basis of this analysis, they set general goals and grade-level objectives. By analyzing the best papers, they

were able to select strategies that the best students used and also used these as model pieces of writing.

Teachers also filled out a form for students that told them what was good about the writing and what they might do to improve. In order to help them focus their instruction, teachers also answered a series of questions about students' writing:

- What knowledge and skills are reflected in the students' writing?
- What challenges does the student face?
- What areas does she/he need to develop more fully?
- What interventions or supports would assist this student in meeting the challenges she/he faces? (What can the teacher do to help the student grow as a writer?) (Webber, Nelson, & Woods, 2000, p. 45)

struction and assess students' writing. Such a system enables a teacher to base instruction on assessment.

Describing key characteristics of good writing is somewhat subjective. First of all, you as a teacher need to have a sense of the characteristics of good writing at your grade level. One way of doing this is to examine the best pieces of writing in your class to determine what traits make these pieces of writing especially effective. Although you can do this for your class, it is even more effective when done on a schoolwide or districtwide basis. To help you with the process, visit the Web site of Profiles Network. Profiles Network has a system for examining students' writing, one that teachers at all levels can participate in. Profiles Network also provides a list of traits for several different kinds of writing, along with student samples at each grade level.

The main element in effective writing as determined by Profiles Network and Six Traits Plus, a popular writing assessment system, is content. These are the ideas or information that the piece conveys or, for narrative, the story that it tells. The remainder of the characteristics have to do with form, the way the content is presented. Form can be subdivided into organization, word choice, sentence construction, and mechanics. A final element is voice, which reflects the individual personality of the author.

To help students become aware of the components of good writing, invite them to tell what they think these components are. Write their responses on the board and create a web of the elements. Their responses will tell you what they

The Six Traits Plus analytical model for assessing and teaching writing is made up of: Ideas, the heart of the message; Organization, the internal structure of the piece; Voice, the personal tone and flavor of the author's message; Word Choice, the vocabulary a writer chooses to convey meaning; Sentence Fluency, the rhythm and flow of the language; Conventions, the mechanical correctness; and Presentation, how the writing actually looks on the page.

think the important elements are and, by implication, where they put their efforts when they are writing. Share samples of good writing with students. Discuss with students what it is about these pieces that makes them effective. This will help students broaden their concept of what good writing is (Spandel, 2001). Provide an overview of the characteristics, but then focus on them one by one. You can start with any trait that you want, but because content is key, most teachers start with that one.

To help students become familiar with the traits and to provide practice for assessing writing, have students assess the writing of unknown writers. You might start with published writers who have works on the students' level. One good source would be from periodicals designed for young people. For third-graders, for instance, look at samples from *Weekly Reader* and *Scholastic Magazine*, third edition. If you don't subscribe to these and they are not available in your school library, sample articles are usually available on the publishers' Web sites. Collect pieces of writing that illustrate key elements in writing. Collect both good examples and bad examples so that you can show how the two differ. After students have had some practice assessing the writing of others, have them assess their own writing (Spandel, 2001). The key characteristics should be translated into a rubric (see Figure 2.7 in Chapter 2). Although a generic rubric is helpful, rubrics geared to each major kind of writing would be more effective because they would offer more specific guidance. In addition, different types of writing have different demands. Focusing on key elements, the most effective rubrics are concise and contain only three to six evaluative criteria. Each evaluative criterion must encompass a teachable skill. For instance, evaluative criteria for a how-to piece might include clear description of steps; list of needed materials; effective, sequential organization; and correct use of mechanics. All of these criteria are teachable.

If possible, students should be involved in constructing rubrics. This gives them a sense of ownership and a better understanding of what is expected of them. In one study, students involved in rubric creation improved in both their writing and their ability to apply criteria to their own writing and that of their writing partners (Boyle, 1996).

So that they can more readily assess their progress over time, students should have a place to store and keep track of their completed works, works in progress, and future writing plans. File folders make convenient, inexpensive portfolios. Two for each student are recommended—one for completed works and one for works in progress. The works-in-progress folder should also contain a listing of the key characteristics of good writing, an editing checklist, a list of skills mastered, a list of topics attempted, and a list of possible future topics.

The works-completed folder, or portfolio, provides a means for examining the student's development. If all drafts of a piece are saved, the teacher can see how the student progressed through the writing steps. A comparison of current works with beginning pieces will show how the writer has developed over the course of the year. Careful examination of the portfolio's contents should reveal strengths and weaknesses and provide insights into interests and abilities. While reading

Voice is the distinctive style or personality that writers put into their work. To foster voice, Simmons (1996) suggests that we read and respond as readers and not as teachers. Our initial reading should be directed to what the student is saying and how he is saying it. Students also need to see models of pieces that have a distinctive voice and time to develop voice.

through the portfolio, the teacher might try to ascertain whether a student is finding his or her own voice, has a pattern of interests, is showing a bent for certain kinds of writing, is applying certain techniques, and is being challenged to grow and develop. The teacher then decides what will best help the student progress further.

Students should also examine their portfolios with a critical eye. What have they learned? What topics have they explored? What pieces do they like best? What kinds of writing do they enjoy most? What are some signs of growth? What questions do they have about their writing? What would help them become better writers? Are there some kinds of writing that they have not yet attempted but would like to try? Of course, teacher and student should confer about the portfolio, reviewing past accomplishments, planning future goals, discussing current concerns, and setting up future goals and projects. (For more information on portfolio assessment, see Chapter 2.)

# TECHNOLOGY AND WRITING

Using a computer results in better writing, especially for less accomplished writers (Bangert-Downs, 1993). Less adept writers seem to be motivated by the added engagement that a word processing program offers. Using a computer may also lead to more collaboration. Because it makes the student's writing more visible, this seems to lead to discussions about writing between the teacher and student and among students (Farnan, 1998; Dahl & Dickinson, 1986). Word processing programs have taken the drudgery out of revising. No longer is it necessary to recopy a piece just because a revision has been made. Computer editing programs allow the user to move words, phrases, sentences, or whole passages; eliminate unwanted words and other elements; and revise elements with a minimum of effort.

Text-to-speech word processing programs such as *Write: Outloud* (Don Johnston), *Dr. Peet's Talk/Writer* (Interest-Driven Learning), and *Special Writer Coach* (Tom Snyder) say the words that students type in. These programs are especially helpful for students with impaired vision and for very young students. They can also be used by students who have difficulty detecting errors in their writing. Students who reread a written piece without detecting a dropped *-ed* or *-ing*, missing words, or awkward phrases often notice these errors when they hear the computer read the piece aloud. *Write: Outloud* is doubly helpful because it has a talking spell checker.

> Word processing makes students' text readily visible, so it is easier for the teacher to take a quick look at the students' work. This visibility makes peer conferencing and collaboration easier (Zorfass, Corley, & Remy, 1994).

> Generally, it is advisable for students to compose their first drafts with pencil and paper because they are faster at writing than they are at typing.

## Desktop Publishing

As the last step in the writing process, publishing is often ignored. However, it is the step that gives purpose to writing. **Desktop publishing,** as its name suggests, provides publishing opportunities where none existed before. With it, students can produce high-quality posters, banners, signs, forms, classroom or school newspapers, reports, and newsletters for clubs. They can also illustrate stories or write

> ■ **Desktop publishing** is the combining of word processing with layout and other graphic design features so that the user can place print and graphic elements on a page.

stories based on illustrations. In some programs, they can insert background music, sound effects, animation, and speech. Two programs that include these features are described below.

*Ultimate Writing and Creativity Center (The Learning Company).* Based on the writing process, has suggestions for prewriting activities and tips for editing, revising, and composing. Has photos, art, music, and sound effects that can be added to stories. Also has a presentation feature. Has a speech capability that reads stories. Appropriate for grades two and up.

*Stanley's Sticker Stories (Edmark).* Provides characters known as stickers, scenes, and background music. Characters can be animated. A dictionary tells what the character is doing: sitting, riding, etc. Shows the word and says it. Elements are used to create a story. Story can also be read aloud. Students who cannot write can record their stories. Excellent tool for creating stories or building vocabulary. Would be especially helpful to ELLs. Appropriate for K–2.

Perhaps desktop publishing's greatest advantage is that it leads to more polished writing. Without any coercion by the teacher, students take one last look at their pieces before having them printed out. Often, they discover a misspelled word, an awkward phrase, or erroneous punctuation that would have otherwise gone unnoticed.

## E-Mail

One of the most popular features of the Internet is e-mail. Surprisingly, e-mailing friends is a favorite activity for young people. Being an immediate form of communication, e-mail is motivating to students. It is also a critical skill, as more and more adults use it to keep in touch with friends and to communicate at work. When discussing e-mailing, compare it to the traditional postcard and letter. Share with students how you go about composing an e-mail. Note that e-mail is less formal but that the correct use of the mechanics and spelling are still important.

Discuss the use of a subject heading for e-mail and the importance of typing the address accurately and the convenience of the address book. Discuss, too, including digital photos or illustrations and attachments. Emphasize the importance of courtesy and safety. With parental permission, you might have students e-mail you and each other. E-mail might be used for practical purposes, such as communicating with members of the literature circle or submitting a project or homework assignment. You might also arrange for students to have keypals in other schools. Sources of keypals are listed below.

IECC-Intercultural E-mail ClassroomConnections
    http://www.iecc.org
ePALS Classroom Exchange
    http://www.epals.com/
Mighty Media Keypals Club
    http://www.mightymedia.com/keypals/

---

**USING TECHNOLOGY**

Kidspiration (Inspiration) uses questions and illustrations to prompt students' writing. Has a speech component that reads students' writing. **http://www. inspiration.com**

---

Eckhoff (1983) examined the effects on children's writing of two different basals: one written in a simplified style, the other composed primarily of children's literature. Students who read the simplified basal tended to write in simplified style. Those who read basal stories written in a more elaborate style wrote more complex pieces. Students also picked up the stylistic devices that they encountered.

# READING HELPS WRITING

Frequent reading is associated with superior writing. This fact was borne out by the results of several studies reviewed by Stotsky (1983). Students who were assigned additional reading improved as much or more in expository writing as those who studied grammar or were assigned extra writing practice. It should be noted that the students who improved did engage in writing tasks. Improved writing resulted only when students also engaged in writing.

Reading also has an impact on fiction writing. At the end of a four-year longitudinal study, fourth-graders who had listened to, read, and talked about children's literature in preparation for writing performed better than a control group (Mills, 1974). At the first-grade level, poetry was used to sharpen the students' observations and oral descriptions. Sequence was presented through a dramatization of "The Three Little Pigs," and later, students retold the story. At the third-grade level, the students discussed the settings in *Crow Boy* (Yashima, 1955), *Evan's Corner* (Hill, 1967), and *Little Toot* (Gramatky, 1939), and then created a fictional piece with an emphasis on setting.

Students can also learn stylistic features from their reading. After a trip to the zoo, one first-grade teacher read *The Day Jimmy's Boa Ate the Wash* (Noble, 1980) to the class. The book begins with the query "How was your trip to the zoo?" and goes on to recount a series of amazing and amusing incidents. A student also began his piece with "How was your trip to the zoo?" However, the rest of his work told how one class member became lost and was found watching the tigers. The boy used *The Day Jimmy's Boa Ate the Wash* to shape his piece but not to determine its content (Franklin, 1988). The stylistic device of using an opening question was borrowed, but the content was original.

Students have a better chance of learning about writing through reading if they "read like a writer," which means that as they read, they notice the techniques the author uses to create a story. This process is enhanced if students respond to their reading in journals. As they begin to look at character's motives and other story elements, they might then begin to incorporate them in their own writing (Hiebert et al., 1998). It also helps if students take note of authors' techniques during discussions of books read. Teachers might make specific recommendations of pieces that students could use as models or sources of techniques. For example, one of Beverly Cleary's or Arnold Lobel's works might help a student who is attempting to write conversational prose.

# A FULL MENU

Students should engage in a full range of writing activities. With guidance, everyone can and should write poetry, plays, and stories. How can we tell what our limits are unless we try? Exploring a new genre helps students understand that particular form and provides them with a different kind of writing experience.

**TABLE 10.2** Suggested writing activities

**Academic**
Book review/book report
State competency test
Web site

**Business/economic**
Seeking information
Ordering a product

**Civic/personal development letters**
Letter to the editor
Making a suggestion
Requesting help
Seeking information

**Everyday/practical**
Directions
List
Message (computer, telephone)
Notice
Sign

**Social**
E-mail
Friendly letter
Postcard
Thank-you note
Get-well card and note
Special occasion card and note
Invitation
Fan letter

**General communication**
Announcement
Newsletter

**Newspaper**
Ad
Feature
Letter to editor
News story
Photo essay/caption

**Creative**
Story
Poem/verse
Play/script

**Personal**
Diary
Journal

**Writing to learn**
Descriptions of characters, persons, places, events, experiments
Comparisons of characters, places, events, issues, processes
Explanation of processes, events, causes, and effects
Diary of events
Journal of observation
Summary of information
Synthesis of several sources of information

Another advantage is that the skills learned in one mode often transfer to other modes. Writing poetry improves word choice and figurative language. Writing plays helps improve dialogue when writing fiction. Fictional techniques enliven expository writing.

Budding writers need a full menu of writing experiences. They should write everything from postcards and thank-you notes to poetry, the most demanding kind of writing. Table 10.2 contains some of the kinds of writing activities that might be introduced in grades K–4. It is not a definitive list and offers only suggestions. It should be adapted to fit the needs of your students and your school district's curriculum.

## HELP FOR STRUGGLING READERS AND WRITERS

Although word processing programs offer assistance to all writers, they are particularly helpful to struggling readers and writers, especially if they have text-to-speech capability. Hearing their compositions read out loud helps students note errors or awkward portions of their pieces that they may not otherwise have detected. For students who have serious writing problems, prediction software such as *Co: Writer*

**TABLE 10.3** Sample comparison/contrast frame paragraphs

African and Asian elephants have many similarities. Both African and Asian elephants are _____ .

Both _____ .

However, there are several differences between African and Asian elephants. African elephants _____ ,

but Asian elephants _____ .

African elephants _____ .

However, Asian elephants _____ .

As you can see, African and Asian elephants differ in the way they look and how they act.

(Don Johnston) can be highly beneficial. *Co: Writer*, which is designed to be used with word processing software, predicts what the writer will say next. For instance, after a letter or two have been typed, *Co: Writer* lists words beginning with that letter. The student can select the whole word and it will be inserted. If the student can't read the words, *Co: Writer* will pronounce them. After the first word has been inserted, *Co: Writer* will predict the next word. *Co: Writer* is helpful for students who have physical difficulty typing in words and struggling readers who know what they want to say but who have serious writing and reading difficulties.

Struggling writers also benefit from suggestions provided in teacher and peer conferences. These serve as scaffolds directing them where and how to revise (Dahl & Farnan, 1998).

Think sheets, as explained earlier in the chapter, would also be of benefit to struggling writers, as would direct instruction in writing techniques and the use of frames. Frames are partly written paragraphs, which the students complete. A frame for comparison–contrast paragraphs is presented in Table 10.3. As struggling writers gain in skill, frames can be faded.

All too often, struggling writers judge that they have nothing worth putting down on paper. To show struggling writers that they have something to say, find out in which areas they are experts. Do they know a lot about raising a puppy, making cookies, or playing basketball? Encourage them to read to find out about favorite topics and to write in their areas of expertise (Hiebert et al., 1998).

# ESSENTIAL STANDARDS

The essential standards translate the information presented in this chapter into relatively specific student objectives so that you will be better able to apply the instructional program discussed. However, the standards are flexible. Feel free to add or modify standards or move standards from one grade level to another. The standards should be tailored to meet the needs of your particular teaching situation.

### Kindergarten
*Students will*

- use drawings, letters, and phonetically spelled words to tell stories, respond to literature, recount experiences, and tell someone what to do.
- begin to use spacing between words, capitalization, punctuation, and other conventions.

### First grade
*Students will*

- write letters, lists, captions, directions, explanations, simple narratives, and responses to literature.
- write narratives that have a beginning, middle, and end and show a sense of story.
- use invented spellings.
- write in sentences and use capital letters and end punctuation marks.
- begin to revise, edit, and proofread.

### Second and third grades
*Students will*

- write letters, directions, explanations, reports, opinions, narratives, and responses to literature.
- write narratives that have a beginning, middle, and end and show a sense of story.
- write in complete sentences and use correct end punctuation, commas in a series, and quotation marks. Students will capitalize proper nouns.
- use varied sentence patterns and conventional spelling.
- use stylistic devices such as dialogue.
- use one or two details and/or examples to develop an idea.
- show a sense of audience.
- revise, edit, and proofread.

### Fourth grade
*Students will*

- write letters, directions, explanations, reports, opinions, narratives, and responses to literature.
- write narratives that have more complex plots and more fully developed characters.

- use varied sentence patterns.
- use descriptive words and vivid verbs.
- follow basic rules of capitalization and punctuation.
- use storytelling techniques, such as building suspense and writing a surprise ending.
- use a number of details and/or examples to develop an idea.
- write multiparagraph pieces that contain an introduction, development, and conclusion.
- use dialogue and other stylistic devices.
- show increased sense of audience.
- revise text by adding, deleting, rearranging, and expanding text.
- use a rubric to evaluate and revise their writing.

 ## ASSESSMENT

In addition to the assessment measures discussed in this chapter, use the devices presented in Chapter 2. The portfolios and holistic and analytic devices de-

### ACTION PLAN

1. Use writing samples and observations of students at work to asses students' current writing development and needs.
2. Based on students' needs, provide guided writing instruction to students.
3. Use discussion, brainstorming, clustering, freewriting, and other techniques to prepare students for writing. Also encourage students to collect topic ideas in journals.
4. Model and discuss the process of composing. Use conferences, wordless books, drawings, models of stories, student research, reading, or other devices to aid students as they compose. If necessary, use frames or specific guidelines, such as those provided in Cognitive Strategy Instruction in Writing, but fade their use as students grow more proficient.
5. Model the process of revising and editing. Provide practice by having students analyze and revise sample pieces. Provide guidance for peer revising and self-revising. Stress revising to make pieces more interesting and more informative.
6. Provide opportunities to publish so that students are motivated to write and gain a sense of audience.
7. Model and explain the process of composing reports. Provide extensive guidance.
8. Guide students as they use word processing programs and construct multimedia presentations.
9. Plan a full-range of writing activities. Create a program that balances students' need to engage in a variety of writing tasks with their need to write on topics of personal interest.
10. Prepare students for local, state, and national assessments. However, don't spend an excessive amount of time practicing for the kinds of writing they will be tested on.
11. Monitor students' progress and make necessary adjustments in the program.

scribed in that chapter should prove to be especially useful. Also, observe students in writing workshop. Note how they approach writing and carry out their writing activities. Do they have strategies for getting started and developing their pieces? Do they see themselves as competent writers? If not, what might be done to build their sense of competence?

## SUMMARY

1. Writing evolves from the prespeech gestures children make and from the language they hear and later use and develops in stages. Instruction should be geared to students' stage of writing development. Needed writing strategies should be identified, presented, practiced, and applied.

2. Once viewed primarily as a product, writing today is viewed as both process and product. Major processes involved in writing include prewriting (topic selection, planning, and rehearsing), composing, revising, editing, and publishing.

3. Essential techniques for teaching writing include modeling, conferencing, sharing, and direct teaching of skills and strategies.

4. Improving writing requires knowing what the characteristics of good writing are. Characteristics of good writing can be translated into rubrics or checklists that help students better understand the requirements of a piece of writing and provide guidance for assessment and revi-

sion. Portfolios in the form of file folders are recommended for storing students' writing and keeping track of it.

5. Although the emphasis in writing instruction is on content, form is also important. Good form improves content. A balanced writing program should include instruction and exploration of a variety of narrative and expository forms.

6. Instruction in composing and mechanical skills should be geared to students' current needs and should be continuing and systematic, including daily instruction as well as on-the-spot aid when problems arise.

7. Good readers tend to be good writers and vice versa. Also, students who read more tend to be better at writing. Their writing reflects structures and stylistic elements learned through reading. Through reading, they also pick up ideas for topics.

## EXTENDING AND APPLYING

1. Observe a group of elementary school students as they write. Note how they go about prewriting, composing, revising, and editing. What strategies do they use? How effectively do they employ them? What other strategies might they use?

2. Try writing for a short period of time three to five days a week to gain insight into the process. If possible, have conferences with a colleague. Note your strengths and areas that need work.

3. Examine a student's permanent writing folder. Track the student's growth. Note gains and needs as well as the types of topics the student has explored and the kinds of writing the student has done. With the student, make plans for future activities.

4. Plan a writing lesson. Using the process approach, focus on topic selection and planning. If possible, teach the lesson. Give an overview of the results of the lesson.

## DEVELOPING A PROFESSIONAL PORTFOLIO

Keep a portfolio of your writing, especially professional pieces such as articles that you have written and class newsletters or other student projects that you have guided. Also include a videotape and/or copy of a lesson plan completed for Item 4 in Extending and Applying above or another writing lesson. Keep documents for any special writing projects that you conducted with your students.

## DEVELOPING A RESOURCE FILE

Maintain a collection of published and unpublished pieces that might be used to illustrate various writing techniques. Also collect pieces of writing that might be used by students to practice assessing or revising writing. Maintain a list of possible topics and rubrics.

# 11

# Diversity in the Classroom

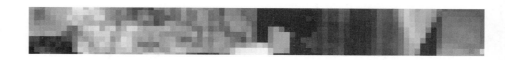

*F*or each of the following statements related to the chapter you are about to read, put a check under "Agree" or "Disagree" to show how you feel. Discuss your responses with classmates before you read the chapter.

|  |  | *Agree* | *Disagree* |
|---|---|---|---|
| **1** | By and large, techniques used to teach average students also work with those who have special needs. | _____ | _____ |
| **2** | Labeling students as reading disabled, learning disabled, or at risk is harmful. | _____ | _____ |
| **3** | Economically disadvantaged children may have difficulty learning to read because their language is inadequate when they begin school. | _____ | _____ |
| **4** | It is best to teach English-as-a-second-language students to read in their native language. | _____ | _____ |
| **5** | Even students with serious reading or other learning disabilities should be taught in the regular classroom. | _____ | _____ |

*O*ur nation is the most culturally diverse in the world. Dozens of languages are spoken in our schools, and dozens of cultures are represented. Adding to that diversity is the trend toward inclusion. Increasingly, students who have learning or reading disabilities, visual or hearing impairments, emotional or health problems, or other disabilities are being taught in regular classrooms. Because these children have special needs, adjustments may have to be made in their programs so that they can reach their full potential. Adjustments also need to be made for children who are economically disadvantaged or who are still learning English. The gifted and talented also have special needs and require assistance to reach their full potential.

What has been your experience teaching children from other cultures or children who are just learning to speak English? What has been your experience with students who have special needs? Think of some special needs students you have known. What provisions did the school make for these students? Could the school have done more? If so, what? What are some adjustments that you make now or might make in the future for such students?

## LINGUISTICALLY AND CULTURALLY DIVERSE STUDENTS

Strickland (1998) recommends using talk to foster students' understanding. "Engage students in literature study groups, group discussion, partner activities, and research groups. Plan activities where talk is used along with reading and writing as a tool for learning" (p. 402).

It is important to value and build on every student's culture. Children from diverse cultures may not see the connection between their culture and school. First and foremost, it is essential that teachers become acquainted with the children's culture, especially if the teachers' backgrounds are different from those of the children they teach (Strickland, 1998). Reading, discussions with the children, visits to homes, and interaction with those who are knowledgeable about the various cultures represented in the classroom are some informal ways of obtaining information. The teacher should constantly seek to know the literary heritage of the cultures, especially how literacy is used. For example, according to Taylor and Dorsey-Gaines (1988), African American families may read for a wide range of purposes, but the school often fails to reinforce the purposes for reading and writing taught in the home. According to Goldenberg (1994), parents of Hispanic students have high academic aspirations for their children, but the school may not realize this.

Schools in the United States are highly individualistic in their teaching and learning styles, evaluation procedures, and norms. Many students, particularly African Americans, Hispanics, and American Indians, are group oriented (Banks & Banks, 1997). Cooperative learning might help these students learn more effectively.

Understanding students' cultural background can lead to more effective teaching. Cultural groups might socialize their children in such a way and have expectations that put children at a disadvantage when they attend school. For instance, children of Mexican immigrants are taught to be passive around adults. They are also discouraged from showing off what they know (Valdes, 1996). However, in the typical public school classroom, students are expected to be assertive and demonstrate their knowledge. As a result of a lack of assertiveness and a failure to display what they know, children of Mexican immigrants were judged to be lacking in skills and background knowledge and were placed in lower reading groups.

**USING TECHNOLOGY**

Some sites devoted to providing information about particular cultures include:

Africa Online
http://www.
africaonline.com/
AfricaOnline/kidsonly.
html/

Asian Studies
http://coombs.anu.
edu. au/WWWVL-
AsianStudies.html

## BILINGUAL LEARNERS

There are currently more than 4.5 million public school children in the United States whose native language is not English (U.S. Department of Education, 1998). Moreover, that number is increasing rapidly. More than 10 percent of all elementary school children have been classified as Limited English Proficient. Nearly half of all LEP students are concentrated in grades K–3 (Kindler, 2002). LEP is "the legal term for students who were not born in the United States or whose native language is not English and who cannot participate effectively in the regular curriculum because they have difficulty speaking, understanding, reading, and writing English" (Office of Bilingual Education, 1998, p. 3). However, this text will use the term ELL (English Language Learner). About 75 percent of ELLs attend high-poverty schools. For many ELL students, schooling is a struggle.

The largest proportion of ELLs are Latinos. Latino students compose 15 percent of students in kindergarten through high school, a proportion projected to increase to 25 percent by 2025. The number of Latino students in public schools is steadily increasing. Latinos compose three-quarters of all students enrolled in Limited English Proficient (LEP) programs, although not all Latino students have limited English proficiency (ERIC Clearinghouse on Urban Education, 2001). Achievement is hindered by poverty, lack of participation in preschool programs, attendance at poor schools, and limited English proficiency (ERIC Clearinghouse on Urban Education, 2001).

## Overview of a Program for English Language Learners

The question of how ELL students should be taught to read and write strikes at the core of what reading is, that is, a language activity. Using prior experience and knowledge of language, the reader constructs meaning. Common sense and research (Fillmore & Valdez, 1986) dictate that the best way to teach reading and writing to ELLs is to teach them in their native language. Learning to read and write are complex tasks that involve the total language system: the semantic, syntactic, and phonological. Until children have a basic grasp of the meaning of a language, they will be unable to read it. Even if they are able to sound out the words, they have no meaning for them.

The prestigious Committee on the Prevention of Reading Difficulties in Young Children recommends teaching ELL students to read in their native language while, at the same time, teaching them to speak English as a second language (Snow, Burns,

**ADAPTING INSTRUCTION for *ENGLISH LANGUAGE LEARNERS***

If students are taught in their native language as they are learning English, they can also get the assistance of their families. Parents will be able to help students with their assignments when the instruction is in their native language (Freeman & Freeman, 1998).

English learners should be involved in reading and writing English as soon as possible. "Written language is fixed. It does not speed past the way oral language does. So when teachers read big books, students acquiring English can follow along and start to make connections between the print and the new language they are acquiring" (Freeman & Freeman, 1998, p. 412).

In California, which is home to 1.5 million ELLs, students are provided with one year of sheltered English immersion. Parents can request waivers to keep their children in bilingual programs. However, the school need not offer bilingual education unless at least twenty waivers have been granted at a particular grade level.

If possible, students should be taught to read and write in their native language.

**ADAPTING INSTRUCTION for *ENGLISH LANGUAGE LEARNERS***

See pp. 437–438 for suggestions for using the language-experience approach to teach ELLs.

**BUILDING LANGUAGE**

Keep a file of pictures and artifacts that might be used to help explain a topic. Have a file for fruits that might include pictures or plastic replicas of fruits. When you mention the fruit, hold up a representation of it. This helps all learners but is especially helpful to ELLs. Your picture file might be electronic and stored on your hard drive or a disk. When needed, it can be flashed on a screen or printed out and held up.

**ADAPTING INSTRUCTION for *ENGLISH LANGUAGE LEARNERS***

The social environment of a classroom is important for language learning. Wong (1991, cited in Cummins, 1994) recommends: "Those situations that promote frequent contacts are the best, especially if the contacts last long enough to give learners ample opportunity to observe people using the language for a variety of communication purposes. Those which permit learners to engage in the frequent use of the language with speakers are even better" (p. 54).

& Griffin, 1998). Once they have a sufficient grasp of English and of basic reading in their native language, they can then learn to read in English. This type of program has several advantages. First of all, children build a solid foundation in their native tongue. With language development, thinking skills are enhanced, concepts are clarified and organized, and children learn to use language in an abstract way. Because they are also learning math, science, and social studies in their native language, background experience is being developed.

### ■ ESL Only

Not all ELLs have access to a bilingual program. If the only program offered is one that teaches the students English as a second language, it is best to delay formal reading instruction until the children have a reasonable command of English (Snow, Burns, & Griffin, 1998). However, students can engage in shared reading, complete language-experience stories, and read predictable books as they learn English. They should also be encouraged to write as best they can. As they gain proficiency in oral English, they can tackle increasingly complex reading and writing tasks. Their oral-language skills will support their reading and writing, and their reading and writing will reinforce and build oral-language skills.

The classroom teacher's role is to support the efforts of these bilingual and/or ESL professionals by meeting regularly with them and mutually planning activities that will enhance students' progress. Even after students have finished the ESL program, they still require special language-development activities. Some adjustments that might be made to adapt the classroom instruction to ELL's needs are described in the paragraphs that follow.

### ■ Build Language

The ELL students' greatest need is to develop skills in understanding and using English. Special emphasis should be placed on school-type language. As students learn English, they first acquire functional structures that allow them to greet others, make conversational statements, and ask questions. This type of everyday communication is heavily contextualized and is augmented by gestures, pointing at objects, and pantomiming. It takes approximately two years for students to become socially proficient in English (Cummins, 2001). However, schooling demands academic language, which is more varied and abstract and relatively decontextualized. This is the language in which math procedures and subject matter concepts are explained. Proficiency in academic English may take up to five years or more. Even though ELL students may seem proficient in oral English, they may have difficulty with academic language. Mastery of conversational English may mask deficiencies in important higher-level language skills (Sutton, 1989). Because of the time required to acquire academic language, English learners may not demonstrate their true abilities on achievement and cognitive ability tests administered in English.

Increasing the amount of oral language in the classroom enhances English speaking. Structure conversations at the beginning of the school day and at other convenient times to talk about current events, weather, hobbies, sports, or other topics of interest. Encourage students to participate in discussions and provide opportunities for them to use "language for a broad variety of functions, both social and academic" (Allen, 1991, p. 362).

A reading program for ELL students should include children's books. "Children's books can provide a rich input of cohesive language, made comprehensible by patterned language, predictable structure, and strong, supportive illustrations" (Allen, 1994, pp. 117–118). Children's books can be used as a stimulus for discussion, show objects that ELL students may not be familiar with, and build concepts. Books that are well illustrated and whose illustrations support the text are especially helpful. A predictable book such as *Cat on the Mat* (Wildsmith, 1982) repeats the simple pattern "The _____ sat on the mat." Eric Carle's *Have You Seen My Cat?* repeats the question pattern "Have you seen my _____ ?" Such books build knowledge of basic syntactical patterns as well as vocabulary. After reading texts of this type, students might use the patterns in their oral language and writing.

To facilitate understanding of oral language, add illustrative elements to discussions. Use objects, models, and pictures to illustrate vocabulary words that might be difficult. Role-play situations and pantomime activities. When talking about rocks in a geology unit, bring some in and hold them up when mentioning their names. When discussing a story about a tiger, point to a picture of the tiger. When introducing a unit on magnets, hold up a magnet every time you use the word; point to the poles each time you mention them. Supplement oral directions with gestures and demonstrations. Think of yourself as an actor in a silent movie who must use body language to convey meaning.

### ■ Use Print

Use print to support and expand the oral-language learning of English learners. Label items in the room. Write directions, schedules, and similar information about routines on the chalkboard. As you write them, read them orally (Sutton, 1989). Also encourage students to write:

> Provide experiences in which language is greatly contextualized (as, for example, a field trip, a science experiment, role playing, planning a class party, solving a puzzle). Use print materials with these activities as a natural extension of the oral language generated: write a class language experience report about the field trip; record information on a science chart; write dialogues or captions for a set of pictures; make lists of party items needed; follow written directions to find a hidden treasure. (p. 686)

### ■ Adapt Instruction

Compare the child's native language with English and note features that might cause difficulty; then provide help in those areas. For example, some major phonological differences between Spanish and English are noted in Table 4.8. Morphological and other differences are summarized in Table 11.1 (O'Brien, 1973). Other differences between Spanish and English include a lack of contractions in Spanish and confusion caused by idiomatic expressions, such as "shoot down the street," and "call up a friend." Another difference has to do with relationships between speakers

Shared readings from a big book, choral readings, and songs can be used to develop oral-language fluency. Scripts, dramatized stories, and readers' theater might also be used.

Before students read a piece, activate their prior knowledge. Because of cultural and linguistic differences, students might not realize that they have background to bring to a story or article. Also, emphasize comprehension over pronunciation (Chamot & O'Malley, 1994).

**ADAPTING INSTRUCTION for *ENGLISH LANGUAGE LEARNERS***
Because of limited English, ELLs may have difficulty fully explaining what they know about a selection they have read. They may mispronounce words whose meanings they know. The key element is whether students are getting meaning from these words, not whether they are pronouncing them correctly. In one study, students who were good readers in Spanish and were becoming proficient readers in English were not given instruction in comprehension because the teachers wrongly believed that their mispronunciations were a sign of weak decoding skills (Moll, Estrada, Diaz, & Lopez, 1980, cited in García, Pearson, & Jiménez, 1994).

**TABLE 11.1** Areas of special difficulty for native speakers of Spanish

| Phonological | Morphological | Syntactical |
|---|---|---|
| *Fewer vowel sounds:* no short *a* (*hat*), short *i* (*fish*), short *u* (*up*), short double *o* (*took*), or *schwa* (*sofa*) <br><br> *Fewer consonant sounds:* no /j/ (*jump*), /v/ (*vase*), /z/ (*zipper*), /sh/ (*shoe*), /ŋ/ (*sing*), /hw/ (*when*), /zh/ (*beige*) | *de* (of) used to show possession: *Joe's pen* becomes *the pen of Joe* <br><br> *mas* (more) used to show comparison: *faster* becomes *more fast* | use of *no* for *not*: He no do his homework. <br> no *s* for plural: my two friend <br> no auxiliary verbs: She no play soccer. <br> adjectives after nouns: the car blue <br> agreement of adjectives: the elephants bigs <br> no inversion of question: Anna is here? <br> articles with professional titles: I went to the Dr. Rodriguez. |

Adapted from C. A. O'Brien, *Teaching the Language-Different Child to Read,* Columbus, OH: Merrill, 1973.

and listeners. In Hispanic cultures, for example, it is customary to avert one's eyes when speaking to persons in authority. However, for many cultural groups, the opposite is true. Students learning English should learn the cultural expectations of the language along with vocabulary and syntax.

Adapt lessons to meet the needs of English learners. When teaching a reading lesson, examine the text for items that might cause special problems. Pay particular attention to the following items:

- *Vocabulary.* What vocabulary words might pose problems for ELLs? Unfamiliar vocabulary is a major stumbling block for ELLs. There may be a number of common English words that ELLs may not be familiar with.
- *Background of experience.* What background is needed to understand the selection? Coming from diverse lands, ELLs may not have the experiences assumed by the selection to be read.
- *Syntax.* Does the selection use sentence patterns that the student might have difficulty with? Is there a heavy use of contractions?
- *Semantics.* Might certain figures of speech or idiomatic expressions cause confusion?
- *Culture.* What cultural items might cause problems in understanding the selection? For instance, some ELL students from traditional cultures might have difficulty understanding the casual relationship that children in the mainstream culture have with authority figures.

The teacher does not have to attempt to present all potentially confusing items. Those most important to a basic understanding of the selection should be chosen. Some potentially difficult items might be discussed after the story has been read.

Of course, as with any group of students, care must be taken to explain to English learners concepts and vocabulary that could hinder their understanding, as well as to build background and activate schemata. Before students read a piece, activate their prior knowledge.

The first reading of a selection should be silent. Because English learners are still learning English, the temptation is to have them read orally. However, this turns the reading lesson into a speech lesson. Plan legitimate activities for purposeful oral rereading after the selection has been read silently and discussed.

Chances are English Language Learners will read more slowly than native speakers of English. Because they are learning the language, it will take longer to process. In addition, until their recognition of English words becomes automatic, they may have to translate words from English into their native tongue. Seeing the word *cow*, the student may have to search his lexicon for the Spanish equivalent of *cow*, *vaca*. The extra step slows down the reading.

### ■ Use a Language-Experience Approach

A language-experience approach avoids the problem of unfamiliar syntax and vocabulary because children read selections that they dictate. Some students might dictate stories that contain words in both English and their native tongue. This should be allowed and could be an aid as the student makes the transition to English.

Although students are learning to read in English, they should still be encouraged to read in their native tongue if they are literate in that language. In the classroom library, include books written in the various languages of English learners. Because Spanish is spoken by a large proportion of the U.S. population, a number of books are published in Spanish, including both translations and original works. Most of the major educational and children's book publishers offer translations of favorite books.

Fortunately, English Language Learners have several strategies they can use to foster comprehension. One strategy is the use of cognates. Cognates are words that are descended from the same language or form. The word for *electricity* in Spanish is *electricidad*. Seeing the word *electricity*, the Spanish-speaking reader realizes that it means the same thing as *electricidad*. Native speakers of Spanish may not realize how many Spanish words have English cognates (see Table 11.2). You might model the process by demonstrating how cognates help you to read Spanish words.

**TABLE 11.2**  High-Frequency Spanish Cognates

| | | | | |
|---|---|---|---|---|
| artista | diferente | fruta | mágico | papá |
| autor | difícil | gigante | mayo | perfecta |
| bebé | elefante | gorila | minuto | rápido |
| biografía | enciclopedia | grado | música | teléfono |
| carácter | eléctrica | hipopótamo | necesita | tigre |
| carro | familia | importante | nota | tomate |
| causa | famoso | insecto | número | uniforme |
| contento | foto | jirafa | oficina | vegetales |
| describir | favorito | mamá | página | zoológico |

## *Exemplary Teaching*

### *Developing Content Knowledge and Language Skills*

Recently arrived from Southeast Asia, Nora's command of English is limited. Realizing that Nora and several of her ELL classmates will have difficulty with the concept of the water cycle if it is presented in the typical manner, the teacher uses a heavily illustrated big book to present the concept. In her lesson, she will build language as well as content knowledge. Her content objective is that students will be able to represent the water cycle in a series of drawings. Her language objective is that students will be able to explain the water cycle orally in simple sentences. As she reads the brief sentences in the big book, Nora's teacher tracks print. When she comes to key content words such as

clouds, she points to the illustration of the clouds.

After reading the book, she shows the students gestures for clouds, rain, and other content words. For guided practice, she has students mime or say key words when she points to pictures that illustrate them. As an application, she gives students a booklet that has sentences that describe the four phases of the rain cycle. Students are asked to draw illustrations for the sentences. To assess students, she notes at various points of the lesson whether students can identify key words or illustrate the sentences describing the water cycle. Students are also asked to retell the description of the water cycle (Echevarria, 1998).

---

**USING TECHNOLOGY**

Little Explorers Picture Dictionary
**http://www.
enchantedlearning.
com/Dictionary.html**
Features nearly 2,000 illustrated dictionary entries. Each word is used in a meaningful example sentence. Most entries have links to a related Web site. There are English, English–Spanish, English–French, English–German, English–Italian, English–Japanese, and English–Portuguese versions. This site also provides illustrations and articles on numerous topics in both English and Spanish.

When responding to questions or retelling a story, students should be encouraged to use their native language if they cannot respond in English. Being able to use their native language helps students to express ideas that they might not have the words for in English. If you don't speak the student's native language, you might ask the student to translate for you. If the student is unable to translate, perhaps another student in the class can do so (Kamil & Bernhardt, 2001). One way of building vocabulary is to create a word wall or charts of words in English and Spanish or other languages. If the class is about to read a selection about snakes, you might list key words such as *snakes, poisonous, prey, fangs,* and *skin* in English and in the native language of the ELL students. The ELL students can help you with the words in their native language (Kamil & Bernhardt, 2001).

Informational text, by the way, may be easier for English Language Learners to read than narrative text. This is especially true if the informational text is developing topics with which ELL students are familiar. In addition, informational text tends to be more culture free than narrative text, so ELLs are not puzzled by unfamiliar customs (Kamil & Bernhardt, 2001).

## Using Technology to Assist English Language Learners

Software programs and Web sites that have a speech component can be helpful to ELLs. *Usborne's Animated First Thousand Words* has a dictionary that illustrates words and says them in both English and Spanish. Printed words also appear in English and Spanish. *Usborne's Animated First Thousand Words* has a variety of challenging games and activities for learning and reinforcing words. Students select any one of thirty-five scenes and have a choice of five games for each of the scenes. Students can hear words read aloud, see them depicted with illustrations, match words to pictures, sort words, and practice saying words by having a word read, recording the word, and comparing their recording to the original version. *Usborne's Animated First Thousand Words* provides excellent practice for both struggling readers and ELLs. This is an excellent resource for English learners.

## INCLUSION

Inclusion means teaching disabled students within the general education classroom and may require making accomodations and modifications. **Inclusion** fits in with current trends in teaching literacy. Recommended practices for inclusion include cooperative learning, self-management, strategy instruction, direct instruction, and goal setting (King-Sears & Cummings, 1996), all of which are emphasized in this text because they are effective practices for all students. The stress on self-selected reading and the workshop approach to reading and writing, which are emphasized in this text, also lend themselves to inclusion. In addition, assistive technology has made it possible for students to compensate for a variety of handicapping conditions.

*T*eaching students with disabilities to read and write may mean adapting techniques and using technology but is mostly a matter of acceptance and caring.

■ **Inclusion** is the practice of educating within the classroom all students, including those with special needs. In full inclusion, all support services are provided within the classroom setting. In partial inclusion, the student may be pulled out of the classroom for special instruction.

### Title 1 and Remedial Programs

Increasingly, Title 1 and remedial specialists are moving toward an inclusive model, which means that remedial instruction is often conducted within the classroom instead of in a resource room. To obtain the best results for the children in Title 1 or remedial programs, it is important for teachers and specialists to confer regularly. All involved benefit from these conferences. The classroom teacher obtains insight into the student's problem and techniques for later use in the classroom; the specialist learns information about the child's functioning in a group and can enlist the classroom teacher's help in providing opportunities for having the child apply skills. The student, of course, benefits by getting the best from both professionals. Conducting remediation in the classroom has many advantages. The classroom teacher is less isolated and spends more time working with other professionals. In addition, disabled readers prefer working in the regular classroom and spend more time reading books and less time on worksheets. Having additional assistance in the classroom also means greater individualization (Gelzheiser & Meyers, 1990).

## INTERVENTION PROGRAMS

An ounce of prevention is worth a pound of cure. Over the last decade, a number of programs have been created that are designed to help those students who are most at risk of failing to learn to read and write. Because of its dramatic but well-documented success, one such program, Reading Recovery, is now being implemented in every state. In the United States, 81 percent of Reading Recovery students, not including students who dropped out or did not complete at least sixty lessons due to absenteeism, were able to read at the average level of their classmates after twelve to twenty weeks of instruction (Lyons, 2000)

Table 11.3 presents an overview of a Reading Recovery lesson. For a complete description of Reading Recovery, see *Reading Recovery: A Guidebook for Teachers in Training* (Clay, 1993b).

### Other Intervention Programs

Although Reading Recovery is an outstanding program, it is costly to implement. However, there are a number of other highly successful early intervention programs that do not require extensive training and may be implemented with small groups of students by the classroom teacher, Title 1 instructor, or remedial specialist. These include Early Intervention in Reading, a program in which the first-grade teacher

> To provide students with disabilities with a high-quality education, federal law requires that students with disabilities be included in state- and districtwide assessments, with or without accommodations. Alternate assessments must be developed for students who cannot participate in regular assessments. The IEP was also changed to ensure that students with disabilities would have access to the regular education curriculum (Individuals with Disabilities Act Amendments of 1997).

> The intent of many remedial programs is to help students catch up so that they can then learn with their peers. However, some practices represent a slow-it-down, make-it-more concrete approach. Having a low estimate of students' ability to progress, the pace of the work is slowed down and students might even be retained (McGill-Franzen, 1994).

| **TABLE 11.3** | Overview of a Reading Recovery lesson |
|---|---|
| *Reading familiar stories* | Student reads one or more familiar books to build fluency. |
| *Taking a running record of yesterday's book* | The teacher analyzes the student's performance as she or he reads the book introduced in yesterday's lesson. |
| *Working with letters* | Magnetic letters are used at various points in the lesson to provide instruction in letter–sound relationships. |
| *Writing a story or message* | The student, under the teacher's guidance, composes a one-sentence or longer story related to an experience the student has had or a book read during the lesson. The story is cut up and taken home to be read for practice. |
| *Reading a new book* | Carefully chosen so as to present an appropriate level of challenge, the new book is introduced by the teacher before being read orally by the student. |

Drawn from *Partners in Learning: Teachers and Children in Reading Recovery* by C. A. Lyons, G. S. Pinnell, & D. E. DeFord, New York: Teachers College Press, 1993.

spends twenty minutes a day working with five to seven of the lowest-achieving students (Hiebert & Taylor, 2000; Taylor, Strait, & Medo, 1994) and the Boulder Project, in which Title 1 teachers work with small groups of low-achieving students (Hiebert, 1994; Hiebert & Taylor, 2000).

## Intervention in Basal Programs

Today's basals make provisions for struggling readers. One advantage of these programs is that they are closely tied to the core program. The core program and the intervention program are mutually reinforcing so that struggling readers are given maximum assistance. Harcourt (Farr et al., 2001) provides a parallel intervention program that follows the same theme as the anthology and introduces some of the same vocabulary. However, the intervention reader is written on a lower level and is decodable. Selections in the intervention program reinforce high-frequency words and key phonics patterns. Each lesson is accompanied by instruction in a key skill and practice and application activities. Directed reading lessons are specially geared to struggling readers. The selection is read in short chunks with lots of guidance by the teacher.

## Lessons from Early Intervention Programs

What lessons can be learned from these intervention programs? Although they differ on specifics, all stress the importance of providing ample opportunity for students to read materials on the appropriate level, teaching students to be strategic readers, monitoring their progress, evaluating the program, providing in-service training, and having strong leadership. Programs at the early levels also have a strong decoding component. Most important of all, the programs have a strong belief in the ability of at-risk children to succeed, a belief that the programs have convincingly confirmed.

## HELP FOR STRUGGLING READERS AND WRITERS

As you have undoubtedly noticed, most of the techniques presented in this chapter are the same as those discussed in previous chapters. In general, the techniques that work with achieving readers also work with students who are at risk. The chief difference in working with achieving and at-risk students is making appropriate adaptations and modifications. Based on the major principles covered in this chapter and the exemplary intervention programs reviewed, the following framework for an intervention program has been adapted from *Building Words* (Gunning, 2001). This framework has been designed to provide a basis for planning an intervention program that can be taught by the classroom teacher. The program is designed for students who lack proficiency with word analysis skills and strategies. Skills range

**ADAPTING INSTRUCTION for *STRUGGLING READERS and WRITERS***
In some schools that have been designated as being underperforming and that have not made adequate progress according to No Child Left Behind guidelines, students will be eligible for supplementary tutoring. Information about schools and services available can be obtained from your state department of education.

In Early Steps, a one-to-one program that emphasizes direct, systematic instruction in phonemic awareness and phonics, the lowest achievers did particularly well. Through direct instruction in word patterns and sorting and encouraging invented spelling, Early Steps may have been reaching some of the kinds of students who needed a more intensive, more explicit approach to phonics than that offered by Reading Recovery (Santa & Høien, 1999).

from working with phonemic awareness and initial consonants through working with multisyllabic words. However, the program can be adapted to focus on comprehension by introducing comprehension strategies and vocabulary instead of phonics or syllabic patterns.

## Building Literacy: A Classroom Intervention Program

### ■ Goals and Objectives

Objectives should be those that are most likely to result in maximum improvement in literacy.

### ■ Direct, Systematic Instruction

Struggling readers and writers need direct, systematic instruction geared to their strengths. High-quality instructional techniques emphasized in this text feature word building; guided reading, including text walk; shared reading; language experience, including shared writing and interactive writing; and use of graphic organizers and reciprocal teaching.

### ■ Selecting Students

Select students with the greatest needs in reading and writing. Depending on students' levels, use an informal reading inventory and/or assessment devices from Appendix B. Also use observation, samples of students' work, and portfolios, if available.

### ■ Size of Group

A group of six or seven is the maximum size that can be taught effectively. However, the more serious the difficulties, the smaller the group should be.

### ■ Scheduling Instruction

Intervention instruction is most beneficial when it's in addition to the instruction already provided. Students who are behind need more instructional time if they are expected to catch up. Before school, after school, and summer programs are recommended. However, if this is not practical, arrange intervention sessions when they would best fit into the daily schedule. You might hold intervention sessions when the rest of the class is engaged in sustained reading, working at learning centers, or working on individual or group projects. Intervention groups should be scheduled every day, if possible, but not less than three times a week. Sessions can last from twenty to forty-five minutes, with forty minutes being the recommended duration.

### ■ Materials

Use high-interest materials. Select materials that are attractive, are well illustrated, and don't have a whole lot of print on a page. Make sure that materials are on the appropriate level of difficulty. Books, listed in Appendix A, especially those listed under the Easy category, could be used as a starting point. Also, have students use technology, such as talking software, to help them overcome learning difficulties.

## ■ Evaluation

Continuously monitor students' progress. Keep records of books read and conduct a running record or modified IRI monthly or weekly, if possible. Observe and make note of student's daily progress. Maintain a portfolio of work samples. Periodically, at least once a month, review each student's progress and make any necessary adjustments.

## ■ Parental Involvement

Let the parents know about the program. Keep them informed about the children's progress. Also, enlist their support. Students in the program should read twenty minutes a night at least four times a week. Discuss with parents how they might help their children fulfill this requirement. Parents might also volunteer to help out. They might work with the rest of the class while you are teaching the intervention group. Or they may work with individuals on experience stories or listen to them read.

## ■ Professional Support

Discuss your program with the principal and enlist her or his support. Also, talk it over with other professionals. They may have suggestions for improvement or may provide assistance should serious problems arise.

## ACTION PLAN

1. Plan and implement a program that provides for all students.
2. Modify assignments as necessary to meet any special needs that students have.
3. Provide extra instruction or alternate instruction for students who are not making progress.
4. For English Language Learners, build language as you build literacy. Build on background knowledge and skills that students bring to class. Make use of cognates, for instance. If possible, students should be taught to read in their first language. When they are taught to read in English, be aware of differences between English and the child's native language so special attention can be paid to elements that are likely to pose problems.
5. If students are struggling, intervene early. If intervention programs are not available, create your own. Set aside a period of the day when you can work with struggling readers.
6. Monitor the progress of students who are not achieving adequately and make adjustments as necessary.

### ■ Parts of a Building Literacy Lesson

A Building Literacy lesson should include certain key elements. At a minimum, there should be a review of past material, an introduction or extension of a new skill or strategy and opportunity to apply that skill or strategy by reading a selection. If time allows, there should be a writing activity. Conclude the session with a brief activity chosen by the student: a game, computer time, or reading of a riddle or verse, for instance. Students should also have a take-home activity, such as a book or periodical to read or reread.

## SUMMARY

1. Because of the multicultural nature of our nation and the trend to include disabled students in the regular classroom, schools are becoming increasingly pluralistic and require a focus on the diverse backgrounds and needs of all children.
2. There are more than 4.5 million public school children whose English language skills are so limited that they will have difficulty learning in classrooms where English is spoken. These students should be taught to read in their native language.

Instruction should be adapted to promote understanding and foster language.
3. Inclusion entails making modifications and adaptations so as to foster the literacy development of special needs students.
4. Reading Recovery and other intervention programs have demonstrated that, given the right kind of instruction, children at risk for failure can be successful.

## EXTENDING AND APPLYING

1. Interview the special education, Title 1, or remedial reading specialist at the school where you teach or at a nearby elementary school. Find out what kinds of programs the school offers for special education, Title 1, and remedial students.
2. Observe a classroom in which remedial or special education instruction is offered according to the inclusion model. What arrangements have the specialist and the classroom teacher made for working together? What are the advantages of this type of arrangement? What are some of the disadvantages?
3. Investigate the culture of a minority group that is represented in a class you are now teaching or

that you may be teaching in the future. Find out information about the group's literature, language, and customs. How might you use this information to plan more effective instruction for the class? Plan a lesson using this information. If possible, teach the lesson and evaluate its effectiveness.
4. Plan a reading lesson for a student with a reading disability. Obtain material that is of interest to the student but that is on his or her reading level. If possible, teach the lesson and evaluate its effectiveness.

## DEVELOPING A PROFESSIONAL PORTFOLIO

Teach a lesson as suggested in Item 4 of Extending and Applying above and record it on a video or CD-ROM and/or keep a copy of the plan for the lesson. Reflect on the effectiveness of the lesson. Experiment with the language-experience approach, cooperative grouping, or other techniques and approaches that have been shown to be effective with ELL students. Summarize and reflect on your use of the techniques.

## DEVELOPING A RESOURCE FILE

Maintain a bibliography of books and other materials that you might use to teach students who have special needs. Also maintain a bibliography of multicultural literature that would be appropriate for the age level that you teach.

# 12

# Creating and Managing a Literacy Program

## ANTICIPATION GUIDE

*F*or each of the following statements related to the chapter you are about to read, put a check under "Agree" or "Disagree" to show how you feel. Discuss your responses with classmates before you read the chapter.

|  |  | *Agree* | *Disagree* |
|---|---|---|---|
| **1** | Students should be heterogeneously rather than homogeneously grouped for reading instruction. | _____ | _____ |
| **2** | Teaching small groups of students with common needs is just about the best way to provide for individual differences. | _____ | _____ |
| **3** | Ultimate responsibility for the progress of struggling readers rests with the classroom teacher. | _____ | _____ |
| **4** | Without parental support, literacy programs have a greatly diminished chance for success. | _____ | _____ |
| **5** | Instruction in the use of the Internet should be a part of the literacy program. | _____ | _____ |
| **6** | Educators have been oversold on the educational value of technology. | _____ | _____ |

## USING WHAT YOU KNOW

*T*he best teachers are caring individuals who have solid knowledge of their field, broad knowledge of children and how they learn, and a firm grasp of effective teaching strategies. In addition, they must be skilled managers. They must have goals and objectives and the means to meet them. They must make wise and efficient use of their resources: time, materials, and professional assistance. They must also have positive interactions with students, administrative and supervising staff, resource personnel, parents, and the community at large. Clearly, a tall order.

Think of some teachers you have had who were excellent managers. What management strategies did they use? What routines did they devise to keep the class running smoothly? As you read this chapter, try to visualize how you might implement those strategies and principles. Also think about the components of a successful literacy program. What elements would such a program have?

## CONSTRUCTING A LITERACY PROGRAM

Previous chapters provided the building blocks for a literacy program. Constructing a program means assembling the blocks in some logical way and then reassembling them when necessary. Effective programs have some common features, such as a philosophy that all children can learn to read, high expectations for students, objectives that are specific and clearly stated, varied and appropriate materials, effective teaching strategies, motivation, building a sense of community, efficient use of time and increased time on task, continuous monitoring of progress, involvement of parents, cooperation among staff, a consistent program that builds on past learnings, prevention and intervention as necessary, and a process for evaluating the program (Hiebert et al., 1998; Hoffman, 1991; Samuels, 1988).

Construction of a literacy program starts with the students. The program should be built on their interests, their cultures, their abilities, and the nature of the community in which they live. To build an effective program, you need to ask: "What are the children's needs? What are their interests? What aspirations do their parents have for them? What literacy skills do they need in order to survive and prosper now and in the future?"

After acquiring as much information as you can about your students and their community, you should consider your philosophy of teaching reading and writing. Do you prefer a top-down or a bottom-up approach or an interactive approach? Will you use direct systematic instruction, an opportunistic approach, or a combination of approaches? Will you use a basal, children's books, or some sort of combination? What role will technology play in your program?

### Setting Goals

Once you have acquired some basic information about students and have clarified your philosophy of teaching reading and writing, you can start setting goals. In setting goals, you might consider the objectives set forth in this text, the school and school district's curriculum framework, and state and national standards, and mandated assessments, such as those required by Reading First. Setting goals should be a collaborative activity among the staff in a school. Teachers need to create a shared vision of what they want their literacy program to do and what shape it will take. Once they agree on common objectives, they can begin planning activities that help them meet those objectives and select the kinds of assessment devices that will keep them aware of how they are doing and flag problem areas.

Although research suggests that literacy programs should have specific objectives, teachers should take a broad view of literacy and also set broad goals (Au & Mason, 1989). These goals should include reading for enjoyment as well as building reading and writing skills to meet the demands of school and society. In addition, specific objectives should be established that lead to fulfilling the goals.

Ultimately, goals and objectives will be determined by the needs of the students. A goal for fourth-graders who will be reading a great deal of content-area material, for example, may be to have them learn summarizing skills. A goal for second-

> "A clear understanding of a school's shared goals is the cornerstone to successful reading programs" (Hiebert et al., 1998, p. 3).

**USING TECHNOLOGY**

Developing Educational Standards offers a wealth of information about curriculum frameworks and standards and provides links to each state so that you can examine your state's standards. Also has links to national standards in all subject fields. **http://edstandards. org/Standards.html**

graders who are struggling with phonics might be to have them improve their automatic application of skills.

## Choosing Materials

Goals and philosophy lead naturally into a choice of materials and activities. For instance, one teacher may elect to use children's books together with a holistic approach to phonics. A second might use a specialized basal, such as *Reading Mastery* (Distar), which focuses on phonic elements. Both approaches have the same goals but reflect different philosophies.

Regardless of philosophy, materials should be varied and should include children's books, both fiction and informational. Because children's interests and abilities are diverse, the selection should cover a wide variety of topics and include easy as well as challenging books. There should also be reference books, children's magazines and newspapers, pamphlets, menus, telephone books, and directions for activities as diverse as planting seeds and operating the classroom computer.

Supplementary materials, such as a VCR and videocassette library, tape recorders and audiocassettes, and computers and software, including CD-ROM and videodiscs, should also be available. There should also be access to the Web. (Additional information on the use of computers and today's technology in a literacy program is offered at the end of this chapter.) Basals and other commercial materials should be on hand if the teacher chooses to use them.

## Selecting Techniques and Strategies

The heart of the instructional program is the quality of the teaching. Effective teachers will have mastered a variety of techniques that they can adapt to fit the needs of their students. Some basic techniques for teaching literacy are listed in Table 12.1.

Teachers must also decide when it is time to substitute one technique or approach for another. For instance, if regular inductive phonics lessons are not working, the teacher might try a word-building approach or speech-to-print phonics. The important point is that the teacher chooses the techniques to be used and makes adjustments when necessary.

Some key student strategies are listed in Table 12.2. It is important to teach students a variety of strategies: Research suggests that, because of the novelty factor, changing strategies enhances achievement.

Teachers' knowledge of techniques should be metacognitive. Not only should they know how to teach the techniques, they should also know where and when to use them. For example, a group of students who need a maximum of structure and assistance should be taught within a DRA framework. As their work habits improve, the DR–TA can be introduced to foster independence. Later, reciprocal teaching might be employed.

## Building Motivation

Strategy instruction should also include affective factors so that students become engaged learners. Engaged learners possess the necessary cognitive tools, but they are also excited about learning. Without motivation, "the difficult work of cognitive learning does not occur rapidly, if it occurs at all" (Guthrie & Wigfield, 1997, p. 3). To foster engagement, the teacher involves students, helps them set goals, pro-

| TABLE 12.1    Essential techniques for teaching literacy | |
|---|---|
| **Technique** | **Appropriate Grade Level** |
| Reading to students | All grades |
| Shared or assisted reading | Primary grades/remedial |
| Language experience | Primary grades/remedial |
| Inductive phonics lesson | Primary grades/remedial |
| Word building | Primary grades/remedial |
| Pattern approach to syllabication | Grade 2 and up |
| Morphemic analysis | Grade 3 and up |
| Direct instructional lesson for skills and strategies | All grades |
| Modeling | All grades |
| Think-aloud lesson | All grades |
| DRA | All grades |
| DR–TA | All grades |
| Guided reading | All grades |
| Text walk | All grades |
| Cooperative learning | All grades |
| Literature discussion groups | All grades |
| ReQuest | Grade 3 and up |
| Reciprocal teaching | All grades |
| KWL Plus | All grades |
| I-Search | Grade 2 and up |
| Responsive elaboration | All grades |
| Process approach to writing | All grades |

vides them with choices, and, in general, helps them understand what they are doing and why so that they are motivated to apply strategies.

In a series of studies on effective instruction, Pressley (2001) discovered that motivation had a significant impact on students' learning. Motivation, the researcher discovered, is mainly a matter of creating a positive and encouraging but challenging environment. Students get the feeling that they're valued and competent and that they are engaged in interesting, worthwhile learning activities. The following characteristics are also featured (Boothroyd, 2001):

- Variety of techniques are used. Techniques are matched to students' needs.
- Routines and procedures are well established. The classroom is orderly.
- Effort is emphasized. Praise and reinforcement are used as appropriate.
- The teacher builds a sense of excitement and enthusiasm
- Cooperation rather than competition is emphasized.
- Manipulatives and hands-on activities are prominent. However, the activities are minds-on and have legitimate learning goals.

## Building a Sense of Community

In an effective literacy program, the teacher focuses on building a community of learners. Traditionally, the focus in schools has been on the individual. As the im-

**TABLE 12.2**   Learning strategies and related instructional techniques

| | Student's Learning Strategies | Teacher's Instructional Techniques |
|---|---|---|
| *Preparational* | Activating prior knowledge<br>Previewing<br>Predicting<br>Setting purpose | Brainstorming<br>Discussion<br>KWL<br>DRA and DR–TA<br>Guided reading<br>Text walk<br>Modeling<br>Direct instruction<br>Reciprocal teaching, ReQuest<br>Think-alouds<br>Responsive elaboration |
| *Selecting/organizing* | Selecting important or relevant details<br>Main idea<br>Summarizing<br>Questioning<br>Using graphic organizers | Think-alouds<br>DRA and DR–TA<br>Guided reading<br>Modeling<br>Direct instruction<br>Reciprocal teaching<br>KWL<br>Discussing<br>Responsive elaboration |
| *Elaborational* | Inferring<br>Evaluating<br>Applying<br>Imaging | Direct instruction<br>DRA and DR–TA<br>Guided reading<br>Modeling<br>Think-alouds<br>Reciprocal teaching<br>Discussing<br>KWL<br>I-Search<br>Responsive elaboration |
| *Monitoring/metacognitive* | Monitoring for meaning<br>Using fix-up strategies | Think-alouds<br>Modeling<br>Reciprocal teaching<br>Direct instruction |
| *Word recognition* | Using pronounceable word parts<br>Using analogies<br>Sounding out words<br>Using context<br>Using morphemic analysis<br>Using syllabic analysis<br>Using the dictionary<br>Integrating word-attack skills | Modeling<br>Word building<br>Direct instruction<br>Think-alouds<br>Responsive elaboration |

Adapted from Jones, Palincsar, Ogle, & Carr, 1986.

portance of learning from others through scaffolding, discussion, cooperative learning, and consideration of multiple perspectives has become apparent, we see that the focus must be on group learning and building a community of learners. In an ideal community of learners, all students' contributions are valued. Activities and

It is essential that teachers build communities of learning so that we learn from each other as we learn about each other (Peterson, 1992).

One source of help for struggling readers and the rest of the class, too, is tutors. Tutors should be screened, trained, supervised, and appreciated. See the following article for excellent suggestions for using volunteers: B. A. Wasik, (1999). Reading coaches: An alternative to reading tutors. *The Reading Teacher, 52,* 653–656.

To make better use of time, avoid teaching students what they already know and stop having them practice skills they have mastered. When introducing new words for a selection, do not spend time on those that are already familiar. One study found that students already knew 80 percent of the words recommended for instruction in the basal materials (Stallman et al., 1990). If the unknown words are words that students recognize when they hear them but do not know in print, do not waste time teaching the meanings. Emphasize the phonic form of the words, which is the unknown element.

discussions are genuine because students feel that they are a valuable part of the learning community.

## MANAGING A LITERACY PROGRAM

A teacher of literacy must be an efficient manager, determining how to handle physical set-up, materials, time, paid classroom assistants, and volunteers. With the current emphasis on inclusion and collaboration, the teacher must also coordinate his or her efforts with a number of specialists: the special education teacher, Title 1 personnel, the reading consultant, and the bilingual and ESL teachers. The teacher must consult with the school social worker, nurse, vice principal, principal, and supervisory personnel and enlist the support of parents.

### Using Time Efficiently

Research clearly indicates that the more time students spend engaged in learning activities and the more content they cover, the more they learn (Berliner, 1985; Brophy & Good, 1986; Rosenshine & Stevens, 1984). The amount of time spent on reading varies greatly; states or local districts often specify a minimum. In one study, time set aside for reading ranged from 47 to 118 minutes (Guthrie, 1980). Thus some students receive more than twice as much instruction as others. For primary grades, aim for a minimum of 90 minutes for literacy instruction, but 120 is more desirable. For the fourth grade, aim for a minimum of 60 minutes, but 90 is more desirable.

### ■ Pacing

Proper pacing plays a key role in literacy achievement (Barr, 1974; Clay, 1993b). Teachers must eliminate those activities that have limited or no value. They should critically examine every activity, asking whether it results in effective learning or practice. Also, eliminate unnecessary seatwork. Use cooperative learning, have students read self-selected books, and have them work at learning centers. Well-planned centers can provide excellent opportunities for exploration and skills application. To be effective, each center should have a specific objective. The key is to arrange a sequence of valuable activities that students can perform without teacher direction. If some of the planned activities involve partners or small groups, students can obtain feedback and elaboration from each other. Figure 9.6 describes two sample centers (Ford, 1994).

### Providing for Individual Differences

With inclusion, today's classrooms are more diverse than ever. In first grade, the range of achievement in a class can be expected to be two or more years; in fourth grade, four years or more; (Kulik, 1992). One way of providing for individual differences is to use organizational plans such as reading and writing workshop, which were explained in Chapters 9 and 10. A second technique is to give extra help to low-achieving students. They might be given one-on-one or small-group instruction before or after school, on Saturdays, or in special summer programs. A third technique is to adapt or modify the program to meet individual needs. Adaptations have been discussed throughout the text and include providing added instruction, easier materials, specialized aids to learning, changing the learning environment, or using assistive technology. A fourth technique is to use varied, **flexible grouping.** Possible groups include whole-class groups, guided reading groups, temporary skills groups, cooperative learning, and interest groups.

### ■ Whole-Class Grouping

**Whole-class instruction** can be efficient and build a sense of community. Reading aloud to students, shared reading, and introducing new concepts and strategies lend themselves to whole-class instruction. Reading and writing workshops begin and end with whole-class activities. As discussed in Chapter 9, some teachers also have their students read certain core texts or selections as a whole group. Preparation for reading the selection is provided to the whole class. Anticipating difficulties that students might have with the text, the teacher develops background knowledge, activates schema, builds vocabulary, sets a purpose, and creates interest in the selection. Although the initial preparatory instruction may be the same for all students, students might read the text in different ways. This is known as tiered instruction. When using tiered instruction, the same concept or skill is taught but teachers adjust the level of difficulty of materials, how the materials are to be presented, how much help is provided, or the difficulty level of the assignment. Higher-achieving students read independently. Others can receive varying degrees of assistance. The teacher might spend additional time reviewing vocabulary, reading a portion of the selection to get the students started, or guiding students through the selection section by section. For children who have more serious reading problems, the teacher might use shared or assisted reading or allow them to listen to a taped version of the selection or view it on CD-ROM.

After the selection has been read, the whole class discusses it. Having read and discussed a story together builds community among students. However, it should be emphasized that although the selection might have been easy or just slightly challenging for some students, it was probably very difficult for others. For this reason, whole-group reading of selections should be used sparingly, and some teachers might choose not to use it at all. If used, whole-group reading of selections should be balanced by providing lower-achieving students with opportunities to read on their instructional or independent levels.

Using **tiered instruction,** today's basals have extensive suggestions for providing for individual differences. In one basal series (McGraw-Hill), the whole class experiences the main selection *Lon Po Po: A Red-Riding Hood Story from China* (Young, 1989) through the use of tiered instruction. There is a preparatory discussion before the selection is read. A tape is available for students who can't read the story on their own. For students who are on level, there are suggestions for guided reading. The best readers read the selection on their own. After the story has been read, the class discusses it as a whole. Follow-up activities are differentiated by level. All of

**Grouping** is the practice of dividing students into classes or within classes by age, ability, achievement, interests, or some other criterion.

■ Because **flexible grouping** allows students to be in a variety of groups, some based on need, some on interest, some on personal choices, they are not tracked into a low, average, or above-average group. Flexible grouping also makes it easier for specialists to work with small groups of students. While the specialist is working with one small group, the classroom teacher can be working with another group (Ogle & Fogelberg, 2001).

■ **Whole-class instruction** is the practice of teaching the entire class at the same time. Although whole-class grouping is efficient and builds a sense of community, it does have disadvantages. Teaching tends to be teacher-centered, there is less opportunity to provide for individual differences, and students have less opportunity to contribute (Radencich, 1995).

■ In **tiered instruction** (Radencich, Beers, & Schumm, 1993), students are exposed to the same selection in the first tier. However, the selection might be read aloud to students who are unable to read the selections on their own. In the second tier, students are grouped according to reading proficiency so that even the poorest readers have material on their level.

the activities have to do with newspapers. However, they differ in difficulty level. In their next lesson, students read leveled books. Below-level students read *Who's Afraid of the Wolf?*, average readers read *Return of the Wolf*, and the best readers read *Peter and the Wolf*. Because the average readers had a guided lesson for *Lon Po Po*, they read their selection independently. This gives the teacher time to have guided lessons with the struggling readers and the highest-achieving readers.

One flaw in the system is that the lowest-level book might be too difficult for some of the students. In that case, the teacher will need to form a fourth group or differentiate instruction in some other way. The strength of this scheme is that the theme unifies the class, so when the teacher reads a story about wolves to the class, all are being prepared for the selections they will read. Later, all will be able to write on related topics. Other basal series have similar plans for providing for individual differences. The trade-off of this plan is that the students who need to read the most are reading the least. The average and the above-average readers read the core selection and then in subsequent lessons read leveled books. However, the struggling readers listen to the core selection because it is too difficult for them to read, even with some guidance. As a result, they read less than the average and above-average readers. As the teacher, you would need to decide whether the benefit of being part of the whole class and listening to a high-quality selection is worth the loss in reading time.

Another series (Harcourt) offers alternative selections for poor readers. The alternative story is easier to read but incorporates some of the same vocabulary as the anthology selection. The teacher can introduce vocabulary for both selections at the same time. The alternative story also incorporates the same themes and is in the same genre as the anthology selection.

### ■ Guided Reading

In guided reading, students are grouped by reading proficiency (Fountas & Pinnell, 1996, 2001). The groups meet on a daily basis for ten to thirty minutes or more. The teacher may organize as many groups as she believes are necessary, but the more groups assembled, the less time there is for each one. As a practical matter, three or four groups are the most that can be handled efficiently. Grouping, however, is flexible. When appropriate, students are moved into other groups.

### ■ Temporary Skills Groups

In **skills** or strategies **groups,** students are grouped based on the need for a particular skill or strategy. Once the skill has been mastered, the group is disbanded. For example, if a number of students are having difficulty monitoring their comprehension, you might group them for lessons and practice sessions on how to use strategies in this area. Make sure that skills or strategies groups provide for special needs that high-achieving students have so that the groups are not stigmatized as being remedial (Radencich, 1995).

### ■ Study Buddies

Pairs of students can work together in a variety of ways—for example, as reading partners who take turns reading to each other, as study buddies who work on an

▌Ability groups tend to be inflexible. Once students have been placed in a group, they tend to stay there. This is especially true of slow learners. One group of students who were tracked into the below-average group in kindergarten stayed there throughout their elementary school years (Rist, 1970).

■ A **skills group** is a temporary group, sometimes known as an *ad hoc* group, that is formed for the purpose of learning a skill or strategy.

assignment together, or as peer editors who read and comment on each other's written pieces.

## ■ Interest Groups

In **interest groups,** students who are interested in a particular topic, author, or genre join together. For example, groups can be set up to discuss particular categories of famous people, such as inventors, entertainers, sports figures, or scientists. Students who select famous inventors would form one group. Those electing to study scientists, a second group, and so on. Each student in the group decides on a particular person to study. The group creates questions to be answered and uses trade books and other sources to gather information. The students work together in cooperative-group style. One advantage of this type of grouping is that it includes students with diverse abilities and acts as a counterbalance to ability or achievement grouping. It also provides students with choice.

■ An **interest group** is a group formed on the basis of students' mutual interest.

## ■ Regrouping

Regrouping is the practice of reassigning students from several classes on the same grade level so each teacher has students who are on the same approximate reading level. If the reading, special ed, and other specialists agree to take groups, this can result in groups that are relatively small in size. A variation of regrouping is the Joplin plan in which students from different grade levels are regrouped. Regrouping, when properly implemented, has been shown to increase achievement (Slavin, 1987a) and is growing in popularity. Regrouping on an informal basis can also be effective. Two fifth-grade teachers might agree that one will take the lowest-level and the other will take the highest-level students. This cuts down on the range of pupils and number of groups. Disadvantages of regrouping include time lost going from class to class and lack of flexibility in the schedule: Students must move into their groups at a certain time.

Grouping can be harmful to self-esteem. Students who are placed in low-achieving groups see themselves as poor readers and so does everyone else, especially if the groups remain unchanged (Hiebert, 1983). Students in the low-achieving group are also deprived of peer models of high performance.

## ■ Balanced Grouping

Grouping patterns should be balanced and flexible. At times, it is best for the class to work as a whole; at other times, small groups or pairs work best, and students should also have some experience working individually. By employing several patterns, the teacher gives students the opportunity to mix with a greater variety of other students, and there is less of a chance that lower-achieving students will brand themselves as "slow" learners. The foundation of balanced grouping lies in the building of a sense of community. Realizing that they are valued and have a common purpose, students are better able to work with each other.

## ■ Advantages and Disadvantages of Grouping

Grouping reduces the variability in achievement and so makes it easier for the teacher to target instruction to the students' needs. The teacher is better able to move at a faster pace for achieving students and provide more focused and added review and practice for struggling readers. However, grouping can be harmful to the self-concepts of struggling readers, who may begin to see themselves as slow learners. Students in the lowest groups are also deprived of the opportunity to learn from the exam-

Grouping can result in gains of an extra two or three months on reading achievement tests. However, grouping is only effective when instruction is tailored to the group (Kulik, 1992). There is no gain when students are placed in groups but all are taught essentially the same material in the same way. It is also essential that students be assessed frequently and that group placement be changed when called for.

ple and ideas of achieving readers. There is also a danger that low expectations will be set for struggling readers and that they will be given activities that are geared to lower-level skills so that they are deprived of opportunities to develop high-level thinking skills (Barr & Dreeben, 1991).

## Continuous Monitoring of Progress

■ **Monitoring** refers to the assessment of students' progress to see whether they are performing adequately. Reading First requires formal monitoring at least three times a year.

A near universal finding of research on effective teaching is that it is essential to know where students are (Hoffman, 1991). **Monitoring** should be continuous but does not necessarily entail formal testing. Observing, periodically checking portfolios, and administering informal checks can provide knowledge about students' progress. Such continuous monitoring assumes that if something is lacking in the students' learning, the program will be modified. Skills and strategies that have been forgotten will be retaught; processes that have gone off on the wrong path will be rerouted. If materials prove to be too dull or too hard, substitutions will be made. If a child needs extra time to learn, it will be supplied. Such adjustments are especially important for slow learners.

## Involving Parents

**INVOLVING PARENTS**

Parent involvement is essential. Goldenberg (2001) found that the more teachers involved parents with their children's program, the higher the children's scores in reading. Parents of children involved in an intensive home-school program were overwhelmingly satisfied with the program; some 90 percent reported completing activities with their children (Campbell & Ramey, 1995).

Parents have a right to be kept informed about their child's literacy program. As a practical matter, keeping them up to date, especially if the program is a new one, will forestall complaints due to misunderstanding and will build support.

Study after study shows that even the most impoverished and least educated parents have high aspirations for their children (Wigfield & Asher, 1984). Unfortunately, however, today's parents have less time to spend with their children. About 24 percent of U.S. families are headed by single parents, and more than 50 percent of mothers of school-age children work outside the home. According to one report, the average American mother spends less than half an hour a day talking or reading with her children; fathers spend less than fifteen minutes (U.S. Department of Education, 1986).

However, if systematic efforts are made, most parents will pitch in. Prior to changes made to improve the effectiveness of the program in an impoverished elementary school in Southern California, teachers incorrectly assumed that parents would lack the time, ability, or motivation to help their children (Goldenberg, 1994). Although the parents were not well educated, they had high aspirations for their children. The school sent home reading materials and suggestions for ways in which the materials might be used. Even though parents were interested and supportive, merely making suggestions at the beginning of the year wasn't enough. The teachers found that it was important to use follow-up notes, phone calls, and regular homework assignments. With follow-through and monitoring, parents began providing assistance and students' achievement increased. The lesson is clear. The school must establish and maintain contact with parents. Quarterly report cards and PTA notices are a start, but more is necessary. Encourage students to take their papers home to show their parents and to read to their parents from their basals and/or trade books. This is especially important for novice readers. After students have finished a level in their basals or completed a trade book, help them prepare a passage to read to their parents.

A key step in communicating with parents is to keep them informed about your program when changes are made. Parents may expect instruction to be the way it was when they were in elementary school. If they understand how a program works, they will be more inclined to support it, which helps ensure the program's success. The school might also hold open houses and special meetings to explain the program. Letters in which the teacher describes what students are studying and why and how parents can help should be sent home periodically. Parents want to help their children but may not know what to do. Provide suggestions specific to the current unit, as well as more general ones with more far-reaching consequences. For example, reading to a child is a powerful technique for developing language and for developing a close relationship with the child. Parents can also provide a place and a time for the child to study, even if it is just a relatively quiet corner in a small apartment. Psychological support is more important than physical space.

## Working with Other Professionals

Mirroring the trend toward cooperative and group learning activities, today's model of effective literacy instruction is one of cooperation and collaboration. The classroom teacher works closely with other classroom teachers, sharing expertise, experience, and resources. In many schools, teachers meet not only to plan programs but also to support each other and to explore new developments in the field. In some schools, for instance, teachers meet to discuss the latest children's books. With the emphasis on inclusion, classroom teachers are also working more closely with the special education teacher, the reading–language arts consultant, and other specialists.

Because of the emphasis on using children's books and technology in the literacy program, it is important for classroom teachers to work with the media specialist. A well-balanced reading program must have a continuous supply of children's books. Media specialists can hold story hours, teach library skills, conduct book talks, help students use computers that are housed in the library, arrange special displays, and help children find appropriate books. They may even be able to provide loans to the classroom library and can keep teachers informed about the latest children's books. Classroom teachers can assist by letting the media specialist know when they plan to ask students to obtain books on certain topics or suggest that students read books by a certain author so that the necessary materials can be assembled.

Because students with special needs are being included in many classrooms, classroom teachers will be collaborating with special education teachers, reading teachers, and other learning specialists. Through collaboration, classroom teachers can obtain services and materials for special needs students and also learn teaching and management techniques that will help them more effectively in-

**USING TECHNOLOGY**
The Partnership for Family Involvement in Education (PFIE) produces a number of publications that focus on joining together employers, educators, families, and community organizations to improve schools. Compact for Reading has specific suggestions for ways in which parents can help their children in reading.
**http://ed.gov/pubs/ parents/pfie.html**

**USING TECHNOLOGY**
To increase communication with parents and to provide help with homework, supply students and parents with an e-mail address where they can get in touch with you or explain the homework assignment on the school's voice mail. Also create a Web page that contains information valuable to parents.
**http://www. readingonline.org/ home.html**

In one elementary school in Connecticut, the writing strategies taught by the learning disabilities specialist were so effective that they were adopted by the whole school. Through collaboration, classroom teachers learned about effective strategies and learning disabilities teachers increased their knowledge of the curriculum.

struct these students. Often, the techniques used and strategies taught work well with all students, so some of these might be used with the whole class.

Collaboration works best when the professionals involved meet regularly, establish common goals, and are flexible but work diligently to meet their common goals and make adjustments as necessary. Carefully planned and implemented collaboration can result in improved learning for both the special needs students and the rest of the class.

## LITERACY AND TECHNOLOGY

Increasingly, technology is becoming a major source of information. Today, being literate means being able to use technology to gather, organize, and report information.

### Using the Internet

**USING TECHNOLOGY**

A thorough but easy-to-understand explanation of techniques for searching on the Web is Worlds of Searching. **http://www. worldsofsearching.org/**

The Internet hosts a vast reservoir of learning activities. The state of California, for instance, has produced a number of CyberGuides. CyberGuides use Web-based activities to help students extend and apply their understanding of literary selections at all grade levels.

WebQuests are similar to CyberGuides. A WebQuest is an inquiry-based learning task that makes use of Internet resources (Dodge, 2001). The best WebQuests engage students as active learners and foster higher-level learning skills. Tasks range from obtaining information, answering intriguing questions, solving mysteries, syn-

*G*etting information from the Internet is an essential literacy skill.

thesizing data from several sources, creating a product or plan, persuading others, building self-knowledge, analyzing events or issues, or making reasoned judgments. Typical WebQuests might include giving a report on suggestions for recycling, comparing the biographies of two authors after visiting their sites, creating an illustrated report of an endangered species, and keeping a journal of a simulated journey.

Because sites are already set up for students, they make efficient use of students' time. Students don't spend a lot of time surfing the Net. Because the sites are chosen by the teacher, they are high quality and safe and geared to the teacher's instructional objectives and students' reading level. Listed below are suggested steps for creating a WebQuest.

**USING TECHNOLOGY**
CyberGuides is found at
Chttp://www.sdcoe.k12.
ca.us/score/cyk3.html.

## ◼ Steps in Creating a WebQuest

**Step 1: Stating objectives.**　What is it that you want students to know or be able to do as a result of the WebQuest? You might want them to be able to write a poem, obtain biographical data about a favorite author, or learn how coins are minted.

**Step 2: Finding appropriate sites.**　Find sites that would enable students to achieve their learning objective. For instance, if the goal is to have them write a poem, you might select sites that contain a variety of poems and explain how poems are created and which provide templates for the creation of easy-to-compose poems.

**Step 3: Organize the WebQuest.**　Create a guide that explains the purpose of the WebQuest and how to implement it. For each site that they visit, students might be provided a brief overview as well as questions to be answered or a task to be completed. The questions or tasks should foster higher-level thinking as well as basic understanding. The Quest should go beyond merely having students retell information.

**Step 4: Establish outcome activities.**　Decide what you want students to do to use this knowledge or skill that they have gained through engaging in this WebQuest. Will they make a plan for recycling? Will they share information with other students?

**Step 5: Assessing the WebQuest.**　Using a rubric or other assessment device, evaluate the students' learning and also the effectiveness of the WebQuest. Did they attain the Quest's learning objectives? Did the WebQuest spark interest and higher-level thinking? How might it be improved?

## ◼ Lists of Sites

There are thousands of sites designed for elementary school students. Here is a list of recommended sites:

- ◼ *Awesome Library:* Provides links to 22,000 carefully reviewed resources for students of all ages. The browser is available in a dozen languages and has a translation feature.
  http://www.awesomelibrary.org

Today's reading programs also offer extensive resources on the Internet. Scott Foresman, for instance, offers an Internet Workshop **http://www.sfreading. com** for each selection in their basal readers. Each workshop is briefly introduced, a link is provided to an approved site, and a worksheet accompanies each workshop.

- *Berit's Best Sites for Children:* One of the oldest and most reliable lists of sites for children in primary grades. Compiled by a librarian.
http://www.cochran.com/theodore/beritsbest/

- *Enchanted Learning:* Features a wealth of information about animals and other topics. Also has a variety of activities and illustrations that can be printed out. Materials are in English and Spanish. Has a Little Explorer's Picture dictionary in both English and Spanish.
http://www.enchantedlearning.com

- *Kathy Schrock's Guide for Educators: Home Page:* A popular site for teachers. Compiled by a school librarian who has also created a collection for students.
http://school.discovery.com/schrockguide/

- *Kid Info/School Subjects:* A student-created site. Arranged by subject area, and linked to many of the best educational sites on line.
http://www.kidinfo.com/School_Subjects.html

- *PBS Teachersource:* Sites selected for curriculum content, arranged by subject areas.
http://www.pbs.org/teachersource/recommended/rec_links.shtm

- *700+ Great Sites from ALA:* Compiled by members of the American Library Association. For students, teachers, librarians, and parents.
http://www.ala.org/parentspage/greatsites/

- *700+ Sites: Planet Earth and Beyond:* Lists a variety of sites that explore science topics, such as animals, earth, and weather.
http://www.ala.org/parentspage/greatsites/earth.html

### ■ Talking Web Sites

With the appropriate software, Web sites can be made to talk. Cast ereader (http://www.cast.org) reads aloud text from the Internet or word processing programs. Awesome Talking Library (http://www.awesomelibrary.org) also has software that reads Web sites. The software from Awesome Talking Library is free if downloaded and is very easy to use. It has variable reading speeds as well as a variety of reading voices. Students can have the whole Web site read or just portions of it. They may, for instance, just want to have a word or two spoken. Both pieces of software provide access to materials that struggling readers or novice readers might not be able to read on their own.

### ■ Outstanding Internet Resource

Read Write Think (http://www.readwritethink.org/), which might just be the best literacy site on the Internet, is sponsored by the International Reading Association (IRA), the National Council of Teachers of English (NCTE), and the Marco Polo Education Foundation. The site features a wide variety of lessons in virtually every skill area and on levels from K to 8. Lessons are based on IRA/NCTE standards-based lessons and integrate Internet content into the learning activity. Each lesson includes a detailed instructional plan and includes student-ready materials such as worksheets, interactives, and Web resources. The site also features outstanding resources for teachers.

### ■ Internet Projects for the Classroom

The Internet offers a multitude of opportunities for projects. Projects that incorporate the use of the Internet in the classroom can be found on the following sites:

- *Global SchoolNet Foundation*
  http://www.gsn.org
- *Pitsco Online Collaborative Projects*
  http://www.pitsco.com/p/Resources/resframe.htm
- *Knickknacks: Collaborative Education on the Internet*
  http://home.talkcity.com/academydr/nicknacks/

### ■ Electronic Mail

Because of ease and speed, **electronic mail** (e-mail) is one of the most popular features on the Internet. It benefits teachers in two ways. It's an excellent means for communicating with other professionals, and it can be used to foster students' writing. Through e-mail, students can work with students in other classes and other schools and can communicate with their teachers and even submit written assignments. Students can also communicate with key-pals.

Just as letter writing is an important skill, so, too, is e-mail. In addition to the skills of traditional letter writing, students need to know the mechanics of sending e-mail, the importance of getting the address right and using an address book, and how to write a heading announcing the subject of an e-mail. For more information on composing e-mail, see Chapter 10.

### ■ Issues of Safety

For all its potential value, the Internet can be a source of harm to young people. Essentially, the Internet is unregulated, so objectionable material is available. Filtering software can be used to restrict access to some objectionable sites. Software that keeps track of sites that have been visited is also available. There is also the issue of security. Unfortunately, some adults have used the Internet to prey on children. The best defense is to supervise students using the Internet and to educate them and their parents about the dangers of the Internet and precautions that might be taken. In many schools, parents and students sign an agreement in which they agree to use the Internet ethically and responsibly. Students also need to be supervised when using the Internet. As a practical matter, monitors should be set up so that teachers can readily see what students are viewing.

## Other Uses of Computers

With advances in technology, there have been dramatic improvements in the power of computers and quality of educational software. In addition to providing

> ■ **Electronic mail** (e-mail) is the sending of notes or messages by means of computer.

> **USING TECHNOLOGY**
> ePALS Classroom Exchange provides opportunities for classroom-to-classroom communication. It has more than 10,000 participating classrooms in nearly one hundred countries. **http://www.epals. com/**

> Teachers in 94 percent of public schools monitor Internet use, and 74 percent of schools have blocking or filtering software. Nearly two-thirds of schools also have an honor code relating to Internet use. Virtually all schools have an acceptable use policy (Cattagni & Westnat, 2001).

> **USING TECHNOLOGY**
> For more information about filtering or blocking devices, contact **http://www.neosoft. com/parental- control/.**

■ A **simulation** is a type of computer program that presents activities or gives the feel of the real experience.

a portal to the Internet, computers have four major educational uses, which sometimes overlap. They provide practice, tutorial instruction, and **simulations** and can also be used as tools. A particularly useful tool for students is Kidspiration. Designed for students in grades K–35, Kidspiration (Inspiration) provides illustrations that students can use to brainstorm ideas or illustrate their writing pieces. It also has templates for creating semantic webs and prompts for writing. Speech capability enables students to hear what they have written.

## Getting the Most out of Computers

Computer software, like other educational materials, requires teacher guidance. Students have to be prepared to complete the activity offered by the software or site they are about to visit. They must have their background knowledge activated, have a purpose for completing the assignment, and know how to read the material. Should they read it fast or slow? Should they read it in parts or as a whole? They also have to know how to use any learning aids that might be built into the program. After students have completed the activity, give them the opportunity to discuss what they have learned, clarify misconceptions, integrate new and old information, and extend and apply their learning.

### ■ Teacher Tools

Technology has also created a variety of valuable tools for the teacher. For instance, using *Wynn Reader* (Arkenstone), the teacher can make adaptations in electronic text. Text can be added, deleted, or simplified. Study aids, such as voice notes, and a built-in dictionary are available. *Worksheet Magic Plus* (Teacher Support Software) makes it possible to create fifteen different kinds of practice activities including crossword puzzles and word searches. *Inspiration* (Inspiration Software) can be used by both students and teachers to make graphic organizers. The software includes thirty-five graphic organizer templates and 1,250 pieces of clip art. Presentation software such as *PowerPoint* (Microsoft) or *Keynote* (Apple) can be used by both teachers and students to make slides, transparencies, and computer presentations. Software such as *Front Page* (Microsoft) can be used in the construction of Web pages.

## Other Technologies

Audio and audiovisual technologies can be used to motivate children to read or to expand children's understanding and appreciation of a selection. For poor readers, audiovisual aids may provide access to a piece of literature that they would not be able to read on their own.

### ■ Audio Technologies

Audio versions of books have three advantages (Rickelman & Henk, 1990). Although warmth and interaction are missing in an electronic reading, it can be played over and over by the student. In addition, it often includes sound effects, may be dramatized, and may even have been recorded by the author of the work. Because of their superior sound quality, CD versions are preferred to taped ones but may not be available for certain titles.

### ■ Audiovisual Technologies

Films and videocassettes are available for a wide variety of children's books. There are hundreds of children's books on video, including *Frog and Toad Are Friends* (Churchill Media), *Cinderella* (Playhouse Video), *Mufaro's Beautiful Daughters* (Weston Woods), and *Following the Drinking Gourd* (SRA Group).

## LITERACY IN TODAY'S AND TOMORROW'S WORLD

Increasingly, literacy will include the ability to use computers and other high-technology devices. Students need to know how to use resources such as the Internet and how to construct multimedia reports. They also need to understand how to get the most out of interactive encyclopedias and other sophisticated sources of information. Computer literacy still requires traditional skills: the ability to read with understanding, to write coherently, and to think clearly. However, today's technology also requires a higher level of literacy. Internet searches allow students to obtain greater amounts of data on a particular topic, including data published that day. Students need the skills to skim and scan data so that they can quickly select information that is relevant and important. A key reading skill for the era of the information superhighway

> **USING TECHNOLOGY**
> WWW 4 Teachers provides a host of easy-to-use tools. With Quiz Star, the teacher can create online quizzes. With Web Worksheet Wizard the teacher can create Web pages. Using Project Poster, students can create Web pages. TrackStar enables teachers to create Web site projects that are based on a series of links to other sites. Teachers may customize already existing Tracks. RubiStar allows teachers to customize any one of several dozen rubrics. NoteStar is designed to help students take notes from online sources.
> **http://4teachers.org/**

*D*uring in-service sessions, teachers learn about the latest developments in literacy instruction.

**FIGURE 12.1**

## Checklist for an Effective Literacy Program

Directions: To read each question, insert the phrase "Do I" before it (e.g., Do I read aloud regularly?). Then circle the appropriate response. If you are not in the teaching situation described, respond as though you were. When finished, analyze your answers. What are your strengths? What are some areas in which you might need improvement?

| Teaching Practices: General | Never | Seldom | Often | Usually |
|---|---|---|---|---|
| Read aloud regularly | 1 | 2 | 3 | 4 |
| Directly teach key strategies and skills | 1 | 2 | 3 | 4 |
| Model reading and writing processes | 1 | 2 | 3 | 4 |
| Use think-alouds to make reading and writing processes explicit | 1 | 2 | 3 | 4 |
| Provide adequate guided practice | 1 | 2 | 3 | 4 |
| Provide opportunities for application | 1 | 2 | 3 | 4 |
| Integrate reading, writing, listening, and speaking | 1 | 2 | 3 | 4 |

| Teaching Practices: Comprehension/Study Skills | | | | |
|---|---|---|---|---|
| Build background and activate prior knowledge | 1 | 2 | 3 | 4 |
| Set or encourage the setting of purposes | 1 | 2 | 3 | 4 |
| Present a variety of comprehension strategies | 1 | 2 | 3 | 4 |
| Teach monitoring/strategic reading | 1 | 2 | 3 | 4 |
| Provide adequate practice/application | 1 | 2 | 3 | 4 |

| Teaching Practices: Word Recognition | | | | |
|---|---|---|---|---|
| Provide systematic instruction in major skill areas: phonics, context clues, syllabication, morphemic analysis, dictionary skills | 1 | 2 | 3 | 4 |
| Provide systematic instruction in use of major cueing systems: phonics, syntactic, semantic | 1 | 2 | 3 | 4 |
| Encourage the use of a variety of decoding strategies | 1 | 2 | 3 | 4 |
| Provide opportunities for students to read widely so skills become automatic | 1 | 2 | 3 | 4 |

| Teaching Practices: Content Area | | | | |
|---|---|---|---|---|
| Use high-quality content-area texts | 1 | 2 | 3 | 4 |
| Supplement content-area texts with informational books and nonprint materials | 1 | 2 | 3 | 4 |
| Provide texts on appropriate levels of difficulty or make adjustments | 1 | 2 | 3 | 4 |
| Present skills and strategies necessary to learn from informational texts | 1 | 2 | 3 | 4 |

| Teaching Practices: Writing | | | | |
|---|---|---|---|---|
| Encourage self-selection of topics | 1 | 2 | 3 | 4 |
| Use a process approach | 1 | 2 | 3 | 4 |
| Provide guided instruction in writing strategies | 1 | 2 | 3 | 4 |

FIGURE 12.1

## Checklist for an Effective Literacy Program *(continued)*

|  | Never | Seldom | Often | Usually |
|---|---|---|---|---|
| Provide frequent opportunities for writing | 1 | 2 | 3 | 4 |
| Provide opportunities to compose in a variety of forms | 1 | 2 | 3 | 4 |

### Materials

| | Never | Seldom | Often | Usually |
|---|---|---|---|---|
| Use a variety of print materials | 1 | 2 | 3 | 4 |
|   Children's books, fiction and nonfiction | 1 | 2 | 3 | 4 |
|   Supplementary materials | 1 | 2 | 3 | 4 |
|   Basal series | 1 | 2 | 3 | 4 |
|   Periodicals | 1 | 2 | 3 | 4 |
|   Real-world materials | 1 | 2 | 3 | 4 |
|   Pamphlets, brochures | 1 | 2 | 3 | 4 |
|   Pupil-written works | 1 | 2 | 3 | 4 |
| Use a variety of nonprint materials | 1 | 2 | 3 | 4 |
|   Tape recorder/CD player | 1 | 2 | 3 | 4 |
|   VCR/DVD | 1 | 2 | 3 | 4 |
|   Computer software | 1 | 2 | 3 | 4 |
|   Web sites | 1 | 2 | 3 | 4 |
|   Games | 1 | 2 | 3 | 4 |
| Adapt materials to students' needs | 1 | 2 | 3 | 4 |
| Provide materials for slow as well as bright students | 1 | 2 | 3 | 4 |
| Evaluate materials before using them | 1 | 2 | 3 | 4 |
|  | 1 | 2 | 3 | 4 |

### Evaluation

| | Never | Seldom | Often | Usually |
|---|---|---|---|---|
| Set goals and objectives (standards) for the program | 1 | 2 | 3 | 4 |
| Align standards (objectives) and assessment | 1 | 2 | 3 | 4 |
| Collect formal and informal data to use as a basis for evaluating the program | 1 | 2 | 3 | 4 |
| Encourage self-assessment | 1 | 2 | 3 | 4 |
| Assess data-collection instruments in terms of validity and reliability | 1 | 2 | 3 | 4 |
| Assemble a portfolio for each student | 1 | 2 | 3 | 4 |
| Share assessment data with students and parents | 1 | 2 | 3 | 4 |
| Use assessment data to improve instruction for each student and to improve program | 1 | 2 | 3 | 4 |

### Organization/Management

| | Never | Seldom | Often | Usually |
|---|---|---|---|---|
| Provide for individual differences | 1 | 2 | 3 | 4 |
| Use a variety of grouping strategies | 1 | 2 | 3 | 4 |
| Use time and materials efficiently | 1 | 2 | 3 | 4 |

is the ability to decide quickly and efficiently whether an article or other document merits reading. With so much more information available, it is essential that time is not wasted reading texts that are not pertinent or worthwhile.

Having more data to work with means that students must be better at organizing information, evaluating it, drawing conclusions, and conveying the essence of the information to others. They also need cognitive flexibility to make use of the growing amounts of information in proposing diverse solutions to the increasingly complex problems sure to arise in the coming years.

## PROFESSIONAL DEVELOPMENT

To keep up with the latest developments in the fields of reading and writing instruction, it is necessary to be professionally active—to join professional organizations, attend meetings, take part in staff-development activities, and read in the field. The International Reading Association (100 Barksdale Road, Newark, DE 19714) and the National Council of Teachers of English (1111 Kenyon Road, Urbana, IL 61801) are devoted to professional improvement in reading and the language arts. For elementary school teachers, the IRA publishes the widely read periodical *The Reading Teacher* and the NCTE publishes *Language Arts*. Both organizations have local and state chapters and sponsor local, state, regional, and national conferences.

As with any other vital endeavor, teachers should set both long-term goals and short-term professional objectives, asking such questions as the following:

- Where do I want to be professionally five years from now?
- What steps do I have to take to get there?
- What are my strengths and weaknesses as a teacher of reading and writing?
- How can I build on my strengths and remediate my weaknesses?
- What new professional techniques/skills or areas of knowledge would I most like to learn?

The answers should result in a plan of professional development.

Filling out the checklist in Figure 12.1 will help you create a profile of your strengths and weaknesses as a reading/writing teacher. The checklist covers the entire literacy program and incorporates the major principles covered in the text. As such, it provides a review of the book as well as a means of self-assessment.

### USING TECHNOLOGY

National Council of Teachers of English provides teaching suggestions, sample lesson plans, and sample units. Also has a number of forums through which teachers can exchange ideas.
**http://www.ncte.org/**

International Reading Association provides a wealth of information on the teaching of reading and writing.
**http://www.reading. org/**

Kathy Schrock's Guide for Educators is an award-winning resource.
**http:// schooldiscovery.com/ schrockguide/**

## ESSENTIAL STANDARDS

### Kindergarten and first grade
*Students will*

- operate a computer in order to run easy-to-use educational software.
- use a simple word processing system and a simple desktop publishing system.
- use audio tape recorders to play and record information.

## Second and third grades

*Students will*

- operate a computer in order to run basic educational software.
- use a basic word processing system and a basic desktop publishing system.
- compose e-mail and communicate with other students.
- use selected bookmarked sites to gather information.
- use audio tape recorders to play and record information.
- use technology ethically and responsibly.

## Fourth grade

*Students will*

- operate a computer in order to run advanced educational software.
- use an advanced word processing system and an advanced desktop publishing system.

> **USING TECHNOLOGY**
> An excellent source of Internet sites for professional development is *The Prentice Hall Directory of Online Resources* (Bigham & Bigham, 1998).

## ACTION PLAN

1. Obtain basic information about your students' culture and their literacy strengths and needs.
2. Construct a program based on the nature of students that you will be teaching. Set goals and objectives.
3. Obtain materials and select teaching techniques and activities that will help you reach those goals.
4. Build motivation by helping students experience the joy of successful learning. Build a classroom community in which students help each other learn.
5. Use time efficiently and provide for individual differences. Use a variety of types of grouping. However, make sure that grouping is flexible so that students can move back and forth between groups and there is no stigma to being in certain groups.
6. Make sure that students, especially the struggling readers, are given materials and instruction at their level each day.
7. Continuously monitor progress with both formal and informal instruments. Make sure that instruction is guided by assessment.
8. Involve parents in their children's learning. Use a variety of techniques to keep them informed about their children's progress. Provide specific suggestions for things they might do to help their children. Make use of their talents and knowledge in the classroom by having them give presentations and help out through tutoring, translating, or performing other tasks.
9. Work cooperatively with the media specialist, the learning disabilities teacher, the reading teacher, and other professionals. Coordinate efforts so that students receive maximum benefit.
10. Make use of technology to foster literacy and guide students so that they learn to use technology as a literacy tool.
11. Evaluate your program and make adjustments as needed.
12. Create a plan for professional development. Include long-term goals and short-term objectives. Keep up with the professional literature, take courses, attend workshops and conferences, observe highly effective teachers, and join a study group to further your professional development.

- use a database to organize information.
- compose e-mail and communicate with other students.
- use CD-ROM and online encyclopedias, databases, and other electronic reference sources.
- use a variety of Internet sites to gather information.
- use audio tape recorders to play and record information.
- use technology ethically and responsibly.

## SUMMARY

1. The construction of a literacy program starts with consideration of the needs and characteristics of students, the parents' wishes, and the nature of the community. General goals and specific objectives are based on these factors.
2. Other elements in the construction of a literacy program include: high-quality teaching, use of varied materials, continuous monitoring of students' progress, involvement of parents, efficient management of time and resources, provision for individual differences, and collaborating with other professionals.

3. Technology should be integrated into the literacy program. Effective use of the Internet requires instruction in efficient searching techniques and the ability to judge the relevance and reliability of information. In addition to yielding a connection to the Internet, computers provide practice, tutorial instruction, and simulations and are a powerful literacy tool. Audio and audiovisual technologies can be used to motivate students.

## EXTENDING AND APPLYING

1. Set up goals and objectives for a reading/language arts program that you are now teaching or plan to teach. Discuss your goals and objectives with a colleague or classmate.
2. Complete the checklist in Figure 12.1. If you are not teaching now, answer it on the basis of how you believe you will conduct yourself when you are a teacher. According to the results, what are your strengths and weaknesses?
3. Respond to the questions about professional goals and objectives on page 525. Based on these responses and your responses to the checklist in Figure 12.1, plan a series of professional development activities.
4. For a week, keep a record of the activities in your reading/language arts class. Which seem to be

especially valuable? Which, if any, seem to have limited value or take up excessive amounts of time? Based on your observations, construct a plan for making better use of instructional time. If you are not teaching now, arrange to observe a teacher who has a reputation for having a well-managed classroom. Note the strategies that the teacher uses to keep the class running smoothly and to make efficient use of time.
5. Assess the parental involvement component of your literacy program. Based on your assessment and the suggestions made in this chapter, make any changes that seem to be needed.

## DEVELOPING A PROFESSIONAL PORTFOLIO

Keep a record of experiences that you have had with technology. This might include Web sites that you set up or helped set up, video productions that you have supervised, or audio tapes that you or your students have created. Note any special training that you have had with technology. Also include lesson plans in which you made effective use of technology.

## DEVELOPING A RESOURCE FILE

Start and maintain a file of Internet sites or titles of software and other technological devices that seem to be especially valuable for the grade level that you teach or plan to teach.

# Appendix A

# Graded Listing of 1200+ Children's Books

• Designates outstanding books.
N Designates nonfiction.

## Reading Level: Caption/Frame

### Beginning Preprimer 1

Arnosky, Jim. *Crinkleroot's 25 Mammals Every Child Should Know*. Bradbury, 1994, 25 pp. N

Arnosky, Jim. *Mouse Colors*. Houghton Mifflin, 2001, 46 pp.

Asch, Frank. *Little Fish, Big Fish*. Scholastic, 1992, 16 pp.

Asch, Frank. *Short Train, Long Train*. Scholastic, 1992, 24 pp.

Brown, Craig. *My Barn*. Greenwillow, 1991, 20 pp.

Brown, Rick. *What Rhymes with Snake?* Tambourine, 1994, 24 pp.

•Cameron, Alice. *The Cat Sat on the Mat*. Houghton Mifflin, 1994, 30 pp.

Carle, Eric. *Do You Want to Be My Friend?* Harper, 1971, 30 pp.

•Carle, Eric. *Have You Seen My Cat?* Scholastic, 1987, 24 pp.

Coxe, Molly. *Whose Footprints?* Crowell, 1990, 36 pp.

Davenport, Zoe. *Animals*. Ticknor & Fields, 1995, 10 pp. N

Davenport, Zoe. *Garden*. Ticknor & Fields, 1995, 10 pp. N

Demarest, Chris. *Honk!* Boyds Mill Press, 1998, 15 pp.

Feder, Jane. *Table, Chair, Bear, A Book in Many Languages*. Ticknor & Fields, 1995, 27 pp.

Gardner, Beau. *Guess What?* Lothrop, Lee & Shepard, 1985, 21 pp.

Gomi, Taro. *My Friends*. Chronicle Books, 1990, 32 pp.

Gomi, Taro. *Who Hid It?* Millbrook Press, 1991, 22 pp.

Grejniec, Michael. *What Do You Like?* North-South Books, 1992, 28 pp.

Grundy, Lynn N. *A Is for Apple*. Ladybird Books, 1980, 26 pp.

Hutchins, Pat. *1 Hunter*. Greenwillow, 1982, 22 pp.

Lillie, Patricia. *Everything Has a Place*. Greenwillow, 1993, 22 pp.

Maris, Ron. *My Book*. Puffin, 1983, 30 pp.

Marshall, Janet. *Look Once, Look Twice*. Ticknor & Fields, 1995, 52 pp.

McMillan, Bruce. *One, Two, One Pair*. Scholastic, 1991, 30 pp.

McMillan, Bruce. *Beach Ball-Left, Right*. Holiday House, 1992, 28 pp.

McMillan, Bruce. *Mouse Views: What the Class Pet Saw*. Holiday House, 1993, 30 pp.

Paterson, Bettina. *My First Wild Animals*. HarperCollins, 1989, 24 pp. N

Rathmann, Peggy. *Good Night, Gorilla*. Putnam, 1994, 34 pp.

Rotner, Shelley, & Kreisler, Ken. *Faces*. Simon & Schuster, 1994, 24 pp.

Rubinstein, Gillian. *Dog In, Cat Out*. Ticknor & Fields, 1993, 28 pp.

Strickland, Paul. *One Bear, One Dog*. Dutton, 1997, 24 pp.

Tafuri, Nancy. *Have You Seen My Duckling?* Greenwillow, 1984, 24 pp.

Tafuri, Nancy. *Who's Counting?* Greenwillow, 1986, 22 pp.

Wallwork, Amanda. *No Dodos*. Scholastic, 1993, 24 pp.

Weiss, Nicki. *Sun Sand Sea Sail*. Greenwillow, 1989, 29 pp.

•Wildsmith, Brian. *Cat on the Mat*. Oxford, 1982, 16 pp.

Wildsmith, Brian. *What a Tail!* Oxford, 1983, 16 pp.

Wildsmith, Brian. *Toot, Toot*. Oxford, 1984, 16 pp.

Wood, Jakki. *Animal Parade*. Bradbury Press, 1993, 26 pp.

## Reading Level: Preprimer 1

### Easy High-Frequency Words

Accorsi, William. *Billy's Button*. Greenwillow, 1992, 20 pp.

Agee, John. *Flapstick*. Dutton, 1993, 20 pp.

Appelt, Kathy. *Elephants Aloft*. Harcourt, 1993, 28 pp.

Aruego, Jose, & Dewey, Ariane. *We Hide, You Seek*. Greenwillow, 1979, 30 pp.

Asch, Frank. *Moonbear's Books*. Simon & Schuster, 1993, 12 pp.

Asch, Frank. *Earth and I Are Friends*. Harcourt, 1994, 28 pp.

Avery, Maryjean Watson, & Avery, David M. *What Is Beautiful?* Tricycle, 1995, 20 pp.

Barton, Byron. *Where's Al?* Houghton Mifflin, 1972, 30 pp.

Beck, Ian. *Five Little Ducks*. Holt, 1992, 24 pp.

Berenstain, Stan, & Berenstain, Jan. *Inside Outside Upside Down*. Random House, 1968, 27 pp.

Berenstain, Stan, & Berenstain, Jan. *Bears on Wheels*. Random House, 1969, 32 pp.

Bernal, Richard. *Night Zoo*. Contemporary, 1989, 18 pp.

Blackstone, Stella. *Bear in a Square*. Barefoot Books, 1998, 30 pp.

Bloome, Suzanne. *The Bus for Us*. Boyds Mill Press, 2001, 24 pp.

Bond, Michael. *Paddington's Opposites*. Viking, 1991, 32 pp.

Carle, Eric. *Do You Want to Be My Friend?* HarperCollins, 1976, 30 pp.

Carroll, Kathleen Sullivan. *One Red Rooster*. Houghton Mifflin, 1992, 21 pp.

Casey, Patricia. *My Cat Jack*. Candlewick Press, 1994, 24 pp.

Christelow, Eileen. *Five Little Monkeys Jumping on the Bed*. Clarion, 1989, 32 pp.

Clarke, Gus. *EIEIO: The Story of Old MacDonald Who Had a Farm*. Lothrop, Lee & Shepard, 1992, 24 pp.

Cousins, Lucy. *What Can Rabbit See?* Tambourine, 1991, 16 pp.

Cousins, Lucy. *Maisy Goes to School*. Candlewick, 1992, 36 pp.

Cox, Mike, & Cox, Chris. *Flowers*. Aro, 1979, 22 pp.

Crews, Donald. *School Bus*. Greenwillow, 1984, 32 pp. N

Crowther, Robert. *Who Lives in the Country?* Candlewick, 1992, 12 pp.

Crume, Marion. *Do You See Mouse?* Silver Burdett, 1995, 28 pp.

de Regniers, Beatrice Schenk. *Going for a Walk*. HarperCollins, 1961, 1993, 24 pp.

Duffy, Dee Dee. *Barnyard Tracks*. Boyds Mill Press, 1992, 29 pp.

Edwards, Frank B. *New at the Zoo*. Firefly, 1998, 24 pp.

Ellwand, David. *Emma's Elephant & Other Favorite Animal Friends*. Dutton, 1996, 32 pp. N

Fleming, Denise. *In the Tall, Tall Grass*. Holt, 1991, 30 pp.

Florian, Douglas. *A Winter Day*. Greenwillow, 1988, 22 pp.

Ginsburg, Mirra. *The Chick and the Duckling*. Simon & Schuster, 1972, 24 pp.

Ginsburg, Mirra. *Asleep, Asleep*. Greenwillow, 1992, 22 pp.

Gomi, Taro. *Where's the Fish?* Morrow, 1977, 24 pp.

Greene, Carol. *Snow Joe*. Children's Press, 1982, 30 pp.

Greene, Carol. *Shine, Sun!* Children's Press, 1983, 30 pp.

Hague, Michael. *Teddy Bear, Teddy Bear*. Morrow, 1993, 16 pp.

Hall, Kristen, & Flaxman, Jessica. *Who Says?* Children's Press, 1990, 29 pp.

Hall, Nancy. *The Mess*. Children's Press, 1990, 29 pp.

Henkes, Kevin. *SHHHH*. Greenwillow, 1989, 20 pp.

Hoban, Tana. *One Little Kitten*. Greenwillow, 1979, 22 pp.

Hutchins, Pat. *Rosie's Walk*. Simon & Schuster, 1968, 30 pp.

Hutchins, Pat. *What Game Shall We Play?* Greenwillow, 1990, 22 pp.

Inkpen, Mick. *Kipper's Book of Opposites*. Harcourt, 1994, 16 pp.

Jonas, Ann. *Now We Can Go*. Greenwillow, 1986, 23 pp.

Jonas, Ann. *Where Can It Be?* Greenwillow, 1986, 30 pp.

Keats, Ezra Jack. *Kitten for a Day*. Four Winds, 1974, 30 pp.

Kopper, Lisa. *Daisy Thinks She's a Baby*. Knopf, 1994, 23 pp.

Kraus, Robert. *Whose Mouse Are You?* Simon & Schuster, 1970, 28 pp.

Lillegard, Dee. *Where Is It?* Children's Press, 1984, 30 pp.

Lindgren, Brabo. *Sam's Ball*. Morrow, 1983, 28 pp.

Mandel, Peter. *Red Cat, White Cat*. Holt, 1994, 24 pp.

Mansell, Dom. *My Old Teddy*. Candlewick Press, 1991, 24 pp.

Maris, Ron. *Is Anyone Home?* Greenwillow, 1985, 30 pp.

•Martin, Bill, Jr. *Brown Bear, Brown Bear, What Do You See?* Holt, 1967, 24 pp.

Marzollo, Jean. *Ten Cats Have Hats*. Scholastic, 1994, 20 pp.

Matthias, Catherine. *Out the Door*. Children's Press, 1982, 31 pp.

Matthias, Catherine. *Over-Under*. Children's Press, 1984, 29 pp.

McKissack, Patricia C. *Who Is Who?* Children's Press, 1983, 30 pp.

McKissack, Patricia. *Who Is Coming?* Children's Press, 1986, 20 pp.

McKissack, Patricia, & McKissack, Fredrick. *Bugs!* Children's Press, 1988, 30 pp. **N**

McMillan, Bruce. *One Sun*. Holiday House, 1990, 30 pp.

McMillan, Bruce. *Play Day, A Book of Terse Verse*. Holiday House, 1991, 30 pp.

Miller, Margaret. *Whose Hat?* Greenwillow, 1988, 36 pp.

Miller, Margaret. *Who Uses This?* Greenwillow, 1990, 37 pp. **N**

Miller, Margaret. *Whose Shoe?* Greenwillow, 1991, 36 pp. **N**

Morris, Ann. *Tools*. Lothrop, Lee & Shepard, 1992, 32 pp. **N**

Morris, Ann. *I Am Six*. Silver Press, 1995, 28 pp.

Namm, Diane. *Little Bear*. Children's Press, 1990, 24 pp.

Namm, Diane. *Monsters!* Children's Press, 1990, 28 pp.

Packard, Mary. *Surprise!* Children's Press, 1990, 24 pp.

Paparone, Pamela. *Five Little Ducks*. North-South, 1995, 26 pp.

Pasternac, Susana. *In the City*. Scholastic, 1994, 16 pp.

Peek, Merle. *Roll Over! A Counting Song*. Clarion, 1980, 24 pp.

Perkins, Al. *The Ear Book*. Random House, 1968, 28 pp.

Petrie, Catherine. *Joshua James Likes Trucks*. Children's Press, 1982, 32 pp.

Pienkowski, Jan. *Weather*. Simon & Schuster, 1975, 22 pp. **N**

Pomerantz, Charlotte. *Where's the Bear?* Greenwillow, 1984, 32 pp.

Raffi. *Wheels on the Bus*. Crown, 1988, 28 pp.

Raffi. *Five Little Ducks*. Crown, 1989, 30 pp.

Raschka, Chris. *Yo! Yes!* Orchard, 1993, 24 pp.

Rayner, Mary. *Ten Pink Piglets*. Dutton, 1994, 22 pp.

Rees, Mary. *Ten in a Bed*. Little, Brown, 1988, 24 pp.

Reese, Bob. *Crab Apple*. Aro, 1979, 20 pp.

Reese, Bob. *Little Dinosaur*. Aro, 1979, 20 pp.

Reese, Bob. *Sunshine*. Aro, 1979, 20 pp.

Rose, Agatha. *Hide and Seek in the Yellow House*. Viking, 1992, 24 pp.

Ruane, Joanna. *Boats, Boats, Boats*. Children's Press, 1990, 28 pp. N.

Shaw, C. G. *It Looked Like Spilt Milk*. HarperCollins, 1947, 30 pp.

Siddals, Mary McKenna. *Tell Me a Season*. Houghton Mifflin, 1997, 26 pp. **N**

Smith, Mavis. *Fred, Is That You?* Little, Brown, 1992, 20 pp.

Snow, Pegree. *A Pet for Pat*. Children's Press, 1984, 32 pp.

Steptoe, John. *Baby Says*. Lothrop, Lee & Shepard, 1988, 24 pp.

Stobbs, William. *Gregory's Dog*. Oxford, 1987, 16 pp.

Stott, Dorothy. *Kitty and Me*. Dutton, 1993, 12 pp.

Stott, Dorothy. *Puppy and Me*. Dutton, 1993, 12 pp.

Tafuri, Nancy. *Early Morning in the Barn*. Greenwillow, 1983, 21 pp.

Tafuri, Nancy. *Rabbit's Morning*. Greenwillow, 1985, 24 pp.

Tafuri, Nancy. *Do Not Disturb*. Greenwillow, 1987, 21 pp.

Tafuri, Nancy. *Spots, Feathers, and Curly Tails*. Greenwillow, 1988, 28 pp.

Tafuri, Nancy. *The Ball Bounced*. Greenwillow, 1989, 22 pp.

Tafuri, Nancy. *This Is the Farmer*. Greenwillow, 1994, 24 pp.

Wildsmith, Brian. *My Dream*. Oxford, 1986, 16 pp.

•Williams, Sue. *I Went Walking*. Harcourt, 1989, 30 pp.

Winter, Susan. *I Can*. Kindersley, 1993, 32 pp.

Wong, Olive. *From My Window*. Silver Burdett Press, 1995, 32 pp.

Wood, Leslie. *The Frog and the Fly*. Oxford University Press, 1997, 16 pp.

Wylie, Joanne, & Wylie, David. *A Fishy Alphabet Story*. Children's Press, 1983, 24 pp.

Ziefert, Harriet. *The Turnip*. Penguin, 1996, 30 pp.

## Reading Level: Preprimer 2

Ancona, George, & Ancona, Mary Beth. *Handtalk Zoo*. Simon & Schuster, 1989, 32 pp.

Asch, Frank. *Just Like Daddy*. Simon & Schuster, 1981, 30 pp.

Auster, Benjamin. *I Like It When*. Raintree, 1990, 24 pp.

Ballard, Peg, & Klinger, Cynthia. *Fun! The Sound of Short U*. Child's World, 2000, 24 pp.

Barton, Byron. *Bones, Bones, Dinosaur Bones*. Crowell, 1990, 30 pp. **N**

Barton, Byron. *The Wee Little Woman*. HarperCollins, 1995, 32 pp.

Barton, Byron. *My Car*. Greenwillow, 2001, 32 pp. **N**

Bennett, David. *One Cow Moo Moo!* Holt, 1990, 28 pp.

Blackstone, Margaret. *This Is Baseball*. Holt, 1993, 30 pp.

Boivin, Kelly. *Where Is Mittens?* Children's Press, 1990, 32 pp.

Brown, Margaret. *Where Have You Been?* Scholastic, 1952, 32 pp.

Brown, Margaret Wise. *Four Fur Feet*. Hyperion, 1961, 1994, 21 pp.

Brown, Ruth. *A Dark, Dark Tale*. Dial Press, 1981, 28 pp.

Bullock, Kathleen. *She'll Be Comin' Round the Mountain*. Simon & Schuster, 1993, 32 pp.

Carle, Eric. *Papa, Please Get the Moon for Me*. Picture Book Studio, 1986, 26 pp.

Cebulash, Mel. *Willie's Wonderful Pet*. Scholastic, 1972, 28 pp.

Cohen, Caron Lee. *Where's the Fly?* Greenwillow, 1996, 28 pp.

Coxe, Molly. *Cat Traps*. Random House, 1996, 32 pp.

Coxe, Molly. *Big Egg*. Random House, 1997, 32 pp.

Crews, Donald. *Flying*. Greenwillow, 1986, 32 pp.

Dabcovich, Lydia. *Sleepy Bear*. Dutton, 1982, 22 pp.

DePaola, Tomie. *Andy, That's My Name*. Simon & Schuster, 1973, 30 pp.

DePaola, Tomie. *The Wind and the Sun*. Silver Press, 1995.

Dodds, Ann Dayle. *Wheel Away*. HarperCollins, 1989, 28 pp.

Duffy, Dee Dee. *Forest Tracks*. Boyds Mill Press, 1996, 28 pp.

Economos. *Let's Take the Bus*. Raintree, 1989, 24 pp.

Evans, Katie. *Hunky Dory Found It*. Dutton, 1994, 28 pp.

•Ford, Miela. *Little Elephant*. Greenwillow, 1994, 20 pp. **N**

Ford, Miela. *Bear Play*. Greenwillow, 1995, 20 pp.

Giganti, Paul, Jr. *How Many Snails?* Greenwillow, 1988, 22 pp.

Ginsburg, Mirra. *Across the Stream*. Greenwillow, 1982, 21 pp.

Ginsburg, Mirra. *Asleep, Asleep*. Greenwillow, 1992, 22 pp.

Gomi, Taro. *Coco Can't Wait*. Morrow, 1984, 30 pp.

Gordon, Sharon. *What a Dog*. Troll, 1980, 32 pp.

Gordon, Sharon. *The Jolly Monsters*. Troll, 1988, 28 pp.

Greeley, Valerie. *Where's My Share?* Simon & Schuster, 1990, 32 pp.

Gregorich, Barbara. *Nine Men Chase a Hen*. School Zone, 1984, 16 pp.

Grejniec, Michael. *Albert's Nap*. North-South Books, 1995, 30 pp.

Greydanus, Rose. *Let's Get A Pet*. Troll, 1988, 32 pp.

Hale, Irina. *How I Found a Friend*. Viking, 1992, 27 pp.

Hamm, Diane Johnston. *How Many Feet in the Bed?* Simon & Schuster, 1991, 27 pp.

Hamsa, Bobbie. *Animal Babies*. Children's Press, 1985, 30 pp. **N**

Herman, Gail. *My Dog Talks*. Scholastic, 1995, 29 pp.

Herman, Gail. *Teddy Bear for Sale*. Scholastic, 1995, 29 pp.

Hill, Eric. *Where's Spot?* Putnam, 1980, 22 pp.

Hill, Eric. *Spot's First Walk*. Putnam's, 1981, 22 pp.

Hindley, Judy. *The Big Red Bus*. Candlewick Press, 1995, 24 pp.

Hort, Lenny. *The Seals on the Bus*. Holt, 2000, 28 pp.

Hutchins, Pat. *Little Pink Pig*. Greenwillow, 1994, 28 pp.

Jonas, Ann. *Splash*. Greenwillow, 1995, 22 pp.

Jones, Carol. *This Old Man*. Houghton Mifflin, 1990, 48 pp.

Kalan, Robert. *Jump, Frog, Jump*. Greenwillow, 1981, 1995, 30 pp.

Kalan, Robert. *Stop, Thief*. Greenwillow, 1993, 22 pp.

Klingel, C., & Noyed, Robert B. *Pumpkins*. The Child's World, 2001, 24 pp. **N**

Krauss, Ruth. *The Carrot Seed*. HarperCollins, 1945, 24 pp.

Krauss, Ruth. *The Happy Day*. HarperCollins, 1949, 28 pp.

Langstaff, John. *Oh, A-Hunting We Will Go*. Atheneum, 1974, 26 pp.

Leemis, Ralph. *Mister Momboo's Hat*. Dutton, 1991, 18 pp.

Lewison, Wendy Cheyette. *"Buzz" Said the Bee*. Scholastic, 1992, 30 pp.

Lillegard, Dee. *Sitting in My Box*. Dutton, 1989, 28 pp.

Maccarone, Grace. *Cars, Cars, Cars*. Scholastic, 1995, 24 pp.

Maris, Ron. *Are You There, Bear?* Greenwillow, 1984, 32 pp.

Martin, Bill, Jr., & Archambault, John. *Here Are My Hands*. Holt, 1987, 24 pp.

Matthias, Catherine. *I Love Cats*. Children's Press, 1983, 32 pp.

McDaniel, Becky Bring. *Katie Did It*. Childrens Press, 1983, 30 pp.

McMillan, Bruce. *Super Super Superwords*. Lothrop, Lee & Shepard, 1989, 27 pp. **N**

Milgrim, David. *Why Benny Barks*. Random House, 1994, 30 pp.

Milios, Rita. *Bears, Bears, Everywhere*. Children's Press, 1988, 32 pp.

Miller, Virginia. *Eat Your Dinner*. Candlewick Press, 1992, 24 pp.

Minarik, Else Holmelund. *It's Spring*. Greenwillow, 1989, 18 pp.

Modesitt, Jeanne. *Mama, If You Had a Wish*. Green Tiger Press, 1993, 26 pp.

Mora, Pat. *Listen to the Desert*. Clarion, 1994, 22 pp.

Morris, Ann. *Shoes Shoes Shoes*. Lothrop, Lee & Shepard, 1995, 29 pp. **N**

Morris, Ann. *Work*. Lothrop, Lee & Shepard, 1998, 29 pp. **N**

Moss, Sally. *Peter's Painting*. Mondo, 1995, 24 pp.

Mueller, Virginia. *Monster Can't Sleep*. Whitman, 1986, 22 pp.

Neasi, Barbara J. *Just Like Me*. Children's Press, 1984, 30 pp.

Nichol, B. P. *Once: A Lullaby*. Greenwillow, 1986, 22 pp.

Nodset, Joan L. *Who Took the Farmer's Hat?* HarperCollins, 1963, 28 pp.

Ogburn, Jacqueline K. *The Noise Lullaby*. Lothrop, Lee & Shepard, 1995, 22 pp.

Paxton, Tom. *Going to the Zoo*. Morrow, 1996, 29 pp.

Raffi. *Down by the Bay*. Crown, 1987, 32 pp.

Raffi. *Shake My Sillies Out*. Crown, 1987, 32 pp.

Rockwell, Anne. *Sweet Potato Pie*. Random House, 1996, 32 pp.

Serfozo, Mary. *Who Said Red?* Simon & Schuster, 1988, 28 pp.

Dr. Seuss. *The Foot Book*. Random House, 1968, 28 pp.

Smith, Mavis. *Look Out*. Puffin, 1991, 16 pp.

Snow, Pegeen. *Eat Your Peas, Louise*. Children's Press, 1993, 30 pp.

Tafuri, Nancy. *The Brass Ring*. Greenwillow, 1996, 30 pp.

Tafuri, Nancy. *Silly Little Goose!* 2001, 31 pp.

•Tolstoy, Alexei. *The Great Big Enormous Turnip*. Franklin Watts, 1968, 28 pp.

Vaughn, Marcia. *Hands Hands Hands*. Mondo, 1986, 1995, 16 pp.

Waddell, Martin. *Squeak-A-Lot*. Greenwillow, 1991, 29 pp.

Walsh, Ellen Stoll. *Hop Jump*. Harcourt, 1993, 26 pp.

Walsh, Ellen Stoll. *Pip's Magic*. Harcourt, 1994, 29 pp.

West, Colin. *One Day in the Jungle*. Candlewick Press, 1995, 16 pp.

West, Colin. *"I Don't Care!" Said the Bear*. Candlewick, 1996, 27 pp.

Wheeler, Cindy. *Marmalade's Nap*. Knopf, 1983, 21 pp.

Wildsmith, Brian. *Brian Wildsmith's Puzzles*. Franklin Watts, 1971, 28 pp.

Yoshi. *The Butterfly Hunt*. Picturebook Studio, 1990, 24 pp.

Ziefert, Harriet M. *Pushkin Meets the Bundle*. Atheneum, 1998, 30 pp.

## Reading Level: Preprimer 3

Alborough, Jez. *Duck in the Truck*. HarperCollins, 2000, 30 pp.

Anholt, Catherine. *Good Days, Bad Days*. Putnam, 1991, 24 pp.

Asch, Frank. *Water*. Harcourt, 1995, 25 pp.

Austin, Virginia. *Say Please*. Candlewick Press, 1994, 26 pp.

Baker, Alan. *White Rabbit's Color Book*. Kingfisher Books, 1994, 22 pp.

Brown, Craig. *City Sounds*. Greenwillow, 1992, 24 pp.

Brown, Craig. *In the Spring*. Greenwillow, 1994, 24 pp.

Brown, Laurie Krasny. *Rex and Lilly Schooltime*. Little, Brown, 1997, 32 pp.

Browne, Anthony. *I Like Books*. Knopf, 1989, 18 pp.

Browne, Anthony. *Things I Like*. Knopf, 1989, 18 pp.

Bullock, Kathleen. *She'll Be Comin' Round the Mountain*. Simon & Schuster, 1993, 32 pp.

Butterworth, Nick, & Inkpen, Mick. *Just Like Jasper*. Little, Brown, 1989, 28 pp.

Butterworth, Nick, & Inkpen, Mick. *Jasper's Beanstalk*. Little, Brown, 1993, 24 pp.

Calhoun, Mary. *While I Sleep*. Morrow, 1992, 30 pp.

Cobb, Annie. *Wheels*. Random House, 1996, 32 pp. **N**

Crews, Donald. *Freight Train*. Greenwillow, 1978, 22 pp. **N**

Dodds, Dayle Ann. *Shape of Things to Come*. Candlewick, 1994, 16 pp.

Donnelly, Liza. *Dinosaur Days*. Scholastic, 1987, 30 pp. **N**

Emberley, Ed. *Go Away, Big Green Monster*. Little, Brown, 1992, 30 pp.

Fleming, Denise. *Count*. Holt, 1992, 30 pp.

Florian, Douglas. *A Beach Day*. Greenwillow, 1990, 32 pp.

Gomi, Taro. *Who Ate It?* Millbrook Press, 1991, 22 pp.

Gordon, Sharon. *What a Dog*. Troll, 1980, 32 pp.

Hamm, Diane Johnston. *Rockabye Farm*. Simon & Schuster, 1992, 24 pp.

Hobsson, Sally. *Chicken Little*. Simon & Schuster, 2000, 26 pp.

Holub, Joan. *Scat, Cats*. Viking, 2001, 30 pp.

Hort, Lenny. *The Seals on the Bus*. Holt, 2000, 28 pp.

Imai, Miko. *Sebastian's Trumpet*. Candlewick Press, 1995, 24 pp.

Jakob, Donna. *My New Sandbox*. Hyperion, 1996, 30 pp.

Janina, Domanska. *Busy Monday Morning*. Greenwillow, 1985, 30 pp.

Janovitz, Marilyn. *Is It Time?* North-South Books, 1994, 24 pp.

Koch, Michelle. *Hoot Howl Hiss*. Greenwillow, 1991, 22 pp.

Kulman, Andrew. *Red Light Stop, Green Light Go*. Simon & Schuster, 1993, 24 pp.

Leman, Jill, & Leman, Martin. *Sleepy Kittens*. Tambourne, 1993, 24 pp.

Maccarone, Grace. *Oink! Moo! How Do You Do?* Scholastic, 1994, 20 pp.

Maris, Ron. *I Wish I Could Fly*. Greenwillow, 1986, 30 pp.

McDonnell, Flora. *I Love Animals*. Candlewick Press, 1994, 24 pp.

McMillan, Bruce. *Puffins Climb, Penguins Rhyme*. Harcourt, 1995, 30 pp.

Medearis, Angela Shelf. *Here Comes the Snow*. Scholastic, 1996, 29 pp.

Miller, Margaret. *Guess Who?* Greenwillow, 1994, 36 pp.

Miller, Margaret. *My Five Senses*. Simon & Schuster, 1994, 22 pp. **N**

Minarik, Else Holmelund. *It's Spring*. Greenwillow, 1989, 18 pp.

Modesitt, Jeanne. *Mama, If You Had a Wish*. Green Tiger Press, 1993, 26 pp.

Neasi, Barbara J. *Just Like Me*. Children's Press, 1984, 30 pp.

Noll, Sally. *Watch Where You Go*. Greenwillow, 1990, 30 pp.

Novak, Matt. *Elmer Blunt's Open House*. Orchard, 1992, 22 pp.

Ogburn, Jacqueline K. *The Noise Lullaby*. Lothrop, Lee & Shepard, 1995, 22 pp.

Parnall, Peter. *Feet!* Simon & Schuster, 1988, 26 pp. **N**

Paschkis, Julie. *So Sleepy, So Wide Awake*. Holt, 1994, 32 pp.

•Peek, Merle. *Mary Wore Her Red Dress and Henry Wore His Green Sneakers*. Clarion, 1985, 22 pp.

Phillips, Joan. *Tiger Is a Scaredy Cat*. New York. Random, 1986, 32 pp.

Pirotta, Saviour. *Little Bird*. Tambourine, 1992, 32 pp.

Pomerantz, Charlotte. *Flap Your Wings and Try*. Greenwillow, 1989, 22 pp.

Raffi. *Everything Grows*. Crown, 1989, 28 pp.

Raffi. *Tingalayo*. Crown, 1989, 30 pp.

Raffi. *Spider on the Floor*. Crown, 1993, 28 pp.

Rehm, Karl, & Koike, Kay. *Left or Right?* Clarion, 1991, 24 pp.

Reiser, Lynn. *Any Kind of Dog*. Greenwillow, 1992, 20 pp.

Rockwell, Anne. *Boats*. Dutton, 1982, 22 pp. **N**

Rockwell, Anne. *Cars*. Dutton, 1984, 22 pp. **N**

Rockwell, Anne. *Willy Can Count*. Arcade, 1989, 24 pp.

Rockwell, Anne. *Sweet Potato Pie*. Random House, 1996, 32 pp.

Roe, Eileen. *All I Am*. Bradbury Press, 1990, 22 pp.

Roffey, Maureen. *Here, Kitty Kitty*. Random House, 1991, 22 pp.

Rohman, Eric. *My Friend Rabbit*. Roaring Brook Press, 2002, 30 pp.

Rotner, Shelley, & Kreisler, Ken. *Citybook*. Orchard, 1994, 29 pp.

Runcie, Jill. *Cock-A-Doodle-Doo*. Simon & Schuster, 1991, 30 pp.

Russo, Marisabina. *Time to Wake Up*. Greenwillow, 1994, 22 pp.

Dr. Seuss. *The Foot Book*. Random House, 1968, 24 pp.

Sheppard, Jeff. *Splash, Splash*. Simon & Schuster, 1994, 40 pp.

Sill, Cathryn. *About Birds: A Guide for Children*. Peachtree, 1991, 30 pp. **N**

Stickland, Paul. *All about Trucks*. Gareth Stevens, 1988, 16 pp. **N**

Stobbs, William. *There's a Hole in My Bucket*. Oxford, 1982, 24 pp.

Testa, Fulvio. *If You Take a Paintbrush, A Book of Colors*. Dial, 1982, 24

Truus. *What Kouka Knows*. Lothrop, Lee & Shepard, 1992, 24 pp.

Vaughn, Marcia. *Hands Hands Hands*. Mondo, 1986, 1995, 16 pp.

Walsh, Ellen Stoll. *Hop Jump*. Harcourt, 1993, 26 pp.

Walter, Virginia. *"Hi, Pizza Man!"* Orchard, 1995, 30 pp.

West, Colin. *"Pardon?" Said the Giraffe*. HarperCollins, 1986, 16 pp.

Wildsmith, Brian, & Wildsmith, Rebecca. *Wake Up, Wake Up*. Harcourt, 1993, 16 pp.

Wiseman, B. *Morris the Moose*. HarperCollins, 1959, 32 pp.

Ziefert, Harriet. *Sleepy Dog*. Random House, 1984, 32 pp.

Ziefert, Harriet. *Say Good Night*. Viking Kestrel, 1987, 30 pp.

Ziefert, Harriett. *Gingerbread Boy*. Viking, 1995, 29 pp.

Ziefert, Harriet. *I Swapped My Dog*. Houghton Mifflin, 1998, 22 pp.

## Reading Level: Primer

Albee, Sarah. *I Can Do It*. Random House, 1997, 30 pp.

Alborough, Jez. *Duck in the Truck*. HarperCollins, 2000, 30 pp.

Aldis, Dorothy. *Hiding*. Viking, 1993, 30 pp.

Alexander, Martha. *You're a Genius, Blackboard Bear.* Candlewick Press, 1995, 22 pp.

Aliki. *Hush Little Baby.* Simon & Schuster, nd, 30 pp.

Aliki. *My Five Senses.* Crowell, 1962, 1989, 32 pp. **N**

Anholt, Catherine, & Anholt, Laurence. *All About You.* Viking, 1991, 26 pp.

Armstrong, Jennifer. *Sunshine, Moonshine.* Random House, 1997, 28 pp. **N**

Arnold, Kataya. *Knock, Knock, Teremok.* North-South, 1994, 24 pp.

Arnosky, Jim. *Deer at the Brook.* Lothrop, Lee & Shepard, 1986, 24 pp. **N**

Asch, Frank. *The Last Puppy.* Simon & Schuster, 1980, 24 pp.

Asch, Frank. *Moongame.* Simon & Schuster, 1984, 28 pp.

Averill, Esther. *Fire Cat.* HarperCollins, 1960, 64 pp.

Baker, Keith. *Who Is the Beast?* Harcourt, 1990, 32 pp.

Bang, Molly. *Delphine.* Morrow, 1988, 24 pp.

Barton, Byron. *Dinosaurs, Dinosaurs.* Crowell, 1989, 36 pp. **N**

Barton, Byron. *The Little Red Hen.* HarperCollins, 1993, 28 pp.

Bender, Robert. *The Preposterous Rhinoceros or Alvin's Beastly Birthday.* Holt, 1994, 24 pp.

Berends, Polly Berrien. *"I Heard," Said the Bird.* Dial, 1995, 29 pp.

Bogacki, Tomek. *The Story of a Blue Bird.* Farrar, Straus & Giroux, 1998, 24 pp.

•Bonsall, Crosby. *And I Mean It, Stanley.* HarperCollins, 1974, 32 pp.

Bonsall, Crosby. *Who's Afraid of the Dark?* HarperCollins, 1980, 32 pp.

Bornstein, Ruth. *Little Gorilla.* Clarion, 1976, 28 pp.

Bornstein, Ruth Lercher. *Rabbit's Good News.* Clarion Books, 1995, 28 pp.

Brenner, Barbara. *Annie's Pet.* Bantam, 1989, 32 pp.

Brenner, Barbara. *Too Many Mice.* Bantam, 1992, 32 pp.

Brisson, Pat. *Benny's Pennies.* Doubleday, 1993, 28 pp.

Brown, Margaret Wise. *Big Red Barn.* HarperCollins, 1956, 1989, 30 pp.

Buckley, Helen E. *Grandfather and I.* Lothrop, Lee & Shepard, 1994, 22 pp.

Bucknall, Caroline. *One Bear All Alone, A Counting Book.* Bucknall, 1985, 20 pp.

Burningham, John. *Aldo.* Crown, 1991, 30 pp.

Calemenson, Stephanie. *It Begins with an A.* Hyperion, 1993, 28 pp.

Capucilli, Alyssa. *Biscuit.* HarperCollins, 1997, 26 pp.

Capucilli, Alyssa Satin. *Bathtime for Biscuit.* HarperCollins, 1998, 32 pp.

Carle, Eric. *The Secret Birthday Message.* HarperCollins, 1971, 22 pp.

Carle, Eric. *Today Is Monday.* Philomel, 1993, 18 pp..

Carle, Eric. *Little Cloud.* Philomel, 1996, 24 pp.

Carle, Eric. *Hello, Red Fox.* Simon & Schuster, 1998, 27 pp.

Carlson, Judy. *Here Comes Kate!* Raintree, 1989, 31 pp.

Carter, Penny. *A New House for the Morrisons.* Viking, 1993, 32 pp.

Coffelt, Nancy. *Good Night, Sigmund.* Harcourt, 1992, 26 pp.

Coulter, Hope. *Uncle Chuck's Truck.* Bradbury, 1993, 24 pp.

Cousins, Lucy. *Za-Za's Baby Brother.* Candlewick, 1995, 24 pp.

Crebbin, June. *The Train Ride.* Candlewick Press, 1995, 24 pp.

Dale, Nora. *The Best Trick of All.* Raintree, 1989, 22 pp.

de Brunhoff, Laurent. *Babar's Little Circus Story.* Random House, 1988, 32 pp.

Demi. *Find Demi's Sea Creatures.* Putnam & Grosset, 1991, 36 pp. **N**

de Regniers, Beatrice Schenk. *How Joe the Bear and Sam the Mouse Got Together.* Lothrop, Lee & Shepard, 1990, 28 pp.

Dobkin, Bonnie. *Just a Little Different.* Children's Press, 1993, 30 pp.

Dorros, Arthur. *Alligator Shoes.* Puffin, 1982, 22 pp.

Driscoll, Laura. *The Bravest Cat! The True Story of Scarlett.* Grosset & Dunlap, 1997, 32 pp. **N**

Dubowski, Cathy East, & Dubowski, Mark. *Snug Bug.* Grossett & Dunlap, 1995, 32 pp.

Dunbar, Joyce. *A Cake for Barney.* Orchard, 1987, 30 pp.

Dunbar, Joyce. *Seven Sillies.* Western, 1993, 30 pp.

•Eastman, P. D. *Are You My Mother?* Random House, 1960, 64 pp.

Eastman, P. D. *Go, Dog, Go.* Random House, 1961, 64 pp.

Ehlert, Lois. *Growing Vegetable Soup.* Harcourt, 1987, 30 pp.

Ehlert, Lois. *Planting a Rainbow.* Harcourt, 1988, 28 pp.

Ehlert, Lois. *Color Zoo.* Lippincott, 1989, 28 pp.

Ehlert, Lois. *Feathers for Lunch.* Harcourt, 1990, 26 pp.

Ehlert, Lois. *Fish Eyes, A Book You Can Count On.* Harcourt, 1990, 32 pp.

Elting, Mary, & Folsom, Michael. *Q Is for Duck.* Houghton Mifflin, 1980, 60 pp.

Emberley, Rebecca. *Let's Go. A Book in Two Languages.* Little, Brown, 1993, 23 pp.

Flack, Marjorie. *Ask Mr. Bear.* Simon & Schuster, 1932, 32 pp.

Fleming, Denise. *In the Tall, Tall Grass.* Holt, 1991, 30 pp.

Fleming, Denise. *Lunch.* Holt, 1992, 28 pp.

Florian, Douglas. *Nature Walk.* Greenwillow, 1989, 28 pp.

Florian, Douglas. *A Carpenter.* Greenwillow, 1991, 22 pp.

Fowler, Alan. *Seeing Things.* Children's Press, 1995, 31pp.

Fox, Mem. *Hattie and the Fox.* Bradbury Press, 1987, 30 pp.

Fox, Mem. *Time for Bed.* Harcourt, 1993, 28 pp.

Fox, Mem. *Zoo Looking.* Mondo, 1996, 27 pp.

Galdone, Paul. *Henny Penny.* Clarion, 1968, 30 pp.

•Gelman, Rita Golden. *More Spaghetti, I Say!* Scholastic, 1977, 30 pp.

Geraghty, Paul. *Slobcat.* Simon & Schuster, 1991, 30 pp.

Gerstein, Mordicai. *Follow Me!* Morrow, 1983, 30 pp.

Giganti, Jr., Paul. *Each Orange Had 8 Slices, A Counting Book.* Greenwillow, 1992, 22 pp.

Ginsburg, Mirra. *Good Morning, Chick.* Greenwillow, 1980, 32 pp.

Goennel, Heidi. *My Day.* Little, Brown, 1988, 28 pp.

Goennel, Heidi. *My Dog.* Orchard, 1989, 26 pp.

Goennel, Heidi. *I Pretend.* Tambourine, 1995, 29 pp.

Goldstone, Bruce. *The Beastley Feast.* Holt, 1998, 30 pp.

Greenfield, Eloise. *Honey, I Love.* HarperCollins, 1978, 16 pp.

Gretz, Susanna. *Duck Takes Off.* Four Winds, 1991, 24 pp.

Gretz, Susanna. *Rabbit Rambles On.* Four Winds, 1992, 24 pp.

Hale, Sara Joseph. *Mary Had a Little Lamb.* Scholastic, 1990, 26 pp.

Harrison, David L. *Wake Up, Sun.* Random House, 1986, 32 pp.

Hawkins, Colin, & Hawkins, Jacqui. *I Know an Old Lady Who Swallowed a Fly.* Putnam, 1987, 22 pp.

Hayes, Sarah. *This Is the Bear.* HarperCollins, 1986, 24 pp.

Hayes, Sarah. *Nine Ducks Nine.* Lothrop, Lee & Shepard, 1990, 24 pp.

Hayes, Sarah. *This Is the Bear and the Scary Night.* Walker, 1992, 24 pp.

Herman, Gail. *What a Hungry Puppy!* Grosset & Dunlap, 1993, 32 pp.

Hill, Eric. *Spot Goes to the Circus.* Putnam, 1986, 22 pp.

Hines, Anna Grossnickle. *What Joe Saw.* Greenwillow, 1994, 30 pp.

Holub, Joan. *Scat, Cat.* Viking, 2001, 30 pp.

Horse, Harry. *A Friend for Little Bear.* Candlewick, 1996, 30 pp.

Hughes, Shirley. *Hiding.* Candlewick, 1994, 16 pp.

Hutchins, Pat. *Clocks and More Clocks.* Simon & Schuster, 1970, 30 pp.

Hutchins, Pat. *The Doorbell Rang.* Greenwillow, 1986, 24 pp.

Hutchins, Pat. *Shrinking Mouse.* Greenwillow, 1997, 24 pp.

Isadora, Rachel. *Listen to the City.* Putnam, 2000, 28 pp.

Jackson, Ellen. *Brown Cow, Green Grass, Yellow Melon Sun.* Hyperion, 1995, 27 pp.

•Johnson, Crockett. *A Picture for Harold's Room.* HarperCollins, 1960, 64 pp.

Jones, Maurice. *I'm Going on a Dragon Hunt.* Simon & Schuster, 1987, 30 pp.

Joyce, William. *George Shrinks.* HarperCollins, 1985, 28 pp.

Kandoian, Ellen. *Maybe She Forgot.* Dutton, 1990, 28 pp.

Kasza, Keiko. *The Pigs' Picnic.* Putnam, 1988, 28 pp.

Kasza, Keiko. *When the Elephant Walks.* Putnam's, 1990, 26 pp.

Kennedy, Jimmy. *Teddy Bears' Picnic.* Holt, 1992, 28 pp.

Klingel, C., & Noyed, Robert B. *Pigs.* The Child's World, 2001, 24 pp. **N**

Koch, Michelle. *By the Sea.* Greenwillow, 1991, 22 pp.

Konigsburg, E. L. *Samuel Todd's Book of Great Colors.* Atheneum, 1990, 24 pp.

Kraus, Robert. *Leo the Late Bloomer.* Simon & Schuster, 1971, 28 pp.

Kraus, Robert. *Come Out and Play, Little Mouse.* Greenwillow, 1987, 28 pp.

Landstrom, Olaf, & Landstrom, Lena. *Will Gets a Haircut.* R & S Books, 1993, 24 pp.

Lewison, Wendy Cheyette. *Going to Sleep on the Farm.* Dial, 1992, 22 pp.

Lionni, Leo. *Little Blue and Little Yellow.* Astor-Honor, 1959, 36 pp.

Lionni, Leo. *Color of His Own.* Knopf, 1975, 28 pp.

Lipniacka, Ewa. *Asleep at Last.* Crocodile Books, 1993, 12 pp.

Lopshire, Robert. *Put Me in the Zoo.* Random, 1960, 61 pp.

Lunn, Carolyn. *Bobby's Zoo.* Children's Press, 1989, 31 pp.

Maccarone, Grace. *"What Is THAT?" Said the Cat.* Scholastic, 1995, 28 pp.

Martin, Bill, Jr. *Polar Bear, Polar Bear, What Do You Hear?* Holt, 1991, 24 pp.

Mayer, Mercer. *There's a Nightmare in My Closet.* Dial, 1968, 28 pp.

McGuire, Richard. *Night Becomes Day.* Viking, 1994, 32 pp.

McNaughton, Colin. *Suddenly.* Harcourt, 1995, 24 pp.

McPhail, David. *Lost!* Little, Brown, 1990, 28 pp.

Medearis, Angela Shelf. *Here Comes the Snow.* Scholastic, 1996, 29 pp.

Merriam, Eve. *The Hole Story.* Simon & Schuster, 1995, 32 pp.

Minarik, Else Holemelund. *The Little Girl and the Dragon.* Greenwillow, 1991, 20 pp.

Moore, Inga. *A Big Day for Little Jack.* Candlewick Press, 1994, 24 pp.

Morley, Carol. *Farmyard Song.* Simon & Schuster, 1994, 24 pp.

Most, Bernard. *Hippopotamus Fun.* Harcourt, 1994, 31 pp.

Noll, Sally. *That Bothered Kate.* Greenwillow, 1991, 30 pp.

Oppenheim, Joanne. *Wake Up, Baby.* Bantam, 1990, 32 pp.

Oppenheim, Joanne. *The Show and Tell Frog.* Bantam, 1992, 32 pp.

Phillips, Joan. *My New Boy.* Random House, 1986, 32 pp.

Philpot, Lorna, & Philpot, Graham. *Amazing Anthony Ant.* Random House, 1993, 22 pp.

Raschka, Chris. *Can't Sleep.* Orchard, 1995, 32 pp.

Rathmann, Peggy. *Ruby the Copycat.* Scholastic, 1991, 27 pp.

Reiser, Lynn. *Bedtime Cat.* Greenwillow, 1991, 20 pp.

Robart, Rose. *The Cake That Mack Ate.* Kids Can Press, 1991, 24 pp.

Rockwell, Anne. *On Our Vacation.* Dutton, 1989, 30 pp.

Rockwell, Anne. *What We Like.* Simon & Schuster, 1992, 24 pp.

Roe, Eileen. *With My Brother.* Simon & Schuster, 1991, 29 pp.

Rotner, Shelley. *Pick a Pet.* Orchard Books, 1999, 28 pp.

Schade, Susan. *Toad on the Road.* Random House, 1992, 32 pp.

Schindel, John, & O'Malley, Kevin. *What's for Lunch?* Lothrop, Lee & Shepard, 1994, 21 pp.

Serfozo, Mary. *There's a Square, A Book about Shapes.* Scholastic, 1996, 32 pp.

•Dr. Seuss. *Green Eggs and Ham.* Random House, 1960, 62 pp.

•Dr. Seuss. *Ten Apples Up on Top.* Random House, 1961, 62 pp.

•Dr. Seuss. *Hop on Pop.* Random House, 1963, 64 pp.

Shaw, Nancy. *Sheep in a Jeep.* Houghton Mifflin, 1986, 32 pp.

Sis, Peter. *Going Up.* Greenwillow, 1989, 19 pp.

Sis, Peter. *An Ocean World.* Greenwillow, 1992, 21 pp.

Soman, David. *One of Three.* Orchard, 1991, 28 pp.

Stadler, John. *Cat at Bat.* Dutton, 1979, 32 pp.

Stadler, John. *Hooray for Snail!* HarperCollins, 1984, 32 pp.

Stadler, John. *Snail Saves the Day.* Crowell, 1985, 32 pp.

Stadler, John. *Cat at Bat Is Back.* Dutton, 1991, 32 pp.

Stevenson, James. *If I Owned a Candy Factory.* Greenwillow, 1968, 1989, 28 pp.

Stoeke, Janet Morgan. *A Hat for Minerva Louise.* Dutton, 1994, 22 pp.

Strub, Susanne. *My Cat and I.* Morrow, 1993, 26 pp.

Sweeney, Jacqueline. *Lou Goes Too!* Marshall Cavendish, 2000, 32 pp.

Taylor, Barbara. *A Day at the Farm.* Dorling Kindersley, 1998, 32 pp. **N**

Tibo, Gilles. *Simon and the Boxes.* Tundra Books, 1992, 22 pp.

Titus, Eve. *Kitten Who Couldn't Purr.* Morrow, 1991, 22 pp.

Tripp, Valerie. *Baby Koala Finds a Home.* Children's Press, 1987, 24 pp.

Waddell, Martin. *When the Teddy Bears Came.* Candlewick, 1994, 24 pp.

Walsh, Ellen Stoll. *Mouse Paint.* Harcourt, 1989, 30 pp.

Walsh, Ellen Stoll. *Mouse Count.* Harcourt, 1991, 28 pp.

Watson, John. *We're the Noisy Dinosaurs.* Candlewick Press, 1992, 26 pp.

Weiss, Nicki. *Where Does the Brown Bear Go?* Greenwillow, 1989, 22 pp.

Westcott, Nadine Bernard. *I Know an Old Lady Who Swallowed a Fly.* Little, Brown, 1980, 28 pp.

Westcott, Nadine Bernard. *The Lady with the Alligator Purse.* Little, Brown, 1988, 22 pp.

Wikler, Linda. *Alfonse, Where Are You?* Crown, 1996, 28 pp.

Wilson, Sarah. *Muskrat, Muskrat, Eat Your Peas.* Simon & Schuster, 1989, 27 pp.

Yolen, Jane. *Mouse's Birthday.* Putnam, 1993, 26 pp.

Young, Ruth. *Who Says Moo?* Viking, 1994, 28 pp.

Ziefert, Harriet. *Jason's Bus Ride.* Puffin, 1987, 32 pp.

Ziefert, Harriet. *Strike Four.* Viking, 1989, 32 pp.

Ziefert, Harriet. *Dark Night, Sleepy Night.* Penguin, 1993, 32 pp.

Ziefert, Harriet. *The Little Red Hen.* Puffin, 1995, 32 pp.

Ziefert, Harriet. *Oh, What a Noisy Farm!* Tambourine, 1995, 27 pp.

Ziefert, Harriet. *The Snow Child.* Viking, 2000, 28 pp.

Zimmermann, H. Werner. *Henny Penny.* Scholastic, 1989, 28 pp.

Zolotow, Charlotte. *Sleepy Book.* HarperCollins, 1958, 26 pp.

## Reading Level: First Grade

Adler, David A. *Young Cam Jansen and the Double Beach Mystery.* Viking, 2002, 32 pp.

Alborough, Jez. *Where's My Teddy?* Candlewick Press, 1992, 24 pp.

Aliki. *We Are Best Friends.* Greenwillow, 1982, 28 pp.

Allen, Johnathan. *My Dog.* Gareth Stevens, 1987, 30 pp.

Allen, Pamela. *Who Sank the Boat?* Coward-McCann, 1982, 28 pp.

Arnold, Marsha. *Quick, Quack, Quick!* Random House, 1996, 32 pp.

Arnold, Tedd. *Green Wilma.* Dial, 1993, 30 pp.

Arnosky, Jim. *Come Out, Muskrats.* Lothrop, Lee & Shepard, 1989, 22 pp. **N**

Asch, Frank. *Bear Shadow.* Simon & Schuster, 1985, 28 pp.

Asch, Frank. *Goodbye House.* Simon & Schuster, 1986, 28 pp.

Ashforth, Camilla. *Horatio's Bed.* Candlewick, 1992, 24 pp.

Axworthy, Anni. *Along Came Toto.* Candlewick Press, 1993, 22 pp.

Ayers, Beryl. *Lucky Duck.* ERA Publications, 1995, 29 pp.

Baker, Alan. *Gray Rabbit's Odd One Out.* Kingfisher, 1995, 23 pp.

Baker, Barbara. *One Saturday Morning.* Dutton, 1994, 48 pp.

Baker, Barbara. *Digby and Kate and the Beautiful Day.* Dutton, 1998, 48 pp.

Barton, Byron. *Airport.* HarperCollins, 1982, 32 pp.

Beaton, Clare. *How Big Is a Pig?* Barefoot Books, 2000, 24 pp.

Beck, Ian. *Home before Dark.* Scholastic, 1997, 30 pp.

Blocksma, Mary. *Yoo Hoo, Moon.* Bantam, 1992, 32 pp.

Bogacki, Tomek (1998). *The Story of a Blue Bird.* Farrar, Straus, Giroux, 24 pp.

Bogan, Paulette. *Spike.* Putnam's, 1998, 28 pp.

Bogan, Paulette. *Spike in the Kennel.* Putnam, 2001, 30 pp.

Bonsall, Crosby. *The Case of the Cat's Meow.* HarperCollins, 1965, 64 pp.

Borden, Louise. *Caps, Hats, Sock, and Mittens.* Scholastic, 1992, 24 pp.

Brandenberg, Franz. *Otto Is Different.* Greenwillow, 1985, 21 pp.

Brenner, Barbara. *The Plant That Kept on Growing.* Bantam, 1996, 29 pp.

Breslow, Susan, & Blakemore, Sally. *I Really Want a Dog.* Dutton, 1990, 37 pp.

•Bridwell, Norman. *Clifford the Small Red Puppy.* Scholastic, 1972, 28 pp.

Brown, Marc. *Arthur's Reading Race.* Random House, 1995, 24 pp.

Brown, Margaret Wise. *Little Donkey, Close Your Eyes.* HarperCollins, 1957, 1985, 1995, 26 pp.

Burningham, John. *Mr. Gumpy's Outing.* Henry Holt, 1970, 32 pp.

Byars, Betsy. *My Brother Ant.* Viking, 1996, 32 pp.

Capucilli, Alyssa Satin. *Inside a Barn in the Country.* Scholastic, 1995, 27 pp.

Carle, Eric. *The Very Hungry Caterpillar.* Philomel, 1969, 22 pp.

Carle, Eric. *The Very Lonely Firefly.* Philomel, 1995, 26 pp.

Carlstom, Nancy White. *I'm Not Moving, Mama.* Simon & Schuster, 1990, 28 pp.

Cauley, Lorinda Bryan. *What Do You Know?* Putnam, 2001, 30 pp.

•Cerf, Bennett. *Bennett Cerf's Book of Animal Riddles.* Random House, 1964, 62 pp.

Chapman, Cheryl. *Snow on Snow on Snow.* Dial, 1994, 29 pp.

Child, Lydia Maria. *Over the River and Through the Woods, A Song for Thanksgiving.* HarperCollins, 1993, 28 pp.

Clements, Andrew. *Dolores and the Big Fire.* Simon & Schuster, 2002, 32 pp.

Cole, Joanna. *It's Too Noisy.* Crowell, 1989, 28 pp.

Collins, Pat Lowery. *Don't Tease the Guppies.* Putnam, 1994, 30 pp.

Cowen-Fletcher. *Mama Zooms.* Scholastic, 1993, 30 pp.

Crews, Donald. *Night at the Fair.* Greenwillow, 1998, 22 pp.

Cummings, Pat. *Angel Baby.* Lothrop, Lee & Shepard, 2000, 22 pp.

Cushman, Doug. *Inspector Hopper.* HarperCollins, 2000, 64 pp.

Degen, Bruce. *Daddy Is a Dooodlebug.* HarperCollins, 2000, 28 pp.

Denton, Kady MacDonald. *Would They Love a Lion?* Kingfisher, 1995, 24 pp.

de Regniers, Beatrice Schenk. *May I Bring a Friend?* Simon & Schuster, 1964, 42 pp.

Dodds, Dayle Ann. *Color Box.* Little, Brown, 1992, 26 pp.

Durant, Alan. *Snake Supper.* Western, 1995, 30 pp.

Dussling, Jennifer. *Stars.* Grosset & Dunlap, 1996, 32 pp. **N**

Edwards, Pamela Duncan. *Warthog Paint, A Messy Color Book.* Hyperion, 2001, 30 pp.

Edwards, Richard. *Something's Coming.* Candlewick Press, 1995, 24 pp.

Ehlert, Lois. *Snowballs.* Harcourt, 1995, 32 pp.

Falwell, Cathryn. *Feast for Ten.* Clarion, 1993, 29 pp.

Fanelli, Sara. *My Map Book.* HarperCollins, 1995, 24 pp.

Fowler, Allan. *Hearing Things.* Children's Press, 1991, 31 pp. **N**

French, Vivian. *Oliver's Vegetables.* Orchard, 1995, 22 pp.

Frith, Michael. *I'll Teach My Dog 100 Words.* Random, 1973, 26 pp.

Gackenbach, Dick. *Claude Has a Picnic.* Clarion, 1993, 30 pp.

Galdone, Paul. *The Gingerbread Boy.* Clarion, 1975, 40 pp.

Geisel, Theodor. *Great Day for Up.* Random House, 1974, 64 pp.

Gerstein, Mordicai. *The Sun's Day.* HarperCollins, 1989, 28 pp.

Goennel, Heidi. *The Circus.* Tambourine, 1992, 26 pp.

Gretz, Susanna, & Sage, Alison. *Teddy Bears at the Seaside.* Simon & Schuster, 1972, 1989, 30 pp.

Guarino, Deborah. *Is Your Mama a Llama?* Scholastic, 1989, 27 pp.

Harrison, Joanna. *Dear Bear.* Carolrhoda, 1994, 29 pp.

Hassett, John and Ann. *Cat up a Tree.* Houghton Mifflin, 1998, 29 pp.

Hazen, Barbara Shook. *Stay, Fang.* Atheneum, 1990, 28 pp.

Heller, Nicholas. *Happy Birthday, Moe Dog.* Greenwillow, 1988, 21 pp.

Hendrick, Mary Jean. *If Anything Ever Goes Wrong with the Zoo.* Harcourt, 1993, 27 pp.

Himmelman, John. *The Day-off Machine.* Silver Press, 1990, 22 pp.

Himmelman, John. *A Guest Is a Guest.* Dutton, 1991, 28 pp.

Ho, Mingfong. *Hush! A Thai Lullby.* Orchard, 1996, 30 pp.

•Hoff, Syd. *Danny and the Dinosaur.* HarperCollins, 1958, 64 pp.

Hoff, Syd. *Oliver.* HarperCollins, 1960, 64 pp.

•Hoff, Syd. *The Horse in Harry's Room.* HarperCollins, 1970, 32 pp.

Hoff, Syd. *Barkley.* HarperCollins, 1975, 32 pp.

Hoff, Syd. *Albert the Albatross.* HarperCollins, 1988, 32 pp.

Hoff, Syd. *Mrs. Brice's Mice.* HarperCollins, 1988, 32 pp.

•Howe, James. *The Day the Teacher Went Bananas.* Dutton, 1984, 28 pp.

Hutchins, Pat. *Don't Forget the Bacon.* Greenwillow, 1976, 28 pp.

Hutchins, Pat. *Tidy Titch.* Greenwillow, 1986, 24 pp.

Hutchins, Pat. *Silly Billy.* Greenwillow, 1992, 26 pp.

Hutchins, Pat. *Three-Star Billy.* Greenwillow, 1994, 27 pp.

Hutchins, Pat. *Shrinking Mouse.* Greenwillow, 1997, 26 pp.

Inkpen, Mick. *Kipper's Toybox.* Harcourt Brace Jovanovich, 1992, 24 pp.

Jakob, Donna. *My Bike.* Hyperion, 1994, 30 pp.

Janovitz, Marilyn. *Look Out, Bird!* North-South, 1994, 30 pp.

Johnson, Angela. *Do Like Kyla.* Orchard Books, 1990, 27 pp.

Johnson, Angela. *Shoes Like Miss Alice's.* Orchard Books, 1995, 26 pp.

Johnson, Suzanne C. *Fribbity Ribbit.* Knopf, 2001, 32 pp.

Jonas, Ann. *The Trek.* Greenwillow, 1985, 27 pp.

•Keats, Ezra Jack. *Whistle for Willie.* Puffin, 1964, 29 pp.

Kessler, Leonard. *Old Turtle's Riddle and Joke Book.* Greenwillow, 1986, 48 pp.

Kimmel, Eric A. *The Gingerbread Man.* Holiday House, 1993, 28 pp.

Kuskin, Karla. *Which Horse Is William?* Greenwillow, 1959, 1987, 21 pp.

Lenski, Lois. *Sing a Song of People.* Little, Brown, 1965, 1987, 28 pp.

Lillie, Patricia. *Floppy Teddy Bear.* Greenwillow, 1995, 29 pp.

Lobel, Arnold. *Grasshopper on the Road.* HarperCollins, 1978, 62 pp.

Mayer, Mercer. *There's Something in My Attic.* Dial, 1988, 29 pp.

McGeorge, Constance W. *Boomer Goes to School.* Chronicle Books, 1996, 24 pp.

McGovern, Ann. *Too Much Noise.* Houghton Mifflin, 1967, 40 pp.

Milios, Rita. *The Hungry Billy Goat.* Children's Press, 1989, 30 pp.

Milstein, Linda. *Coconut Mon.* Tambourine, 1995, 29 pp.

Minarik, Else Holmelund. *Little Bear's Visit.* HarperCollins, 1961, 64 pp.

Minarik, Else Holmelund. *A Kiss for Little Bear.* HarperCollins, 1968, 32 pp.

Most, Bernard. *If the Dinosaurs Came Back.* Harcourt, 1978, 25 pp.

Most, Bernard. *Pets in Trumpets and Other Word-Play Riddles.* Harcourt, 1991, 32 pp.

Munsch, Robert N. *The Dark.* Annick Press, 1989, 28 pp.

Nerlove, Miriam. *I Meant to Clean My Room Today.* Macmillan, 1988, 26 pp.

Nims, Bonnie Larkin. *Where Is the Bear?* Whitman, 1988, 20 pp.

Nims, Bonnie Larkin. *Where Is the Bear in the City?* Whitman, 1992, 20 pp.

Noble, Trinka Hakes. *The Day Jimmy's Boa Ate the Wash.* Dial, 1980, 26 pp.

Numeroff, Laura. *Dogs Don't Wear Sneakers.* Simon & Schuster, 1993, 27 pp.

O'Donnell, Peter. *Carnegie's Excuse.* Scholastic, 1992, 24 pp.

Oppenheim, Joanne. *"Not Now!" Said the Cow.* Bantam, 1989, 32 pp.

Oppenheim, Joanne. *The Donkey's Tale.* Bantam, 1991, 32 pp.

•Parish, Peggy. *Dinosaur Time.* HarperCollins, 1974, 32 pp. **N**

Poland, Janice. *A Dog Named Sam.* Dial, 1995, 40 pp.

Rayner, Shoo. *My First Picture Joke Book.* Viking, 1989, 30 pp.

Robins, Joan. *Addie's Bad Day.* HarperCollins, 1993, 32 pp.

Rockwell, Anne. *Fire Engines.* Dutton, 1986, 22 pp. **N**

Rogers, Paul, & Rogers, Emma. *Quacky Duck.* Little, Brown, 1995, 23 pp.

Roth, Susan L. *Creak, Thonk, Bump, A Very Spooky Mystery.* Simon & Schuster, 1996, 30 pp.

Rowe, John. *Rabbit Moon.* Picture Book Studio, 1992, 22 pp.

Rylant, Cynthia. *Mr. Putter and Tabby Walk the Dog.* Harcourt, 1994, 38 pp.

Samuels, Barbara. *Duncan and Dolores.* Bradbury, 1986, 28 pp.

Schade, Susan, & Buller, Jon. *Snug House, Bug House!* Random House, 1994, 39 pp.

Dr. Seuss. *The Cat in the Hat.* Random House, 1957, 62 pp.

Dr. Seuss. *The Cat in the Hat Comes Back.* Random House, 1957, 62 pp.

Dr. Seuss. *One Fish Two Fish Red Fish Blue Fish.* Random House, 1960, 62 pp.

Shapiro, Arnold L. *Who Says That?* Dutton, 1991, 30 pp.

Sheppard, Jeff. *Full Moon Birthday.* Atheneum, 1995, 28 pp.

Simon, Norma. *Fire Fighters.* Simon & Schuster, 1995, 22 pp.

Siracusa, Catherine. *Bingo, the Best Dog in the World.* HarperCollins, 1991, 64 pp.

Slavin, Bill. *The Cat Came Back.* Whitman, 1992, 26 pp.

•Slobodkina, Esphyr. *Caps for Sale.* HarperCollins, 1947, 42 pp.

Snyder, Carol. *One Up, One Down.* Atheneum, 1995, 26 pp.

Spurr, Elizabeth. *The Gumdrop Tree.* Hyperion, 1994, 28 pp.

Stevenson, James. *B, R, R, R, R!* Greenwillow, 1991, 30 pp.

Stevenson, Robert Louis. *The Moon.* HarperCollins, 1984, 27 pp.

Sullivan, Charles. *Numbers at Play, A Counting Book.* Rizzoli, 1992, 40 pp.

Taylor, Livingston, & Taylor, Maggie. *Can I Be Good?* Harcourt, 1993, 30 pp.

Tompert, Ann. *Just a Little Bit.* Houghton Mifflin, 1993, 29 pp.

Torres, Leyla. *Subway Sparrow.* Farrar, Straus, Giroux, 1993, 28 pp.

Trapani, Iza. *The Itsy Bitsy Spider.* Whispering Coyote Press, 1993, 26 pp.

Weiss, Leatie. *My Teacher Sleeps in School.* Puffin, 1984, 28 pp.

Westcott, Nadine Bernard. *Skip to My Lou.* Little, Brown, 1989, 28 pp.

Westcott, Nadine Bernard. *I've Been Working on the Railroad.* Hyperion, 1996, 27 pp.

Williams, Sherley Anne. *Working Cotton.* Harcourt, 1992, 26 pp.

Wong, Herbert Yee. *Eek! There's a Mouse in the House.* Houghton Mifflin, 1992, 24 pp.

Wood, Audrey. *The Napping House.* Harcourt, 1984, 30 pp.

Young, Ruth. *Golden Bear*. Viking, 1992, 26 pp.

Ziefert, Harriet. *The Three Little Pigs*. Puffin, 1995, 30 pp.

Ziefert, Harriet. *The Cow in the House*. Viking, 1997, 30 pp.

Ziefert, Harriet. *The Ugly Duckling*. Puffin, 1997, 30 pp.

## Reading Level: 2A

### Transitional between End of First and Early Second Grade

Abercrombie, Barbara. *Michael and the Cats*. Simon & Schuster, 1993, 18 pp.

Alda, Arlene. *Sheep, Sheep, Sheep, Help Me Fall Asleep*. Doubleday, 1992, 28 pp.

Aliki. *Best Friends Together Again*. Greenwillow, 1995, 28 pp.

Allen, Jonathan. *Who's at the Door?* Tambourine, 1992, 23 pp.

Anholt, Catherine, & Anholt, Laurence. *Come Back, Jack*. Candlewick Press, 1993, 32 pp.

Anholt, Laurence. *The New Puppy*. Western, 1994, 30 pp.

Babbitt, Natalie. *Bub or the Very Best Thing*. HarperCollins, 1994, 27 pp.

Baker, Barbara. *Digby and Kate*. Dutton, 1988, 48 pp.

Baker, Barbara. *Digby and Kate Again*. Dutton, 1988, 48 pp.

Ballard, Robin. *Cat and Alex and the Magic Flying Carpet*. HarperCollins, 1991, 32 pp.

Bancroft, Henrietta, & Van Gelder, Richard G. *Animals in Winter*. HarperCollins, 1997, 32 pp. **N**

Barracca, Debra, & Barracca, Sal. *The Adventures of Taxi Dog*. Dial, 1990, 30 pp.

Bauman, A. F. *Guess Where You're Going, Guess What You'll Do*. Houghton Mifflin, 1989, 32 pp.

Bayer, Jane. *A My Name Is Alice*. Dial, 1984, 26 pp.

Becker, Bonny. *The Quiet Way Home*. Holt, 1995, 24 pp.

Benchley, Nathaniel. *Oscar Otter*. HarperCollins, 1966, 64 pp.

Benjamin, A. H. *What If?* Green Tiger Press, 1996, 24 pp.

Berlan, Kathryn Hook. *Andrew's Amazing Monsters*. Maxwell, 1993, 28 pp.

Bliss, Corinne Demas. *The Shortest Kid in the World*. Random House, 1994, 48 pp.

Brenner, Barbara, & Hooks, William H. *Ups and Downs of Lion and Lamb*. Bantam, 1991, 48 pp.

Bridwell, Norman. *Clifford's Puppy Days*. Scholastic, 1989, 30 pp.

Brown, Craig. *Tractor*. Greenwillow, 1995, 24 pp.

Brown, Marc. *Spooky Riddles*. Random House, 1983, 38 pp. **N**

Brown, Ruth. *Ladybug, Ladybug*. Dutton, 1988, 26 pp.

Burton, Virginia. *The Little House*. Houghton Mifflin, 1942, 40 pp.

Byars, Betsy. *Hooray for the Golly Sisters*. HarperCollins, 1990, 64 pp.

Camp, Lindsay. *Keeping up with Cheetah*. Lothrop, Lee & Shepard, 1993, 24 pp.

Carlson, Nancy. *Arnie and the New Kid*. Viking, 1990, 28 pp.

Caseley, Judith. *Grandpa's Garden Lunch*. Greenwillow, 1990, 20 pp.

Cauley, Lorinda Bryan. *Treasure Hunt*. Putnam's, 1994, 30 pp.

Celsi, Teresa. *The Fourth Little Pig*. Steck Vaughn, 1990, 23 pp.

Clifton, Lucille. *Everett Anderson's Friend*. Holt, 1976, 1992, 20 pp.

Clifton, Lucille. *Three Wishes*. Doubleday, 1992, 28 pp.

Coffelt, Nancy. *Tom's Fish*. Harcourt, 1994, 30 pp.

Cole, Joanna. *Hungry, Hungry Sharks*. Random House, 1986, 48 pp. **N**

Cosgrove, Stephen. *The Fine Family Farm*. Forest House, 1991, 22 pp.

Cowen-Fletcher, Jane. *It Takes a Village*. Scholastic, 1994, 28 pp.

Crews, Donald. *Bigmama's*. Greenwillow, 1991, 30 pp.

Deetlerfs, Renee. *Tabu and the Dancing Elephants*. Dutton, 1995, 27 pp.

Demarest, Chris L. *My Little Red Car*. Boyds Mill Press, 1992, 28 pp.

Demuth, Patrick. *Johnny Appleseed*. Grosset & Dunlap, 1996, 32 pp. **N**

de Regniers, Beatrice Schenk. *It Does Not Say Meow*. Seabury Press, 1972, 40 pp.

DeSaix, Deborah Durland. *In the Back Seat*. Farrar, Straus, Giroux, 1993, 28 pp.

Dinardo, Jeffrey. *The Wolf Who Cried Boy*. Grossett & Dunlap, 1989, 30 pp.

Dobkin, Bonnie. *Truck Stop*. Children's Press, 1994, 30 pp.

Donaldson, Julia. *A Squash and a Squeeze*. Simon & Schuster, 1993, 24 pp.

Ehlert, Lois. *Mole's Hill: A Woodland Tale*. Harcourt, 1994, 30 pp.

Everitt, Betsy. *Frida the Wondercat*. Harcourt, 1990, 30 pp.

Faulkner, Matt. *Jack and the Beanstalk*. Scholastic, 1986, 48 pp.

Flack, Marjorie. *The Story about Ping*. Viking, 1933, 1961, 32 pp.

Fowler, Susi Gregg. *Fog*. Greenwillow, 1992, 30 pp.

Gackenbach, Dick. *Dog for a Day*. Houghton Mifflin, 1987, 30 pp.

Gág, Wanda. *Millions of Cats*. Putnam, 1928, 32 pp.

Galdone, Paul. *The Three Billy Goats Gruff*. Clarion, 1973, 30 pp.

Galdone, Paul. *The Three Little Kittens*. Clarion, 1986, 30 pp.

Gantos, Jack. *Rotten Ralph's Show and Tell*. Houghton Mifflin, 1989, 30 pp.

Garten, Jan. *Alphabet Tale*. Greenwillow, 1994, 52 pp.

Gershator, Phillis. *Sambalena Show-Off*. Simon & Schuster, 1995, 21 pp.

Gibson, Betty. *The Story of Little Quack*. Little, Brown, 1990, 30 pp.

Gillard, Denise. *Music from the Sky*. Groundwood, 2001, 22 pp.

Gilman, Phoebe. *Something from Nothing*. Scholastic, 1992, 28 pp.

Ginsburg, Mirra. *Good Morning, Chick*. Greenwillow, 1980, 32 pp.

Goodman, Susan E. *Pilgrims of Plymouth*. National Geographic Society, 2001, 16 pp.

Graham, Bob. *"Let's Get a Pup!" Said Kate*. Candlewick Press, 2001, 30 pp.

Greenfield, Eloise. *She Come Bringing Me That Little Baby Girl*. HarperCollins, 1974, 1990, 28 pp.

Griffith, Helen V. *Plunk's Dreams*. Greenwillow, 1990, 29 pp.

Hall, Katy, & Eisenberg, Lisa. *Buggy Riddles*. Puffin, 1986, 48 pp. **N**

Halpern, Shari. *I Have a Pet*. Simon & Schuster, 1994, 30 pp.

Harwayne, Shelley. *Jewels, Children's Play Rhymes*. Mondo, 1995, 21 pp.

Havill, Juanita. *Jamaica's Find*. Scholastic, 1986, 31 pp.

Havill, Juanita. *Jamaica's Blue Marker*. Houghton Mifflin, 1995, 28 pp.

Hazen, Barbara. *Fang*. Atheneum, 1987, 28 pp.

Hazen, Barbara. *Good-Bye, Hello*. Atheneum, 1995, 28 pp.

Hess, Debra. *Wilson Sat Alone*. Simon & Schuster, 1994, 27 pp.

Hoban, Lillian. *Arthur's Funny Money*. HarperCollins, 1981, 64 pp.

Hoff, Syd. *Sammy the Seal*. HarperCollins, 1959, 64 pp.

Hoff, Syd. *Duncan the Dancing Duck*. Clarion Books, 1994, 32 pp.

Hoff, Syd. *The Lighthouse Children*. HarperCollins, 1994, 32 pp.

Howard, Elizabeth Fitzgerald. *The Train to Lulu's*. Bradbury Press, 1988, 30 pp.

Howard, Ellen. *The Big Seed*. Simon & Schuster, 1993, 27 pp.

Howard, Jane R. *When I'm Sleepy*. Dutton, 1985, 22 pp.

Howard, Jane R. *When I'm Hungry*. Dutton, 1992, 22 pp.

Howe, James. *There's a Dragon in My Sleeping Bag*. Atheneum, 1994, 26 pp.

Hubbard, Patricia. *My Crayons Talk*. Holt, 1996, 24 pp.

Hurwitz, Johanna. *New Shoes for Silvia*. Morrow, 1993, 28 pp.

Ivimey, John W. *Three Blind Mice*. Clarion, 1987, 30 pp.

Jensen, Kiersten. *Possum in the House*. Gareth Stevens, 1989, 31 pp.

Johnson, Angela. *When I Am Old with You*. Orchard, 1990, 28 pp.

Johnson, Angela. *The Leaving Morning*. Orchard Books, 1992, 28 pp.

Johnson, Crockett. *Harold and the Purple Crayon*. HarperCollins, 1955, 1993, 61 pp.

Johnson, Paul Brett, & Lewis, Celeste. *Lost*. Orchard, 1995, 32 pp.

Jones, Rebecca C. *Matthew and Tilly*. Dutton, 1991, 28 pp.

Jordan, Helene J. *How a Seed Grows*. HarperCollins, 1960, 1992, 30 pp. **N**

Kasza, Keiko. *The Rat and the Tiger*. Putnam, 1993, 29 pp.

Keats, Ezra Jack. *The Snowy Day*. Viking, 1962, 32 pp.

Keats, Ezra Jack. *Louie*. Greenwillow, 1975, 32 pp.

Kent, Jack. *The Caterpillar and the Polliwog*. Simon & Schuster, 1982, 28 pp.

Kessler, Leonard. *Here Comes the Strikeout*. HarperCollins, 1966, 64 pp.

Kessler, Leonard. *Kick, Pass, and Run*. HarperCollins, 1966, 64 pp.

Kessler, Leonard. *Super Bowl*. Greenwillow, 1980, 56 pp.

Kessler, Leonard. *The Big Mile Race*. Greenwillow, 1983, 47 pp.

Ketteman, Helen. *Not Yet, Yvette*. Whitman, 1992, 22 pp.

Kimmel, Eric A. *Anansi and the Moss-Covered Rock*. Holiday House, 1988, 28 pp.

Kimmel, Eric A. *I Took My Frog to the Library*. Viking, 1990, 24 pp.

Kimmel, Eric A. *The Old Woman and Her Pig*. Holiday, 1992, 30 pp.

Kraus, Robert. *Phil the Ventriloquist*. Greenwillow, 1989, 28 pp.

Krensky, Stephen. *Lionel at Large*. Dial, 1986, 56 pp.

Lee, Huy Voun. *At the Beach*. Holt, 1994, 26 pp.

Lillegard, Lee. *My Yellow Ball*. Dutton, 1993, 29 pp.

Ling, Mary. *See How They Grow, Butterfly*. Dorling Kindersley, 1992, 21 pp. **N**

•Lobel, Arnold. *Frog and Toad Together*. HarperCollins, 1971, 64 pp.

Lobel, Arnold. *Owl at Home*. HarperCollins, 1975, 62 pp.

Lobel, Arnold. *Mouse Soup*. HarperCollins, 1977, 62 pp.

•Lobel, Arnold. *Days with Frog and Toad*. HarperCollins, 1979, 64 pp.

Mangas, Brian. *Follow That Puppy!* Simon & Schuster, 1991, 29 pp.

Mann, Kenny. *I Am Not Afraid*. Bantam, 1993, 28 pp.

Marshall, James. *Fox Be Nimble*. Penguin, 1992, 48 pp.

Martin, Bill, Jr., & Archambault, John. *Chicka Chicka Boom Boom*. Simon & Schuster, 1989, 30 pp.

•Mozelle, Shirley. *Zack's Alligator*. HarperCollins, 1989, 64 pp.

Marzollo, Jean. *Pretend You're a Cat*. Dial, 1990, 26 pp.

Marzollo, Jean. *Snow Angel*. Scholastic, 1995, 28 pp.

Mayer, Mercer. *There's an Alligator under My Bed*. Dial, 1987, 30 pp.

McCully, Emily Arnold. *The Grandma Mix-up*. HarperCollins, 1988, 64 pp.

McDermott, Gerald. *Anansi the Spider: A Tale from the Ashanti*. Holt, 1972, 34 pp.

McDermott, Gerald. *Zomo the Rabbit: A Trickster Tale from West Africa*. Harcourt, 1992, 30 pp.

McPhail, David. *The Day the Sheep Showed Up*. Scholastic, 1998, 32 pp.

Miles, Betty. *Tortoise and the Hare*. Simon & Schuster, 1998, 32 pp.

Moore, Inga. *Six-Dinner Sid*. Simon & Schuster, 1991, 28 pp.

Morris, Ann. *On the Go*. Lothrop, Lee & Shepard, 1990, 29 pp. **N**

Mullins, Patricia. *Dinosaur Encore*. HarperCollins, 1992, 23 pp. **N**

Murphy, Jill. *A Quiet Night In*. Candlewick Press, 1994, 24 pp.

Murphy, Stuart J. *Lemonade for Sale*. HarperCollins, 1998, 31 pp.

Narahashi, Keiko. *I Have a Friend*. Simon & Schuster, 1987, 27 pp.

Naylor, Phyllis Reynolds. *Ducks Disappearing*. Atheneum, 1997, 30 pp.

Neitzel, Shirley. *The Bag I'm Taking to Grandma's*. Greenwillow, 1995, 30 pp.

Ness, Caroline. *Let's Be Friends*. HarperCollins, 1995, 16 pp.

Novak, Matt. *Mouse TV*. Orchard, 1994, 27 pp.

Numeroff, Laura Joffe. *If You Give a Mouse a Cookie*. HarperCollins, 1985, 30 pp.

Numeroff, Laura. *If You Give a Pig a Pancake*. HarperCollins, 1998, 30 pp.

Oppenheim, Joanne. *Left & Right*. Harcourt, 1989, 29 pp.

Parish, Peggy. *Amelia Bedelia Helps Out*. Greenwillow, 1979, 64 pp.

Paul, Ann Whitford. *Shadows Are About*. Scholastic, 1992, 29 pp.

•Penner, Lucille. *Dinosaur Babies*. Random House, 1991, 32 pp. **N**

Prater, John. *Once Upon a Time*. Candlewick, 1993, 24 pp.

Rabe, Tish. *On Beyond Bugs! All about Insects*. Random, 1999, 44 pp.

Raffi. *Baby Beluga*. Crown, 1990, 30 pp.

Reiser, Lynn. *The Surprise Family*. Greenwillow, 1994, 28 pp.

Rey, H. A. *Curious George*. Houghton Mifflin, 1941, 54 pp.

Roberts, Bethany. *A Mouse Told His Mother*. Little, Brown, 1997, 32 pp.

Robinson, Fay. *Recycle That!* Children's Press, 1995, 32 pp. **N**

Rotner, Shelley, & Kreisler, Ken. *Nature Spy*. Simon & Schuster, 1992, 26 pp. **N**

Rounds, Glen. *The Three Billy Goats Gruff*. Holiday House, 1993, 29 pp.

•Rylant, Cynthia. *Henry and Mudge, The First Book*. Simon & Schuster, 1990, 40 pp.

Rylant, Cynthia. *Poppleton Everyday*. Scholastic, 1997, 48 pp.

Schwartz, Alvin. *All of Our Noses Are Here and Other Noodle Tales*. HarperCollins, 1985, 64 pp.

Sendak, Maurice. *Where the Wild Things Are*. HarperCollins, 1964, 36 pp.

Serfozo, Mary. *Who Wants One?* Simon & Schuster, 1989, 32 pp.

Shannon, David. *Duck on a Bike*. Blue Sky Press, 2002, 28 pp.

Sharmat, Marjorie. *Mitchell Is Moving*. Simon & Schuster, 1978, 46 pp.

Sharmat, Marjorie. *I'm the Best*. Holiday House, 1991, 29 pp.

Shelby, Anne. *The Someday House*. Orchard, 1996, 27 pp.

Showers, Paul. *Look at Your Eyes*. HarperCollins, 1992, 32 pp. **N**

Simms, Laura. *The Squeaky Door*. Crown, 1991, 27 pp.

Simon, Norma. *Cats Do, Dogs Don't*. Whitman, 1986, 29 pp. **N**

Siracusa, Catherine. *No Mail for Mitchell*. Random House, 1990, 32 pp.

•Slepian, Jan, & Seidler, Ann. *The Hungry Thing*. Scholastic, 1967, 30 pp.

•Slepian, Jan, & Seidler, Ann. *The Hungry Thing Returns*. Scholastic, 1990, 28 pp.

Stadler, John. *The Adventures of Snail at School*. HarperCollins, 1993, 64 pp.

Stevenson, James. *Will You Please Feed Our Cat?* Greenwillow, 1987, 30 pp.

Sykes, Julie. *This and That*. Farrar, Straus and Giroux, 1996, 24 pp.

Thomas, Abigail. *Pearl Paints*. Holt, 1994, 29 pp.

Van Leeuwen, Jean. *Tales of Amanda Pig*. Dial, 1983, 56 pp.

Walsh, Ellen Stoll. *You Silly Goose*. Harcourt, 1992, 30 pp.

Wheeler, Cindy. *Bookstore Cat*. Random House, 1994, 32 pp.

Whybrow, Ian. *Quacky Quack-Quack*. Simon & Schuster, 1991, 24 pp.

Wilcox, Cathy. *Enzo the Wonderfish*. Ticknor & Fields, 1983, 30 pp.

Wildsmith, Brian. *Goat's Trail*. Knopf, 1986, 30 pp.

Winthrop, Elizabeth. *Best Friends' Club*. Harcourt, 2000, 24 pp.

Wolff, Patricia Rae, & Root, Kimberley. *The Toll-Bridge Troll*. Harcourt, 1995, 21 pp.

Wormel, Mary. *Hilda Hen's Search*. Harcourt, 1994, 28 pp.

Wormell, Mary. *Hilda Hen's Happy Birthday*. Harcourt, 1995, 28 pp.

Yoshi. *Who's Hiding Here?* Picture Book Studio, 1987, 32 pp.

Ziefert, Harriet. *Pete's Chicken*. Tambourine, 1994, 32 pp.

Ziefert, Harriet. *The Magic Porridge Pot*. Puffin, 1997, 30 pp.

Ziefert, Harriet. *The Ugly Duckling*. Puffin, 1997, 30 pp.

Zimmerman, Andrea, & Clemesha, David. *The Cow Buzzed*. HarperCollins, 1993, 28 pp.

Zion, Gene. *Harry the Dirty Dog*. HarperCollins, 1956, 28 pp.

Zion, Gene. *No Roses for Harry*. HarperCollins, 1958, 28 pp.

## Grade 2B Books

Alcott, Susan. *Young Amelia Earhart: A Dream to Fly*. Troll, 1992, 32 pp. **N**

•Allard, Harry, & Marshall, James. *Miss Nelson Is Missing*. Houghton Mifflin, 1985, 32 pp.

Arnosky, Jim. *Otters under Water*. Putnam, 1992, 24 pp. **N**

Arnosky, Jim. *Every Autumn Comes the Bear*. Putnam, 1993, 28 pp. **N**

Atwell, Debbie. *River*. Houghton Mifflin, 1999, 28 pp. **N**

Baehr, Patricia. *Mouse in the House*. Holiday, 1994, 29 pp.

•Bang, Molly. *The Paper Crane*. Greenwillow, 1985, 29 pp.

•Bemelmans, Ludwig. *Madeline*. Penguin, 1939, 44 pp.

Benjamin, Alan. *Buck*. Simon & Schuster, 1993, 24 pp.

Blume, Judy. *Freckle Juice*. Bantam Doubleday Dell, 1971, 47 pp.

Blume, Judy. *The One in the Middle Is the Green Kangaroo*. Bantam Doubleday Dell, 1981, 39 pp.

Boegehold, Betty D. *A Horse Called Starfire*. Bantam, 1991, 32 pp.

Bos, Burny. *More from the Molesons*. North-South Books, 1995, 46 pp.

Branley, Franklyn M. *Day Light, Night Light*. HarperCollins, 1998, 32 pp. **N**

Brenner, Barbara. *Wagon Wheels*. HarperCollins, 1978, 64 pp.

Brown, Marc. *Arthur's Pet Business*. Little, Brown, 1990, 30 pp.

Burton, Marilee Robin. *My Best Shoes*. Tambourine, 1994, 22 pp.

Chermayeff, Ivan. *Fishy Facts*. Harcourt Brace, 1994, 29 pp. **N**

Christian, Mary Blount. *Swamp Monsters*. Dial, 1983, 56 pp.

Coerr, Eleanor. *The Josephina Story Quilt*. HarperCollins, 1986, 64 pp.

Coerr, Eleanor. *Chang's Paper Pony*. HarperCollins, 1988, 64 pp.

Cole, Joanna, & Calmeson, Stephanie. *Why Did the Chicken Cross the Road? And Other Riddles Old and New*. Morrow, 1994, 64 pp. **N**

Cosby, Bill. *The Best Way to Play*. Scholastic, 1997, 33 pp.

Cosby, Bill. *The Meanest Thing to Say*. Scholastic, 1997, 33 pp.

Cristaldi, Kathryn. *Baseball Ballerina*. Random, 1992, 48 pp.

DeFelice, Cynthia. *Clever Crow*. Atheneum, 1998, 30 pp.

Demuth, Patricia Brennan. *Achoo!* Grosset & Dunlap, 1997, 30 pp. **N**

de Paola, Tomie. *Charlie Needs a Cloak*. Prentice-Hall, 1973, 27 pp.

Disalvo-Ryan, Dyanne. *City Green*. Morrow, 1994, 30 pp.

Dorflinger, Carolyn. *Tomorrow Is Mom's Birthday*. Whispering Coyote Press, 1994, 28 pp.

•Dorros, Arthur. *Abuela*. Dutton, 1991, 36 pp.

Dorros, Arthur. *This Is My House*. Scholastic, 1992, 29 pp. **N**

Dorros, Arthur. *Radio Man*. HarperCollins, 1993, 32 pp.

Dubowski, Cathy East, & Dubowski, Mark. *Pretty Good Magic*. Random, 1987, 48 pp.

Ehlert, Lois. *Red Leaf, Yellow Leaf*. Harcourt, 1992, 31 pp.

Fleischman, Paul. *Time Train*. HarperCollins, 1991, 30 pp.

Fowler, Allan. *The Biggest Animal Ever*. Children's Press, 1992, 30 pp. **N**

Fowler, Allan. *Frogs and Toads and Tadpoles, Too*. Children's Press, 1992, 32 pp. **N**

Fowler, Allan. *The Upside-Down Sloth*. Children's Press, 1993, 32 pp. **N**

Fowler, Allan. *What Magnets Can Do*. Children's Press, 1993, 32 pp. **N**

Fowler, Allan. *Woolly Sheep and Hungry Goats*. Children's Press, 1993, 32 pp. **N**

Fowler, Allan. *The Best Way to See a Shark*. Children's Press, 1995, 31 pp. **N**

Freeman, Don. *Corduroy*. Viking, 1968, 32 pp.

Galdone, Paul. *Little Red Riding Hood*. McGraw-Hill, 1974, 29 pp.

Gibbons, Gail. *Farming*. Holiday House, 1988, 30 pp. **N**

Giff, Patricia Reilly. *Today Was a Terrible Day*. Viking, 1985, 25 pp.

Giff, Patricia Reilly. *Watch Out, Ronald Morgan*. Viking, 1985, 25 pp.

Giff, Patricia Reilly. *The Secret at the Polk Street School*. Dell, 1987, 72 pp.

Graves, Bonnie. *The Best Worst Day*. Hyperion, 1996, 64 pp.

Haas, Jessie. *Chipmunk!* Greenwillow, 1993, 21 pp.

Hadithi, Mwenye. *Baby Baboon*. Little, Brown, 1993, 28 pp.

Hall, Katy, & Eisenberg, Lisa. *Sheepish Riddles*. Dial, 1996, 48 pp. **N**

Hartman, Gail. *As the Roadrunner Runs, A First Book of Maps*. Bradbury, 1994, 30 pp. **N**

Hennessy, B. G. *Road Builders*. Penguin, 1994, 28 pp. **N**

Heo, Yumi. *Father's Rubber Shoes*. Orchard, 1995, 29 pp.

Hoban, Lillian. *Arthur's Pen Pal*. HarperCollins, 1976, 64 pp.

Hoban, Russell. *Bread and Jam for Frances*. HarperCollins, 1964, 31 pp.

Hoberman, Mary Ann. *One of Each*. Little, Brown, 1997, 30 pp.

Hoffman, Mary. *Boundless Grace*. Dial, 1995, 24 pp.

Hopkins, Lee Bennett (Ed.). *Surprises*. HarperCollins, 1986, 64 pp.

Howard, Elizabeth Fitzgerald. *Aunt

*Flossie's Hats (and Crab Cakes Later)*. Houghton Mifflin, 1991, 31 pp.

Jaffe, Nina. *Sing, Little Sack!* Bantam, 1993, 48 pp.

Johnson, Angela. *Julius*. Orchard, 1993, 30 pp.

Johnson, Dolores. *What Kind of Baby-Sitter Is This?* Simon & Schuster, 1991, 32 pp.

Johnson, Doug. *Never Babysit the Hippopotamuses*. Holt, 1993, 28 pp.

Jones, Rebecca C. *Great Aunt Martha*. Dutton, 1995, 30 pp.

Kasza, Keiko. *Grandpa Toad's Secrets*. Putnam's, 1995, 30 pp.

Keats, Ezra Jack. *Pet Show!* Simon & Schuster, 1972, 32 pp.

Koontz, Michal Robin. *Chicago and the Cat*. Dutton, 1993, 30 pp.

Kramer, Sydelle. *Wagon Train*. Grosset & Dunlap, 1997, 48 pp. **N**

Kuskin, Karla. *Roar and More*. HarperCollins, 1956, 1990, 42 pp.

Kuskin, Karla. *Something Sleeping in the Hall*. HarperCollins, 1985, 64 pp.

•Kuskin, Karla. *Soap Soup and Other Verses*. HarperCollins, 1992, 64 pp.

Kuskin, Karla. *City Dog*. Clarion, 1994, 27 pp.

Legge, David. *Bamboozled*. Scholastic, 1994, 30 pp.

Levy, Elizabeth. *Schoolyard Mystery*. Scholastic, 1994, 45 pp.

Lionni, Leo. *Swimmy*. Knopf, 1963, 28 pp.

Maestro, Marco, & Maestro, Giulio. *What Do You Hear When Cows Sing and Other Silly Riddles?* HarperCollins, 1996, 48 pp. **N**

Marshall, James. *George and Martha Rise and Shine*. Houghton Mifflin 1976, 44 pp.

Marzollo, Jean. *Soccer Sam*. Random, 1987, 48 pp.

Marzollo, Jean. *School Days: I Spy, A Book of Picture Riddles*. Scholastic, 1992, 28 pp. **N**

McConnachie, Brian. *Elmer and the Chickens vs. the Big Leagues*. Crown, 1992, 30 pp.

McDonald, Megan. *Is This a House for Hermit Crab?* Orchard, 1990, 26 pp.

•McGovern, Ann. *Stone Soup*. Scholastic, 1968, 32 pp.

McKean, Thomas. *Hooray for Grandma Jo!* Crown, 1994, 28 pp.

Meddaugh, Susan. *Tree of Birds*. Houghton Mifflin, 1990, 30 pp.

Miller, Montzalee. *My Grandmother's Cookie Jar*. Price/Stern/Sloan, 1987, 26 pp.

Mills, Claudia. *Gus and Grandpa at Basketball*. Farrar, Straus & Giroux, 2001, 48 pp.

Moss, Marissa. *Mel's Diner*. Troll, 1994, 30 pp.

Most, Bernard. *A Dinosaur Named after Me*. Harcourt, 1991, 32 pp.

Murphy, Stuart J. *Lemonade for Sale*. HarperCollins, 1998, 31 pp.

Noll, Sally. *I Have a Loose Tooth*. Greenwillow, 1992, 30 pp.

Numeroff, Laura Joffe. *If You Give a Moose a Muffin*. HarperCollins, 1989, 30 pp.

Oechsli, Kelly. *Mice at Bat*. HarperCollins, 1986, 64 pp.

Oppenheim, Joanne. *"Uh-Oh!" Said the Crow*. Bantam, 1993, 32 pp.

Parish, Peggy. *Thank You, Amelia Bedelia*. HarperCollins, 1964, 30 pp.

Parkinson, Curtis. *Tom Foolery*. Bradbury, 1993, 30 pp.

Penner, Lucille Recht. *The True Story of Pocahontas*. Random House, 1994, 48 pp. **N**

Pilkey, Dav. *When Cats Dream*. Orchard, 1992, 29 pp.

•Platt, Kin. *Big Max*. HarperCollins, 1965, 64 pp.

Rabe, Tish. *On Beyond Bugs! All about Insects*. Random House, 1999, 44 pp. **N**

Reneaux, J. J. *Why Alligator Hates Dog, A Cajun Folktale*. August House, 1995, 26 pp.

Rotner, Shelley. *Wheels Around*. Houghton Mifflin, 1995, 29 pp. **N**

Ryden, Hope. *Joey, the Story of a Baby Kangaroo*. Tambourine, 1994, 38 pp. **N**

Rylant, Cynthia. *The Relatives Came*. Bradbury, 1985, 28 pp.

Rylant, Cynthia. *The Case of the Troublesome Turtle*. Greenwillow Books, 2001, 48 pp.

Sanfield, Steve. *Bit by Bit*. Philomel, 1995, 28 pp.

Sendak, Maurice. *Chicken Soup with Rice*. HarperCollins, 1962, 32 pp.

Sharmat, Marjorie Weinman. *Nate the Great and the Musical Note*. Coward-McCann, 1990, 48 pp.

Sharmat, Marjorie Weinman. *Nate the Great and the Tardy Tortise*. Delacorte, 1995, 41 pp.

Sharmat, M. W. *Nate the Great Saves the King of Sweden*. Delacorte, 1998, 48 pp.

Slote, Elizabeth. *Nellie's Grannies*. Tambourine Books, 1993, 30 pp.

Smith, Mavis. *A Snake Mistake*. HarperCollins, 1991, 28 pp.

Soto, Gary. *Too Many Tamales*. Putnam, 1993, 32 pp.

Stevenson, James. *Fun No Fun*. Greenwillow, 1994, 30 pp.

Teague, Mark. *The Field beyond the Outfield*. Scholastic, 1992, 30 pp.

Teague, Mark. *Pigsty*. Scholastic, 1994, 30 pp.

Viorst, Judith. *Alexander and the Terrible, Horrible, No Good, Very Bad Day*. Atheneum, 1972, 28 pp.

Waber, Ira. *Ira Sleeps Over*. Scholastic, 1972, 46 pp.

Waggoner, Karen. *The Lemonade Babysitter*. Little, Brown, 1992, 29 pp.

Wallace, Karen. *Duckling Days*. DK, 1999, 32 pp. **N**

Welch, Willy. *Playing Right Field*. Scholastic, 1995, 29 pp.

Wells, Rosemary. *Lucy Comes to Stay*. Dial, 1994, 26 pp.

Wildsmith, Brian. *The Owl and the Woodpecker*. Oxford University Press, 1971, 30 pp.

Williams, Vera B. *A Chair for My Mother*. Greenwillow, 1982, 28 pp.

Wolff, Ferida. *Seven Loaves of Bread*. Tambourine, 1993, 29 pp.

Wu, Norbert. *Fish Faces*. Holt, 1993, 28 pp. **N**

Wyler, Rose, & Ames, Gerald. *Magic Secrets*. HarperCollins, 1990, 64 pp. **N**

Yee, Wong Herbert. *Mrs. Brown Went to Town*. Houghton Mifflin, 1996, 28 pp.

Yolen, Jane. *Owl Moon*. Philomel, 1987,

Zoehfeld, Kathleen Weidner. *What Lives in a Shell?* HarperCollins, 1994, 26 pp. **N**

**Challenging Reading Level:
Grade 3 Reading Level
(Interest Level: Grade 2)**

Choi, Sook Nyul. *The Best Older Sister*. Delacorte, 1997, 47 pp.

Kline, Suzy. *Song Lee and the Hamster Hunt*. Viking, 1994, 52 pp.

Kline, Suzy. *Mary Marony and the Chocolate Surprise*. Putnam, 1995, 86 pp.

Kline, Suzy. *Marvin and the Mean Words*. Putnam, 1997, 81 pp.

Milne, A. A. *Winnie-The-Pooh*. Bantam Doubleday Dell, 1926, 161 pp.

Stevenson, James. *Sam the Zamboni Man*. Greenwillow, 1998, 29 pp.

### Third-Grade Books

**Easy Reading Level: Grade 2
(Interest Level: Grade 3)**

Alphin, Elaine Marie. *A Bear for Miguel*. HarperCollins, 1996, 64 pp.

Bolognese, Don. *Little Hawk's New Name*. Scholastic, 1995, 48 pp.

•Bulla, Clyde Robert. *The Chalk Box Kid*. Random House, 1987, 57 pp.

•Bunting, Eve. *December*. Harcourt, 1997, 28 pp.

Dorros, Arthur. *Ant Cities*. HarperCollins, 1987, 32 pp. **N**

Hopkins, L. B. (Ed.). *Questions, Poems of Wonder*. HarperCollins, 1992, 64 pp. **N**

Lundell, Margo. *A Girl Named Helen Keller*. Scholastic, 1995, 48 pp. **N**

Osborne, Mary Pope. *Afternoon on the Amazon*. Random House, 1995, 67 pp.

Penner, Lucille Recht. *Sitting Bull*. Grosset & Dunlap, 1995, 48 pp. **N**

•Dr. Seuss. *The Cat's Quizzer*. Random House, 1976, 62 pp. **N**

Smith, Christine. *How to Draw Cartoons*. Gareth Stevens, 1997, 24 pp. **N**

**Average Reading Level: Grade 3 (Interest Level: Grade 3)**

Aardema, Verna. *Anansi Does the Impossible! An Ashanti Tale*. Atheneum, 1997, 28 pp.

Adler, David A. *A Picture Book of Benjamin Franklin*. Holiday, 1990, 32 pp. **N**

Adler, David A. *A Picture Book of Harriett Tubman*. Holiday, 1992, 32 pp. **N**

Adler, David A. *A Picture Book of Rosa Parks*. Holiday House, 1993, 32 pp. **N**

•Angelou, Maya. *Kofi and His Magic*. Clarkson Potter, 1996, 38 pp. **N**

•Arnosky, Jim. *Crinkleroot's Guide to Knowing Butterflies and Moths*. Simon & Schuster, 1996, 32 pp. **N**

Asimov, Isaac. *Why Are Whales Vanishing?* Gareth Stevens, 1992, 24 pp. **N**

Ball, Jacqueline. *Do Fish Drink? First Questions and Answers about Water*. Time Life, 1993, 48 pp. **N**

Barrett, Judi. *Cloudy with a Chance for Meatballs*. Atheneum, 1978, 30 pp.

Bourgeois, Paulette, & Clark, Brenda. *Franklin Forgets*. Scholastic, 2000, 29 pp.

Bloom, Valerie. *Fruits: A Caribbean Counting Poem*. Holt, 1992, 26 pp.

Bottner, Barbara. *Nana Hannah's Piano*. Putnam's, 1996, 32 pp.

Branley, Franklyn M. *The Planets in Our Solar System (Rev.)*. HarperCollins, 1987, 32 pp. **N**

Calmenson, Stephanie. *The Frog Principal*. Scholastic, 2001, 28 pp.

Choi, Yangsook. *New Cat*. Farrar, Straus & Giroux, 1999, 28 pp.

Clifford, Eth. *Flatfoot Fox*. Houghton Mifflin, 1995, 47 pp.

•Cohen, Barbara. *Molly's Pilgrim*. Bantam Doubleday Dell, 1983, 41 pp.

•Cole, Joanna. *The Magic School Bus and the Electric Field Trip*. Scholastic, 1997, 48 pp. **N**

•Dalgliesh, Alice. *Courage of Sarah Noble*. Scribner's, 1954, 54 pp.

Darling, Kathy. *Rain Forest Babies*. Walker, 1996, 32 pp. **N**

Demuth, Patricia Brennan. *In Trouble with Teacher*. Dutton, 1995, 73 pp.

Duffey, Betsy. *How to Be Cool in Third Grade*. Viking, 1993, 69 pp.

Duffey, Betsy. *Hey, New Kid*. Viking, 1996, 89 pp.

Ganeri, Anita. *I Wonder Why . . . Camels Have Humps and Other Questions about Animals*. Reader's Digest, 1993, 32 pp.

Garay, Luis. *The Long Road*. Tundra, 1997, 28 pp.

Garland, Sherry. *My Father's Boat*. Scholastic, 1998, 30 pp.

George, Jean Craighead. *Arctic Son*. Hyperion, 1997, 30 pp.

Gershator, David, & Gershator, Phillis. *Palampam Day*. Marshall Cavendish, 1997, 24 pp.

Gerstein, Mordicai. *Behind the Couch*. Hyperion, 1996, 57 pp.

Gibbons, Gail. *Weather Words and What They Mean*. Holiday House, 1990, 30 pp.

•Gibbons, Gail. *Marshes and Swamps*. Holiday House, 1998, 30 pp. **N**

Giff, Patricia Reilly. *A Glass Slipper for Rosie*. Viking, 1997, 73 pp.

•Guthrie, Donna, Bentley, Nancy, & Arnsteen, Katy Keck. *Young Author's Do-It-Yourself Book: How to Write, Illustrate, and Produce Your Own Book*. Millbrook Press, 1994, 64 pp. **N**

Hautzig, Deborah. *Beauty and the Beast*. Random House, 1995, 32 pp.

•Hodge, Deborah. *Whales, Killer Whales, Blue Whales and More*. Kids Can Press, 1997, 32 pp. **N**

Johnson, Dolores. *Grandma's Hands*. Marshall Cavendish, 1998, 30 pp.

Karas, G. Brian. *The Nature of the Beast*. Tambourine, 1996, 30 pp.

Kimmel, Eric A. *Easy Work! An Old Tale!* Holiday House, 1998, 30 pp.

Lafferty, Peter. *Why Do Balls Bounce? First Questions and Answers about How Things Work*. Time Life, 1995, 48 pp. **N**

Leedy, Loreen. *Mapping Penny's World*. Holt, 2000, 30 pp.

Levitin, Sonia. *Boom Town*. Orchard

Books, 1998, 30 pp.

Lindbergh, Reeve. *Nobody Owns the Sky*. Candlewick Press, 1996, 22 pp. **N**

•Markle, Sandra. *Outside and Inside Bats*. Atheneum, 1997, 40 pp. **N**

McCourt, Lisa. *The Goodness Gorillas*. Health Communications, 1997, 29 pp.

Meddaugh, Susan. *Cinderella's Rat*. Houghton Mifflin, 1997, 32 pp.

Medina, Tony. *Deshawn Days*. Lee and Low, 2001, 30 pp.

Miller, Debbie E. *Are Trees Alive?* Walker, 2002, 30 pp. **N**

Mitchell, Rhonda. *The Talking Cloth*. Orchard, 1997, 26 pp.

Naylor, Phyllis Reynolds. *I Can't Take You Anywhere*. Atheneum, 1997, 32 pp.

Osborne, Mary Pope. *Ghost Town at Sundown*. Random House, 1997, 73 pp.

Petersen, P. J. *The Sub*. Dutton, 1993, 86 pp.

Peterson-Fleming, Judy, & Fleming, Bill. *Puppy Training and Critters, Too*. Tambourine, 1996, 40 pp. **N**

Polacco, Patricia. *Aunt Chip and the Great Triple Creek Dam Affair*. Philomel, 1996, 36 pp.

Reynolds, Marilynn. *The New Land*. Orca, 1997, 30 pp.

Riggio, Anita. *Secret Signs along the Underground Railroad*. Boyds Mill Press, 1997, 28 pp.

Ripley, Catherine. *Why Does Popcorn Pop? And Other Kitchen Questions*. Firefly Books, 1997, 32 pp. **N**

Sanders, Scott Russell. *A Place Called Freedom*. Simon & Schuster, 1997, 28 pp.

Shannon, David. *The Rain Came Down*. Scholastic, 2000, 30 pp.

•Silverstein, Shel. *Where the Sidewalk Ends*. HarperCollins, 1974, 166 pp. **N**

Slepian, Jan, & Seidler, Ann. *The Hungry Thing Goes to a Restaurant*. Scholastic, 1992, 30 pp.

Stewart, Dianne. *Gift of the Sun: A Tale from South Africa*. Farrar, Straus & Giroux, 1996, 24 pp.

Stolz, Mary. *King Emmett the Second*. Greenwillow, 1991, 56 pp.

Teague, Mark. *The Secret Shortcut*. Scholastic, 1996, 24 pp.

Van Leeuwen, Jean. *Fourth of July on the Plains*. Dial, 1997, 30 pp.

Warner, Gertrude C. *The Boxcar Children: Mystery Behind the Wall*. Albert Whitman, 1973, 127 pp.

Wood, Audrey. *The Flying Dragon*

*Room.* Scholastic, 1996, 28 pp.

Yezerski, Thomas F. *Together in Pinecone Patch.* Farrar, Straus & Giroux, 1998, 30 pp.

Yolen, Jane. *Sleeping Ugly.* Coward, McCann & Geoghegan, 1981, 64 pp.

Zoehfeld, Kathleen Weidner. *How Mountains Are Made.* HarperCollins, 1995, 32 pp. **N**

Zoehfeld, Kathleen Weidner. *Dinosaurs Big and Small.* HarperCollins, 2002, 33 pp. **N**

### Challenging Reading Level: Grade 4 (Interest Level: Grade 3)

•Ada, Alma Flor. *My Name Is Maria Isabel.* Simon & Schuster, 1993, 57 pp.

Adler, David A. *A Picture Book of Thurgood Marshall.* Holiday, 1997, 32 pp. **N**

Bond, Michael. *A Bear Called Paddington.* Houghton Mifflin, 1958, 128 pp.

Brown, Marc. *Arthur Makes the Team.* Little, Brown, 1998, 61 pp.

Cleary, Beverly. *Muggie Maggie.* Avon, 1990, 70 pp.

Gibbons, Gail. *Recycle! A Handbook for Kids.* Little, Brown, 1992, 28 pp. **N**

•Gibbons, Gail. *Planet Earth/Inside Out.* Morrow, 1995, 26 pp. **N**

Harrison, Michael, & Stuart-Clark, Christopher. *The New Oxford Treasury of Children's Poems.* Oxford University Press, 1995, 174 pp.

Hickox, Rebecca. *The Golden Sandal: A Middle Eastern Cinderella Story.* Holiday House, 1998, 28 pp.

Honeycutt, Natalie. *Juliet Fisher and the Foolproof Plan.* Bradbury Press, 1992, 133 pp.

•Lindberg, Becky Thoman. *Thomas Tuttle, Just in Time.* Whitman, 1994, 111 pp.

MacDonald, Betty. *Mrs. Piggle-Wiggle.* HarperCollins, 1947, 119 pp.

Penner, Lucille Recht. *Monster Bugs.* Random House, 1996, 48 pp. **N**

Steig, William. *Sylvester and the Magic Pebble.* Simon & Schuster, 1969, 30 pp.

Zoehfeld, Kathleen Weidner. *Terrible Tyrannosaurus.* HarperCollins, 2001, 30 pp. **N**

### Fourth-Grade Books

### Easy Reading Level: Grade 1 (Interest Level: Grade 4)

Schwartz, Alvin. *In a Dark Dark Room.* HarperCollins, 1984, 62 pp.

### Easy Reading Level: Grade 2 (Interest Level: Grade 4)

•Bulla, Clyde Robert. *Shoeshine Girl.* Crowell, 1975, 84 pp.

•Shea, George. *Amazing Rescues.* Random House, 1992, 48 pp. **N**

### Easy Reading Level: Grade 3 (Interest Level: Grade 4)

Abbott, Tony. *Danger Guys.* HarperCollins, 1994, 69 pp.

Adler, David A. *Lou Gehrig, The Luckiest Man.* Harcourt Brace, 1997, 30 pp. **N**

•Avi. *Man from the Sky.* Knopf, 1980, 117 pp.

Ballard, Robert. *Finding the Titanic.* Scholastic, 1993, 48 pp. **N**

•Berends, Polly. *The Case of the Elevator Duck.* Random House, 1973, 60 pp.

Blume, Judy. *Blubber.* Dell, 1974, 153 pp.

Bunting, Eve. *Train to Somewhere.* Houghton Mifflin, 1996, 32 pp.

Clymer, Eleanor. *The Trolley Car Family.* Scholastic, 1947, 216 pp.

Danziger, Paula. *Amber Brown Goes Fourth.* Putnam, 1995, 101 pp.

Donnelly, Judy. *Tut's Mummy Lost... And Found.* Random House, 1988, 48 pp. **N**

Giff, Patricia Reilly. *Shark in School.* Delacorte, 1994, 103 pp.

Hall, Lynn. *Barry, The Bravest Saint Bernard.* Random House, 1973, 48 pp. **N**

Hest, Amy. *When Jessie Came across the Sea.* Candlewick Press, 1997, 36 pp.

Hooks, William H. *The Girl Who Could Fly.* Macmillan, 1995, 51 pp.

Little, Emily. *The Trojan Horse, How Greeks Won the War.* Random House, 1992, 48 pp. **N**

Louie, Ai-Ling. *Yeh-Shen: A Cinderella Story from China.* Philomel, 1982, 28 pp.

•Lundell, Margo (retold by). *Lad, a Dog.* Scholastic, 1997, 44 pp.

MacLachlan, Patricia. *Skylark.* HarperCollins, 1994, 87 pp.

O'Connor, Jim. *Comeback! Four True Stories.* Random House, 1992, 48 pp. **N**

•Penner, Lucille Recht. *Twisters.* Random House, 1996, 46 pp. **N**

Pinkwater, Daniel. *Mush: A Dog from Space.* Atheneum, 1995, 40 pp.

Prelutsky, Jack. *The Beauty of the Beast.* Knopf, 1997, 100 pp. **N**

Rylant, Cynthia. *Best Wishes.* Richard C. Owen, 1992, 32 pp. **N**

•Sachar, Louis. *Wayside School Is Falling Down.* Avon, 1989, 179 pp.

Sachar, Louis. *Wayside School Gets a Little Stranger.* Avon, 1995, 168 pp.

•Shuter, Jane. *The Ancient Egyptians.* Heinemann, 1997, 32 pp. **N**

Sobol, Donald J. *Encyclopedia Brown Saves the Day.* Bantam, 1970, 114 pp.

Steptoe, John. *Creativity.* Houghton Mifflin, 1997, 28 pp.

•Wells, Robert E. *What's Faster than a Speeding Cheetah?* Whitman, 1997, 29 pp. **N**

Willis, Meredith Sue. *Marco's Monster.* HarperCollins, 1996, 118 pp.

Wilson, Nancy Hope. *Old People, Frogs, and Albert.* Farrar, Straus & Giroux, 1997, 58 pp.

### Average Reading Level: Grade 4 (Interest Level: Grade 4)

Aardema, Verna. *Why Mosquitoes Buzz in People's Ears.* Dial, 1975, 21 pp.

•Ada, Alma Flor. *The Gold Coin.* Atheneum, 1991, 32 pp.

Allen, Eugenie. *The Best Ever Kids' Book of Lists.* Avon, 1991, 117 pp. **N**

Arnold, Eric. *Volcanoes! Mountains of Fire.* Random House, 1997, 64 pp. **N**

•Atwater, Richard, & Atwater, Florence. *Mr. Popper's Penguins.* Little, Brown, 1938, 139 pp.

•Banks, Kate. *The Bunnysitters.* Random House, 1991, 63 pp.

Ben-Ezer, Ehud. *Hosni the Dreamer.* Farrar, Straus & Giroux, 1997, 2 8 pp.

Brown, Don. *Alice Ramsey's Grand Adventure.* Houghton Mifflin, 1997, 32 pp. **N**

Brown, Jeff. *Flat Stanley.* HarperCollins, 1964, 44 pp.

Burnie, Richard. *Masterthief: Catch the Crook and Solve the Crime.* Johnathan Cape, 2000, 30 pp.

•Butterworth, Oliver. *The Enormous Egg.* Little, Brown, 1956, 169 pp.

Choi, Yangsook. *The Name Jar.* Knopf, 2001, 30 pp.

Christopher, Matt. *The Dog That Pitched a No-Hitter.* Little, Brown, 1988, 32 pp.

•Christopher, Matt. *Baseball Turnaround.* Little, Brown, 1997, 122 pp.

Clement, Frank. *Counting on Frank.* Gareth Stevens, 1991, 30 pp.

•Clifford, Eth. *Help! I'm a Prisoner in the Library.* Scholastic, 1979, 96 pp.

Cooper, Floyd. *Coming Home: From the Life of Langston Hughes.* Philomel, 1994, 30 pp. **N**

•Coote, Roger. *The Earth*. Smithmark, 1997, 32 pp. **N**

Costain, Meredith, & Collins, Paul. *Welcome to China*. Chelsea House, 2002, 32 pp. **N**

Donati, Annabelle. *Animal Record Holders*. Western, 1993, 32 pp. **N**

Earle, Sylvia. *Hello, Fish*. National Geographic Society, 1999, 30 pp. **N**

Earth Works Group. *50 Simple Things Kids Can Do to Save the Earth*. Andrew & McMeel, 1990, 156 pp. **N**

Engel, Trudie. *We'll Never Forget You, Roberto Clemente*. Scholastic, 1996, 106 pp. **N**

•Flackam, Margery. *Creepy, Crawly Caterpillars*. Little, Brown, 1996, 32 pp. **N**

Flournoy, Valerie. *The Patchwork Quilt*. Dial, 1985, 29 pp.

Fritz, Jean. *The Cabin Faced West*. Puffin, 1958, 124 pp.

Fritz, Jean. *And Then What Happened, Paul Revere?* Coward, McCann & Geoghegan, 1973, 48 pp. **N**

•Gardiner, John Reynolds. *Stone Fox*. HarperCollins, 1980, 71 pp.

Gregory, Christiana. *The Winter of the Red Snow: The Revolutionary War Diary of Abigail Jane Stewart*. Scholastic, 1996, 167 pp.

Gutelle, Andrew. *Baseball's Best*. Random House, 1990, 48 pp. **N**

•Hanly, Sheila. *The Big Book of Animals*. Dorling Kindersley, 1997, 48 pp. **N**

Harrison, David L. *Rivers: Nature's Wonderous Waterways*. Boyds Mill Press, 2002, 30 pp.

Hermes, Patricia. *The Starving Time. Elizabeth's Diary, Book Two*. Scholastic, 2001, 110 pp.

Hopkinson, Deborah. *Birdie's Lighthouse*. Atheneum, 1997, 29 pp.

Hughes, Carol. *Toots and the Upside-Down House*. Random, 1996, 143 pp.

Hurwitz, Johanna. *Aldo Applesauce*. Morrow, 1979, 127 pp.

James, Mary. *Shoebag Returns*. Scholastic, 1996, 144 pp.

•Kerr, Daisy. *Knights & Armor*. Franklin Watts, 1997, 39 pp. **N**

•Kerr, Daisy. *Medieval Town*. Franklin Watts, 1997, 39 pp. **N**

Kirk, Daniel. *Humpty Dumpty*. Putnam, 2000, 32 pp.

Kramer, S. A. *Basketball's Greatest Players*. Random, 1997, 48 pp. **N**

Kramer, S. A. *Wonder Women of Sports*. Grosset & Dunlap, 1997, 48 pp. **N**

•Krumgold, Joseph. *And Now Miguel*. Crowell, 1953, 245 pp.

Lauber, Patricia. *You're Aboard Spaceship Earth*. HarperCollins, 1996, 32 pp. **N**

Lears, Laurie. *Becky the Brave*. Whitman, 2002, 28 pp.

Levy, Elizabeth. *A Mammoth Mix-Up*. HarperCollins, 1995, 87 pp.

Lindgren, Astrid. *Pippi Longstocking*. Puffin, 1950, 160 pp.

Lottridge, Celia Barker. *The Wind Wagon*. Silver Burdett, 1995, 56 pp.

•MacLachlan, Patricia. *Sarah, Plain and Tall*. HarperCollins, 1985, 58 pp.

McGinty, Alice B. *The Jumping Spider*. Rosen, 2002, 24 pp.

•Mead, Alice. *Junebug*. HarperCollins, 1995, 102 pp.

Minahan, John A. *Abigail's Drum*. Pippin, 1995, 64 pp.

•Moss, Cynthia. *Elephant Woman: Cynthia Moss Explores the World of Elephants*. Atheneum, 1997, 42 pp. **N**

Murphy, Jim. *West to a Land of Plenty, The Diary of Teresa Angelino Viscardi*. Scholastic, 1998, 204 pp.

Nathan, Emma. *What Do You Call a Group of Hippos? And Other Animal Groups*. Blackbirch, 2000, 24 pp. **N**

O'Connor, Jim. *Jackie Robinson and the Story of All-Black Baseball*. Random House, 1989, 48 pp. **N**

•Petty, Kate. *I Didn't Know That the Sun Is a Star and Other Amazing Facts about the Universe*. Copper Beech Books, 1997, 32 pp. **N**

Phillips, Louis. *Keep 'em Laughing, Jokes to Amuse and Annoy Your Friends*. Viking, 1996, 60 pp. **N**

Press, Judy. *The Kids' Natural History Book*. Williamson, 2000, 144 pp. **N**

Richards, Julie. *Howling Hurricanes*. Chelsea House, 2002, 32 pp. **N**

•Rylant, Cynthia. *The Van Gogh Cafe*. Harcourt, 1995, 53 pp.

•Sachs, Marilyn. *The Bears' House*. Puffin Books, 1971, 67 pp.

Seabrooke, Brenda. *The Care and Feeding of Dragons*. Dutton, 1998, 120 pp.

Shreve, Susan. *Joshua T. Bates in Trouble Again*. Knopf, 1997, 90 pp.

Simon, Seymour. *Seymour Simon's Book of Trucks*. HarperCollins, 2000, 32 pp. **N**

Singer, Beth Wolfensberger. *Lefty, a Handbook for Left-Handed Kids*. Addison Wesley Longman, 1997, 64 pp. **N**

Soto, Gary. *The Cat's Meow*. Scholastic, 1987, 78 pp.

Spinner, Stephanie, & Weiss, Ellen. *The Weebie Zone*. HarperCollins, 1996, 76 pp.

•Stoops, Eric D., Martin, Jeffrey L., & Stone, Debbie Lynne. *Whales*. Sterling, 1995, 80 pp. **N**

Taylor, Mildred D. *The Gold Cadillac*. Dial, 1987, 43 pp.

Van Laan, Nancy. *In a Circle Long Ago*. Knopf, 1995, 128 pp.

•Walker, Jane. *Fascinating Facts about Volcanoes*. Millbrook, 1994, 32 pp. **N**

Wallner, Alexandra. *Laura Ingalls Wilder*. Holiday, 1997, 32 pp. **N**

Warnock-Kinsey, Natalie, & Kinsey, Helen. *The Bear That Heard Crying*. Cobblehill/Dutton, 1993, 28 pp.

•White, E. B. *Charlotte's Web*. HarperCollins, 1952, 184 pp.

•Wilder, Laura Ingalls. *Little House in the Big Woods*. HarperCollins, 1932, 238 pp.

•Wilkinson, Philip. *Spacebusters: The Race to the Moon*. Dorling Kindersley, 1998, 48 pp. **N**

Woodruff, Elvira. *Awfully Short for the Fourth Grade*. Bantam Doubleday Dell, 1989, 142 pp.

Yangsook, Choi. *The Name Jar*. Knopf, 2001, 30 pp.

**Challenging Reading Level: Grade 5 (Interest Level: Grade 4)**

Avi. *The Barn*. Orchard, 1994, 106 pp.

•Awan, Shaila. *The Burrow Book*. Dorling Kindersley, 1997, 19 pp. **N**

Bateman, Teresa. *The Ring of Truth*. Holiday House, 1997, 28 pp.

Baum, L. Frank. *The Wizard of Oz*. Puffin, 1900, 1988, 188 pp.

Bernhard, Emery, & Bernhard, Durga. *Prairie Dogs*. Harcourt, 1997, 29 pp. **N**

Bishop, Nic. *Animal Flight*. Houghton Mifflin, 1997, 32 pp. **N**

•Dahl, Roald. *James and the Giant Peach*. Puffin, 1961, 126 pp.

•Facklam, Margery. *The Big Bug Book*. Little, Brown, 1994, 32 pp. **N**

Mahy, Margaret. *The Five Sisters*. Viking, 1997, 80 pp.

McCully, Emily Arnold. *The Bobbin Girl*. Dial, 1996, 30 pp.

•McKay, Hilary. *Dog Friday*. Simon & Schuster, 1994, 133 pp.

•Taylor, Mildred. *Roll of Thunder. Hear My Cry*. Puffin, 1976, 275 pp.

# Informal Assessment of Key Skills and Strategies

Name _____     Total number correct _____

Date _____     Estimated level _____

| Word Pattern Survey | | | |
|---|---|---|---|
| 1. go _____ | 21. game _____ | 41. spark _____ | 61. through _____ |
| 2. me _____ | 22. tree _____ | 42. stair _____ | 62. straight _____ |
| 3. see _____ | 23. wide _____ | 43. shore _____ | 63. enough _____ |
| 4. I _____ | 24. road _____ | 44. curl _____ | 64. clue _____ |
| 5. no _____ | 25. use _____ | 45. steer _____ | 65. edge _____ |
| 6. hat _____ | 26. goat _____ | 46. park _____ | 66. strong _____ |
| 7. wet _____ | 27. save _____ | 47. purse _____ | 67. suit _____ |
| 8. sit _____ | 28. wheel _____ | 48. clear _____ | 68. thought _____ |
| 9. hop _____ | 29. mine _____ | 49. storm _____ | 69. flood _____ |
| 10. fun _____ | 30. cute _____ | 50. charge _____ | 70. breathe _____ |
| 11. ran _____ | 31. chain _____ | 51. chalk _____ | 71. calm _____ |
| 12. men _____ | 32. speak _____ | 52. brook _____ | 72. clothes _____ |
| 13. win _____ | 33. slide _____ | 53. crown _____ | 73. knock _____ |
| 14. got _____ | 34. toast _____ | 54. join _____ | 74. soft _____ |
| 15. bug _____ | 35. blind _____ | 55. should _____ | 75. fault _____ |
| 16. drop _____ | 36. plane _____ | 56. stew _____ | 76. tough _____ |
| 17. jump _____ | 37. steel _____ | 57. bounce _____ | 77. height _____ |
| 18. sand _____ | 38. drive _____ | 58. crawl _____ | 78. laugh _____ |
| 19. ship _____ | 39. broke _____ | 59. broom _____ | 79. earth _____ |
| 20. lunch _____ | 40. price _____ | 60. pound _____ | 80. brought _____ |

Directions: Give one copy of the survey to the student and keep one for marking. Mark each response + or –. Start with the first item for all pupils. Say to the student, "I am going to ask you to read a list of words to me. Some of the words may be hard for you, but read as many as you can." Stop when the student gets five in a row wrong. The survey tests four levels. Each level has twenty items as follows: 1–20: easy long-vowel and short-vowel patterns; 21–40: long-vowel patterns; 41–60: r-vowel and other vowel patterns /aw/, /ŌŌ/, /ŎŎ/, /ow/, /oy/; 61–80, irregular and low-frequency patterns. Students are proficient at a level if they get 80 percent or more correct at that level. Students should be instructed at a level if they get more than 4 out of 20 wrong at that level.

From T. Gunning (1996). *Teacher's Guide for Word Building, Book A.* New York: Phoenix Learning Resources. Reprinted by permission of Galvin Publications.

Name _____     Score _____

Date _____

## Syllable Survey

| | | | | | | |
|---|---|---|---|---|---|---|
| 1. sunup | ____ | 18. distant | ____ | 35. creature | ____ |
| 2. inside | ____ | 19. prevent | ____ | 36. audience | ____ |
| 3. ago | ____ | 20. museum | ____ | 37. pleasant | ____ |
| 4. open | ____ | 21. several | ____ | 38. spaghetti | ____ |
| 5. under | ____ | 22. building | ____ | 39. information | ____ |
| 6. farmer | ____ | 23. probably | ____ | 40. voyage | ____ |
| 7. finish | ____ | 24. modern | ____ | 41. confusion | ____ |
| 8. mistake | ____ | 25. monument | ____ | 42. neighborhood | ____ |
| 9. thunder | ____ | 26. opposite | ____ | 43. studio | ____ |
| 10. morning | ____ | 27. message | ____ | 44. allowance | ____ |
| 11. reward | ____ | 28. success | ____ | 45. microphone | ____ |
| 12. famous | ____ | 29. struggle | ____ | 46. auditorium | ____ |
| 13. mumble | ____ | 30. repeat | ____ | 47. available | ____ |
| 14. spider | ____ | 31. recognize | ____ | 48. disappointment | ____ |
| 15. chicken | ____ | 32. survive | ____ | 49. bulletin | ____ |
| 16. rocket | ____ | 33. appreciate | ____ | 50. moisture | ____ |
| 17. magnet | ____ | 34. antelope | ____ | | |

*Directions:* Give one copy of the survey to the student and keep one for marking. Mark each response + or −. Start with the first item for all pupils. Say to the student, "I am going to ask you to read a list of words. Some of the words may be hard for you, but read as many as you can." Stop when the student gets five in a row wrong. A score of 45 or above indicates that the student is able to decode multisyllabic words. A score between 40 and 44 indicates some weakness in decoding multisyllabic words. A score below 40 indicates a definite need for instruction and practice in decoding multisyllabic words. A score of 5 or below suggests that the student may be deficient in basic decoding skills. Give the Word Pattern Survey.

# EMERGENT LITERACY ASSESSMENT

The paper-and-pencil assessment measures are designed so that they can be administered to groups of youngsters. However, groups should be kept small, and, if time allows, the assessment measures should be administered individually.

## Letter Recognition

To administer the Letters survey, distribute a copy of the survey and a strip of cardboard about the size of a ruler that can be used as a marker so that students have no difficulty focusing on a row of possible responses. Explain the purpose of the assessment. Say to students, "I want to see how many letters you know. Look at your papers. You will see rows of letters. I am going to say the name of a letter, and then I'm going to ask you to make a ring around that letter. Let's do the first one for practice. Find the ball." (The pictured items are used instead of numerals to help students find the right rows.) "Now put your markers under the ball." (Check to make sure all are on the sample row.) "Now find the letter *X* and make a ring around it. Here is what the letter *X* looks like." (Write it on the chalkboard.) "Find it and make a ring around it." (Check to make sure that all have drawn a ring around the *X*.)

"Now move your marker down to the row that has a cat. Look at the letters in that row, and draw a ring around the letter *S.*" Using this same procedure, have students draw a ring around the following:

| | |
|---|---|
| 1. S | 11. s |
| 2. A | 12. a |
| 3. B | 13. b |
| 4. R | 14. r |
| 5. M | 15. m |
| 6. O | 16. o |
| 7. T | 17. t |
| 8. E | 18. e |
| 9. G | 19. g |
| 10. K | 20. k |

To administer the test individually, point to the first letter in Row 1 and ask the student to say the letter's name. Then go to the next letter. Continue to do this until you reach the letter *Q*. At that point, you will have checked all twenty-six uppercase letters. Follow this same procedure for assessing knowledge of lowercase letters. Start with the letter *n* in Row 11 and continue to *q*. However, discontinue testing if the student misses five letters in a row or if it is obvious that he doesn't know the letters.

When given as an individual measure, the Letters survey requires that letters be identified, a more difficult task than recognizing the letters, which is what is involved in a group administration. If a student has difficulty identifying letters, switch to the administration that you would use with a group, asking him to draw a ring around the letter that you name, and see if he knows the letters on a recognition level. A score of 8 out of 10 is adequate.

## Survey of Rhyming Sounds

To administer the measure, distribute copies of the Rhyming survey. Explain to students the purpose of the measure and then give them directions. Say, "I want to see if you can tell when words rhyme. Words rhyme if they have the same ending sound. For example, *Bill* and *Jill* rhyme because they both have an 'il' sound. *Book* and *took* rhyme because they both have an 'ook' sound. Find the top row of pictures on your paper. We want to see which one rhymes with the first one. Put your marker under the row that begins with a ring. *Ring* is the name of the first picture. Now point to each of the other three pictures in the row as I say their names: *ball, king, shoe*. Which one, *ball, king*, or *shoe*, rhymes with *ring*? The answer is *king*. That is why the picture of the king has a ring drawn around it. *Ring* and *king* rhyme. They both have an 'ing' sound. Now move your marker down to the next row, the row that begins with a house. Point to the house. *House* is the name of the first picture. Now let's see which of the three other pictures in that row rhymes with *house*. Point to the pictures as I say their names: *bed, dog, mouse*. Which one rhymes with *house*? *Bed, dog,* or *mouse*? Draw a ring around the picture whose name rhymes with *house*. Did you draw a ring around the mouse? *Mouse* is the right answer. *Mouse* and *house* rhyme. They both end with an 'ouse' sound."

Administer the ten test items. Identify the pictures in each row and remind students to draw a ring around the picture in each row whose name rhymes with the name of the first picture, but provide no other assistance. Individual administration of the Rhyming survey is identical to group administration. A score of 8 out of 10 indicates a good grasp of rhyme.

## Beginning Sounds Survey

To administer this assessment, distribute copies of the Beginning Sounds survey and explain its purpose to students. Say, "I want to see if you can tell whether two words begin alike. Words begin alike if they begin with the same sound. The words *tie* and *ten* begin alike because they begin with the same sound: /t/. The words *pen* and *pet* begin alike because they begin with the same sound: /p/. Look at the row of pictures at the top of your paper. Find the top row of pictures. We want to see which one begins with the same sound as the first one. Put your marker under the row that begins with a nail. *Nail* is the name of the first picture. Now point to each of the other three pictures in the row as I say their names: *bike, car, net*. Which one, *bike, car*, or *net*, begins with the same sound as *nail*? Which begins with an /n/ sound? The answer is *net*. That is why the net has a ring drawn around it. *Nail* and *net* begin with the same sound. They both begin with an /n/ sound. Now move your marker down to the next row, the row that begins with a dog. Point to the dog. *Dog* is the name of the first picture. Now let's see which of the three other pictures in that row begins with the same sound as *dog*. Point to the pictures as I say their names: *wagon, deer, pin*. Which one begins with the same sound as *dog*? Which begins with a /d/ sound? *Wagon, deer*, or *pin*? Draw a ring around the picture whose name begins with the same sound as *dog*. Did you draw a ring around the deer? Deer is the right answer. *Deer* and *dog* begin with the same sound. They both begin with a /d/ sound."

Administer the ten test items. Identify the pictures in each row and remind students to draw a ring around the picture in each row whose name begins with the same sound as the first picture in that row. (Individual administration of the Beginning Sounds survey is the same as group administration.) A score of 8 out of 10 indicates a good grasp of beginning sounds.

## Beginning Consonant Correspondences Survey

To administer the survey of Beginning Consonant Correspondences, distribute copies of the survey and explain its purpose. Say, "I want to see if you can tell which letters are used to spell the beginning sounds of words. For instance, the letter *f* is used to spell the sound /f/ that you hear at the beginning of *five*. The letter *h* is used to spell /h/, the sound that you hear at the beginning of *hand*. Sometimes, two letters are used to spell a sound. The letters *th* are used to spell the sound that you hear at the beginning of *thorn*.

"Look at the zebra and the row of letters at the top of your paper. Put your marker under that row. I'll say the name of the picture again, and you listen to its beginning sound: *zebra*. Then choose from the four letters in the row the one that spells the beginning sound of *zebra*. Listen carefully. Which of the four letters, *r, b, z*, or *f*, spells the first sound in *zebra*? Which letter spells /z/? The answer is *z*. That's why a ring has been drawn around it. The letter *z* spells the /z/ sound you hear at the beginning of *zebra*."

Help students complete the second sample item. Then administer the twenty test items. Identify the pictures for each test item and have students draw a ring around the letter that spells the first sound of the picture's name.

To give this assessment individually, cover up the illustrations and start with the letter *y* in row 1. Have the student say the sound that each letter stands for or supply a word that begins with that letter. The first sixteen items encompass all the beginning consonant correspondences assessed in the group administration. (For *c*, accept a /k/ or /s/ sound or word. For *g*, accept a /g/ or /j/ sound or word.) To assess knowledge of initial digraph correspondences, have students say the sound that each digraph in row 17 represents. Or students may supply a word that begins with the digraph being assessed. A score of 16 out of 20 shows that students have begun to master initial consonant correspondences.

Name _____    Uppercase score _____ /10

Date _____    Lowercase score _____ /10

## Letters

**Circle the letter that your teacher says.**

| A. | | O | X | R | U |
|---|---|---|---|---|---|
| 1. | | N | S | D | C |
| 2. | | I | T | A | P |
| 3. | | B | J | V | Z |
| 4. | | W | G | K | R |
| 5. | | X | M | H | U |
| 6. | | E | O | F | L |
| 7. | | Y | Q | B | T |
| 8. | | S | R | E | C |
| 9. | | I | G | X | Z |
| 10. | | P | W | H | K |
| 11. | | n | s | d | c |
| 12. | | i | t | a | p |
| 13. | | b | j | v | z |
| 14. | | w | g | k | r |
| 15. | | x | m | h | u |
| 16. | | e | o | f | l |
| 17. | | y | q | b | t |
| 18. | | s | e | r | c |
| 19. | | i | g | x | z |
| 20. | | p | w | h | k |

From T. Gunning (1994). *Teacher's Guide for Word Building: Beginnings.* New York: Phoenix Learning Resources. Reprinted by permission of Galvin Publications.

Name _____     Score _____ /10

Date _____

## Rhyming

In each row, say the name of the first picture. Then find the picture whose name rhymes with the name of the first picture. Draw a ring around the picture that has the rhyming name.

A.

B.

1.

2.

3.

4.

5.

6.

7.

8.

9.

10.

From T. Gunning (1994). *Teacher's Guide for Word Building: Beginnings*. New York: Phoenix Learning Resources. Reprinted by permission of Galvin Publications.

Name _____       Score _____ /10

Date _____

## Beginning Sounds

In each row, say the name of the first picture. Then find the picture whose name begins with the same sound. Draw a ring around the picture whose name begins with the same sound as the first one.

A.

B.

1.

2.

3.

4.

5.

6.

7.

8.

9.

10.

From T. Gunning (1994). *Teacher's Guide for Word Building: Beginnings.* New York: Phoenix Learning Resources. Reprinted by permission of Galvin Publications.

Name _____    Score _____ /20

Date _____    Items missed _____

## Beginning Consonant Correspondences

Circle the letter or letters that spell the first sound of the name of the picture.

| | | | | | |
|---|---|---|---|---|---|
| A. | | r | b | (z) | f |
| B. | | l | c | g | y |
| 1. | | y | b | m | k |
| 2. | | j | z | g | s |
| 3. | | c | w | n | b |
| 4. | | d | r | v | t |
| 5. | | p | f | h | z |
| 6. | | t | h | k | x |
| 7. | | l | j | s | w |
| 8. | | n | f | r | g |

*(continued)*

| 9. | | t | f | d | s |
| 10. | | k | l | z | m |
| 11. | | p | w | r | d |
| 12. | | y | c | f | g |
| 13. | | d | l | c | r |
| 14. | | w | r | c | n |
| 15. | | b | t | j | f |
| 16. | | p | y | h | l |
| 17. | | wh | th | ch | sh |
| 18. | | th | ch | sh | wh |
| 19. | | th | sh | ch | wh |
| 20. | | ch | th | wh | sh |

From T. Gunning (1994). *Teacher's Guide for Word Building: Beginnings.* New York: Phoenix Learning Resources. Reprinted by permission of Galvin Publications.

# References

## Professional

Achilles, C. M., Finn, J. D., & Bain, H. P. (1997–1998). Using class size to reduce the equity gap. *Educational Leadership, 54*(8), 40–43.

Adams, M. J. (1990). *Beginning to read: Thinking and learning about print: A Summary*, Cambridge, MA: MIT Press.

Adams, M. J. (1994). Modeling the connections between word recognition and reading. In R. B. Ruddell, M. R. Ruddell, & H. Singer (Eds.), *Theoretical models and processes of reading* (4th ed.) (pp. 838–863). Newark, DE: International Reading Association.

Adams, M. J. (2001). Alphabetic anxiety and explicit, systematic phonics instruction: A cognitive science perspective. In S. B. Neuman & D. K. Dickinson (Eds.), *Handbook of early literacy research* (pp. 66–80). New York: Guilford.

Adams, M. J., & Higgins, A. W. F. (1985). The growth of children's sight vocabulary: A quick test with educational and theoretical implications. *Reading Research Quarterly, 20,* 262–281.

Adoption Guidelines Project. (1990). Workbooks. In *Adoption Guidelines Project, a guide to selecting basal reading programs.* Urbana: University of Illinois, Center for the Study of Reading.

Afflerbach, P. (1990). The influence of prior knowledge on expert readers' main idea construction strategies. *Reading Research Quarterly, 25,* 31–46.

Afflerbach, P., & VanSledright, B. (2001). Hath! Doth! What? Middle graders reading innovative history text. *Journal of Adolescent & Adult Literacy, 44,* 696–707.

Afflerbach, P. P., & Johnston, P. H. (1986). What do expert readers do when the main idea is not explicit? In J. F. Baumann (Ed.), *Teaching main idea comprehension* (pp. 49–72). Newark, DE: International Reading Association.

Ahlmann, M. E. (1992). Children as evaluators. In K. S. Goodman, L. B. Bird, & Y. M. Goodman (Eds.), *The whole language catalog: Supplement on authentic assessment* (p. 95). Santa Rosa, CA: American School Publishers.

Allen, V. (1991). Teaching bilingual and ESL children. In J. Flood, J. M. Jensen, D. Lapp, & J. R. Squire (Eds.), *Handbook of research on teaching the English language arts* (pp. 356–364). New York: Macmillan.

Allen, V. G. (1994). Selecting materials for the reading instruction of ESL children. In K. Spangenberg-Urbschat, & R. Pritchard (Eds.), *Kids come in all languages: Reading instruction for all ESL students* (pp. 108–131). Newark, DE: International Reading Association.

Allen, V. G., Freeman, E. B., Lehman, B. A., Scharer, P. L. (1995). Amos and Boris: A window on teachers' thinking about the use of literature in their classrooms. *The Reading Teacher, 48,* 384–390.

Almasi, J. F., O'Flahavan, J. F., & Arya, P. (2001). A comparative analysis of student and teacher development in more and less proficient discussions of literature. *Reading Research Quarterly, 36,* 96–120.

Altwerger, B., Edelsky, C., & Flores, B. M. (1987). Whole language: What's new? *The Reading Teacher, 41,* 144–154.

Alvermann, D. E., & Phelps, S. F. (1994). *Content area reading and literacy: Succeeding in today's diverse classrooms.* Boston: Allyn & Bacon.

Alvermann, D. E.,Young, J.P., Weaver, D., Hinchman, K. A., Moore, D. W., Phelps, S. F., Thrash, & E. C., Zaleewski, P. (1996). Middle and high school students' perceptions of how they experience text-based discussions: A multicase study. *Reading Research Quarterly, 31,* 244-267.

Anderson, G., Higgins, D., & Wurster, S. R. (1985). Differences in the free-reading books selected by high, average, and low achievers. *The Reading Teacher, 39,* 326–330.

Anderson, L. (1981). *Student responses to seatwork: Implications for the study of students' cognitive processing* (Research Series No. 102). East Lansing: Michigan State University, The Institute for Research on Teaching.

Anderson, R. C. (1984). Role of the reader's schema in comprehension, learning, and memory. In R. C. Anderson, J. Osborn, & R. J. Tierney (Eds.), *Learning to read in American schools: Basal readers and content texts* (pp. 469–482). Hillsdale, NJ: Lawrence Erlbaum.

Anderson, R. C. (1990, May). *Microanalysis of classroom reading instruction.* Paper presented at the annual conference on reading research, Atlanta.

Anderson, R. C., Hiebert, E. H., Scott, J. A., & Wilkinson, I. A. G. (1985). *Becoming a nation of readers: The report of the commission on reading.* Washington, DC: National Institute of Education.

Anderson, R. C., Wilson, P. T., & Fielding, L. G. (1988). Growth in reading and how children spend their time outside of school. *Reading Research Quarterly, 23,* 285–303.

Andre, M. E. D. A., & Anderson, T. H. (1978–1979). The development and evaluation of a self-questioning study technique. *Reading Research Quarterly, 14,* 605–623.

Anthony, H. M., Pearson, P. D., & Raphael, T. E. (1989). *Reading comprehension research: A selected review* (Technical Report No. 448). Champaign: University of Illinois, Center for the Study of Reading.

Appel, R. & Vermeer, A. (1996). Speeding up the acquisition of Dutch vocabulary by migrant children. Uitbreiding van de Nederlandse woordenschat van allochtone leerlingen in het basisonderwijs, *Pedagogische Studieen 73,* 82–92.

Applebee, A. N. (1978). *The child's concept of story: Ages two to seventeen.* Chicago: University of Chicago Press.

Applebee, A. N., Langer, J. A., & Mullis, I. V. S. (1988). Who reads best? *Factors related to reading achievement in grades 3, 7, and 11.* Princeton, NJ: Educational Testing Service.

Arciero, J. (1998, October). *Strategies for shared text reading responses.* Paper presented at Connecticut Reading Association meeting, Waterbury.

Armbruster, B. B., & Anderson, T. H. (1981). *Content area textbooks* (Technical Report No. 23). Champaign: University of Illinois, Center for the Study of Reading.

Arnold, C. (2001). *Did you hear that?* Watertown, MA: Charlesbridge.

Aronson, E. (1978). *The jigsaw classroom.* Beverly Hills: Sage.

Asch, S., & Nerlove, H. (1967). The development of double function terms in children: An exploratory investigation. In

J. P. Cecco (Ed.), *The psychology of thought, language, and instruction* (pp. 283–291). New York: Holt, Rinehart & Winston.

Atwell, N. (1987). *In the middle*. Portsmouth, NH: Boynton/Cook.

Atwell, N. (1990). *Coming to know: Writing to learn in the intermediate grades*. Portsmouth, NH: Heinemann.

Au, K. H. (1994). Portfolio assessment: Experiences at the Kamehameha elementary education program. In S. W. Valencia, E. H. Hiebert, & P. P. Afflerbach (Eds.), *Authentic reading assessment: Practices and possibilities* (pp. 103–126). Newark, DE: International Reading Association.

Au, K. H., & Mason, J. M. (1989). Elementary reading programs. In S. B. Wepner, J. T. Feeley, & D. S. Strickland (Eds.), *The administration and supervision of reading programs* (pp. 60–75). New York: Teachers College Press.

Australian Ministry of Education. (1990). *Literacy profiles handbook*. Victoria, Australia: Author.

Ausubel, D. P. (1959). Viewpoints from related disciplines: Human growth and development. *Teachers College Record, 60,* 245–254.

Ausubel, D. P. (1960). The use of advance organizers in the learning and retention of meaningful verbal material. *Journal of Educational Psychology, 51,* 267–272.

Bader, L. A. (2002). *Reading and language inventory* (4th ed.). Upper Saddle River, NJ: Prentice Hall.

Bagge-Rynerson, B. (1994). Learning good lessons: Young readers respond to books. In T. Newkirk (Ed.), *Workshop 5: The writing process revisited* (pp. 90–100). Portsmouth, NH: Heinemann.

Baker, L., & Brown, A. L. (1984). Metacognitive skills and reading. In P. D. Pearson, R. Barr, M. L. Kamil, & P. Mosenthal (Eds.), *Handbook of reading research* (pp. 353–394). New York: Longman.

Bangert-Downs, R. L. (1993). The word processor as an instructional tool: A meta-analysis of word processing in writing instruction. *Review of Educational Research, 63,* 69–93.

Banks, J. A., & Banks, C. A. M. (1997). *Multicultual education* (2nd ed.). Boston: Allyn & Bacon.

Barr, R. (1974). Instructional pace differences and their effect on reading acquisition. *Reading Research Quarterly, 9,* 526–554.

Barr, R., & Dreeben, R. (1991). Grouping students for reading instruction. In R. Barr, M. L. Kamil, P. Mosenthal, & P. D. Pearson (Eds.), *Handbook of reading research* (Vol. II, pp. 885–910). New York: Longman.

Bartlett, F. C. (1932). *Remembering*. Cambridge: Cambridge University Press.

Barton, P. E. (2001). *Raising achievement and reducing gaps: Reporting progress toward goals for academic achievement*. Available online at http://www.negp.gov/issues/publication/negpdocs/negprep/rpt_barton/barton_paper.pdf

Bauman, G. A. (1990, March). *Writing tool selection and young children's writing*. Paper presented at the spring conference of the National Conference of Teachers of English, Colorado Springs, CO.

Baumann, J. F. (1986). The direct instruction of main idea comprehension ability. In J. F. Baumann (Ed.), *Teaching main idea comprehension* (pp. 133–178). Newark, DE: International Reading Association.

Baumann, J. F., & Duffy, A. M. (1997). *Engaged reading for pleasure and learning: A report from the National Reading Research Center*.

Baumann, J. F., Hoffman, J. V., Duffy-Hester, A. M., Ro, J. M.

(2001). "The First R" yesterday and today: U.S. elementary reading instruction practices reported by teachers and administrators. *Reading Research Quarterly, 35,* 338–377.

Baumann, J. F., & Ivey, G. (1997). Delicate balances: Striving for curricular and instructional equilibrium in a second-grade, literature/strategy-based classroom. *Reading Research Quarterly, 32,* 244–275.

Baumann, J. F., & Serra, J. K. (1984). The frequency and placement of main ideas in children's social studies textbooks: A modified replication of Braddock's research on topic sentences. *Journal of Reading Behavior, 16,* 27–40.

Bear, D. (1995). *Word study: A developmental perspective based on spelling stages*. Paper presented at the annual meeting of the International Reading Association, Anaheim, CA.

Bear, D., & Barone, D. (1989). Using children's spellings to group for word study and directed reading in the primary classroom. *Reading Psychology, 10,* 275–292.

Bear, D. R., Invernizzi, M., Johnston, F., & Templeton, S. (1996). *Words their way: Word study for phonics, vocabulary, and spelling instruction*. Upper Saddle River, NJ: Merrill.

Bear, D. R., & Templeton, S. (1998). Explorations in developmental spelling: Foundations for learning and teaching phonics, spelling, and vocabulary. *The Reading Teacher, 52,* 222–242.

Beaver (1997). *Developmental reading assessment*. Parsippany, NJ: Celebration Press.

Beck, I. L., & McKeown, M. G. (1983). Learning words well—a program to enhance vocabulary and comprehension. *The Reading Teacher, 36,* 622–625.

Beck, I. L., & McKeown, M. G. (2001). Text talk: Capturing the benefits of read-aloud experiences for young children. *The Reading Teacher, 55,* 10–20.

Beck, I. L., McKeown, M. G., & Kucan, L. (2002). *Bringing words to life: Robust vocabulary instruction*. New York: Guilford Press.

Beck, I. L., McKeown, M. G., & Omanson, R. C. (1987). The effects and uses of diverse vocabulary instructional techniques. In M. G. McKeown & M. E. Curtis (Eds.), *The nature of vocabulary acquisition* (pp. 147–163). Hillsdale, NJ: Lawrence Erlbaum.

Beck, I. L., Omanson, R. C., & McKeown, M. G. (1982). An instructional redesign of reading lessons: Effects on comprehension. *Reading Research Quarterly, 17,* 462–481.

Benson, V., & Cummins, C. (2000). *The power of retelling: Developmental steps for building comprehension*. Bothell, WA: Wright Group/McGraw-Hill.

Bereiter, C., & Scardamalia, M. (1982). From conversation to composition: The role of instruction in a developmental process. In R. Glass (Ed.), *Advances in instructional psychology* (Vol. 2, pp. 1–64). Hillsdale, NJ: Lawrence Erlbaum.

Berk, L. E. (1997). *Child development* (4th ed.). Boston, MA: Allyn & Bacon.

Berkowitz, S. J. (1986). Effects of instruction in text organization on sixth-grade students' memory for expository text. *Reading Research Quarterly, 21,* 161–178.

Berliner, D. C. (1981). Academic learning time and reading achievement. In J. T. Guthrie (Ed.), *Comprehension and teaching: Research reviews* (pp. 203–226). Newark, DE: International Reading Association.

Berliner, D. C. (1985). Effective classroom teaching: The necessary but not sufficient condition for developing exemplary schools. In G. R. Austin & H. Gartier (Eds.), *Research on exemplary schools* (pp. 211–234). New York: Academic Press.

Biemiller, A. (1994). Some observations on acquiring and using reading skill in elementary schools. In C. K. Kinzer, & D. J. Leu (Eds.), Multidimensional aspects of literacy research, theory, and practice. *Forty-third Yearbook of the National Reading Conference* (pp. 209–216). Chicago, IL: National Reading Conference.

Bigham, V. S., & Bigham, G. (1998). *The Prentice Hall directory of online educational resources.* Paramus, NJ: Prentice Hall.

Birnbaum, R. K. (1999). *NewPhonics.* Pittsford, NY: NewPhonics Literacy System.

Bissex, G. L. (1980). *GNYS AT WRK.* Cambridge, MA: Harvard University Press.

Bjorklund, B., Handler, N., Mitten, J., & Stockwell, G. (1998, October). *Literature circles: A tool for developing students as critical readers. writers, and thinkers.* Paper presented at the forty-seventh annual conference of the Connecticut Reading Association, Waterbury.

Blachman, B. A., Tangel, D. M., Ball, E., Black, R., & McGraw, C. K. (1994). Kindergarten teachers develop phonological awareness and word recognition skills: A two-year intervention with low-income, inner-city children. *Reading and Writing: An Interdisciplinary Journal, 11,* 239–273.

Blachowicz, C. L. Z. (1977). Cloze activities for primary readers. *The Reading Teacher, 31,* 300–302.

Blachowicz, C. L. Z., & Fisher, P. (2000). Vocabulary instruction. In M. L. Kamil, P. B. Mosenthal, P. D. Pearson, & R. Barr (Eds.), *Handbook of Reading Research* (Vol. III, pp. 503–523). Mahwah, NJ: Erlbaum.

Bloom, B. (Ed.). (1957). *Taxonomy of educational objectives.* New York: McKay.

Blum, I. H., Koskinen, P. S., Tennant, S., Parker, E. M., Straub, M., & Curry, C. (1995). Using audiotaped books to extend classroom literacy instruction into the homes of second-language learners. *Journal of Reading Behavior, 27,* 535–564.

Board of Directors of International Reading Association (1999). High-stakes assessments in reading. *The Reading Teacher, 53,* 257–264.

Boehm, A. E. (1971). *Boehm test of basic concepts manual.* New York: Psychological Corporation.

Bond, G. L., & Dykstra, R. (1967). The cooperative research program in first-grade reading instruction. *Reading Research Quarterly, 2,* 1–142.

Bond, G. L., & Dykstra, R. (1967). The cooperative research program in first-grade reading instruction. *Reading Research Quarterly, 2,* 1–142.

Boothroyd, K. (2001, December). *Being literate in urban third-grade classrooms.* Paper presented at the annual meeting of the National Reading Conference, San Antonio, TX.

Borders, S., & Naylor, A. P. (1993). *Children talking about books.* Phoenix, AZ: Oryx.

Boyle, C. (1996). *Efficacy of peer evaluation and effects of peer evaluation on persuasive writing.* Unpublished master's thesis, San Diego State University, San Diego, CA.

Bransford, J. D., Stein, B. S., Shelton, T. S., & Owings, R. A. (1981). Cognition and adaptation: The importance of learning to learn. In J. Harvey (Ed.), *Cognition, social behavior, and the environment.* Hillsdale, NJ: Lawrence Erlbaum.

Brewster, P. G. (Ed.). (1952). *Children's games and rhymes.* Durham, NC: Duke University Press.

Bridge, C. A., Winograd, P. N., & Haley, D. (1983). Using predictable materials vs. preprimers to teach beginning sight words. *The Reading Teacher, 36,* 884–891.

Bristow, P. S., Pikulski, J. J., & Pelosi, P. L. (1983). A comparison of five estimates of reading instructional level. *The Reading Teacher, 37,* 273–279.

Bromley, K. D (1998). *Language arts: Exploring connections* (3rd ed.). Boston: Allyn & Bacon.

Brophy, J. E., & Good, T. L. (1970). Teachers' communication of differential expectations for children's classroom performance: Some behavioral data. *Journal of Educational Psychology, 61,* 365–375.

Brophy, J. E., & Good, T. L. (1986). Teacher behavior and student achievement. In M. E. Wittrock (Ed.), *Handbook of research on teaching* (pp. 328–375). New York: Macmillan.

Brown, A. L. (1985). *Reciprocal teaching of comprehension strategies: A natural history of one program for enhancing learning* (Technical Report No. 334). Champaign: University of Illinois, Center for the Study of Reading.

Brown, A. L., & Day, J. D. (1983). Macrorules for summarizing text: The development of expertise. *Journal of Verbal Learning and Verbal Behavior, 22*(1), 1–14.

Brown, C. S., & Lytle, S. L. (1988). Merging assessment and instruction: Protocols in the classroom. In S. M. Glazer, L. W. Searfoss, & L. M. Gentile (Eds.), *Reexamining reading diagnosis: New trends and procedures* (pp. 94–102). Newark, DE: International Reading Association.

Brown, H., & Cambourne, B. (1987). *Read and retell.* Portsmouth, NH: Heinemann.

Brown, K. J. (2000). What kind of text—For whom and when? Textual scaffolding for beginning readers. *The Reading Teacher, 53,* 292–307.

Bruce, B. (1980). Plans and social actions. In R. J. Spiro, B. C. Bruce, & W. F. Brewer (Eds.), *Theoretical issues in reading comprehension* (pp, 367-384). Hillsdale, NJ: Erlbaum.

Bruck, M. (1992). Persistence of dyslexics' phonological awareness deficits. *Developmental Psychology, 28,* 874–886.

Bruner, J. (1975). The ontogenesis of speech acts. *Journal of Child Languages, 2,* 1–40.

Bruner, J. (1986). *Actual minds, possible worlds.* Cambridge, MA: Harvard University Press.

Brynildssen, S. (2000). *Vocabulary's influence on successful writing.* ERIC Clearinghouse on Reading English and Communication. Bloomington, IN: ERIC Digest D157.

Bunce, B. H. (1995).*Building a language-focused curriculum for the preschool classroom, Volume II: A planning guide.* Baltimore: Brookes.

Burns, J. M., & Richgels, D. S. (1989). An investigation of task requirements associated with the invented spelling of 4-year-olds with above average intelligence. *Journal of Reading Behavior, 21,* 1–14.

Bus, A. G., & van Ijzendoorn, M. H. (1999). Phonological awareness and early reading: A meta-analysis of experiential training studies. *Journal of Educational Psychology, 91,* 403–414.

Bush, C., & Huebner, M. (1979). *Strategies for reading in the elementary school* (2nd ed.). New York: Macmillan.

Button, K., Johnson, M. J., & Furgeson, P. (1996). Interactive writing in a primary classroom. *The Reading Teacher, 49,* 446–454.

Byrne, B. (1992). Studies in the acquisition procedure for reading: Rationale, hypotheses, and data. In P. B. Gough, L. C. Ehri, & R. Treiman (Eds.), *Reading acquisition* (pp. 1–35). Hillsdale, NJ: Lawrence Erlbaum Associates.

Calfee, R., & Hiebert, E. (1991). Classroom assessment of reading. In R. Barr, M. L. Kamil, P. Mosenthal, & P. D. Pearson (Eds.), *Handbook of reading research* (Vol. II, pp. 281–309). New York: Longman.

Calkins, L. (2001). *The art of teaching reading.* Portsmouth, NH: Heinemann.

Calkins, L. M. (1986). *The art of teaching writing.* Portsmouth, NH: Heinemann.

Calkins, L. M. (1994). *The art of teaching writing* (new ed.). Portsmouth, NH: Heinemann.

Calkins, L. M., & Harwayne, S. (1991). *Living between the lines.* Portsmouth, NH: Heinemann.

Campbell, F. A., & Ramey, C. T. (1995). African American students at middle adolescence: Positive effects of early intervention. *American Educational Research Journal, 32,* 743-772.

Campbell, R. (Ed.). (1998). Looking at literacy learning in preschool settings. In R. Campbell (Ed.), *Facilitating preschool literacy* (pp. 70–83). Newark, DE: International Reading Association.

Campbell, R. (2001). *Read-alouds with young children.* Newark, DE: International Reading Association.

Carbo, M. (1997). *What every principal should know about teaching reading: How to raise test scores and nurture a love of reading.* Syosset, NY: National Reading Styles Institute.

Carbo, M., Dunn, R., & Dunn, K. (1986, 1991). *Teaching students to read through their individual learning styles.* Boston: Allyn & Bacon.

Carlson, N. R., & Buskist, W. (1997). *Psychology: The science of behavior* (5th ed.). Boston: Allyn & Bacon.

Carnine, D., Kameenui, E. J., & Coyle, G. (1984). Utilization of contextual information in determining the meaning of unfamiliar words. *Reading Research Quarterly, 19,* 188–204.

Carnine, D., Silbert, J., & Kameenui, E. J. (1990). *Direct instruction in reading.* Columbus, OH: Merrill.

Carr, E., Dewitz, P., & Patberg, J. P. (1989). Using cloze for inference training with expository text. *The Reading Teacher, 42,* 380–385.

Carr, K. S. (1983). The importance of inference skills in the primary grades. *The Reading Teacher, 36,* 518–522.

Cartwright, C. P., Cartwright, C. A., & Ward, M. E. (1989). *Educating special learners.* Belmont, CA: Wadsworth.

Cattagni, A., & Westnat, E. F. (2001). *Internet access in U. S. public schools and classrooms: 1994–2000.* Washington, DC: U.S. Department of Education, National Center for Educational Statistics. Available online at http://nces.ed.gov/pubs2001/2001071.pdf

Center for the Study of Reading. (1990). *Suggestions for the classroom: Teachers and independent reading.* Urbana: University of Illinois Press.

Chall, J. S. (1967). *Learning to read: The great debate.* New York: McGraw-Hill.

Chall, J. S. (1983a). *Learning to read: The great debate* (rev. ed.). New York: McGraw-Hill.

Chall, J. S. (1983b). *Stages of reading development.* New York: McGraw-Hill.

Chall, J. S. (1987). Two vocabularies for reading: Recognition and meaning. In M. G. McKeown & M. E. Curtis (Eds.), *The nature of vocabulary acquisition* (pp. 7–17). Hillsdale, NJ: Lawrence Erlbaum.

Chall, J. S. (1996). *Stages of reading development* (2nd ed.). Fort Worth, TX: Harcourt Brace.

Chall, J. S., Bissex, G. L., Conard, S. S., & Harris-Sharples, S. H. (1996). *Qualitative assessment of text difficulty: A practical guide for teachers and writers.* Cambridge, MA: Brookline.

Chall, J. S., & Dale, E. (1995). *The new Dale-Chall readability formula.* Cambridge, MA: Brookline.

Chamot, A. U., & O'Malley, J. M. (1994). Instructional approaches and teaching procedures. In K. Spangenberg-Urbschat & R. Pritchard (Eds.), *Kids come in all languages: Reading instruction for ESL students* (pp. 82–107). Newark, DE: International Reading Association.

Chapman, J. W., Tunmer, W. E., & Prochnow, J. E. (2001). Does success in the reading recovery program depend on developing proficiency in phonological-processing skills? A longitudinal study in a whole language instructional context. *Scientific Studies of Reading, 5,* 141–176.

Chard, N. (1990). How learning logs change teaching. In N. Atwell (Ed.), *Coming to know: Writing to learn in the intermediate grades* (pp. 61–68). Portsmouth, NH: Heinemann.

Chicago Public Schools. (2000). *Rubrics.* Available online at http://intranet.cps.k12.il.us/Assessments/Ideas_and_Rubrics/ideas_and_rubrics.html

*Children's books in print 2002* (Annual). New York: Bowker.

Christenbury, L., & Kelly, P. (1983). *Questioning: A path to critical thinking.* Urbana, IL: National Council of Teachers of English.

Christie, J. F. (1990). Dramatic play: A context for meaningful engagements. *The Reading Teacher, 43,* 542–545.

Clarke, L. K. (1988). Invented vs. traditional spelling in first graders' writings: Effects on learning to spell and read. *Research in the Teaching of English, 22,* 281–309.

Clay, M. M. (1972). *Reading: The patterning of complex behavior.* Auckland, New Zealand: Heinemann.

Clay, M. M. (1975). *What did I write?* Auckland, NZ: Heinemann.

Clay, M. M. (1982). *Observing young readers.* Portsmouth, NH: Heinemann.

Clay, M. M. (1985). *The early detection of reading difficulties* (3rd ed.). Auckland, New Zealand: Heinemann.

Clay, M. M. (1991). *Becoming literate: The construction of inner control.* Portsmouth, NH: Heinemann.

Clay, M. M. (1993a). *An observation survey of early literacy achievement.* Portsmouth, NH: Heinemann.

Clay, M. M. (1993b). *Reading Recovery: A guidebook for teachers in training.* Portsmouth, NH: Heinemann.

Clay, M. M. (2000). *Running records for classroom teachers.* Portsmouth, NH: Heinemann.

Cline, R. K. J., & Kretke, G. L. (1980). An evaluation of long-term SSR in the junior high school. *Journal of Reading, 23,* 503–506.

Cole, A. D. (1998). Beginner-oriented texts in literature-based classrooms: The segue for a few struggling readers. *The Reading Teacher, 51,* 488–501.

Collins, A., & Smith, E. (1980). *Teaching the process of reading comprehension* (Technical Report No. 182). Urbana: University of Illinois, Center for the Study of Reading.

Collins, J. L. (1998). *Strategies for struggling writers.* New York: Guilford Press.

Colorado Department of Education (2002). *Scoring rubrics.* Available online at: http://www.cde.state.co.us/cdeassess/as_rubricindex.htm

Combs, M. (1987). Modeling the reading process with enlarged texts. *The Reading Teacher, 40,* 422–426.

Community Update. (2001). *Reading by leaps and bounds.* Community Update, Issue No. 86, p. 4. Available online at http://www.ed.gov/G2K/community/01–04.pdf

Conard, S. S. (1990). *Change and challenge in content textbooks.* Paper presented at the annual conference of the International Reading Association, New Orleans.

Connelly, B., Johnston, R. S., & Thompson, G. B. (1999). The influence of instructional approaches on reading procedures. In G. B. Thompson & T. Nicholson (Eds.), *Learning to read: Beyond phonics and whole language* (pp. 103–123). New York: Teacher's College Press.

Cook, V. (2001). *Second language learning and language teaching* (3rd ed). New York: Oxford University Press.

Cooper, C. R., & Odell, L. (1977). *Evaluating writing: Describing, measuring, judging*. Urbana, IL: National Council of Teachers of English.

Cooper, P. D. (1996). *Intervention literacy instruction for hard-to-teach students in grades 3–6*. Paper presented at the annual meeting of the International Reading Association, New Orleans.

Cooper, P. D., & Pikulski, J. J. (2001). *Houghton Mifflin reading*. Boston: Houghton Mifflin.

Courtney, A. M., & Abodeb, T. L. (1999). Diagnostic-reflective portfolios. *The Reading Teacher, 52*, 708–714.

Cox, C., & Many, J. E. (1992). Towards an understanding of the aesthetic stance towards literature. *Language Arts, 66,* 287–294.

Cox, C., & Zarillo, J. (1993). *Teaching reading with children's literature*. New York: Merrill.

Crafton, L. K. (1991). *Whole language: Getting started . . . moving forward*. Katonah, NY: Richard C. Owen.

Crawford, P., & Shannon, P. (1994). "I don't think these companies have much respect for teachers": Looking at teacher's manuals. In P. Shannon & K. Goodman (Eds.), *Basal readers: A second look* (pp. 1–18). Katonah, NY: Richard C. Owen.

Cummins, J. (1994). The acquisition of English as a second language. In K. Spangenberg-Urbschat & R. Pritchard (Eds.), *Kids come in all languages: Reading instruction for all ESL students* (pp. 36–62). Newark, DE: International Reading Association.

Cummins, J. (2001). Assessment and intervention with culturally and linguistically diverse learners. In S. R. Hollins & J. V. Tinajero (Eds.), *Literacy assessment of second language learners* (pp. 115–129). Boston: Allyn & Bacon.

Cunningham, J. W., & Foster, E. O. (1978). The ivory tower connection: A case study. *The Reading Teacher, 31*, 365–369.

Cunningham, J. W., & Moore, D. W. (1986). The confused world of main idea. In J. F. Baumann (Ed.), *Teaching main idea comprehension* (pp. 1–17). Newark, DE: International Reading Association.

Cunningham, P. M. (1978). Decoding polysyllabic words: An alternative strategy. *Journal of Reading, 21*, 608–614.

Cunningham, P. M. (1998). The multisyllabic word dilemma: Helping students build meaning, spell, and read "big" words. *Reading and Writing Quarterly: Overcoming Learning Disabilities, 14*, 189–218.

Cunningham, P. M., & Allington, R. L. (1999). *Classrooms that work: They can all read and write* (2nd ed.). New York: Longwood.

Cunningham, P. M., & Allington, R. L. (2003). *Classrooms that work: They can all read and write* (3rd ed.). Boston: Allyn & Bacon.

Cunningham, P. M., & Cunningham, J. W. (1992). Making words: Enhancing the invented spelling-decoding connection. *The Reading Teacher, 46*, 106–115.

Curtis, M. E. (1987). Vocabulary testing and vocabulary instruction. In M. G. McKeown & M. E. Curtis (Eds.), *The nature of vocabulary acquisition* (pp. 37–51). Hillsdale, NJ: Lawrence Erlbaum.

Dahl, K. (1992). Kidwatching revisited. In K. S. Goodman, L. B. Bird, & Y. M. Goodman (Eds.), *The whole language catalog: Supplement on authentic instruction* (p. 50). Santa Rosa, CA: American School Publishers.

Dahl, K., & Farnan, N. (1998). *Children's writing: Perspectives from research*. Newark, DE: International Reading Association & National Reading Conference.

Dale, E., & O'Rourke, J. (1971). *Techniques of teaching vocabulary*. Chicago: Field.

D'Arcy, P. (1989). *Making sense, shaping meaning: Writing in the context of a capacity-based approach to learning*. Portsmouth, NH: Boynton/Cook.

Davis, F. B. (1968). Research on comprehension in reading. *Reading Research Quarterly, 3*, 449–545.

Davis, G., Jackson, J., & Johnson, S. (2000, May). *Guided writing: Leveling the balance*. Paper presented at the annual meeting of the International Reading Association, Indianapolis.

Davis, Z. T., & McPherson, M. D. (1989). Story map instruction: A road map for reading comprehension. *The Reading Teacher, 43*, 232–240.

Day, J. P. (2001). How I became an exemplary teacher (Although I'm really still learning just like anyone else). In M. Pressley, R. L. Allington, R. Wharton-McDonald, C. C. Block, & L. M. Morrow (Eds.), *Learning to read: Lessons from exemplary first-grade classrooms* (pp. 48–69). New York: Guilford.

DeFord, D. E. (1985). Validating the construct of theoretical orientation in reading instruction. *Reading Research Quarterly, 20*, 351–367.

Deighton, L. C. (1959). *Vocabulary development in the classroom*. New York: Columbia University Press.

Devine, T. G. (1986). *Teaching reading comprehension: From theory to practice*. Boston: Allyn & Bacon.

Dewitz, P., Carr, E. M., & Patberg, J. P. (1987). Effects of inference training on comprehension and comprehension monitoring. *Reading Research Quarterly, 22*, pp. 99–121.

Dickinson, D. K., & Smith, M. W. (1994). Long-term effects of preschool teachers' book reading on low-income children's vocabulary and story comprehension. *Reading Research Quarterly, 29*, 104–122.

Dillon, J. T. (1983). *Teaching and the art of questioning*. Bloomington, IN: Phi Delta Kappa.

Dodge, B. (2001). *FOCUS: Five rules for writing a great WebQuest*. Available online at http://www.iste.org/L&L/archive/vol28/no8/featuredarticle/dodge/index.html

Dole, J. S., Duffy, G. G., Roehler, L. R., & Pearson, P. D. (1991). Moving from the old to the new: Research on reading comprehension. *Review of Educational Research, 61*, pp. 239–264.

Donahue, P. A., Finnegan, R. J., Lutkus, A. D., Allen, N. R., & Campbell, J. R. (2001). *The nation's report card: Fourth-grade reading 2000*. Washington, DC: U.S. Department of Education.

Donahue, P. A., Voekl, K. E., Campbell, J. R., & Mazzeo, J. (1999). *NAEP 1998 report card for the nation and the states*. Washington, DC: U.S. Department of Education.

Donovan, C. A., &. Smolkin, L. B. (2001). Genre and other factors influencing teachers' book selection for science instruction. *Reading Research Quarterly, 36*, 421–440.

Dooling, D. J., & Lachman, R. (1971). Effects of comprehension on retention of prose. *Journal of Experimental Psychology, 88*, 216–222.

Dorion, R. (1994). Using nonfiction in a read-aloud program: Letting the facts speak for themselves. *The Reading Teacher, 47*, 616–624.

Douglas, M. P. (1989). *Learning to read: The quest for meaning.* New York: Teacher's College Press.

Dowhower, S. L. (1987). Effects of repeated reading on second-grade transitional readers' fluency and comprehension. *Reading Research Quarterly, 22,* 389–406.

Dressel, J. H. (1990). The effects of listening to and discussing different qualities of children's literature on the narrative writing of fifth graders. *Research in the Teaching of English, 24,* 397–414.

Duffelmeyer, F. A. (1985). Main ideas in paragraphs. *The Reading Teacher, 38,* 484–486.

Duffelmeyer, F. A., & Duffelmeyer, B. B. (1979). Developing vocabulary through dramatization. *Journal of Reading, 23,* 141–143.

Duffy, G. G. (2002). The case for direct explanation of strategies. In C. C. Block & M. Pressley (Eds.), *Comprehension instruction: Research based best practices* (pp. 28–41). New York: Guilford.

Duffy, G. G., & Roehler, L. R. (1987). Improving reading instruction through the use of responsive elaboration. *The Reading Teacher, 40,* 514–520.

Duffy, R. (1994). It's just like talking to each other: Written conversation with five-year-old children. In N. Hall & A. Robinson (Eds.), *Keeping in touch: Using interactive writing with young children* (pp. 31–42). Portsmouth, NH: Heinemann.

Duke, N. (2000). IRA outstanding dissertation award for 2000: Print environments and experiences offered to first-grade students in very low and very high SES school districts. *Reading Research Quarterly, 35,* 456–457.

Durgunoglu, A. Y., & Oney, B. (2000). *Literacy development in two languages: Cognitive and sociocultural dimensions of cross-language transfer.* A Research Symposium on High Standards in Reading for Students from Diverse Language Groups: Research, Practice & Policy. Washington, D.C.: Office of Bilingual Education and Minority Languages Affairs, U. S. Department of Education. Available online at http://www.ncbe.gwu.edu/ncbepubs/symposia/reading/reading3.html

Durkin, D. (1993). *Teaching them to read* (6th ed.). Boston: Allyn & Bacon.

Dykstra, R. (1974). Phonics and beginning reading instruction. In C. C. Walcutt, J. Lamport, & G. McCracken (Eds.), *Teaching reading: A phonic/linguistic approach to developmental reading* (pp. 373–397). New York: Macmillan.

Echevarria, J. (1998). *Teaching language minority students in elementary schools.* Washington, DC, and Santa Cruz, CA: Center for Research in Education, Diversity & Excellence.

Eckhoff, B. (1983). How reading affects children's writing. *Language Arts, 60,* 607–616.

Edelsky, C. (1994). Exercise isn't always healthy. In P. Shannon & K. Goodman (Eds.), *Basal readers: A second look* (pp. 19–34). Katonah, NY: Richard C. Owen.

Editorial Projects in Education. (2001). Quality counts 2001, A better balance. *Education Week on the Web.* Available online at http://www.educationweek.org/sreports/qc01

Educate the Children. (2001). *NLS activity resource sheet, Year 2, Term 2, Strand W 5.* Available online at http://www.standards.dfee.gov.uk/local/literacy/PDF/oa077.pdf

Education Department of Western Australia. (1994). *Writing resource book.* Melbourne, Australia: Longman.

Eeds, M., & Wells, D. (1989). Grand conversations: An exploration of meaning construction in literature study groups. *Research in the Teaching of English, 23,* 4–29.

Ehri, L. C. (1991). Development of the ability to read words. In R. Barr, M. L. Kamil, P. Mosenthal, & P. D. Pearson (Eds.), *Handbook of reading research* (Vol. II, pp. 383–417). New York: Longman.

Ehri, L. C. (1994). Development of the ability to read words: Update. In R. B. Ruddell, M. R. Ruddell, & H. Singer (Eds.), *Theoretical models and processes of reading* (4th ed.) (pp. 323–358). Newark, DE: International Reading Association.

Ehri, L. C. (1998). Research on learning to read and spell: A personal-historical perspective. *Scientific Studies of Reading, 2,* 97–114.

Ehri, L. C., & McCormick, S. (1998). Phases of word learning: Implications for instruction with delayed and disabled readers. *Reading and Writing Quarterly: Overcoming Learning Disabilities, 14,* 135–163.

Ehri, L. C., Nunes, S. R., Willows, D. M., Schuster, B. V., Yaghoub-Zadeh, Z., Shanahan, T. (2001). Phonemic awareness instruction helps children learn to read: Evidence from the National Reading Panel's meta-analysis. *Reading Research Quarterly, 36,* 250–287.

Elbro, C., Bornstrom, I., & Petersen, D. K. (1998). Predicting dyslexia from kindergarten: The importance of the distinctiveness of phonological representations of lexical items. *Reading Research Quarterly, 33,* 36-60.

Elkind, D. (1981). *The hurried child.* Reading, MA: Addison-Wesley.

Elkonin, D. B. (1973). Reading in the USSR. In J. Downing (Ed.), *Comparative reading* (pp. 551–579). New York: Macmillan.

Elley, W. B. (1989). Vocabulary acquisition from listening to stories. *Reading Research Quarterly, 24,* 174–187.

Elley, W. B. (1992). *How in the world do students read?* The Netherlands: IEA.

Emig, J. (1971). *The composing processes of twelfth-graders.* Urbana, IL: National Council of Teachers of English.

Enz, B. (1989). *The 90 per cent success solution.* Paper presented at the International Reading Association annual convention, New Orleans.

ERIC Clearinghouse on Urban Education. (2001). Latinos in school: Some facts and findings. *ERIC Clearinghouse on Urban Education Digest, No. 162.* New York: Teachers College, Institute for Urban and Minority Education. Available online at http://eric-web.tc.columbia.edu/digests/dig162.html

Ericson, L., & Juliebo, M. F. (1998). *The phonological awareness handbook for kindergarten and primary teachers.* Newark, DE: International Reading Association.

Estes, T., & Vaughn, J. (1985). *Reading and learning in the content classroom* (2nd ed.). Boston: Allyn & Bacon.

Fader, D. (1977). *The new hooked on books.* New York: Berkley.

Farnan, N. (1996). Connecting adolescents and reading: Goals at the middle level. *Journal of Adolescent & Adult Literacy, 39,* 436–445.

Farr, R. (1991). Current issues in alternative assessment. In C. P. Smith (Ed.), *Alternative assessment of performance in the language arts: Proceedings* (pp. 3–17). Bloomington, IN: ERIC Clearinghouse on Reading and Communication Skills and Phi Delta Kappa.

Farr, R., & Carey, R. F. (1986). *Reading: What can be measured?* Newark, DE: International Reading Association.

Farr, R., & Farr, B. (1990). *Integrated assessment system.* San Antonio, TX: Psychological Corporation.

Farr, R. et al. (2001). *Collections.* Orlando, FL: Harcourt.

Feitelson, D., Kita, B., & Goldstein, Z. (1986). Effects of reading series stories to first-graders on their comprehension and use of language. *Research on the Teaching of English, 20*, 339–356.

Ferreiro, E. (1986). The interplay between information and assimilation in beginning literacy. In W. H. Teale & E. Sulzby (Eds.), *Emergent literacy* (pp. 15–49). Norwood, NJ: Ablex.

Ferreiro, E. (1990). Literacy development: Psychogenesis. In Y. M. Goodman (Ed.), *How children construct literacy* (pp. 12–25). Newark, DE: International Reading Association.

Ferreiro, E., & Teberosky, A. (1982). *Literacy before schooling.* Portsmouth, NH: Heinemann.

Fielding, L. G., Wilson, P. T., & Anderson, R. C. (1986). A new focus on free reading: The role of trade books in reading instruction. In T. E. Raphael (Ed.), *The contexts of school-based literacy* (pp. 149–160). New York: Random House.

Fielding-Barnsley, R. (1997). Explicit instruction of decoding benefits children high in phonemic awareness and alphabet knowledge. *Scientific Studies of Reading, 1*(1), 85–98.

Fields, M. W., Spangler, K., & Lee, D. M. (1991). *Let's begin reading right: Developmentally appropriate beginning literacy* (2nd ed.). New York: Macmillan.

Fillmore, L. W., & Valdez, C. (1986). Teaching bilingual learners. In M. E. Wittrock (Ed.), *Handbook of research on teaching* (pp. 648–685). New York: Macmillan.

Fisher, C., & Natarelli, M. (1982). Young children's preferences in poetry: A national survey of first, second, and third graders. *Research in the Teaching of English, 16*, 339–355.

Fitzgerald, J. (1989). Research on stories: Implications for teachers. In K. P. Muth (Ed.), *Children's comprehension of text: Research into practice* (pp. 2–36). Newark, DE: International Reading Association.

Flexner, S. B., & Hauck, L. C. (1994). *The Random House dictionary of the English language* (2nd ed., rev.). New York: Random House.

Flood, J., Medcaris, A., Hasbrouk, J. E., Paris, S., Hoffman, J., Stah, Stah, S., Lapp, D., Tinejero, J. V., & Wood. K. (2001). *McGraw-Hill reading.* New York: McGraw-Hill.

Foorman, B. R., Fletcher, J. M., Francis, D. J., Schatschneider, C., Mehta, P. (1998). The role of instruction in learning to read: Preventing reading failure in at-risk children. *Journal of Educational Psychology, 90*, 37–55.

Ford, M. P. (1994). *Keys to successful whole group instruction.* Paper presented at the annual conference of the Connecticut Reading Association, Waterbury.

Fountas, I. C. (1994). *Little readers for guided reading teacher's manual.* Boston: Houghton Mifflin.

Fountas, I. C., & Pinnell, G. S. (1996). *Guided reading: Good first teaching for all children.* Portsmouth, NH: Heinemann.

Fountas, I. C., & Pinnell, G. S. (1999). *Matching books to readers: Using leveled books in guided reading, K–3.* Portsmouth, NH: Heinemann.

Fountas, I. C., & Pinnell, G. S. (2001). *Guiding readers and writers grades 3–6.* Portsmouth, NH: Heinemann.

Fowler, A., Palumbo, L. C., Liss-Bronstein, L., Wilder, T. D., Lavalette, M., & Gillis, M. (2002). *Enhancing oral language.* New Haven, CT: RESC Alliance.

Franklin, E. A. (1988). Reading and writing stories: Children creating meaning. *The Reading Teacher, 42*, 184–190.

Fredericks, A. D. (1986). Mental imagery activities to improve comprehension. *The Reading Teacher, 40*, 78–81.

Freeman, Y. S., & Freeman, D. E. (1998). Effective literacy practices for English learners. In C. Weaver (Ed.), *Practicing what we know: Informed reading instruction* (409–438). Urbana, IL: National Council of Teachers of English.

Fry, E. (1977a). *Elementary reading instruction.* New York: McGraw-Hill.

Fry, E. (1977b). Fry's readability graph: Clarifications, validity, and extension to level 17. *Journal of Reading, 21*, 242–252.

Fry, E. (December 1993–January 1994). Commentary: Do students read better today? *Reading Today,* p. 33.

Gage, F. C. (1990). *An introduction to reader-response issues: How to make students into more active readers.* Paper presented at the annual meeting of the Connecticut Reading Conference, Waterbury.

Gallo, D. R. (1985). Teachers as reading researchers. In C. N. Hedley & A. N. Baratta (Eds.), *Contexts of reading* (pp. 185–199). Norwood, NJ: Ablex.

Gambrell, L. B. (1980). Think time: Implications for reading instruction. *The Reading Teacher, 34*, 143–146.

Gambrell, L. B., & Bales, R. J. (1986). Mental imagery and the comprehension monitoring performance of fourth- and fifth-grade poor readers. *Reading Research Quarterly, 21*, 454–464.

Gambrell, L. B., Codling, R. M., & Palmer, B. M. (1996). *Elementary student's motivation to read. Reading Research Report No. 52.* Athens, GA: National Reading Research Center.

Gambrell, L. B., Wilson, R. M., & Gantt, W. N. (1981). Classroom observations of good and poor readers. *Journal of Educational Research, 24*, 400–404.

Gans, R. (1940). *Study of critical reading comprehension in intermediate grades: Teacher's College contributions to education, No. 811.* New York: Bureau of Publications, Teachers College, Columbia University.

García, G. E., Pearson, P. D., & Jiménez, R. T. (1994). *The at-risk situation: A synthesis of reading research.* Champaign, IL: University of Illinois, Center for the Study of Reading.

Garner, R. (1994). Metacognition and executive control. In R. B. Ruddell, M. R. Ruddell, & H. Singer (Eds.), *Theoretical models and processes of reading* (4th ed.), (pp. 715–756). Newark, DE: International Reading Association.

Garner, R., Hare, V. C., Alexander, P., Haynes, J., & Winograd, P. (1984). Inducing use of a text lookback strategy among unsuccessful readers. *American Educational Research Journal, 21*, 789–798.

Garner, R., MacCready, G. B., & Wagoner, S. (1984). Readers' acquisition of the components of the text lookback strategy. *Journal of Educational Psychology, 76*, 300–309.

Gaskins, I. W. (1998). *What research suggests are ingredients of a grades 1–6 literacy program for struggling readers.* Paper presented at International Reading Association Convention, Orlando.

Gaskins, I. W., Ehri, L. C., Cress, C., O'Hara, C., & Donnelly, K. (1996–1997). Procedures for word learning: Making discoveries about words. *The Reading Teacher, 50*, 312–327.

Gelzheiser, L. M., & Meyers, J. (1990). Special and remedial education in the classroom: Theme and variation. *Reading, Writing, and Learning Disabilities, 6*, 419–436.

Gensemer, E. (1998). *Teaching strategies for taking charge of task, text, situation, and personal characteristics.* Paper presented at International Reading Association Convention, Orlando.

Gibson, E. J., Gibson, J. J., Pick, A. D., & Osser, H. (1962). A developmental study of the discrimination of letter-like forms. *Journal of Comparative and Physiological Psychology, 55*, 897–906.

Gibson, E. J., & Levin, H. (1974). *The psychology of reading.* Cambridge, MA: MIT Press.

Gibson, E. J., Osser, H., & Hammonds, M. (1962). The role of grapheme-phoneme correspondence in the perception of words. *American Journal of Psychology, 75,* 554–570.

Gibson, E. J., Osser, H., & Pick, A. (1963). A study in the development of grapheme-phoneme correspondences. *Journal of Verbal Learning and Verbal Behavior, 2,* 142–146.

Gibson, L. (1989). *Literacy learning in the early years: Through children's eyes.* New York: Teachers College Press.

Gipe, J. P. (1980). Use of a relevant context helps kids learn. *The Reading Teacher, 33,* 398–402.

Glass, G. G. (1976). *Glass analysis for decoding only: Teacher's guide.* Garden City, NY: Easier to Learn.

Gold, J., & Fleisher, L. S. (1986). Comprehension breakdown with inductively organized text: Differences between average and disabled readers. *Remedial and Special Education, 7,* 26–32.

Goldenberg, C. (1994). Promoting early literacy development among Spanish-speaking children: Lessons from two studies. In E. H. Hiebert & B. M. Taylor (Eds.), *Getting reading right from the start* (pp. 171–200). Boston: Allyn & Bacon.

Goldenberg, C. (2001). Making schools work for low income families in the 21st century. In S. B. Neuman & D. K. Dickinson (Eds), *Handbook of early literacy research* (pp. 211–231). New York: Guilford.

Golick, M. (1987). *Playing with words.* Markham, ONT: Pembroke.

Goodman, K. S. (1974). Miscue analysis: Theory and reality in reading. In J. E. Merritt (Ed.), *New horizons in reading* (pp. 15–26). Newark, DE: International Reading Association.

Goodman, K. S. (1986). *What's whole in whole language?* Portsmouth, NH: Heinemann.

Goodman, K. S. (1994). Forward: Lots of changes, but little gained. In P. Shannon & K. Goodman (Eds.), *Basal readers: A second look* (pp. xiii–xxvii). Katonah, NY: Richard C. Owen.

Goodman, K. S. (1994). Reading, writing, and written texts: A transactional sociopsycholinguistic view. In R. B. Ruddell, M. R. Ruddell, & H Singer (Eds.), *Theoretical models and processes of reading* (4th ed.) (pp. 1093–1130). Newark, DE: International Reading Association.

Goodman, Y. M. (1985). Kidwatching: Observing children in the classroom. In A. Jagger & M. T. Smith-Burke (Eds.), *Observing the language learner* (pp. 9–18). Newark, DE: International Reading Association.

Gordon, C. J. (1985). Modeling inference awareness across the curriculum. *Journal of Reading, 28,* 444–447.

Gordon, C. J. (1989). Teaching narrative text structure: A process approach to reading and writing. In K. P. Muth (Ed.), *Children's comprehension of text: Research into practice* (pp. 79–102). Newark, DE: International Reading Association.

Goswami, U. (2001). Early phonological development and acquisition of literacy. In S. B. Neuman & D. K. Dickinson (Eds), *Handbook of early literacy research* (pp. 111–125). New York: Guilford.

Gough, P. B. (1985). *One second of reading: Postscript.* In H. Singer & R. R. Ruddell (Eds.), Theoretical models and processes of reading (3rd. ed.) (pp. 687–688). Newark, DE: International Reading Association.

Gough, P. B., & Hillinger, M. L. (1980). Learning to read: An unnatural act. *Bulletin of the Orton Society, 30,* 179–196.

Gough, P. B., Juel, C., & Griffith, P. L. (1992). Reading, spelling, and the orthographic cipher. In P. B. Gough, L. C. Ehri, &

R. Treiman (Eds.), *Reading Acquisition* (pp. 35–48). Hillsdale, NJ: Lawrence Erlbaum.

Gough, P. B., Larson, K. C., & Yopp, H. (2001). *The structure of phonemic awareness.* Unpublished paper. Austin: University of Texas.

Graesser, A., Golding, J. M., & Long, D. L. (1991). Narrative representation and comprehension. In R. Barr, M. L. Kamil, P. Mosenthal, & P. D. Pearson (Eds.), *Handbook of reading research* (Vol. II, pp. 171–205). New York: Longman.

Graesser, A. C., & Bertus, E. L. (1998). The construction of causal inferences while reading expository texts on science and technology. *Scientific Studies of Reading, 2*(3), 247–269.

Graves, D. H. (1975). Examination of the writing processes of seven-year-old children. *Research in the Teaching of English, 9,* 221–241.

Graves, D. H. (1983). *Writing: Teachers and children at work.* Exeter, NH: Heinemann.

Graves, M. F. (1987). Roles of instruction in fostering vocabulary development. In M. G. McKeown & M. E. Curtis (Eds.), *The nature of vocabulary acquisition* (pp. 165–184). Hillsdale, NJ: Lawrence Erlbaum.

Graves, M. F., & Dykstra, R. (1997). Contextualizing the first-grade studies: What is the best way to teach children to read? *Reading Research Quarterly, 32,* 342–344.

Graves, M. F., & Hammond, H. K. (1980). A validated procedure for teaching prefixes and its effect on students' ability to assign meaning to novel words. In M. Kamil & A. Moe (Eds.), *Perspectives on reading research and instruction* (pp. 184–188). Washington, DC: National Reading Conference.

Graves, M. F., Juel., C., Graves, B. B. (2001). *Teaching reading in the 21st century* (2nd ed.). Boston: Allyn & Bacon.

Gray, W.S., & Holmes, E. (1938). *The development of meaning vocabulary in reading,* Chicago: Publications of the University of Chicago.

Greenlaw, M. J. (1983). Reading interest research and children's choices. In N. Roser & M. Frith (Eds.), *Children's choices: Teaching with books children like* (pp. 90–92). Newark, DE: International Reading Association.

Greenwald, E. A., Persky, H. R., Campbell, J. R., Mazzeo, J. (1999). NAEP Writing Report Card for the Nation and the States. *Education Statistics Quarterly, 1*(4), 23–28.

Griffith, P. L., & Olson, M. W. (1992). Phonemic awareness helps beginning readers break the code. *The Reading Teacher, 45,* 516–523.

Grunwald Associates. (2001). *Children, families and the Internet.* Available online at http://www.grunwald.com/survey/survey_content.html

Gunning, T. (1975). *A comparison of word attack skills derived from a phonological analysis of frequently used words drawn from a juvenile corpus and an adult corpus.* Unpublished doctoral dissertation, Temple University, Philadelphia.

Gunning, T. (1982). Wrong level test: Wrong information. *The Reading Teacher, 35,* 902–905.

Gunning, T. (1990). *How useful is context?* Unpublished study, Southern Connecticut State University, New Haven.

Gunning, T. (1994). *Word building book D.* New York: Phoenix Learning Systems.

Gunning, T. (1995). Word building: A strategic approach to the teaching of phonics. *The Reading Teacher, 48,* 484–488.

Gunning, T. (1996). *Choosing and using books for beginning readers.* Paper presented at the annual meeting of the Connecticut Reading Conference, Waterbury.

Gunning, T. (1998a). *Assessing and correcting reading and writing difficulties.* Boston: Allyn & Bacon.

Gunning, T. (1998b). *Best books for beginning readers.* Boston: Allyn & Bacon.

Gunning, T. (1999). *Decoding behavior of good and poor second grade students.* Paper presented at the annual meeting of the National Reading conference, Orlando.

Gunning, T. (2000a). *Assessing the difficulty level of material in the primary grades: A study in progress.* Paper presented at the annual meeting of the National Reading Conference, Scottsdale, AZ.

Gunning, T. (2000b). *Best books for building literacy for elementary school children.* Boston: Allyn & Bacon.

Gunning, T. (2000c). *Phonological awareness and primary phonics.* Boston: Allyn & Bacon.

Gunning, T. (2001). *An analysis of second graders' attempts to read multisyllabic words.* Paper presented at the annual meeting of the National Reading Conference, San Antonio, TX.

Gunning, T. (2002). *Assessing and correcting reading and writing difficulties* (2nd ed.). Boston: Allyn & Bacon.

Guthrie, J. T. (1980). Research views: Time in reading programs. *The Reading Teacher, 33,* 500–502.

Guthrie, J. T., & Wigfield, A. (1997). Reading engagement: A rationale for theory and teaching. In J. Guthrie & A. Wigfield (Eds.), *Motivating readers through integrated instruction* (pp. 1–12). Newark, DE: International Reading Association.

Gutkin, R. J. (1990). Sustained reading. *Language Arts, 67,* 490–492.

Hackett, J. K., Moyer, R. H., & Adams, D. K. (1989). *Merrill science.* Columbus, OH: Merrill.

Hagerty, P., Hiebert, E., & Owens, M. (1989). Students' comprehension, writing, and perceptions in two approaches to literacy instruction. In S. McCormick & J. Zutell (Eds.), *Thirty-eighth yearbook of the National Reading Conference* (pp. 453–459). Chicago: National Reading Conference.

Hague, S. A. (1989). Awareness of text structure: The question of transfer from L1 and L2. In S. McCormick & J. Zutell (Eds.), *Cognitive and social perspectives for literacy research and instruction* (pp. 55–64). Chicago: National Reading Conference.

Halstead, J. W. (1988). *Guiding gifted readers.* Columbus, OH: Ohio Psychology.

Hammond, D. W. (2001). *The essential nature of teacher talk and its effect on students' engagement with expository text.* Paper presented at the annual meeting of the International Reading Association, New Orleans.

Hansen, J. (1981). The effects of inference training and practice on young children's reading comprehension. *Reading Research Quarterly, 16,* 391–417.

Hansen, J., & Pearson, P. D. (1980). *The effects of inference training and practice on young children's comprehension* (Technical Report No. 166). Urbana: University of Illinois, Center for the Study of Reading.

Hansen, J., & Pearson, P. D. (1982). *Improving the inferential comprehension of good and poor fourth-grade readers* (Report No. CSR-TR-235). Urbana: University of Illinois, Center for the Study of Reading (ERIC Document Reproduction No. ED 215–312).

Harcourt Educational Measurement (2000). *Some things parents should know about testing: A series of questions and answers.* Available online at http://www.hbem.com/library/parents.htm

Hare, V. C., & Borchardt, K. M. (1984). Direct instruction of summarization skills. *Reading Research Quarterly, 20,* 62–78.

Harmon, J. M. (1998). Constructing word meanings: Strategies and perceptions of four middle school learners. *Journal of Literacy Research, 30,* 561–599.

Harper, L. (1997). *The writer's toolbox: Five tools for active revision instruction.* Language Arts, 74, 193–200.

Harris, A. J., & Jacobson, M. D. (1982). *Basic reading vocabularies.* New York: Macmillan.

Harris, A. J., & Sipay, E. R. (1990). *How to increase reading ability* (9th ed.). New York: Longman.

Harris, T. L., & Hodges, R. E. (1995). *The literacy dictionary, the vocabulary of reading and writing.* Newark, DE: International Reading Association.

Harste, J. C., Short, K. G., & Burke, C. (1988). *Creating classrooms for authors: The reading-writing connection.* Portsmouth, NH: Heinemann.

Harste, J. C., Woodward, V. A., & Burke, C. L. (1984). *Language stories and literacy lessons.* Portsmouth, NH: Heinemann.

Hartman, D. K. (1994). The intertextual links of readers using multiple passages: A postmodern semiotic/cognitive view of meaning making. In R. B. Ruddell, M. R. Ruddell, & H. Singer (Eds.), *Theoretical models and processes of reading* (4th ed.) (pp. 616–636). Newark, DE: International Reading Association.

Harvey, S. (1998). *Nonfiction matters: Reading, writing, and research in grades 3–8.* York, ME: Stenhouse.

Hayes, D. A., & Tierney, R. J. (1982). Developing readers' knowledge through analogy. *Reading Research Quarterly, 17,* 256–280.

Heath, S. B. (1991). The sense of being literate: Historical and cross-cultural features. In R. Barr, M. L. Kamil, P. Mosenthal, & P. D. Pearson (Eds.), *Handbook of reading research,* (Vol. II, pp. 3–25). New York: Longman.

Hehir, T. (1994). *Learning disabilities: A national responsibility.* Paper presented at the meeting of the National Center for Learning Disabilities, Washington, DC.

Heimlich, J. E., & Pittelman, S. D. (1986). *Semantic mapping: Classroom applications.* Newark, DE: International Reading Association.

Helbig, A., & Perkins, A. (2001). *Many peoples, one land: A guide to new multicultural literature for children and young adults.* New York: Greenwood.

Henderson, E. H. (1981). *Learning to read and spell.* DeKalb: Northern Illinois University Press.

Henderson, E. H. (1990). *Teaching spelling.* Boston: Houghton Mifflin.

Hendrick, J. (2001). *The whole child: Developmental education for the early years* (7th ed.). Boston: Allyn & Bacon.

Henry, M. K. (1990). Reading instruction based on word structure and origin. In P. G. Aaron & R. M. Joshi (Eds.), *Reading and writing disorders in different orthographic systems* (pp. 25–49). Dordrecht, Netherlands: Kluwer Academic Publishers.

Herman, P. A., Anderson, R. C., Pearson, P. D., & Nagy, W. E. (1987). Incidental acquisition of word meanings from expositions with varied text features. *Reading Research Quarterly, 22,* 263–284.

Hidi, S., & Anderson, V. (1986). Producing written summaries: Task demands, cognitive operations, and implications for instruction. *Review of Educational Research, 56,* 473–493.

Hiebert, E. (1983). An examination of ability grouping for reading instruction. *Reading Research Quarterly, 18,* 231–255.

Hiebert, E. H. (1994). A small-group literacy intervention with Chapter 1 students. In E. H. Hiebert & B. M. Taylor (Eds.), *Getting reading right from the start* (pp. 85–106). Boston: Allyn & Bacon.

Hiebert, E. H. (1999). Text matters in learning to read. *The Reading Teacher, 52,* 552–566.

Hiebert, E. H., Pearson, P. D., Taylor, B. M., Richardson, V., & Paris, S. G. (1998). *Every child a reader.* Ann Arbor: University of Michigan School of Education, Center for the Improvement of Early Reading Achievement.

Hiebert, E. H., & Taylor, B. M. (2000). Beginning reading instruction: Research on early interventions. In M. L. Kamil, P. B. Mosenthal, P. D. Pearson, & R. Barr (Eds.), *Handbook of Reading Research* (Vol. III, pp. 455–482). Mahwah, NJ: Erlbaum.

Hiebert, E. H., Valencia, S. W., & Afflerbach, P. P. (1994). Definitions and perspectives. In S. W. Valencia, E. H. Hiebert, & P. P. Afflerbach (Eds.), *Authentic reading assessment: Practices and possibilities* (pp. 6–25). Newark, DE: International Reading Association.

Hildreth, G. (1936). Developmental sequences in name writing. *Child Development, 7,* 291–303.

Hildreth, G. (1950). *Readiness for school beginners.* New York: World.

Hirsch, E. D. (1987). *Cultural literacy: What every American needs to know.* Boston: Houghton Mifflin.

Hoffman, J. V. (1991). Teacher and school effects in learning to read. In R. Barr, M. L. Kamil, P. Mosenthal, & P. D. Pearson (Eds.), *Handbook of reading research* (Vol. II, pp. 911–950). New York: Longman.

Hoffman, J. V. (1992). Critical reading/thinking across the curriculum: Using I-charts to support learning. *Language Arts, 69,* 121–127.

Hoffman, J. V., Assaf, L. C., & Paris, S. G. (2001). High-stakes testing in reading: Today in Texas, tomorrow? *The Reading Teacher, 54,* 482–492.

Hoffman, J. V., McCarthney, S. J., Elliott, B., Bayles, D. L., Price, D. P., Ferree, A., Abbott, J. A. (1998). The literature-based basal in first-grade classroom: Savior, Satan, or same-old, same-old? *Reading Research Quarterly, 33,* 168–197.

Holdaway, D. (1979). *The foundations of literacy.* New York: Ashton Scholastic.

Homa, L. L. (2000). *The elementary school library collection: A guide to books and other media, phases 1-2-3* (22nd ed.). Williamsport, PA: Brodart.

Hornsby, P., Sukarna, P., & Parry, J. (1986). *Read on: A conference approach to reading.* Portsmouth, NH: Heinemann.

Hotchkiss, P. (1990). Cooperative learning models: Improving student achievement using small groups. In M. A. Gunter, T. H. Estes, & J. H. Schwab (Eds.), *Instruction: A models approach* (pp. 167–184). Boston: Allyn & Bacon.

Howard, M. (1998). *Current, best strategies to enhance your reading instruction.* Bellevue, WA: Bureau of Education & Research.

Huck, C. S. (1989). No wider than the heart is wide. In J. Hickman & B. E. Cullinan (Eds.), *Children's literature in the classroom: Weaving Charlotte's web* (pp. 252–262). Needham Heights, MA: Christopher-Gordon.

Hyman, R. T. (1978). *Strategic questioning.* Englewood Cliffs, NJ: Prentice-Hall.

Idol, L., & Croll, V. (1985). Story mapping training as a means of improving reading comprehension. *Learning Disability Quarterly, 10,* 214–229.

Individuals with Disabilities Act Amendments of 1997. 20 U.S.C. 1400 et seq.

International Reading Association. (1988). *New directions in reading instruction.* Newark, DE: Author.

International Reading Association. (1999). *High stakes assessments in reading: A position statement of the International Reading Association.* Newark, DE: Author.

International Reading Association (2002). *What is evidence based reading? A position statement of the International Reading Association.* Newark, DE: Author.

International Reading Association & National Association for the Education of Young Children. (1998). Learning to read and write: Developmentally appropriate practices for young children. *The Reading Teacher, 52,* 193–216.

Invernizzi, M., Meier, J. D., Swank, L., & Juel, C. (2001). *PALS-K, Phonological awareness literacy screening, 2000–2001.* Charlottesville: University of Virginia.

Irwin, P. A., & Mitchell, J. N. (1983). A procedure for assessing the richness of retellings. *Journal of Reading, 26,* 391–396.

Jenkins, J. R., Matlock, B., & Slocum, T. A. (1989). Approaches to vocabulary instruction. *Reading Research Quarterly, 24,* 215–235.

Jett-Simpson, M. (Ed.). (1990). *Toward an ecological assessment of reading progress.* Schofield: Wisconsin State Reading Association.

Jiganti, M. A., & Tindall, M. A. (1986). An interactive approach to teaching vocabulary. *The Reading Teacher, 39,* 444–448.

Jiménez, R. T. (1997). The strategic reading abilities and potential of five low-literacy Latina/o readers in middle school. *Reading Research Quarterly, 32,* 224–243.

Johns, J. L. (1997). *Basic reading inventory* (7th ed.). Dubuque, IA: Kedall/Hunt.

Johnson, D. D., Moe, A. J., & Baumann, J. F. (1983). *The Ginn word book for teachers: A basic lexicon.* Lexington, MA: Ginn.

Johnson, D. D., & Pearson, J. D. (1984). *Teaching reading vocabulary* (2nd ed.). New York: Holt, Rinehart & Winston.

Johnson, D. W., & Johnson, R. T. (1994). *Learning together and alone: Cooperative, competitive, and individualistic learning* (4th ed.). Boston: Allyn & Bacon.

Johnson, M. S., & Kress, R. A. (1965). *Developing basic thinking abilities.* Unpublished manuscript, Temple University, Philadelphia.

Johnson, M. S., Kress, R. A., & Pikulski, J. J. (1987). *Informal reading inventories* (2nd ed.). Newark, DE: International Reading Association.

Johnson, N. L. (1995). *The effect of portfolio design on student attitudes toward writing.* Unpublished master's thesis, San Diego State University, San Diego, CA.

Johnston, F. R. (1999). The timing and teaching of word families. *The Reading Teacher, 53,* 64–75.

Johnston, F. R. (2001). The utility of phonic generalizations: Let's take another look at Clymer's conclusions. *The Reading Teacher, 55,* 132–150.

Johnston, P. (1997). *Constructive evaluation of literacy* (2nd ed.). New York: Longman.

Johnston, P. H., & Rogers, R. (2001). Early literacy development: The case for "informed assessment." In S. B. Neuman & D. K. Dickinson (Eds.), *Handbook of early literacy research* (pp. 377–389). New York: Guilford.

Joint Task Force on Assessment. (1994). *Standards for the assessment of reading and writing.* Newark, DE: International

Reading Association and Urbana, IL: National Council of Teachers of English.

Jones, B, F., Palincsar, A. S., & Ogle, D. S., &. Carr, E. G (Eds.), (1986). *Strategic teaching and learning: Cognitive instruction in the content areas* (pp. 73–91). Alexandria, VA: ASCD.

Jongsma, E. (1980). *Cloze instruction research: A second look.* Newark, DE: International Reading Association.

Jordan, G. E., Snow, C. E., & Porche, M. V. (2000). Project ease: The effect of a family literacy project on kindergarten students' early literacy skills. *Reading Research Quarterly, 35,* 524–546.

Juel, C. (1994). *Learning to read and write in one elementary school.* New York: Springer-Verlag.

Juel, C., & Minden-Cupp, C. (2000). Learning to read words: Linguistic units and instructional strategies. *Reading Research Quarterly, 35,* 458–492.

Juel, C., & Roper-Schneider, D. (1985). The influence of basal readers on first-grade reading. *Reading Research Quarterly, 20,* 134–152.

Jurek, D. (1995). *Teaching young children.* Torrance, CA: Good Apple.

Kaissen, J. (1987). SSR/Booktime: Kindergarten and first grade sustained silent reading. *The Reading Teacher, 40,* 532–536.

Kameenui, E. J., Dixon, R. C., & Carnine, D. W. (1987). Issues in the design of vocabulary instruction. In M. E. McKeown & M. E. Curtis (Eds.), *The nature of vocabulary instruction* (pp. 129–145). Hillsdale, NJ: Lawrence Erlbaum.

Kamhi, A. G., & Catts, H. W. (1999). Language and reading: Convergences and divergences. In H. W. Catts and A. G. Kamhi (Eds.), *Language and reading disabilities* (pp. 1–24). Boston: Allyn & Bacon.

Kamil, M. L., & Bernhardt, E. B. (2001). Reading instruction for English language learners. In M. F. Graves, C. Juell, & B. Graves, *Teaching reading in the 21st century* (pp. 460–503). Boston: Allyn & Bacon.

Kawakami-Arakaki, A., Oshiro, M., & Farran, D. (1989). Research to practice: Integrating reading and writing in a kindergarten curriculum. In J. Mason (Ed.), *Reading and writing connections* (pp. 199–218). Boston: Allyn & Bacon.

Keene, E. O., & Zimmermann, S. (1997). *Mosaic of thought: Teaching reading comprehension in a reader's workshop.* Portsmouth, NH: Heinemann.

Kibby, M. W. (1989). Teaching sight vocabulary with and without context before silent reading: A field test of the "focus of attention" hypothesis. *Journal of Reading Behavior, 21,* 261–278.

Kibby, M. W. (1993). What reading teachers should know about reading proficiency in the U.S. *Journal of Reading, 37,* 28–40.

Kimmel, S., & MacGinitie, W. H. (1984). Identifying children who use a perseverative text processing strategy. *Reading Research Quarterly, 19,* 162–172.

Kindler, A. (2002). *Survey of the states' limited English proficient students and available educational programs and services 2000–2001 summary report.* Washington, DC: Office of English Language Acquisition, Language Enhancement, and Academic Achievement for Limited English Proficient Students. Available online at http://www.ncela.gwu.edu/ncbepubs/reports/

King-Sears, M. E., & Cummings, C. S. (1996). Inclusive practices of classroom teachers. *Remedial and Special Education, 17,* 217–225.

Klesius, J. P., & Griffith, P. L. (1996). Interactive storybook reading for at-risk learners. *The Reading Teacher, 49,* 552–560.

Kletzien, S. B. (1991). Strategy use by good and poor comprehenders reading expository text of differing levels. *Reading Research Quarterly, 26,* 67–86.

Koskinen, P. S., Gambrell, L. B., Kapinus, B. A., & Heathington, B. S. (1988). Retelling: A strategy for enhancing students' reading comprehension. *The Reading Teacher, 41,* 892–896.

Kucan, L., & Beck, I. L. (1996). Thinking aloud and reading comprehension research: Inquiry, instruction, and social interaction. *Review of Educational Research, 67,* 271–299.

Kuhn, M. R., & Stahl, S. A. (2000). *Fluency: A review of developmental and remedial practices* (CIERA-Report 2-008). Ann Arbor: CIERA/University of Michigan, School of Education (ERIC Document Reproduction Service No. ED438 530). Available online at http://www. ciera.org/library/reports/index.html

Kulik, J. A. (1992). *An analysis of the research on ability grouping: Historical and contemporary perspectives.* Storrs: The National Research Center on the Gifted and Talented, University of Connecticut. (ERIC Document Reproduction Service No. ED350 777).

Kutpier, K., & Wilson, P. (1993). Updating poetry preferences: A look at the poetry children really like. *The Reading Teacher, 47,* 28–35.

Laberge, D., & Samuels, S. J. (1974). Toward a theory of automatic information processing in reading. *Cognitive Psychology, 6,* 293–323.

Langer, J. A. (1986). Reading, writing, and understanding: An analysis of the construction of meaning. *Written Communication, 3,* 219–266.

Langer, J. A. (1999). *Beating the odds: Teaching middle and high school students to read and write well.* Albany, NY: National Research Center on English Learning and Achievement. (ERIC Document Reproduction Service No. ED435 993).

Langer, J. A., Applebee, A. N., Mullis, I. V. S., & Foertsch, M. A. (1990). *Learning to read in our nation's schools: Instruction and achievement in 1988 at grades 4, 8, and 12.* Princeton, NJ: Educational Testing Service.

Law, B., & Eckes, M. (2002). *The more than just surviving handbook: ESL for every classroom teacher.* Winnipeg, MAN: Portage & Main Press.

Learning Media. (1991). *Dancing with the pen: The learner as writer.* Wellington, New Zealand: Ministry of Education.

Lehr, S., & Thompson, D. L. (2000). The dynamic nature of response: Children reading and responding to Maniac Magee and The Friendship. *The Reading Teacher, 53,* 480–493.

Lensmire, T. (1994). *When children write: Critical re-visions of the writing workshop.* New York: Teachers College Press.

Leseman, P. P. M., & deJong, P. F. (1998). Home literacy: Opportunity, instruction, cooperation and social-emotional quality predicting early reading achievement. *Reading Research Quarterly, 33,* 294–318.

Leslie, L., & Caldwell, J. (2001). *Qualitative reading inventory-3.* New York: Addison Wesley Longman.

Leu, D. J. (2000). Exploring literacy on the Internet. *The Reading Teacher, 53,* 424–429.

Leung, C. B. (1992). Effects of word-related variables on vocabulary growth through repeated read-aloud events. In C. K. Kinzer & D. J. Leu (Eds.), *Literacy research, theory, and practice: Views from many perspectives* (pp. 491–498). Chicago: National Reading Conference.

Liberman, I. Y., & Shankweiler, D. (1991). Phonology and beginning reading: A tutorial. In L. Rieben & C. A. Perfetti (Eds.), *Learning to read: Basic research and its implications* (pp. 3–18). Hillsdale, NJ: Lawrence Erlbaum.

Lima, C. W., & Lima, J. A. (2002). *A to zoo subject access to children's picture books* (6th ed.). New Providence, NJ: Bowker.

Lindamood, P., & Lindamood, P. (1998). *The Lindamood phoneme sequencing program for reading, spelling, and speech: LIPS.* Austin, TX: Pro-ed.

Linden, M., & Wittrock, M. C. (1981). The teaching of reading comprehension according to the model of generative learning. *Reading Research Quarterly, 17,* 44–57.

Linebarger, D. L. (2000). *Summative evaluation of* Between the Lions: *A final Report to the WGBH Educational Foundation.* Kansas City: University of Kansas. Available online at http://pbskids.org/lions/about/report/BTL_Report.pdf

Lipson, M. Y. (1984). Some unexpected issues in prior knowledge and comprehension. *The Reading Teacher, 37,* 760–764.

Lipson, M. Y., Valencia, S. W., Wixson, K. K., & Peters, C. W. (1993). Integration and thematic teaching and learning. *Language Arts, 70,* 252–263.

Lipson, M. Y., & Wixson, K. K. (1997). *Assessment and instruction of reading disability: An interactive approach* (2nd ed.). New York: HarperCollins.

Lukens, R. J. (1995). *A critical handbook of children's literature* (5th ed.). New York: HarperCollins.

Lyons, C. (2000). *Reading Recovery in the United States: More than a decade of data.* Available online at http://readingrecovery.org/rr/rrusa.htm

Maclean, M., Bryant, P., & Bradley, L. (1987). Rhymes, nursery rhymes, and reading in early childhood. *Merrill Palmer Quarterly, 33,* 255–281.

Madden, N. (2000, February). Meeting the expository challenge with SFA. *Success Stories,* p. 6. Available online at http://www.successforall.net/current/newsletters.htm

Maimon, E. P., & Nodine, B. F. (1979). Measuring syntactic growth: Errors and expectations in sentence-combining practice with college freshmen. *Research in the Teaching of English, 12,* 233–244.

Manning, G. L., & Manning, M. (1984). What models of recreational reading make a difference? *Reading World, 23,* 375–380.

Many, J. E. (1990). The effect of reader stance on students' personal understanding of literature. In J. Zutell & S. McCormick (Eds.), *Literacy theory and research: Analyses from multiple paradigms* (thirty-ninth yearbook of the National Reading Conference) (pp. 51–63). Chicago: National Reading Conference.

Many, J. E. (1991). The effects of stance and age level on children's literary responses. *Journal of Reading Behavior, 21,* 61–85.

Manzo, A. V. (1969). The ReQuest procedure. *Journal of Reading, 13,* 123–126.

Manzo, A. V., & Manzo, V. C. (1993). *Literacy disorders.* Fort Worth, TX: Harcourt Brace Jovanovich.

Maria, K. (1990). *Reading comprehension instruction: Issues and strategies.* Parkton, MD: York Press.

Maria, K., & MacGinitie, W. (1987). Learning from texts that refute the reader's prior knowledge. *Reading Research and Instruction, 26,* 222–238.

Martin, M. (1995). *Spelling in the kindergarten.* Paper presented at the annual meeting of the International Reading Association, Anaheim.

Martinez, M., & Teale, W. H. (1987). The ins and outs of a kindergarten writing program. *The Reading Teacher, 40,* 444–451.

Marzano, R. J., & Marzano, J. S. (1988). *A cluster approach to elementary vocabulary instruction.* Newark, DE: International Reading Association.

Mason, J. M., Peterman, C. L., & Kerr, B. M. (1988). *Fostering comprehension by reading books to kindergarten children* (Technical Report No. 426). Champaign: University of Illinois, Center for the Study of Reading.

Matthews, M. W., & Kesner, J. E. (2000). The silencing of Sammy. *The Reading Teacher, 53,* 420–421.

McArthur, T. (Ed.). (1992). *The Oxford companion to the English language.* New York: Oxford University.

McClure, A. A., Harrison, P., & Reed, S. (1990). *Sunrises and songs: Reading and writing poetry in an elementary classroom.* Portsmouth, NH: Heinemann.

McClure, A. A., & Kristo, J. V. (Eds.). (1994). *Inviting children's responses to literature.* Urbana, IL: National Council of Teachers of English.

McCormick, S. (1992). Disabled readers' erroneous responses to inferential comprehension questions: Description and analysis. *Reading Research Quarterly, 27,* 55–77.

McCoy, K. M., & Pany, D. (1986). Summary and analysis of oral reading corrective feedback research. *The Reading Teacher, 39,* 548–554.

McCracken, R. A. (1991). *Spelling through phonics.* Grand Forks, ND: Pegusis.

McGee, L. M. (1995). Talking about books with young children. In N. L. Roser & M. G. Martinez (Eds.), *Book talk and beyond* (pp. 105–115). Newark, DE: International Reading Association.

McGee, L. M., & Tompkins, G. E. (1981). The videotape answer to independent reading comprehension activities. *The Reading Teacher, 34,* 427–433.

McGill-Franzen, A. (1994). Compensatory and special education: Is there accountability for learning and belief in children's potential? In E. H. Hiebert & B. M. Taylor (Eds.), *Getting reading right from the start: Effective early literacy interventions* (pp. 13–35). Boston: Allyn & Bacon.

McKenna, M. C., & Kerr, D. J. (1990). Measuring attitude toward reading: A new tool for teachers. *The Reading Teacher, 43,* 626–639.

McKeown, M. G. (1993). Creating effective definitions for young word learners. *Reading Research Quarterly, 28,* 16–32.

McLane, J. B., & McNamee, G. D. (1990). *Early literacy.* Cambridge, MA: Harvard University Press.

McLaughlin, B., August, D., Snow, C., Carlo, M., Dressier, C., White, C., Lively. T., & Lippman, D. (2000). *Vocabulary knowledge and reading comprehension in English language learners.* Final Performance Report. Washington, DC: Office of Educational Research and Improvement. Available online at http://www.ncela.gwu.edu/ncbepubs/symposia/reading/6august.pdf

McMahon, S. (1997). Book clubs: Contexts for students to lead their own discussions. In S. I. McMahon & T. E. Raphael (Eds.), *The book club connection: Literacy learning and classroom talk* (pp. 89–106). New York: Teachers College Press.

McMaster, J. C. (1998). "Doing" literature: Using drama to build literacy. *The Reading Teacher, 51,* 574–584.

McNamara, T. P., Miller, D. L., & Bransford, J. D. (1991). Mental models and reading comprehension. In R. Barr, M. L. Kamil, P. Mosenthal, & P. D. Pearson (Eds.), *Handbook of reading research* (Vol. II, pp. 490–511). New York: Longman.

McNeil, J. D. (1987). *Reading comprehension: New directions for classroom practice* (2nd ed.). Glenview, IL: Scott, Foresman.

Medley, D. M. (1977). *Teacher competence and teacher effectiveness:*

*A review of process-product research.* Washington, DC: American Association of Colleges for Teacher Education.

Menke, P. J., & Pressley, M. (1994). Elaborative interrogation: Using "why" questions to enhance the learning from text. *Journal of Reading, 37*, 642–645.

Mesmer, H. A. (1999). Scaffolding a crucial transition using text with some decodability. *The Reading Teacher, 53,* 130–142.

Metsala, J. L. (1999). The development of phonemic awareness in reading-disabled children. *Applied Psycholinguistics, 20,* 149–158.

Meyer, B. J. F., & Rice, G. E. (1984). The structure of text. In P. D. Pearson, R. Barr, M. L. Kamil, & P. Mosenthal (Eds.), *Handbook of reading research* (pp. 319–351). New York: Longman.

Meyers, K. L. (1988). Twenty (better) questions. *English Journal, 77*(1), 64–65.

Mills, E. (1974). Children's literature and teaching written composition. *Elementary English, 51*, 971–973.

Moats, L. C. (2000). *Speech to print: Language essentials for teachers.* Baltimore: Brookes.

Moldofsky, P. B. (1983). Teaching students to determine the central story problem: A practical application of schema theory. *The Reading Teacher, 38*, 377–382.

Moore, D. W., & Moore, S. A. (1986). Possible sentences. In E. K. Dishner, T. W. Bean, J. E. Readence, & D. W. Moore (Eds.), *Reading in the content areas: Improving classroom instruction* (2nd ed.) (pp. 174–179). Dubuque, IA: Kendall/Hunt.

Moore, D. W., Moore, S. A., Cunningham, P. M., & Cunningham, J. W. (1986). *Developing readers and writers in the content areas.* New York: Longman.

Morrow, L. M. (1985). Reading and retelling stories: Strategies for emergent readers. *The Reading Teacher, 38*, 871–875.

Morrow, L. M. (1988). Young children's responses to one-to-one story readings in school settings. *Reading Research Quarterly, 23*, 89–107.

Morrow, L. M. (1997). *Literacy development in the early years: Helping children read and write* (3rd ed.). Boston: Allyn & Bacon.

Morrow, L. M., & Asbury, E. B. (2001). Patricia Loden. In M. Pressley, R. L. Allington, R. Wharton-McDonald, C. C. Block, & L. M. Morrow (Eds.), *Learning to read: Lessons from exemplary first-grade classrooms* (pp. 184–202). New York: Guilford.

Mosenthal, J. H. (1990). Developing low-performing, fourth-grade, inner-city students' ability to comprehend narrative. In J. Zutell & S. McCormick (Eds.), *Literacy theory and research: Analyses from multiple paradigms* (thirty-ninth yearbook of the National Reading Conference) (pp. 275–286). Chicago: National Reading Conference.

Moustafa, M. (1995). Children's productive phonological recoding. *Reading Research Quarterly, 30*, 464–476.

Moustafa, M., & Maldonado-Colon, E. (1999). Whole-to-part phonics instruction: Building on what children know to help them know more. *The Reading Teacher, 52*, 448–458.

Mullis, I. V. S., Campbell, J. R., & Farstrup, A. E. (1993). *Executive summary of the NAEP 1992 reading report card for the nation and the states.* Princeton, NJ: Educational Testing Service.

Murphy, L. L., Plake, B. S., Impara, J. C., & Spies, R. A. (Eds.). (2003). *Tests in print VI.* Lincoln, NE: University of Nebraska Press.

Murray, B. A. (1998). Gaining alphabetic insight: Is phoneme manipulation skill or identity knowledge causal? *Journal of Educational Psychology, 90*, 461–475.

Murray, D. (1979). The listening eye: Reflections on the writing conference. *College English, 41*, 13–18.

Murray, D. M. (1989). *Expecting the unexpected: Teaching myself—and others—to read and write.* Portsmouth, NH: Boynton/Cook.

Muschla, G. R. (1993). *Writing workshop survival kit.* West Nyack, NY: Center for Applied Research in Education.

Muter, V., & Snowling, M. (1998). Concurrent and longitudinal predictors of reading: The role of metalinguistic and short-term memory skills. *Reading Research Quarterly, 33*, 320–337.

Muth, K. D. (1987). Teachers' connection questions: Prompting students to organize text ideas. *Journal of Reading, 31*, 254–259.

Nagy, W. E. (1988). *Teaching vocabulary to improve reading comprehension.* Newark, DE: International Reading Association.

Nagy, W. E., & Anderson, R. C. (1984). How many words are there in printed English? *Reading Research Quarterly, 19*, 304–330.

Nagy, W. E., Anderson, R. C., & Herman, P. A. (1987). Learning word meanings from context during normal reading. *American Educational Research Journal, 24*, 237–270.

Nagy, W. E., & Herman, P. A. (1987). Breadth and depth of vocabulary knowledge: Implications for acquisition and instruction. In M. G. McKeown & M. E. Curtis (Eds.), *The nature of vocabulary acquisition* (pp. 19–35). Hillsdale, NJ: Lawrence Erlbaum.

Nagy, W. E., & Scott, J. A. (2000). Vocabulary processes. In M. L. Kamil, P. B. Mosenthal, P. D. Pearson, & R. Barr (Eds.), *Handbook of Reading Research* (Vol. III, pp. 269–284). Mahwah, NJ: Erlbaum.

Nation, K., & Hulme, C. (1997). Phonemic segmentation, not onset-rime segmentation, predicts early reading and spelling skills. *Reading Research Quarterly, 32*, 154–167.

National Association of State Boards of Education. (1992). *Winners all: A call for inclusive schools.* Alexandria, VA: Author.

National Center for Educational Statistics. (1998). *The condition of education.* Washington, DC: U.S. Department of Education.

National Center on Education and the Economy & The University of Pittsburgh. (1997). *Performance standards, Vol. 1, Elementary school.* Washington, DC: New Standards.

National Center on Education and the Economy & The University of Pittsburgh, (2001). *Speaking and listening for preschool through third grade.* Washington, DC: New Standards, AZ.

Nessel, D. (1987). The new face of comprehension instruction: A closer look at questions. *The Reading Teacher, 40*, 604–606.

Neuman, S. B. (1997). *Getting books in children's hands: A study of access to literacy.* Paper presented at National Reading Conference, Scottsdale.

New Standards Primary Literacy Committee. (1999). *Reading and writing grade by grade: Primary literacy standards through third grade.* Washington, DC: National Center on Education and the Economy & The University of Pittsburgh.

Newmann, F. M., & Wehlage, G. G. (1993). Five standards of authentic instruction. *Educational Leadership, 50*(7), 8–12.

Nicholson, T., & Whyte, B. (1992). Matthew effects in learning new words while listening to stories. In C. K. Kinzer & D. J. Leu (Eds.), *Literacy research, theory, and practice: Views from many perspectives* (pp. 499–501). Chicago: National Reading Conference.

Noyce, R., & Christie, J. F. (1989). *Integrating reading and writing instruction in grades K–8*. Boston: Allyn & Bacon.

Nua Internet Surveys. (2001). *How many online?* Available online at http://www.nua.ie/surveys/how_many_online/index.html

Oakhill, J., & Yuill, N. (1996). Higher-order factors in comprehension disability: Processess and remediation. In C. Cornoldi & J. Oakhill (Eds.), *Reading comprehension difficulties: Process and intervention* (pp. 69–92). Mahwah, NJ: Erlbaum.

O'Brien, C. A. (1973). *Teaching the language-different child to read*. Columbus, OH: Merrill.

Ogle, D., & Fogelberg, E. (2001). Expanding collaborative roles of reading specialists: Developing an intermediate reading support program. In V. J. Risko & K. Bromley (Eds), *Collaboration for diverse learners: Viewpoints and practices*. Newark, DE: International Reading Association.

Ogle, D. M. (1989). The know, want to know, learn strategy. In K. D. Muth (Ed.), *Children's comprehension of text* (pp. 205–223). Newark, DE: International Reading Association.

Oken-Wright, P. (1998). Transition to writing: Drawing as a scaffold for emergent writers. *Young Children, 53*(2), 76–81.

Olson, J. L. (1987). Drawing to write. *School Arts, 87*(1), 25–27.

O'Rourke, J. P. (1974). *Toward a science of vocabulary development*. The Hague: Mouton.

Otto, B. (2001). *Language development in early childhood*. Upper Saddle River, NJ: Prentice Hall.

Owens, R. E. (2001). *Language development* (5th ed.). Boston: Allyn & Bacon.

Palincsar, A. S., & Brown, A. L. (1986). Interactive teaching to promote independent learning from text. *The Reading Teacher, 39*, 771–777.

Palincsar, A. S., Winn, J., David, Y., Snyder, B., & Stevens, D. (1993). Approaches to strategic reading instruction reflecting different assumptions regarding teaching and learning. In L. J. Meltzer (Ed.), *Strategy assessment and instruction for students with learning disabilities: From theory to practice* (pp. 247–292). Austin, TX: Pro-Ed.

Paratore, J. R. (1995). Implementing an intergenerational literacy project: Lessons learned. In L. M. Morrow (Ed.), *Family literacy: Connections in schools and communities* (pp. 37–53). Newark, DE: International Reading Association.

Paris, S. G., Wasik, B. A., & Turner, J. C. (1991). The development of strategic readers. In R. Barr, M. L. Kamil, P. Mosenthal, & P. D. Pearson (Eds.), *Handbook of reading research* (Vol. II, pp. 609–640). New York: Longman.

Parsons, L. (1990). *Response journals*. Portsmouth, NH: Heinemann.

Pearson, P. D. (1985). Changing the face of reading comprehension instruction. *The Reading Teacher, 38*, 724–738.

Pearson, P. D., & Camperell, K. (1994). Comprehension of text structures. In R. B. Ruddell, M. R. Ruddell, & H. Singer (Eds.), *Theoretical models and processes of reading* (4th ed.) (pp. 448–568). Newark, DE: International Reading Association.

Pearson, P. D., & Gallagher, M. C. (1983). The instruction of reading comprehension. *Contemporary Educational Psychology, 8*, 317–345.

Pearson, P. D., & Johnson, D. D. (1978). *Teaching reading comprehension*. New York: Holt, Rinehart & Winston.

Perfetti, C. A. (1985). *Reading ability*. New York: Oxford University Press.

Perfetti, C. A. (1992). The representation problem in reading acquisition. In P. B. Gough, L. C. Ehri, & R. Treiman (Eds.), *Reading acquisition* (pp. 145–174). Hillsdale, NJ: Lawrence Erlbaum.

Peters, E. E., & Levin, J. R. (1986). Effects of a mnemonic imagery strategy on good and poor readers' prose recall. *Reading Research Quarterly, 21*, 179–192.

Peterson, R. (1992). *Life in a crowded place: Making a learning community*. Portsmouth, NH: Heinemann.

Petty, W., Herold, C., & Stoll, E. (1968). *The state of the knowledge of the teaching of vocabulary* (Cooperative Research Project No. 3128). Champaign, IL: National Council of Teachers of English.

Pike, K., Compain, R., & Mumper, J. (1994). *New connections: An integrated approach to literacy*. New York: HarperCollins.

Pine, J. M. (1994). The language of primary caregivers. In C. Gallaway and B. Richards (Eds.), *Input and interaction in language acquisition* (pp. 15-37). Cambridge: Cambridge University Press.

Pinnell, G. S., & Fountas, I. C. (1998). *Word matters*. Portsmouth, NH: Heinemann.

Pinnell, G. S., & Fountas, I. C. (2002). *Leveled books for readers grades 3–6*. Portsmouth, NH: Heinemann.

Pinnell, G. S., Pikulski, J. J., Wixson, K.K., Campbell, J. R., Gough, P. B., & Beatty, A. S. (1995) *Listening to children read aloud*. Washington, DC: U.S. Department of Education, National Center for Education Statistics.

Plake, B. S., Impara, J. C., & Spies, R. A. (Eds.). (2003). *The fifteenth mental measurements yearbook*. Lincoln, BE: University of Nebraska Press.

Platt, P. (1978). Grapho-linguistics: Children's drawings in relation to reading and writing skills. *The Reading Teacher, 31*, 262–268.

Popham, W. J. (2000). *Modern educational measurement: Practical guidelines for educational leaders*. Boston: Allyn & Bacon.

Prawat, R. S. (1989). Promoting access to knowledge, strategy, and disposition in students: A research synthesis. *Review of Educational Research, 59*, 1–41.

Pressley, M. (1994). *What makes sense in reading instruction according to research*. Paper presented at the annual meeting of the Connecticut Reading Association, Waterbury.

Pressley, M. (2002). Comprehension strategies instruction: A turn-of-the-century status report. In C. C. Block & M. Pressley (Eds.), *Comprehension instruction: Research-based best practices* (pp. 11–27). New York: Guilford.

Pressley, M., Allington, R. L., Wharton-McDonald, R., Block, C. C., & Morrow, L. M. (2001). The nature of first-grade instruction that promotes literacy achievement. In M. Pressley, R. L. Allington, R. Wharton-McDonald, C. C. Block & L. M. Morrow (Eds.), *Learning to read: Lessons from exemplary first-grade classrooms* (pp. 48–69). New York: Guilford.

Pressley, M., Borkowski, J. G., Forrest-Pressley, D., Gaskins, I. W., & Wiley, D. (1990). *Cognitive strategy instruction that really improves children's academic performance*. Cambridge, MA: Brookline Books.

Pressley, M., Borkowski, J. G., Forrest-Pressley, D., Gaskins, I. W., & Wiley, D. (1993). Closing thoughts on strategy instruction for individuals with learning disabilities: The good information-processing perspective. In L. Meltzer (Ed.), *Strategy assessment and instruction for students with learning disabilities: From theory to practice* (pp. 355–377). Austin, TX: Pro-Ed.

Pressley, M., Johnson, C. J., Symons, S., McGoldrick, J. A., & Kurita, J. A. (1989). Strategies that improve children's memory and comprehension of what is read. *Elementary School Journal, 89,* 3–32.

Pressley, M., Wharton-McDonald, R., Mistretta-Hampston, J., & Echevarria, M. (1998). Literacy instruction in 10 fourth- and fifth-grade classrooms in upstate New York. *Scientific Studies of Reading, 2,* 159–194.

Probst, R. (1988). Dialogue with a text. *English Journal, 77*(1), 32–38.

Prochaska, J. O., Norcross, J. C., & DiClemente, D. C. (1994). *Changing for the good.* New York: Avon.

Purcell-Gates, V. (1997). Stories, coupons, and the TV guide: Relationships between home literacy experiences and emergent literacy knowledge. *Reading Research Quarterly, 31,* 406–428.

QuanSing, J. (1995, May). *Developmental teaching and learning using developmental continua as maps of language and literacy development which link assessment to teaching.* Paper presented at the annual meeting of the International Reading Association, Anaheim, CA.

Radencich, M. C. (1995). *Administration and supervision of the reading/writing program.* Boston: Allyn & Bacon.

Radencich, M. C., Beers, P. G., & Schumm, J. S. (1993). *A handbook for the K–12 resource specialist.* Boston: Allyn & Bacon.

Raines, S., & Isbell, R. (1994). *Stories: Children's literature in early education.* Albany, NY: Delmar.

Ramey, C. T., & Campbell, F. A. (1991). Poverty, early-childhood education, and academic competence: The Abecederian experiment. In A. Huston (Ed.), *Children reared in poverty* (pp. 190–221). New York: Cambridge University Press.

Ramos, F., & Krashen, S. (1998). The impact of one trip to the public library: Making books available may be the best incentive for reading. *The Reading Teacher, 51,* 614–615.

Raphael, T. E. (1984). Teaching learners about sources of information for answering questions. *The Reading Teacher, 28,* 303–311.

Raphael, T. E. (1986). Teaching question/answer relationships, revisited. *The Reading Teacher, 39,* 516–522.

Raphael, T. E., & Boyd, F. B. (1997). When readers write: The book club writing component. In S. I. McMachon & T. E. Raphael (Eds.), *The book club connection: Literacy learning and classroom talk* (pp. 69–88). New York: Teachers College Press.

Raphael, T. E., & Englert, C. S. (1989). Integrating reading and writing instruction. In P. Winograd, K. K. Wixson, & M. Y. Lipson (Eds.). *Improving basal reading instruction* (pp. 231-255). New York: Teachers College Press.

Raphael, T. E., & Englert, C. S. (1990). Writing and reading: Partners in constructing meaning. *The Reading Teacher, 43,* 388–400.

Raphael, T. E., Englert, C. S., & Kirschner, B. W. (1989). Acquisition of expository writing skills. In J. M. Mason (Ed.), *Reading and writing connections* (pp. 261–290). Boston: Allyn & Bacon.

Rashotte, C. A., & Torgesen, J. K. (1985). Repeated reading and reading fluency in learning disabled children. *Reading Research Quarterly, 20,* 180–188.

Read, C. (1971). Pre-school children's knowledge of English phonology. *Harvard Educational Review, 41,* 1–34.

Reading Recovery Council of North America. (2001). *Reading recovery: Basic facts.* http://www.readingrecovery.org/ReadingRecoveryInfo/BasicFacts.htm

Reinking, D., & Rickman, S. S. (1990). The effects of computer-mediated texts on the vocabulary learning and comprehension of intermediate-grade readers. *Journal of Reading Behavior, 22,* 395–411.

Reutzel, D. R., & Cooter, R. B. (1991). Organizing for effective instruction: The reading workshop. *The Reading Teacher, 44,* 548-555.

Reutzel, D. R., & Cooter, R. B. (1992). *Teaching children to read: From basals to books.* New York: Macmillan.

Rhodes, L. K. (1990, March). *Anecdotal records: A powerful tool for ongoing literacy assessment.* Paper presented at the National Council of Teachers of English spring conference, Colorado Springs, CO.

Rhodes, L. K., & Dudley-Marling, C. (1988). *Readers and writers with a difference: A holistic approach to teaching learning-disabled and remedial students.* Portsmouth, NH: Heinemann.

Richgels, D. J. (2001). Invented spelling, phonemic awareness, and reading and writing instruction. In S. B. Neuman & D. K. Dickinson (Eds), *Handbook of early literacy research* (pp. 142–155). New York: Guilford.

Richgels, D. S., McGee, L. M., & Slaton, E. A. (1989). Teaching expository text structure in reading and writing. In K. D. Muth (Ed.), *Children's comprehension of text* (pp. 167–184). Newark, DE: International Reading Association.

Richgels, D. S., & Wold, L. S. (1998). Literacy on the road: Backpacking partnerships between school and home. *The Reading Teacher, 52,* 18–29.

Rickelman, R. J., & Henk, W. A. (1990). Reading technology: Children's literature and audio/visual technologies. *The Reading Teacher, 43,* 682–684.

Riley, J. (1996). *The teaching of reading.* London: Paul Chapman.

Rimer, S. (1990, June 19). Slow readers sparkling with a handful of words. *The New York Times,* pp. B1, B5.

Rinehart, S. D., Stahl, S. A., & Erickson, L. G. (1986). Some effects of summarization training on reading and studying. *Reading Research Quarterly, 21,* 422–438.

Rist, R. (1970). Student social class and teacher expectations. The self-fulfilling prophecy in ghetto education. *Harvard Educational Review, 40,* 411–451.

Rittle-Johnson, B., & Siegler, R. S. (1999). Learning to spell: Variability, choice, and change in children's strategy use. *Child Development, 70,* 332–348.

Rodriguez, T. A. (2001). Teaching ideas: From the known to the unknown: Using cognates to teach English to Spanish-speaking literates. *The Reading Teacher, 54,* 744–746.

Rose, M. C., Cundick, B. P., & Higbee, K. L. (1983). Verbal rehearsal and visual imagery: Mnemonic aids for learning disabled children. *Journal of Learning Disabilities, 16,* 352–354.

Rosenblatt, L. (1978). *The reader, the text, the poem.* Carbondale: Southern Illinois University Press.

Rosenblatt, L. (1991). Literature—S. O. S.! *Language Arts, 68,* 444–448.

Rosenblatt, L. M. (1990). Retrospect. In E. S. Farrell & J. R. Squire (Eds.), *Transactions with literature: A fifty-year perspective* (pp. 97-107). Urbana, IL: National Council of Teachers of English.

Rosenblatt, L. M. (1994). The traditional theory of reading and writing. In R. B. Ruddell, M. R. Ruddell, & H. Singer (Eds.), *Theoretical models and processes of reading* (4th ed.) (pp. 1057–1092). Newark, DE: International Reading Association.

Rosenshine, B., & Meister, C. (1994). Reciprocal teaching: A review of the research. *Review of Educational Research, 64,* 479–530.

Rosenshine, B., Meister, C., & Chapman, S. (1996). Teaching students to generate questions: A review of the intervention studies. *Review of Educational Research, 66*, 181–221.

Rosenshine, B., & Stevens, R. (1984). Classroom instruction in reading. In P. D. Pearson, R. Barr, M. L. Kamil, & P. Mosenthal (Eds.), *Handbook of reading research* (Vol. II, pp. 745–798). New York: Longman.

Routman, R. (1991). *Invitations: Changing as teachers and learners K–12*. Portsmouth, NH: Heinemann.

Rowand, C. (2000). Teacher use of computers and the Internet in public schools. *Education Statistics Quarterly, 2*(2), 72–75. Available online at http://www.asd.com/asd/

Ruddell, M. R. (1992). Integrated content and long-term vocabulary learning with the vocabulary self-collection strategy. In E. K. Dishner, T. W. Bean, J. E. Readence, & D. W. Moore (Eds.), *Reading in the content areas: Improving classroom instruction* (3rd ed.) (pp. 190–196). Dubuque, IA: Kendall/Hunt.

Ruddell, R. B. (1995). Those influential literacy teachers: Meaning negotiators and motivators. *The Reading Teacher, 48*, 454–463.

Ruddell, R. B., & Boyle, O. F. (1989). A study of cognitive mapping as a means to improve summarization and comprehension of expository text. *Reading Research and Instruction, 29*(1), 12–22.

Ruddell, R. B., & Ruddell, M. R. (1995). *Teaching children to read and write: Becoming an influential teacher*. Boston: Allyn & Bacon.

Rumelhart, D. (1980). Schemata: The building blocks of cognition. In R. J. Spiro, B. C. Bruce, & W. F. Bruner (Eds.), *Theoretical issues in reading comprehension* (pp. 33–58). Hillsdale, NJ: Lawrence Erlbaum.

Rumelhart, D. (1984). Understanding understanding. In J. Flood (Ed.), *Understanding reading comprehension* (pp. 1–20). Newark, DE: International Reading Association.

Sadow, M. K. (1982). The use of story grammar in the design of questions. *The Reading Teacher, 35*, 518–522.

Sadowski, M., & Paivio, A. (1994). A dual coding view of imagery and verbal processes in reading comprehension. In R. B. Ruddell, M. R. Ruddell, & H. Singer (Eds.), *Theoretical models and processes of reading* (4th ed.) (pp. 582–601). Newark, DE: International Reading Association.

Salinger, T. (2001). Assessing the literacy of young children: The case for multiple forms of evidence. In S. B. Neuman & D. K. Dickinson (Eds), *Handbook of early literacy research* (pp. 390–418). New York: Guilford.

Samuels, S. J. (1979). Decoding and automaticity: Helping poor readers become automatic at word recognition. *The Reading Teacher, 41*, 756–760.

Samuels, S. J. (1988). Characteristics of exemplary reading programs. In S. J. Samuels & P. D. Pearson (Eds.), *Changing school reading programs: Principles and case studies* (pp. 3–9). Newark, DE: International Reading Association.

Samuels, S. J. (1994). Toward a theory of automatic information processing in reading revisited. In R. B. Ruddell, M. R. Ruddell, & H. Singer (Eds.), *Theoretical models and processes of reading* (4th ed.) (pp. 816–837). Newark, DE: International Reading Association.

Santa, C. (1989). *Comprehension strategies across content areas*. Paper presented at the annual conference of the New England Reading Association, Newport, RI.

Santa, C. (1994, October). *Teaching reading in the content areas*. Paper presented at the International Reading Association's Southwest Regional Conference, Little Rock, AR.

Santa, C. M. (1988). *Reading opportunities in literature*. Unpublished manuscript.

Santa, C. M., & Høien, T. (1999). An assessment of Early Steps: A program for early intervention. *Reading Research Quarterly, 34*, 54–79.

Savin, H. B. (1972). What the child knows about speech when he starts to learn to read. In J. F. Kavanagh & I. G. Mattingly (Eds.), *Language by ear and by eye* (pp. 319–326). Cambridge, MA: MIT Press.

Scanlon, D. M., Velluntino, F. R., Small, S. G., & Fanuele, D. P. (2001). *Severe reading difficulties: Can they be prevented? A comparison of prevention and intervention approaches*. Paper presented at the annual convention of the American Educational research association, New Orleans.

Scardamalia, M., & Bereiter, C. (1986). Research on written composition. In M. C. Wittrock (Ed.), *Handbook of research on teaching* (pp. 778–863). New York: Macmillan.

Scardamalia, M., Bereiter, C., & Goelman, H. (1982). The role of production factors in writing ability. In M. Nystrand (Ed.), *What writers know: The language, process, and structure of written discourse* (pp. 173–210). New York: Academic.

Schatz, E. K., & Baldwin, R. S. (1986). Context clues are unreliable predictors of word meanings. *Reading Research Quarterly, 21*, 439–453.

Schickedanz, J. A. (1999). *Much more than the ABCs: The early stages of reading and writing*. Washington, DC: National Association for the Education of Young Children.

Schnorr, J. A., & Atkinson, R. C. (1969). Repetition versus imagery instructions in the short- and long-term retention of paired associates. *Psychonomic Science, 15*, 183–184.

Schunk, D. H., & Zimmerman, B. J. (1997). Developing self-efficacious readers and writers: The role of social and self-regulatory processes. In J. T. Guthrie & A. Wigfield (Eds.), *Reading engagement: Motivating readers through integrated instruction* (pp. 34–50). Newark, DE: International Reading Association.

Scott, T. (1998). *Using content area text to teach decoding and comprehension strategies*. Paper presented at the annual meeting of the International Reading Association, Orlando.

Searfoss, L. W., & Readence, J. E. (1994). *Helping children learn to read* (3rd ed.). Boston: Allyn & Bacon.

Shany, M. T., & Biemiller, A. (1995). Assisted reading practice: Effects on performance for poor readers in grades 3 and 4. *Reading Research Quarterly, 30*, 382–395.

Shearer, B. (1999). *The vocabulary self-collection strategy (VSS) in a middle school*. Paper presented at the forty-ninth annual meeting of the National Reading Conference, Orlando.

Shefelbine, J. (1990). A syllabic-unit approach to teaching decoding of polysyllabic words to fourth- and sixth-grade disabled readers. In J. Zutell & S. McCormick (Eds.), *Literacy theory and research: Analyses from multiple paradigms* (thirty-ninth yearbook of the National Reading Conference) (pp. 223–229). Chicago: National Reading Conference.

Shefelbine, J., & Calhoun, J. (1991). Variability in approaches to identifying polysyllabic words: A descriptive study of sixth graders with highly, moderately, and poorly developed syllabication strategies. In S. McCormick & J. Zutell (Eds.), *Learner factors/teacher factors: Issues in literacy research and instruction* (pp. 169–177). Chicago: National Reading Conference.

Shefelbine, J., & Newman, K. K. (2000). *SIPPS (systematic instruction in phoneme awareness, phonics, and sight words): Challenge level*. Concord, CA: Developmental Studies Center.

Short, K. G. (1990, March). *Using evaluation to support learning in a process-centered classroom.* Paper presented at the spring conference of the National Council of Teachers of English, Colorado Springs, CO.

Shuy, R. (1973). Nonstandard dialect problems: An overview. In J. L. Laffey & R. Shuy (Eds.), *Language differences: Do they interfere?* (pp. 3–16). Newark, DE: International Reading Association.

Silvaroli, N. J., & Wheelock, A. (2001). *Classroom reading inventory* (9th ed.). New York: McGraw-Hill.

Simmons, J. (1990). Portfolios as large-scale assessment. *Language Arts, 67,* 262–268.

Simmons, J. (1990). What writers know with time. *Language Arts, 73,* 602–605.

Simmons, J. (1996). What writers know with time. *Language Arts, 73,* 602–605.

Sinatra, G. M., Brown, K. J., & Reynolds, R. E. (2002). Implications of cognitive resource allocation for comprehension strategies instruction. In C. C. Block & M. Pressley (Eds.), *Comprehension instruction: Research-based best practices* (pp. 62–76). New York: Guilford.

Sinatra, R. C., Stahl-Gemeke, J., & Berg, D. N. (1984). Improving reading comprehension of disabled readers through semantic mapping. *The Reading Teacher, 38,* 22–29.

Sinatra, R. C., Stahl-Gemeke, J., & Morgan, N. W. (1986). Using semantic mapping after reading to organize and write original discourse. *Journal of Reading, 30,* 4–13.

Singleton, S. (1997). The creation of a basal program: A collaborative effort. In J. Flood, S. B. Heath, & D. Lapp (Eds.), *Handbook of research on teaching literacy through the communicative and visual arts* (pp. 869–871). New York: Simon & Schuster Macmillan.

Skillings, M. J., & Ferrell, R. (2000). Student-generated rubrics: Bringing students into the assessment process. *The Reading Teacher, 53,* 452–455.

Skjelfjord, V. J. (1976). Teaching children to segment words as an aid to learning to read. *Journal of Learning Disabilities, 9,* 39–48.

Slater, W. H., & Graves, M. F. (1989). Research on expository text. Implications for teachers. In K. D. Muth (Ed.), *Children's comprehension of text* (pp. 140–166). Newark, DE: International Reading Association.

Slavin, R. E. (1987a). Ability grouping and student achievement in elementary schools: A best-evidence synthesis. *Review of Education Research, 57,* 293–336.

Slavin, R. E. (1987b). Cooperative learning and the cooperative school. *Educational Leadership, 45*(3), 7–13.

Slavin, R. E. (1997–1998). Can education reduce societal inequity? *Educational Leadership, 55*(4), 6–10.

Sloan, G. D. (1984). *The child as critic* (2nd ed.). New York: Teachers College Press.

Smith, E. L., & Anderson, C. W. (1984). Plants as producers: A case study of elementary science teaching. *Journal of Research in Science Teaching, 21,* 685–698.

Snider, M. A., Lima, S. S., DeVito, P. J. (1994). Rhode Island's literacy portfolio assessment project. In S. Valencia, E. H. Hiebert, & P. P. Afflerbach (Eds.), *Authentic reading assessment: Practices and possibilities* (pp. 71–88). Newark, DE: International Reading Association.

Snow, C. E., Burns, M. S., & Griffin, P. (1998). *Preventing reading difficulties in young children.* Washington, DC: National Academy Press.

Snow, C. E., Dickinson, D. K., & Tabors, P. O. (2002). The home-school study of language and literacy development.

Available online at http://gseweb.harvard.edu/~pild/homeschoolstudy.htm

Spandel, V. (2001). *Creating writers through 6-trait writing assessment and instruction.* New York: Longman.

Spandel, V., & Stiggins, R. J. (1997). *Creating writers: Linking writing assessment and instruction* (2nd ed.). New York: Longman.

Spires, H. A., & Donley, J. (1998). Prior knowledge activation: Inducing engagement with informational texts. *Journal of Educational Psychology, 90,* 249–260.

Squire, J. R. (1994). Research in reader response, naturally interdisciplinary. In R. B. Ruddell, M. R. Ruddell, & H. Singer (Eds.), *Theoretical models and processes of reading* (4th ed.) (pp. 637–652). Newark, DE: International Reading Association.

Stahl, S. A. (1990). *Responding to children's needs, styles, and interests.* Paper presented at the thirty-fifth annual convention of the International Reading Association, Atlanta.

Stahl, S. A. (1998). Teaching children with reading problems to decode: Phonics and "not-phonics" instruction. *Reading and Writing Quarterly: Overcoming Learning Disabilities, 14,* 165–188.

Stahl, S. A., & Fairbanks, M. M. (1986). The effects of vocabulary instruction: A model-based meta-analysis. *Review of Educational Research, 56,* 72–110.

Stahl, S. A., Heubach, K., & Crammond, P. (1997). Fluency-Oriented Reading Instruction. (Reading Research Report No. 79). Athens, GA: National Reading Research Center (ERIC Document Reproduction Service No. ED 405 554).

Stahl, S. A., & McKenna, M. M. (2002). *The concurrent development of phonological awareness, word recognition, and spelling.* Atlanta: The University of Georgia, Center for the Improvement of Early Reading Achievement. Available online at http://www.ciera.org/library/archive/2001-07/200107.htm

Stahl, S. A., Osborne, J., & Lehr, F. (1990). *Beginning to read: Thinking and learning about print: A summary.* Urbana: Center for the Study of Reading, University of Illinois at Urbana-Champaign.

Stahl, S. A., Richek, M. A., & Vandeiver, R. J. (1991). Learning meaning vocabulary through listening: A sixth-grade replication. In J. Zutell & S. McCormick (Eds.), *Learner factors/teacher factors: Issues in literacy research and instruction* (pp. 185–192). Chicago: National Reading Conference.

Stallman, A. C., Commeyras, M., Kerr, B., Reimer, K., Jiménez, R., & Hartman, D. K. (1990). Are "new" words really new? *Reading Research and Instruction, 29,* 12–29.

Stauffer, R. G. (1969). *Directing reading maturity as a cognitive process.* New York: Harper & Row.

Stauffer, R. G. (1970). *Reading-thinking skills.* Paper presented at the annual reading conference at Temple University, Philadelphia.

Stecher, B. M., Barron, S., Kaganoff, T., & Goodwin, J. (1998). *The effects of standards-based assessment on classroom practices: Results of the 1996–97 RAND survey of Kentucky teachers of mathematics and writing* (CSE Technical Report 482). Los Angeles: University of California, Los Angeles, Graduate School of Education & Information Studies, Center for the Study of Evaluation, National Center for Research on Evaluation, Standards and Student Testing (CRESST) and RAND Education.

Steffler, D. J., Varnhagen, C. K., Friesen, C. K., & Treiman, R. (1998). There's more to children's spelling than the errors they make: Strategic and automatic processes for one-syllable words. *Journal of Educational Psychology, 90,* 492–505.

Steinmetz, S. (Ed.). (1999). *Random House Webster's unabridged dictionary of the English language* (2nd ed.). New York: Random House.

Sternberg, R. J. (1987). Most vocabulary is learned from context. In M. G. McKeown & M. E. Curtis (Eds.), *The nature of vocabulary acquisition* (pp. 89–105). Hillsdale, NJ: Lawrence Erlbaum.

Sternberg, R. J., & Powell, J. S. (1983). Comprehending verbal comprehension. *American Psychologist, 38,* 878–893.

Sticht, T. G., & James, J. H. (1984). Listening and reading. In P. D. Pearson, R. Barr, M. L. Kamil, & P. Mosenthal (Eds.), *Handbook of reading research* (pp. 293–317). New York: Longman.

Stoll, D. R. (1997). *Magazines for kids and teens* (2nd ed.). Newark, DE: International Reading Association.

Stotsky, S. (1983). Research of reading/writing relationships: A synthesis and suggested directions. *Language Arts, 60,* 568–580.

Strickland, D. S. (1998). Educating African-American learners at risk: Finding a better way. In C. Weaver (Ed.), *Practicing what we know: Informed reading instruction* (pp. 394–408). Urbana, IL: National Council of Teachers of English.

Strickland, D. S., & Taylor, D. (1989). Family storybook reading: Implications for children, curriculum, and families. In D. S. Strickland & L. M. Morrow (Eds.), *Emerging literacy: Young children learn to read and write* (pp. 27–33). Newark, DE: International Reading Association.

Sulzby, E. (1985). Children's emergent reading of favorite storybooks: A developmental study. *Reading Research Quarterly, 20,* 458–481.

Sulzby, E. (1989a). Appendix 2.1, Forms of writing and rereading from writing, Example list. In J. M. Mason (Ed.), *Reading and writing connections* (pp. 51–63). Boston: Allyn & Bacon.

Sulzby, E. (1989b). Assessment of writing and of children's language while writing. In L. Morrow & J. Smith (Eds.), *The role of assessment and measurement in early literacy instruction* (pp. 83–109). Englewood Cliffs, NJ: Prentice-Hall.

Sulzby, E., Barnhart, J., & Hieshima, J. A. (1989). Forms of writing and rereading from writing: A preliminary report. In J. M. Mason (Ed.), *Reading and writing connections* (pp. 31–50). Boston: Allyn & Bacon.

Sulzby, E., & Teale, W. (1991). Emergent literacy. In R. Barr, M. L. Kamil, P. Mosenthal, & P. D. Pearson (Eds.), *Handbook of reading research* (Vol. II, pp. 727–757). New York: Longman.

Sulzby, E., Teale, W., & Kamberelis, G. (1989). Emergent writing in the classroom: Home and school connections. In D. S. Strickland & L. M. Morrow (Eds.), *Emerging literacy: Young children learn to read and write* (pp. 63–79). Newark, DE: International Reading Association.

Sundbye, N. (1987). Text explicitness and inferential questioning: Effects on story understanding and recall. *Reading Research Quarterly, 22,* 82–98.

Sutherland, Z., & Arbuthnot, M. H. (1986). *Children and books* (7th ed.). Glenview, IL: Scott, Foresman.

Sutton, C. (1989). Helping the nonnative English speaker with reading. *The Reading Teacher, 42,* 684–688.

Sweet, A. P. (1997). Teacher perceptions of student motivation and their relation to literacy learning. In K. Guthrie & A. Wigfield (Eds.), *Reading engagement: Motivating readers*

*through integrated instruction* (pp. 86–101). Newark, DE: International Reading Association.

Taba, H. (1965). The teaching of thinking. *Elementary English, 42,* 534–542.

Tabors, P. O. (1997). *One child, two languages: A guide for preschool educators of children learning English as a second language.* Baltimore: Brookes.

Taylor, B. M., Strait, J., & Medo, M. A. (1994). Early intervention in reading: Supplemental instruction for groups of low-achieving students provided by first-grade teachers. In E. H. Hiebert & B. M. Taylor (Eds.), *Getting reading right from the start* (pp. 85–106). Boston: Allyn & Bacon.

Taylor, D., & Dorsey-Gaines, C. (1988). *Growing up literate: Learning from inner-city families.* Portsmouth, NH: Heinemann.

Taylor, H. H. (2001, March). Curriculum in Head Start. *Head Start Bulletin No. 67,* p. 2. Available online at http://www.headstartinfo.org/publications/hsbulletin67/hsb67_00.htm

Taylor, K. K. (1986). Summary writing by young children. *Reading Research Quarterly, 21,* 193–208.

Taylor, M. A. (1990, March). *Exploring mythology and folklore: The macrocosm and microcosm.* Paper presented at the spring conference of the National Council of Teachers of English, Colorado Springs, CO.

Teale, W. H., & Sulzby, E. (1986). *Emergent literacy: Writing and reading.* Norwood, NJ: Ablex.

Temple, C., Martinez, M., Yokota, J., & Naylor, A. (1998). *Children's books in children's hands: An introduction to their literature.* Boston: Allyn & Bacon.

Temple, C., Nathan, R., Temple, F., & Burris, N. A. (1993). *The beginnings of writing* (3rd ed.). Boston: Allyn & Bacon.

Terry, A. (1974). *Children's poetry preferences.* Urbana, IL: National Council of Teachers of English.

Tetewsky, S. J., & Sternberg, R. J. (1986). Conceptual and lexical determinants of nonentrenched thinking. *Journal of Memory and Language, 25,* 202–225.

Texas Instrument Foundation, Head Start of Greater Dallas, Southern Methodist University. (1996). *Leap into a brighter future.* Paper presented at Head Start's third national research conference, Dallas. Available online at http://www.ti.com/corp/docs/company/citizen/foundation/leapsbounds/leap.pdf

Texas State Board of Education (2000). *Summary of decodable text in conforming first grade programs.* Austin: Author. Available online at http://www.tea.state.tx.us/Textbooks/materials/decodtxt.htm

Thompson, A. (1990). Thinking and writing in learning logs. In N. Atwell (Ed.), *Coming to know: Writing to learn in the intermediate schools* (pp. 35–51). Portsmouth, NH: Heinemann.

Thompson, G. B., Cottrell, D. S., & Fletcher-Finn, C. M. (1996). Sublexical orthographic–phonological relations early in the acquisition of reading: The knowledge sources account. *Journal of Experimental Child Psychology, 62,* 190–222.

Thonis, E. (1983). *The English-Spanish connection: Excellence in English for Hispanic children through Spanish language and literacy development.* Compton, CA: Santillana, OESE (2002). Available online at http://www.ed.gov/offices/OESE/earlyreading/

Thorndike, R. L. (1973). Reading as reasoning. *Reading Research Quarterly, 9,* 135–147.

Thorndyke, P. (1977). Cognitive structures in comprehension and memory of narrative discourse. *Cognitive Psychology, 9,* 77–110.

Tiedt, P. M., & Tiedt, I. M. (2002). *Multicultural teaching: A handbook of activities, information, and resources* (6th ed.). Boston: Allyn & Bacon.

Tierney, R. J., Carter, M. A., & Desai, L. E. (1991). *Portfolio assessment in the reading-writing classroom.* Norwood, MA: Christopher-Gordon.

Tierney, R. J., Readence, J. E., & Dishner, E. K. (1995). *Reading strategies and practices: A compendium* (4th ed.). Boston: Allyn & Bacon.

Tompkins, G. E., & Yaden, D. B. (1986). *Answering questions about words.* Urbana, IL: National Council of Teachers of English.

Topping, K. (1987). Paired reading: A powerful technique for parent use. *The Reading Teacher, 40,* 608–609.

Topping, K. (1989). Peer tutoring and paired reading: Combining two powerful techniques. *The Reading Teacher, 42,* 488–494.

Topping, K. (1998). Effective tutoring in America Reads: A reply to Wasik. *The Reading Teacher, 52,* 42–50.

Torgesen, J. K., Wagner, R. K., Rashotte, C. A. (1994). Longitudinal studies of phonological processing and reading. *Journal of Learning Disabilities, 27,* 276–286.

Torgesen, J. K., Wagner, R. K., Rashotte, C. A., Burgess, S. R., & Hecht, S. A. (1997). The contributions of phonological awareness and rapid automatic naming ability to the growth of word reading skills in second to fifth grade children. *Scientific Studies of Reading, 1,* 161–185.

Touchstone Applied Science Associates (1994). *DRP handbook.* Brewster, NY: Author.

Touchstone Applied Science Associates. (1997). *Text sense, summary writing, teacher's resource manual.* Brewster, NY: Author.

Trabasso, T., & Magliano, J. P. (1996). How do children understand what they read and what can we do to help them? In M. F. Graves, P. van den Broek, & B. M. Taylor (Eds.), *The first R, every child's right to read* (pp. 160–188). New York: Teachers College Press & International Reading Association.

Trelease, J. (2001). *The new read-aloud handbook* (5th ed.). New York: Penguin.

Trussell-Cullen, A. (1994). *Celebrating the real strategies for developing non-fiction reading and writing.* Paper presented at the annual meeting of the Connecticut Reading Association, Waterbury.

Tunnell, M. O., & Jacobs, J. S. (1989). Using "real" books: Research findings on literature-based reading instruction. *The Reading Teacher, 42,* 470–477.

Turbill, J. (1982). *No better way to teach writing!* Rozelle, Australia: Primary English Teaching Association.

Tyson, E. S., & Mountain, L. (1982). A riddle or pun makes learning words fun. *The Reading Teacher, 36,* 170–173.

U.S. Department of Education (2002a). *Early Reading First: Frequently asked questions.* Available online at http://www.ed.gov/offices/OESE/earlyreading/faq. html

U.S. Department of Education (2002b). *Guidance for the Reading First program.* Washington, DC: Author.

U.S. Department of Education (2002c). *Head Start regulations, Part 1304.21.* Available online at http://www.acf.hhs.gov/programs/hsb/peformance/index.htm

U.S. Department of Education. (2002d). *Reading first criteria for review of state applications.* Available online at http://www.ed.gov/offices/OESE/readingfirst/grant.html

U.S. Department of Education. (2002e). *The No Child Left Behind Act of 2001.* Available online at http://www.ed.gov/legislation/ESEA02/

U.S. Department of Education (Office of Bilingual Education and Minority Languages Affairs). (1998). *Facts about limited English proficient students.* Available online at http://www.ed.gov/offices/OBEMLA/index.html

U.S. Department of Education (Office of Special Education and Rehabilitative Services). (2000). *Twenty-second annual report to Congress on the implementation of the Individuals with Disabilities Education Act.* Washington, DC: Government Printing Office.

Valdes, G. (1996). *Con Respeto: Bridging the distances between culturally diverse families and schools: An ethnographic portrait.* New York: Teachers College Press.

Valencia, S. W. (1990). Assessment: A portfolio approach to classroom reading assessment: The whys, whats, and hows. *The Reading Teacher, 43,* 338–340.

Valencia, S. W., & Place, N. A. (1994). Literacy portfolios for teaching, learning, and accountability: The Bellevue literacy assessment project. In S. W. Valencia, E. H. Hiebert, & P. P. Afflerbach (Eds.), *Authentic reading assessment: Practices and possibilities* (pp. 134–156). Newark, DE: International Reading Association.

Valencia, S. W., & Wixson, K. W. (2001). Inside English/language arts standards: What's in a grade? *Reading Research Quarterly, 36,* 202–217.

van den Broek, P., & Kremer, K. E. (2000). The mind in action: What it means to comprehend during reading. In B. Taylor, M. F. Graves, & P. van den Broek (Eds.), *Reading for meaning: Fostering comprehension in the middle grades* (pp. 1–31). New York: Teachers College Press.

Vandervelden, M. C., & Siegel, L. S. (1997). Phonological recoding and phoneme awareness in early literacy; A developmental approach. *Reading Research Quarterly, 30,* 854–876.

Vaughn, S., Klinger, J., & Schumm, J. (n. d.). *Collaborative strategy instruction: A manual to assist with staff development.* Miami: University of Miami.

Vellutino, F. R., & Scanlon, D. M. (2001). Emergent literacy skills. Early instruction and individual differences as determinants of difficulties in learning to read: The case for early intervention. In S. B. Neuman & D. K. Dickinson (Eds.), *Handbook of early literacy research* (pp. 295–321). New York: Guilford.

Venezky, R. L. (1965). *A study of English spelling-to-sound correspondences on historical principles.* Unpublished doctoral dissertation, Stanford University, Stanford, CA.

Venezky, R. L. (1999). *The American way of spelling.* New York: Guilford.

Verhallen, M., & Schoonen, R. (1993). Vocabulary knowledge of monolingual and bilingual children. *Applied Linguistics, 14,* 344–363.

Vernon-Feagans, L., Hammer, C. S., Miccio, A., & Manlove, E. (2001). Early language and literacy skills in low-income African-American and Hispanic children. In S. B. Neuman & D. K. Dickinson (Eds). *Handbook of early literacy research* (pp. 192–210). New York: Guilford.

Vukelich, C. (1990). Where's the paper? Literacy during dramatic play. *Childhood Education, 66,* 205–209.

Vygotsky, L. S. (1962). *Mind and society: The development of higher psychological processes.* Cambridge, MA: MIT Press.

Vygotsky, L. S. (1978). *Thought and language.* Cambridge, MA: MIT Press.

Vygotsky, L. S. (1987). The development of scientific concepts in childhood. In R. F. Rieber & A. S. Carton (Eds.), *The collected works of L. S. Vygotsky* (N. Mnick, Trans.) (Vol 1, pp. 167–241). New York: Plenum.

Walpole, S. (1998–1999). Changing texts, changing thinking:

Comprehension demands of new science textbooks. *The Reading Teacher*, 52, 358–369.

Watson, A. J. (1984). Cognitive development and units of print in early reading. In J. Downing & R. Valten (Eds.), *Language awareness and learning to read* (pp. 93–118). New York: Springer-Verlag.

Weber, E., Reed, B., & Woods, R. (1997). *Profiles: Windows on writing*. Flint, MI: Genesee Intermediate School District.

Weber, R. M., & ; Longhi-Chirlin, T. (2001). Beginning in English: The growth of linguistic and literate abilities in Spanish-speaking first graders. *Reading Research and Instruction*, 41, 19–50.

Weinstein, C., & Mayer, R. (1986). The teaching of learning strategies. In M. C. Wittrock (Ed.), *Handbook of research on teaching* (pp. 315–327). New York: Macmillan.

Wells, G. (1986). *The meaning makers: Children learning language and using language to learn*. Portsmouth, NH: Heineman.

West, J., Denton, K., & Germino-Hausken, E. (2000). *Early childhood longitudinal study: Kindergarten class of 1998–99*. Washington, DC: National Center for Educational Statistics. Available online at http://nces.ed.gov/pubsearch/pubsinfo. asp?pubid=2000070

Westby, C. E. (1999). Assessing and facilitating text comprehension problems. In H. W. Catts and A. G. Kamhi (Eds.), *Language and reading disabilities* (pp. 154–223). Boston: Allyn & Bacon.

Wharton-McDonald, R. (2001). Teaching writing in first grade: Instruction, scaffolds and expectations. In M. Pressley, R. L. Allington, R. Wharton-McDonald, C. C. Block, & L. M. Morrow (Eds.), *Learning to read: Lessons from exemplary first-grade classrooms* (pp. 70–91). New York: Guilford.

White, T. G., Power, M. A., & White, S. (1989). Morphological analysis: Implications for teaching and understanding vocabulary growth. *Reading Research Quarterly*, 24, 283–304.

White, T. G., Sowell, J., & Yanagihara, A. (1989). Teaching elementary students to use word-part clues. *The Reading Teacher*, 42, 302–308.

Wigfield, A. (1997). Children's motivations for reading and writing engagement. In J. Guthrie & A. Wigfield (Eds.), *Motivating readers through integrated instruction* (pp. 14–33). Newark, DE: International Reading Association.

Wigfield, A., & Asher, S. R. (1984). Social and motivational influences on reading. In P. D. Pearson, R. Barr, M. L. Kamil, & P. Mosenthal (Eds.), *Handbook of reading research* (pp. 423–452). New York: Longman.

Wilde, S. (1995). *Twenty-five years of inventive spelling: Where are we now?* Paper presented at the annual meeting of the International Reading Association, Anaheim, CA.

Williams, J. P. (1986a). Identifying main ideas: A basic aspect of reading comprehension. *Topics in Language Disorders*, 8, 1–13.

Williams, J. P. (1986b). Research and instructional development on main idea skills. In J. F. Baumann (Ed.), *Teaching main idea comprehension* (pp. 73–95). Newark, DE: International Reading Association.

Wilson, P. (1986). *Voluntary reading*. Paper presented at the annual convention of the International Reading Association, Philadelphia.

Wilson, P. (1992). Among nonreaders: Voluntary reading, reading achievement, and the development of reading habits. In C. Temple & P. Collins (Eds.), *Stories and readers: New perspectives on literature in the elementary classroom* (pp. 157–169). Norwood, MA: Christopher-Gordon.

Winne, R. H., Graham L., & Prock, L. (1993). A model of poor readers' text-based inferencing: Effects of explanatory feedback. *Reading Research Quarterly*, 28, 536–566.

Winograd, P. N. (1984). Strategic difficulties in summarizing text. *Reading Research Quarterly*, 19, 404–425.

Withers, C. (Ed.). (1948). *A rocket in my pocket: The rhymes and chants of young Americans*. New York: Holt.

Wixson, K. K. (1983). Questions about a text: What you ask about is what children learn. *The Reading Teacher*, 37, 287–293.

Wixson, K. K. , & Dutro, E. (1998). Standards for primary-grade reading: An analysis of state frameworks. (CIERA Report #3-001). Available online at http://www.ciera.org/ciera/publications/report-series/

Wolf, M., & Katzir-Cohen, T. (2001). Reading fluency and its intervention. *Scientific Studies of Reading*, 5, 211–238.

Wong, B. Y. L., & Wong, R. (1986). Study behavior as a function of metacognitive knowledge about critical task variables: An investigation of above average, average, and learning disabled readers. *Learning Disabilities Research*, 1, 101–111.

Worthy, J., & Broaddus, K. (2001). Fluency beyond the primary grades: From group performance to silent, independent reading. *The Reading Teacher*, 55, 334–343.

Yaden, D. B., Tam, A., Madrigal, P., Brassell, D., Massa, J., Altamirano, S., & Armendariz, J. (2001). Early literacy for inner-city children: The effects of reading and writing interventions in English and Spanish during the preschool years. (CIERA Article #00–04). Available online at http://www.ciera.org/ciera/publications/report-series/

Yokota, J. (Ed.). (2001). *Kaleidoscope, a multicultural booklist for grades K–8* (3rd ed.). Urbana, IL: National Council of Teachers of English.

Yopp, H. K. (1988). The validity and reliability of phonemic awareness tests. *Reading Research Quarterly*, 23, 159–199.

Yopp, R. H., & Yopp, H. K. (1992). *Literature-based reading activities*. Boston: Allyn & Bacon.

Zarnowski, M. (1990). *Learning about biographies: A reading-and-writing approach for children*. Urbana, IL: National Council of Teachers of English.

Zeno, S. M., Ivens, S. H., Millard, R. T., & Duvvuri, R. (1995). *The educator's word frequency scale*. Brewster, NY: Touchstone Applied Science Associates.

Zill, N., & West, J. (2001). *Entering kindergarten: A portrait of American children when they begin school*. Washington, DC: U.S. Department of Education, Office of Educational Research and Improvement. Available online at http://nces.ed.gov/pubs2001/2001035

Zinsser, W. (1988). *Writing to learn*. New York: Harper & Row.

Zorfass, J., Corley, P., & Remy, A. (1994). Helping students with disabilities become writers. *Educational Leadership*, 51(7), 62–66.

Zwaan, R. A., & Graesser, A. C. (1998). Introduction to special issue of SSR: Constructing meaning during reading. *Scientific Studies of Reading*, 2(3), 195–198.

## Children's Books and Periodicals

Aardema, V. (1975). *Why mosquitoes buzz in people's ears: A West African folk tale*. New York: Dial.

Aiken, J. (1962). *Wolves of Willoughby Chase*. New York: Dell.

Albee, S. (1997). *I can do it*. New York: Random House.

Alexander, A. (1961). *Boats and ships from A to Z*. New York: Rand McNally.

Avi. (1994). *The barn*. New York: Orchard.

Baldwin, D., & Lister, C. (1984). *Your five senses*. Chicago: Children's Press.

Bang, M. (1985). *The paper crane*. New York: Greenwillow.

Barracca, S. (1990). *The adventures of taxi dog*. New York: Dial.

Barton, B. (1982). *Airport*. New York: Crowell.

Bauer, C. (1984). *Too many books*. New York: Viking.

Berger, M., & Berger, G. (1995). *What do animals do in winter?* Nashville, TN: Ideals Children's Books.

Bridwell, N. (1972). *Clifford the small red puppy*. New York: Scholastic.

Brink, C. (1935). *Caddie Woodlawn*. New York: Macmillan.

Brown, A. (2001). *Hoot and holler*. New York: Knopf.

Brown, J. G. (1976). *Alphabet dreams*. Englewood Cliffs, NJ: Prentice-Hall.

Burchard, P. (1999) *Lincoln and slavery*. New York: Antheneum.

Burnford, S. (1961). *Incredible journey*. New York: Bantam.

Burton, L. L. (1942). *The little house*. Boston: Houghton Mifflin.

Byars, B. (1970). *Summer of the swans*. New York: Viking.

Cameron, A. (1994). *The cat sat on the mat*. Boston: Houghton Mifflin.

Carle, E. (1969). *The very hungry caterpillar*. New York: Philomel.

Carle, E. (1973). *Have you seen my cat?* New York: Watts.

Carle, E. (1987). *Papa, please get the moon for me*. New York: Simon & Schuster.

Choi, Y. (2001). *The name jar*. New York: Knopf.

Christian, A., & Felix, A. (1997). *Can it really rain frogs? The world's strangest weather events*. New York: John Wiley & Sons.

Cleary, B. (1975). *Ramona the brave*. New York: Morrow.

Cleary, B. (1981). *Ramona Quimby, age 8*. New York: Morrow.

Cole, J. (1992). *Magic school bus on the ocean floor*. New York: Scholastic.

Coxe, M. (1996). *Cat traps*. New York: Random House.

Crews, D. (1984). *Schoolbus*. New York: Greenwillow.

Curtis, F. (1977). *The little book of big tongue twisters*. New York: Harvey House.

Dalgliesh, S. (1954). *Courage of Sarah Noble*. New York: Scribner's.

Danziger, P. (1995). *Amber Brown goes fourth*. New York: Putnam.

Degen, B. (1983). *Jamberry*. New York: Harper & Row.

dePaola, T. (1973). *Andy: That's my name*. Englewood Cliffs, NJ: Prentice-Hall.

Douglas, B. (1982). *Good as new*. New York: Lothrop.

Eastman, P. D. (1960). *Are you my mother?* New York: Random House.

Egan, R. (1997). *From wheat to pasta*. Danbury, CT: Children's Press.

Ellwand, D. (1996). *Emma's elephant & other favorite animal friends*. New York: Dutton.

Emberley, E. (1987). *Cars, boats, planes*. New York: Little, Brown.

Enderle, J., & Tessler, S. G. (1996). *Francis, the earthquake dog*. San Francisco: Chronicle Books.

Eth, C. (1995). *Flatfoot Fox and the case of the bashful beaver*. Boston: Houghton Mifflin

Everitt, B. (1998). *Up the ladder, down the slide*. New York: Harcourt Brace.

Farmighetti, R. (Ed). *(1999). The world almanac*. New York: Newspaper Enterprise.

Fletcher, R. J. (1997). *Spider boy*. New York: Clarion.

Folsom, M., & Folsom, M. (1986). *Easy as pie*. New York: Clarion.

Freeman, D. (1978). *A pocket for Corduroy*. New York: Viking.

Friedman, I. (1984). *How my parents learned to eat*. New York: Houghton Mifflin.

Fritz, J. (1982). *Will you sign here, John Hancock?* New York: Coward.

Gág, W. (1928). *Millions of cats*. New York: Coward.

Galdone, P. (1974). *Little Red Riding Hood*. New York: Clarion.

Galdone, P. (1975). *The gingerbread boy*. New York: Clarion.

Garten, J. (1964). *The alphabet tale*. New York: Random House.

Geisel, T. S. (Dr. Seuss). (1957). *The cat in the hat*. New York: Random House.

Geisel, T. S. (Dr. Seuss). (1961). *The cat in the hat comes back*. New York: Random House.

Geisel, T. S. (Dr. Seuss). (1974). *There's a wocket in my pocket*. New York: Beginner.

Gershator, D., & Gershator, P. (1997). *Palampam Day*. New York: Marshall Cavendish.

Gibbons, G. (1972). *Recycle: A handbook for kids*. Boston: Little, Brown.

Gibbons, G. (1992). *Recycle! A handbook for kids*. Boston: Little, Brown.

Goodall, J. S. (1988). *Little Red Riding Hood*. New York: Macmillan.

Grahame, K. (1966). *The reluctant dragon*. New York: Holiday House.

Gramatky, H. (1939). *Little Toot*. New York: Putnam.

Greydanus, R. (1988). *Let's get a pet*. New York: Troll.

Hamilton, V. (1985). *The people could fly*. New York: Knopf.

Haushner, R. (1994). *What food is this?* New York: Scholastic.

Hazen, B. S. (1999). *That toad is mine*. New York: HarperCollins.

Hill, E. S. (1967). *Evan's corner*. New York: Holt, Rinehart & Winston.

Hill, L. S. (1997). *Farms feed the world*. Minneapolis: Carolrhoda Books.

Hoban, L. (1981). *Arthur's funny money*. New York: HarperCollins.

Hoban, R. (1964). *Bread and jam for Frances*. New York: Harper & Row.

Hutchins, P. (1976). *Don't forget the bacon!* New York: Mulberry.

Hutchins, P. (1987). *Rosie's walk*. New York: Simon & Schuster.

Hyman, T. S. (1983). *Little Red Riding Hood*. New York: Holiday House.

Ivimey, J. W. (1987). *The complete story of the three blind mice*. New York: Clarion.

Johnson, A. (1992). *The leaving morning*. New York: Orchard Books.

Keats, E. J. (1962). *The snowy day*. New York: Viking.

Keats, E. J. (1964). *Whistle for Willie*. New York: Viking.

Komori, A. (1983). *Animal mothers*. New York: Philomel.

Krauss, R. (1945). *The carrot seed*. New York: Harper.

Kremetz, J. (1986). *Jamie goes on an airplane*. New York: Random House.

L'Engle, M. (1962). *A wrinkle in time*. New York: Farrar, Straus & Giroux.

Lessem, D. (1997). *Supergiants: The biggest dinosaurs*. Little, Brown.

Lewis, C. S. (1950). *The lion, the witch, and the wardrobe*. New York: Macmillan.

Lewison, W. C. (1992). *Buzz said the bee*. New York: Scholastic.

Lobel, A. (1970). *Frog and toad are friends*. New York: Harper & Row.

Louie, A. (1982). *Yeh-Shen: A Cinderella story from China*. New York: Philomel.

Lowry, L. (1990). *Number the stars*. Boston: Houghton Mifflin.

Lutz, N. J. (2001). *Frederick Douglas.* Broomall, PA: Chelsea House.

Macdonald, F. (2001) *The world in the time of Marco Polo.* Broomall, PA: Chelsea House.

Maitland, B. (2000). *Moo in the morning.* New York: Farrar, Straus & Giroux.

Malam, J. (1998). *Leonardo DaVinci.* Minneapolis, MN: Carolrhoda.

Martin, B., Jr. (1983). *Brown bear, brown bear, what do you see?* New York: Holt.

Mason, A. (1997). *If you were there, Viking times.* New York: Simon & Schuster.

Mathieu, J. (1993). *Big Joe's trailer truck.* New York: Random House.

McCloskey, R. (1941). *Make way for ducklings.* New York: Viking.

McGovern, A. (1968). *Stone soup.* New York: Scholastic.

McKissack, P., & McKissack, F. (1988). *Bugs.* Chicago: Children's Press.

McMillam, B. (2001). *Days of the ducklings.* Boston: Houghton Mifflin.

Minark, E. H. (1961). *Little Bear's visit.* New York: HarperCollins.

Modesitt, J. (1990). *The story of z.* Saxonville, MA: Picture Book Studio.

Most, B. (1991). *A dinosaur named after me.* Orlando, FL: Harcourt.

Musgrove, M. (1976). *Ashanti to Zulu.* New York: Dial.

Naylor, P. (1991). *Shiloh.* New York: Atheneum.

Naylor, P. (1996). *Fear Place.* New York: Alladin.

Naylor, P. (1997). *Ducks disappearing.* New York: Atheneum.

Nedobeck, D. (1981). *Nedobeck's alphabet book.* Chicago: Children's Press.

Neff, M. M. (1990). Legends: How Gordie Howe was a hockey star in his youth and also when he was a grandpa. *Sports Illustrated for Kids, 2*(2), 48.

Noble, T. H. (1980). *The day Jimmy's boa ate the wash.* New York: Dial.

Parks, K. (2002). *The world book of facts.* New York: World Almanac Books.

Paulsen, G. (1991). *Woodsong.* New York: Puffin.

Petrie, C. (1983). *Joshua James likes trucks.* Chicago: Children's Press.

Phillips, L. (1997). *Ask me anything about dinosaurs.* New York: Avon.

Polacco, P. (2001). *The keeping quilt* (rev.). New York: Simon & Schuster.

Pomerantz, C. (1987). *How many trucks can a tow truck tow?* New York: Random House.

Potter, B. (1908). *The tale of Peter Rabbit.* London: Warne.

Rathman, P. (1995). *Officer Buckle and Gloria.* New York: Putnam's.

Richards, J. (2002) *Howling hurricanes.* Broomall, PA: Chelsea House.

Robbins, K. (1999). *Big rigs: Giants of the highway.* New York: Atheneum.

Rockwell, A. (1984). *Cars.* New York: Dutton.

Rolfer, G. (1990). Game day. *Sports Illustrated for Kids, 2*(8), 25.

Rylant, C. (1985). *The relatives came.* New York: Bradbury.

Schade, S. (1992). *Toad on the road.* New York: Random House.

Segal, L. (1973). *All the way home.* New York: Farrar, Straus & Giroux.

Sendak, M. (1963). *Where the wild things are.* New York: Harper & Row.

Shaw, N. (1986). *Sheep in a jeep.* Boston: Houghton Mifflin.

Shaw, N. (1992). *Sheep on a ship.* Boston: Houghton Mifflin.

Shaw, N. (1996). *Sheep in a shop.* Boston: Houghton Mifflin.

Shuter, J. (1997). *The ancient Egyptians.* Portsmouth, NH: Heineman.

Shuter, J. (1997). *The ancient Greeks.* Des Plaines, IL: Heinemann.

Slepian, J., & Seidler, A. (1992). *The hungry thing goes to a restaurant.* New York: Scholastic.

Snow, P. (1984). *A pet for Pat.* Chicago: Children's Press.

Sobol, D. (1961). *The Wright brothers at Kitty Hawk.* New York: Dutton.

Souza, D. M. (1998). *Fish that play tricks.* Minneapolis: Carolrhoda.

Speare, E. (1958). *The witch of Blackbird Pond.* Boston: Houghton Mifflin.

Stevenson, R. L. (1967). *Treasure island.* Feltham, ENG: Hamlyn.

Stevenson, R. L. (1985). *A child's garden of verses.* London: Longman.

Stille, D. R. (2002). *Fire trucks.* Mankato, MN: Compass Point Books.

Stolz, M. (1992). *Stealing home.* New York: HarperCollins.

Stone, L. M. (1985). *Antarctica.* Chicago: Children's Press.

Stone, L. M. (1998). *Brown bears.* Minneapolis: Lerner.

Thompson, S. E. (1998). *Built for speed: The extraordinary, enigmatic cheetah.* Minneapolis: Lerner.

White, E. B. (1952). *Charlotte's web.* New York: Harper & Row.

Wilder, L. I. (1932). *Little house in the big woods.* New York: HarperCollins.

Wildsmith, B. (1982). *Cat on the mat.* New York: Oxford University Press.

Wildsmith, B. (1988). *Squirrels.* New York: Oxford University Press.

Williams, M. (1926). *The velveteen rabbit.* New York: Doubleday.

Yashima, T. (1955). *Crow boy.* New York: Viking.

Yee, H. W. (1996). *Mrs. Brown went to town.* Boston: Houghton Mifflin.

Young, E. (1989). *Lon Po Po: A Red-Riding story from China.* New York: Philomel.

Young, M. (1999). Guinness book of world records. New York: Sterling.

Ziefert, H. (1984). *Sleepy dog.* New York: Random House.

Ziefert, H. (1998). *I swapped my dog.* Boston: Houghton Mifflin.

Zion, G. (1956). *Harry the dirty dog.* New York: Harper & Row.

# Index

## Photo Credits